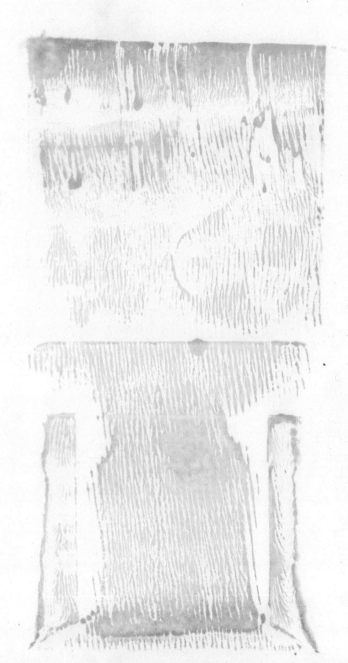

IVC

THE GREEK ATOMISTS
AND EPICURUS

THE GREEK ATOMISTS
AND EPICURUS

A Study

By CYRIL BAILEY, M.A.

NEW YORK / RUSSELL & RUSSELL

FIRST PUBLISHED IN 1928
REISSUED, 1964, BY RUSSELL & RUSSELL
A DIVISION OF ATHENEUM PUBLISHERS, INC.
L. C. CATALOG CARD NO: 64-11844
ISBN: 0-8462-0427-4
PRINTED IN THE UNITED STATES OF AMERICA

PREFACE

AS a natural sequel to an edition of the text of Epicurus I attempted a general exposition of his system. But as soon as one sets about that task it becomes clear that it would be incomplete and unsatisfactory without an account of the Atomic philosophers who preceded him. This book is therefore intended as a study of the development of Atomism in Greece and of its embodiment in the comprehensive system of Epicurus. An attempt has been made to put together from the scattered remains which we possess the theories of the three Atomic philosophers, to set them in relation to one another and to deal with some of the problems which inevitably arise in considering them. I cannot claim to be a philosopher, still less a man of science. There will therefore be found little criticism from an external philosophic point of view and little attempt to indicate, except incidentally, parallels or differences between the ancient and modern Atomic theories. What I have tried to do is to understand as far as possible the minds of these Greek thinkers and to set out their thoughts from the inside. The 'plain man's' exposition of what Epicurus intended to be the 'plain man's' philosophy may at least prove a useful basis for the criticism of others more learned in science and philosophy.

I have tried as far as possible to let the three philosophers tell their own story in their own words, when they have been preserved, and failing that to use the accounts and comments given by ancient writers. Happily, except perhaps for

Leucippus, there is a sufficient quantity of material preserved, but it is necessary to piece it together. It is often tempting to try to bridge over gulfs by conjecture and to attribute to the philosophers theories and ideas which their recorded beliefs seem to suggest. Some of their modern critics have in their enthusiasm gone too far in this direction, and I have tried to resist the temptation except in places where I felt confident that the ground was sure.

My debt to many modern writers will be sufficiently indicated in the foot-notes, but a special word of sincere acknowledgement is due to Hermann Diels and Hermann Usener for the collection of the material on which this account is based, and, among critics to Carlo Giussani, Dr. Ettore Bignone, and Professor John Burnet. I wish also to express my gratitude to the Trustees of the Jowett Copyright Fund for their assistance towards the publication of this volume.

C. B.

October, 1926.

CONTENTS

CONTENTS

PART II. EPICURUS

APPENDICES

Abbreviations used in foot-notes

*E. G. P.*3 = *Early Greek Philosophy*, J. Burnet, 3rd edition, 1920.

D. = *Die Fragmente der Vorsokratiker*, H. Diels, 3rd edition, 1912. Under each author the quotations are divided into A. references to life and teaching, B. fragments.

U. = *Epicurea*, H. Usener, 1887.

C. B. = *Epicurus*, C. Bailey, 1926.

INTRODUCTION

TO the modern mind few facts in the history of human thought are probably more astonishing than that the cardinal theories, on which two great branches of science, astronomy and chemistry, are now respectively built, should have been propounded by Greek philosophers only to be abandoned and lie dormant for centuries. The notion of a helio-centric world, the germ of which was contained in the speculations attributed to the Pythagorean Philolaus, was completed in the third century by Aristarchus of Samos, yet produced no effect on scientific thought, till the truth was rediscovered by Copernicus. And though the Atomic Theory of Leucippus and Democritus in the form in which it was adopted by Epicurus, became widely known in Greece and at one period still more widely at Rome, it was even so regarded rather as the eccentric adjunct of a popular theory of morals than as a scientific explanation of the world. It was totally eclipsed throughout the Middle Ages by the physical speculations of Aristotle which rested on the older notion of the four 'elements', and had to wait for its partial revival by Gassendi and its modern rediscovery by Dalton. Yet, though the world so long refused it, its association with one of the noblest works of Latin poetry and its own intrinsic interest in the light of modern scientific theories make it worth while to attempt to put together its history. It has for us a double interest as a theory with which we can find ourselves in greater sympathy than with most of its competitors, and also as a peculiarly fascinating product of the subtle and penetrating Greek genius, making its way with acute observation certainly, but with little that can be called experiment, into the inner secrets of nature.

Atomism 'flourished' in Greece for a period of about 150 years, from 430 B.C. to 280 B.C. During the whole of this period there was something like an Atomic school, working at the theory, handing down traditions and developing new points with greater or less activity, but three great names stand out as landmarks in the course of its evolution, those of Leucippus, Democritus and Epicurus. If in passing through their hands the theory had remained unaltered, if, as some critics have thought, it were impossible to distinguish the original ideas of Leucippus from the additions and expansions of Democritus, and if Epicurus, as it used to be said, had in reality adopted the theory of Democritus without change to serve as a physical base to his moral system, it might be possible to treat of Atomism as a single whole. But the careful research of modern scholars, and in particular the work of Diels, Usener, and Giussani has shown that this is not the case. The theory until it left Epicurus remained always vital, capable of new developments and applications, admitting not merely of greater refinements in the working out of detail but also of a securer co-ordination as a whole. No better proof of this growth could be given than a comparison of the extant fragments and notices of Leucippus with the poem of Lucretius. The same fundamental theory is indeed recognized, and certain doctrines have been transmitted with singular tenacity, but the crudeness of the earlier theory has been refined away, and the whole system has been so elaborated in detail and unified in structure as to have been in fact completely transformed; Atomism then must be regarded as a theory in process of development. Moreover, so widely different were the three men in personal character and in the attitudes with which they approached their work that it is essential that they should be treated of separately. Leucippus with the humility of a pioneer regards himself as the mediator between the rival theories of his predecessors, and having formulated the fundamental principle of atomism, sets himself to work out some of its consequences with a certain naïve insight, but without any serious attempt at the creation of a complete system. Democritus, the man of encyclopaedic learning and universal interests, taking over the theory from Leucippus, develops and systematizes it on every side, weaving it into a vast but loosely constructed philosophy, which ranged in an all-embracing spirit over the world and human life. Epicurus is primarily a moralist, a preacher of a Gospel of life, who cares nothing for knowledge and learning as such. But he does care greatly, and that not only from a moral point of view, for a materialist theory of the universe, based upon a complete trust in the validity of sensation, and in such a theory Atomism takes its natural place on the physical side. He simplifies in places, elaborates in others, has a minute eye for consequential details and a singular power of visualizing effects: above all he welds together physics, morals, and psychology into a consistent system based on a single principle. It is therefore impossible to group together in a single account a theory developed on such different lines and approached from such different points of view, and though, in telling the story of Atomism it will be necessary to some extent to trace and retrace the same ground, yet such are the divergences between its three exponents that there should be no danger of monotony. But beyond Epicurus it is not profitable or indeed possible to follow the history of Atomism: it is true that his followers attempted to develop his sytem in certain outlying provinces, especially in the spheres of Logic and Rhetoric (both of them subjects banned by the Master), yet so great was their respect for the authority of his name that the first care of the school was to preserve intact, without addition or subtraction, the heritage which he had handed down to them. It is owing to this scrupulous conscientiousness of his disciples that we can accept the poem of Lucretius, written more than two hundred years after the death of Epicurus, as a certain record of his doctrines.

For similar reasons it is impossible, in the case at any rate of Democritus and Epicurus, to deal merely with the physical theory of Atomism and neglect the rest of their work; such an abstraction would give a false impression not merely of the philosophers but of the development of Atomism itself. For in some respects the most interesting feature in its history is the way in which, starting as a physical cosmogony—one in the long series of speculations of the early Greek philosophers—afterwards, as the range of philosophy widened or the centre of interest shifted, it gradually became co-ordinated in a greater whole. In Democritus indeed its position is perhaps rather one of juxtaposition than of co-ordination; though it is closely connected, for instance, with his metaphysical scepticism, it is not so easy to trace its relation to his moral theory, still less to those manifold and diverse subjects which filled the books of his Tetralogies. But with Epicurus the change is very marked. Epicureanism is indeed a very different thing from Atomism. Morals, psychology, and physics are all grouped together in a system which is a whole. And Atomism is not loosely attached to the other fields of interest, but penetrates them all and is penetrated by them. The theories of psychology, even of morals, rest directly on an Atomic basis, and the theories of Atomism in turn are controlled and conditioned by the fundamental principles of psychology. For this reason I have had no scruple in treating generally of the many fields of Democritus' activity and in regarding Atomism in its last stage as a part of the wider Epicureanism.

In reading or writing the history of Greek Atomism, it is impossible not to have an eye on modern science. Yet the temptation to see closer parallels than actually exist and to read modern ideas into ancient speculation is very real and must be resisted. It must always be remembered that ancient speculation is a very different matter from modern research: at its best it rested in the main on *a priori* reasoning, and though observation and even experiment may have given some knowledge of detail, they had little place in the development of the larger fundamental theories. And not only do methods differ, but the fundamental conceptions of the atom in the ancient theory and modern chemistry are widely divergent. The Greeks conceived a perfectly hard unalterable body, incapable of entering into any combination except by juxtaposition or at most entanglement: modern chemistry conceives an elastic changeable body, which in the fusion of chemical combination merges its material identity in a new substance. The ancient theory conceived of infinite atoms all of homogeneous material; the modern chemist assigns a materially different atom to each of his numerous elements, though indeed in its latest developments chemical physics seems to be coming back to the notion of an ultimate homogeneous germ of all the elements. These are some of the differences which should put any writer but an expert in modern science upon his guard. He cannot forbear from time to time to note coincidences, or apparent coincidences,[1] between the ancient and the modern ideas, but a complete comparison of the two, fascinatingly interesting as it would be, must be left to others. For myself, I shall endeavour simply to tell the story of Atomism in Greece, hoping that it may possibly inspire some expert in modern chemistry to add the missing chapter with an authoritative hand. But even a layman may assert without contradiction that it was the Greeks who put the questions which modern science is still endeavouring to answer: had their problems been different, the whole course of European scientific thought might never have existed.

[1] Many such interesting coincidences have been remarked in Dr. J. Masson's *Lucretius, Epicurean and Poet*.

PART I

THE ATOMISTS

I
THE ANTECEDENTS OF ATOMISM

NO important system of thought has ever appeared in the world as the 'special creation' of its founder, wholly detached from what has gone before: it must have its roots in the speculations and discoveries of many predecessors, which have been advancing unconsciously towards one solution. This solution could not have been anticipated and may often at the moment pass unrecognized, yet to one looking back it is seen to be the inevitable outcome of previous thought. So it certainly was with the Greek theory of the atomic constitution of the universe; it was no brilliant and isolated invention, but the natural issue of the long series of speculations of the early physical philosophers. Alike the nature of the problems which they had set themselves to solve—problems which grew in complexity, as each new thinker made his fresh contribution of difficulties—and the general trend of the answers they gave, pointed to Atomism as the ultimate conclusion, and Leucippus, who had the genius to perceive this, regarded himself not so much as a conspicuous innovator, but rather as the reconciler of the rival theories of his predecessors. In order then to understand both the form and the content of the system of the Atomists, it is necessary to inquire briefly into the main lines of previous speculation, with a view to determining the problem which they inherited and the given conditions of its solution.

The history of early Greek speculation has often been written,[1] and it is not my purpose to attempt any general description or estimate of it; it is only intended here to inquire into it in so far as it led up to Atomism. It will therefore be

[1] It is almost superfluous to refer to Zeller's *Philosophie der Griechen*, to Gomperz, *Greek Thinkers* (vol. i in English Translation by L. Magnus), and to Professor Burnet's *Early Greek Philosophy* (3rd edition, 1920); to the last work in particular this Chapter owes very much.

necessary to abstract from the theories of the earlier thinkers what is relevant to this purpose and to neglect other elements which lie apart from it; but there is the less danger that a false picture will thus be given, because what is essential for the present discussion is in fact just the kernel of their speculations. For the ultimate problem lying at the back of them all is the inquiry, what is the nature (φύσις) of the world? It is no doubt true that this question was in origin religious rather than physical;[1] cosmogony sprang from religion and brought forth cosmology. It is not therefore surprising that a theological undercurrent is discernible in the theories of many of the early philosophers and that from time to time it comes prominently to the surface; Epicurus himself,[2] some three centuries after Thales, still finds it necessary to implore his disciple to beware of 'myth' and cling to 'physiology'. Yet from the first moment that it comes into view,[3] philosophy is seen to be honestly endeavouring to free science from the prejudices of religion and to regard nature as a purely physical existence. Thus the intention of the early thinkers, when they posed the question 'what is the nature of the world?' was to suggest an inquiry into the ultimate material substance of which it was composed. It is therefore on their answers to this fundamental question, given in the long debate which ensued, that attention must be concentrated; for those answers constitute in fact the antecedents of Atomism.

Lucretius, whose poem preserves the doctrines of Atomism in a more expanded form than any other extant document, devotes a large section of his first book[4] to the criticism of the predecessors of the Atomists. This section has for us the peculiar interest that, based as it certainly is on an

[1] The connexion of theology and physical science in the early Greek philosophers is well brought out in Mr. F. M. Cornford's *From Religion to Philosophy*, though I cannot agree with his notion of the origin of the conception of φύσις and think that he overrates the importance of the religious element in the philosophers of the ·scientific tradition'.

[2] e.g. Ep. ii, § 87.

[3] See Gomperz, *Greek Thinkers*, Chap. I.

[4] i. 635–920.

Epicurean work,[1] it represents the orthodox tradition of the Atomic school. In this aspect its main value lies not so much in its criticism, which is often delivered from an unsympathetic and dogmatic Epicurean point of view, but in its preservation of the Atomists' conception of the steps by which their own system was approached. Lucretius recognizes in previous speculation three stages. In the first the answer to the ultimate problem of the constitution of the world is given as a single 'element'[2] or substance, and of this stage Heraclitus[3] is made typical. In the second stage he places philosophers who postulated as the ultimate basis two or more elements, and associates it with the name of Empedocles,[4] who believed the world to be composed of all the four. Finally, as the nearest approach to Atomism—though in some respects its opposite pole—he places the theory of Anaxagoras, which stands alone in its unique originality. This division is not merely arbitrary, but does in fact represent clearly enough the natural process of development from Monism to a greater and greater Pluralism, of which in a sense Atomism was the culmination, and it will therefore be more than a mere matter of convenience to follow it. At the same time the separation of the early philosophers into schools, though based on logical as well as local and historical grounds, must not be exaggerated: for there is a vital connexion running all through their speculations. Each new stage of thought arises out of the criticism of its predecessor;

[1] Possibly the Ἐπιτομὴ τῶν πρὸς τοὺς φυσικούς (D.L. x. 27). The main bulk of Lucretius' poem is probably based on Epicurus' Μεγάλη Ἐπιτομή (see Giussani, *Stud. Lucr.* p. 10), but it is improbable that that work contained systematic criticism of other philosophers.

[2] The word 'element' (στοιχεῖον) is first used by Plato. The idea may have come from the Pythagoreans and is explicit in Empedocles (*E. G. P.*3, p. 228, n. 1).

[3] That Heraclitus is really taken as a type is, I think, clear from the fact that some of Lucretius' criticism—and in particular that of the notion of condensation and rarefaction (647–54)—is not applicable to his theory, but to those of others of the Monists.

[4] In this section Lucretius expressly states (716) that Empedocles is only a type, and recognizes (763, 770) two distinct schools among the upholders of the theory of the four elements.

indeed even constructive thinking is sometimes intended as a form of attack. But usually this is not so: a constructive period will be followed by a period of criticism and out of it again arises new construction on a fresh basis. It will therefore be necessary not merely to consider the prominent representatives of the three main constructive stages, but also those other philosophers, who by a largely negative and critical attitude prepared the way for the next development. Parmenides, and later on Zeno and Melissus, are as important precursors of Atomism, as Heraclitus, Empedocles, and Anaxagoras.

§ 1. *The Monists*

Under the title of Monists may roughly be grouped together those philosophers who held that the primary substance, out of which the world was made, was one. Their speculations were throughout guided by the ultimate desire for unification, a feeling perhaps rather than a reasoned conclusion that behind all the infinite variety and changeableness of the world around them there must be some one permanent substance, which did not vary or change. But though all held this fundamental belief in common, their theories are marked by a growing sense of difficulty in the monistic explanation. After its apparently first confident enunciation by Thales, arises an ill-disguised feeling of dissatisfaction: it is easy enough to suppose an ultimate unity, but much more difficult to explain how multiplicity can have arisen from it, and how both the one fundamental substance and the many forms in which it appears can be equally real. Two periods may be clearly distinguished: the first consists of the 'School of Miletus', all closely dependent on one another, Thales, Anaximander and Anaximenes, the second is represented by the independent and original theory of Heraclitus of Ephesus. To these must be added the strange doctrine of Parmenides of Elea, which in its thoroughgoing Monism and its relentless disregard of the appearances of normal experience, really reduced Monism to an absurdity and prepared the way for a solution on different lines.

Though considerable information is extant with regard to Thales himself and his doings, his journey to Egypt and importation to Ionia of Egyptian geometry,[1] his political importance and his plea for Ionian federation, and his famous prediction of the eclipse of the sun, very little indeed is known about his philosophical views. For the present purpose practically all that can be counted certain is the bare statement that he said the primary substance was water.[2] Why he selected water and how he explained the creation of other things from water we do not know. Aristotle suggests that he was led to his conclusion by observing that the 'nourishment of all things is moist and that even the hot is created from the moist and lives by it', and further 'that the seeds of all things are in their nature moist', but this looks rather like the reasoning of a later age, after physiological interests had arisen. It is perhaps more probable that he selected water because as a matter of commonplace observation it seemed most likely to be able to give rise to other things. He saw it not only in a liquid state, but in a solid form as ice and also in an 'airy' condition, as he would probably have said, as vapour. Such observation would have led him to conclude that it might change also into other solids, hardening into earth and rock, and passing through the medium of 'air' even into fire itself. It is most unfortunate that we have no further trustworthy information as to his theories, for it seems impossible in view of the subtle reasoning of his immediate successor that he can have been content with the mere enunciation of his belief. As it is, it must simply be accepted as the foundation of the Ionic speculation. We may notice as a survival of the theological interest—though too much has been made of it—the statement attributed to Thales that 'all things are full of gods';[3] the same sort of animism seems to be implied in his argument that 'the magnet is alive, because it moves iron'.[4]

---

[1] For an examination of these traditions see *E. G. P.*3, pp. 41–7.

[2] Arist. *Metaphys. A.* 3.983 b; D.A. 1 2. Aristotle states that Thales said water was the 'material cause', but he is speaking of course in his own terminology.

[3] Arist. *de Anima, A.* 5. 411 a; D.A. 22.   [4] Ibid. *A.* 2. 405 a; D.A. 22.

ANAXIMANDER, who is described as a 'companion' of Thales, which means probably a member of the same group united by philosophical interests, though not so versatile a man, would appear to have been a far more audacious and subtle thinker. He developed something like a system of the heavenly bodies,[1] explaining their nature and their relations to one another, he formed a new view of the earth and its position in the world, and propounded a theory of the creation of animals and man, which has, perhaps over-enthusiastically, been recognized as the forerunner of modern ideas of Evolution. In dealing with the main problem, he would seem to have adopted from Thales the general notion of a single primary substance and then to have set himself deliberately to consider of what nature it must be, and what were the fundamental conditions of its existence. The idea that most forcibly impressed itself on him was that it must be 'infinite'[2] (ἄπειρον), 'boundless', that is to say in extent. As he looked at the world around him he saw that there was a continual 'strife of opposites': the hot and the cold appear to be at war with one another, so too the moist and the dry. The result is a continual destruction and waste. If then there is to be material to keep this destructive warfare going, and to repair its losses, there must, so to speak, be an eternal stock to draw upon 'in order that becoming may not fail'.[3] The primary substance then, whatever else it may be, must be something without limit: it must never be possible to get to the end of it: it must be 'boundless'. Moreover, it must for the same reason be eternal: it is, as he said,[4] 'deathless and ageless'. Is it possible then to describe its material character? Can it be, as Thales had thought, water, or indeed any one of the things of ordinary experience? Emphatically not, Anaximander replied, for 'these things are hostile to one another; air is cold, water is moist, fire is hot, and if any one of these were infinite, it must even

---

[1] For a very brief treatment of these subordinate interests see § 4 of this Chapter.   [2] Diog. Laert. ii. 1; D. 1.

[3] Aet. 1. 3. 3; D. 14 ἵνα μηδὲν ἐλλείπῃ ἡ γένεσις.

[4] Hipp. *Ref.* i. 6. 1; D. 11.

now have put an end to all the others'.[1] What the material nature of 'the boundless' is Anaximander does not say; he was content to leave it indefinite. Later philosophers, speaking of it in their own accustomed phraseology, called it 'indeterminate matter'[2] or something 'distinct from the elements',[3] or even with greater precision 'a nature between air and fire or air and water'.[4] Such phraseology is anachronistic, as it implies a distinction of the 'elements', though it may to some extent express Anaximander's idea. The 'boundless' was apparently conceived as outside all the worlds, a vast envelope,[5] as it were, enclosing them, out of which they were created and into which they would ultimately be destroyed.[6] Not content with this general idea, Anaximander went on to specify the way in which 'worlds', which he conceived of as innumerable,[7] were created out of 'the boundless'. There was in the 'boundless' eternal motion,[8] which brought the worlds into being by means of the 'separating out of opposites':[9] this seems to mean that a constant jostling inside the 'boundless' shook out 'the opposites'. An interesting reference explains the process and its consequences:[10] 'something able to beget hot and cold was separated off from the eternal at the creation of this world, and out of this a circle of flame grew up round the air enclosing the earth, as the bark grows round the tree'. A piece of the 'boundless', we must understand, was shaken off and separated itself into the two opposites, the hot and the cold; the cold composed the earth in the centre and the 'fiery circle' gave birth to the heavenly bodies. Similarly

---

[1] Arist. *Phys.* Γ. 5. 204b.   [2] Arist. *Met.* Λ. 2. 1069b.

[3] Arist. *Phys.* Γ. 5. 204 b παρὰ τὰ στοιχεῖα.

[4] Alex. Aphrod. in Arist. *Metaph.* A. 6. 988 a; D. 16 τὴν μεταξὺ φύσιν ἀέρος τε καὶ πυρός, ἢ ἀέρος τε καὶ ὕδατος.

[5] Hipp. *Ref.*, l.c. πάντας περιέχειν τοὺς κόσμους.

[6] Aet. 1. 3. 3. D. 14.

[7] Ibid. ἀπείρους κόσμους. Burnet (*E. G. P.*3 58 ff.) has shown that this must mean infinite coexisting, not successive worlds.

[8] Hipp. *Ref.* i. 6. 2; D.A. 11.

[9] Arist. *Phys.* A. 4. 187 a ἐκ τοῦ ἑνὸς ἐνούσας τὰς ἐναντιότητας ἐκκρίνεσθαι. D. 16.   [10] Theophrastus in Ps.-Plut. *Strom.* 2.

other worlds would be formed, though in their case it might be a different pair of 'opposites' which were 'separated out'. In such worlds 'the opposites' would be in a continual state of strife, sometimes the one, sometimes the other gaining the upper hand, but at last 'they make reparation and satisfaction to one another for their injustice according to the appointed time';[1] the balance is exactly restored, the 'world' is destroyed and 'the opposites' merged again in the boundless. This picturesque description of the birth and death of worlds passes perhaps a little outside the main problem of the ultimate matter, but it greatly assists in the understanding of Anaximander's general notion, and contains the germs of many cosmogonical ideas which persisted through the whole of early speculation and take their place in the theories of the Atomists.

It seems at first sight a retrogression that after the singular insight of Anaximander ANAXIMENES should have gone back on the idea that the primary substance was one of the things known to experience and selected 'Air'.[2] But an examination of his theory shows that it was really an advance on Thales and even on Anaximander himself.[3] Anaximander's difficulty had been that he could not see how any of the known substances could change into the others, and for this reason he had spoken of his 'boundless' as being neither one nor the other of them. But if any satisfactory explanation of this change could be given, it might be possible to return to a theory less arbitrary and more like that of Thales. This explanation Anaximenes found in 'thickening and thinning out',[4] or as we should say, rarefaction and condensation. All things were formed of air, but the differences between them were due to the presence of more or less air in a greater or less state of compression: in other words the difference between things was quantitative, not qualitative. The diffi-

---

[1] Simpl. in Arist. *Phys.* A. 2. 184 (24. 13); D. 9.
[2] Simpl. in Arist. *Phys.* A. 2. 184 (24. 26) (Theophrastus); D.A. 5.
[3] See *E. G. P.*3, 73 ff.
[4] Simpl. l.c. διαφέρειν δὲ μανότητι (also called ἀραίωσις, Plut. *Strom.* 3; D. 6) καὶ πυκνότητι κατὰ τὰς οὐσίας.

culty of Thales' theory was avoided and moreover it was now possible to conceive of a fundamental substance, which was really homogeneous, while Anaximander's 'boundless', which contained the 'opposites', would seem to have had the character of a mixture. What then was Anaximenes' 'air' and how did he conceive its changes? His notion was a very delicate one and deserves appreciation. He appears to have worked from the analogy of the human body. 'Even as our soul, which is air, holds us together, so breath and air encompass the whole world.'[1] Moreover, he observed the curious fact that if we breathe out with our lips tightly pressed the breath feels comparatively cold, but much warmer, if the mouth be wide open.[2] From this he drew the conclusion that air condensed is cold, but rarefied it becomes hot, and on this fact he founded his theory of the formation of other things from air. 'When air is most even ($\delta\mu o\lambda\omega\tau\alpha\tau o\varsigma$ i.e. as we might say, in a normal state), it is invisible to the sight',[3] and this is the reason that we do not see air as such, 'but it is made visible by the cold and the hot, the moist and the moving', or as we should perhaps more naturally say, when it becomes hot or cold or moist or moving. Hence extending his notion gradually beyond our immediate experience of air he could say that 'when it is thinned it becomes fire, when thickened, wind and then cloud, and if still more thickened, water, and then earth, and then stones'.[4] The theory was indeed based on elementary observation and then carried by conjecture beyond its limits: on the one hand the air seemed to 'thin out' into the fiery bodies in the heavens, on the other to thicken into clouds,[5] which in their turn produced rain: it required no great stretch of the imagination to conceive the process continuing and creating solid earth and even stones. In his new idea then Anaximenes had shown not merely how a single homogeneous substance,

---

[1] Quoted by Aet. i. 3, 4; D.B. 2.
[2] Plut. *de Prim. Frig.* 7, 947 F; D.B. 1.
[3] Hipp. *Ref.* i. 7. 2 ; D.A. 7. [4] Simpl. in Arist. *Phys.* l.c.
[5] Hipp. *Ref.* i. 7. 7. D.A. 7. $\sigma v\nu\epsilon\lambda\theta\delta\nu\tau\alpha$ $\delta\grave{\epsilon}$ $\kappa\alpha\grave{\iota}$ $\dot{\epsilon}\pi\grave{\iota}$ $\pi\lambda\epsilon\hat{\iota}o\nu$ $\pi\alpha\chi\upsilon\nu\theta\acute{\epsilon}\nu\tau\alpha$ $\nu\acute{\epsilon}\phi\eta$ $\gamma\epsilon\nu\nu\hat{\alpha}\sigma\theta\alpha\iota$ $\kappa\alpha\grave{\iota}$ $o\ddot{\upsilon}\tau\omega\varsigma$ $\epsilon\grave{\iota}\varsigma$ $\ddot{\upsilon}\delta\omega\rho$ $\mu\epsilon\tau\alpha\beta\acute{\alpha}\lambda\lambda\epsilon\iota\nu.$

such as Thales had conceived, might create the rest without losing its own identity, but had also incidentally accounted for the creation of Anaximander's 'opposites' without having to suppose them already existent in the 'boundless': hot and cold, moist and dry are all produced by quantitative difference in the compression of air. It is not without cause that Anaximenes was regarded in antiquity as the culmination of the Milesian School,[1] for though at first sight his theory seems so much less far-sighted than that of Anaximander, it is seen ultimately to be a more logical working out of the fundamental idea of the school and to be free from the difficulties involved in the theories of both his predecessors.

The Milesian School then had established the main idea of the single primary substance, out of which all else was created, had shown that this must be unlimited in extent, and had suggested various means by which the different substances of experience might come into being. But though their theories had thus enunciated principles which were to prove of great and lasting importance, they were yet beset with great difficulties, two of which seem to have made themselves almost immediately felt. In the first place the assumption that the primary substance exists as something external to the worlds—an infinite store of matter, as it were, parts of which might be broken off to form worlds— is at once unnatural and uneconomical. Secondly, the Milesians had themselves betrayed a sense of the difficulty of passing from this one primary substance to the many things of sensation: Anaximander's 'boundless' containing the 'opposites' could not really be homogeneous, and Anaximenes' expedient of quantitative difference suggested an unreality about other substances which were actually only compressed or rarefied air. It was apparently with these difficulties that HERACLITUS of Ephesus set himself primarily to deal. Though he disclaims all connexion with his predecessors and despises the speculation of philosophers[2] no less than the ignorance of the mob,[3] proclaiming himself the

[1] See E. G. P.3, p. 78.
[2] frs. 16–18 Bywater; D.B. 40, 129, 108.   [3] fr. 5 Bywater; D.B. 17.

possessor of a unique secret, which men are yet 'unable to understand, when they first hear it',[1] it is nevertheless clear not merely that the Milesians had set him his problem, but that his solution,[2] for all its originality, has a close kinship to theirs. The great 'discovery' on which Heraclitus so prides himself was the identity of the One and the Many: 'out of all one and out of one all'.[3] The implication of this rather cryptic statement must be found in the speculations of his predecessors: it is not sufficient, Heraclitus says in effect, to suppose some external One, from which the substance of the world is supplied; rather it is the world itself which is One, and its unity is in fact constituted by the very multiplicity of things, which at first sight seems to destroy it. In the world, as he insisted, we see perpetual flux and constant change: 'all things pass away, and nothing abides',[4] they are like the current of a river, whose water changes at every moment so that 'you cannot step into the same river twice'.[5] Yet behind this unceasing flow and constant alteration there is permanence; the ever-shifting things of experience are but the parts of an abiding whole. Nor again is the 'strife', which had seemed to Anaximander an 'injustice', inconsistent with the universal unity: it is indeed its essential condition; 'war is the father of all and the king of all'.[6] The world is a 'harmony of opposing tensions',[7] just as the straining of its parts against each other and against the hands produces the efficiency of the bow, and the tension and reaction of its strings give the harmonious note of the lyre.

So far the 'discovery' sounds mystic and its statement dogmatic, but Heraclitus knew what it meant, and it is

[1] *fr.* 2 Bywater; D.B. 1.

[2] It is more difficult to give a succinct account of Heraclitus' cosmology than of those of his predecessors. This is not so much due to lack of information or the obscurity of his fragments, but because, as Burnet has ably shown, all the parts of his system—cosmogony, astronomy, psychology, and as far as it goes, ethics—are closely knit up together and abstraction is consequently harder.   [3] *fr.* 59 Bywater; D.B. 10.

[4] Plut. *Theaet.* 152 e; *Crat.* 401 d, 402 a.

[5] *fr.* 41 Bywater; D.B. 91.   [6] *fr.* 44 Bywater; D.B. 53.

[7] *fr.* 45 Bywater; D.B. 51 παλίντροπος ἁρμονίη.

easier to grasp his idea when it is translated into physical terms. What then is this One which is also All? As the true successor of the Milesians Heraclitus conceived his One as a primary substance out of which everything else was made, and selected fire: 'the world was ever and is and shall be an everliving fire'.[1] Just as Thales had probably based his theory of water as the primal matter on the observation of its changes, and Anaximenes, as we know, had argued for air on the analogy of the human breath, so without doubt Heraclitus' selection of fire was not arbitrary: for the flame seems at once to illustrate the idea of the single world with its ever-shifting material. We see the fuel passing into the flame and disappearing, and at the other end issues the smoke, yet the flame itself, ever shifting in shape and position, preserves a constant identity as long as fuel is supplied it. So it is with the world, whose existence Heraclitus conceived pictorially as 'an upward and a downward path',[2] like the lap of the Greek racecourse. At the head is the eternal fire itself, on the downward path,[3] as heat becomes extinguished, the fire changes into moisture, and the moisture in its turn hardens into earth. Then begins the upward path; the earth again liquifies into water, and the water evaporating and passing again into the fire[4] supplies the fuel to keep it ever alight. How does this process take place? Is it really a change of matter, so that there is not in fact a single fundamental substance, or is it a quantitative change, such as Anaximander conceived or something else? The answer, though highly important, is not very easy to give. Tradition[5] certainly speaks of 'thickening and thinning out' in connexion with Heraclitus' theory, and Lucretius'[6] criticism assumes it, but on the one hand the accounts of Heraclitus

---

[1] *fr.* 20 Bywater; D.B. 30.

[2] *fr.* 69 Bywater; D.B. 60.   [3] See D.L. ix. 9; D.A. 1.

[4] ἀναθυμίασις is the characteristic word used by Heraclitus both of the process of the 'upward path' and of the kindling of the dry light of the soul (*frs.* 41, 42 Bywater; D.B. 12).

[5] So Theophrastus (*Phys. Op.* 1; D. 475, apud Simpl. in Arist. *Phys.* A. 2. 184 (23. 33); D.A. 5) and Diogenes Laertius, l.c. 8.

[6] i. 645–54.

do not rest on good authority and there has probably been confusion with the theory of Anaximander, on the other Lucretius though nominally attacking Heraclitus yet probably intends to cover the whole of the Monists. More light can be obtained from certain fragments describing Heraclitus' 'cosmology',[1] which seems just to be the concrete manifestation of the 'upward and downward path'. The eternal fire appears in the world as the sun: his fire 'is first transformed into sea'[2] through the intermediate stage of the 'fiery waterspout',[3] which itself is due to the 'kindling and extinction of clouds'.[4] Water[5] then passes into earth (the process of freezing would act as an indication, as well as the observation of sea-shells and fossil fish inland attributed to Xenophanes).[6] Earth again becomes sea by means of the rivers, and the sea once more is taken up by evaporation to pass again into the light of the sun. Thus in the course of a 'great year' the whole world is renewed. The idea is now far more definite but it is still doubtful whether Heraclitus could have said whether he conceived the changes as qualitative or quantitative. He would have insisted that the eternal fire was the one reality, the source and goal of all matter: other things were not indeed condensed or rarified fire, nor yet had they independent reality: they existed only in relation to fire, he might have said, as its fuel or its smoke.

Throughout the whole world then is this double motion, to fire and from fire, and it is the exact balance of the movements which preserves the equilibrium of the world and ensures its eternity: 'all things are given in exchange for fire, and fire for all things, even as goods are exchanged for gold and gold for goods',[7] and the permanence of all is preserved because all things observe their own 'measures', 'the fire is kindled in due measures and in due measures extinguished'.[8]

[1] Burnet's argument (*E. G. P.*3, pp. 148 ff.) on this point seems convincing.
[2] *fr.* 21 Bywater; D.B. 31.
[3] πρηστήρ: compare *Lucr.* vi. 423–50.   [4] Aet. iii. 3. 9; D.A. 14.
[5] *fr.* cit. D.B. 31 θαλάσσης δὲ τὸ μὲν ἥμισυ γῆ, τὸ δὲ ἥμισυ πρηστήρ.
[6] Hipp. *Ref.* 1. 14; Xenophanes D.A. 33.
[7] *fr.* 22 Bywater; D.B. 90.
[8] *fr.* 20 Bywater; D.B. 30: cf. *fr.* 29 Bywater; D.B. 94.

Nor is this true merely of the world as a whole, but of all in it. The sea, for instance, is 'half earth, and half fiery waterspout': half of it, that is, is just ceasing to be fire and becoming sea, the other half is ceasing to be sea and becoming earth. If there were not this 'tension of opposites', the world would cease to be: if the upward path, for instance, were to gain the victory over the downward, all would end in a great conflagration.[1] Thus it turns out that Anaximander's 'opposites' are in all cases the two aspects of a single process: 'the cold is getting warm, the warm cold, the moist is becoming dry, and the parched is becoming damp'.[2] And their 'strife', the pulling of the two processes in opposite directions, is in fact just the 'harmony which gives the world its permanence'. 'Homer was wrong in saying "would that Strife might perish from among gods and men": if his prayer were heard, all things would pass away.'[3]

In this somewhat fantastic—or perhaps we should say mystic—theory Heraclitus felt that he had finally satisfied the conditions required by his predecessors. He had shown that there was a primary substance which was yet not external to the world, that it was in the fullest physical sense One but that yet the Many were but forms of it, and that the Strife, which had proved a stumbling-block to Anaximander, was just the condition of that equilibrium which ensured the world's eternity. It was not without cause that he could look down on the ignorance of the multitude and say that 'wisdom is apart from other things'.[4] Heraclitus has for us a double interest; for not only was his theory the culmination of the Ionian Monism, but long afterwards he became an object of special veneration to the Stoics, the permanent rivals of the Epicureans. They perceived naturally enough in his speculations an anticipation of their own belief in the

[1] Certain authorities actually attribute the doctrine of the ἐκπύρωσις to Heraclitus, but Burnet (*E. G. P.*³ 158 ff.) has shown that it is a hopeless contradiction of the main principles of his system and must be a Stoic accretion.

[2] *fr.* 39 Bywater; D.B. 126.

[3] *fr.* 43 Bywater.   [4] *fr.* 18 Bywater; D.B. 108.

'divine spark of fire',[1] which was alike the 'soul of the world'
and the soul of man. It was undoubtedly for this reason in
a great measure that Lucretius[2] selected Heraclitus as the
type of the Monists. Some of his criticism is certainly beside
the mark: he attributes to Heraclitus[3] the notion of rarefaction and condensation and complains that he does not
admit the existence of a void[4]—a point which did not arise
in discussion till after Heraclitus' day. But in two respects
at least his observations are of value, for they mark the
weakness of the Monist position not merely from an atomic
point of view, and suggest the problems which immediately
arose from it and were to be the material for the work of the
next generation. Firstly, he argues in effect, if the primal
substance is one, other things must differ from it either in
quantity or quality: if in quantity,[5] then their own existence
is unreal; you would only get more or less concentrated
'fire': if in quality,[6] then Monism is a delusion, for there are
other existences which are not in fact 'fire'. Secondly,[7] with
a slight shifting of his ground, he complains that to maintain
that everything else is only a disguised form of the one
primary substance, is to attack the validity of the senses: they
recognize 'fire', but fail to see that all else is really 'fire' too.
As will be seen,[8] Heraclitus was apparently ready to accept
this position, but it marks the first avowal of scepticism, and
the beginning of the discussion of the source and validity of
knowledge: for the first time 'wisdom' declares itself 'apart
from other things'.

Among the Monists may best be included a philosopher,
who, although he was in fact the founder of a new school, yet
brought the Monist theory to a culmination, because he

[1] Unfortunately they also interpreted his doctrines in their own terminology
and even attributed to him ideas which he cannot have held, such as those of
the λόγος and the ἐκπύρωσις, and one of the chief difficulties of understanding our doxographical tradition about Heraclitus is the necessity for
disentangling Stoic elements: see Burnet.

[2] i. 635–704. [3] 647 ff. [4] 655 ff.
[5] 650–1. [6] 665–71. [7] 690–700.
[8] Sext. *adv. Math.* vii. 126; D.A. 16: cf. *fr.* 132 Bywater; D.B. 46.
See § 4, p. 58.

made it for ever impossible. PARMENIDES of Elea was indeed
one of those thinkers, whose work seems to be mostly
negative: he follows out the old idea to its logical conclusion,
and that conclusion proves impossible for any one to accept;
yet because it shows the weakness of the old, it also sets the
conditions for the new, and may be, as Parmenides' theory
was, the starting-point of more than one line of inquiry.
While the later Ionians were engaged in their endeavours
to reconcile the existence of the one primary substance with
the many substances of experience, there had been among
them a wandering philosopher, whose thoughts had turned
mostly to religion. The chief work of XENOPHANES of Colophon was his *Satires* or *Silloi*, in which he had attacked the
old anthropomorphic polytheism of Homer and Hesiod—
the Olympian religion—and proclaimed that there was 'One
god, the greatest among both gods and men, like unto mortals
neither in form nor in thought'.[1] This was not however,
as it sounds, a proclamation of a monotheistic religion, but
had its direct relation to Ionian physical speculation. The
'one god' was in fact, as Aristotle[2] tells us, the whole world,
and the import of his aphorism was just that, while his contemporaries were looking for some external substance—for
he preceded Heraclitus—from which the many might be
supplied, Xenophanes insisted that the world itself was one.

That Parmenides was in any sense a pupil of Xenophanes,
as the doxographers tell us,[3] is improbable, but it is quite
likely that the older philosopher in the course of his wander-
ings visited Elea and may have influenced the younger. At
any rate it was this notion of the actual Unity of the World
itself which Parmenides determined to work out to its logical
conclusion. It has been noticed that Heraclitus had already
expressed himself sceptical as to evidence of the senses, and
was inclined to appeal from them to the reason of the mind.
Parmenides threw himself whole-heartedly into this sceptical
position: at the outset of his poem[4] he boldly declares that

[1] D.B. 23.   [2] *Metaphys. A.* 5. 986 b.
[3] Simpl. in Ar. *Phys.* A. 2. 184 (22. 27); D.A. 7—derived from
Theophrastus.   [4] D.B. 1, l. 29.

there are two 'Ways', the Way of Truth, which is reached only by the mind, and the Way of 'the Opinions of mortals, in which is no true confidence at all', which is based upon sensation. The poem proceeds to expound both 'Ways', and the views of the world at which they respectively arrive, but it is clear even from such fragments as we possess that the Way of Truth is alone Parmenides' own view, the Way of Opinion is only expounded to show its falsity.[1] What then is the Way of Truth? 'That It is and that it cannot not be is the path of Persuasion, who is the companion of Truth, but that It is not and that it must needs not be, this way I tell thee is a path wherein is no learning at all. For that which is not thou canst not know—for that cannot be—no nor utter it. For the same thing can be thought and can be.'[2] The main proposition here contained that what is, is, and what is not, is not, appears at first sight both indisputable and unprofitable, but the clue to the riddle lies in the last clause. Parmenides' test of reality is 'thought' (νοεῖν), or rather, according to the essentially material notions of early Greek philosophy, 'visualization': 'for it must needs be that what can be spoken of and thought is: for it is possible for it to be, but it is not possible for what is nothing to be'.[3] What then can be thought or 'visualized'? Clearly, since once more the whole train of previous philosophy may be taken as a sure guide, matter or body. 'It is' then means neither more nor less than the existence of matter or body: it exists to the full and it alone exists: empty space unoccupied by matter does not exist, empty space is nothing, for nothing cannot, in Parmenides' sense, be 'thought'. In other words the world is solid body, pure matter, a corporeal *plenum*. Here then, Parmenides seems to say, is the logical conclusion of the Ionian hypothesis: if anything is seriously meant by the statement that the world is one, it must be that it is a continuous homogeneous body and nothing else.

[1] For the controversy as to what Parmenides intended by the Way of Opinion see *E. G. P.*3, pp. 182 ff., and Cornford, pp. 218 ff.

[2] D.B. 4, l. 3 ; 5.

[3] D.B. 6. I follow Burnet's interpretation as against Diels.

Nor does Parmenides shrink from the consequences of his conclusions, but proclaims them with cheerful confidence. 'If what is is, it can never have come into being or pass away, for what can there have been before or after it?'[1] It is eternal. Indeed what was and what shall be do not exist: what is, is now: past and future are an illusion and time itself a dream. Moreover, the world being absolutely continuous body, 'it is not divisible, for it is alike all over':[2] the apparent separation of things from one another is but a fallacy of the senses. Nor can it move, for motion implies empty space, which is nothing and does not exist:[3] it therefore does not change and there is no 'becoming or passing away',[4] no birth nor death. Nor is it infinite in extent:[5] for it is complete in itself and 'lacks nothing' outside itself. It is in fact 'complete on every side, like in bulk to a perfect sphere, equal from the centre in every direction'.[6] Parmenides' world is thus a finite, eternal, indivisible, immovable, spherical, corporeal mass: motion, change, variety, birth, and death, all that we know by the experience of our senses are mere delusions. It is no longer strange to learn that he 'expelled the senses from the way of Truth';[7] for thought had certainly led to conclusions very far from the 'opinion' of the senses.

The theory of Parmenides was indeed the death-blow of Monism, for it showed conclusively that no further progress could be made in this direction. The expedients of the later Ionians for preserving the unchangeable One and at the same time reconciling it with the ever-changing Many had been shown to fail, because they in reality involved the abandonment of the fundamental principle of Unity. The strict following out of this principle could only lead to a view of Unity, which was wholly divorced from experience, and seemed to be entirely devoid of fruitful results. Yet Parmenides' theory was in effect a turning-point in the history of Greek philosophy. It had in the first place shown for the first time the importance of logical thought: a theory

---

[1] D.B. 8, ll. 3–14.   [2] Ibid., l. 22.   [3] Ibid., l. 26.
[4] Ibid., l. 27.   [5] Ibid., l. 32.   [6] Ibid., l. 42.
[7] Ps. Plut. *Strom.* 5; D.A. 22.

could not henceforward be accepted, until its full consequences had been thought out and weighed. It was again the starting-point for further speculations on the part of Parmenides' Eleatic disciples, which were to lead along the peculiar lines of the master's thought to consequences of great importance. But above all, it pointed to the inevitable direction of future development: 'philosophy must now cease to be monistic or cease to be corporealist'.[1] The old belief in matter as the sole reality, on which Parmenides' own system rested, was too strong to be broken down yet: philosophy chose the line of least resistance and ceased to be monistic. It is not without significance that the view of the world which Parmenides expounded—or more probably exposed—in the Way of Opinion, was a dualism, based on the complementary 'substances' of Light and Darkness.

§ 2. The Pluralists—Empedocles

The theory of Parmenides had made it impossible any longer to maintain the single homogeneous substance as the primary basis of the world, because the variety and complexity of phenomena could not by this means be accounted for. Thinkers began to search for a solution on new lines, and it is not hard to perceive the form which new theories must take. Indeed it had almost been suggested by the theory of Heraclitus, whose notion of 'fire which was not fire', when it took the forms of the moist and the solid, was but a thinly disguised pluralism. If variety could not be produced by a single primary substance, it might be explained by the assumption of two or more such substances, which by their mixture could secure complexity in derivative compounds without themselves altering or losing their primary homogeneity. Accordingly a number of such theories sprang up, in which the substances selected by the older philosophers were coupled together in pairs. Lucretius notices[2] among such dualistic speculations the combinations of air and fire (Oenopides of Chios), earth and moisture

[1] *E. G. P.3*, p. 180.　　　[2] i. 712–13.

(Xenophanes), and doubtless the changes were rung also on the other possible conjunctions. But a dualism did not open up much greater possibility of variation than the old monism, and the more complete form of pluralism was soon propounded by EMPEDOCLES of Agrigentum, who assumed as the foundation of the world the four 'primary substances', earth, air, fire, and water.[1] The striking character of Empedocles' personality, at once politician, physician, prophet, magician, and mystic, and the great poetical merit of the work in which he expounded his system, admired[2] and indeed imitated long after by Lucretius, have perhaps gained for his theory a greater fame than it deserves. But it was an important step in the long dialogue and suggested conceptions of lasting value, supplying indeed the main basis for the physical theory of Aristotle.

Philosophically Empedocles appears to have regarded himself as a mediator between the system of Parmenides and the evidence of the senses.[3] He admits indeed their insecurity as witnesses of the truth,[4] and urges his disciple not to trust to any one sense rather than another,[5] but at the same time he warns him not to 'refuse his trust to any of the bodily parts, by which there is a path for understanding': the supremely important thing is to 'consider everything in the way in which it is clear'. If we are to press this rather vague 'theory of knowledge', it seems to mean that the understanding is to be the final judge, but its data must come through sense, and sense-evidence after careful consideration must be accepted. In this spirit Empedocles takes Parmenides' conception of the world and asks in what respect it must be modified to correspond with the evidence of the senses. But though Parmenides' position may be his immediate starting-point, he also desires without doubt to place himself in immediate relation with the Ionian Monists. Of his four 'primary substances' Water was the ultimate matter of Thales; Fire of Heraclitus; Earth played a large

[1] D.B. 17, l. 18: see also D.B. 6, where the four substances are introduced under allegorical names.   [2] i. 731-3.
[3] See *E. G. P.*3, p. 227.   [4] D.B. 2.   [5] D.B. 4, ll. 9 ff.

part as a derivative in all the systems, and though Empedocles' Air is no longer the misty or vaporous air (ἀήρ) of
Anaximenes, but the clear Air of the Atmosphere (αἰθήρ), it
was no doubt suggested by it. Further, it may be noticed
that the four new primary substances correspond exactly
to Anaximander's pairs of opposites, the hot and the cold
(i.e. air), the moist and the dry. Empedocles thus clearly
wished his solution to stand in close connexion with the
speculations of all his prominent predecessors.

The four 'primary substances' are all of them, of course,
to be conceived of as purely material or bodily, just as were
the substances of the Monists. But each of them now is
absolutely homogeneous with itself, indestructible, and unchangeable: each bears the marks of eternity which Parmenides had assigned to 'the whole'. In other words Empedocles had reached the conception of an 'element'[1]
(στοιχεῖον): compound things could be separated into matter
which in its turn might be compound, and so on, but ultimately you would come to two or more of the 'four' and beyond
them separation could not proceed. The conception was of
the utmost importance, not only for the Atomic Theory, but
indeed for all future chemical and physical science: though
Empedocles' 'elements' have long ceased to be regarded as
such, the conception still survives. These elements then by
their combinations produced the things of sense: earth
mingling with water, for instance, might make mud, fire and
water vapour and so on. But it soon becomes clear that even
with four elements, the possibilities of difference in compound bodies are greatly limited: this difficulty Empodocles
solved by another of the far-sighted conceptions, which are
really his contribution to knowledge—the elements could
mingle,[2] he saw, in different proportions. Thus the bones
of animals,[3] he thought, were composed of four parts of fire

[1] Empedocles did not himself use the word, but it is constantly employed
by the critics and doxographers, and it is a considerable economy to follow
them.
[2] Gomperz, p. 233, has called attention to the importance of this point.
[3] D.B. 96.

to two of earth and two of water, while in flesh and blood [1]
the three were mingled in equal proportions. By this means
a far greater variety of combinations was made possible and
indeed Empedocles thought that he could thus account for
the whole infinite complexity of phenomena. What we know
then as the birth and death of things is a delusion, in so far
as it implies an actual coming of something into being and
an annihilation: for, as he says, laying down definitely for
the first time the great principle which was really assumed
even in the speculation of his predecessors and was to be
handed on to the Atomists: 'it cannot be that anything should
be created out of that which is not at all, and that that which
is should utterly perish is impossible and unheard of'.[2]
Therefore 'there is no birth of any of mortal things, no, nor
any end of accursed death, but only the mingling and change
of things mingled, and the name of birth is given to this by
men'.[3] The apparent creation of a new thing is only the
coming together of 'elements' which before were separate,
or a shifting of their positions (διάλλαξις) so as to form a
different compound: this again is a conception which was
to be very fruitful in future speculation. Moreover, since
'no part of the whole is empty or overfull',[4] since, that is,
there is no space (the influence of Parmenides is again
visible) and matter is equally distributed over the whole,
the 'shifting of positions' must be regarded as a kind of
kaleidoscopic change, in which the bits of the various elements take each other's places, much as matter has sometimes been conceived to move in 'ether'. All creation and all
dissolution is but a readjustment of the positions of the
particles of the four 'elements'.

Such is the general trend of Empedocles' theory, in which
the influence of the recently established studies of physiology
and medicine is clear enough, leading to an interest in the
structure of individual substances and bodies no less than

---

[1] D.B. 98. These examples illustrate the growing interest in physiology
and medicine, which had a still greater influence, as will be seen, on the
theories of Empedocles' contemporary Anaxagoras.

[2] D.B. 12.   [3] D.B. 8.   [4] D.B. 13.

in the macrocosm of the universe. But Empedocles, like his predecessors, threw his theory into the picturesque form of a great world-process, and it is necessary to consider this briefly, as it exhibits more clearly his relation to previous thinkers and especially to Parmenides. Like him Empedocles conceived of the world as a sphere, 'the spherical and round, rejoicing in its circular solitude'.[1] Within this sphere in origin were all the elements in perfect mixture, mingling one with another in harmony, and as yet there was nothing of a world such as we know, 'there neither the swift limbs of Helios are descried, no, nor the shaggy might of earth nor the sea'.[2] There was no 'division nor unrighteous strife in his (the world's) limbs, but he was equal on every side and quite boundless'[3]—unlike the limited sphere of Parmenides. But besides the four 'elements', Empedocles imagined two other existences, which from his usual manner of speaking of them,[4] he clearly conceived of as equally corporeal, 'accursed Strife, equal in weight everywhere, and Love equal in length and breadth'; the scrupulous reference to weight, length, and breadth seems to proclaim them as the same in kind with the 'elements'. Of these two Love is that which makes for harmony,[5] that is, 'the union of unlikes' (there seems to be a trace of Heraclitus' influence here), and Strife that which makes for discord, the separation of unlikes and the union of like to like. All the six substances were equal and eternal: 'for all these are equal and alike in years, and each has rule over his own prerogative, and to each is his own character. And besides these there is nought that cometh into being or passeth away. . . . They are themselves and nought else (i.e. perfectly pure), but running through one another (i.e. mingling) they become

---

[1] D.B. 27, l. 4.   [2] Ibid., l. 2.

[3] D.B. 27a, 28.

[4] e.g. D.B. 17, ll. 19, 20, which follow immediately after the list of the four 'elements' and suggesting no trace of a distinction in kind between them and Love and Strife.

[5] Once again the influence of physiology is apparent as Empedocles expressly says (l. 22) that Love is 'she who is known as implanted in the limbs of mortals'.

now one thing, now another, yet are ever unceasingly alike.'[1] In the original period of the perfect mixture Love is wholly within the Sphere, mingling with the four and causing their mingling with one another: Strife on the other hand is wholly outside it on the 'extreme bounds of the circle'.[2] But in course of time in accordance with the 'mighty oath'[3] of destiny, 'when Strife had grown to greatness in the limbs of the god', that is, had begun to make its way from outside into the mixture, then 'all the limbs of the god were shaken in turn'.[4] The mixture began to separate out into its constituent elements, and like to join like: 'earth increases its own bulk, and air increases air',[5] and Love which had held the mixture together was gradually driven out of the Sphere. When the process was complete and Strife reigned supreme, the four 'elements' would be wholly distinct. Then would set in the reaction: Love would come back and Strife retire, so that the unlike would again unite with unlike, until at last it returned once more to the perfect mixture from which it started. Thus it will be seen that there are four recurring stages in the world's history, (1) perfect Love, (2) Strife prevailing, (3) perfect Strife, (4) Love prevailing. Now a world of mortal things like ours could not come into being in the first and third periods, either when all the 'elements' were completely mixed or when they were absolutely separated: it can be created and exist only in the second and fourth periods, the intermediate times, when both forces are at work: 'twofold is the birth of mortal things and twofold its passing away: for one generation the coming together of all things brings to birth and destroys, and the other is nourished and scattered as they spread apart again.'[6] Empedocles went into great detail of the differences in creation at these two periods, describing for instance in the case of animals how in the period when Love was gradually gaining the upper hand over Strife, separate limbs would be created which joined themselves in fantastic combinations,[7] but when Strife was vanquishing

---

[1] D.B. 17, ll. 27 ff.   [2] D.B. 35, l. 10.   [3] D.B. 30.   [4] D.B. 31.
[5] D.B. 37.   [6] D.B. 17, ll. 3 ff.   [7] D.B. 57, 59.

Love, indistinguishable and sexless beasts appeared, which gradually separated into distinction of sex and kind. It is not worth while to follow out these ingenious but rather grotesque speculations, but it is worth noting that Empedocles probably placed our present world in the second period, when Strife was entering in and separating the previously mixed elements.

Lucretius' criticism of Empedocles and the pluralists—even if considerable latitude of generalization be allowed him on the understanding that he is dealing with a 'school' and not a single theory—is on the whole of less value than his comment on the Monists. The complaints that they assume motion without allowing empty space,[1] and that they permit infinite division,[2] which ultimately spells destruction, are really anachronistic and are delivered from the Atomist point of view, and a large section of comment[3] is more applicable to the theory of Heraclitus than to that of Empedocles. But there are at least two criticisms which are cogent and help us to estimate the true position of Empedocles. In the first place he argues that the four primal substances are too 'soft'[4] (*mollia*) to act as a basis to the world: we are familiar with earth, air, fire, and water and we see them constantly changing and perishing: the real primal substances cannot be like in constitution to the 'mortal' things of experience. Secondly he maintains that,[5] if these four 'elements' actually change into other things, then they are not real elements, but if they always retain their nature in combination, then they can make nothing else but themselves: in other words, there is still the same difficulty as there was with Monism; you cannot account for change and complexity without destroying the immutable character of the elements. These two criticisms taken together do in fact exhibit the real weakness of the theory of the 'four elements'. On the one hand it has destroyed the old idea of fundamental unity, for it leaves the world fourfold in character, and the permanence of its new basis is very doubtful: on the other hand its pluralism is not

[1] i. 742 ff.   [2] 746 ff.   [3] 782 ff.
[4] 753 ff.   [5] 763 ff.

thoroughgoing enough, for it is in reality no easier to explain the world as we know it with four 'elements' than with one. The true solution must at once offer a greater permanence and unity, it must be more Monistic; and it must also afford far greater possibilities of complex combination and consequent variety, it must be an infinitely more genuine pluralism. Yet Empedocles' theory was at least a step out of the Parmenidean *impasse*: it showed the direction in which speculation must now move and suggested incidentally a number of new interests and novel conceptions, which were to be of lasting value.

§ 3. *The Pluralists—Anaxagoras*

The highly ingenious and in many ways far-sighted theory of Anaxagoras of Clazomenae, who although Empedocles' senior in years,[1] published his work later, stands in a sense alone in the history of Greek scientific thought. No other theory directly led up to it, and, as far as we know, he had no followers. Yet on the one hand it very markedly brought speculation a stage nearer Atomism, on the other it was equally clearly the outcome of the conditions of thought in his time. Empedocles had shown that the only hope of progress lay in abandoning a strict Ionian monism, which Parmenides' logic had shown to be impossible, and assuming a pluralism in the ultimate constituents. The world of sensible things, with all its variety and movement and change, could not be accounted for by the postulate of a single continuous substance underlying them: it could better be explained by supposing four ultimate elements. Yet even they were not sufficient, a more thoroughgoing pluralism was required. Anaxagoras[2] was prepared to meet this requirement without reserve, his pluralism was absolutely complete: 'he said that the first-beginnings were infinite'.[3] We

---

[1] Arist. *Metaphys. A.* 3. 984 a; D.A. 43 τῇ μὲν ἡλικίᾳ πρότερος ὢν τούτου, τοῖς δ' ἔργοις ὕστερος, ἀπείρους εἶναί φησι τὰς ἀρχάς.

[2] It will be noticed that in many points my account of Anaxagoras' theory differs from those ordinarily given : I have attempted to justify it in Appendix I.

[3] See n. 1.

are no longer, that is, to think of the primary existence as
a single mass of homogeneous substance, nor even of four
such masses capable of breaking up and intermingling with
one another in different proportions, but rather of an unlimited number of small particles. Nor are these 'seeds' of
things homogeneous in substance and quality, but again
almost infinitely different—for there are 'seeds' corresponding to every known form of corporeal matter. In other words
all existing things are formed of 'particles like to wholes'
(ὁμοιομέρειαι), so that, as Lucretius[1] explains in the rather
crude form in which he first sets out the theory, 'he thinks
that bones are made of very small and tiny bones and flesh of
small and tiny pieces of flesh, and blood is created of many
drops of blood coming together in union, and that gold
again can be built up of grains of gold, and the earth grow
together of little earths, that fire is made of fires and water
of water-drops, and all the rest he pictures and imagines in
the same way'. This is the utmost limit of pluralism in a
double sense: for not merely are the particles infinite in
number (and indeed every particle is infinitely divisible[2]),
but there is almost infinite variety in the nature of their
substance—a variety only limited by that of the world of
experience: the old notion of unity seems to be thrown to
the winds. Nor again, if this simple and reckless pluralism
were the whole truth of Anaxagoras' view, would it account
at all, as Lucretius[3] points out, for the phenomena of change:
for if bread, for instance, be entirely composed of minute
particles of bread-substance and nothing else, how can it
ever, when we eat it, become, as it clearly does, our flesh
and blood?

Now it was exactly this question of the phenomena of
change which was Anaxagoras' own great interest: for the
physiological and medical investigations of the new schools
of Magna Graecia and Sicily had transferred the scene of
action, as it were, from heaven to the human body, and
focussed attention on alteration and development. At the
same time the logical monism of Parmenides was still influ-

[1] i. 835 ff.   [2] D.B. 3, see below, p. 37.   [3] 859 ff.

ential enough to secure the recognition as the very starting-point of inquiry of the principle of the permanence of matter: 'nothing is created out of nothing'. If then Anaxagoras' theory is to be rightly understood, it must be viewed much more as an attempt to reconcile the observed changes of matter with an assured underlying permanence than as a protest in favour of complete pluralism against the Monism of the Ionians and the tentative advance of Empedocles. For it is indeed a far more subtle speculation than it is represented as being by Lucretius and most of its modern critics. Anaxagoras faithfully repeats the ultimate principle of Parmenides, 'it is impossible, he says, for what is not to be',[1] but from this premise he is led to a conclusion very different from that of Parmenides. He applied the principle at once in the field of physiology. There he observed that the food which we eat is apparently transformed into flesh, blood, bones, and so on, and he asked himself how this can be.[2] In appearance the process involves the perishing of one substance and the creation of another, but this is inconsistent with the root-principle: 'how',[3] he exclaims in one of the few extant fragments, 'could hair be created out of what is not hair or flesh out of what is not flesh?' It is impossible, and the only explanation of the phenomenon is that hair and flesh and the rest must already have been present in the food. With this start Anaxagoras constructed a theory of the constitution and behaviour of the universe and all it contains, based on the widest possible extension of the conclusion he had thus reached: 'there is a portion ($\mu o \hat{\iota} \rho a$) of everything in everything'.[4] It seemed to him as he saw the vast number of apparent transformations of substance in the world around him that everything must have in it the potentiality of changing into anything else, and this could only be the case if it already contained everything in itself.

But at this point his theory appeared to be contradicted by the evidence of the senses. We observe concrete things

---

[1] D.B. 3.
[2] Simpl. in Arist. *Phys. Γ.* 4. 203; D.A. 45: cf. Aet. i. 3. 5; D.A. 46.
[3] D.B. 10.   [4] Simpl. in Arist. *Phys. A.* 2. 184 (27. 2); D.A. 41.

as homogeneous wholes. If we take a piece of bread and crumble it up even into minute particles, these particles remain bread and nothing else. But if the reason why bread when eaten can produce flesh and blood is in truth that it already contains them, then, as Lucretius[1] urged in his naïve criticism, we ought to perceive drops of blood when we grind corn, and milk when we cut up the grass on which the cattle graze: how is it that we do not? Because, answered Anaxagoras, 'everything is and was most manifestly (ἐνδηλό- τατα) those things of which it has most in it'.[2] It is quite true that bread contains in it portions of everything, but because the portions of bread greatly exceed in number and bulk those of any other thing, it has throughout the appearance and character of bread and nothing else. The subordinate portions, even those of the bodily substances which bread may become, are so minute and so scattered in among the prevailing portions of bread, that they not merely are not perceived but never could be perceptible or manifest (ἔνδηλα)— they are, in fact, as a later commentator puts it in his own phraseology only, 'perceptible in thought'.[3]

Here Anaxagoras might well have stopped, and indeed many critics think he did, but his thought was nothing if not thoroughgoing. Just as he extended his discovery that portions of bodily substances were latent in food to the wide generalization that there is a portion of everything in everything, so here having noted that the smallest perceptible particle of bread was still bread, he pushed his view to its logical conclusion. There is, he held, no limit to division: 'there is no least of what is small, but always a smaller';[4] you can go on dividing and dividing and never reach a particle so minute that after it you come to nothing: 'there are an equal number of portions in the great and the small',[5] for in both the portions are infinite. This acceptance of infinite divisibility creates a new difficulty: for how then can there still be portions of 'everything in everything'? If you only

[1] i. 881.   [2] Simpl. in Arist. *Phys.* l.c.
[3] λόγῳ θεωρητά, Aet. i. 3. 5; D.A. 46.
[4] D.B. 3.   [5] D.B. 6.

go on dividing long enough you must come to particles of pure bread or pure flesh or blood. If Anaxagoras had had no other idea of composition than mere juxtaposition, there would be no escape from this difficulty: infinite division would be incompatible with the belief in 'everything in everything': for sooner or later, though it might be far below the ken of the senses, you must reach particles which will no longer contain everything, indeed ultimately particles which will be but one thing. Modern critics have adopted many expedients to escape from this *impasse*, but there is, as far as I can see, only one way out of it and that is the supposition that the ultimate constitution of things is not a mere juxta-position of particles, but a fusion in which the identity of the individual particle is merged in the identity of the whole; not, to use Anaxagoras' own terms, a mere combination (σύγκρισις), but a mixture (σύμμιξις). There is good evidence[1] to show that this was in fact Anaxagoras' solution. In the ulti-mate constitution of matter 'all things' were mixed together in a fusion, and the concrete world of experience consists of substances made up of bits of this fusion combined not now in a fresh fusion, but in juxtaposition. These bits, which Anaxagoras called 'the seeds' of things, or more technically the 'homoeomeries', were not, of course, like the atoms of the later theory, irreducible minima: they might be split up and divided to infinity, but seeing that they contained 'all things' in fusion, however much they might be so divided, the very smallest particle would still contain all things, would still be a 'seed' or 'homoeomery'. Thus the principle of infinite division was made reconcilable with the belief that 'there is a portion of everything in everything'.

The 'things' thus fused in the 'seeds' were just the con-crete substances of the world of sense, and at this point Anaxagoras shows that he wished his theory to embrace the ideas of his predecessors: for included among these 'things' are the 'opposites' of Anaximander, the cold and the hot, the moist and the dry, and so on, and the elements of Empe-docles, as well as all other substances, bone, flesh, gold,

[1] See Appendix I.

wood, rock, &c., which are met with in the experience of sense. But the seeds, though all absolutely alike in being a fusion of all things, differed in character according to proportions in which the 'things' were fused in them: there would thus be a 'gold-seed', for instance, containing the fusion of all things, but dominated by the presence of gold, a 'bone-seed' in which bone was in the ascendant: once again each 'seed' 'is those things of which it has most of it'. And in this difference of character between seed and seed lies the explanation of the phenomena of change. The compound body consists of 'seeds' united in combination (σύγκρισις): once again in the compound there are 'seeds' of all things, but its character is determined by the prevailing 'seed': bread has seeds in which every other 'thing' in turn prevails, but the majority of its 'seeds' are those in which bread prevails, and the other 'seeds', minute and scattered, are latent and never perceptible, so that the whole has the character of bread. Nor are the alien 'seeds' equal in number: there are more 'seeds' of one kind than another even among those in a minority: more of those substances into which the whole substance is liable to change, or rather which it is able to produce out of itself, and fewer of others. Bread has most 'bread-seeds', then next most of 'flesh-seeds' and 'bone-seeds', and so on, and very few, say, of 'gold-seeds' and 'rock-seeds'. Hence when violent external force is applied, as in the process of eating, the alien 'seeds' are 'separated out' (ἐκκρίνεται) from the compound substance and joining the like-seeds in the body become part of a new substance in which now they are in turn the prevailing 'thing'. In this way it is possible to understand the apparent birth of a new substance without imagining it to be created out of the non-existent: birth is only the breaking up (διάκρισις) of a previous compound and the union of the latent 'seeds' in it in a new compound (σύγκρισις). The theory is subtle and complicated but clear: the individual 'seeds' (σπέρματα) have portions (μοῖραι) of all things in fusion, but in each some one thing prevails: the compound body is formed of seeds in juxtaposition, but in each body 'seeds' of one kind are in the majority with others latent among them themselves varying in number and kind. By this highly ingenious system, which has been greatly misinterpreted by his critics, Anaxagoras felt that he had satisfied the conditions required of it: he had accounted for variety and change without destroying ultimate permanence by the admission of creation or destruction.

Like Empedocles, Anaxagoras was not content with his physical system without working it out in an account of the universe and the creation of ordered worlds from it. It is the more important to consider this briefly, because not only have we more copious information about it than about other parts of the system, but it is in fact the necessary antecedent of the physical theory: without it the notion of the 'seeds', their character and combinations would be a merely arbitrary assumption. The 'ultimate substance' of the universe, in Anaxagoras' view, is just the original fusion ($\mu\epsilon\hat{\imath}\gamma\mu\alpha$) of the portions of all things: 'all things were together infinite in bulk and in smallness: for the small too was infinite. And since all things were together, no one thing was manifest owing to its smallness'.[1] The fusion was complete, and the fused particles of all things indistinguishable. Yet even here, though every part of the fusion contained all things, different 'things' prevailed in different parts, and in the mixture as a whole 'mist and sky ruled, for they are the greatest in the universe both in bulk and size': the universal fusion, that is, was, like all other things, 'those things of which it had most in it'. But there was one 'thing' which did not enter into the universal fusion, and this was 'Mind' ($\nu o\hat{\upsilon}\varsigma$),[2] which Anaxagoras conceived of as a corporeal substance, much of the same nature as Empedocles' Love and Strife. 'Mind' remained 'alone by itself', not that it was apart altogether from the mixture, but though it was disseminated in it, it did not fuse with the other 'things' but kept pure. 'Mind', then, wherever it was present caused a movement of extreme swiftness,[3] which took the form of a rotation,[4] first of all of a small portion of matter, then of more

[1] D.B. 1.   [2] D.B. 12.   [3] D.B. 9.   [4] D.B. 12.

and more in an ever-increasing whirl. As the result of this movement bits of the fused mass were caught up in the whirl and 'separated off', and these bits were of course the 'seeds'. Each portion as being a part of the fusion contained everything, but according to the part of the mass from which it came, differed in its prevailing thing: the portions separated off were thus the 'seeds of all things, having every kind of form and colour and savour (ἡδονή)'.[1] The next step is that the 'seeds' are separated apart from one another:[2] those of different kinds tended to come away from one another. Then like joined like:[3] 'seeds' of the same kind came together and formed the compound bodies of the world; yet not even then were they absolutely alone but took with them in lesser proportions 'seeds' of all other things. The new compound body contains again 'seeds' of all things, but is 'that of which there is most in it'. The detailed process of world-formation is like that described by earlier thinkers, but has Anaxagoras' own stamp: the first things[4] to be separated off are mist and sky, which prevailed in the original fusion. Then 'from clouds water is separated off, from water earth, and from earth stones are solidified by the cold'.[5] Gradually these separated elements began to form themselves into a world, 'the dense and the moist and the cold and the dark come together where the earth is now, and the thin and the warm and the dry (and the light) went out to the farther part of the ether'[6] and these formed the heavenly bodies. Thus our world was created and of course a similar process is taking place in other parts of the universe as well, nor is even our world complete, for 'the rotation goes on and will go on more and more'.[7] Not only then is there a complete parallelism between the nature of the macrocosm and that of the 'seed', but the nature of the 'seed' is the necessary outcome of its origin as a casual fragment of the universal fusion, broken off in the whirl.

Lucretius' criticism of Anaxagoras is largely vitiated by his misunderstanding of its true import. Starting, as was

[1] D.B. 4, § 1.   [2] D.B. 13.   [3] D.B. 14.   [4] D.B. 2.
[5] D.B. 16.   [6] D.B. 15.   [7] D.B. 12.

seen above, from the notion that Anaxagoras' main contention was that compound things were constituted of particles
'each exactly resembling the whole' (a misinterpretation of
homoeomeria), he then charges him with trying to avoid
the difficulty of change by the poor expedient of supposing
that 'all things are mingled in all things',[1] and criticizing
this idea in its crudest form complains that in that case substances ought to give some indication of the alien matter
which they contain. But, as has been shown, it was just this
question of change which was Anaxagoras' primary interest
and the theory which he proposed to meet it was far more
subtle than the naïve 'expedient' suggested by Lucretius.
Whether it was that Epicurus and his followers felt that
Anaxagoras' theory was dangerously like their own and in
their efforts to discredit it intentionally distorted its meaning,
we cannot tell: in any case their traditional criticism is beside
the mark. There is, however, one point in Lucretius' attack
which is of interest and value. He complains once more,[2]
as he did in the case of Empedocles, that the primary particles
which Anaxagoras supposed, being like in character to compound things, are 'too feeble' (*nimis imbecilla*). Here he
touches on a real weakness in the theory: if ultimate particles
are to be permanent they cannot be like in character to the
things which are constantly coming into being and passing
away: as Anaximander saw long before, the primary substance cannot be 'water or air or fire or anything else'. Such
criticism leads at once to an atomic conclusion: if primary
particles are to be the secret of creation, they must be, like
Anaximander's 'boundless', something lying behind all
created things, different from and prior to them all.

The theory of Anaxagoras takes us from the infinitely
great to the infinitely small. No longer does he set up as the
ultimate matter some one all-pervading substance, but an
infinite number of minute particles, each in their turn containing infinitely tinier 'portions' of all concrete things fused
together in a homogeneous whole. Ionian Monism is completely deserted and the half-hearted pluralism of Empe-

[1] i. 875 ff.   [2] i. 847 ff.

docles is scouted as insufficient to account alike for the variety of things and for the changes of experience. With the adoption of an infinite pluralism the way is definitely prepared for Atomism. Yet for all its nearness in this respect, the theory of Anaxagoras is in others the very antipodes of Atomism. Anaxagoras wholly abandoned any thought of fundamental unity, except in so far as all the 'seeds' had once been part of a single universal fusion of 'everything'. It was the distinguishing note of Atomism to return once more to a fundamental unity, not by seeking, as did the earlier philosophies, for a single ultimate 'nature', but by postulating an absolute homogeneity of substance in the infinite particles and referring variety to difference in their shape and combinations. Anaxagoras again insisted on infinite division: so great was his fear of admitting a dissolution which might result in annihilation that he postulated an infinite progress to smaller and smaller. Atomism, believing permanence to be as essential to a right conception of the universe as unity insisted on a minimum: unless there were a limit to division, annihilation, it held, must result, because there could be no stability. The contrasts of the two systems are instructive· the very logical completeness of Anaxagoras' theory suggested the points in which it was practically untenable. After all, for all its ingenuity and consistency, the theory is complicated and arbitrary: it must make way for a system at once more economical and more acceptable to common sense.

It is well at this point to pause for a moment in order briefly to summarize the progress of thought hitherto and to consider what was the main problem which lay before the contemporaries of Anaxagoras. The original question of Thales 'what is the ultimate matter of which the world is composed?' had led to a series of answers so varied and complex that it is not easy at once to disentangle the thread of logical advance which does in fact run through these varied speculations. In the first stages a strong feeling—in origin doubtless religious—had led thinkers to proclaim the fundamental unity of the world and to look for it in some one homogeneous and continuous substance. But it was soon realized that this insistence on the physical reality of the One made it impossible to explain the normal appearance of the Many: if there is but one substance, how can there be variety and change? To obviate this difficulty various expedients were suggested—a boundless indefinite substance outside the world, which, when its nature is analysed, appears to be more like a mixture of many things than one, or a process of rarefaction and condensation, which however will not produce the Many, but only more or less of the One. Similarly the 'upward and downward path' of Heraclitus is seen to be little else than a disguised pluralism, and the strict logic of Parmenides shows that if the doctrine of the One is to be seriously maintained, it involves the denial of all the most common experiences of sensation, of the separation and division of things, of motion and of change.

Monism is accordingly abandoned and experiments made in pluralistic theories. At first, with Empedocles, pluralism seemed not to go far enough: for while on the one hand it had successfully destroyed the fundamental unity, yet it could not sufficiently account for multiplicity and change. To meet this comes the infinite pluralism of Anaxagoras, which in a most uneconomical theory of the ultimate nature of the world, seems to sweep away altogether any idea of an underlying unity.

It is clear that thought cannot stop here: a more satisfactory theory must be evolved. What is required is a system which can in some way reconcile this 'strife of opposites' which has run through the whole debate. It must establish a pluralism which will explain variety and change, yet preserve a fundamental unity: it must allow separation and division, yet insist on permanence: it must maintain the infinity and eternity of the universe, yet explain the creation and destruction of a limited world. In short, as the Eleatic Melissus observed,[1] stoutly maintaining the Parmenidean Monism against the ideas of the pluralists: 'if there were many, they would be bound to be each one of them such as

[1] D.B. 8.

I say the one is': the only kind of pluralism is one in which each particle may have the unity and permanence of the Parmenidean whole. This, as Burnet[1] has pointed out, is in reality the exact formula of Atomism, and the way is now prepared for Leucippus.

§ 4. *Subordinate Problems*

Hitherto the theories of the early philosophers have been considered only in so far as by their main ideas they led up to the central notion of Atomism. But side by side with these main ideas there had gradually developed a mass of speculation dealing with many topics more or less closely related to them and spreading, as almost every philosopher in turn added some new sphere of investigation, over a wide field of thought and inquiry. It has already been necessary to observe how they all supplemented their general notion of the universe with some more or less exact speculation as to the process by which the world was created, speculation which in many cases throws considerable light on the main idea of the ultimate form of existence. Not content with this from the first they elaborated their notions of the world with a wealth of usually disconnected conjectures as to the causes of individual phenomena terrestrial and celestial. Even Thales is credited with views on such diverse topics as the causes of eclipses, of the Nile flood, and of the action of the magnet, and very soon every respectable philosopher was expected to have his views as to the disposition and movements of the heavenly bodies, meteorological phenomena and a variety of normal and abnormal occurrences on earth. Soon too speculation arose as to certain wider and more vital problems more closely related to the main developments of thought. Worlds, it was held, or at any rate our world was developed out of a primary substance or substances or fusion: what was the ultimate cause which set the process in motion? Or again, when the answers of philosophers as to the constitution of the universe became more and more remote from

[1] *E. G. P.3*, p. 328.

the apparent experience of everyday life, they asked, not unnaturally, what is the source of our knowledge? Does it come through the senses or by thought? And this led to the kindred question, what is the nature of our senses and our mind and what is their relation to the outer world and to its ultimate truths? With the great mass of speculations relating to terrestrial and celestial[1] phenomena it would be outside the scope of the present work to attempt to deal: for although they too find their place in the theories of the Atomists and Epicurus and must be briefly considered there, they lie for the most part outside the main current of thought, and conjecture is usually so sporadic that previous ideas cannot in any definite way be said to have led up to the views of Leucippus and Democritus. On the other hand the broader problems of the ultimate cause, the processes of perception and thought and the theory of knowledge lie so close to the main questions and played so large a part in the views of the Atomists and above all of Epicurus, that it is necessary to make some attempt to gather up shortly the threads of previous speculation.

A. *The efficient cause.*

The question of the efficient cause of the creation of a world or worlds out of the primary substance did not at once emerge into prominence as a scientific problem. This apparent reticence on a point which afterwards became of primary importance is no doubt due to the origin of philosophy in religion.[2] The primary substance is itself regarded at first not as so much inanimate matter which must be worked on by an outside power and set in motion in order to produce change and so creation, but rather as a kind of living thing with half-mysterious powers, which by the force which is in it can move and change. 'Everything',[3] said Thales in this spirit, 'is full of gods', for he thought, as Aristotle

---

[1] For speculations on astronomical and meteorological subjects see especially O. Gilbert, *Die meteorologischen Theorien des griechischen Alterthums.*

[2] See Cornford, op. cit., and especially pp. 4 ff.

[3] Arist. *de Anima, A.* 5. 411a; D.A. 22.

explains, that 'soul is mingled in the whole': the primary substance is indeed not merely the body out of which the world is made, but also the soul which animates and moves it. And this semi-theological attitude persisted throughout the speculations of the pre-Atomic philosophers, more or less prominent according to the personal bent of the individual thinkers, but never wholly abandoned. Thus Xenophanes, the bitter opponent of traditional mythology, yet speaks of the world, whose intrinsic unity he proclaimed, as 'one god', and the same theological conception is apparent in the 'perfect sphere' of Parmenides. But side by side with this theological notion, as it were painfully emerging from it by degrees, arises the more strictly scientific conception of the world, in which it was felt that causes must be sought for in phenomena themselves regarded as a natural and not a supernatural manifestation. It is not easy to trace the growth of the scientific idea, partly because it never wholly separates itself from religion, and partly because no steady development can be found in a series of philosophers whose points of view at all periods differed so widely that a recent writer[1] has felt justified in distinguishing a scientific from a mystic tradition among them. Our authorities too are vague on the point, but we can at least discover the main ideas which were current and so realize the problem which lay before the more definitely materialist thinkers of the Atomic School. Nothing is more remarkable than the complex interaction of the two impulses, religious and scientific, and the strange contrasts of attitude which they exhibit.

The Milesian thinkers are at once nearest in time to the early religious conceptions out of which philosophy springs, and also the most determined in their efforts to get free from it. With all of them the primary substance is described in definitely material terms, the 'water' of Thales, the 'air' of Anaximenes, even the 'boundless' of Anaximander, which, as has been seen, is to be regarded as a material body intermediate in nature between what were later known as the elements. And so, when we look among the records of their

[1] Cornford, op. cit.

theories for a trace of the efficient cause of creation, we find similarly that it is stated to be 'eternal motion'.[1] Here at the outset of speculation is an idea which was to be of lasting value: the primary substance is regarded as something which in its own nature is static, and it is the action of motion upon it which causes the breaking up and mingling and revolution which gives rise to the creation of ordered worlds (κόσμοι). We seem too to be dealing with a definitely physical conception, intended to explain creation as the work of natural causes working within material body. And yet, if examination is to be pressed a little farther, the result does not appear by any means so certain. In the first place, as Burnet[2] has shown in the case of Anaximander, it is not likely that the Milesians themselves spoke of 'eternal motion': this is rather the interpretation of their ideas in the terminology of a later age, accustomed to look to motion as the cause of change. In the second, even if they had the idea of motion as the immediate efficient cause, it is clearly necessary to go behind it and ask 'what was the cause of the motion?' We cannot in the case of the Milesians give any definite answer, but if Anaximander's own account of the process of creation be examined, hints may certainly be discovered of a rather different underlying conception. The 'opposites' 'separate out' from the 'boundless' and the world is maintained in equilibrium by their strife duly held in balance; 'they make reparation and satisfaction to one another for their injustice according to the appointed time'.[3] This language, as Cornford[4] has pointed out, is really animistic, if not definitely theological: its mythical counterpart is to be found in the legends of the division of the universe between the gods, and the real underlying idea is that of 'due portion' (μοῖρα). We seem then to have a physical conception set, as it were, in a religious background, but implicitly, at any rate, the notion of a primary motion has been established.

[1] Κίνησις ἀΐδιος. Of Anaximander, Hipp. *Ref.* i. 6. 2; D. 11; of Anaximenes, Simpl. in Arist. *Phys. A.* 2. 184 (24. 26); D.A. 5.
[2] *E. G. P.*3, p. 61.
[3] Simpl. in Arist. *Phys. A.* 2. 184 (24. 13); D. 9.   [4] pp. 10 ff.

The arbitrary and almost mystic theory of Heraclitus
might well prepare us to find in him a definitely religious
conception of the efficient cause. It is therefore at first sight
astonishing that the doxographers[1] attribute to him the
notion of necessity (ἀνάγκη) as the ultimate controlling force:
for 'necessity' in the hands of Democritus becomes the
equivalent of 'natural law', the most fully scientific conception in Greek philosophy, associated with a complete determinism. Can it be that in Heraclitus there was anything
resembling this notion? Again, a closer examination considerably weakens the confident statement of the doxographers. In the first place notice its application[2] to the
fantastic notion of the upward and downward path, the
'exchange' of all things with fire: in connexion with so
arbitrary a theory, definitely opposed to the experience of
normal sensation, it is impossible that 'necessity' can have
anything like the idea of 'natural law': it is at most, as it will
be seen to be in some of Heraclitus' successors, an extraneous
and arbitrary power, a kind of deus ex machina, called in to
produce results which would otherwise seem improbable.
Secondly, it may be observed that in both passages 'necessity'
is connected with 'destiny' (εἱμαρμένη): now 'destiny'[3] is a
much more clearly religious conception, and suggests at
once the arbitrary external force. And when we look to
Heraclitus' own fragments for an explanation, it appears at
once in the same conception of the 'due portion' of things
which was seen in Anaximander to have a direct origin in
religious notions: 'the fire is kindled in due measures and
in due measures extinguished:'[4] 'the sun will not exceed
his due measures'.[5] 'Necessity', 'destiny', is but a physical

---

[1] Aet. i. 27. 1; D.A. 8 : Ἡράκλειτος πάντα καθ᾽ εἱμαρμένην, τὴν δὲ
αὐτὴν ὑπάρχειν καὶ ἀνάγκην.   Simpl. in Arist. Phys. A. 2. 184 (23. 33);
D.A. 5 ; ποιεῖ δὲ καὶ τάξιν τινὰ καὶ χρόνον ὡρισμένον τῆς τοῦ κόσμου
μεταβολῆς κατά τινα εἱμαρμένην ἀνάγκην.
[2] This is its context in the passage from Simplicius.
[3] Aetius' identification of Heraclitus' εἱμαρμένη with λόγος in a passage
(i. 28. 1; D.A. 8) where he is avowedly following Poseidonius may be dismissed as an obvious Stoic interpretation.
[4] D.B. 30.   [5] D.B. 94.

application of the old religious equilibrium. Yet, for all that, since it so presented itself to later commentators, it is not unreasonable to see in Heraclitus the germ of the notion of 'necessity' emerging from a religious background, just as with the Milesians appeared the first traces of 'eternal motion'.

In Parmenides the same notion of 'necessity' as an extraneous force binding the world into certain definite forms appears again. Parmenides' 'One' was of course motionless and external: no cause is therefore required to start the motion which leads to creation, but, on the other hand, as a kind of violent contradiction of the views of his predecessors, he announces[1] that it is just 'Necessity' which ordains that the world shall be motionless. When it is seen that 'necessity' appears in his poems also as 'the due measure'[2] (Μοῖρα) and 'Justice'[3] (Δίκη), and that the doxographers[4] identify it not only with 'destiny' (εἱμαρμένη) but also with 'providence' (πρόνοια), it is clear that the conception is more definitely theological than it was in Heraclitus: the constraining force is super-physical and its action is arbitrary. Similarly in Empedocles we hear of 'Necessity'[5] and also of 'the mighty oath'[6] as the controlling cause of the succession of Strife and Love, an even more clearly personified expression of the theological notion.

Yet for all his theological and mystical bent Empedocles gives us also the germ of new ideas, and that in two directions. Firstly, although 'Necessity' and 'The mighty oath' lie in the background as the ultimate forces of the universe, yet he is not content, like his predecessors, to make them the immediate efficient causes of the changes which bring about the creation of the world. As if he saw that such a cause must be looked for in the physical constitution of the universe itself, he attributes the actual alterations in the whole to the action of the physical causes, Strife and Love. They, like the four elements, are corporeal existences, part of the physical structure of the universe itself; they act indeed

---

[1] D.B. 8, l. 30.   [2] Ibid., l. 37.   [3] Ibid., l. 14.
[4] Aet. i. 25. 3; D.A. 32.
[5] Arist. de Gen. et Corr. B. 6. 334 a.   [6] D.B. 30, l. 3.

under the control of the 'mighty oath', but are in themselves within and a part of the material whole. Fantastic as it may be, this notion is clearly an advance towards the conception of 'natural law' and of a world controlled, immediately at any rate, by the principles and constitution of its own being. Secondly, in Empedocles for the first time appears the conception of 'chance'[1] ($\tau \acute{\nu} \chi \eta$): 'the air',[2] he says in the course of his explanation of creation, 'sank down upon the earth, for thus it happened to be running at that time', and a similar account was given of the 'accidental' putting together of animals. Here we seem to have a notion of the casual action of the natural world, and although he was blamed for it both by Plato[3] and Aristotle,[4] the idea is clearly an attempt to get away from the religious conception of an invariable arbitrary guidance, and was destined to play a considerable part in the system of Epicurus.

Anaxagoras in this respect as in others stands largely alone, yet he more definitely carries out the scientific tendency begun by Empedocles. Motion he definitely establishes as the cause of the creation of worlds out of the 'mixture', and even more clearly seeks the cause of motion in something which is itself a part of the physical universe. The old religious bias may perhaps be seen in a weakened form in his selection for this purpose of 'mind', yet, as has been noticed, he understood 'mind' as something purely corporeal. Just as in his main theory, in spite of its great unlikeness to Atomism, Anaxagoras opened the way to a complete pluralism, so in his scientific conception of the world he drew very close to the materialism of Democritus.

The Atomists then received the problem of the efficient cause in a somewhat complex form. Science had as yet by no means shaken itself free of religion: the notion of a mysterious and arbitrary controlling force constraining the world into certain forms almost by its own whim, and the idea of the partition of the universe between contending 'natures' held in balance by a kind of supernatural compact

---

[1] D.B. 103.　　　[2] D.B. 53.　　　[3] *Laws*, x. 889 b; D.A. 48.
[4] *Phys. B.* 8. 198 b.

were both close to the surface in the speculation of their predecessors. On the other hand there were adumbrations of more purely physical conceptions, in which the controlling force lay within the physical world and was itself a part of it. And here the choice seemed threefold: it might be that there were physical principles subordinate to, yet closely connected with, an external controlling force like Empedocles' 'Love and Strife' or Anaxagoras' 'Mind', or that the effects of nature were produced by an as yet ill-defined 'chance', or that there was a supreme 'destiny' or 'necessity', manifested indeed in the physical world and universal in it, yet in itself not an unconditional sequence of causality but still a somewhat arbitrary constraint. It was one of the most important contributions of the Atomists to philosophical thought that they were able out of these contradictory data to evolve something like a genuinely scientific principle of law.

B. *The Senses and the Mind.*

It is clear that the two remaining problems, that of the nature of our senses and our mind and the processes of their perception and thought, and that of the validity of these processes as a criterion of truth are closely connected, and the views held of either must to a considerable extent be affected by the attitude adopted towards the other. Yet, as has been recently pointed out,[1] the connexion between metaphysics and psychology among the Greek philosophers is not nearly as intimate as might be expected, and it is quite possible to consider the two questions separately. It will be convenient therefore to deal first with the senses and the mind and their activities, and then with theories of the cognition of truth. Both play an integral part in the views of the Atomists and lie at the very root of the system of Epicurus.

A theory of sensation is attributed first to Parmenides,[2]

---

[1] Beare, *Greek Theories of Elementary Cognition*, p. 2 : the full and interesting account of the views of Empedocles and Anaxagoras in this work is of great value.

[2] Theophrastus, *de Sensu*, 1 ff.; D.A. 46—the chief authority throughout for the details of the theory of perception.

but seeing that it is derived from that part of his poem which dealt with the Way of Opinion, and probably therefore represents not his own views but those of the Pythagoreans,[1] and that the theory agrees in the main with that of Empedocles, he may in a brief survey be neglected: but he must be remembered as evidence that the elaborate theory of Empedocles does not stand alone at the very outset of inquiry, but that there had been considerable previous speculation, as indeed we otherwise know from the accounts which have survived of the views of Alcmaeon of Croton.[2] For the present purpose, however, it will be sufficient to summarize the theories of Empedocles and Anaxagoras, as they will show the ideas prevalent among the contemporaries of the Atomists.

The views of Empedocles are of course conditioned by his general theory, according to which all concrete things are made of the combination of the four elements 'running through' each other:[3] each piece, that is, of one of the elements had in it pores or cracks into which pieces of the other entered. Sensation then must be produced in the same way: there are, he thought, 'emanations'[4] ($\dot{a}\pi o\rho\rho o a\acute{\iota}$) constantly being given off by 'all things that are created', and these emanations enter into the pores of other created things. Sensation does not of course result on all occasions, but only —and this was the cardinal point in Empedocles' theory— when like meets like,[5] when the 'emanation' that is, 'fits'[6] exactly into the pore which it enters. The whole notion is thus essentially physical and material and sensation of every kind rests ultimately upon touch,[7] of which, like most of the other early Greek philosophers, he gives no special account, thinking doubtless that its nature was too obvious to require explanation.

The general idea may best be illustrated from Empedocles' explanation of vision, of which we have a full account

[1] See *E. G. P.*3, p. 184.
[2] See D., pp. 131 ff.; *E. G. P.*3. 193–6; Beare, pp. 11, 93, 130, 160, 180, 203, 251. [3] D.B. 21. 13–14. [4] D.B. 89.
[5] D.B. 90; Theophr. 2; D.A. 86. [6] Ibid. 7. [7] Ibid. 9.

in Theophrastus and several important fragments of Empedocles himself. It is based,[1] like all early theories, on a primitive analysis of the eye itself as consisting of a fiery element (of which we are conscious when we 'see stars'), and a watery element surrounding it: it is however noticeable that Empedocles makes no use of the observation of the image in the pupil, which plays a large part in other theories.[2] The eye, like all other things, is compounded of the four elements;[3] the fire is set in the middle, and an elaborate description[4] shows how it is protected from the surrounding water by 'delicate tissues', which have fine pores through which the fire may pass, like the flame in a lantern. Of the four elements like then perceives like: 'for with earth we see earth, with water water, and with air divine air, and with fire destroying fire',[5] the incoming emanations fitting, we must suppose, into the pores of the corresponding element. Empedocles further realized that what we see is really colour, and he appears to have recognized four primary colours,[6] white, black, red, green, corresponding to the four elements out of which all colours were composed:[7] it is at any rate clear that he held that the dark element of water in the eye perceived dark things,[8] and the fiery element light things. So far the eye is regarded as purely passive, perceiving the emanations which fitted respectively into the pores of the several elements: but there is no doubt that Empedocles also held the view that the fire in the eye passed outwards and as it were actively grasped things.[9] It is a little difficult to reconcile the two theories, and accounts of Empedocles' view may have been contaminated by the similar theory of Plato,[10] but we seem here to have a first trace of the distinction between mere passive 'seeing' and active 'looking' which was to become so prominent in the psychology of Epicurus. He further recognized that the eyes of different

[1] Beare, pp. 9, 10.   [2] Ibid., p. 15.   [3] Theophr. 7.
[4] D.B. 84.   [5] D.B. 109.   [6] Stob. *Ecl.* 1. 16. 3.
[7] D.B. 71.   [8] Theophr. 7.
[9] D.B. 84, l. 11; and Arist. *de Sensu*, 2. 437 b.
[10] *Timaeus*, 45 b: see Beare, p. 17; and *E. G. P.*3 248.

animals and even of different persons were differently constituted and therefore better or worse suited to perceive different
things:[1] they may even perceive the same thing differently,
an admission which was to have important consequences.

The other senses were explained by Empedocles on the
same general lines. Hearing[2] was caused by 'emanations' of
air hitting upon a 'fleshy twig' (σάρκινος ὄζος) inside the ear,
which then oscillated like a 'gong' (κώδων) to 'like sounds'.
Smell[3] is closely connected with respiration: as we breathe
we draw in 'emanations' and if they fit into similar pores in
the nostrils, the sense of smell is stimulated. Of taste and
touch we have no special record,[4] but must suppose that
Empedocles maintained his general idea of the emanations
and pores and the principle that like perceives like.

More important for our purpose is the statement[5] that
'he speaks in the same way about understanding and ignorance. For understanding (τὸ φρονεῖν) is due to similars, and
ignorance to dissimilars, understanding being regarded as
the same as perception or very similar to it'. Thought, that
is, is like sensation a purely physical and material function,
both in process and result—a view which was to have vast
consequences in the completely material system of the
Atomists. Unfortunately we possess no account, if indeed
Empedocles ever gave one, of the details of the process,
but we may suppose that he carried out his main principles
logically, for we are told[6] that 'according to men's difference
of formation their understanding differs' and that the man[7]
in whom all four elements were most equally combined was
wisest—for he would be able to think about most things.
Similarly in a famous line[8] Empedocles declares that 'the
blood around the heart is the thinking part', for in the blood
the four elements are equally mixed. It is strange that from the
outset such a very crude physical psychology should have

---

[1] Theophr. 8: cf. D.B. 108.
[2] Ibid. 9: cf. D.B. 99; Beare, pp. 95–9.
[3] Ibid. Beare, 133–6.   [4] Theophr. 9; Beare, 161–3.
[5] Theophr. 9, 10.   [6] D.B. 108.   [7] Theophr. 11.
[8] αἷμα γὰρ ἀνθρώποις περικάρδιόν ἐστι νόημα D.B. 105.

appeared satisfactory, but its persistence shows how natural such materialistic views were to the Greek mind: the atomic psychology would not have caused to contemporaries the shock which it gives to the modern reader.

For Anaxagoras' theories of sensation we have far less detailed and more sporadic information, but certain facts stand out which are sufficient to illustrate both the similarity and the divergence of the views held in the latter half of the fifth century. In the first place he asserted, apparently in intentional opposition to Empedocles, that perception [1] was due not to 'similars' but to 'opposites'. This he illustrated from the primary sense of touch: [2] a body which is of the same temperature as our own body does not give us any sensation of hot or cold, but only one which is itself hotter or colder; we are influenced by the temperature which is 'contrary to' our own. Such perception of contraries is of course always possible on Anaxagoras' general theory that 'all things have a portion of everything', for there will then be present in each of the sense-organs the contraries of all they may have to perceive. His idea [3] may also have been dictated by his doctrine that 'mind', which controls all sensation, itself never enters the mixture and is therefore, in a sense, the 'contrary' of all else. He further noted as a kind of corollary the very interesting observation that 'all perception involves pain: [4] for the touch of the unlike always produces pain'. This he proves from the painful effect of excessively bright lights or loud sounds: we seem to have an anticipation of the modern notion of the part played by irritation in perception. [5]

In reference to vision in particular, with regard to which, as usual, fuller details have been preserved than about the other senses, Anaxagoras differed again from Empedocles in basing his views on the image [6] (ἔμφασις) seen in the pupil

[1] Theophr. *de Sensu*, 27; D.A. 92.

[2] Ibid. 28.

[3] So Beare, p. 37, but the relation of νοῦς to αἴσθησις and of νοῦς in the universe to the human mind are by no means clear.

[4] Theophr. 29.   [5] See *E. G. P.*3, 274.   [6] Theophr. 27.

of the eye (κόρη), and found confirmation for his general theory in the observation that the image 'is reflected in a part of the eye not of the same but of a different colour'. The reason then that most animals see better by day than by night is that the night is 'more uniform in colour with their eyes': but there are some animals with specially gleaming eyes who see better at night, not, as Empedocles thought, because the fire in the eyes then issues forth, but again because of the contrast in colour between eye and object. In his treatment of the other senses there is little that is remarkable, except another curious anticipation of modern ideas in the statement that we hear 'because the sound passes right through to the brain',[1] which makes us wish for further information as to Anaxagoras' physiology, and the strange notion[2] that the larger the animal and therefore its organs of perception, the greater will be its perceptive powers, 'for the large animals hear great sounds and those from a distance, while the small sounds escape them, but the small animals hear only small sounds and those near by'.

Anaxagoras' psychology was of course conditioned by his general conception of 'mind' as the one element which always remained pure and never entered the mixture, and we have practically no information as to its details, but he seems, according to Aristotle,[3] to have held that it was present 'in all animals great and small, noble and of small repute'. He believed[4] that 'soul' (ψυχή) and mind (νοῦς), that it is to say, the elements in the living organism which respectively perceive and think, were one in kind, but that the mind, as the ultimate cause of motion, was supreme and 'the beginning of all things'. This identification we have already noticed in Empedocles, but the distinction seems clearly made for the first time. If however it is right to understand Anaxagoras' whole idea of 'mind' as of something corporeal, there is no advance on the definitely material and physical conception of sensation and mental processes which his predecessor maintained.

---

[1] Ibid. 28.
[3] de Anima, A. 2. 404 b; D.A. 100.
[2] Ibid. 29, 30.
[4] Ibid. 405 a.

The Atomists thus inherited in the field of psychology an entirely material idea of the mind and senses and of the processes of sensation and thought, a belief that both processes were in ultimate analysis identical, a supreme confidence in touch as the basis of all sensation and a consequent notion of 'effluences' from the objects of perception. The main controversy which remained over was the question whether perception was due to 'similars' or 'opposites'. As in the main theory of the universe, so here the Atomic solution was looked on as a reconciliation of opposing views.

C. *Theory of Knowledge.*

The problems which centre round what we are accustomed to call the Theory of Knowledge appear in a comparatively simple form in the early philosophers and are concerned only, as is natural, with the question of the validity of the evidence of the senses. This problem arose for them inevitably in two ways, firstly, out of their general theories of the ultimate nature of the Universe, for when theory propounded a view which was obviously at variance with the straightforward experience of the senses, it was necessary to account in some way for this divergence, and secondly, but never in an acute form before the time of the Atomists, from the special theories which they held concerning the processes of sense-perception.

To the philosophers of the Milesian school the question did not apparently occur, or at least, if it presented itself to them, we have no record of their answers. But the theory of Heraclitus at once raised it in an acute form: for, as Lucretius[1] points out in the course of his criticism, if we say that the senses correctly recognize fire, but are mistaken about everything else in the world—for all other things are in reality fire just as much—we violently impugn their veracity. That Heraclitus himself was aware of this difficulty is clear from his own saying, 'the eyes are bad witnesses for men,[2] so are the ears of those who have barbarous (i.e.

[1] i. 693–700.   [2] Bywater 4; D.B. 107.

uninstructed) souls':[1] another fragment seems to represent him as saying deliberately that 'the sight makes errors',[2] though he seems also to have admitted that 'the eyes are more exact witnesses than the ears'.[3] In opposition to the senses Heraclitus set up 'reason'[4] (λόγος) as the true guide, and the commentators explain this to mean 'not reason of any sort but the divine reason which is common to men'. We must, however, be cautious about accepting this explanation, as there is little doubt that the accounts of Heraclitus' doctrine have been largely contaminated by the teaching of the Stoics,[5] who recognized in him the germs of their own theories and were apt to ascribe their own beliefs to him. It is probably safest to admit that we do not know certainly what Heraclitus meant by Logos—perhaps it was just his own account of the universe, of which he speaks in the fragment[6] of introduction which has come down to us. But it is clear that we have here in an unmistakable form the seeds of scepticism of the senses, and the opposition of a higher truth to be obtained by thought.

It is not surprising in view of the general theory of Parmenides, which appears to maintain its relentless Monism in the teeth of all ordinary observations, to be told that he 'expels the senses from the way of truth',[7] and to find that he is reckoned by the doxographers[8] among those philosophers who said flatly that sensations were false. It is not only a necessary corollary of his views, but is completely consonant with his opposition of the Way of Truth and the Way of Opinion: indeed in speaking of the latter himself, he seems to make an intentional contrast between the senses and reason: 'let not custom full of experience constrain thee along this road, to turn upon it a careless eye or sounding ear

---

[1] βαρβάρους ψυχὰς ἐχόντων which Sextus, who quotes the fragment, explains (*adv. Math.* vii. 126; D.A. 16) as meaning βαρβάρων ἐστὶ ψυχῶν ταῖς ἀλόγοις αἰσθήσεσι πιστεύειν.

[2] Bywater 132; D.B. 46.   [3] Bywater 15; D.B. 101 a.

[4] Sextus, l.c.   [5] See *E. G. P.*3, p. 142.

[6] Bywater 2; D.B. 1: see *E. G. P.*3, p. 133, n. 1.

[7] [Plut.] *Strom.* 5; D.A. 22.

[8] Aet. iv. 9. 14: cf. Philodem. *Rhet. fr.* inc. 3. 7; D.A. 49.

or tongue, but judge by reason the much-disputed proof spoken by me'.[1] Scepticism initiated by Heraclitus becomes complete in Parmenides.

Empedocles in this respect as in his general system represents a reaction from the overstrained views of Parmenides. There is no very clear record of his metaphysic, but it seems possible to reconstruct it to some extent from his fragments: it turns out to be, as we should expect, a rather curious combination of common sense and mysticism. Sextus[2] informs us that Empedocles held that 'the criterion of truth was not the senses, but the right word (ὀρθὸς λόγος), and that of the right word part was divine and might not be revealed, part mortal and capable of revelation'. This looks at first sight like a modification of the Heraclitean position: the senses are no longer called false but they cannot be taken as sure evidence: the truth is contained in Empedocles' own inspired account. But a rather closer investigation seems to show that with Empedocles the opposition is not so much between the senses and the mind, as between human faculties altogether and a divine truth. The feebleness of man's faculties is put clearly enough near the beginning of the poem: 'Straitened[3] are the powers spread over the bodily members (i.e. the powers of perception and sensation), and many are the sudden woes which blunt men's careful thoughts (μέριμναι): they behold a brief part of life that is no life[4] and with short shrift rise up and fly away like smoke, persuaded of that only on which each has chanced, as they are driven hither and thither, though each boasts that he hath found the whole: but verily this is not to be looked upon nor heard by man nor grasped by his mind'. It is clearly not the senses only which are disparaged but the mind as well: man's whole view is limited and his faculties too feeble to find out the truth alone. Yet part of 'the true word' may be learnt by man, 'and thou', says the poet to his reader, 'since thou hast turned aside into this path, shalt learn, yet no more than the wit of man can compass'. Man's business

---

[1] D.B. 1. 34–7.   [2] vii. 122; D.B. 2 praef.   [3] D.B. 2.
[4] Reading ζωῆς ἀβίου with Scaliger: see *E. G. P.*3, p. 204, n. 3.

then, apart from such divine inspiration as Empedocles claimed for himself, is 'careful thought'; the fools are those who 'have not far-minded thoughts'.[1] And 'careful thought' consists in the right use of the faculties we possess, diligent investigation with them all and the checking of one by the other: 'come now, search with all thy powers in what way each thing is clear.[2] Hold not sight in greater trust than hearing, nor set thy echoing ear above the instruction of thy tongue (i.e. taste) and restrain not thy belief in any other of thy bodily parts ($\gamma\nu\acute{\iota}\omega\nu$), by which there is a way ($\pi\acute{o}\rho os$) for understanding, but consider each thing in the way in which it is clear'. The senses then are not wholly false, but they must be used for active investigation: we must look and not merely see: 'look upon it with thy mind, he says elsewhere,[3] and sit not wondering with thine eyes'. There seems to be the same distinction which was noticed in Empedocles' theory of perception between the active and passive use of the senses. It is reasonable then to maintain that in comparison with Heraclitus and Parmenides, Empedocles does in a very large measure rehabilitate the senses: the mere passive experience of the normal man is of little value, but when the senses are used in active investigation with 'careful thought', man may hope to attain something of divine truth. His faculties are weak but not useless: common sense is set in a religious background.

It might be expected that Anaxagoras with his belief in 'mind' standing apart from all other things and never entering the mixture and his theory of the hidden portions of 'everything in everything' would take up a profoundly sceptical position as to the evidence of the senses. And accordingly the doxographical tradition[4] tells us bluntly that he said the senses were false. But once again the examination of the few extant fragments which bear on the point seems very considerably to modify this conclusion. He did indeed say that 'owing to their weakness we are not able to discern

[1] $\delta o\lambda\iota\chi\acute{o}\phi\rho ov\epsilon s$ $\mu\acute{\epsilon}\rho\iota\mu\nu\alpha\iota$ D.B. 11.
[2] D.B. 4. 9–13.　　　　　　　　[3] D.B. 17, l. 21.
[4] Aet. iv. 9. 1; D.A. 96.

the truth',[1] but Sextus, who has preserved this fragment, has given a very interesting illustration of its meaning, which puts us on the right track. Suppose, he says, that we take two coloured liquids and pour from one into the other drop by drop, our sight will not be able to discern the gradual alteration of colour, although it takes place in fact. Here we have a direct link with the general theory: our senses,[2] Anaxagoras would seem to say, can tell us the prevailing thing in a compound body, but cannot discern the portions of all other things hidden in it. And it is in this sense that we must understand the famous paradox with which Anaxagoras[3] used to illustrate the opposition of thought and appearance: 'snow is white; but snow is congealed water; water is black: therefore snow is black': we know, that is, from the fact of this change that snow must have in it black 'seeds', which if it melts will give the prevailing colour to water, but our sight cannot perceive them: they can only perceive the colour of which snow 'has most in it'. Anaxagoras' scepticism is certainly not complete: the senses are accurate as far as they go, and what they tell us is true, but they do not go far enough, they cannot tell us the underlying reality which we know by reason to be there. Yet in spite of their imperfection, they are of the greater value in investigation and indeed the only guide: for we read in another fragment, which would, till we understand Anaxagoras' position, appear to be almost a flat contradiction of that from which we started, that 'things perceived ($\phi\alpha\iota\nu\acute{o}\mu\epsilon\nu\alpha$) are the vision of the unseen';[4] our investigation, that is, of what is below the ken of the senses, must proceed from and be guided by the evidence which they can give us. So far from a complete scepticism, this is not so very remote from the position of Epicurus himself: Anaxagoras' complaint of 'the instrument' is not that it is a bad one, but that it is not sharp enough.

The predecessors of the Atomists exhibit then a strong movement towards scepticism of sense-evidence followed by

[1] Sext. vii. 90; D.B. 21.   [2] See *E. G. P.*3, p. 274.
[3] Sext. *Pyrrh. Hypot.* i. 33; D.A. 97.   [4] D.B. 21 a.

a partial reinstatement: from the attitude 'the senses are false and must be expelled from the way of truth' they reach the later position, 'the senses are not of themselves safe tests of truth, but they are of great value as instruments in investigation'. Nor is this change difficult to explain in the light of the general progress of thought. The theories of the Monists do not rest on observation or investigation, but are rather based on *a priori* reasoning about the universe and its nature. Such reasoning led naturally enough to results which were not only remote from the normal evidence of the senses, but often at variance with it. Under these conditions the evidence of perception must necessarily be disparaged and truth supposed to reside either in the unfettered use of reason or in a divine inspiration. But with the growth in Sicily and Magna Graecia of a more minute and terrestrial scientific interest, and especially with the establishment of the medical schools, observation and experiment are brought into prominence, and in these the senses, actively investigating and testing results, are of paramount importance. When philosophy takes the infinitely small as its starting-point, it will trust necessarily to the instrumentality of the senses. This attitude is of course most clearly marked in Anaxagoras, who took as his basis of investigation the phenomena of physiology and nutrition: for him though the senses could not teach all, nothing could be learnt without them. By the time of the Atomists then the extreme of scepticism was over: they breathed an atmosphere in which the senses were not indeed regarded as the final court of appeal, but were at least the most important of witnesses.[1]

[1] It will be noticed that in this chapter no account has been given of the Pythagoreans, whose theory of the origin of things in 'numbers' undoubtedly influenced the Eleatics and through them may have inspired the root-idea of Atomism. In a very brief sketch of the antecedents of Atomism it seemed best to deal only with the more concrete theories of the physicists, whom, as we may fairly judge from Lucretius, Epicurus regarded as his true predecessors.

II

LEUCIPPUS

§ 1. *Life and Writings*

IN dealing with the predecessors of the Atomists it has been sufficient to consider their theories apart from their personal history and character. But of the three great figures in the Atomic tradition it would naturally be interesting to know more. Unfortunately, though it is possible to form a fairly accurate picture both of Democritus and of Epicurus, Leucippus[1] remains wrapped in considerable obscurity. That he was the founder of the Atomic School in Greece and that he did not owe his theory to any extraneous source, there seems no reasonable ground for doubting. There was indeed a curious tradition[2] extant among later writers that the Atomic theory originated from a certain 'Mochus', a Phoenician philosopher, said to have lived 'about the time of the Trojan War', and one authority[3] goes so far as to say that he himself in the fourth century A.D. was actually acquainted with disciples of Mochus' school. Modern authorities are inclined to reject this story as a fable, and probably rightly, but in view of this suggestion of oriental influence it is interesting to realize that at an early date Indian philosophers had arrived at an atomic explanation of the Universe. The doctrines of this school[4] were expounded in the Vaicesika Sûtra and interpreted by the aphorisms of Kanada. While, like the Greek Atomists, they

---

[1] See *E. G. P.*3, pp. 330 ff., for a discussion of the questions concerning the life of Leucippus and his position in the history of philosophy: compare also Dyroff, *Demokritstudien*, § 1.

[2] See Strabo, xvi, p. 757; Sext. Emp. *adv. Math.* ix. 363; D. (Democritus) A. 55; Iambl. *Vit. Pythag.* 14.

[3] Iambl. l.c.

[4] See A. B. Keith, *Indian Logic and Atomism*, especially pp. 208–32; also Mabilleau, *Histoire de la Philosophie Atomistique*, Book I; Colebrooke, *Miscellaneous Essays*.

reached atomism through the denial of the possibility of infinite division and the assertion that indivisible particles must ultimately be reached in order to secure reality and permanence in the world, there are very considerable differences between the Indian doctrine and that of the Greeks. The Vaicesika atoms are not all ultimately homogeneous, but atoms of different kinds are assumed corresponding to the four elements, earth, water, air, and ether: qualities are attributed to them varying according to the substance to which they correspond, and they are conceived of as elastic in structure. Kanada works out the idea of their combinations in a detailed system, which reminds us at once of the Pythagoreans and in some respects of modern science, holding that two atoms combined in a binary compound and three of these binaries in a triad which would be of a size to be perceptible to the senses. All these differences make the suggestion of borrowing improbable: moreover, the latest writer[1] on the subject is not inclined to put the Indian works as early as previous scholars had done, and states that there is no proof of the atomic doctrine in India until after contact with the Greek kingdom of Bactria. He even discusses the question whether the Indian doctrine is derived from the Greek, but admits elsewhere[2] that the works as we have them presuppose much previous discussion. If there was then an old atomic tradition in India, it may be that some inkling of it had penetrated to Greece, either, as the legend of 'Mochus' would suggest, by way of Phoenicia, or possibly through the Ionian colonies,[3] but there is certainly no reason for supposing that Leucippus owed any direct debt to it, or that he is other than an 'original' thinker in the sense that he evolved his Atomism for himself as the direct outcome of the theories of his Greek predecessors.

The discrepancies in tradition as to Leucippus' origin and training are almost as great as those about the birthplace of

[1] Keith, op. cit., p. 17.

[2] p. 1.

[3] The strange story of the instruction of Democritus by the wise men in Xerxes' army (see p. 110) may point in the same direction.

Homer. The first difficulty which has to be met is startling: Epicurus[1] in one of his many letters to his disciples asserted that 'there never was such a person as a philosopher Leucippus', and certain modern critics[2] have been inclined to accept his statement literally. But we need not in fact attach much importance to it: Epicurus[3] was intensely jealous for his own originality, and invariably attempted to discredit all from whom he might be supposed to have derived his doctrines. In at least one other passage[4] of his own works he seems to be making a direct criticism on a doctrine specially attributed by the authorities to Leucippus, and we may reasonably interpret his denial of Leucippus' existence as a rather more vehement assertion than usual of his own independence. Aristotle,[5] moreover, undoubtedly regarded him as the founder of the Atomic theory, and so also did Theophrastus.[6] Further, Diogenes of Apollonia,[7] whose theories are ridiculed in *The Clouds* of Aristophanes (423 B.C.), shows distinct traces of Atomism; since Democritus' *floruit* cannot be placed before 420 B.C., Diogenes must have drawn on some earlier Atomic source than Democritus, and this can hardly be other than Leucippus. This argument not only confirms the existence of Leucippus, but practically settles the question of his date. We may therefore safely conclude that Leucippus existed, that he was the inventor of the Atomic system, and that he 'flourished' about 430 B.C. or a little earlier.

His native place was variously given in antiquity as Elea, Abdera, and Miletus.[8] There is little doubt that the last tradition is correct. The suggestion of Abdera is due to

---

[1] Diog. Laert. x. 13; D.A. 2.

[2] E. Rohde, *Jahrbuch für Klass. Philol.* cxxiii, p. 742, and more recently Brieger (*Hermes*, xxxvi, pp. 166 sq.).

[3] See Part II, Chap. I, p. 226.　　　　　　　　　[4] Ep. ii, § 89.

[5] e.g. *Metaphys. A.* 4. 985 b; D.A. 6 Λεύκιππος δὲ καὶ ὁ ἑταῖρος αὐτοῦ Δημόκριτος.

[6] Diog. Laert. ix. 46; D. (Democritus) 33.

[7] *E.G.P.*[3], p. 331.

[8] D.L. ix. 30; D.A. 1. That Μήλιος is a mere mistake for Μιλήσιος is shown by other references, e.g. Simpl. in Arist. *Phys. A.* 2. 184 (28. 4); D.A. 8.

confusion, or at least association, with Democritus and the Atomic School, which grew up there, possibly founded by Leucippus himself. The idea that he came from Elea is more interesting and must be connected with the tradition that he was a disciple of the Eleatic School and 'heard' Zeno.[1] Burnet[2] is inclined to think that this may be true and that Leucippus actually visited Elea, possibly as a result of the Milesian revolution in 450 B.C. In any case the influence upon his philosophy of the teaching of Zeno and the younger Eleatics is clear, and we may perhaps in this connexion note the further tradition preserved by Tzetzes[3] that he was a pupil of Melissus, whose Eleatic criticism so strikingly foreshadowed the Atomic theory. If then we may think of Leucippus as a native of Miletus who visited Elea, we may without indulging any fanciful speculation recognize powerful influences on his thought. We know that the old Milesian School did not wholly die out, and in the intensely physical character of his system and the absence of all mysticism, Leucippus does indeed appear as the inheritor of their 'scientific tradition': on the other hand, though Atomism is the very antipodes of the theory of Parmenides,[4] the founder of the Eleatic School, it shows evident traces of the criticism of Zeno and Melissus.[5] It does not always happen that a man's philosophy reflects the history of his life so clearly as would seem to be the case with Leucippus.

Of his writings we know little or nothing. If we may trust Theophrastus, he was the author of 'The Greater World-system' (Μέγας Διάκοσμος), as the full exposition of the Atomic theory came to be known in the School, though other authorities, perhaps with greater probability, assign it to Democritus: for it seems more likely that we should attribute to Leucippus the main outlines of the theory, and to the School culminating in Democritus its working out in detail.

[1] D.L. l.c.; Clem. *Strom*. i. 64. 353; D.A. 4; [Galen] *Hist. Philos.* 3; D.A. 5.   [2] *E. G. P*.3, p. 331.   [3] *Chil*. ii. 980; D.A. 5.
[4] Cf. Simpl. in Arist. *Phys. A*. 2. 184 (28. 4); D.A. 8.
[5] Especially in the idea that pluralism can only secure permanence, if it rejects the possibility of infinite division: see p. 72.

On the other hand we may safely believe that Leucippus originated many of the principal technical terms of Atomism,[1] which are credited to him in the doxographical tradition. There is also expressly assigned to him a sentence out of a work on 'The Mind',[2] though it again, with its emphatic assertion of the supremacy of 'necessity', reads more like Democritus than Leucippus. There is therefore nothing extant of Leucippus' own work on which it is possible to build, and the difficulty of forming any exact view as to his theories is greatly increased, when the accounts of his theory are examined, for in nearly all the references he is coupled with Democritus and no distinction is drawn between them. It has in consequence been the usual practice of writers on the Atomic theory to group them together and credit them both with the whole of the system. This is however a very unsatisfactory plan and clearly ought not to be adopted, if it is possible to avoid it. For it cannot be doubted that in fact the theory must have undergone considerable modification and development in its transition through the School from Leucippus to Democritus, and the strongly marked character of the later philosopher with his insatiate love of investigation and his encyclopaedic knowledge and interests make it certain that he would not have been content to accept a ready-made system without development and expansion. Happily it is not really necessary to accept the confusion. For on the one hand there is a vast mass of doctrine, apart from the very considerable fragments of his own writing, which is expressly attributed to Democritus and not to Leucippus, on the other not merely is it possible to detect certain points[3] in which Leucippus held distinctly different opinions from those afterwards put forward by Democritus, but by a fortunate chance Aristotle[4]

[1] See those collected by Diels in B.1.

[2] D.B. 2: οὐδὲν χρῆμα μάτην γίνεται, ἀλλὰ πάντα ἐκ λόγου τε καὶ ὑπ' ἀνάγκης.

[3] e.g. the idea of the μέγα κενόν, Hipp. Ref. 1. 12; D.A. 10, see p. 92, a view of the origin of thunder, Aet. iii. 3. 10; D.A. 25 (cf. Democritus, D.A. 93), and theories as to the shape and inclination of the earth.

[4] Metaphys. l.c., and de Gen. et Corr. A. 8. 325 a; D.A. 7.

himself in two very important passages of reference and criticism speaks expressly of Leucippus. The work of Diels in separating out the references which belong specially to Leucippus is of immense value, and that he has not exercised a merely arbitrary choice is shown by the very definite picture which they present of Leucippus as the founder of the main principles of Atomism and a person with a marked genius for the invention of striking and often quaint technical terms in contrast to the more universal and more detailed diligence of Democritus. It is not then without justification that Leucippus[1] may be dealt with separately and an attempt made to estimate the general principles which he laid down and the extent to which he carried the development of the Atomic system. It must not however be supposed that great contrasts will appear between him and his disciple: they stand to one another rather as the pioneer and the enthusiastic and energetic follower.

§ 2. *The Atomic Theory*

It has already been hinted that Leucippus regarded himself, and was generally considered in antiquity, not so much as the founder of a great hypothesis, which was the fullest answer that the ancient world could give to the original question of Thales, but rather in the more humble capacity of a mediator between the diverse views of his predecessors and in particular between the two Schools of thought which as the result of the long debate were left in sharp opposition, the Eleatic Monism of the successors of Parmenides, and the Pluralism of Empedocles and Anaxagoras. Atomism is in fact presented to us as a reconciliation of those many antinomies which had sprung up in the course of earlier discussion, the One and the Many, change and permanence, division and continuity, the senses and thought. It is in

---

[1] Among modern writers Lafaist, *Dissertation sur la philosophie atomistique*, is, as far as I know, alone in attempting a separate treatment of Leucippus and Democritus, but Dyroff, op. cit., § 1, has drawn attention to important points of difference, and in particular to a difference of spirit, which is borne out by Diels' division of the extant references.

this aspect that it is approached in a most valuable passage of Aristotle,[1] which clearly sets out the relation of Leucippus to his predecessors and will therefore form the best basis for the consideration of his theory.

Leucippus and Democritus have come to a conclusion about all things for the most part by the same method and with the same view, making their starting-point what naturally comes first. For some of the older philosophers (sc. the Eleatics) held that reality was necessarily one and immovable: for empty space does not exist, and motion would be impossible, unless there were empty space apart from matter; nor could many things exist, unless there were something to separate them.

Aristotle then goes on to explain the Eleatic criticism on the pluralists, to state the view of the extreme Monists, and to point out that, if one appeals to the facts, such a view seems little short of madness. He then resumes:[2]

but Leucippus (we may mark this special mention of the founder of the School) thought he had a theory, which should be consistent with sense-perception and not do away with coming into being or destruction or motion or the multiplicity of things. He agreed so far with appearances, but to those who hold the theory of the One, on the ground that there could be no motion without empty space, he admitted that empty space is not real, and that nothing of what is real is not real: for the real in the strict sense is an absolute *plenum*. But the *plenum* is not one, but there is an infinite number of them, and they are invisible owing to the smallness of their bulk. These move in empty space (for there is empty space), and by their coming together produce coming into being and by their separation destruction. . . . But out of the One in the strict sense multiplicity could not be produced, nor unity in the full sense out of the Many, for that is impossible.

This very suggestive passage may be considered first in the light of previous speculation. Aristotle's last sentence puts exactly the position which had been reached with regard to the central problem of the ultimate existence. The strict Monism of Parmenides not merely could not account for the creation of the Many, but actually denied their existence except as an illusion of the senses, and even the laxer Monism

---

[1] *de Gen. et Corr.* A. 8. 324 b 35; D.A. 7.
[2] Ibid. 325 a 23.

of the Ionians and Heraclitus could not explain the Many except by a virtual abandonment of unity. On the other the main weakness of the current pluralistic theories was just that they destroyed the fundamental 'One': neither the 'sphere' of Empedocles, in which the four elements were mingled by Love, nor Anaxagoras' 'mixture 'of 'portions' were in any sense homogeneous. How then did Leucippus propose to meet this difficulty? Exactly on the lines suggested by the aphorism of Melissus. The ultimate 'nature'[1] was, he said, an infinite number of small particles, pluralism is absolute, but yet they are 'one', and that in two senses. In the first place the ultimate matter, though existing in this infinitely discrete form, is yet absolutely homogeneous: all the infinite particles are exactly similar in substance and there is therefore but one ultimate 'nature': 'their nature they say is one, as if each one of them were, for instance, a separate piece of gold'.[2] Secondly, and this is rather the line of thought which Aristotle reproduces here, each one of the particles is in itself a 'One': for to it, as Melissus postulated, may be applied all the attributes of the Parmenidean 'One': it is an absolute corporeal *plenum*, sheer matter and nothing else, it is absolutely indivisible,[3] entirely without motion inside itself, unchangeable, eternal. In other words, as Aristotle puts it with epigrammatic clearness: 'the real in the strict sense is an absolute *plenum*; but this *plenum* is not one, but there is an infinite number of them'. In this way then Leucippus thought that he had solved the problem of the One and the Many. He established a unity which yet allowed infinite multiplicity, a multiplicity which yet provided to the full an underlying unity. The unity which thought demanded was satisfied, and yet the multiplicity to which the senses bore witness was shown to be true.

---

[1] For the old Ionian word φύσις as applied to Atomism see Simpl. in Arist. *Phys.* Θ 9. 265 b ταῦτα γὰρ (*sc.* the atoms) ἐκεῖνοι φύσιν ἐκάλουν.

[2] Arist. *de Caelo, A*. 7. 275b; D.A. 19: cf. *Phys.* Γ. 4. 203a τὸ κοινὸν σῶμα πάντων ἐστὶν ἀρχή.

[3] The justification of these epithets will become clearer when the nature of the atoms is discussed in § 3.

Moreover, this unlimited pluralism was not, like that of Anaxagoras, uneconomical in assuming an infinite variety in the substance of the ultimate constituents: it had all the economy of the Monist theories, for in substance all the infinite particles were one.

Now this supposition of an infinitely discrete ultimate matter raises at once the question of division, which was another form in which the root-problem had recently presented itself. Anaxagoras, as has been seen, supposed his 'seeds' or particles of the original 'mixture' to be infinitely divisible, and Empedocles and the upholders of the 'element' theory had taken up the same attitude. Infinity in number had not yet been thought of apart from endless division and subdivision. It was against this supposition that the younger Eleatics, in defence of Parmenidean Monism, had chiefly directed their attack. Zeno,[1] whose arguments[2] were probably aimed primarily at the mathematical pluralism of the Pythagoreans, had argued in effect, that if we say that a thing is infinitely divisible we must mean that it is composed of an infinite number of points or units. But what are these points: have they themselves magnitude or not? If they have not, then their addition to or subtraction from something else can make no difference: things will be infinitely small, indeed non-existent: if they have magnitude, then they must themselves be divisible into smaller parts, and so on *ad infinitum*; everything will be made of an infinite number of units and will therefore be infinitely great. Either conclusion is absurd. That the first of these contentions was also used in a more popular form against the materialistic systems of pluralism maintained by Empedocles and Anaxagoras is clear from its employment in that context by Lucretius:[3] infinite division, it was held, destroys permanence: things could be frittered away from less and less to nothing, and the process of creation, which is always slower

---

[1] D.B. 1 and 2.   [2] See *E. G. P.*3, p. 362.
[3] i. 746 ff., 844 ff., which refer back to the fuller exposition of the argument in 540–64. Lucretius also employs the other half of Zeno's argument against the notion of infinite division in i. 615 ff.

than that of destruction, would be impossible. Against these criticisms of the pluralistic view Leucippus guarded himself in the only possible way by supposing that there is after all a limit to division. Things may be divided again and again into smaller and smaller parts even far below the ken of the senses, but ultimately a point is reached at which further division is impossible: you come at last to ultimate particles of matter which are indivisible (ἀδιαίρετα) or 'atoms' (ἄ-τομα). This conclusion Leucippus seems to have claimed as a deduction from experience: 'They (i.e. Leucippus and Democritus) abandoned division to infinity on the ground that we cannot divide to infinity and by this means guarantee the perpetual continuity (τὸ ἀκατάληκτον) of division, and said that bodies consisted of indivisible particles';[1] that is, that as in our experience there is a limit to the extent to which we can subdivide, because particles became so small that they pass out of the ken of the senses, so Leucippus supposed it was with the ultimate physical realities: there is a 'least possible' for existence, just as there is a least possible for perception. The line of argument is quite consonant, as will be seen, with Leucippus' general attitude to the relation of sense-perception to truth, and it reads like a first adumbration of the very elaborate argument of Epicurus[2] on the same topic. However he reached his conclusion, Leucippus could now reply both to the dialectic of Zeno and to the more popular form of his arguments. To Zeno he could now say that there is a fixed unit of existence: and though these units are still infinite in number, in any given thing the number of them is limited, they could (theoretically at least) be counted, and therefore so far from nullifying the magnitude of things,[3] they form the ultimate basis for the calculation of size. And to the less scientific objectors he could say, as Lucretius does again and again, that the conception of infinite particles as the ultimate substratum, so far from annulling the permanence of matter,

---

[1] Simpl. in Arist. *Phys*. Z. 1. 231 a; D.A. 13.
[2] Ep. i, §§ 55–9.
[3] Compare again Epicurus' argument on the subject in Ep. i, §§ 55–9.

is now its surest guarantee: for each one of these ultimate particles is indivisible and eternal, and they provide a point beyond which further dissolution is impossible, the stopping-point for destruction and the starting-point for creation. Thus a discrete infinity is reconciled with permanence: there are infinite particles, but thanks to their very essential character, the world can never be frittered away into nothing-ness. What had been the chief weapon against previous pluralistic systems, becomes for Atomism its stronghold of defence.

But there was yet another objection to which this theory of the existence of matter in the form of infinite discrete particles was liable. If they are discrete, there must be something to separate them (διάστημα): if they are to move—and without motion they cannot combine to form things or shift their position so as to change things—there must be something external to them for them to move in. What is this something? The Pythagoreans,[1] who with their doctrine of the infinitely divisible had been confronted with this problem, had thought of air as lying between the particles of matter, but since the theory of Empedocles had shown that air was an element, as corporeal in substance as earth or fire or water, this answer was no longer possible. Par-menides had seen that the only answer could be 'empty space', but, profoundly convinced as he was that the only existence was that of body, he had denied the existence of empty space altogether: it was 'nothing' (οὐδέν). The world was a corporeal *plenum*, there was no division between parts of matter but all was a continuous whole, neither was there any possibility of motion. Melissus had more recently en-forced this position as part of his attack on pluralism: 'Nor is there anything empty (κενεόν): for the empty is nothing and that which is nothing cannot be: nor does it (*sc.* the world) move: for it has nowhere to withdraw to (ὑποχωρῆσαι), but it is full. For if there were anything empty, it would withdraw into the empty: but as the empty is not, it has nowhere to withdraw to.'[2] Leucippus was prepared to meet

[1] See *E. G. P.*3, p. 289.　　　　　　[2] D.B. 7, § 7.

this difficulty perfectly boldly: he affirmed, using Melissus' own terms, that 'the elements are the full and the empty',[1] or, as Diogenes[2] puts it, 'the universe is the full and the empty', that is, that it is as necessary to conceive of unoccupied space separating the particles of matter as it is to postulate the particles of matter themselves. How then did he answer the metaphysical difficulty of the Milesians? His reply was extremely subtle, and if it seems to us something of a quibble, this is due not so much to Leucippus, as to the persistence of the philosophical tradition which had hitherto refused to acknowledge reality, except in the form of matter. He admitted, as is made clear in Aristotle's exposition, that empty space is 'not real' ($\mu\dot{\eta}$ $\check{o}\nu$): the only fully real existence is matter, 'the completely full' ($\pi\alpha\mu\pi\lambda\hat{\eta}\rho\epsilon\varsigma$). But, he said, though empty space is not in this sense a real thing, it none the less exists: 'the real exists not a whit more than the not real, empty space no less than body.'[3] In effect Leucippus had introduced a new conception of reality: in the old sense empty space is not real, for it has not the most elementary attribute of matter, it cannot touch or be touched. But it none the less exists: we must form a new idea of existence, something non-corporeal, whose sole function is to be where the fuller reality is not, an existence in which the full reality, matter, can move and have its being. He thus established the necessary requirement for his conception of a discrete infinity of matter; the particles of body were indeed separated by the empty. At the same time, it must be observed, he had protected himself against a possible charge of dualism: if he were taxed with having, like the materialistic pluralists, destroyed the fundamental unity of the universe by the admission of two 'existences', matter and space, he could reply that he still held that there was but one full reality: the other 'existence' was, as it were, but the negation of this reality ($\tau\grave{o}$ $\mu\grave{\eta}$ $\check{o}\nu$), but it did nevertheless exist. For the moment his success was to have conquered in the

---

[1] Arist. *Metaphys. A.* 4. 985 b; D.A. 6.
[2] D.L. ix. 30; D.A. 1, &c.
[3] Arist. ibid.: cf. Simpl. in Arist. *Phys. A.* 2. 184 (28. 4); D.A. 8.

dialectical debate with the Eleatics, but for the permanent progress of thought he had achieved the far greater triumph of establishing the conception of non-corporeal existence: it is, as Burnet[1] has pointed out, a strange achievement for the founder of the great materialist school of antiquity to have been 'the first to say distinctly that a thing might be real without being a body'.

In all these different ways Leucippus had shown himself the mediator, and had reconciled the oppositions which had played so large a part in previous debate. He had shown how the One might also be the Many, he had shown that there might be a discrete infinity and yet a limit to division, he had exhibited the existence of empty space without refusing to acknowledge matter as the single reality. But he had of course done much more than this, for he had discovered a theory of the Universe, which was not only in itself remarkable in its penetration, but was to prove capable of development and application with a completeness which was impossible to any of its predecessors. To realize this it is necessary to leave the negative conception of Leucippus as a mediator and to inquire into the positive doctrines of his theory and its application as an explanation of the world.

§ 3. *Atoms and Space: the creation of things*

The main principles of the theory of Leucippus have so far established the conception of small discrete particles of homogeneous body separated by and situated in empty space. It is a long step from this to the infinitely complex and varied world of phenomena, and it is necessary at this point to ask how he conceived the nature of the two constituents and by what process they were enabled so to combine as to create the things of experience.

First, both atoms and space are infinite, the atoms in number, space in extent. This might be deduced from the belief that the universe itself was infinite,[2] in which Leucippus followed the Ionians and Melissus,[3] who had revolted

[1] *E. G. P.*[2], p. 389.
[2] D.L. ix. 31; D.A. 1.   [3] D.B. 3.

on this point from the strict conception of Parmenides. But it would appear that Leucippus[1] argued rather from the infinite variety of phenomena to the infinite number of the atoms, and from that the infinite extent of space follows directly: for in a limited space, infinity of particles could only be obtained by infinite subdivision.

Of the nature of space there was but little to be said: all that Leucippus could predicate of it is that it is 'empty' (κενόν), or as he seems to have put it in one of those quaint terms which he invented for the Atomic theory, 'porous'[2] (μανόν). The use of this term is instructive, for it makes it clear that he was thinking always of the intervals (διαστήματα) between particles of matter. Later on[3] there is some confusion between two possible senses of 'space'. The mathematical sense of extension, though it is sometimes attributed to the Atomists, was always too abstract a conception for them, but they did vary between thinking of space as the whole extent of the universe, some parts of which were occupied by matter, and on the other hand as the 'empty' parts, the intervals between body. But it is clear that by Leucippus at any rate only the latter meaning is intended: 'space' is the sum total of those parts of the whole, which at any given moment are not occupied by matter. Body and space are mutually exclusive, and together they make up the sum total of the universe.

On the nature of the atoms—the only form of the full existence of matter—there is naturally much more detail. Their two essential characteristics have already been noticed. They are in the first place all absolutely homogeneous in substance: there is only one primary matter, although it exists in the form of infinite discrete particles: here Leucippus places himself of course in the strongest possible

---

[1] This is certainly the argument which Leucippus adduced for the infinite shapes of the atoms (Arist. *de Gen. et Corr. A.* 1. 315 b; D.A. 9) and therefore *a fortiori* for their infinite number, and its method is supported by the argument from sensation noticed above in favour of a limit to division.

[2] Arist. *Metaphys. A.* 4. 985 b; D.A. 6.

[3] See Part II, Chap. III, p. 294.

contrast to Anaxagoras, and by this condition establishes his own claim to have secured the unity of the fundamental matter. Secondly, they are indivisible: this attribute is no less essential, for it is again the condition of permanence. But of this idea there is considerable elaboration. Not merely did Leucippus speak normally of the atoms as indivisible (ἀδιαίρετα) or 'uncuttable' (ἄτομα), but looking at them sometimes rather from the point of view of their substance or consistency, he described them as solid[1] (στέρεα) or full (πυκνά, πλήρη), or, using another of his peculiarly descriptive technical terms, as 'compact' (ναστά).[2] He appears also to have given two 'causes' for the indivisibility of the atoms, which are in fact rather in the nature of further descriptions, but serve to bring out the idea more clearly. The first cause is that 'they cannot be acted upon',[3] a notion subsequently elaborated by Democritus: this does not mean of course that an atom could not be affected as a whole, for that would preclude motion and so combination, but that it cannot be internally altered as regards its essential nature or shape: it is in fact an amplification or explanation of the attribute of solidity; the atom is absolutely hard sheer matter and nothing can change its structure—for change of structure, as will be seen, implies the presence of void. The second 'cause' is more characteristic and interesting: the atoms are indivisible 'because they are small and have no parts'.[4] Here there seems in the first place to be a thought of the parallel of sense-experience by which Leucippus is said to have been first led to the conception of the atom: in the perceptible world the smaller a thing is, the more difficult it is to divide it into parts, and the *minimum* of perception cannot be so divided at all without its passing altogether out of the range of sensation. So with the atom, the *minimum* of physical existence: its indivisibility is directly due to its smallness.

[1] Arist. *Metaphys. A.* 4. 985 b; D.A. 6.

[2] Simpl. in Arist. *Phys. A.* 2. 184 (28. 4); D.A. 8: τὴν τῶν ἀτόμων οὐσίαν ναστὴν καὶ πλήρη ὑποτιθέμενος. The word is unusual and is used of a kind of close-pressed cake or bread.

[3] τὴν ἀπάθειαν, ibid. in Arist. *Phys. Z.* 1. 231 a; D.A. 13.

[4] τὸ·σμικρὸν καὶ ἀμερές, ibid

We may notice incidentally that Democritus by no means agreed on this point. The statement that 'the atoms have no parts' looks at first sight dangerous, for the Eleatic critics might well fasten on it and argue that 'that which has no parts has no magnitude', and that therefore Leucippus' atom was not in reality a physical existence at all. And indeed it is clear that later criticism did attack the statement, and Epicurus had to defend the Atomic position in a very elaborate argument.[1] But to Leucippus no such difficulty occurred, for to himself his meaning was quite plain. He did not mean that the atom had no parts in the mathematical sense, for it had of course extension. He applied the term in a purely physical sense, and meant that it had no separable parts: 'they have no share in the void:'[2] there is in their internal structure no 'interval' (διάστημα) of space. Indeed we might not unfairly translate the word he uses (ἀμερές) as 'indivisible into parts'. Once again the alleged 'cause' is only an amplification of the original epithet 'indivisible', indeed of the word 'atom'. The atom then is indivisible and solid, unchangeable and a single inseparable whole: it is in all these respects the microcosm of the Parmenidean 'One'.

The ultimate particles then are all alike in texture, and alike in being indivisible and unalterable. How then can they produce the countless variety of phenomena? Such difference in their products must be due to some differences in themselves. These differences Leucippus[3] recognized to be three and expressed them once more in his own quaint technical terms 'rhythm' (ῥυσμός), 'touching'[4] (διαθιγή), and 'turning' (τροπή). Aristotle explains these terms to mean

[1] That already referred to in Ep. i. 55–9.

[2] ἀμοίρους τοῦ κενοῦ, Simpl. in Arist. *de Caelo*, A. 7. 275; D.A. 14.

[3] Arist. *Metaphys.* l.c.

[4] Beare, op. cit., p. 37, n. 2, inclines to the suggestion that διαθιγή is a dialectical form of διαθήκη = διάθεσις, 'position in order', but though this meaning would undoubtedly correspond better to Aristotle's explanation τάξις, the contact with neighbouring atoms is so vital an element in Atomic composition that we may well suppose that the old derivation from √θιγ is correct and that Leucippus thought of order or arrangement as 'contact on either side'.

respectively 'shape' (σχῆμα), 'arrangement' (τάξις) and 'position' (θέσις), and adds an apt illustration[1] from the letters of the alphabet, which he probably derived from Democritus: A differs from N in shape, A N from N A in arrangement, and ⊐ (the older form of Z) from H in position (i.e. it is H turned on its side). We may conclude then that 'rhythm' is the internal arrangement of parts (of course not separable parts) or 'shape', 'touching' is the position of an atom with regard to other atoms in a series or conglomeration, and 'turning' the position of an atom with regard to itself. These three differences were sufficient according to Leucippus' view to account for all the infinite variety of phenomena: for by the combination of the three differences an infinite complexity of permutations can be formed. Thus, if we may continue Democritus' illustration with the three shapes ANH we might have as combinations A N H, A H N, A ⊐ N, Ɐ H N, &c. Later on the members of the Atomic School worked out in detail the special ways in which these differences caused difference of sensational effect, and Democritus in particular seems to have had especial pleasure in elaborating this part of the theory; they do not appear to have made much use of 'turning', but roughly speaking accounted for the direct differences of shape, sound, smell, and taste in compound things by differences in the shape of component atoms, and difference in colour in particular by difference in arrangement. Leucippus probably left the notion general, except that he did expressly state that the atoms which went to compose fire were of spherical shape,[2] doubtless as being the most mobile.

On the other hand there was one detail on which Leucippus insisted with less than his usual foresight. So eager was he to be certain that these elementary differences would account without difference in substance for all the variety of phenomena that he was not content merely to postulate

---

[1] The illustration seems unsatisfactory as it appears in the manuscripts, but Diels has successfully explained it after Wilamowitz by means of the older forms of the letter Z written as ⊐.

[2] Arist. de Caelo, Γ. 4. 303 a; D.A. 15.

difference of shape in the atoms, but asserted that the number of different shapes was infinite. Two reasons are suggested for this conclusion, both of them interesting and illustrative of the general attitude of the Atomists: 'since they thought truth lay in appearance, and the things of appearance were infinite and contrary to one another, they made the shapes (of the atoms) infinite'.[1] Here we have once again the common-sense revolt against the theoretical unity of Eleaticism: the world is infinitely various and that must imply infinite variety in that quality in its ultimate constituents which gives rise to the difference of phenomena. It may be objected that this supposition is really contradictory of the fundamental economy of Atomism,[2] for by mere change of order and position it would be possible to suppose a world created of atoms homogeneous in shape as well as substance. But Leucippus was opposing Empedocles and Anaxagoras, and it was natural that having once established the fundamental unity of substance he should feel himself bound to take every opportunity of securing variety in other ways. The second is an *a priori* reason which perhaps savours more of the metaphysical mind of Democritus than the matter-of-fact Leucippus: 'he believed the number of shapes to be infinite because there was no reason why any one of them should be of one shape rather than another'.[3] It has been pointed out that this in reality proves nothing more than that it is impossible to predict the shape of any given atom:[4] their shapes are unassignable but not necessarily infinite. But it is fully in accordance with the anti-teleological attitude of the Atomists and they may well have felt it cogent. The shapes then are infinite in number. Later criticism perceived the difficulty that since,[5] after a certain limit of permutation, difference of shape can only be secured by increase of size, infinity of shapes must mean that some

---

[1] Arist. *de Gen. et Corr.* A. 315 b; D.A. 9.

[2] See Mabilleau, op. cit., p. 192.

[3] Simpl. in Arist. *Phys. A.* 2. 184 (28. 4); D.A. 8: τῶν ἐν αὐτοῖς σχημάτων ἄπειρον τὸ πλῆθος διὰ τὸ μηδὲν μᾶλλον τοιοῦτον ἢ τοιοῦτον εἶναι.

[4] Mabilleau, l.c.   [5] See Epicurus, *Ep.* i., § 56; Lucr. ii. 481 ff.

atoms will be of great size and therefore perceptible to the
senses, which is a contradiction of Leucippus'[1] own express
assertion that the atoms are 'invisible owing to the smallness
of their size'. Democritus[2] indeed appears not to have shrunk
from this consequence, and boldly stated that some atoms
were 'very large', but Epicurus realizing the objection which
had escaped his predecessors limited the number of shapes.

For Leucippus the shapes of the atoms were definite[3] but
unlimited in number, and by this difference together with
those of position and arrangement the atoms were completely
adapted to form an infinite variety of compound bodies
varying in effect for every kind of sense-perception. Aristotle clearly suggests the range of possibility: 'by changes in
its composition the same thing can seem the opposite to
different people, and can be altered by a small addition and
seem entirely new, if one part of it is shifted: for a tragedy
and a comedy might be written with the same letters'.[4]

How then did this combination of atoms to form things
come about? For so far we have only the conception of
infinite atoms existing in an empty void which separates
them. Aristotle's[5] general summary gives us the main idea:
the atoms 'move in empty space . . . and by their coming
together produce coming into being and by their separation
destruction'. Of what nature is this motion and what is its
origin? The two questions are closely linked together but
neither of them is easy to answer. In the first place it seems
clear that the motion was eternal: the atoms are never in the
accounts which are extant said to 'be' or to 'rest' in the void,
but always to be moving.[6] In the systems of Empedocles

[1] Arist. de Gen. et Corr. A. 8. 325 a; D.A. 7.

[2] Dionys. apud Eus. P. E. xiv. 23. 3; D. (Democr.) A. 43: see p. 127.

[3] ἀπείροις ὡρίσθαι σχήμασι, Arist. de Gen. et Corr. A. 8. 325 b; D.A. 7.

[4] Ibid. 315b; D.A. 9. The illustration from letters is a very favourite one
with Lucretius (i. 197, 823 ff., 912 ff.) and may well go back, like the
previous example, to Democritus.   [5] de Gen. et Corr. A. 325a; D.A. 7.

[6] κινεῖσθαι, Arist. de Caelo, Γ. 2. 300b; D.A. 16; Alex. in Metap. A. 4. 985b;
D.A. 6; Hipp. Ref. 1. 12; D.A. 10; φέρεσθαι, Arist. de gen. et Corr. A. 325 a;
D.A. 7; Simpl. in Arist. Phys. A. 2. 184 (28. 4); D.A. 8; Simpl. in Arist.
de Caelo, A. 7. 275; D.A. 14.

and Anaxagoras the original state of the mass of matter had been regarded as static and compact, and it required the advent of the extraneous forces of Love and Strife or Mind to enter in and cause motion which should separate and break up and so make the start of creation. But in Leucippus' conception this was not so: no extraneous force was required to break up the original matter, for it had always existed in the form of separate particles, and no extraneous force was required to set the particles in motion. There never was a condition of things in which the atoms were at rest in the void: they had been in motion from all time.

What then was the direction of this motion? This is a much more difficult question. Epicurus,[1] who certainly attributed weight to the atoms, held that their 'natural' motion was 'downwards', a view which required much explanation with reference to an infinite space, and Democritus[2] too had some notion of a connexion of weight and motion. But there seems to be no trace of such an idea in Leucippus. The nearest indication of his conception seems to be given by Simplicius:[3] 'the atoms move in the void and catching each other up jostle together' (ἐπικαταλαμβανούσας ἀλλήλας συγκρούεσθαι). This was of course in all forms of the Atomic theory regarded as the actual condition of atomic motion caused by the collisions of moving atoms and the succession of blows which sent them flying in all directions, but Epicurus certainly conceived of a theoretic condition in which before a single collision had occurred the atoms were all moving in the same direction without catching each other up. This however is due to his belief in weight as the cause of motion, and it seems safest and most in harmony with the accounts to suppose that Leucippus did not distinguish any two stages, but that for him the condition of jostling and collision was from the first 'natural'; in other words that the eternal motion of the atoms was always in all directions.[4]

[1] See Ep. i, §§ 60, 61.   [2] See Chap. III, pp. 128 ff.
[3] In Arist. de Caelo, A. 7. 275; D.A. 14.
[4] See E. G. P.3, p. 340, and the general discussion of the whole question in Chap. III, § 4, pp. 138 ff.

Such a conclusion would be quite in harmony with the argument about the infinite shapes of the atoms: for, as Leucippus might say, 'there is no reason why motion should be in one direction more than in another'.

If this be the true account of the character of the atomic motion, it is necessary to inquire what is its cause. Aristotle sarcastically complains that Leucippus supplied no answer to this question: 'they say that motion is eternal: but what it is and why it is they do not say nor do they explain the cause why it is in one direction more than another':[1] and again 'the explanation of motion, whence or how it belongs to the bodies, they indolently omitted':[2] his complaint is echoed by the commentators.[3] Now if the character of the motion attributed to the atoms has been rightly interpreted, we might reply to part of Aristotle's question that the reason why Leucippus did not explain why the motion was in one direction more than another was that he did not conceive it to be so. But there remains the more important question of the cause of motion at all, and it is obvious that we have thus come back upon the old difficulty of the efficient cause.[4] Seeing that this was one of the traditional problems of the philosophers, it seems at first sight unlikely that Leucippus should have avoided giving a reply, and indeed our own difficulty in dealing with the authorities is not that there is no answer, but that there are too many. Some of these may certainly be put out of court: Leucippus cannot have said that the motion was 'due to force' ($\beta\acute{\iota}\alpha$):[5] this, as another commentator[6] points out, rightly describes the motion resulting from the atomic collision, but not the primary and eternal, or, as Aristotle calls it, the 'natural' motion. Nor again could he have described it as an 'undesigned ($\mathring{\alpha}\pi\rho\sigma\nu\acute{o}\eta\tau\sigma\nu$) and fortuitous ($\tau\upsilon\chi\alpha\acute{\iota}\alpha\nu$) motion':[7] this is a confusion with the

[1] ἀλλὰ διὰ τί καὶ τίνα οὐ λέγουσιν οὐδ' εἰ ὡδὶ ⟨ἢ⟩ ὡδὶ τὴν αἰτίαν. *Metaphys. Λ.* 6. 1071 b; D.A. 18.

[2] *Metaphys. A.* 4. 985 b; D.A. 6.

[3] e.g. Alex. commenting on this passage; D.A. 6.

[4] See Chap. I, pp. 46–52.

[5] Simpl. in Arist. *de Caelo, Γ.* 2. 300 b; D.A. 16.

[6] Alex. in *Metaphys. A.* 4. 985 b; D.A. 6.   [7] Aet. i. 4. 1; D.A. 24.

Atomic descriptions of the concourse of atoms which 'happens' to form a world. If Leucippus gave any answer to the question at all, it must have been that the cause of motion was 'necessity': there are traces of this answer in the doxographers,[1] and in the only aphorism[2] attributed to Leucippus, he is recorded as saying that 'nothing occurs at random, but everything for a reason (ἐκ λόγου) and by necessity'. This was certainly the answer of Democritus, and if Leucippus gave it, he meant by necessity, as Democritus did, not the arbitrary external force, which his predecessors had called in to produce any effect which was otherwise unaccountable, but rather that the atoms in moving obeyed the law of their own being. The conception of natural law becomes far more explicit in Democritus, but there is little doubt that in his whole system, Leucippus too was striving for it and trying to exclude arbitrary and external forces as far as he possibly could. And if it be said that from our point of view it seems arbitrary to assume motion as an essential part of the nature of the original matter, Leucippus was after all only returning to the notion of the Ionian Monists. But perhaps for this very reason it is safest to assume that Aristotle is literally correct and that Leucippus did not assign any cause for the original motion. As Burnet[3] has ingeniously argued, it was when motion had to be introduced as the cause of the separation of an originally compact mass, whose nature was to be continuous and motionless, that it was necessary to explain its origin. Leucippus might well suppose that having demonstrated the existence of a world in which matter was already discrete, it was unnecessary to account further for motion: the existence of empty space was, as it were, itself the cause of motion as it was of separation. Motion was eternal and therefore 'natural': you cannot ask for its cause any more than you can for the reason why the primary matter existed in the form of particles. However this may be, the uncertainty with regard to Leucippus on

[1] Hipp. *Ref.* i. 12; D.A. 10 speaks of the process of world-formation as taking place διὰ τὴν ἀνάγκην, and similarly complains that Leucippus does not state what this ἀνάγκη is.   [2] D.B. 2.   [3] *E. G. P.*³, p. 341.

this point is not due merely to the accident of tradition: it is one of the many signs that Atomism was as yet in its infancy. It was not till later developments that the solution appeared or even the difficulty was clearly comprehended.

The primary result of motion is collision between the atoms: 'they move in the void striking one another and jostling'.[1] And collision may have two results: either the colliding atoms recoil and fly off again moving in new directions, or they may become entangled with one another, and this entanglement is the first beginning of the creation of things. The two processes are well described by Simplicius:[2] 'they move in the void and catching each other up jostle together, and some recoil in any direction that may chance, and others become entangled with one another in various degrees according to the symmetry of their shapes and sizes and positions and order, and they remain together and thus the coming into being of composite things is effected'. The atoms which recoil may of course at some future time enter into combination, when they light upon a 'symmetry' better suited to them, but it must be noted that the Atomists always assume at any given moment a large number of 'free' atoms moving about independently of combinations: indeed the 'odds', so to speak, are always large against the meeting of atoms with the right shape and position and order to form things. But from time to time such combination does take place and it is important to understand its character clearly.

The most usual description of it is certainly 'entanglement',[3] which seems to express the idea elaborated in the above account: a projection, for instance, in one atom will catch in a depression in another, an atom arriving in a certain position will fit in to an already formed nucleus, an atomic group in a certain order will fit on to another group: all the 'differences' of the atoms, shapes, position, and arrange-

---

[1] Alex. l.c.; D.A. 6.   [2] de Caelo, 242. 15; D.A. 14.
[3] περιπλέκεσθαι, Arist. de Gen. et Corr. A. 325 a; D.A. 7; Simpl. in Arist. de Caelo, A. 7. 275; D.L. ix. 30; D.A. 1; συμπλοκή, Arist. de Caelo, Γ. 4. 303 a; D.A. 15.

ment come into play as determining factors. The general idea is clear but there are two points of special importance about the atomic combinations, which are brought out by Aristotle's comments on Leucippus.[1] In the first place the atoms 'act and are acted upon as they chance to touch one another: for in this respect they are not one '. Similarly later on in the same passage he states that 'creation comes about by touching '. The sole relation between atom and atom is that of contact: it is contact which can repel them from one another and make them fly apart again, and contact no less which is their form of union, if they remain together. In other words, the atoms never so unite as to merge into one another or lose their identity in a new 'one' which they so form. However closely they may be packed, however exactly their shapes fit into one another, there is always between each of them an 'interval' of empty space. This notion is of paramount importance for the understanding of the ancient Atomic theory and stands in marked contrast to modern ideas. For the ancients the combination of atoms was always merely that of juxtaposition. Anaxagoras,[2] as we have seen, in his theory of the 'mixture' came somewhere near the notion of a complete fusion, in which the identity of the original constituents is lost in the new substance, and such is of course the root-notion of the modern theory of chemical combination. But for Leucippus and his followers such a conception was impossible: indeed it would be a contradiction of the most fundamental principles, for it would be an alteration of the primary substance, which would of necessity destroy the ultimate permanence of reality. The atoms then in juxtaposition produce what is for appearance a 'one ': but it is not so in reality, for it is not continuous matter, but matter in tiny particles aggregated together but separated by intervals of empty space, between every one of them. 'Out of the One in the strict sense multiplicity could not be produced, nor unity in the full sense out of the Many, for that is impossible.'[3]

[1] *de Gen. et Corr. A.* 325 a; D.A. 7.
[2] See Chap. I, pp. 38 ff.　　　　　　　[3] Arist. *de Gen. et Corr.* l.c.

A second point of hardly less importance is vouched for, as far as Leucippus is concerned, only by a casual mention in Aristotle:[1] 'all things are created', he says, 'by the entanglement of the atoms and their oscillation' (περιπάλαξις). The word looks again like one of Leucippus' peculiarly descriptive technical terms, and though the doctrine only reached its full importance in Democritus or even in Epicurus, there seems no reason for denying its suggestion to Leucippus. The motion of the atoms is eternal; therefore even when they are in contact with one another in a compound body, even physically linked by their projections to one another, their motions still continue. The atoms continue to perform tiny trajects, greater or less according to the texture of the compound, colliding with one another in infinitesimal periods of time, and recoiling again to another collision: every compound body, every 'thing' that we perceive by the senses is in a constant state of internal atomic vibration. This extraordinarily penetrating idea, which seems indeed a wonderful anticipation of the beliefs of modern science, was destined to play an important part in atomic theories of motion:[2] it does not appear that Leucippus worked out its consequences, but we may fairly trust to Aristotle's statement that he had the idea.

When once the compound is formed, the void in its composition is the determining factor in its fate: 'it is owing to the void that dissolution and destruction take place and likewise increase too, through the entrance of solid particles (*sc.* atoms)'.[3] Aristotle compares the idea to Empedocles' notion of the pores, to which indeed Leucippus may have owed much of his physics, and it is not difficult to understand. Into the tiny intervals of empty space in the compound new atoms will enter in their flight from outside. Occasionally their 'shape or position or order' will fit them to become entangled in their turn and increase the bulk of the compound: as long as this happens the thing grows.

[1] *de Caelo, Γ.* 4. 303 a; D.A. 15.
[2] Especially in Epicurus: see Part II, Chap. V, pp. 331 ff.
[3] Arist. *de Gen. et Corr.* l.c.

But sometimes a particle unsuited to join the compound may enter in a space-interval with such velocity that its force will split up the compound body, loosen the hold of the original atoms and break up their juxtaposition: if the dissolution thus effected is comparatively light, the dislocation may be only momentary, or perhaps only a part of the compound may be broken off and a lessening or decay (φθίνειν) be caused, which is the reverse of the process of growth. But it may be, especially if the compound has already been weakened by many such 'blows' that the new force will be strong enough to break it up altogether: then will follow dissolution: the compound body will be destroyed, will cease to exist, and the atoms which composed it will again become 'free' or enter into some new compound. Creation, growth, decay, destruction are thus the successive stages in the history of the compound body, each being a form of atomic 'combination' or 'dissolution'.[1] But even apart from these irruptions from without, the compound body may also suffer change, the result not now of the entrance of new atoms, but of a shifting of the position or order of those which already compose it.[2] As the result of an external blow or merely by a kaleidoscopic shifting in the course of the internal vibration, the absolute or relative positions of the component atoms may be altered, and then a change will take place in the body which will be felt in its sensational effect: the shape, or colour, or sound, or smell, or taste of the thing will be altered. Once again the details of this idea were worked out later, but Leucippus seems to have laid the foundation.

The whole conception of the nature of the atoms, their motions and combinations is extraordinarily subtle and full of insight. When it is realized that it comes from a pioneer, succeeding to theories so very different in character, it is remarkable that he should have been able not merely to reach the main conception by means of which they might

---

[1] Arist. *de Gen. et Corr. A.* 315 b; D.A. 9. διακρίσει μὲν καὶ συγκρίσει γένεσιν καὶ φθοράν. Aristotle, though he correctly describes the process, seems to be using the technical terms of Anaxagoras.

[2] Ibid. τάξει δὲ καὶ θέσει ἀλλοίωσιν.

be reconciled, but to work it out into so delicate and yet economical an explanation of the fundamental nature of the universe. Much still remained to be done in the way of development and addition—not always felicitous—but all the main ideas of the nature and conduct of the atoms are there from the first in the theory of Leucippus.

§ 4. *Cosmogony : the creation of worlds*

In the first chapter it seemed best not to enter into the particulars of the early cosmogonies, because they can easily be studied elsewhere and the mass of detail involved would have obscured the main issues. For the same reason it will be sufficient here to note the source of Leucippus' principal ideas as we come to them, and to take his cosmogony as a starting-point, the basis on which later upholders of the Atomic theory had to build. A full account of his main views on the creation of worlds is given by Diogenes[1] and is confirmed in some details by an abstract of part of the 'Greater World-system' which has survived and by a few notices in the doxographers. It is to some extent expressed in the terms of a later age, but no doubt preserves the ideas of Leucippus accurately enough, and here and there has traces embedded in it of what must have been his own phraseology:

He says that the whole is infinite; that part of it is full and part empty, and these are the elements. Out of these are formed an infinite number of worlds and into these they are dissolved. The worlds are produced in this way; a large number of atoms of all kinds of shapes are carried by severance from the boundless (κατ' ἀποτομὴν ἐκ τοῦ ἀπείρου) into a great void: they gather together and form into a single whirl (δίνη), in which they collide with one another and circle round in all sorts of ways, and separate apart, like joining like. And when they can no longer whirl round in equilibrium owing to the congestion, the fine bodies go into the outer void, as if sifted out; but the rest remain together and becoming entangled, unite their motions with one another and form a kind of first spherical compound mass: and this mass stands apart as a sort of membrane, enclosing in itself atoms of all

[1] D.L. ix. 31, 2; D.A. 1.

kinds. And as they whirl round in virtue of the resistance of the centre, the membrane all round becomes thin, as the contiguous bodies always flow together owing to the contact throughout the whirl. And thus the earth is brought into being, when the particles, which are carried towards the centre, remain together. And once more the enclosing membrane is increased, as bodies outside separate out and join it:[1] and as it moves on in the whirl, it adds to itself whatever it touches. Some of these bodies cohere and make a compound mass, at first watery and muddy, but afterwards becoming dry, as they move round with the whirl of the whole system, and then catching fire, they form the material for the heavenly bodies.

At this point the account goes on to deal with astronomical questions and the conformation of our earth and its consequences in a passage which will best be considered separately, and then concludes: 'and just like the creation of the worlds,[2] so also their growth and waning and passing away take place owing to some kind of necessity, but what this is he does not make clear'.

There are many points in this account which require comment, and, if it is possible to get a clear idea of Leucippus' conception, it will lay the best foundation for the understanding of later theories. The underlying notion of the infinite 'whole' as consisting of the two 'elements', 'the full' and 'the empty', is of course derived directly from the root-principle of atomism, and it is quite clear that here, 'the empty' is regarded as that which is, where matter is not; the two 'elements' are mutually exclusive. But it must be remembered that owing to the eternal movement of the atoms, 'the full' and 'the empty' are constantly changing places: a spot which is occupied one moment will be empty the next and vice versa. Leucippus follows the lead of all previous philosophers except Heraclitus and Parmenides in holding that our 'world' is not unique, but only one of many, indeed an infinite number of similar worlds. For him this would be a natural deduction from the infinity of the atoms and space: there is no reason why atoms should gather to

---

[1] Reading ἐπέκκρισιν with Diels, 2nd ed.
[2] The plurals γενέσεις, αὐξήσεις, &c., seem to demand κόσμων for κόσμου.

form a world at one time or in one part of space any more
than at another time and place: but the idea forms part of
the cosmogonical tradition, and we find it already in Anaximander.[1] The next point is curious and shows Leucippus'
tenacity of tradition. It seems that he held the notion that
in origin the atoms moved in empty space united in a mass
of matter which he speaks of as 'the boundless'[2] (τὸ ἄπειρον).
This notion is not of course essential to Atomism, indeed it
is repugnant to it, for the atoms in the pre-cosmic state are
far more naturally conceived, as in later theories, as freely
dispersed throughout the whole of infinite space. But
Leucippus doubtless wished to attach his new theory to
previous views, and intended to recall both Anaximander's
conception of 'the boundless' and the more recent 'Mixture'
of Anaxagoras. None the less, it would not be right to
conceive Leucippus' atomic mass as a full corporeal *plenum*:
even in this original condition there must be an interval of
'the empty' between atom and atom and also movement.
From this conglomerated mass from time to time a large
number of atoms are 'severed and fall into a great void',[3]
a portion, that is of hitherto unoccupied space, which is
therefore suitable for the creation of a world. Diogenes'
phraseology at this point suggests that he is quoting Leucippus' own words, and once again the idea of the breaking off
of a mass of atoms recalls Anaximander's 'separating out of
opposites' from 'the boundless', and more closely the breaking away of 'seeds' in Anaxagoras' theory. When Atomism
became more free from tradition, this consequential conception of 'the boundless' likewise disappeared.

The idea of the 'whirl' (δίνη) is characteristic of the
Atomic School at all its stages, but the account given by

---

[1] [Plut.] *Strom.* 2; D. 10 (Anaximander).

[2] Gomperz, *G. T.*, p. 335, renders κατ' ἀποτομὴν ἐκ τοῦ ἀπείρου
'severing themselves from the infinite vacuum', but it is hard to attach any
meaning to this, and 'the boundless' must surely be the concentrated mass of
matter, as in the theories of Anaximander and Anaxagoras.

[3] εἰς μεγὰ κενόν certainly does not mean, as some critics have rendered it,
'into *the* great void'.

Diogenes of its formation and development is obscure. Some of the difficulties to which it gives rise will be better considered in the light of the theories of Democritus, but the general picture can be grasped. The conception of a 'whirl' is in fact already found in Anaxagoras, for with him[1] it was a rotatory motion which was originally communicated by 'mind' to portions of the 'mixture' and was maintained after they had broken off to form a world. The notion is no doubt derived from the actual appearance of the heavens as the inside of a hollow sphere, in which the heavenly bodies move in circles.

As to the cause of the 'whirl'—the reason, that is, why this mass of atoms should develop a circular motion, Leucippus once again, as in regard to the original motion of the atoms, could only say, if he did indeed assign a reason at all,[2] that it was 'necessity', by which here too he probably meant not an arbitrary force but the natural process of cause and effect. The atoms moved according to a law of their own being: they would unite in the void in all sorts of formations and one of these might be a 'whirl': if it was, a 'cosmos' resulted.

The 'vortex' once formed, four stages are apparently distinguished. In the first stage the motion of the 'whirl' affects all the atoms uniformly, but they still retain their original motion as well and move about 'colliding and circling in all sorts of ways'. The general result is expressed in terms familiar in the cosmology of Anaxagoras: the atoms are 'separated out' (διακρίνεται) and 'like joins like'. Now for Anaxagoras the meaning is clear enough: the 'likeness' is that of substance, seeds similar in their prevailing substance are sifted out from the 'mixture' and come together: but what can be the meaning for the Atomists, whose primary particles are all absolutely homogeneous in substance? The reference must be to the only points in which there can be

---

[1] See pp. 40 ff.

[2] Diogenes' complaint looks like an echo of the dissatisfaction of Aristotle as to the efficient cause, and we must not attach too much importance to his statement that Leucippus attributed the creation of worlds to ἀνάγκη: see above, p. 90.

difference between atoms, regarded individually, namely, shape and size.[1] Those of similar shape come together: the larger join the larger, the smaller the smaller. The conception is clearly brought out by the famous illustration which is attributed to Democritus, but was probably a common-place of the Atomists: 'for among animals[2] too like herds with like, doves with doves, and cranes with cranes, and so on with other beasts: and similarly in the case of inanimate things, as we can see with seeds in a sieve and pebbles on the shore: for in the whirling (δῖνος) of the sieve beans range themselves apart with beans and barley with barley and wheat with wheat, and by the motion of the waves large stones are driven to the same place with other large stones and round with round, just as if the similarity among them had an attractive force'. The reference in the last example to size and shape as the determining elements is explicit, and there is an exact parallel to the first effect of the whirl.

The second and third stages are more difficult to understand, but are not, I think, really confused in thought. The atoms in their original free motion outside the whirl were 'in equilibrium' (ἰσόρροπα): that is, as Burnet[3] has clearly shown, their 'tendency to move in one direction is exactly equal to the tendency in any other'. But now the uniform direction of the whirl has produced a congestion (πλῆθος), which impedes the free exercise of the original motion in all directions. The result is that the 'fine', that is the 'smaller', atoms are, by a characteristic atomic conception which is used to explain all upward motion,[4] caught between the larger atoms and 'squeezed out'[5] into the outer void. The larger atoms remain behind and 'stay together':[6] interlacing

---

[1] See Liepmann, *Die Mechanik der Leucipp-Democritischen Atome*, p. 27.

[2] D. (Democritus) B. 164.

[3] *E. G. P.*3, p. 345. There is no question here of weight, nor is there, I think, in any other part of Leucippus' theory: Democritus first spoke of 'heavier' and 'lighter' atoms in a sense which needs explanation: see pp. 128 ff.

[4] The σοῦς, Arist. *de Caelo*, Δ. 6. 313 a; D. (Democritus) A. 62.

[5] Diogenes says 'sifted out' (διαττώμενα), but the corresponding account in Aet. i. 4. 2; D.A. 24 has the characteristic atomic term ἐξεθλίβετο.

[6] συμμένειν, the technical word for compound bodies.

and uniting their motions (συγκατατρέχειν), they form into 'the first spherical body'. At the end then of the second stage we must conceive the 'whirl' as filled with more or less compactness by this mass of the larger atoms, separated of course by intervals of void, retaining individually something of their former motion in all directions, but all affected by the single rotatory motion of the whirl. This mass is described picturesquely by Leucippus as a 'membrane' (ὑμήν), which 'stands apart' (ἀφίστασθαι) as an individual formation amid the indiscriminate movement of the surrounding universe: it contains in itself atoms of every size and shape.

In the third stage the effect of the rotatory motion becomes still more definite, and modern criticism has done much to elucidate the rather cryptic phraseology of our account. The whirl, as Aristotle[1] tells us, was always conceived by the philosophers who spoke of it on the analogy of an eddy of wind or water. From this two results follow: in the first place it must be thought of as horizontal, not vertical, so that motion from the centre outwards or vice versa is not motion 'up' or 'down'. In the second, it must not be thought of either as a conglomeration of disconnected and independent atoms or bits of compound matter, moved in rotation by an external force, nor on the other as possessing the complete connexion or rigidity of a revolving solid wheel or plate. Its component parts are independent in the sense that they are always intersected by intervals of empty space, but they are connected owing to the contact (ἐπίψαυσις) of contiguous atoms which holds good throughout the whirl. In other words the 'spherical' mass is a revolving body with the kind of elasticity which might belong, for example, to a wheel made of chain-mail—indeed even that would be too rigid an illustration, and the notion of the water-eddy gives the best idea. This being so the rotatory motion is

---

[1] *de Caelo*, B. 13. 295 a; Burnet, *E. G. P*.3 346 has completely defended Leucippus against Gomperz's charge of blindness in not perceiving and using the idea of 'centrifugal force'. His explanation of the character of the whirl and of the 'resistance of the middle' (ἡ τοῦ μέσου ἀντέρεισις) seem to me convincing.

quickest and strongest at the outer edge, and there it is impossible for any atom or atomic nucleus to resist the whirl. Thanks to the chain of contiguous atoms the motion is communicated from the outer edge towards the centre, but the nearer it approaches the centre, the weaker and slower it becomes: at the centre itself there is a possibility of complete 'resistance' to the rotation. Just then as might be the case with sticks thrown into an eddy of water, the larger atoms and the more solid of the atomic nuclei[1] now formed tend in proportion to their bulk to gather towards the centre: their size[2] gives them the capacity of resisting the whirl and they gather together where resistance is most easy. Two consequences follow. On the one hand the outer part of the membrane is thinned, as in it are left only those 'finer' and 'smaller' bodies which offer least resistance and are carried on by the vortex, on the other the comparatively unmoving mass in the centre becomes more and more compact and forms what for the first time may be described as 'an earth'. A marked distinction now arises between this central body and the outer 'membrane', which, although always in contact with it owing to the atomic 'contiguity', yet becomes more markedly independent both in character and position.

The last stage is concerned solely with the development of the outer 'membrane'. It receives no more accessions from within the sphere and is indeed in itself wholly rarified, containing only the 'finest' of the bodies: but as it whirls round it attracts 'bodies'—again probably, both atoms and atomic nuclei—from the outer universe. These are caught up in the whirl, and uniting into compounds with one another, form large masses, which gradually drying and even igniting owing to the rapidity of the whirl, become the fiery substance of sun, moon, and stars. The cosmos is then com-

---

[1] I do not think with Burnet that in this stage we are any longer dealing solely with 'larger and smaller *atoms*'; the second stage has clearly led to the formation of atomic nuclei and compounds, and in the third 'bodies' must be held to include both.

[2] As will be seen it is at this point in the system that Democritus begins to speak of 'heavier' and 'lighter' bodies.

plete, and a 'world', as we know it, has been evolved. The account does not add, as Leucippus must have held, that the interval between the outer membrane and the earth is filled up and the link of contact supplied by the intervening air.

In Leucippus' cosmogony there are, as has been incidentally noticed, many features which recall the ideas of Anaxagoras and even go back to the earlier speculations of the Ionian philosophers. It may indeed be called 'reactionary'[1] in the sense that Leucippus undoubtedly desired here, as elsewhere, to attach himself closely to previous philosophical tradition. But it is surely remarkable that with all this conservatism he has been able to present the process of world creation in the vortex in a manner essentially his own, developed naturally from his own main contentions and gaining thereby a coherence and a scientific character which it never before possessed. The whirl itself is no longer a causeless, superimposed form of motion, but one of the many which result naturally from the free atomic movement; and its effects are no longer arbitrary, but deduced with a high degree of accurate imagination from the data of its character: the joining of 'like to like', the aggregation of the larger earth-particles in the centre, the rush of the light ether-particles to the outer rim are now all accounted for by a 'necessity' which is not an extraneous power, but the natural manifestation of causation. His originality consists not in a wholly new imagination, but in the brilliant adaptation of previous notions to his own main position, and the explanation of them by its means. Those who are interested in the anticipation of modern ideas may notice a distinct resemblance throughout to the main conceptions of the 'nebular hypothesis', and will be struck again with the notion of the drying and ignition of solid bodies owing to the rapidity of the motion of the whirl. In short Leucippus' cosmogony is not an attempt to break away from previous tradition, but to harmonize that tradition with new conditions. It shows a very notable faculty of adjustment and is not without prophetic insight.

[1] E. G. P.3, p. 347.

We may now proceed to the details of the world thus formed which are mostly derived from the small section in Diogenes' account previously omitted: 'the orbit of the sun is outermost, that of the moon nearest the earth, those of the other heavenly bodies between these two. All of them catch fire owing to the rapidity of their motion and the sun also receives flame from the stars; but the moon has but a small share in the fire. And the sun and moon are eclipsed (and the obliquity of the zodiac is caused[1]) by the inclination of the earth towards the south; and the northern regions are always under snow and are cold and frozen. The sun is eclipsed rarely and the moon continually because their orbits are uneven'. The earth then is the centre of the world. The geocentric idea was held by all the early philosophers, except the Pythagoreans, who believed in a 'great fire' in the centre. Leucippus did not oppose the general tradition, and by placing the earth in the centre could also explain how it was held at rest by the 'resistance of the centre', and so being motionless remain solid and moist. In orbits at various distances from the earth revolved the moon, the stars, and the sun. This was a direct contradiction of the traditional view, which placed the orbit of the stars outside that of the sun, but it was held by Anaximander[2] and Leucippus' reason for adopting it was doubtless that, as the sun gives more light than the stars, it must be more completely on fire and must therefore be placed where the speed of the 'whirl' is greatest. It is clear from the theory of eclipses, as due to the passing of sun and moon behind the raised northern parts of the world, that all three orbits were regarded as horizontal to the earth and not, as was usually conceived, perpendicular: the whole 'whirl' must therefore be imagined as lying in a horizontal plane. No distinction is made between fixed stars and planets, although this again had long been observed. The statement that the sun is 'also kindled (ἐκπυροῦσθαι) by the stars' is not easy to interpret, but was no doubt intended

---

[1] These words are not in the manuscripts, but can be supplied with certainty.

[2] Aet. ii. 15. 6; D. (Anaximander) 18.

to explain its superior brightness, and is probably connected with his general atomic view: just as 'the membrane' caught up particles from the void to form fuel for the heavenly bodies generally, so presumably the sun in its orbit attracted fire from the neighbouring stars—but the notion is not clear without further explanation than we possess. The moon does not apparently get her light from the sun, as even Anaximander[1] had held, but simply has 'less of the fire'. There is much that seems wilfully childish in all this, but possibly a fuller account of Leucippus' reasons would make it clear why in so many instances he went back to very antiquated notions.

Almost more puerile is his idea of the earth's shape and position and the consequences. The earth itself is 'drum-shaped',[2] that is of the flat shape which we associate rather with the tambourine: the shape of the earth was always a traditional matter of controversy among the cosmologists, and Leucippus once more returns to a notion of Anaximander,[3] who described the earth as 'the drum of a column'. It was tilted up towards the north and down towards the south, because the atmosphere[4] in the southern parts was warm and therefore thin in texture, that in the north chilled and frozen, and therefore more solid and better able to support the earth: the notion is again primitive, but Leucippus manages to support it in relation to his general atomic and cosmological theories. To this tilting of the earth are due the eclipses of sun and moon, which occur when they pass behind the northern regions, and similarly the cycle of the zodiac seems oblique apparently because the earth itself is tilted in relation to it: Anaximenes[5] had already used the same idea to explain night, but that Leucippus should have had recourse to this ancient notion of eclipses is the more remarkable since both Empedocles and Anaxagoras had

---

[1] D.L. ii. 1; D. (Anaximander) 1.
[2] τυμπανοειδής, Aet. iii. 10. 4; D.A. 26.
[3] Aet. iii. 10. 2; D. (Anaximander) 25.
[4] Aet. iii. 12. 1; D.A. 27.
[5] Arist. *Meteor.* B. 1. 354 a; D (Anaximenes) A. 14.

rightly explained them. The more frequent eclipse of the moon is due to the greater proximity of its orbit to the earth and its consequent comparative shortness.

Leucippus no doubt also discussed meteorological phenomena in the traditional manner of the early philosophers, but all that survives to us is his explanation of thunder, which is mainly of interest because it is markedly different from that of Democritus: 'when fire that is caught in very thick clouds falls out, it produces a loud clap of thunder'.[1] Once again this simple belief comes from Anaximander.

In comparison with the brilliance and originality of Leucippus' main atomic theory, his cosmology seems disappointing and lacking in independence. Not only does he show an extreme tenacity in retaining the views of previous thinkers, but, at any rate in the details of his world-system, a wilful perverseness in neglecting recent ideas and returning to the antiquated notions of Anaximander and Anaximenes. Burnet[2] indeed believes his whole cosmology to be based on Ionian ideas and would account for it on the ground that Leucippus was unwilling to accept a cosmology from the Eleatics, who, though their views had been so divergent from his own, had yet suggested Atomism to him, and wishing his theories to be consistently divergent from those of the Pluralists, was necessarily driven back on to those of the Ionians. But surely, if the analysis given above be at all correct, we must draw a great distinction between the main theory of the creation of the world and the subsequent astronomical details. In the former, although there is no doubt much that suggests, and is intended to suggest, the old Ionian views, it is impossible to deny either the very close relation of Leucippus' system to that of Anaxagoras, or the ingenuity with which previous theories are adapted to suit the new conditions of Atomism. As far as this main theory is concerned, it would be truer to say that Leucippus, just as in his Atomic theory itself, wished to appear as the mediator between his predecessors. He accordingly constructed an account in which many conceptions were meant

---

[1] Aet. iii. 3. 10; D.A. 25.   [2] *E. G. P.*[3], p. 339.

to recall the views of earlier philosophers, both of the old Monists and more particularly of Anaxagoras. But for all its reminiscences the whole is conceived directly on the basis of his own Atomic theory, and the more closely we inquire into details the more apparent becomes the insight with which it was worked out: it has possibly seemed unduly crude to the critics, because it has not been fully understood. But the details of the world-system stand altogether on a different plane and do often show a blindness which is certainly unworthy of the rest of his theory. He not only disregards the theories of the Pythagoreans who, by abandoning the notion of a geocentric world, had made an advance in science comparable in antiquity only to Atomism itself, but, what is more serious in the light of his ideas of creation, he makes no use at all of the often far-sighted theories of Empedocles and Anaxagoras. It is indeed difficult to account for this blindness, but the subsequent history of Atomism would suggest that the true explanation is that while his primary interest lay in the first principles of the Atomic theory and in the main outlines of cosmology, he was comparatively indifferent to astronomical details, and was content to accept current popular notions without considering the more serious conjectures of his contemporaries: there are not wanting traces of a similar attitude both in Democritus and Epicurus.

§ 5. *The soul, sensation, and theory of knowledge*

Certain notices have come down to us concerning Leucippus' theories on psychology and metaphysic—to use modern terms. In each case he is associated with Democritus and it is a little difficult to know how far the views may not really be rather due to the latter: on the analogy of other parts of the system, where we have more explicit information, it is probably safe to attribute to Leucippus the first outline of ideas which Democritus subsequently elaborated.

The soul (ψυχή) had been conceived by the early philosophers as the cause of life in the body and also, after they began to reflect on the subject, as the cause of sensation. They regarded it as distributed over the body and of course as a material existence just like everything else. They were therefore from the first interested in discussing the substance of which it was composed. Anaximander, for what reason we do not know, described it as 'like air'[1] (ἀερώδης), and Anaximenes, wishing no doubt to associate the soul with the primal substance, definitely stated that it was 'airy'[2] (ἀερία). Heraclitus for the same reason called it an 'exhalation'[3] (ἀναθυμίασις), the word by which he described the passing of all other substances into the primal fire. Anaxagoras[4] had gone back on the older idea that it was 'like air', but Leucippus[5] returned to Heraclitus' notion that it was fire. His reason is characteristic and typical of the way in which he adapted previous notions to his own general theory: fire was composed of spherical atoms, and Leucippus decided that it must be spherical atoms also which made the soul: 'because "rhythms"[6] of this kind can most easily penetrate through everything and can move other things as they move themselves'. The idea is naïve, but ingenious. The spherical shape is the least able to remain at rest and therefore the most mobile: fire in the external world and the soul within us are the most mobile things we know: therefore they must both be composed of spherical atoms and be alike in substance. Moreover, a spherical shape can not only move itself but also move anything in which it may be contained: the spherical soul-atoms distributed over the body and rolling about move the limbs, much as a marble will move a small doll, and in this way it is the soul which 'gives living things their power of movement'. The intense materialism of the idea seems strange to us, but if it once be granted, the reasoning is acute and was destined to hold its place with Democritus.

Aristotle[7] has preserved another doctrine of Leucippus'

[1] Aet. iv. 3. 2; D. (Anaximander) 29.
[2] Philopon. in Arist. de Anima, Prooem.; D. (Anaximenes) A. 23.
[3] Arist. de Anima, A. 2. 405 a.; Aet. iv. 3. 12; D. (Heraclitus) A. 15.
[4] Aet. iv. 3. 1; D. (Anaxagoras) A. 93.
[5] Arist. de Anima, A. 2. 404 a; D.A. 28.
[6] ῥυσμούς, i.e. 'shapes', Leucippus' own technical term: see p. 79.
[7] l.c.

which is equally interesting: he thought 'that respiration is the limit (ὅρος) of life'—that is, that when respiration ceases, so does life.

'For as surrounding matter presses together our bodies and squeezes out atoms of the shape which cause motion in living creatures because even by themselves they can never remain still (i.e. the spherical atoms), assistance comes from without when other atoms of the same kind enter in in respiration. For these also prevent those which are already in the living creatures from being separated out, by assisting in driving back that which is pressing and contracting them. And they live as long as they are able to do this.'

The general idea of the importance of respiration to life comes no doubt from Empedocles,[1] but once more Leucippus has ingeniously modified the notion of its process and function on atomic lines. The relation of the surrounding atmosphere to the living creature is conceived as closely parallel to that of the outer universe to the created world: it is at once a source of supply and a danger. The body is at every moment subject to blows, which tend to disrupt it and 'squeeze out' atoms from its structure, the spherical soul-atoms as much as others. But for long it is able by respiration to take in fresh supplies of soul-atoms, which not only add to its vitality and maintain the power of motion, but also act as a kind of buffer to those already within the body against the continuing attacks. But either through some sudden blow of tremendous force, or by the gradual reversal of the balance, the attack ultimately gains the upper hand: respiration fails, the supply of soul-atoms ceases, and life passes from the body. The whole idea is a special and careful application of Leucippus'[2] general theory of growth, decay, and destruction.

Leucippus is also credited by the authorities with having originated the famous theory of vision, which was so prominent in the Atomic theory. Once more Empedocles is certainly the source. It will be remembered that the theory of Empedocles,[3] that vision was due to the fitting of effluences

[1] See his elaborate account of the process in D. (Empedocles) B. 100.
[2] See p. 88.   [3] See Chap. I, § 3, p. 54.

from things into the pores of the eyes, like perceiving like, stood apart from the general current of ideas of vision, in that it took no account of the image in the pupil (ἔμφασις). Leucippus adopting the general notion that perception must be due to contact and that therefore there must be some 'effluence' from the object to the eye, was, thanks to the atomic theory, able both to explain what this effluence was and to connect it with the image seen in the eye. He said that 'idols [1] (εἴδωλα) flow off, similar in shape to the objects from which they flow, that is to say, visible things, and fall into the eyes of the persons seeing and that sight results in this way'. This brief account may be a little amplified from our general knowledge of Atomism. The idea which he held generally of the constant efflux of atoms from things, broken off or squeezed out by blows external and internal, enabled Leucippus to explain without difficulty how effluences might arise. Moreover, he could now show that these effluences would bear a direct relation to the thing from which they came: for they would be in fact, as was more carefully explained later on, a sort of thin atomic film arising from the surface of the visible object, and therefore exactly 'similar to it in shape'. This film or 'idol' he conceived as traversing the intervening space, entering the eye and then itself becoming the ocular image (ἔμφασις). The idea is as yet crude: it was to be greatly refined and modified by Democritus, but Epicurus, anxious to leave as little chance as possible for error in perception, returned to an idea not far removed from that of Leucippus. We are told briefly that Leucippus explained the other senses too as 'alterations of the body',[2] and may suppose that in their case also he worked out the main atomic ideas of the nature of the effluences and their action on the senses. More important is the attribution to him of the belief that 'thought too takes place when "idols" come in from without: for neither sensation nor thought can grasp anything (ἐπιβάλλειν) apart from the "idol" which falls upon them'.[3] The identification of the processes of sensation and

[1] Alex. in Arist. de Sensu, B. 438 a; D.A. 29.
[2] Aet. iv. 8. 5; D.A. 30.
[3] Ibid. iv. 8. 10; D.A. 30.

thought was, as has been seen, traditional, and Leucippus characteristically took it over and worked it out on his own theory: the 'thought-image' was to run through all the versions of the atomic theory, carrying with it an essentially material view of the mental processes and a continuous habit of regarding thought as a kind of 'visualization'. Once more Leucippus appears as at once reconciler and pioneer.

With regard to Leucippus' view of the validity of sense-perception and the means of obtaining true knowledge it is very difficult to speak with certainty. It might well be expected in view of his theory that sensation is effected not by any direct contact or communication between object and percipient but by the medium of 'idols' and effluences, which might be altered in their transit, that he would be sceptical in regard to the information of sense-perception. And indeed the doxographers do attribute to him in common with Democritus the very definite doctrine that the qualities perceived by sense exist only 'by convention [1] (νόμῳ), that is to say, by opinion (δόξῃ) and our sensations (πάθεσι): for nothing is true or comprehensible except the first elements, atoms, and void. For these alone exist by nature (φύσει), and all else are the properties (συμβεβηκότα) of these differing from one another according to position and order and shape'. Now this we know to be very nearly the position of Democritus [2] reached as the result of a long process of thought and involving something like the distinction between primary and secondary qualities. Of all this there is no other trace in the records of Leucippus, and it seems much more like the subtle refinement and distinction which is so characteristic of Democritus and so much less usual with his master. Moreover, we have Aristotle's [3] definite statement, when he is discussing the shapes of the atoms, that it was because Leucippus saw the infinite variety of things and 'thought that the truth lay in appearance' that he attributed infinite differences of shape to the atoms too. The two positions are not of course inconsistent, and Leucippus may well have held

[1] Aet. iv. 9. 8; D.A. 32.   [2] See Chap. III, § 8, pp. 177 ff.
[3] de Gen. et Corr. A. 315 b; D.A. 9.

something the same position as Anaxagoras, that the senses were, if properly used, safe guides to the discovery of truth, but could not in themselves give full and accurate information. Such a general conclusion would be both in harmony with his predecessors and a natural accompaniment of an atomic theory of reality, it may even have led Leucippus to make the distinction between 'conventional' and 'natural' existences, but that he held any such precise doctrine as that here attributed to him, seems unlikely. Again he was probably content with a general attitude and the careful working out of distinctions was the work of Democritus.

§ 6. *Conclusion*

The main points in Leucippus' Atomic theory have now been traversed and it remains to form some general conclusion as to its value and importance. Leucippus' work may be viewed either with reference to the past or to the future. There has been much discussion as to his place in the chain of early thinkers and the true relation of his theory to those of the preceding Schools. The most recent English writer[1] concludes that 'so far as his general theory of the physical constitution of the world is concerned . . . it was derived entirely from Eleatic and Pythagorean sources, while the detailed cosmology was in the main a more or less successful attempt to make the older Ionian beliefs fit into this new physical theory'. If the foregoing analysis has been at all correct, it may fairly be said that this conclusion is in both its inferences too narrow. If it was the Eleatic criticism of the theories of the Pythagoreans which led Leucippus logically to an Atomic solution of the problems before him, yet the whole physical setting of his theory and the view it implied of the physical substratum of existence was a direct inheritance from the Ionian Monists and the Pluralists. On the other hand though in the details of his cosmology he showed a perverse preference for the antiquated beliefs of Anaximander and Anaximenes, yet his main conception of the 'whirl' and the process by which within it an ordered world

[1] Burnet, *E. G. P.*3, p. 349.

came into being has much more affinity to the theory of Anaxagoras. Finally, in his speculations on psychology and the process of sensation he undoubtedly took Empedocles as his guide. It would, I think, be a truer view of Leucippus to regard him in all parts of his system, as antiquity did, as the mediator in the long dispute, who was able to reconcile opposing schools by a new solution of the antimonies which divided them. Thus he reconciled the 'One' of Parmenides and the Eleatics with the 'Many' of the Pluralists by the conception of a permanent substratum which though not continuous, is homogeneous, one in substance, though not in extension. He satisfied the criticism which the Eleatics had aimed at the Pythagoreans by maintaining that matter was infinite in extent, and existed in the form of infinite particles, but was yet not infinitely divisible. He saw that the only solution of the *impasse* of Monism was the admission of the existence of empty space, yet he agreed with the strictest Monists that it was not 'real' or 'full existence'. In all these ways he seems not merely the logical successor of a single School, whose tenets were mostly negative in tendency, but the inheritor and critic of them all, who by a single far-sighted conjecture went far to remove the difficulties over which they differed. And if it be asked what were his greatest positive contributions to the history of thought, the answer would be that they were two: firstly, the introduction of a new conception of reality which showed 'how body must be regarded if we take it to be the ultimate reality',[1] and secondly, the formulation of a Pluralistic theory of the constitution of the world, which was infinitely more economical than that of Anaxagoras and maintained at the same time the unity of homogeneity. He had given the most fully satisfactory answer to the original question of Thales.

For the future he had laid down the lines on which a new and fruitful speculation might proceed. He had found a basis for the understanding of the physical world, whose possibilities were only gradually unfolded. He had established the main principles of the Atomic theory and had gone far too, as well

[1] Ibid.

as we can judge, in the working out of its application in detail both with regard to the nature of the ultimate particles of matter and the manner of their combinations and in his ideas of the creation and structure of the world. No doubt there was much left for his successors to do. The theory must be amplified and elaborated in detail: gaps must be filled up and on many points, where Leucippus' speculation was obviously crude and unsatisfying, alterations must be made. Democritus was to work this physical hypothesis into something like a universal system, to think out its metaphysical principles and to connect it—albeit loosely—with a philosophy of life. But however much his successors added, altered, and improved, the main outlines of the Atomic theory in antiquity remained always those which were sketched by Leucippus. His name was obscured later by the fame of his great disciple, and modern science, when it propounded an Atomic theory of the world, assumed the airs of a new discoverer, but none the less Leucippus deserves all the credit due to the pioneer, the first founder of Atomism.

III

DEMOCRITUS

§ 1. *Life and writings*

DEMOCRITUS is a far less shadowy figure than Leucippus and the air of mystery which hangs over his life is due rather to his own strange personality than to our lack of information. There is no reason to doubt the almost universal tradition that his birthplace was Abdera[1] in Thrace: the alternative statement that he was a Milesian must be due either to confusion with Leucippus or to a desire to associate him with the Milesian School, just as Leucippus himself was said to have been born at Elea. His date is practically fixed by his own assertion in the 'Lesser World-system'[2] that he was 'a young man in the old age of Anaxagoras, being forty years his junior'. This would tally well enough with Apollodorus' assertion[3] that he was born in the eightieth Olympiad (460–457 B.C.), and his 'floruit' might then be placed about 420 B.C., which would be quite consistent with the most probable view of his relations with Leucippus—that he was his pupil and about ten years younger. The assertion[4] that he was born in the third year of the seventy-seventh Olympiad (470–469 B.C.), though more definite, would make him rather older than is probable, while the wild statement[5] that Democritus and Anaxagoras were both contemporaries of Heraclitus, born at the outset of the fifth century, only serves to show how untrustworthy our tradition can be in matters of chronology.

Many stories of his life have come down to us, some fanciful, but others out of which it seems possible to construct a plausible account. His father, whose name is given variously as Hegesistratus or Athenocritus or Damasippus, was apparently a man of wealth and position in Abdera and

---

[1] e.g. D.L. ix. 34; D.A. 1; Suidas, s.v. Δημόκριτος, D.A. 2.
[2] D.L. ix. 41.   [3] Ibid.   [4] Of Thrasylus, ibid.
[5] Euseb. *Chron. Cyrill. c. Jul.* 1. 13; D.A. 4.

is said to have entertained Xerxes on his march through Thrace. According to the story[1] Xerxes left some of his household with his host, and they instructed Democritus in his youth in oriental astronomy and 'theology': but unless we suppose that they remained in Hegesistratus' household for at least twenty-five years it is impossible to credit this legend and it must be supposed to have arisen to account for Democritus' early interest in orientalism. On his father's death,[2] Democritus, who was the third son, is said to have taken the ready money as his portion of the inheritance and to have spent it all in travelling, for which he had a passion.[3] We are told that he visited Egypt and learnt mathematics from the priests, and then turning eastward went to Persia and even to India, where he conversed with 'the naked philosophers'. There is nothing improbable in these distant travels, and their influence may be traced clearly enough in the very wide scope of the writings attributed to him. A large number of mathematical works[4] suggest the influence of Egypt, while treatises[5] with such titles as 'Concerning the sacred writings in Babylon', 'Concerning things in Meroe', 'Account of Chaldaea', certainly support the story of travel in Africa and the East. He is said too to have had the habit of going into contemplative retirements,[6] during which he 'lived in tombs', a practice which may well have been derived from Eastern sages, and the attribution to him of uncanny knowledge[7] and the gift of prophecy[8] with regard to the weather points again in the same direction. Though it is difficult to trace any direct oriental influence in the main notions of his philosophy, it adds to the picturesqueness of his character to think of him as the much-travelled man tinged in the eyes of his contemporaries with the mystery of the East.

With regard to his philosophical training authorities seem

---

[1] D.L. ix. 34.   [2] Ibid. 35, &c.
[3] See his own statement D.B. 247, quoted on p. 205.
[4] D.L. ix. 47; D.A. 33.
[5] Ibid. 49.   [6] Ibid. 38.   [7] Ibid. 42.
[8] Clem. *Strom.* vi. 32; Plin. *N. H.* xviii. 341; D.A. 18.

to be agreed that he was a pupil of Leucippus, and indeed it can hardly be otherwise, whether we suppose that he visited him in Miletus, or, as is probable, that Leucippus[1] himself came in later life to Abdera and founded the Atomic School there. There are however several other statements about his education which deserve attention. It was asserted that he also 'heard' Anaxagoras,[2] but though there is nothing in the discrepancy of their age which makes this impossible, nor can we agree with Diogenes that Democritus' statement that Anaxagoras filched his doctrines as to the sun and moon from earlier philosophers makes it inconceivable that he can have been his pupil, it seems hard to imagine when they can have met except during Democritus' very brief visit to Athens. Most likely the statement means little more than that there are traces of Anaxagoras' influence in Democritus' theory. The same is probably the true explanation of the assertion[3] made on the authority of Democritus' contemporary, Glaucus of Rhegium, that he 'heard one of the Pythagoreans': a visit to Magna Graecia is of course a conceivable incident in his travels, and he certainly wrote a work called 'Pythagoras', but little special trace of Pythagoreanism is to be found in his theories, except in so far as Pythagoreanism was in a general sense the forerunner of Atomism. A more interesting story[4] tells that he came to Athens and 'knew Socrates', though owing to his modesty he refrained from making himself known to him: 'I came to Athens', he said himself, 'and no one recognizes me':[5] the influence of Socrates might account for the far greater preponderance of the moral interest in Democritus than in any of his predecessors.

His universal knowledge gained for him among his contemporaries the nickname of 'Wisdom'[6] ($\Sigma o\phi\iota a$), and it is indeed amply justified by the extremely wide scope of his

[1] Gomperz, *Greek Thinkers*, p. 317, definitely asserts this, but evidence seems lacking, except for the obviously incorrect statement that Leucippus was a native of Abdera: see Chap. II, p. 66.   [2] D.L. ix. 34.
[3] Ibid. 38.   [4] Ibid. 36.   [5] Ibid.
[6] Suidas D.A. 2; Clem. *Strom*. l.c.

writings. It would be interesting in this connexion to suppose, as Thrasylus[1] suggested, that he is the philosopher in the pseudo-Platonic *Anterastai*, who compares the philosopher to a pentathlete: 'for indeed he was a pentathlete in philosophy'. His more famous title of 'the laughing philosopher'[2] (*Γελασῖνος*), which became immensely popular in Graeco-Roman times, is said to be due to his good-natured amusement at 'the vain efforts' of men and is illustrated by such stories as that of his interview with Darius.[3] It is generally agreed that he lived to an extraordinary old age: the authorities make him something between 90 and 109 at the time of his death.[4] It was also said[5] that before the end of his life he went blind, or even blinded himself, and maintained that what he could see with the 'soul's eye' was truer and more beautiful than things perceived with the bodily eye. There is another characteristic story that, when he perceived that his faculties were waning, he preferred to die and refused sustenance,[6] but that during the Thesmophoria,[7] which then took place, he prolonged his life by inhaling hot loaves of bread, in order that his sister might not be prevented by mourning for his death from taking part in the festival. Whether it be true or not, the tale well illustrates both his personal fortitude and his kindly feeling for others.

Of Democritus' works we possess a full list arranged by Thrasylus[8] on the model of the Platonic tetralogies. It shows an extraordinary width of interest and something like an encyclopaedic attempt to embrace all knowledge as it existed in his day. It is worth while to notice the titles of some of the works which were of most philosophical importance or suggested problems afterwards dealt with by Epicurus: others will serve to illustrate the variety of his investigations.

[1] D.L. ix. 37.
[2] Suidas, l.c.; Hor. *Ep.* ii. 1. 194; Juvenal, x. 33.
[3] Julian. *Ep.* 37; D.A. 20.
[4] '90' Diod. xiv. 11; D.A. 5: 'over 100' D.L. ix. 39; D.A. 1; '109' Hipparchus, D.L. ibid. 43.
[5] Cic. *Tusc.* v. 39. 114; D.A. 22, &c.
[6] Lucr. iii. 1039; *Ath. Epit.* ii. 46; D.A. 29.
[7] D.L. ix. 43.   [8] Ibid. 45 ff.

(1) Under the head of Ethics, besides the treatise already noticed entitled 'Pythagoras', there was an essay on 'The Lower World' (περὶ τῶν ἐν Ἅιδου), in which he[1] seems to have discussed from the physiological point of view the circumstances under which a man apparently dead might come to life, and the 'Tritogeneia',[2] where he explained the goddess's title as an allegorical reference to the three gifts of prudence, right reason, right speaking, and right action. More important was the work on 'Cheerfulness' (εὐθυμίη) which represented Democritus' moral ideal. (2) In the department of Physics there are four tetralogies, containing the works of greatest interest for the exposition of the Atomic theory. The list begins with the 'Greater World-system', which Theophrastus assigned to Leucippus: it seems on the whole more likely that the complete elaboration of the atomic theory should have been the work of Democritus, but, if the attribution to Leucippus is right, the 'Lesser World-system' (Μικρὸς Διάκοσμος), which follows in the list, may perhaps be regarded as Democritus' own exposition of the theory, the title being chosen with the natural humility of a disciple. Unfortunately such remains as can with certainty be assigned to it, do not give much clue to its contents.[3] The 'Cosmography' and the book 'On Planets' would have worked out his cosmological ideas in detail, and it may be noticed that the title of the last book implies that, unlike Leucippus, Democritus distinguished between planets and fixed stars. In the second tetralogy four important books are included, (a) the first book on Nature (περὶ φύσεως), dealing with the world, (b) the second book on Nature, dealing with Man, (c) On the Mind, (d) On Sensation, these two last being sometimes classed together under the title 'On the Soul'. All these works must of course have been of cardinal importance and together comprised Democritus' teaching on physiology and psychology. Next comes a tetralogy dealing with the 'secondary qualities' of taste and colour and the

---

[1] Procl. *in Remp.* ii. 113; D.B. 1.
[2] *Etym. Orion*, p. 153, 5; D.B. 2: see p. 196.
[3] D.L. ix. 41; D.B. 5.

ultimate differences of atomic 'rhythm' by which they were caused: from these books are preserved some of the most important fragments [1] dealing with the theory of knowledge. The last tetralogy of the Physics dealt mainly with the logical aspect of investigation and contained the 'Guarantees' (Κρατυντήρια), apparently a critical confirmation of the general theory, the 'Idols' or 'Concerning Providence' (titles rather difficult to reconcile, though the book probably dealt with the origin of the belief in the divine ruling of the world owing to the visitations of the 'idols' of supernatural beings), the Logical Canon and certain Problems: fragments of these books have again survived. (3) Next follow a number of unarranged books of Αἰτίαι, which seem to have discussed those miscellaneous problems which were mostly inherited from previous thinkers, and ultimately were grouped together in the sixth book of Lucretius: among them are titles such as 'Causes in the sky', 'Causes in the Air', 'Causes on the Earth', and more special subjects such as 'The Magnet'. (4) The next three tetralogies concern Mathematics and Astronomy, and probably represent the interests which Democritus acquired in his visits to Egypt and the East. Of them practically nothing remains but the titles, except in the case of the 'Parapegma', which seems to have been a kind of Calendar, in which were noted not merely the main astronomical occurrences of the year, but meteorological observations as to the probabilities of the weather which recall the stories of Democritus' uncanny skill as a weather prophet. One fortunately rescued fragment of the 'Geography' [2] contains his idea of the shape of the earth and indicates one of his most marked differences from Leucippus. (5) Two tetralogies on 'Music' succeed, in the first of which he dealt with rhythms and sounds, beautiful and cacophonous, and advanced a theory of poetic inspiration, which subsequently gave rise to considerable exaggerations. [3] In

---

[1] D.B. 6–8. [2] D.B. 15.

[3] Cf. especially Hor. A. P. 296 ' excludit sanos Helicone poetas Democritus '. It would be very interesting to know more of this work, and to be able to judge of its relation to Aristotle's Poetics.

the second tetralogy there was first a criticism of Homer, or rather as it would appear from the fragments,[1] of Homeric words and phraseology, and such strange problems as 'Who was the mother of the swine-herd Eumaeus?' where Democritus' conclusion that she was named 'Poverty' (πενία) seems almost to suggest an allegorical interpretation of the poems. There was also an important discussion on the origin of language, in which Democritus[2] held that names were invented deliberately (θέσει) and not naturally (φύσει). This was a traditional subject of dispute and Epicurus was afterwards to reverse Democritus' decision. (6) Finally there are two more tetralogies of 'Technical Matters', the first of which dealt with medical subjects, such as diet, the second with a variety of topics such as painting, tactics and heavy-armed battle (ὁπλομαχικόν), and agriculture: included in the last work was a discussion[3] of the right arrangement for the plantation of vines, which reappears in Virgil's *Georgics* and *Columella*. To the tetralogies is appended a list of miscellaneous treatises, some of which have been already noticed as indicating oriental interests, others such as the 'Voyage round the Ocean' (περίπλους) and 'Concerning History' (probably 'Investigation' in the old sense) still further widen the range of Democritus' interests. Of the style of his writing Cicero[4] tells us that it was ornate and in the rapidity of its motion and the distinction of its phrasing 'more worthy to be called poetical than the language of comic poets'—a curious and somewhat equivocal compliment. He also assures us that,[5] in contrast to the style of Heraclitus, it was never obscure, a judgement which the extant fragments hardly bear out. Dionysius[6] ranks him with Plato and Aristotle as an exponent of the 'middle style' of composition.

This brief survey of the 'tetralogies' shows at once that Democritus was a man of far greater mental range than Leucippus; his subjects are derived not merely from the

---

[1] D.B. 23–5.   [2] D.B. 26.   [3] D.B. 27.
[4] *de Orat.* i. 11, 49; *Orat.* 20, 67; D.A. 34.
[5] *de Divinatione*, ii. 64. 133; D.A. 34.
[6] *de Comp. Verb.* 24; D.A. 34.

traditional spheres of philosophic thought in Greece, but from many other pursuits and interests of his fellow-country-man and from many sources which he had encountered in his own foreign travels. He seems indeed to have endea-voured to incorporate in his writings something like the whole range of extant knowledge and thought and, as far as possible, to have reduced it to a systematic whole. By far the most important part of this system is undoubtedly the Atomic theory which he had learnt from his master Leucippus: but the wide scope of his own interests and thought had enabled him to set the theory in its relations with other departments of human knowledge and, as it were, to see it in truer pro-portion. Consequently, he is not only able to attach to it a moral theory which, although somewhat vague and inde-pendent, yet contained the germs of a cheerful and good-hearted philosophy of imperturbability, but in dealing with the Atomic theory itself he is more conscious of its relation to other problems, and in particular shows a far deeper in-sight than Leucippus into the metaphysical difficulties which it involved. Moreover, his insatiate curiosity for detail—he was in some aspects a scientific Herodotus—led him to take greater interest in the working out of the minutiae of the Atomic theory and the consequences implied in it. This is particularly noticeable in his treatment of the nature and combination of the atoms, of the 'secondary qualities' ac-quired by compound bodies, and of the exact details of the process of sensation: in all these particulars he shows a subtlety and refinement which was outside the range of the blunter enthusiasm of Leucippus, and in many respects, for all his love of detail proved too much for the patience of Epicurus. Though to Epicurus belongs the credit of having welded all the parts of his system into a whole based on one simple metaphysical principle, yet in many departments the physical and metaphysical sides of Atomism reach their highest point in subtlety of comprehension in Democritus.

One great advantage we possess in dealing with Demo-critus is that there is still extant a very considerable body of his own sayings. Doubt has indeed been thrown on the genuineness of some of these, especially those dealing with the moral theory, but the labour of scholars has made it possible to distinguish the true from the false with a fair degree of certainty. There is also a vastly greater number of references to his theories, containing a wealth of detail, which is sadly lacking in the case of Leucippus. In consequence it is possible to arrive much more nearly at a rational account of his theory as a whole. It will be convenient to preserve the same order of treatment as was adopted with Leucippus, though, as Democritus' theory is a more consistent unity, some overlapping from section to section is inevitable. As far as possible too, I shall endeavour to consider the additions and modifications which Democritus made to his master's theory, and will only go back on the main principles when Democritus put them in a new light, but here again it is hardly possible to avoid some repetition.

§ 2. *The Atomic Theory*

The main outline of the Atomic theory is handed on from Leucippus to Democritus without substantial alteration, but its statement is at once more systematic, more definite, and in some respects more elaborated. At the foundation of the theory lies the same solution of the old problem of the 'ultimate existence', the conception of infinite indivisible particles in an infinite void. 'Democritus thinks', says Aristotle [1] using his own phraseology, 'that the nature of the eternal things is small existences (οὐσίαι) unlimited in number, and in addition to these he assumes space (τόπος) infinite in extent.' This, though it agrees exactly with Leucippus' view, is rather more explicit than any statement attributed to him, and so are the terms he applies to the two fundamentals. He adopted Leucippus' nomenclature and speaks of the ultimate particles as 'atoms' (ἄτομοι) and even 'the compact bodies' (ναστά), and of space similarly as the 'void' (κενόν): but to these he added the name of 'the boundless' [2] (ἄπειρον) for space, and, if we may trust Plutarch,[3] that of 'the

[1] apud Simpl. in Arist. *de Caelo, A.* 10. 279; D.A. 37 : cf. Diog. Laert. ix. 44; D.A 1.   [2] Simpl. l.c.   [3] *adv. Colot.* 8. 1110; D.A. 57.

shapes' (ἰδέαι) for the atoms—a name fully in harmony with
the important part which atomic shape played in his system.
More interesting apparently was his attitude to the old
problem of the existence of empty space with which Leucippus had dealt so ingeniously. Following on his master's
lines he not only admitted body as the only full existence,
but emphasized his belief in his terminology, speaking
habitually of the atoms as 'the real things'[1] (ὄντα): the void
similarly is described not merely with Leucippus as the
'not-real' (τὸ μὴ ὄν), but even as the 'nothing' (οὐδέν), in opposition to which he naïvely invented the term δέν, 'thing', as
a description of the atom. Hence Leucippus' famous defence of the existence of the void in opposition to the Eleatic
view appears in Democritus in the form 'the thing does not
exist any more than the nothing'.[2] Aristotle seems also to
suggest another subtle variation on the part of Democritus,
which, if it can really be attributed to him, greatly cleared
up the conception of the void. Leucippus had been content
to speak of it, as did the Eleatics who denied that it existed
at all, as the 'not-real' or 'non-existent' (μὴ ὄν): according to
Aristotle,[3] Democritus, taking advantage of the distinction
between the two Greek negatives, called it the 'unreal'
(οὐκ ὄν) or the 'nothing' (οὐδέν). He was in this way able to
distinguish the void whose existence he affirmed as stoutly
as Leucippus from absolute non-existence (τὸ μὴ ὄν), and to
dispose of his opponents' objection by phraseology as well as
argument. Though it is not perhaps safe to build too much
on the expression of single passages, Aristotle seems so careful in his use of the negative (οὐ) and the refinement is so
characteristic of Democritus that we may well believe he

---

[1] Arist. *Phys. A.* 5. 188 a; D. 4. 45. [2] Plut. *adv. Colot.* 4. 1108; D.B. 156.
[3] οὐδέν apud Simpl. l.c., οὐκ ὄν Arist. *Phys. A.* 5. 188a; D.A. 45: cf.
Hipp. *Refut.* i. 13; D.A. 40. As against this evidence in Aristotle we must set
μηδέν in Plut. *adv. Colot.* 4. 1108 (D.B. 156), where the negative μή may
well be due to the construction (διορίζεται μὴ μᾶλλον τὸ δὲν ἢ τὸ μηδὲν
εἶναι) and μὴ ὄν in Simpl. in Arist. *Phys. A.* 2. 184 (28. 15); D.A. 38, where
Democritus is specifically associated with Leucippus. I think it is more natural
to suppose that Aristotle's phraseology is right: there seems no reason why
he should have varied the negative, unless Democritus did so himself.

made it: 'space' was not 'the real' (ὄν), not body, neither was it the 'not-real' (μὴ ὄν), that which does not exist at all, but only 'unreal' (οὐκ ὄν). The distinction is a strong reinforcement of what Leucippus meant. His conception of space seems still to hover between two notions: sometimes it is the 'empty' (κενόν), that in which body is not, sometimes 'place' (τόπος), that in which the atoms exist.

Nor was Democritus content in these ways to have given a clearer and more definite form to the main idea of the atomic theory: he strengthened it also with at least three notable additions. It is to him that we first find attributed the fundamental principle on which the whole physical system is subsequently based that 'nothing is created out of the non-existent or is destroyed into the non-existent'.[1] The history of this principle is significant: it was enunciated before Democritus by Melissus. 'That which was, was always and always shall be.[2] For if it had come into being, it must needs be that before it came into being, it was nothing: if then it was nothing, by no means could anything have come to be out of nothing.' In the mouth of Melissus this is an emphatic restatement of Parmenidean Monism: 'it is', the material universe is one, eternal and permanent. And when Democritus places it in the forefront of Atomism, he seems at once to declare his connexion with the Eleatic school and his difference from them. On the one hand he accepts to the full the conception of the unity and eternity of the universe: nothing can be added to it, nothing can be taken away from it, the ultimate substratum of matter neither comes into being nor passes away. Yet for all that he is prepared to show that this unity and eternity is not inconsistent, as the Eleatics had thought, with the multiplicity and variability of phenomena: granted that the unchangeable One is divisible and that its parts can move, thanks to the existence of empty space, it can then give rise to all the variety of the world of experience. From Democritus' time the aphorism appears as the starting-point of Atomism: Epicurus[3] not merely enunciates it, but is prepared to prove it by a kind of

[1] D.L. ix. 44; D.A. 1.　　[2] Melissus, D.B. 1.　　[3] Ep. i, § 38.

'universal induction' from phenomena, and Lucretius,[1] following his lead, gives it his own characteristic turn as a weapon against the religious notion of arbitrary creation by divine beings. In its two parts it is indeed the germ of the modern 'laws' of the 'universality of cause and effect' and the 'permanence of matter'.

Closely connected with this base-principle are two others, hardly less fundamental, which are grouped together in an interesting reference: 'Democritus[2] postulated that the universe was "infinite" (ἄπειρον) because it was not by any means created by any one (or "anything" μηδαμῶς ὑπό τινος). Further he calls it unchangeable and in general describes explicitly what it is altogether. The causes of things now coming into being, he says, have no beginning, but from infinite time back are foreordained by necessity all things that were and are and are to come.' The 'infinity' of the universe is not here, as it is in Leucippus and in other places in Democritus, a spatial infinity, but an infinity of time, eternity. The eternity of the universe is of course an immediate inference from the first principle, indeed, as is seen clearly in the argument of Melissus, it is implied in it: if nothing can be created out of nothing, then the universe can never have been created, it must have existed from all time. Once again an Eleatic notion is adopted by Democritus and henceforth in the Atomic system the eternity of the universe, and by implication of its component parts, 'the causes of things', the atoms and the void, takes its place side by side with the idea of its infinity in extent: as it is spatially boundless, so it is temporally everlasting, without beginning and without end.

Secondly, in the last sentence of this extract and in close connexion with the notion of eternity must be noticed the emphatic statement of the supremacy of 'necessity': 'by necessity are foreordained all things that were and are and are to come'. In the theories of earlier philosophers and in that of Leucippus himself the question of the ultimate efficient cause was only raised in connexion with the pro-

---

[1] i. 150 'nullam rem e nilo gigni *divinitus* unquam'.
[2] Plut. *Strom.* 7; D.A. 39.

blem of motion: here as a base-principle of the nature of the universe is asserted a full and unhesitating determinism. The change is characteristic and important. It has been seen already that Leucippus[1] seems to have asserted in a rather half-hearted manner that 'necessity' was the motive cause, and that by his assertion he intended not, as previous thinkers have done, to introduce an inexplicable external force to explain what could not otherwise be shown to follow from his fundamental principles, but rather to adumbrate the idea familiar to us as that of 'natural law': the ultimate controlling principle is that everything follows the laws of its own being. This notion which Leucippus applied with some hesitation to explain the original motion of the atoms, Democritus now confidently asserts with a much wider, indeed, a universal application: 'necessity ' orders all things, indeed by necessity the whole course of things is foreordained from all eternity: the whole history of the universe is but the inevitable outcome, step by step, of its original and eternal constitution.

In adopting this conception we may suppose that Democritus had two main objects in view. In the first place he wished, as Aristotle[2] himself tells us, to controvert the prevailing idea of 'chance' ($\tau \acute{v} \chi \eta$), which he regarded as a merely loose conception, intellectually and even morally dangerous: 'for, they say, nothing is brought about by chance, but for everything there is a definite cause'. But even more he desired to be rid once and for all of the mysterious, semi-religious external forces, which previous philosophers and even more markedly his own contemporaries had postulated as the efficient causes of their systems: the world, as he conceived it, did not require the intervention of Empedocles' 'Love and Strife' or Anaxagoras' 'Mind' to bring it into being or keep it going: it is a wholly physical existence whose action is purely mechanical, controlled by the law of its own being and nothing more. Not less strongly did he desire to deny a second inheritance from the 'religious' tradition of philosophy, the idea of the 'final cause': the universe is not ruled by design, nor is there, as religion would have men

[1] Chap. II, p. 85.   [2] *Phys. B.* 4. 195b; D.A. 68.

believe, a purpose in the creation of the world or of any of its parts either organic or inorganic. Creation is the undesigned result of inevitable natural processes. The religious tinge which had clung to philosophy from its birth and had recently shown itself in less markedly theological, but still supernatural, forms was to be utterly banished from Atomism and leave it an untrammelled system of natural physics. The consequences of this decision were momentous. In the sphere of physical speculation it introduced for the first time the possibility of a strictly scientific conception of the world, and therefore immensely strengthened the Atomic Theory as a system. Democritus was himself indeed sometimes rather hard put to it to carry out his own principles and found that it involved at any rate large postulates in the root-conceptions: later on, when its psychology was more clearly developed, Atomism found itself beset with many difficulties which must of necessity gather round a purely materialist theory and the expedients invented to overcome them only showed more clearly the fundamental weakness. In the moral sphere too, though Democritus himself shows no traces of having perceived its implication, his rigid assertion of the law of cause and effect led at once to the controversy between free-will and determinism, which is still the most difficult of all the problems concerned with the presuppositions of Ethics. Once again Epicurus, anxious for the practical effectiveness of his moral theory, was led to protest against a universal 'necessity' by means of a naïve physical supposition for the preservation of free-will. But for Democritus himself these inherent difficulties never defined themselves: 'necessity', conceived as 'natural law', was to be the foundation-stone of his system, consistently recognized throughout his exposition of the physical world.[1]

---

[1] An interesting analysis of Democritus' various uses of ἀνάγκη will be found in Goedeckemeyer, *Epikurs Verhältnis zu Demokrit*, pp. 32 ff., but I think he is inclined to underestimate the evidence for a general conception of 'natural law', of which the various meanings of ἀνάγκη which he discovers in Democritus are in reality aspects, though not always perfectly logically deduced.

If then—and there seems no reason to doubt the inferences from the tradition—Democritus in all these points amplified and solidified the main ideas of Atomism, he appears at once as a man of much wider interest and perception than Leucippus. He is not content with a purely physical theory starting from a physical origin and dealing only with underlying problems when they are forced upon his notice, but he has an eye from the first for the metaphysical implications of the new conception of the universe. By a closer analysis of the notion of the 'void' he makes the whole Atomic idea more definite, and by his assertion of the eternity of the universe and the fundamental notion of necessity, he has prepounded a metaphysical basis not merely for Atomism but for any scientific view of the world. And this is in fact the character of his work throughout. He has not the completely co-ordinating mind which would enable him to systematize all his various interests and views in one correlated whole, but his many-sided activities led him into fields unknown to Leucippus, and in particular, as a closer acquaintance with him abundantly shows, he was prepared to think out the presuppositions of the physical theory which he had adopted.

§ 3. *Nature and movement of Atoms: creation of things*

In passing from the general principles of Atomism to the individual parts of the theory we shall find that Democritus once more makes little or no change in the main ideas, but in detail of argument adds, modifies, and alters considerably, always with great subtlety of insight and a clear comprehension of consequences. It is as if a rather crabbed and narrow theory expounded from the inside has passed into the hands of a man of the world who can look at it from many points of view and infuse new life into it. His treatment of the character and behaviour of the atoms is characteristic of his general attitude.

Just as he had insisted in general on the permanence of matter as the basis of physical inquiry, so he seems to press emphatically for the permanence of the individual atoms.

This had of course been part of the teaching of Leucippus,[1] who had argued for the indestructibility of the atoms, firstly owing to their hardness which made them 'incapable of being acted upon' (ἀπαθεῖς), and secondly owing to their smallness, which arose from the fact that they 'had no parts' (τὸ ἀμερές). Democritus' attitude to both these positions is interesting. On the proof from the nature of the atoms he apparently laid great stress. He is represented[2] as repeating Leucippus' statement that the atoms 'could not be acted on owing to their hardness' and making two interesting additions to it. The first is of the nature of an explanation:[3] the atoms not only 'cannot be acted upon', but are 'unchangeable': to the Greek mind[4] 'acting' or 'suffering' always implied 'alteration', and Democritus' new epithet therefore makes Leucippus' meaning plain. He did not mean that an atom cannot be acted upon as a whole, as it is in fact every time that a collision with another atom starts it moving in a fresh direction, but that no external force can change its internal constitution or alter its material substance or shape or size. The idea involved that change is always a form of destruction is insisted on by Aristotle and later plays a prominent part in the atomic theory.[5] A second and more striking addition to the fundamental idea is assigned to Democritus by Plutarch,[6] who speaks of 'existences infinite in number, indivisible and without difference, *unacting* and unacted on'. The negation of activity as well as passivity is at first sight startling, but is in reality closely connected with

[1] See Chap. II, p. 78.
[2] D.L. ix. 44; D.A. 1; Plut. *adv. Colot.* 8; D.A. 57.
[3] D.L. l.c. ἀναλλοίωτα.
[4] See Arist. *de Gen. et Corr. A.* 7 ff.
[5] Compare the oft-repeated maxim of Lucretius, i. 670, &c.:
    nam quodcumque suis mutatum finibus exit,
    continuo hoc mors est illius quod fuit ante.

[6] *adv. Colot.* 8. 1110 F; D.A. 57. οὐσίας ἀπείρους τὸ πλῆθος, ἀτόμους τε κἀδιαφόρους, ἔτι δ' ἀποίους καὶ ἀπαθεῖς. Arist. *de Gen. et Corr. A.* 325b 36. ἀναγκαῖον ἀπαθές τε ἕκαστον λέγειν τῶν ἀδιαιρέτων . . . καὶ μηθενὸς ποιητικὸν πάθους speaks as if the notion was common to the Atomists generally. See the notes in H. H. Joachim's edition (Clar. Press, 1922) for a full discussion of the whole idea.

the idea of 'change'. If a thing can be changed, it can also change something else: if, for instance, it can itself become hot, it will heat anything else with which it comes into contact. Now it was precisely this difficulty of the explanation of acting and being acted upon while at the same time preserving permanence in the substratum which lay at the bottom of many of the problems of the early Greek philosophers. And the solution propounded by the Atomists was that in compound things action and 'passion' were possible because of the existence of the void, which enabled the component atoms to shift their places and change their positions: 'they act and are acted on wherever they happen to be in contact'.[1] But the indivisible atoms themselves which have no mixture of void can neither be changed or change one another. On this line of thought the addition of the active idea that the atoms cannot act is but the logical corollary of the passive notion that they cannot be acted on; 'that which acts and that which is acted upon are alike and the same',[2] as Aristotle reports Democritus to have said. Both conceptions are reinforcements of the idea of the unchangeableness or absolute hardness of the atom.

In all these ways is Leucippus' simple notion of atomic hardness worked out in its wider implications and at the same time very greatly strengthened. But to his second proof of indestructibility based on the size of the atoms Democritus' attitude is strikingly different. Leucippus' argument was indeed open to objections. In the first place it might be argued that extremely small size is in itself no proof of indestructibility. This objection Leucippus had himself to some extent met by stating that by extreme smallness he meant that 'the atom had no parts', that is, was incapable of further subdivision, destruction being regarded as the cleaving of a thing into smaller bits of matter. But this very contention itself is liable to the mathematical objection, which might well have been urged by a member of the Eleatic school, that 'that which has no parts had no

[1] Arist. de Gen. et Cor. A. 8. 325a 32.
[2] Ibid. A. 7. 323b; D.A. 63.

magnitude': the atom, if it is as Leucippus described it, is not really a physical existence at all. Whether these objections had in fact been raised or whether Democritus himself clearly perceived them we cannot tell: but it is certain that the Leucippean argument from size is nowhere attributed to him, and indeed cannot have been used by him. For having once abandoned the idea of smallness as a proof of indestructibility he seems to have gone to the other extreme, and we are informed that he stated that 'some of the atoms were very large'[1] and again that they were 'unlimited not only in number but in size':[2] it is even stated by one authority[3] that he said that 'there might be an atom as big as a world'. To this idea Epicurus perceived the objection that in that case some atoms would be perceptible to the senses, and he was therefore driven to return in a modified form to Leucippus' view that they were very small and 'without parts'. Democritus seems not to have perceived this difficulty and we may notice as a proof of his independence of his master the freedom with which he reverses a conception without hesitation when it was no longer required. It is clear that for proof of the permanence of the atoms he relied entirely on the notion of hardness, explained and reinforced by his own modifications. That a difference on this point between various schools of Atomists was recognized in antiquity is shown by an interesting note of Galen:[4] 'they maintain, he says, that the first bodies cannot be acted on, some, such as the followers of Epicurus, holding that they were unbreakable owing to their hardness, others, such as the school of Leucippus, that they were indivisible owing to their smallness'. The omission of Democritus is curious, and the description of Epicurus' position far from accurate: indeed one almost wonders whether there is not some confusion, for Democritus' position is in fact exactly that which is first described.

Leucippus had assigned to the atoms the 'primary properties' of size and shape; Democritus followed him but once

---

[1] Dionys. apud Eus. *prep. ev.* xiv. 23. 2; D.A. 43.
[2] D.L. ix. 44; D.A. 1.　　　　　　　　[3] Aet. i. 12. 6; D.A. 47.
[4] *de Elem. sec.*; Hipp. i. 2; D.A. 49.

more worked out the implications of his ideas with stricter logic and unhesitating consistency. His striking divergence from Leucippus as regards the size of the atoms has already been noticed: not requiring minuteness as an argument for permanence, he frankly abandoned it and postulated 'very large' atoms. His attitude as regards atomic shape is equally characteristic. Leucippus,[1] holding that the differences in compound things were largely due to differences of shape in the constituent atoms, and observing the great variety in things, had been led to assume many different shapes in the atoms. Democritus, whose ingenious mind conceived a still greater interest than had his master in the mechanical varieties brought about by atomic shape, seems to have followed out the idea to its conclusion and asserted that the number of different atomic shapes was 'infinite'.[2] To him also must probably be assigned the rather strange *a priori* argument on which this conclusion is based, 'that there is no reason that anything should be of one kind rather than another'.[3] Now logically of course infinite differences in shape imply infinite differences in size:[4] for within the limits of the same size there can only be limited differences of shape, and further variety of form cannot be obtained except by increase in bulk. To Leucippus, who relied on the minuteness of the atom for its permanence, this fact, if he had perceived it, would have raised a serious difficulty, but to Democritus, who was prepared to admit the existence of 'very large' atoms, it was not open to the same objection. It was left to Epicurus, returning to the idea of minuteness, to object also to the assumption of infinity of shapes in the

---

[1] See Chap. II, p. 81.

[2] Simpl. in Arist. *Phys.* A. 2. 184 (28. 15); D.A. 38: cf. Simpl. in Arist. *de Caelo*, A. 10. 279; D.A. 37 σχήματα παντοῖα.

[3] Simpl. *Phys.* l.c. διὰ τὸ μηδὲν μᾶλλον τοιοῦτον ἢ τοιοῦτον εἶναι. Simplicius attributes the argument to the school in general and elsewhere (28. 4; D. (Leucippus) A. 8) assigns it specifically to Leucippus, but it sounds more like the generalizing *a priori* proof which would have been adduced by Democritus.

[4] This was perhaps first clearly seen by Epicurus: see the argument in Lucr. ii. 478 ff.

atoms on the ground that it implied infinity of size and therefore the perceptibility of some atoms. Democritus, correcting what he believed to be a mistake of Leucippus' and wishing to secure the utmost variety, held that the atoms had every kind of shape and size.

In the other details of the nature of the atoms Democritus followed his master closely. Like him he conceived all atoms[1] as being absolutely homogeneous in material substance: this is of course an ultimate necessity of Atomism and the only condition by which it can claim a fundamental unity in its account of the world. Similarly he preserved[2] the three 'differences' of the atoms, shape, position, order, as Leucippus had stated them, and expressed them apparently in the same curious terms, 'rhythm', 'turning', and 'touching'. But here a double amplification may be noticed. Being free, as has been seen, to attribute any size to the atoms, he makes far greater use than Leucippus of differences in size and in particular makes it the direct cause of the difference in 'weight' of atoms in the whirl as he himself conceived it.[3] Secondly, since it was a matter which strongly attracted his subtle mind, he worked out with great elaboration the various combinations of the atoms in compounds and the effect produced on sensation by their different shapes and arrangements, paying special attention to varieties in taste and colour.[4] These will be more conveniently considered in treating of his general account of sensation.

There is however one exceedingly difficult problem with regard to Democritus' views which affects not only his conception of the atom but his account alike of the original motion of the atoms and of their behaviour in the cosmic whirl. Did he or did he not assign 'weight' to the atoms as one of their primary properties and make it the cause of their motion? The ancient authorities show considerable discrepancy on this point and it has been hotly debated by

---

[1] The atoms are described as ἀδιάφορα, Plut. *adv. Colot.* 8. 1110; D.A. 57, and more explicitly as ὁμοφυεῖς; Simpl. in Arist. *de Caelo*, Γ 1. 299; D.A. 61. [2] Simpl. in Arist. *Phys. A*. 2. 184 (28. 15); D.A. 38.
[3] See below, p. 132. [4] Theophr. *de Sensu*, 64; D.A. 135.

modern scholars. It will be more convenient to discuss the question in relation to the atomic motion and the cosmic whirl and to assume here that Democritus, like Leucippus, was content to make size and shape the only primary properties of the atom, and that 'weight' in an absolute sense was introduced later into the atomic theory[1]—possibly by Nausiphanes—and only fully acknowledged by Epicurus in close connexion with his general account of atomic motion.

We may therefore proceed to consider Democritus' account of the original Atomic motion, which is the first step in the formation of compound bodies. The information which has reached us is so various and so contradictory that at first sight it seems almost impossible to decide what was in fact his view. But the researches of modern scholars into this difficult subject have very greatly cleared the ground and the practical agreement[2] of their conclusions makes it possible to state a theory of Democritus' position with some confidence. It will be found that it does not in any essential differ from that of Leucippus, but is more explicit.

It is however necessary first to consider what is now generally recognized as the false view. Epicurus in expounding his own theory of atomic motion finds that it originates in the universal downward fall[3] of the atoms through empty space caused by their weight, but refuses to accept the idea[4] that the meeting of atoms was brought about because the heavier, falling more quickly, overtook the lighter: in absolutely empty space, as he points out, where

---

[1] Since Epicurus (Ep. i, § 61: cf. Lucr. ii. 225 ff.) is concerned to argue against a theory that the heavier atoms catch up the lighter in their downward fall in the void, it is clear that the idea of weight as the cause of downward motion must have been introduced into the atomic theory before his time.

[2] See Liepmann, op. cit., Brieger, *Die Urbewegung der Atome und die Weltentstehung bei Leucipp und Demokrit*; Dyroff, *Demokritstudien*, pp. 31–9; Giussani, *Lucretius*, vol. i, p. 134, n. 1; Burnet, *E. G. P.*3, pp. 341 ff. All these writers are in substantial agreement, but the first two hold that weight is an original property of the atoms, though not the cause of motion. Goedeckemeyer, *Epikurs Verhältnis zu Demokrit*, rejects the modern view, but gives no satisfactory explanation of the difficulty.

[3] Ep. i, § 43.   [4] Ibid., § 61.

there can be no resistance at all, bodies whatever their weight will fall at an equal rate. It was usually supposed that he is here arguing against the view of Democritus, who is represented[1] as attributing absolute weight to the atoms and making that, as Epicurus did himself, the cause of an original perpendicular fall. Some of the ancient evidence,[2] which seems to support this view, is undoubtedly contaminated by Epicurean influence, but there are other references which cannot be so lightly dealt with. Thus Simplicius[3] informs us that the Atomists said that 'the atoms moving in virtue of the heaviness ($\beta\alpha\rho\acute{v}\tau\eta\tau\alpha$) that is in them through the void which yields and offers no opposition change their place', and again almost more explicitly: 'they say that the atoms which are all alike in substance have weight ($\beta\acute{\alpha}\rho\sigma\varsigma$), and since some of them are heavier the lighter are squeezed out by them as they sink down and carried upwards, and thus they say that some of them seem light and others heavy ($\beta\alpha\rho\acute{\epsilon}\alpha$)'.[4] Similarly Theophrastus, who states expressly that Democritus 'distinguishes heavy and light according to size',[5] appears to make weight the reason why all the atoms 'have the same impulse of movement',[6] and Cicero seems to express the same view.[7] Far more important are two passages in Aristotle, in one of which[8] he states that 'Democritus says that each of the indivisibles is heavier in proportion to its excess (of bulk)': and in the other after the simple statement that 'the larger of them is heavier',[9] goes on to expound the atomic view that in compound things this direct variation of weight with size does not hold good, for in a compound body of larger size there may be more void, but in the atom, which *ex hypothesi* contains no void, the

[1] e.g. by Zeller, *Ph. d. Gr.* i. 604; Ueberweg, *History of Philosophy*, i. 884.
[2] Pseudo-Plut. i. 4; Galen, *Hist. Phil.* 7 : see Liepmann, op. cit., pp. 19–30.
[3] In Arist. *Phys. Θ.* 9. 265 b; D.A. 58.
[4] In Ar. *de Caelo, Γ.* 1. 299; D.A. 61.   [5] *de Sensu*, 61; D.A. 135.
[6] Ibid. 71.   [7] *de Fin.* i. 6. 17; D.A. 56.
[8] Βαρύτερόν γε κατὰ τὴν ὑπεροχὴν ἕκαστον τῶν ἀδιαιρέτων: *de Gen. et Corr. A.* 8. 326 a; D.A. 60.
[9] *de Caelo, Δ.* 2. 309 a; D.A. 60.

proportion between size and weight must be exact. There seems then a considerable body of evidence both for attributing weight to the atoms and for regarding it as the original cause of motion.

Now with regard to the evidence of Simplicius it might be urged that to some extent he puts himself out of court by his own contradictions,[1] for in spite of his explicit attribution of motion to weight in the passages cited, he elsewhere states[2] that 'the atoms are moved in the boundless void by force', and in a still more remarkable passage[3] he maintains that 'the atoms which are naturally stationary (!) are moved by a blow'. But an argument from inconsistency is never finally satisfactory and there is evidence[4] that the Atomists could regard weight itself as a kind of internal blow. Moreover, we have the express statement of Aristotle that Democritus associated heaviness with size and Theophrastus' suggestion that weight is the cause of motion. But in the first place we may note that Aristotle does not speak of weight as a primary property of the atoms, as is their shape and size, but regards it only as a secondary derivative from size: further he never associates with Democritus the conception of absolute weight, but only speaks of atoms as 'heavier' or 'lighter' than one another. And a closer examination of Simplicius' statement that the Atomists 'say that some *seem* to be light and others heavy' suggests that he too regarded 'weight' not only as a derivative property of the atoms but even in some sense as illusory. Still further light is thrown on the problem by a later passage in the same author,[5] where he explains in regular atomic terms that fire moves upward because it is squeezed out by other bodies and for this reason seems to be light; ' and to these other things weight only seems to belong, and it seems always to be carried towards the centre'.

---

[1] See Liepmann, op. cit., p. 40.   [2] In Arist. *de Caelo*, Γ. 2. 300 b.
[3] In Arist. *Phys. A*. 2. 184 (42. 10); D.A. 47.
[4] $T\hat{\eta}$ τοῦ βάρους πληγῇ, Aet. i. 3. 18; D.A. 47 of Epicurus: cf. Cic. *de Fato*, 20, 46 'aliam enim quandam vim motus habebant a Democrito impulsionis quam plagam ille appellat, a te, Epicure, gravitatis et ponderis'.
[5] Simpl. in. Ar. *de Caelo, A*. 10. 280; D.A. 61.

He is of course speaking here not of atoms but of compound bodies, but the similarity of the two passages suggests that they should be taken together and the last clause provides a valuable clue. For the mention of 'the centre' shows clearly enough that he is thinking of the cosmic whirl in which the 'heavier' bodies are those which are most able to resist the rotatory motion of the whirl and therefore congregate in the centre. Can this idea also be applied to the 'heavier' and 'lighter' atoms? When we come to consider the formation of a cosmos in the whirl, we shall find that the idea[1] is not merely applicable but exactly coincides with the cosmological accounts which have come down to us. It may then safely be inferred with the bulk of recent commentators that though Democritus did indeed speak of 'heavier' and 'lighter' atoms, he did not attribute absolute weight to them,[2] still less did he regard weight as the initial cause of perpendicular motion downwards in the void, but considered it rather as a derivative property from size, acting, not when the atoms were free in the void, but only in the cosmic whirl as a faculty of resisting in a greater or less degree the motion of the whirl itself.

If then the notion of the perpendicular fall owing to weight may finally be dismissed as far as Democritus is concerned, what is the character of the original motion of the atoms and what its cause? Now that the main misconception is cleared away these questions are not so difficult to answer. In the first place there is almost universal agreement that Democritus spoke of the atoms as 'always in motion':[3] there never, that is to say, was a beginning of motion, but as the atoms are themselves eternal, so is their motion. And this motion was not, as motion due to weight must have been, in the one direction downward, but in all directions.[4] Democritus describes it in the characteristic and imaginative term

---

[1] See below, pp. 144–6.
[2] This is explicitly confirmed by Aet. i. 3. 18; i. 12. 6; D.A. 47.
[3] ἀεὶ κινεῖσθαι τὰ πρῶτα σώματα, Arist. de Caelo, Γ. 2. 300 b: cf. Hipp. Ref. i. 13; D.A. 40.
[4] Cf. D.L. ix. 44; D.A. 1: Simpl. in Ar. de Caelo, A. 10. 279; D.A. 37, &c.

'vibration'.[1] The atoms moving about hither and thither up and down and in every way, colliding and jostling with one another from the first, presented the appearance of a great vibrating mass. We gather indeed from Aristotle[2] that the Atomists already made use of the famous illustration, which Lucretius[3] put to such good use, from the motes in a sunbeam: just as they seem to fly to and fro jostling each other aimlessly, meeting and parting in every direction, so do the atoms in the precosmic state. In other words what Epicurus conceived as a second stage in development, when the 'swerve' had converted the downward fall into an infinite series of collisions, is imagined by Democritus as the eternal condition of atomic motion from all time.

And as the cause of this multifarious motion Democritus, probably following Leucippus before him, places 'necessity',[4] the governing cause of everything in the universe. At first sight this seems a contradiction of his own principle, if it has hitherto been rightly explained: for by asserting the supremacy of necessity Democritus meant just that every effect has a cause, but here is an effect, a motion, for which no cause at all is assigned except the universal 'necessity'. Either then he is employing 'necessity' as some of his predecessors had done as an arbitrary expedient to explain what cannot otherwise be accounted for, or he is abandoning his own principle. Some such difficulty seems to be in Aristotle's mind, when he complains[5] that Democritus 'gives up any attempt to explain the cause, and refers everything to necessity'. But already in Leucippus we have seen a hint of the answer to this difficulty: the eternal atomic motion was, in Democritus' view, beyond all causes, and was itself the cause of all. For, if the conception of the eternal being of the universe be not merely of atoms in the void, but of atoms

[1] παλμός, Aet. i. 23. 3; D.A. 47; περιπαλάσσεσθαι, Simpl. in Arist. Phys. Θ. 9. 265 b; D.A. 58.
[2] de Anima, A. 2. 404 a.   [3] ii. 114–41.
[4] Arist. de Gen. Animal. E. 8. 789 b; D.A. 66; D.L. ix. 45, &c.
[5] l.c. the οὗ ἕνεκα here is of course the 'final cause', a notion which was essentially repugnant to Democritus and which his whole conception of ἀνάγκη was intended to controvert : see above, p. 121.

moving in the void, then we have no more right to ask for the cause of movement than we have for the cause of the existence of the atoms and the void themselves.[1] We could only demand the cause of motion, if it were something that supervened on a previous state of rest. Aristotle, in his more sympathetic mood towards Atomism, seems to understand this. In a still more remarkable passage[2] he says that the Atomists 'think that the cause of motion is the void, in the sense that it is that in which motion takes place'. If we think of this in reference to pre-Atomic speculation, we seem to understand what is meant. The great difficulty of Monism and even of the theory of Anaxagoras was how to derive from the original static mass of matter the phenomena of sense-perception, separated things and motion. The Atomists by the introduction of the conception of the void felt that they had solved both these problems: empty space not merely separates pieces of matter, but it enables them to move. Separation and movement to their notion so nearly implied each other, that movement was an essential part of the new conception: it is therefore 'causeless', or, as Democritus preferred to put it, 'necessary'. The very existence of atoms and void carried with it atomic motion.

It remains to consider the other two causes of motion which are suggested by Simplicius, 'force'[3] and 'a blow'.[4] In the light of Cicero's identification[5] of the Democritean 'blow' with Epicurus' notion of weight, it might be possible to explain both these expressions as in reality referring to the natural original motion of the atoms by an internal force or blow which is part of their nature. But seeing that Cicero's

---

[1] This would probably have been Democritus' answer to the charge of inconsistency brought against him by Aristotle, *de Gen. et Corr.* A. 8, 326 ᵇ, where he inquires what is it that moves the atom? if it is some external force, then they are not ἀπαθῆ: if they move themselves, they are not ἄποια (see p. 124). He might have replied 'they are neither moved by an external force, nor do they move themselves: they are of their very nature for ever in motion: a force would be needed not to move them, but to stop them'.

[2] *Phys.* Δ. 7. 214 a.   [3] Simpl. in Arist. *de Caelo*, Γ. 2. 300 b.

[4] Simpl. in Ar. *Phys.* A. 2. 184 (42. 10); D.A. 47.

[5] *de Fato*, 20. 46; D.A. 47.

statement is almost certainly founded on the false conception that Democritus assigned weight as the cause of motion, it is better to disregard it. In that case both expressions will refer not to the original motion of the atoms, but to derivative motions which are logically subsequent, though actually contemporaneous. As the result of their movements in many directions the atoms immediately come into collision with one another, and consequently leaping back start off in new directions: this motion, which is in fact after the first collision normally that of almost all atoms, may well be described as due to 'a blow', as it was by the Epicureans later on. Similarly other atoms meeting may aggregate in small nuclei, uniting together in various degrees of close connexion and forming in fact the first beginnings of compound bodies. But these nuclei will still be in everlasting motion and by the combined force of the movements of the component atoms will develop, as it were, a motion of their own as wholes: this is pre-eminently the case with 'the whirl', a motion formed in this way by an aggregation of atoms and leading by a series of stages to the formation of a cosmos out of the unmeaning jostle of atoms. Now a previously independent atom coming near one of these moving aggregates may, as it were, be caught up into the prevailing motion and go along with it: it may be then said to be moved 'by force'. Again it is a derivative motion, but one so closely following the original movement that it may be regarded as eternally contemporaneous with it. It would thus appear that neither of these terms is to be excluded as erroneous from the account of atomic motion, yet neither of them are in any way inconsistent with the general notion which has been attributed to Democritus. The original motion is due to 'necessity' as part of the constitution of things, but motion by 'force' and 'blows' is immediately derived from it.

It seems then that Democritus did not in his account of atomic motion depart in any essential from the earlier conceptions of Leucippus, but once more we find that the ideas of the earlier philosopher are worked out with greater insight and imagination, especially in regard to the 'vibration' of the atoms one with another, and that the wider implications of the theory and in particular its relation to the underlying idea of 'necessity' are more clearly defined. This is what we should expect, and it is satisfactory to find that Democritus did not in fact make such a wide departure from atomic tradition as would be involved in the conception of absolute weight as the cause of a universal downward motion.

A similar inference must be drawn with regard to Democritus' conception of the union of atoms in compounds, the small nuclei which may prove either the kernels of 'things' or even 'worlds', or turn out to be merely, as it were, abortive attempts. A clear account has fortunately been preserved to us:[1]

the atoms are at war with one another (στασιάζειν) as they move along in the void owing to their dissimilarity and their other differences, and as they move they collide and are interlaced in a manner which makes them touch and be near to one another, but never really produces any single existence out of them: for it is quite absurd to suppose that two or more things could ever become one. The reason why the atoms for a certain time remain in combination (συμμένειν, obviously a technical term) he believes to be because they fit into and grasp one another (διὰ τὰς ἐπαλλαγὰς καὶ τὰς ἀντιλήψεις τῶν σωμάτων): for some of them have uneven sides (σκαληνά), and some are hooked, some are concave, and some convex and others with innumerable varieties of shape. He thinks then that they retain hold of one another and remain in combination until some stronger necessity from what surrounds them comes and shakes them and scatters them apart. And he speaks of this coming into being and its opposite separation not merely with reference to animals, but also plants and worlds and generally about all perceptible bodies.

There are several points in this account which deserve notice both as advances in definiteness and refinement upon Leucippus and also as laying down the lines of subsequent atomic theory. In the first place the idea of the 'war of atoms' due to their dissimilarity of shape recalls the old notion of the repulsion of unlike from unlike and its complement the union of like with like, of which there are abundant traces

[1] Simpl. in Ar. de Caelo, A. 10. 279; D.A. 37.

in the subsequent account of the cosmic whirl: Democritus, though not so anxious as his master to mediate between his predecessors and incorporate their ideas, yet not infrequently shows their influence. More important is his insistence on the exact nature of the union of atoms in compounds: the new creation, the nucleus or compound body is never in the strict sense 'one': the atoms do not coalesce to form a new body, but even in the compound retain their separate nature and are kept apart by a larger or smaller interval of void: 'it is impossible', as Aristotle[1] quotes his saying in its full form, 'for one thing to be made out of two or two out of one', the combination is purely mechanical. A later writer[2] puts the notion very explicitly: 'what seems to be a mixture is in reality a juxtaposition of the atoms with one another at small intervals, each of them preserving its own nature, which it had before the mingling'. Later theory was to insist further that each atom in the compound preserved also its own motion. Complementary to this conception is the idea of the ultimate destruction of the compound by the separation of the atoms owing to some force or blow from outside. This is of course a notion which the Atomists shared with Anaxagoras, but it is here stated with great clearness and was to have ever-increasing prominence. Even more characteristic perhaps of Democritus is the great elaboration of the details of atomic shape and their effect on union. This was indeed the most conspicuous contribution of Democritus to the detail of the atomic theory: he worked it out not merely for a love of its own detail, but, as will be seen later, in careful and elaborate connexion with the resultant effects for sense-perception.

Here again Democritus has elaborated and strengthened the atomic theory with his own peculiar vividness of imagination. There is nothing which is really new, but much that adds freshness and life to the outline of Leucippus. We must now follow out his ideas with regard to the one special form of atomic aggregate, the whirl, which is the cause of the creation of a world.

[1] *Metaphys.Z.*13.1039a; D.A.42.   [2] Alex. *de Mixt.* 2, p. 591; D.A.64.

§ 4. *The Cosmic Whirl—Creation of Worlds*

No considerable additions of detail at this point in the theory are recorded of Democritus, but once again he seems to have worked out and greatly strengthened the underlying ideas. In the last section it was seen how the atoms moving in all directions in the void collided and jostled, and sometimes becoming entangled with one another and remaining in juxtaposition formed new aggregates (ἀθροίσματα) of matter enclosing void. These aggregates would differ in the number of atoms they contained and in the closeness or laxness of their union, and according to these differences would be determined the size and shape, the density and weight of the new compound: such compounds as were made of closely compact atoms with little void would be hard and heavy,[1] those which were composed of comparatively few atoms and much void would be soft and light. It must be supposed too—though there is no direct evidence for it—that Democritus conceived of each of these new aggregates as having its own characteristic motion—the sum, as it were, of the motions of the individual atoms determined alike by the direction of their original motion and by the new motions derived from the successive 'blows' of their collisions. But in no case would such aggregation have any effective result and lead to the formation of a world, except when the aggregate formed fell into the particular motion of a 'whirl' (δίνη). Then by a process which Leucippus had originally indicated and which must be reconsidered in the light of Democritus' main ideas, a 'cosmos' with an earth and air and sky and heavenly bodies would be evolved.

The first question then which must be asked is clearly enough: what is the cause of this atomic 'whirl'? Leucippus' answer, as has been seen, was somewhat vague, but with Democritus the theory becomes far more definite. In the first place we have a very clear statement in Diogenes:[2] 'he said that all things come into being of necessity: for the

---

[1] Arist. *de Caelo*, Δ. 2. 309 a; D.A. 60.
[2] ix. 45; D.A. 1.

whirl is the cause of the creation of all things, the whirl which he calls necessity'. This is emphatic language: Democritus thought then that the whirl was due to the operation of natural laws, was formed by the atoms as the effect of their own character and motion and collisions. And if he did indeed 'call the whirl necessity', we are not to suppose that he meant by that that it was an unexplained postulate, like the original motion of the atoms, but rather an outcome of that motion so striking and important in its results as to deserve the title of 'necessity' *par excellence*. So far this is in exact accord with what would be expected from Democritus' main position: the 'whirl' is a necessary effect of the operation of atomic motion under certain conditions. But Aristotle in the course of his discussion on chance and the 'automatic' seems to suggest another explanation: for he says with unmistakeable reference to the Atomists: 'But there are some who believe "the automatic" to be the cause even of the heaven above us and indeed of all worlds: for they say that the whirl and the motion which separated and arranged the whole in this order are produced automatically',[1] and in another place his commentator[2] remarks with explicit reference to Democritus that 'he seems to produce the whirl automatically and by chance'.

Here it seems as if we had a contradiction not merely of the first account of the cause of the whirl, but of the very root-principles of Democritus' system. Can it be that the thinker who based his system on the axiom that 'nothing comes into being by chance, but that for all things there is a definite cause',[3] yet stated that the cosmic whirl, the most important factor in creation, was brought about 'automatically and by chance', and if he did, what can he have intended by it? Aristotle's evidence is incontrovertible and there can be no serious doubt that Democritus did give these two

---

[1] *Phys. B.* 4. 196 a; D.A. 69 ἀπὸ ταὐτομάτου γὰρ γίγνεσθαι τὴν δίνην καὶ τὴν κίνησιν τὴν διακρίνασαν καὶ καταστήσασαν εἰς ταύτην τὴν τάξιν τὸ πᾶν.

[2] Simpl. in Arist. *Phys. B.* 3. 195; D.A. 67.

[3] Arist. *Phys. B.* 4. 195 b; D.A. 68.

apparently inconsistent accounts of the origin of the whirl, that it was 'necessity', yet came into being 'automatically'. Modern writers who have taken account of this difficulty have for the most part attempted to explain it away. Thus one ingenious critic,[1] who incidentally does not sufficiently distinguish this special movement of the whirl from the atomic motion in general, holds that Aristotle is not here using 'automatic' in his usual sense of a result occurring 'accidentally' (κατὰ συμβεβηκός), that is without reference to the 'final cause' of a thing's existence, but is opposing it to the conception of an external controlling force, such, for instance, as the 'Mind' of Anaxagoras. That the atomic movement is 'automatic' will then mean that it 'originates from itself without a cause', and Democritus will then be stating from another point of view what he had already expressed by saying that the motion of the atoms was due to necessity, namely, that in moving they were simply obeying the law of their own being as by nature *moving particles*: 'necessity' and 'automatism' are in this sense identical in meaning. This is a clever reconciliation, but it cannot possibly be accepted. For in the first place it is perfectly clear in the context that there is no question of atomic motion in general, but only of the specific movement of the whirl, and what is far more important, it is inconceivable that in a passage where Aristotle is endeavouring to determine the precise meaning of 'automatism' and 'chance' and arrives at a definite conclusion, he should in his crucial instance be using the word in a quite different sense.

A more profitable line of approach will be to inquire into Aristotle's conclusions on the point at issue. His whole discussion in the *Physics* is conducted in the language of his own philosophy and he refers the ideas of 'chance' and 'automatism' directly to his conception of the 'final cause' (οὗ ἕνεκα). His conclusion is that 'the automatic' is that which occurs or comes into being 'by accident' (κατὰ συμβεβη-κός), that is, without reference to the final cause, and 'chance' occurrences are a subdivision of 'the automatic' con-

[1] Liepmann, *Die Mechanik der Leucipp-Democritischen Atome*, pp. 34, 35.

cerned with actions which are a matter of deliberate choice (κατὰ προαίρεσιν). Now these cannot of course have been with any exactness the ideas of the Atomists, but they are of value in the present discussion to this extent, that when the Atomists said that the whirl was 'automatic', part of their intention was no doubt to exclude the idea of purpose or design. The atoms did not form themselves into a whirl in order that a cosmos might result: there is no design either on their part or on the part of any extraneous force or power. They fall into the whirl 'accidentally' and the result by a process of strict necessity is a world. Democritus'[1] intention was no doubt anti-teleological: this, as has been seen, was one of his great aims in establishing 'necessity' as the basis of his system, and it remained always a cardinal point in the Atomic tradition that the creation of a world was not the result of design. Cicero[2] speaks of the conglomeration of atoms out of which a cosmos arises as a *concursus fortuitus*, and Lucretius[3] in notable verses puts the position unmistakeably: 'for not by design did the first beginnings of things place themselves each in their order with foreseeing mind, nor indeed did they make compact what movements each should start, but because many of them shifting in many ways throughout the world are harried and buffeted by blows from limitless time, by trying movements and unions of every kind, at last they fall into such dispositions as these, whereby our world of things is created and holds together'. Nor is there of course in this idea of 'the automatic' anything at all inconsistent with the fundamental notion of necessity: the formation of the whirl is the outcome of natural causes, the shape, size, motions, and collisions of the atoms, but it is accidental, entirely undetermined either by purpose or design.

That this was in part Democritus' meaning I have little doubt: but it is not an entirely satisfactory explanation, if only because it is based on Aristotelian conceptions which

[1] This I take to be the view of Zeller and Lange.
[2] *de Nat. Deor.* i. 24. 66: cf. *Tusc.* i. 11. 22, and 18. 42.
[3] i. 1021 ff.

could not have been fully present to him. A far more satis-factory result would be reached, if we could determine his own conception of 'chance' and 'automatism', and this, it appears to me, we are in a position to do.[1] Aristotle[2] informs us that even those who are most fully aware that every effect can be referred to a definite cause—he must include the Atomists, even if they are not the only persons in his mind—yet habitually say that some things are due to chance and others not. The conception of 'chance' then must be con-sistent with that of necessity. And of the nature of this conception Aristotle has most fortunately preserved us a hint: he says[3] that the persons who state that the whirl is produced automatically distinguish its creation from that of animals and plants, 'for it is no chance product which arises from each seed, but from one seed olives and from another a man'. There is here clearly no question of design: that which differentiates the creation of the olive and the man from the creation of a universe is clearly the definite seed: one can say with regard to these seeds that they must pro-duce olive and man, but of the atoms moving in space and colliding it is not possible to say which of them may fall into the whirl: there is nothing peculiar in their nature which determines it. It would seem then that the Atomists had a strict scientific conception of 'chance'; they knew that everything has its cause, 'necessity' is all-controlling, but in many cases we are unable to predict what will happen or to reach back to the cause, and such occurrences we attribute to 'chance'. This idea is strikingly borne out by another passage in the Aristotelian discussion,[4] where he again seems to have Democritus in view: 'the causes from which "chance" results would follow, must be indefinite (ἀόριστα): and this is why chance seems to belong to the indefinite and to be unascertainable (ἄδηλος) to man'. If with this passage we compare the statement of a doxographer[5] that Democritus

---

[1] See Goedeckemeyer, pp. 36 ff.; Mabilleau, pp. 216–18.
[2] *Phys. B.* 4. 195 b.
[3] Ibid. 196 a; D.A. 69. [4] Ibid. 197 a 8.
[5] Theodoret. vi. 15. αἰτία ἄδηλος ἀνθρωπίνῳ λόγῳ.

regarded chance as a 'cause unascertainable for human reason', there seems no longer cause to doubt, but the point is clinched when we find Simplicius[1] speaking of Democritus' conception of 'the automatic' as an 'indefinite cause'. The Atomic conception of 'chance' then is, as we may say, the purely subjective conception which is proper to a scientific view of nature. 'Chance' is no external force which comes in to upset the workings of 'necessity' by producing a cause-less result; it is but a perfectly normal manifestation of that 'necessity', but the limits of the human understanding make it impossible for us to determine what the cause is. There are special conditions—the aggregation of atoms of a certain shape, size, position, order, and movement—which will make for the production of a cosmic whirl, and the whole process is but the carrying out of the universal laws of cause and effect: but we cannot know what these conditions are and therefore we attribute the result to 'chance'. Epicurus, whose notion of the 'swerve' of the atoms 'at no certain time or place' was indeed a contradiction of the universal necessity, was driven to adopt a somewhat different view of chance, but Democritus' conception, so far from being any contra-diction of his fundamental principles, is perfectly consistent with them, and forms a notable example of the consistency and accuracy of his thought. The idea of the origin of the whirl, so far from being confused by him, has been greatly cleared and strengthened: it is produced as the inevitable outcome of natural processes, but it is undesigned and for men unpredictable.

There are no separate accounts given of Democritus' conception of the process of world-formation in the whirl.[2] That which has been already examined in reference to Leucippus must be regarded as holding good for the

---

[1] Simpl. in Arist. *Phys. B.* 4. 196 a.

[2] The account given in Aet. i. 4; D. (Leucippus) 24, is, as Liepmann has shown (pp. 19 ff.), largely contaminated by Epicurean theory: thus it makes no specific mention of the whirl, and speaks of 'the heaviest atoms' as moving 'downwards'. But it is useful in preserving here and there an important technical term.

Atomists in general. But it may in some points be considered afresh in the light of Democritus' general views; in particular it throws much light on the very vexed problem of the place of 'weight' in Democritus' system. It will be remembered that on the one hand in the cosmogony of Leucippus there was no trace of weight either as an efficient cause or a resultant: it is the larger and bulkier atoms which by their expanse are able to offer a resistance to the whirl and so congregate in the centre, the finer and smaller atoms which are squeezed out to the edges and carried round in the full rotatory motion of the vortex. Similarly we have seen reason to agree with the denial of the doxographers of any attribution of absolute weight to the atoms by Democritus, and still more to refuse to admit the assumption of a primary property of weight as the cause of a downward motion leading to the collisions of the atoms and the resultant formation of a whirl. What then can Aristotle mean when he states that 'Democritus says that each of the indivisible particles is heavier according to increase of bulk'[1] (κατὰ τὴν ὑπεροχήν), or elsewhere that 'the greater of them is the heavier'?[2] We are now, I think, in a position at last to answer this question. Three points in the Aristotelian discussion must be noted. (1) He never speaks of the atom, as such, in virtue of its being a piece of solid matter, possessing 'weight', but only of some atoms as being 'heavier' or 'lighter' than others. Indeed in a notable passage[3] he remarks that 'former philosophers have never spoken of absolute weight or lightness but have only used the words relatively. They never say what is "the heavy" or "the light" but only what is "the heavier" or "the lighter" among things that have weight'. In other words the earlier thinkers had no notion of the weight of a thing as a property comparable to its size or shape, but only thought of it as heavier or lighter, that is, offering more or less resistance to an

---

[1] de Gen. et Corr. A. 8. 326 a 9; D.A. 60.

[2] de Caelo, Δ. 2. 309 a; D. ibid: cf. Theophr. de Sensu, 61; D.A. 135.

[3] de Caelo, 308 a: see E. G. P.3, 342, where it is noted that 'weight is never called a "thing", as, for instance, warmth and cold are'.

external moving force. (2) Throughout the discussion Aristotle is thinking of weight in a formed cosmos and regards 'heaviness' as a tendency 'downwards', that is *towards the centre*, and lightness as a tendency upwards, that is, *towards the outside* (πρὸς τὸ ἔσχατον). This notion is not of course strange even to us, for the effect of weight in ordinary practice is motion 'downwards', as we say, towards the earth, even though the absolute direction of such motion is precisely opposite at the antipodes. (3) His main point with regard to Democritus is that heaviness is derivative from and exactly proportionate to size: the larger the atom the heavier.

If now the Aristotelian idea be applied to the atomic cosmogony, as it has been interpreted from Diogenes, it is seen to fit exactly. There is no question of free atoms moving in a boundless void, but of a cosmic whirl in which 'up' and 'down' could mean nothing but towards or from the centre. The 'heavier' atom is precisely that which is 'larger' and therefore moves towards the centre because it is more capable of resisting the extraneous force of the rotatory motion. It is heavier not because of its absolute weight, but only derivatively because larger and therefore more difficult to move: we might in fact say,[1] without stretching the language too far, that the larger atom has greater heaviness, that is greater resisting power, but not more weight. The account thus given is borne out by the contrast which Aristotle[2] quotes from Democritus between the solid atoms, whose heaviness is exactly proportionate to their size, and compound bodies where the comparative weight of things of the same size varies according to the amount of void in their constitution: a piece of wool, for instance, is lighter than a piece of bronze of the same size, because it contains more void. Here we are undoubtedly inside a cosmos and 'heaviness' means tendency towards the centre: but the wool is lighter because it has more void in a given

---

[1] The explanation of this rather difficult point comes more easily to the German commentators who can oppose naturally *das Schwere* and *Gewicht*.

[2] *de Caelo*, Δ. 2. 309 a.

bulk and therefore less sheer matter to drag it, as it were, towards the centre. Aristotle's language is in fact applicable —and only applicable—to the atoms inside the cosmic whirl, and in this conception there appears a reconciliation between the apparently divergent views of the tradition about Democritus. The doxographers are right in denying that Democritus attributed weight to the atoms as a third property together with size and shape—for they are speaking from the Epicurean point of view which thinks of absolute weight as the cause of an original perpendicular downward movement. On the other hand there is no doubt that Democritus did speak, as Aristotle reports him of 'heavier' and 'lighter' atoms, as a derivative quality, immediately dependent on size, and called into being, as it were, in the vortex, as a counteraction of the rotatory motion of the whirl. It is in fact a kind of compendious expression denoting what is clearly implied without it in Diogenes' account of Leucippus' theory.

Like Leucippus Democritus held that worlds were infinite in number,[1] but made important additions to the theory in assuming and elaborating differences between them and introducing details as to their growth, decay, and destruction. These are summed up in an interesting traditional description:[2]

worlds are infinite in number and different in size. In some there is no sun or moon, in some these are larger than those in our world and in others more in number. The distances between worlds are unequal and in some quarters there are more worlds, in others fewer: some are growing, others are reaching their prime, some are decaying or coming into being in one part and failing in another. They are destroyed by one another by colliding. And some worlds are without living creatures and all moisture. . . . A world grows towards its prime, until it can no longer take in any addition from without.

In these ideas there is certainly a freedom of speculation and a boldness of imagination which contrasts effectively with the rather bald and restricted ideas attributed to Leucippus.

---

[1] D.L. ix. 44; D.A. 1.　　　　[2] Hipp. Ref. 1. 13; D.A. 40.

Democritus is prepared not merely to assume an infinity of cosmic whirls in the universe, but, as it were, to sweep all space in his imagination and to postulate the same variety between world and world which he saw between members of the same species of thing within a world. In some quarters of space he shows us worlds close-packed and crowding in on one other, in others they are rarer with large intervals of void tenanted by the free atoms. Internally, too, these worlds differ in structure: Democritus is not bound by his experience of our world with its sun, moon, and stars, but can conceive worlds without sun or moon, or with several, worlds without life or the moisture which could sustain it. There is a fine width of view in all this and it seems to add a dignity to Atomism.

More important perhaps for the subsequent development of the system is the notion of the various stages of growth in the worlds: they are not all 'complete', but some are still increasing, others beginning already to decay. The general idea may perhaps have been suggested by the stages in Empedocles' world caused by the interaction of 'Strife' and 'Love', but it is worked out in a far less arbitrary manner. Particularly notable is the final sentence which contains the germ of all the later theory of growth and decay:[1] a world, like a living organism, continues to grow so long as it is capable of taking in and assimilating extraneous atomic matter, but a period ultimately arrives when this can no longer be so, when the loss of matter exceeds the gain; then decay sets in and ultimately dissolution. The idea that a world may be growing in one part and decaying in another is, I think, peculiar to Democritus, and is a little difficult to understand on atomic principles, but it is a further proof of his vividness of imagination in conceiving differences of condition between the infinite worlds. Democritus too states for the first time the notion of the ultimate destruction of worlds: just as a world has a birth in the cosmic universe,[2] so it must ultimately pass away and dissolve once more into

[1] See especially Lucr. ii. 1105 ff.
[2] A world is both *nativom* and *mortale*, Lucr. v. 235 ff.

its component atoms: they alone are eternal. That this final dissolution may take place internally as the result of the continuation of the process of decay is implied in the account, but Democritus with a fine stretch of the imagination conceives another possibility: just as the ordinary atomic compound may be dissolved as the result of a 'blow' which severs the interlacings of its atoms, so the huge organism of a world may be broken up by collision with another world. The idea is not quite clear, but we are probably not to conceive the worlds as moving in space—a notion for which there is no evidence in the Atomists—but rather as growing in bulk until they jostle a neighbouring world. This seems to be the picture presented in another brief account:[1] 'a world is destroyed when a greater world overcomes a lesser': we may even conceive that the 'greater world' swallows up the component atoms of the smaller in its own organism. Finally we have evidence of a still further pursuit of his idea by Democritus in the notion that the dissolved atoms of a broken world may possibly reunite themselves to form another: 'the worlds of Democritus change into other worlds made out of the same atoms:[2] the worlds thus become the same in form, but not in individuality'.[3] This speculation does not reappear with reference to worlds, but it does curiously enough in connexion with the human body[4]—another proof of the analogous treatment by the atomists of the organisms of the living body and the world. It is probable that the whole idea of growth, decay and destruction was much more elaborated by Democritus than our present accounts would lead us to suppose: there is at any rate enough to show how much Epicurus owed to him on this point, and to prove once again the audacity and penetration of his speculation.

---

[1] Aet. ii. 4. 9; D.A. 84.   [2] Simpl. in Ar. *de Caelo*, A. 10. 280; D.A. 82.
[3] This must, I think, be the meaning of τῷ ἀριθμῷ: the new world constructed out of the old atoms would be the same in substance, but its 'number', so to speak, in the series of worlds would be different. We may compare the famous phrase of Cicero, *de Nat. Deor.* i. 19. 49, about the Epicurean gods: 'nec soliditate quadam nec ad numerum'.   [4] Cf. Lucr. iii. 847–51.

§ 5. *Our World : the heavenly bodies and the earth*

It was noticed with regard to Leucippus' theory of our world and its constitution that he did not appear to have very much interest in the questions which arose, and harked back in a reactionary spirit to the rather crude theories of the early Ionians, neglecting the results of recent and contemporary observation and speculation. In this respect there is considerable evidence for a marked change of attitude on the part of Democritus: indeed we can in this part of the theory point most certainly to definite differences of opinion between the two philosophers. Democritus seems to have had a real interest in these subjects, a much greater respect for views developed since the time of the Ionian school, and, as usual, considerable insight and boldness of speculation on his own account.

In the first place he reversed Leucippus' strange theory as regards the relative position of the orbits of the heavenly bodies, and held that the moon is lowest[1] (i.e. nearest the earth), then the sun, then the fixed stars; as for the planets they are not all at an equal height'. This was a definite advance, and we may notice moreover the explicit distinction between fixed stars and planets, which seems to have been unknown to Leucippus. That he also made use of his conclusion to explain the apparent motions of the heavenly bodies is expressly explained by Lucretius,[2] who tells us that Democritus held that the nearer the orbit of a body to the earth, the less it is affected by the whirl:[3] the motion of the moon then is slowest, that of the sun next, and that of the fixed stars the fastest. Consequently by a common optical delusion the stars appear to us to be stationary, and the sun and moon to be moving in the direction opposite to that of their real motion, the moon faster than the sun. This very ingenious notion, which for long held its place in astronomy, has a peculiar interest for us in that it accords

[1] Hipp. *Ref*. i. 13; D.A. 40.   [2] v. 621 ff.
[3]   quanto quaeque magis sint terram sidera propter,
      tanto posse minus cum caeli turbine ferri. 623–4.

exactly with the view which has been taken of the nature of
the cosmic whirl, and affords another example of the
'resistance of the middle'. Democritus was evidently at
pains to accommodate his astronomical views to his general
theory of the world.

With regard to the nature of the heavenly bodies too
tradition is similarly suggestive of Democritus' care for
general consistency. It will be remembered that Leucippus
had held that sun, moon, and stars were masses of matter
caught up from the exterior universe by the outer membrane
of the world and ignited by the rapidity of their motion in
the whirl. Democritus considers their structure from the
atomic point of view and decides that they are compounded
of smooth and round atoms,[1] as is the soul: the round shape,
as always in the atomic theory, being associated with mobility
and consequently with fire. A curious and interesting passage[2] seems to suggest an attempt to connect this new theory
with Leucippus' notion: 'sun and moon have their own
characteristic motion: at first they had by no means a warm
nature, nor indeed generally speaking very bright, on the
contrary they resembled the nature of the earth. For each
of them first of all was brought into being by a separate
foundation (ὑποβολή) of the world, and afterwards when the
orb of the sun[3] increased in size, fire was taken into it'.
Leucippus' idea of the original earthy nature of sun and
moon is retained, but the change is produced not now by
rotation, but by the inclusion of the round atoms of fire.
The new notion is characteristic, if somewhat clumsy. The
statement of the doxographer[4] that the sun was according to
Democritus a 'red-hot mass or a fiery stone' reads too
suspiciously like Anaxagoras though it would not be inconsistent with the general idea. More suggestive is a
remark of Cicero's[5] that Democritus thought the sun was

---

[1] Diog. Laert. ix. 44; D.A. 1.   [2] Plut. *Strom.* 7; D.A. 39.

[3] This I take to be the meaning of τοῦ περὶ τὸν ἥλιον κύκλου: cf. τῇ
περὶ τὴν γῆν φύσει just above.

[4] Aet. ii. 20. 7 μύδρον ἢ πέτρον διάπυρον; D.A. 87.

[5] *de Fin.* i. 6. 20; D.A. 87.

'large', for it hints at a conflict with the view to which Epicurus was led by his insistence on the validity of the evidence of sense-perception. Two interesting notions about the moon have come down to us, the one as short-sighted as the other is penetrating. The first is an attempt at the explanation of the light of the full moon: 'when she takes up her position in a straight line with him who gives her light (i.e. exactly between the earth and the sun) she takes in and receives the sunlight:[1] so that it is natural that she herself should be seen and show the sun through her (διαφαίνειν)'. This extraordinary notion that the sun's light is seen through the moon is severely criticized by Plutarch, and contrasted unfavourably with the view of Empedocles, who saw rightly enough that this was the position which caused an eclipse of the sun: it does indeed seem strange that Democritus, if he realized that the moon's light was due to the sun, should nevertheless have invented a theory so perverse. On the other hand he seems to have answered the problem why the moon looks so 'earthy'[2] (γεώδης) with singular perspicacity, saying that it was owing to 'the shadow of the lofty parts in it: for the moon has glens and valleys'. Almost equally striking is his theory of the Milky Way, which he describes as 'the joint rays of many tiny continuous stars shining together owing to their dense crowding'.[3] A longer description is even more remarkable, though, since it is attributed also to Anaxagoras, the credit ought not perhaps to be given to Democritus:

The Milky Way is the light of certain stars: for when the sun passes at night under the earth, his light still falls on certain of the stars above the earth: their proper light is then not seen, for it is impeded by the rays of the sun. The shadow of the earth runs up in front of others and keeps them in darkness so that they are not caught by the light of the sun: the proper light of these stars is seen and they are the Milky Way.[4]

This view undoubtedly influenced Democritus' notion of

[1] Plut. *de Fac. in Orb. Lunae*, 16. 929 c; D.A. 89 a.
[2] Aet. ii. 30. 3; D.A. 90. [3] Aet. iii. 1. 6; D.A. 91.
[4] Alex. in Arist. *Meteor. A.* 8. 345 a; D.A. 91.

the shape of the earth. He definitely deserted Leucippus' idea of its 'tambourine-shape' and said that it was 'long-shaped (προμήκης), the length being one and a half times the breadth',[1] a formation which would suit the general contour of the Milky Way. It looks once again as if he were trying to work his detailed account of the world into a consistent whole, instead of the rather haphazard jumble of notions which had satisfied Leucippus. He followed him however in holding that the earth was tilted down towards the south because the atmosphere there was weaker:[2] 'for in the north it is unmixed, but mixed in the south, therefore the earth is weighed down in this part, where it is more luxuriant in fruits and produce.' Whether he used this tilting of the earth, like Leucippus, to explain night and eclipses we have no information: the theory of the Milky Way seems to suggest a more rational view of the sun's daily 'revolution', but his strange notion of the moon's light looks as if Democritus had not advanced much farther than Leucippus in determining the cause of eclipses. The statement that the earth 'was at first wandering because of its smallness and lightness,[3] but in time became thick and heavy and came to a standstill', is exactly in harmony with the theory of the whirl. Altogether the account of the heavenly bodies is a curious combination of insight and stupidity, but at least it seems more consistent both with itself and with Atomism generally than the crude jumble of ideas attributed to Leucippus.

Democritus dealt further with certain phenomena of sky and earth, which may most conveniently be considered here. Comets[4] he curiously explained as an optical illusion produced when two planets are so near together as to produce the 'joint-appearance' (σύμφασις) of a single body. This notion is obviously connected closely with the theory of the Milky Way and it is significant that it too is attributed to

[1] Agathem. i. 1. 2; D.B. 15.
[2] Aet. iii. 12. 2; D.A. 96.
[3] Aet. iii. 13. 4; D.A. 95.
[4] Alex. in Arist. *Meteor. A.* 6. 342 b; D.A. 92.

Anaxagoras jointly with Democritus. The theory of the origin of thunder and lightning is very elaborate and markedly at variance with the crude notion of Leucippus: 'thunder is caused by an uneven combination of atoms forcing the cloud which encloses it in a downward direction:[1] lightning is a collision of clouds owing to which the fire-producing particles gather together as they rub one another through the many void apertures into a single spot and filter through. A thunderbolt is produced when the downward motion is formed in a cloud by fire-producing particles which are purer and finer and more even and, as he writes himself, "close-fitted" (πυκνάρμονα). Waterspouts occur when combinations of fire with more void are caught in places full of void and in a kind of peculiar membrane which surrounds them, and then forming into bodies owing to this mixture of many elements, swoop down upon the deep.' The inclusion of thunderbolts and 'presters' is very characteristic of the traditional meteorology, but the whole idea is once again thought out in atomic terms. Of earthquakes he also gave an explanation: 'the earth is full of water and receives a large quantity of rain-water as well and is moved by this means: for when the water is in excess and the hollow places cannot contain it, it forces its way out and so causes an earthquake'.[2] In other parts of his works Democritus engaged in the ever-popular discussion in antiquity as to the cause of the Nile-floods,[3] and, as a recently discovered papyrus has revealed to us, attempted an explanation of salt-springs.[4] In a separate treatise he gave a detailed exposition of the magnet, the gist of which is that like always attracts like:[5] iron and the magnet are constructed of similar atoms: they tend then towards each other and when they are close the atoms rush from one to the other and fill up void spaces, so that they hold the two substances in contact.

---

[1] Aet. iii. 3. 11; D.A. 93.
[2] Arist. *Meteor. B.* 7. 365 a; D.A. 97.
[3] Aet. iv. 1. 4; D.A. 99.
[4] Hibeh Papyr. 16; Grenfell and Hunt; D.A. 99 a.
[5] Alex. *Quaest.* ii. 23, p. 137; D.A. 165.

Here, as in the cosmogony, we see that the attraction of the old notion of 'like to like' is strong on Democritus, but once again his ideas of atomic shape and size give it a new plausibility. These miscellaneous theories are not perhaps of much value in themselves, but they started certain permanent topics of atomic speculation and reveal the origin of much of that odd conglomeration of discussions which is so prominent in the second letter of Epicurus and the sixth book of Lucretius.

Another great department of inquiry which Democritus pursued 'with the greatest interest and elaboration is that of zoology and physiology. Thrasyllus records three books on these subjects and it so happens that a very considerable body of information[1] has come down to us as to Democritus' theories. It is hard to find in them anything specially atomic and his speculations were no doubt inspired by the same contemporary interest in these matters which gave Anaxagoras the starting-point in physiology for his main theory of the constitution of matter. But there is nothing in the views recorded which is inconsistent with Atomism and it may be taken as certain that Democritus took as much pains to accommodate his theories here to his main principles as he did in the department of Astronomy. The extraordinary width of his interest and the vividness of his insight into detail is again apparent. With regard to human physiology perhaps the most interesting statement is that he believed men were originally sprung from 'water and mud':[2] that is to say, as another account suggests,[3] that they came from the earth, but it was the moist element in it which was the efficient cause. We seem here to be half-way between the old mythological story of Prometheus and the elaborate Epicurean idea of the birth of animals and men from 'wombs rooted in the ground':[4] moreover the hint that he compared the creation of worms from moist earth[5] suggests the origin of an argument which was ultimately to be worked to death

---

[1] See D.A. 139–64.
[2] Censor. 4. 9; D.A. 139.
[3] Aet. v. 19. 6; D. ibid.
[4] Lucr. v. 801 ff.
[5] Lact. *Inst. div.* vii. 7. 9; D. ibid.

by Lucretius.[1] Besides this guess at the origin of our first parents, there are plentiful details as to his theories of generation and conception[2] and of the process of gestation and the nourishment of the infant in the womb[3] which show at any rate acute conjecture: his followers seem to have neglected inquiry on this head. A curious line of inquiry which he seems also to have pursued is the investigation of symptoms of the survival of sensation in the body for a while after the moment of death:[4] his inference would undoubtedly have been to the wholly material character of the soul and its gradual dissolution like that of any other decaying atomic compound.

With regard to other animals we have evidence of elaborate theories advanced by Democritus as to the birth of mules,[5] the growth of the horns of cattle and stags,[6] and even on such apparently minute and obscure topics as spiders and their webs,[7] the eyes of owls,[8] and the crowing of cocks.[9] Another whole book was devoted to 'seeds and plants and fruits', and we have evidence of an interesting theory that plants which grow straight up are shorter-lived than those which grow crooked[10] because it is less easy for the sap to run above the ground than among the roots: this certainly looks as if it were deduced from the general atomic theory of motion. Finally there is a theory that even stones[11] have 'souls' which are the cause of their shaping: this is not of course a return to Ionian hylozoism, but rather a purely materialistic view that 'life' cannot be supposed to begin suddenly in the organic world. It is not without interest in view both of the system of Epicurus and of the theories of some modern physiologists.

[1] ii. 928, &c.
[2] D.A. 140–2.
[3] D.A. 144.
[4] D.A. 160.
[5] Ael. *H. N.* xii. 16; D.A. 151.
[6] Ibid. xii. 18; D.A. 153.
[7] [Arist.] *Hist. anim.* ix. 39. 623; D.A. 150.
[8] Etym. genuin. s.v. γλαῦξ; D.A. 157.
[9] Cic. *de Divin.* ii. 26. 57; D.A. 158.
[10] Theophr. *de Caus. Pl.* ii. 11. 7; D.A. 162.
[11] Albert. Magn. *de Lapid.* i. 1. 4; D.A. 164.

§ 6. *The soul, sensation, and thought*
(a) *Soul and mind.*

Democritus inherited from Leucippus the general conception that the soul (ψυχή) or vital principle was corporeal, that it was of the nature of fire and was, like fire, composed of spherical atoms, for they were the most mobile. These ideas Democritus retained unmodified, but some of the notices on the point are interesting, for they serve at once to bring out the essentially material nature of the conception, and also point to a dawning sense of its difficulties. In his summary of Democritus' doctrines Diogenes[1] has the somewhat startling statement: 'the sun and moon are composed of smooth and spherical particles, and likewise the soul'. The soul that is, is fiery in its nature, therefore it must be composed of the same kind of particles as the fiery heavenly bodies: the presence of the spherical particles give to both their characteristics. Even more astonishing seems the statement of a late authority[2] that 'there is a soul in the stone', which is supported by the assertion of Aetius[3] that 'Democritus said that all things have a share in some kind of soul' (ψυχῆς ποιᾶς). At first sight this looks more like the doctrine of the Stoic school and even seems to anticipate the ideas of modern thinkers about 'mind-stuff', but Democritus probably meant little more by it than that there was present in all things a certain portion of the spherical particles which could produce either fire or the soul, so that in a potential sense they too had a soul. The idea is striking but in reality purely material. Hardly less remarkable is a statement made by Aristotle[4] in reference to Democritus, 'some have thought the soul is fire: for fire too has the finest parts and is the most *bodiless* (ἀσώματον) of all the elements and

---

[1] D.L. ix. 44; D.A. 1. It is noticeable that the word used here is ὄγκων, not ἀτόμων, and it may be that Democritus was thinking not of spherical atoms, but of spherical atomic nuclei. There is good reason for believing that this was the idea of Epicurus.

[2] Albert Magn. *de Lapid.* 1. 1. 4; D.A. 164.

[3] Aet. iv. 4. 7; D.A. 117.

[4] *de Anima, A.* 2. 405 a 5; D.A. 101.

more than anything else is moved and moves other things'. We may perhaps accept the view of a commentator[1] on this passage that 'the term "bodiless" is not used in its full sense (for none of them would say that) but meaning that among bodies it is bodiless owing to the fineness of its parts'. If Aristotle is quoting Democritus and he himself used the word 'bodiless' in however a metaphorical sense, we may imagine that even in his mind there was arising something of the doubt as to the full capacity of any known material substance to produce the soul, which led subsequently to Epicurus' assumption[2] of the 'nameless' element in the soul. Be this as it may, it is clear that Democritus took over Leucippus' account of the soul's structure, and that with regard to the corporeal nature of the soul he was equally explicit. This must not be forgotten when we come to deal with the more intricate questions which arise in reference to his psychology: the more material the interpretation given to his statements, the more likely it is to be right.

Where is this soul, and what are its functions? It has been seen that little more can be safely attributed to Leucippus than that it is in the body and is the cause of the body's motions.[3] This view was also held by Democritus and can now be defined more closely: 'the soul moves the body in which it is situated, even as it is moved itself'.[4] From an interesting passage in Lucretius[5] we learn that Democritus supposed that it was distributed over the body, soul-atoms and body-atoms being placed in alternate juxta-position, a very exact conception, which Epicurus was subsequently at pains to refute. Thus disposed in the body the soul[6] moves it doubtless in the same mechanical manner as was conceived by Leucippus; 'it is capable of movement because of the smallness of its parts and their shape':[7] the

---

[1] Philop., ad loc.; D.A. 101.   [2] See Part II, Chap. VIII, pp. 390 ff.
[3] See Chap. II, § 5.
[4] Arist. *de Anima*, A. 3. 406 b 15; D.A. 104.
[5] iii. 370 ff.
[6] Arist. *de Anima*, l.c.: cf. ibid. A. 5. 409 a 32; D.A. 104 a.
[7] Ibid. 405 a 5; D.A. 101.

spherical shape is again conceived of as the most mobile and it communicates its motions to the body in which it is situated. Aristotle adds a curious illustration: 'he says that Daedalus made his wooden Aphrodite a moving figure by pouring in molten silver;[1] similarly Democritus too speaks, for he says that the indivisible spheres (sc. the spherical particles) move, because it is their nature never to remain still, and drag along with them and set in motion the whole body'. The motion of the soul-atoms actually sets the body in motion.

But this is not the sole function of the soul, for, although our authorities are not explicit on this point, Democritus must also have held that the contact with external bodies moves the soul in the body and so causes sensation. This becomes clearer when we pass to the discussion of the means of knowledge, but we may quote for it at the moment a criticism of Aristotle,[2] which brings out very clearly the corporeal conception: 'since the soul is in all the sentient body, there must be two bodies in the same place, if the soul is a sort of body (σῶμά τι)'. There is here at least the germ of the later Epicurean idea of the soul by its presence in the body communicating sensation to the body, and the notion of the 'two bodies'[3] shows how completely the atomists thought of the soul as corporeal in the same sense as any other part of the body. The same idea is illustrated in an elaboration[4] attributed to Democritus of Leucippus' notion of respiration, which shows clearly how he conceived the relation of the soul-atoms to those of body:

Democritus says that as the result of respiration something occurs to those who breathe, for he argues that it prevents the soul from being squeezed out of the body. . . . He says that the soul and the warm are identical, the first forms of the spherical. When then these atoms are being crowded together owing to the surrounding matter which

[1] ἄργυρον χυτόν here may possibly mean 'quicksilver'.
[2] Ibid. A. 5. 409 a 32; D.A. 104 a.
[3] Aristotle's difficulty is surely solved by Democritus' idea (Lucr. iii. 370 ff.) that soul- and body-atoms are distributed alternately.
[4] Arist. de Resp. 4. 471 b 30; D.A. 106.

squeezes them out, he says that respiration comes in to help. For in the air is a great quantity of atoms such as he calls 'mind' and 'soul'; when then a creature breathes and the air enters in, these come in too and arrest the squeezing motion and prevent the soul in the animals passing out. And this is why life and death depend upon respiration and expiration. For when the pressure of surrounding matter prevails and can no longer be checked by what comes in from without, as the creature cannot breathe, then death results. For death is the departure of atoms of this shape from the body owing to the pressure of their surroundings.

This passage suggests two further points of importance. In the first place the account of death is more explicit than in anything attributed to Leucippus. All through life the soul-atoms are carrying on a kind of contest with the body-atoms which tend to squeeze them out in expiration: but in return fresh soul-atoms are taken in as we breathe from the outer air. At last the contest proves unequal, the soul-atoms are breathed out, no more can be taken in, and the body deprived of the soul, which gave it life and sensation, perishes. This account must be at once modified and supplemented by a curious theory attributed to Democritus[1] that even 'the dead parts of bodies have a share in sensation, because they clearly always have a share in something that is warm and capable of sensation, when the greater part is breathed forth'. That is to say that even when the soul has so effectively been squeezed out of the body that death ensues, there yet lurk in the body enough spherical particles to give it in a faint measure warmth and sensation. The idea, which clearly emphasizes the material picture in Democritus' mind, may be compared with his statement that 'all things have a share in soul',[2] and is said to have been used by him as an explanation of stories of the restoration of the dead to life:[3] 'for not even death, it seems, was a quenching of all the life of the body, but life was let go owing to some blow perhaps or wound, but the bonds of the soul about the marrow still remained rooted and the heart kept the fire of

---

[1] Aet. iv. 4. 7; D.A. 117.   [2] Above, p. 156.
[3] Procl. *in Remp.* ii. 113. 6; D.B. 1.

life stored up in the depth; and because these remained the body regained the extinguished life and proved sufficient for the recreation of soul.' We may perhaps compare the account given by Lucretius [1] of the remnants of life in the limbs of warriors cut off in battle.

So the body dies and the soul likewise perishes, for the mobile round atoms are dispersed in the outer air, indeed, they are not even breathed out all at once or in conjunction. It is not therefore surprising to find that Democritus,[2] like Leucippus, held 'that the soul was mortal (φθαρτή) and was destroyed with the body', though in fact this momentous conclusion receives but little notice in the authorities.

Not less noticeable in the account of respiration is the incidental identification of 'mind' and 'soul', for here we come upon a cardinal point. Both the distinction and the identification are important, and are vouched for in many quotations: 'Democritus', says Aristotle,[3] 'said simply that soul and mind are the same', and the phrase is repeated in later commentators. First as to the distinction: the soul (ψυχή) was thought, as has been seen, to be distributed over the body and to be the cause of sensation and of movement: the mind (νοῦς) on the other hand is considered rather as an aggregate of unmixed soul-atoms, situated in some one part of the body, and to be the cause and seat of thought. This was a traditional conception among the physiologists but here for the first time becomes explicit in atomic terms. In what part of the body the mind was situated was a matter of controversy among philosophers, but we may feel sure that Democritus was in accord with the general atomic tradition that it was in the breast: 'Democritus and Epicurus said that the soul was of two parts, having both the reasoning part (τό λογικόν) situated in the breast (θώραξ) and the unreasoning (τὸ ἄλογον) scattered all through the compound of

[1] iii. 642 ff.
[2] Aet. iv. 7. 4; D.A. 109.
[3] de Anima, A. 2. 404 a. 27; D.A. 101: cf. Philopon. in loc., p. 71. 19; D.A. 113.

the body.'[1] The statement here is loose, for the Atomists would not have spoken of the soul as having 'two parts' and the terms 'reasoning' and 'unreasoning' belong to a later stage of thought, but the general idea of the distinction between 'soul' and 'mind' is clear, and the statement as to the seat of the soul unequivocal. By his identification of 'mind' and 'soul' Democritus meant simply that they were of the same atomic composition: the spherical particles which distributed in the body formed the soul, were gathered together unmixed, as Epicurus later explained, in the breast and so produced that complex form of sensation which is called thought. For, as will be seen later on, Democritus made the complementary identification of sensation and thought: the two processes being due to the movement of similar particles were in fact the same.

This account of the soul is of great interest and importance. It was a first attempt to think out on atomic lines what must always be the most difficult problem for any purely materialistic philosophy, how can sensation and thought and the instruments with which they are performed be explained on a purely corporeal basis? Democritus' answer was tentative and crude and left much to be worked out more completely by Epicurus, but it had laid down the lines for him, and the difficulties which it left over are not more insuperable than those which must be met by any modern attempt to explain the action of the senses and the mind on rigidly material assumptions.

[1] Aet. iv. 4. 6; D.A. 105. Aetius' statement in another passage (iv. 5. 1; D. ibid.) that Democritus held with Hippocrates and Plato that the mind was in the brain must be a mistake. Still less probable is the statement of Sext. vii. 349; D.A. 107, that some following Democritus said that the διάνοια (incidentally not a Democritean term) was in the whole body. Goedeckemeyer (p. 54) is inclined to think that Democritus made no real distinction at all between a perceptive and a rational element, but this is really implied in his use of the words ψυχή and νοῦς, of which there can be no doubt. Mention may just be made of an unauthoritative statement in Hippocr. 23. 1 ff.; D.C. 6, that Democritus placed the seat of thought in the brain, of anger in the heart, and of desire in the liver.

(b) Sensation, the senses, and thought.

In regard to sensation Democritus appears even more conspicuously as the elaborator of the ideas of Leucippus,[1] who had apparently been content with the general notion that the soul was the cause of sensation in the body, though he had invented the theory of the 'idols' as the cause of vision and the cause of thought in the mind. Democritus followed up these clues with much detailed speculation as regards the individual senses and their relation to their objects.

As regards sensation in general we have two interesting statements as to his views. In the first place we are told[2] that it was brought about by a process of 'change' or 'alteration' (τῷ ἀλλοιοῦσθαι), which is quite consistent with the generally material view of the Atomists: the object from without impinges on atoms of soul in the body and disturbs them, altering their positions, and then, as the naïve simplicity of atomic materialism puts it, 'sensation follows'. Here we have the germ of the elaborate description of the genesis of sensation by atomic motion described by Lucretius.[3]

The second statement is the very basis of all atomic sensationalism: 'they make all the objects of sense touchable (ἁπτά):[4] if this is so, each of the other senses is a kind of touch'. In a purely material system there can be no form of communication between one body and another except that of contact: if the spherical atoms of the soul are to be set in motion, it can only be by the touch of another atomic compound. This idea undoubtedly lies at the basis of all

[1] See pp. 101–6.

[2] Theophr. *de Sensu*, 49; D.A. 135. Theophrastus raises the question which side Democritus would take in the question debated by the earlier philosophers whether sensation was caused by 'the like' or 'the unlike', and sets against this statement, which tells in favour of the unlike, Democritus' statement that 'that which acts and that which suffers are alike' (cf. Arist. *de Gen. et corr.* A. 7. 323 b; D.A. 63). But probably Democritus did not raise the question to himself at all.

[3] iii. 246 ff.

[4] Arist. *de Sensu*, 4. 442 a 29; D.A. 119.

the theories of 'idols' and 'effluences' which we meet in the account of the other senses, and to the end the Atomists [1] felt a certain security about the sense of touch which they did not always feel about sight or hearing.

This being so, it might have been expected that Democritus would have devoted some consideration to the sense of touch itself, but beyond a single passage [2] dealing with the sensations of hot and cold, from which it appears that Democritus referred them to differences of size and shape in the atoms composing the object, we have no indication that he discussed it, and Theophrastus [3] in his detailed criticism of the sensation-theory passes it over unnoticed. This notable omission was no doubt in part due to the same naïve spirit of common sense which prompted Democritus in another context [4] to say 'a man is that which we all know'. It may be also, as a recent critic has suggested,[5] that he was half-conscious that the fundamental problem of touch would raise in an acute form the ultimate difficulty of the relation between the physical contact and the psychical sensation. At any rate it is clear that in his account of the other senses his chief concern is always to provide for contact and that this not infrequently gave him trouble.

It is obvious that the sense nearest akin to simple touch is taste, for in taste parts of the body—the tongue and the palate—are brought into immediate contact with the object. They therefore perceive it, just as any part of the body perceives an object which touches it, but that is not all. In something of the same way as the body may have an added sensation of hot or cold from the object touching it, so the tongue and palate have the further sensation which we denote by the epithets, sweet, bitter, sour, salt, &c. Now

[1] Cf. e.g. Lucr. ii. 434–5,
      tactus enim, tactus, pro divum numina sancta,
      corporis est sensus.

[2] Simpl. in Ar. *de Caelo, Γ*. 1. 299; D.A. 120.

[3] *de Sensu*, 49 ff.; D.A. 135.

[4] D.B. 165. We may compare Lucr. i. 422 'corpus enim per se communis dedicat esse sensus'.

[5] Beare, *Greek Theories of Elementary Cognition*, p. 183.

these are not properties or qualities of the atoms, for their only properties are size, shape, and, in the cosmic whirl, weight. Nor are they, according to Democritus, qualities inherent in the atomic compounds: 'none of the other perceptible qualities [1] (*sc.* besides the three primary properties) exists by nature, but they are all experiences (πάθη) of the sense as it changes, and from this arises the sense-perception (φαντασία)'. This idea is of great importance for the understanding of Democritus' sensation-theory: difference of taste is purely subjective and is not inherent in the object: it is brought about by the 'change' in the position of the soul-atoms in the tongue and palate.

But it is not for that reason arbitrary: it is caused by, and is, as it were, the reflex of differences of size and shape in the atoms composing the object. In this point Democritus was apparently greatly interested and worked out in full detail the effect on taste of the different atomic shapes and sizes. Sharp taste,[2] for instance, is produced by small and fine atoms 'with many corners and bends', which penetrate the body and warm it by producing voids in it; 'for that which has most voids most easily becomes warm'. Sweet taste again is due to round and not particularly small shapes, for they penetrate the body but 'not violently or very quickly'. In the same way Democritus explained the minute differences in shape which cause the finer distinctions between the sour, the bitter, the salt, and the pungent.

Now here it is obvious that we have a far more elaborate mechanism than in the simple sense of touch, and the connexion is far less close. For the difference in shape in the atoms of the object produces in the percipient not a simple recognition of such differences, but a difference in his own purely subjective sensation of taste. Moreover, there is here a further possibility of failure of correspondence. The difference of sensation in the percipient is produced by an alteration in the positions of the soul-atoms in tongue and palate. But these may already differ in different individuals

[1] Theophr. *de Sensu*, § 63; D.A. 135: cf. also § 60.
[2] Ibid., § 65: cf. Theophr. *de Caus. Plant.* vi. 1. 6; D.A. 129.

or indeed in the same individual at different times. Hence what is sweet to one animal may seem bitter to another and the same man may differ in his judgement of taste in health and in sickness. 'We must know ', says Theophrastus,[1] 'not merely the active thing but the passive, especially as "the same taste does not appear the same to all", as Democritus says.' For there is nothing to prevent what is sweet to us being bitter to some other animals.' In another passage [2] he gives the physical explanation: ' it is of importance into what conditions of body (ἕξιν) it enters: for this too makes no small difference, because the same thing sometimes produces opposite effects and opposite things the same'. The subjective element in taste is thus greatly emphasized and a real and permanent correspondence between object and percipient considerably endangered. Hence arises the famous saying of Democritus,[3] which will have to be examined when we come to his metaphysical theory: ' Sweet is by convention (νόμῳ) and bitter is by convention.' There are signs of a possible divergence between sensation and truth.

It is evident that the sense of sight is by no means so easy to reduce to terms of touch: the object that you see does not touch your eye and a less immediate form of contact must be found. Leucippus,[4] as has been seen, explained sight by the notion of 'images' or 'idols' (εἴδωλα), which were constantly being thrown off the surface of things, and travelling through the air came into contact with the eye and by stirring the soul-atoms there produced the sensation of sight much as the direct touch of an external body could give the sensation of hot or cold. The authorities [5] who attribute this theory to Leucippus, assign it also to Democritus, and we find it again in this comparatively simple form in Epicurus. The idea of contact is preserved and touch is still the cause

---

[1] de Caus. Plant. vi. 2. 1; D.A. 130.
[2] de Sensu, 67; D.A. 135.
[3] Sext. adv. Math. vii. 136; D.B. 9.
[4] See Chap. II, § 5, p. 103.
[5] Aet. iv. 13. 1; Alex. de Sensu, 24, 14; 56. 12; D. (Leucippus) 29.

of sensation, but the intervention of the 'idols'[1] clearly leaves room for the possibility of error, as the 'image' may be distorted in transit. The difficulties which beset the theory at the outset are many and obvious: Aristotle[2] for instance raises the question why the eye alone should see and not other parts of the body which contain soul-atoms; Theophrastus[3] asks pertinently how two people could see each other, for their 'idols', when they are looking at one another, must collide: Aristotle[4] again ridicules Democritus' statement that if only there were void and nothing else between, we could see 'whether there was an ant in heaven'! These are superficial difficulties, but they point to an underlying weakness.

There is however evidence to show that Democritus himself, in part perhaps aware of some of these difficulties and in part wishing to attach himself to earlier theories of vision, broke away from the strict atomic tradition and elaborated the crude conception of Leucippus. It seems clear[5] that he started from the idea of older thinkers that what is actually seen is the image (ἔμφασις) in the pupil of the eye, and decided that this 'image'[6] was something hard (στερεόν) which entered the 'moist' (ὑγρόν) formation of the eye, and could so easily impress itself. 'For this reason', Theophrastus tells us in an account which seems to retain some of Democritus' own technical words, 'moist eyes are better than dry eyes for seeing, since the outer coat (χιτών) is very thin and compact (πυκνότατος), but the inner parts very spongy (σομφά) and empty of compact and hard flesh, but full of thick and smooth moisture, while the veins in the eyes are straight and devoid of moisture, so that they are of like shape with (ὁμοσχημονεῖν) the impressions. For everything best recognizes what is akin to it (τὰ ὁμόφυλα).' All this seems to bear

---

[1] *Etym. Gen.*; D.B. 123 suggests that Democritus called the 'idols' by the characteristic title δείκελον.

[2] *de Sensu*, 2. 438 a 5; D.A. 121: cf. Theophr. *de Sensu*, 54; D.A. 135.

[3] Ibid. 52.   [4] *de Anima*, B. 7. 419 a 15; D.A. 122.

[5] οἴεται τὸ ὁρᾶν εἶναι τὴν ἔμφασιν, Arist. *de Sensu*, 2. 438 a 6; D.A. 121: cf. Theophr. *de Sensu*, 50; D.A. 135.

[6] Theophr. ibid.

the mark of Democritus' close interest in details, and we may notice that his idea of the hard and dry 'idols' falling on the hard and dry veins and so being recognized by them bears out his general view that 'that which acts and that which is acted upon are alike and the same'.[1] It is the action of like on like.

But what is this 'image' in the eye? Theophrastus [2] gives his account: 'the image (ἔμφασις) is not produced directly in the pupil (κόρη), but the air between the eye and the thing seen is contracted and stamped (συστελλόμενον τυποῦσθαι) by the object seen and the seer; for from everything there is always taking place some effluence (ἀπορροήν)'. He [3] goes on to explain that the image thus stamped on the air is not broken up (θρύπτεσθαι), as the impression (ἐντύπωσις) is like one made on wax. The idea seems to be that the 'effluences' from eye and object meet and contract a portion of the air into a kind of waxy solid on which is then impressed the outline of the object: the image thus formed enters the eye and causes vision. The account is not above suspicion: it seems to be unsupported and one may well suppose that the idea of the contribution of the percipient to the formation of the image may be derived from the theory of Plato,[4] based in its turn on Empedocles' view, but there seems no reason to doubt that Democritus held the notion of the 'impression' (ἀποτύπωσις) as the cause of the image in the pupil, and it is borne out by his corresponding theory of hearing. If we are to conjecture his reason for this elaborate idea, it was probably that he saw that the objects of sense are in three dimensions, or as he would have said 'solid', whereas the image in the eye is of two dimensions, as he might have said 'flat': the transition then must be made somewhere in transit between the object and the eye and the formation of an 'impression' will account for it.

But how can this idea be reconciled with the traditional atomic notion of the 'idols', which Democritus is said to

[1] Arist. de Gen. et Corr. A. 7. 323 b; D.A. 63.
[2] de Sensu, 50; D.A. 135.   [3] 51.
[4] Tim. 45 b. See p. 54.

have held? We have no information on the point and can only suppose, if he did indeed hold the two theories concurrently, that the 'idol' was in fact the 'effluence' from the object—still in three dimensions—and that it formed the two-dimensional impressions on the air. If so, there seem to be new sources of error opened: the 'idol' itself may be distorted in transit, it may produce an incorrect 'impression' of itself, and the 'impression' again may be distorted before it becomes the 'image' in the pupil. But we must be content to be without sufficient knowledge on this point: what is clear is that the 'impression' theory seemed to Epicurus to be too complicated and that he returned to the simpler notion of Leucippus that it was the 'idol' itself which entered the eye.

There is a further point as regards vision which leads to a very characteristically Democritean piece of analysis. If it is asked what it is that sight tells us about an object, the answer is in the first place its size and shape. Now these are real properties of the compound object, as they are of its component atoms. But sight also gives us the sensation of colour, and colour is not, according to Democritus, any more than taste, a quality of things: 'he says', Aristotle [1] tells us, 'that colour does not exist'; it has not, that is to say, the real objective existence of shape and size. It is then, like taste, an 'experience of the sense', [2] a sensation caused by the 'alteration' of the soul-atom in the eye of the percipient due to the particular conformation of the object. Now differences of taste were caused mainly by differences in the shape of the atoms combining to form the object: differences of colour Democritus [3] seems rather to have attributed to their 'position' ($\tau\rho o\pi\acute{\eta}$). The turning of the component atoms

---

[1] de Gen. et Corr. A. 2. 316 a 1; D.A. 123: cf. Aet. i. 15. 8; D.A. 125.

[2] $\pi\acute{a}\theta os$ $\tau\hat{\eta}s$ $a\grave{\iota}\sigma\theta\acute{\eta}\sigma\epsilon\omega s$, Theophr. de Sensu, 61; D.A. 135.

[3] Arist. l.c. $\tau\rho o\pi\hat{\eta}$ $\gamma\grave{a}\rho$ $\chi\rho\omega\mu a\tau\acute{\iota}\zeta\epsilon\sigma\theta a\iota$. This is of course based on Leucippus' account of the three 'differences' of the atoms. Aet. i. 15. 8 introduces here all the three 'differences' of order, shape, and position ($\delta\iota a\tau a\gamma\acute{\eta}$, $\dot{\rho}\nu\theta\mu\acute{o}s$, $\tau\rho o\pi\acute{\eta}$), but he is speaking rather of qualities in general, and we may accept Aristotle's statement that difference of colour was specially produced by difference in position.

upside-down or through a right angle would, that is, produce a different effect of colour on the eye of the percipient.
This general idea Democritus worked out at great length in
a detailed analysis of the various colours and the atomic
conformations which caused them. Theophrastus' account [1]
is again open to suspicion because it attributes difference of
colour to difference of shape in the atoms rather than to
difference of position, but it gives the general notion, and we
may well suppose that Democritus admitted the influence
of shape as well as that of position. There were, he held,
four primary colours, white, black, red, and green.[2] The
sensation of white was caused by smooth atoms, but it
varied in brightness and dullness according to their arrangement (e.g. 'crumbling and friable white objects are made of
atoms round indeed, but slanting in their position to one
another', which brings out the idea of position very clearly),
black is produced by 'rough, angular, and unlike' atoms;
red by 'the same atoms as heat (*sc.* spherical), but larger', and
green by a different arrangement of atoms and void. From
these primary colours by combination Democritus deduced
a detailed scheme of secondary colours: it is not easy to
follow out, largely because of our ignorance of the exact
shades of colour denoted by the Greek words, but it seems
clear that it is not based on any practical consideration of the
mixing of paints, but merely on the aesthetic sensations of
the percipient in looking at natural objects.[3] In all this we
have a further example of Democritus' diligence in the
working out of minutiae, but we are unfortunately left without any indication as to the relation of this theory of colour
to the general theory of vision. We do not know how the
arrangements and positions of the atoms in the objects were

[1] *de Sensu*, 73–8; D.A. 135.

[2] χλωρόν, the light-green of young plants. Modern critics have accepted
Diels' substitution of χλωρόν for ὠχρόν throughout the passage in Theophrastus on the ground that it works out more satisfactorily and that ὠχρόν was
due to confusion with the colour-theory of Empedocles: see Dyroff., op. cit.,
p. 179, n. 1.

[3] So Dyroff, op. cit., p. 179, in a most interesting appendix on Democritus'
colour-system, pp. 176–84.

conveyed by the 'idols' or the 'impressions', and Theophrastus raises a pertinent difficulty when he asks [1] if colour is due, as in the case of green, to the arrangement of atoms and void, how can this be conveyed to the eye; 'for there cannot be an effluence from void'? It must probably be admitted that Democritus had not thought this problem out, but we are left with a sense that the whole theory of vision was very elaborate and complicated and even less calculated than the theory of taste to support Leucippus' naïve trust in the truth of sensation.

The sense of hearing Democritus would appear to have treated in something of the same way. There is unfortunately no specific information surviving of Leucippus' view, but it may be safely assumed that he held the idea attributed to the atomic school [2] in general that 'sound is a body', in other words, that when we utter a sound we eject from our mouth a certain number of atoms combined in a particular formation. This 'body' then travelling through the air and entering the ear of the hearer sets in motion the soul-atoms there, with the result that we hear. But it appears that this simple explanation did not satisfy Democritus, probably, as we may conjecture, because it would not account for the hearing of the same sound at once by many persons, and he introduced a notion parallel to that which he had employed to explain sight. Theophrastus [3] after his elaborate explanation of the theory of vision states that Democritus explained hearing 'in the same way', and a later authority [4] sets this out in detail in curious language which must in part be Democritus' own: 'the air', he says, 'is broken up ($\theta\rho\dot{\upsilon}\pi\tau\epsilon\sigma\theta\alpha\iota$) into bodies of like shape ($\dot{o}\mu o\iota o\sigma\chi\dot{\eta}\mu o\nu a$) and is rolled along together with ($\sigma\upsilon\gamma\kappa\alpha\lambda\iota\nu\delta\epsilon\hat{\iota}\sigma\theta\alpha\iota$) the fragments of voice'. He lays great stress on the likeness of these particles of air and compares the way in which on a beach pebbles of the same size get grouped together or, when a sieve containing cereals is

---

[1] de Sensu, 80; D.A. 135.
[2] σῶμά φασι τὴν φωνήν, Schol. Dionys. Thrac. p. 482; D.A. 127.
[3] de Sensu, 55; D.A. 135.　　　　[4] Aet. iv. 19. 13; D.A. 128.

shaken, the beans and the peas and so on will collect apart. All this is undoubtedly Democritean in argument,[1] and the idea seems to be that the sound particles like the effluence from the objects of vision, or their 'idols', make 'air-impressions'. These disperse and travel in all directions, and then, to continue the account from another source,[2] 'the air enters into the empty space and causes a movement; it enters equally all over the body,[3] but chiefly and above all through the ears, because there it traverses most void and lingers (διαμίμνει) least. For this reason we do not perceive sound in the rest of our body, but only in the ears. And when it is once inside, it is quickly dispersed (equably through the body and does not fall outside it[4])'. The theory thus enunciated seems to give a very close parallel to the account of vision, and the parallel is strengthened by the working out which follows of the most favourable conditions for hearing:[5] 'we hear most acutely, if the outer coat (χιτών) is dense, and the veins empty and as free as possible from moisture and porous (εὔτρητα) throughout all the body, and specially the head and the ears, . . . for thus the sound would come in all together (ἀθρόον) as though entering through much void which is porous and free from moisture'. Again the account is not without ambiguity and confusion, but it shows Democritus' love of the working out of detail. A commentator[6] asks contemptuously how 'a few fragments of breath could fill a theatre which seats 10,000', but his comment seems inappreciative, and Democritus' account, despite its elaboration, goes nearer to solve the problem than the traditional atomic view. At the same time we must again notice that the introduction of a medium in the 'air-

[1] Cf. the similar fragment of Democritus in Sext. *adv. Math.* vii. 116; D.B. 164.

[2] Theophr. *de Sensu,* 55; D.A. 135.

[3] This suggests the answer to Aristotle's difficulty (p. 166) about the theory of vision: Democritus would have said that the εἴδωλα do in fact strike all parts of the body, but only in the eyes meet matter of the right texture to perceive them.

[4] These words are added from a little farther on in Theophrastus' account.

[5] Theophr. l.c. 56.   [6] Aet. iv. 19. 13; D.A. 128.

impression' increases in the sense of hearing too the liability to error.

With regard to the sense of smell our information as to Democritus' view is even more scanty than in the case of the other senses. Lucretius[1] gives the natural atomic view that it was a direct effluence from things, which he curiously regards as proceeding from deep down inside the object as opposed to colour which comes from the surface. Whether Democritus again modified the notion, whether he regarded smell as an 'experience of the sense' like colour and taste or as an effluence like sound is uncertain. Theophrastus[2] complains that he said little in detail about smell except the somewhat mysterious remark that it was caused by 'the thin effluence coming from the heavy things',[3] which without a context is certainly not very easy to interpret. We may perhaps conclude that Democritus was less interested in smell than in the other senses.

Though the five senses have now been dealt with and it has been seen how Democritus, faithful to his first principle, reduces them all to touch, the account of his view of sensation is not yet complete. For to him thought ($\phi\rho\acute{o}\nu\eta\sigma\iota\varsigma$)[4] is sensation, 'and that is change ($\mathrm{\mathring{a}}\lambda\lambda o\acute{\iota}\omega\sigma\iota\varsigma$)', or as it is put more explicitly elsewhere,[5] 'sensations and thoughts ($\nu o\acute{\eta}\sigma\epsilon\iota\varsigma$) are alterations ($\mathring{\epsilon}\tau\epsilon\rho o\iota\acute{\omega}\sigma\epsilon\iota\varsigma$) of the body'. To this we may add the information that 'sensation and thought occur when "idols" ($\epsilon\mathring{\iota}\delta\omega\lambda a$) approach from without'.[6] This is not very explicit, but by the help of the account of the mind already noticed and of later atomic expositions[7] of the idea we can reconstruct his notion with certainty. The mind[8] is exactly like the soul in composition—they are 'the same'—and only

[1] iv. 673 ff.   [2] de Sensu, 82; D.A. 135.
[3] τὸ λεπτὸν ἀπορρέον ἀπὸ τῶν βαρέων: in view of Lucretius' view that smell comes from deep down in things it is tempting to conjecture βαθέων for βαρέων.   [4] Arist. Metaphys. Γ. 5. 1009 b; D.A. 112.
[5] Aet. iv. 8. 5; D. (Leucippus) 30.
[6] Aet. iv. 8. 10; D. (Leucippus) A. 30.
[7] e.g. Lucr. iv. 722 ff.   [8] See p. 160.

differs in that it is a close congregation of the soul-atoms in one part of the body, probably in Democritus' idea in the breast. Certain 'idols' then which are too fine to stir the more distributed soul-atoms on the surface of the body and in the organs of sense and so to produce sensation, pass on within the body until they reach the mind. There, as the soul-atoms are so closely packed, the 'idols' cannot pass by without moving them and the result of this motion is the peculiar kind of sensation which we call thought: it is in its nature exactly parallel to the movements which produce sight or hearing. To this general idea little can be added except an interesting statement in Theophrastus [1] that thought 'takes place when the soul'—note that here the general word 'soul' ($\psi v \chi \acute{\eta}$) is used for the mind—'is equable in its temperature: but if it is too hot or too cold, it changes things ($\mu \epsilon \tau a \lambda \lambda \acute{a} \tau \tau \epsilon \iota v$)'. This curious idea, which again shows Democritus' physiological interests, seems to explain his famous praise [2] of Homer's diction, when he says that 'Hector lay there out of his mind ($\dot{a} \lambda \lambda o \phi \rho o \nu \acute{\epsilon} \omega v$)', a word which Demo-critus thought an exact expression of the effect of anger, which makes the soul too hot and so incapable of true thought. The whole idea is very parallel to what he said of the best conditions for sight and hearing.

It does not seem that Democritus carried his notion of the identity of thought and sensation farther than this. There are of course many difficulties in the conception, one of the most obvious being that which aroused the attention of Lucretius,[3] that thought is not always the result of an external stimulus, but the mind can turn itself spontaneously to one object or another. To meet this and other difficulties Epicurus had greatly to elaborate his psychology, but he retained the root-ideas that mind and soul are the same in their atomic composition and that the processes of sensation and thought are analogous. From Democritus' own point

[1] *de Sensu*, 58; D.A. 135 γίνεται (*sc.* τὸ φρονεῖν) συμμέτρως ἐχούσης τῆς ψυχῆς κατὰ τὴν κρῆσιν.

[2] Arist. *de Anima*, A. 2. 404 a 27; D.A. 101.

[3] iv. 777 ff.

of view we may notice the ingenious economy of his conception: soul and mind are the same; their objects are communicated to them in the same way; thought, like sensation, can be reduced to a purely material contact. The idea is a cardinal one in his system and becomes of great importance in his metaphysics.

The ancient commentators were apt to make fun of Democritus' theory of sensation, and Theophrastus [1] in particular, to whom we owe most of our detailed information, is never weary of asking pertinent and awkward questions: 'if sight is due to an impression on the air, which then comes to us backwards, as it were, why do we not see things the wrong way round (i.e. with the right hand as the left)?' 'when we see several things in the same place, how can their impressions coexist in the same piece of air?' 'why can't you see yourself?' In a similar spirit it would be easy to point to the clumsiness of the theory in detail and the extreme improbability of effluence, 'idols', and air-impressions: or on broader grounds to argue that the purely material theory of Democritus does not really touch the problem which he sets out to solve: it establishes a connexion between object and percipient, but it does not really tell us what thought and sensation, as we know them, are.

But it is more profitable to look at the theory as it stands and inquire into its efficiency from its own point of view. Though gaps and weaknesses have been pointed out (some of which might perhaps be explained if we had fuller knowledge), it is impossible not to admire the consistency of the whole and the economy with which all the different experiences of sensation are reduced to the one central notion of touch. There is thus laid a foundation for belief in the main in the evidence of the senses. On the other hand, in the extremely indirect methods by which in some instances contact is secured and the possibilities of error which they introduce, the way is opened for doubt and scepticism. Theophrastus [2] put his finger on the real weakness of the

[1] *de Sensu*, 52, 53; D.A. 135.   [2] *de Sensu*, 69; D.A. 135.

theory when he complained with regard to Democritus' view of sense-impressions (τὰ αἰσθητά): 'he at once makes them experiences of sensation and assigns them to differences of shape'. He saw, that is, that both object and percipient must contribute something to the act of perception, but he did not satisfactorily distinguish their parts. There was room then for a more carefully thought-out system to be devised by his successors, but in many ways Democritus' rather fanciful notions were a nearer approach to scientific accuracy then the cruder consistency of Epicurus.

§ 7. *The Gods*

The references to Democritus' beliefs as to the gods and religion are scanty and difficult to piece together, but as there are indications of a view which may have led the way for Epicurus, but differed in certain important respects from his theory, it is well to refer to it briefly. That Democritus did not hold the orthodox theory of prayer to the gods, as beings dwelling in the sky who would assist their suppliants, is clear from a fragment [1] in which he says with an obvious note of contempt, 'Some few among educated (λογίων) men lift up their hands to the region where we Greeks now speak of air and say: "Zeus ponders on all things, he knows all and gives and takes away and he is king over all." ' We do not know on what grounds he based this criticism, but if, which will be seen to be doubtful, he believed in the existence of gods, we may safely assume that, like Epicurus, he held that they took no part in the affairs of the world. At the same time Democritus was confronted by the universal belief in the gods and there is evidence to show that he explained this on the lines that might be expected. In the first place he pointed to what he believed to be a false inference from the phenomena of the sky: 'men in old days seeing the occurrences (παθήματα) [2] in the sky, such as thunder and lightning and thunderbolts and the conjunctions of heavenly bodies and the eclipses of sun and moon, dreaded the gods,

---

[1] Clem. *Protr.* 68; D.B. 30.   [2] Sext. ix. 24; D.A. 75.

believing that they were the cause of these things'. This argument becomes prominent in Epicurus. But it does not go far enough, for it is necessary to show how the idea of gods arise in the minds of men at all. This, as we learn from a fragment quoted by Sextus,[1] he accounted for by the entry into men's minds of 'idols': 'certain "idols" draw near men, and of these some are beneficial,[2] others harmful, hence he prays to meet with fortunate (εὐλόγχων) "idols". These are great, of exceeding size, and not easily destroyed,[3] though not indestructible, and they foretell the future to men, being seen and uttering sounds. And the ancients receiving the ιmpression of them imagined that there was a god, though besides these images there was no other god with an indestructible nature'. Here may certainly be recognized the same general idea of the visitation of 'idols' which we know in Epicurean writers,[4] but there appear to be important points of difference. In the first place the mention of harmful images as well as beneficial looks as if Democritus' 'theology' included not only gods in the usual sense, but evil spirits as well: as if in fact it were a 'daemonology' rather than a 'theology'. This has no counterpart in Epicurus. Secondly, Epicurus had no doubt of the existence of gods and believed that the images which visited men came from the persons of divine beings, but the last sentence in the Democritus fragment looks as though he were sceptical of the existence of his 'daemons' apart from the images. Nor do references elsewhere satisfactorily clear up Democritus' position. The statement that he called the gods (or 'daemons') 'idols'[5] and said that the air was full of them, seems to show that he did not believe in any reality beyond the 'idols', but in another passage,[6] in which he is represented as saying that the 'idols' visited animals as well as men, they are

[1] ix. 19; D.B. 166.
[2] Plin. *N. H.* ii. 14; D.A. 76, by personifying this notion produces the ridiculous parody that Democritus said that 'there were only two gods, Punishment and Reward'.
[3] Sext. *adv. Math.* ix. 19 δύσφθαρτα μὲν, οὐκ ἄφθαρτα δέ.
[4] e.g. Lucr. v. 1169 ff.   [5] Anonymi, *Hermippus*, 122; D.A. 78.
[6] Clem. *Strom.* v. 88; D.A. 79.

described as coming 'from the divine being' (ἀπὸ. τῆς θείας οὐσίας)—an expression more in accord with the Epicurean view. Cicero [1] too in a passage of ironical criticism charges him with gross inconsistency in his ideas on the whole question: 'at one time he holds that images endowed with a divine nature exist in the universe, at another he says that the gods are elements of mind (*principia mentis*) which exist in the same universe, at another living images, which are in the habit of helping or harming us, at another certain immense images, so great that they embrace the whole universe on the outside (*extrinsecus*)'. The notion here that the gods are 'elements of mind' should probably be taken in conjunction with an equally mysterious statement [2] that 'mind is god in spherical-shaped fire': the meaning seems to be that the same spherical-shaped particles, which make both fire and soul, and, as has been seen,[3] are breathed in in respiration, form the images of the gods.

On the whole, we must be content to say that we do not know enough of Democritus' theory to explain or criticize it; it is clear however that he held the theory of 'idols' which Epicurus took as the basis of his theology, but he probably differed from Epicurus in thinking that these 'idols' were themselves 'divine' and that there were no 'divine beings' from which they came.

§ 8. *Theory of knowledge*

There is no portion of Democritus' system which has been so much discussed and which still remains so obscure as his conception of the basis on which our knowledge rests. In antiquity it was fully discussed by Aristotle [4] in relation to the theories of the Eleatics, and among later writers it was dealt with by Theophrastus [5] and by Sextus,[6] who has preserved some valuable fragments of Democritus' own writings. Aristotle tends to lay stress on Democritus' belief that truth lay in phenomena and Sextus on his scepticism, while

---

[1] *de Nat. Deor.* i. 43. 120; D.A. 74. [2] Aet. i. 7. 16; D.A. 74.
[3] pp. 156, 158. [4] *de Gen. et corr.* A. 8, 325 b.
[5] *de Sensu*, 49 ff.; D.A. 135. [6] *adv. Math.* vii.

Theophrastus, as has been seen, is mainly concerned with his theories as to the individual senses, which he treats in a very critical spirit. Modern writers are equally at variance. Some are inclined to follow Aristotle in claiming Democritus as a 'phenominalist', others[1] maintain that his foundation is 'rational', while others again have proclaimed him a sceptic.[2] All that can be done here is to make a brief review of the evidence which antiquity has left us and attempt some conclusion from it.

If we turn first to the extant fragments of Democritus, the impression which they leave is that he was a confirmed sceptic. Many of them suggest this in a general form: 'a man must learn on this principle that he is far removed from the truth',[3] 'we know nothing truly about anything, but for each of us his opinion is an influx'[4] (i.e. is conveyed to him by the influx of 'idols' from without), 'to learn truly what each thing is, is a matter of uncertainty',[5] 'in truth we know nothing unerringly, but only as it changes according to the disposition of our body and of the things that enter into it and impinge upon it'[6] (a remark which connects closely with the general theory of sensation), 'we know nothing truly, for the truth lies hidden in the depth'.[7] A more explicit statement of Democritus' line of thought is found in the famous aphorism:[8] 'sweet is by convention and bitter

---

[1] e.g. Natorp, *Forschungen*, 164 ff.

[2] For an interesting reconsideration of the problem see Dyroff, *Demokritstudien*, pp. 80 ff.

[3] γιγνώσκειν χρὴ ἄνθρωπον τῷδε τῷ κανόνι, ὅτι ἐτεῆς ἀπήλλακται, Sext. *adv. Math.* vii. 137; D.B. 6.

[4] ἐτεῇ οὐδὲν ἴσμεν περὶ οὐδενός, ἀλλ' ἐπιρυσμίη ἑκάστοισιν ἡ δόξις, ibid.; D.B. 7.

[5] ἐτεῇ οἷον ἕκαστον γιγνώσκειν ἐν ἀπόρῳ ἐστί, ibid.; D.B. 8.

[6] ἡμεῖς δὲ τῷ μὲν ἐόντι οὐδὲν ἀτρεκὲς συνίεμεν, μεταπῖπτον δὲ κατά τε σώματος διαθήκην καὶ τῶν ἐπεισιόντων καὶ τῶν ἀντιστηριζόντων, ibid. 136; D.B. 9.

[7] ἐτεῇ δὲ οὐδὲν ἴδμεν· ἐν βυθῷ γὰρ ἡ ἀλήθεια, Diog. Laert. ix. 72; D.B. 117.

[8] νόμῳ γλυκὺ καὶ νόμῳ πικρόν, νόμῳ θερμόν, νόμῳ ψυχρόν, νόμῳ χροιή, ἐτεῇ δὲ ἄτομα καὶ κενόν, Sext. *adv. Math.* vii. 135; D.B. 9; quoted also by Diog. Laert. ix. 72; D.B. 117 and Galen, *de Medic. Empir.* 1259. 8. νόμῳ is

by convention, hot by convention, cold by convention, colour by convention; in truth are atoms and void'. Putting these sayings together we seem to have a very strong attack on the validity of the senses and the indications of a fairly thorough-going scepticism, and it is not surprising to be informed by Sextus[1] that Democritus and his followers have 'swept away (ἀνῃρήκασι) phenomena one and all'. And when we compare these sayings with his theory of sensation, their ground becomes clear. The qualities of things which we experience in sensation, hot cold, sweet bitter, red green, are not in Democritus' view actually qualities in things, still less in the atoms that compose them; they are merely 'experiences of our sensation', caused no doubt by differences of shape and position and arrangement in the atoms, but corresponding to no reality and liable to be distorted by the atomic conformation of the sense-organs of the percipient. By means of such sensations we can gain no real knowledge of the nature of things, still less of the ultimate substratum which lies behind them. From a consideration of most of the surviving fragments alone the conclusion that Democritus was a sceptic as to the evidence of the senses would be almost inevitable. And there is one more aphorism which seems to push the position still farther:[2] the senses are represented as addressing the mind and saying 'wretched mind, from us you received your beliefs, yet would you overthrow us? your victory is your own fall'. The mind, that is, receives from the senses the information on which it builds, and if it then denies the validity of the senses, it is annihilating its own validity too. The condemnation appears to be extended to the mind and the processes of thought, and scepticism to be complete: the one solid foundation left is the true existence of the atoms and the void, though of them we can never have direct cognition.

here opposed as so often in Greek thought to φύσει and is almost equivalent in sense to 'in appearance'. Sextus paraphrases νομίζεται . . . εἶναι καὶ δοξάζεται τὰ αἰσθητά.   [1] vii. 369; D.A. 110.

[2] τάλαινα φρήν, παρ' ἡμέων λαβοῦσα τὰς πίστεις ἡμέας καταβάλλεις; πτῶμά τοι τὸ κατάβλημα, Galen, l.c.; D.B. 125.

But there is another side to the picture. In a very interesting reference to Democritus' work 'the Canons' (*sc.* Principles of Investigation) Sextus[1] tells us that he said that there were two kinds of knowledge, that through the senses and that through the mind: the latter 'he calls "legitimate" (γνησίη) and assigns credence to it for the judgement of truth, but that by the senses he calls "bastard" (σκοτίη) and denies its certainty for the determination of truth'. He then proceeds to quote Democritus' own words: 'there are two kinds of knowledge,[2] one legitimate, one bastard: to the bastard belong all these, sight, hearing, smell, taste, touch. But the legitimate is separated from this'. Then, adds Sextus, in preferring the legitimate to the bastard he gives his reason in the words: 'when the bastard can no longer see things smaller and smaller, nor hear nor smell, nor taste, nor perceive by touch, but [it is necessary to investigate] still more subtly, [then the legitimate knowledge comes to the rescue with an instrument of investigation more subtle]'.[3] It is clear that this aphorism must be taken in connexion with the assertion of the true existence of the atoms and the void. They are known not by the senses, but by the mind. The way of the senses is liable to err for it deals with the shifting and changing material which produces our sensations, but the way of the mind, which deals with the ultimate realities is 'legitimate'. Moreover when in the investigation of nature the senses fail and cannot probe into things beyond their ken, then the way of the mind comes in with its 'subtler instrument' and leads to truth. Here seems to be an emphatic reinstatement of the truth of thought as against the evidence of the senses. It is borne out by an interesting

[1] vii. 138. 9; D.B. 11.

[2] γνώμης δὲ δύο εἰσὶν ἰδέαι, ἡ μὲν γνησίη, ἡ δὲ σκοτίη· καὶ σκοτίης μὲν τάδε σύμπαντα, ὄψις, ἀκοή, ὀδμή, γεῦσις, ψαῦσις. ἡ δὲ γνησίη, ἀποκεκριμένη δὲ ταύτης.

[3] ὅταν ἡ σκοτίη μηκέτι δύνηται μήτε ὁρῆν ἐπ᾽ ἔλαττον μήτε ἀκούειν μήτε ὀδμᾶσθαι μήτε γεύεσθαι μήτε ἐν τῇ ψαύσει αἰσθάνεσθαι, ἀλλ᾽ ἐπὶ λεπτότερον ⟨δέῃ ζητεῖν, τότε ἐπιγίνεται ἡ γνησίη ἅτε ὄργανον ἔχουσα τοῦ νῶσαι λεπτότερον⟩. I quote the restoration at the end as given by Diels.

passage of Sextus[1] in which he compares and contrasts Democritus and Plato as both believers, though in different ways, in the reality of the objects of thought ($\tau\grave{\alpha}$ $\nu o\eta\tau\acute{\alpha}$): 'the followers of Plato and Democritus both thought that the only realities were the objects of thought, but Democritus reached this conclusion because there was no physical sub-stratum perceptible to the senses, since the atoms which formed all things by their combinations had a nature devoid of all perceptible qualities, while Plato saw that perceptible things were always coming into being, yet never existed, &c.' The comparison of Democritus and Plato is rather fantastic, seeing the immense difference of their views, but it is significant that a later commentator should have been able to group them together in this way. It seems then that a solid basis for Democritus' view is reached in the truth of thought as to the ultimate realities, the atoms and the void, and this is the ground of Natorp's view that the basis of atomism is rational.

At this point we are met with the statement[2] of Demo-critus that 'the mind and the soul are the same'. It has been seen that the primary reference in this is to their atomic structure, but the analysis of Democritus' psychology has shown further that it conveys with it the conception that their processes of operation are the same: the mind is roused by the influx of 'idols' and its movement results in thought, just as the movement of the soul-atoms similarly produced in the sense-organs results in perception. What is the effect of this belief on the other side of the equation? if the 'objects of thought' are 'true', what of the objects of sensation? Aristotle twice repeats a kind of compressed syllogism of Democritus': 'soul and mind are the same;[3] for the truth is the phenomenon', or in a rather more extended form, 'sensation is thinking, and that is change, therefore the

---

[1] viii. 6; D.A. 59. $\nu o\eta\tau\acute{\alpha}$ is clearly used in different senses of Plato's 'ideas' and Democritus' ultimate realities, the atoms and the void.

[2] See p. 160.

[3] de Anima, A. 2. 404 a 27; D.A. 101. $\tau\alpha\grave{\upsilon}\tau\grave{o}\nu$ $\psi\upsilon\chi\grave{\eta}\nu$ $\kappa\alpha\grave{\iota}$ $\nu o\hat{\upsilon}\nu\cdot$ $\tau\grave{o}$ $\gamma\grave{\alpha}\rho$ $\dot{\alpha}\lambda\eta\theta\grave{e}s$ $e\hat{\iota}\nu\alpha\iota$ $\tau\grave{o}$ $\phi\alpha\iota\nu\acute{o}\mu\epsilon\nu o\nu$.

phenomenon in sensation is necessarily true'.[1] Here seems
at first sight to be something like a reinstatement of sensation, and if so a position would be reached diametrically
opposed to the scepticism which finds expression in Democritus' own sayings as preserved by Sextus.

What then is to be said about this divergence? Critics
have been inclined either to neglect the evidence on the one
side or the other, or to impugn its authenticity, and to proclaim Democritus sceptic, phenomenalist, or rationalist according to preconceived notions; and not a little misunderstanding has arisen from the assumption that he must have
been the precursor of Epicurus in his affirmation of the truth
of sensation. It is clear that his theory was widely different
from that of Epicurus and considerably more subtle, and
it seems possible to put it together even from the scanty and
contradictory evidence which we possess. In the first place
it must be noticed that Democritus nowhere says that
'sensation' is true or that 'thought' is true: the statements
are that 'the objects of thought are true', and that 'the
phenomenon is true'. This gives a clue and a reminder that
in any material system, if we wish to understand it, we must
work from the external to the internal. In Democritus'
atomic materialism the real ultimate existences are the atoms
and the void: the only real knowledge then must be the
knowledge of these, of their character and their behaviour.
Now such knowledge can never be obtained by the senses,
for they are both imperceptible to the senses. They can
only be known to the mind by thought; the process of the
mind inquiring into the nature of the atoms and the void
is 'legitimate', and the objects of its thought here are 'true'.
But how does the mind obtain this knowledge of the atoms
and the void? It has been suggested[2] that Democritus
thought that the mind had direct cognizance of the atoms:

---

[1] *Metaphys. Γ*. 5. 1009 b; D.A. 112. διὰ τὸ ὑπολαμβάνειν φρόνησιν μὲν
τὴν αἴσθησιν, ταύτην δ᾽ εἶναι ἀλλοίωσιν, τὸ φαινόμενον κατὰ τὴν αἴσθησιν
ἐξ ἀνάγκης ἀληθὲς εἶναί φασιν. Cf. also Philopon. in Arist. *de Anima*,
A. 2. 404 a; D.A. 113.

[2] By Brandis: see Mabilleau, op. cit., p. 226.

far too minute to stir the senses, yet individual atoms might stir the subtle combination of pure soul-atoms and so be known, as the objects of sense are by the senses. But for such an idea there is no particle of evidence, and even if the atoms could thus be known directly, certainly the void could not, for it cannot 'move' anything. The knowledge of the ultimate realities by the mind must be based on the knowledge of 'things' by the senses and is in fact an inference from them. 'Diotimus', says Sextus [1] in an important passage, 'said that according to Democritus the "criterion" for the apprehension of things unseen is phenomena'. This is expressed in language more suitable to Epicurus, but its meaning is clear: Democritus held, like Epicurus after him, that the data on which the mind bases its knowledge of the atoms and the void are given by phenomena to the senses. It is no doubt in this sense that Aristotle [2] says with a slight variation of the usual phrase that the Atomists thought 'that the truth was in appearance' ($\tau\hat{\omega}$ $\phi\alpha\acute{\iota}\nu\epsilon\sigma\theta\alpha\iota$): the appearances, that is, presented to the senses in their cognition of phenomena contain the data for the true knowledge of the realities. It is significant too that in introducing one of the most sceptical of Democritus' aphorisms, Sextus [3] points out, by way of showing Democritus' inconsistency, that in the Cratynteria,[4] whence the quotation is taken, he 'undertook to assign to the senses the mastery over belief'. It seems only a small step now to the statement 'the phenomenon is true', and that step is made easier by Democritus' insistence that the soul and the mind are the same, an insistence not due so much to his physical materialism as to the importance for his psychology: the cognition of phenomena by the senses is identical in process with the cognition of the realities by the mind.

But it is still necessary to ask in what sense is the pheno-

---

[1] vii. 140; D.A. 111.   [2] de Gen. et Corr. A. 315 b 9.

[3] vii. 136 ἐν ... τοῖς Κρατυντηρίοις ... ὑπεσχημένος ταῖς αἰσθήσεσι τὸ κράτος τῆς πίστεως ἀναθεῖναι D.B. 9.

[4] Natorp, Forschungen, p. 179, n. 2, points out that the title of the work κρατυντήρια points in the same direction.

menon 'true' and how can this idea be reconciled with the many indications of scepticism in the extant fragments? Perhaps it is possible to get nearest to the answer, if we take the instance of one of the senses, 'sight'. Sight gives us the sensation of an object with size, shape, and colour. Now colour is not, in Democritus' view, a quality of the object, it is 'an experience of our sense': it has no objective reality and exists only 'by convention'; to build on such a sensation can lead only to 'bastard' thinking. But shape and size are real properties of the object as a compound of atoms and the void; they are moreover the properties of the atoms themselves which compose it. In so far then as we attend to the information about these properties and these only, our perception is not misleading, and the 'phenomenon', which is a unity of these properties and weight (also a property of the atoms acquired in the 'whirl') and no others, is 'true'. And here we have the secret of the importance which Democritus attaches to the sense of touch: it alone can give us information as to shape and size without any of the super-added sensations (except those of hot and cold) which are subjective and confuse our cognition of the object. The phenomenon is true then in a double sense: for, if we can put away all these subjective sensations, it gives us the information of what it really is, a compound of void and atoms of a certain size, shape, and weight, and secondly, so regarded, it enables us by inference to have knowledge of the ultimate realities. But the moment these subjective experiences are taken to be a report of an objective reality in the object, the 'bastard path' is entered on and we are led astray in an unreal world. It must be noticed now that it is in close connexion[1] with the aphorism that colour, sweet, bitter, &c., are 'by convention' that we find that most sceptical of all the utterances in which the senses turn upon the mind. The mind is in error and has no foundation when it builds upon the 'experiences of the senses', but when it confines itself to the true 'objects of thought', the atoms and the void, and bases its conclusions upon sensation which

[1] Galen, *de Medic. Empir.* 1259. 8; D.B. 125.

tells of the real properties of things, it is on the 'legitimate path'.

It seems then, if this analysis is correct—and it is only too clear how scanty are the materials for a conclusion—that Democritus was neither a sceptic nor a rationalist, nor a phenomenalist, he does not fit into any of the modern categories; he neither denied nor affirmed the truth of *all* sensation nor of *all* thought; but built up for himself a 'theory of knowledge', subtle and almost paradoxical, but based directly on his atomic conception of the world. The final realities of the universe, the atoms and the void, are real and are capable of being known by the mind. Phenomena are built up of the final realities and retain the primary properties of size and shape: as such they are real and can be known by the senses. The mind may safely make its deduction from phenomena, both because the phenomenon as a unity of these primary properties is real and because sensation—the mere perception of the real phenomenon—is the same as thought. But once go beyond these primary properties, beyond the reality of the phenomenon, and you are attributing to the object what is really the subjective experience of your senses, and thought based on those ' conventions' will lead you nowhere.

This tentative reconstruction of Democritus' ideas is no doubt cruder and more naïve than that put forward by most of his modern critics, but they seem to me to have been led astray by the more abstract thinking of Aristotle and the later Greek philosophers and not to have sufficiently attempted to work out the problem on Democritus' own material lines. Yet, if this account is near the truth, it will be seen that the position of Democritus was difficult and subtle and might well prove an insecure basis for a world-system. This Epicurus seems to have felt and swept it all away in a whole-hearted return to complete trust in sensation.

§ 9. *Ethics*

So far the account of Democritus' theories has been based mainly on descriptions and references in ancient authors with the help of an occasional quotation of Democritus' own words. When we pass to consider his moral theory there is an unexpected change. Very little is told us by the authorities either by way of explanation or criticism, but on the other hand there is a considerable body of sayings [1] attributed to Democritus, contained in an anthology of 'Maxims' (γνῶμαι) and in a collection made by Stobaeus. Of these sayings some deal with fundamental ideas, most range in a discursive spirit over the field of human life, containing criticisms and precepts which might be almost equally applicable, whether he had a base theory or not. The question naturally arises whether he is to be considered as a consistent thinker with a moral system—and if so, how far he suggested lines of thought for Epicurus—or is rather to be regarded as a moralist of the type of Hesiod or Theognis, laying down sporadic precepts for guidance in life. One of his modern critics [2] holds that he had a central system which was in close connexion with his physical theories, and round this built a practical morality, another [3] is inclined to deny him any system at all.

Before, however, any inquiry can be made into Democritus' moral ideas, there is one obvious problem that must be raised. In the physical world, as has been seen,[4] he had emphatically asserted the supremacy of 'necessity' (ἀνάγκη) as the controlling force: 'by necessity are foreordained all things that were and are and are to come'. He intended by this assertion to establish the idea of natural law and to eliminate both the theological conception of the world and the idea of chance. If this notion were to be extended—as

---

[1] It has seemed good in this chapter to quote most of the maxims in full, as they are perhaps less accessible than the more connected writings of Epicurus.

[2] Natorp, *Ethika des Demokritos.*

[3] Dyroff, *Demokritstudien,* pp. 127 ff.   [4] § 2, p. 120.

in strictness it should—to the field of human action, it should result in a pure determinism; and if man's actions are determined, if everything he does is the inevitable outcome of the past, and what he is to do in the future is foreordained, what is the value of a moral theory or indeed even of moral precepts? Strangely enough, this question seems never to have occurred to Democritus' mind. There is no trace of it in any extant fragment or in the authorities, and the precepts are given as though man were perfectly free to obey or disobey them. Still more oddly the figure of 'chance' (τύχη) raises its head again on the moral side, and there are several passages in which it seems to be set in opposition to man's will and foresight: 'men have fashioned an image of chance as a cloak for their own ill-council. For chance rarely fights against prudence, and most things in life keen sight with understanding guides aright';[1] 'the foolish are guided by the gains of chance, but those who have knowledge of such things by those of wisdom';[2] 'chance is a giver of great gifts, but unstable; nature is self-reliant. Therefore by the lesser and certain means it overcomes the greater gift of hope';[3] 'chance spreads before us a banquet of riches, but self-control a banquet of self-sufficiency'.[4] In all these quotations chance is represented as ultimately less efficient than man's effort, but in another passage it is accorded a more important position: 'Courage is the beginning of action, but chance is master of the end.'[5] In each of these passages 'chance' is no doubt used in a loose and popular sense of the unpredictable issue of events, and is not necessarily in contradiction with a fundamental belief in necessity: results are determined by

---

[1] Stob. ii. 8. 16; D.B. 119; N. 29, 30: see pp. 197, 200.
[2] Stob. iii. 4. 71; D.B. 197; N. 33. ἀνοήμονες ῥυσμοῦνται τοῖς τῆς τύχης κέρδεσιν, οἱ δὲ τῶν τοιῶνδε δαήμονες τοῖς τῆς σοφίης.
[3] Stob. ii. 9. 5; D.B. 176; N. 64. τύχη μεγαλόδωρος, ἀλλ' ἀβέβαιος, φύσις δὲ αὐτάρκης· διόπερ νικᾷ τῷ ἥσσονι καὶ βεβαίῳ τὸ μεῖζον τῆς ἐλπίδος.
[4] Stob. iii. 5. 26; D.B. 210; N. 65. τράπεζαν πολυτελέα μὲν τύχη παρατίθησιν, αὐταρκέα δὲ σωφροσύνη.
[5] Stob. iv. 51. 16; D.B. 269; N. 126. τόλμα πρήξιος ἀρχή, τύχη δὲ τέλεος κυρίη.

natural law working itself out, but to man, who cannot fathom all the workings of law, they take the appearance of chance. Nevertheless there is here a striking contrast to the suppression of the idea of chance in the physical theory and it seems to show that Democritus' ethics are largely independent of his physics. The same independence must be assumed in regard to his silence on the fundamental question of determinism. To Epicurus the problem presented itself acutely, and he fights[1] as violently against the 'destiny of the physicists' as he does against the 'myth of the gods': but by the time of Democritus this great question was apparently not even simmering and he proceeds to lay down his directions for the moral life with a simple *naïveté*, unconscious of the problem which he himself had raised by his insistence on the supremacy of 'necessity' in the physical world. His moral precepts are given on the assumption that man is free to act as he will.

It is generally agreed that the key-word to Democritus' moral ideas is 'cheerfulness'[2] ($\epsilon \dot{v} \theta v \mu \acute{\iota} \eta$); it is quoted by the authorities as his conception of the 'end' and occurs in several of the extant fragments. Two fundamental questions arise at once: is 'cheerfulness' to be regarded as the base of Democritus' ethical principles, or is it itself derivative from a wider pleasure-theory, standing to it in the same relation as Epicurus'[3] 'imperturbability' ($\dot{a} \tau a \rho a \xi \acute{\iota} a$) does to his ultimate basis of 'pleasure' ($\dot{\eta} \delta o v \acute{\eta}$)? And if so, is there any link in a general theory of sensationalism between this conception in the moral field and the metaphysic of Democritus' atomism? It is obvious that these questions are of great importance, for if they were both to be answered in the affirmative, Democritus would in ethics as well as in physics be the precursor of Epicurus and the later philosopher's claim to independence could not be sustained.

There is one statement which has come down to us which implies an affirmative answer to both questions. Sextus[4] in

---

[1] See Part II: Chap. V, p. 318.
[2] See D.L. ix. 45; D.A. 1, and several fragments quoted below on p. 192.
[3] See Part II, Chap. X, p. 499.   [4] vii. 140; D.A. 111.

a passage already referred to[1] quotes Diotimus as authority for the belief that Democritus maintained that there were three 'criteria', and that among them 'the criterion of choice and avoidance is the feelings (πάθη)'. If this statement could be confirmed it would be clear that 'cheerfulness' was in Democritus' view only a special form of 'pleasure', and that he held, as Epicurus did, that in the moral field the immediate feeling of pleasure and pain was the test of good and bad: pleasure must be chosen and pain avoided. His whole system would be linked up on a basis of sensation, and 'cheerfulness' must take its place as a derivative notion. But Sextus' statement can certainly not be accepted without question. In the first place the language is wholly that of a later age: the words used, 'criterion' (κριτήριον), 'choice' (αἵρεσις), 'avoidance' (φυγή), 'feeling' (πάθος), are all Epicurean terms, of which there is no evidence elsewhere in connexion with Democritus: indeed they are ideas which at his time before the invention of the Aristotelian terminology were hardly current. Secondly, there is no trace elsewhere in the fragments or the authorities of any such Epicurean link between the moral and the physical theories, and lastly— and this is surely conclusive—it has been seen that Democritus' position as regards the trustworthiness of sensation was far more sceptical than that of Epicurus: the man who held that 'sweet' and 'bitter' are 'by convention' cannot have joined up his moral theories with his physical system on a basis of sensation. It can hardly be doubted that Sextus was led away by the common tendency to associate Democritus with Epicurus, and that here at least their theories were divergent.

It seems necessary then to answer the second question in the negative, but is it still true that Democritus' moral theory was ultimately based on 'pleasure'? There is a fragment[2] of his twice repeated in somewhat different forms:

---

[1] p. 183.

[2] τέρψις καὶ ἀτερπίη οὖρος, Clem. Strom. ii. 139; D.B. 4; N. 3 ὅρος συμφόρων καὶ ἀσυμφόρων τέρψις καὶ ἀτερψίη, Stob. iii. 1. 46; D.B. 188; N. 2.

'Enjoyment and its absence is the limit of the advantageous and disadvantageous.' This might seem to be a counterpart in Democritean language of Sextus' statement as to the 'criterion' and to bring us back again to an ultimate pleasure-theory. But too much emphasis must not be laid upon it. It is quoted in close connexion with the idea of 'cheerfulness' and may well be no more than a practical maxim for its attainment. Other citations tell in the same direction. Diogenes[1] in his summary of Democritus' views says that 'cheerfulness is not the same as pleasure, as some have mistakenly understood it, but a state in which the soul lives peacefully and tranquilly, never disturbed by fear or superstition or any other feeling'. This looks like the preservation of a genuine tradition and makes a clear distinction between 'cheerfulness' and 'pleasure'. We may quote too a somewhat cryptic saying assigned to Democritus himself,[2] which links up the moral idea much more satisfactorily than Sextus' statement with his actual metaphysical theory: 'for all men the same thing is good and true; but pleasant differs for one and another'. There is, that is to say, in the world of knowledge an ultimate truth ('the atoms and the void') and there is in the moral world an ultimate good (sc. presumably 'cheerfulness'), but in both spheres the 'sweet' or 'pleasant' is conventional and differs from man to man. If then pleasure is in Democritus' view an ever-shifting and changing quantity, it is not likely that it would be taken as the ultimate moral basis: indeed it is here definitely contrasted with the universal 'good'.

It may be assumed then that there was no more fundamental idea behind Democritus' notion of 'cheerfulness'. Nor is it probable that he would have described 'cheerfulness', as Diogenes[3] does in his account of him as 'the end' (τέλος): that again is the conception of a later age and implies

[1] ix. 45; D.A. 1.
[2] Dem. 34; D.B. 69; N. 6 ἀνθρώποις πᾶσι τωὐτὸν ἀγαθὸν καὶ ἀληθές· ἡδὺ δὲ ἄλλῳ ἄλλο. Dyroff (op. cit., p. 131) disputes the genuineness of this fragment, but there seems no sufficient ground for rejecting it.
[3] ix. 45; D.A. 1.

a far more logically worked-out system of ethics than the detached aphorisms which we possess would allow us to attribute to Democritus. Indeed, before Socrates had turned men's minds to a systematic inquiry into the moral life, it is improbable that any thinker propounded what could in any real sense be described as an ethical system. 'Cheerfulness' is put forward by Democritus as the state of mind at which men should aim, in a perfectly simple and naïve spirit. Yet on the other hand it is a mistake to regard his aphorisms as a collection of detached ejaculations: it is perfectly possible to trace in the majority of them a connexion with the root-idea of 'cheerfulness' and by grouping them together to form a picture of the life which Democritus would recommend to his disciples. The effort of reconstruction is worth the trouble, if only because there arise in the course of it many ideas which had a prominent place in the later Greek theories and in particular in the ethics of Epicurus. If Epicurus was not indebted to Democritus for the root-notion of his philosophy of pleasure, many incidental traits of the ideal Epicurean may be recognized in the maxims of his predecessor.

We may try first to get a more definite idea of what is meant by 'cheerfulness': Diogenes[1] describes it as 'a state in which the soul lives peacefully and tranquilly, never disturbed by fear or superstition or any other feeling'. Two important points emerge from this. In the first place it is clear that Democritus is thinking solely of a state of mind: the body, as will be seen later, is definitely ranked below the 'soul' by Democritus, and its pleasures are considered only as they affect the soul. Here we have a contrast with the pleasure-theory of Epicurus, which not only takes account of the body, but makes its pleasures and pains the starting-point. On the other hand when we come to the substantive description we have an equally clear anticipation of Epicurus' notion of 'imperturbability' (ἀταραξία) as the true pleasure of the soul, and the mention of fear and superstition as the causes of disturbance is peculiarly significant. Once again

[1] ix. 45; D.A. 1.

we must beware of the possibility of the attribution of Epicurean views by the doxographers to Democritus, but it is clear that the idea of 'cheerfulness' is one of undisturbed serenity rather than of an active and sensational pleasure: the notion is, we might fairly say, Epicurean rather than Cyrenaic. The general idea suggested by Diogenes is borne out by two of the fragments: 'the cheerful man is always inclined to just and lawful deeds, and sleeping and awake he is happy and strong and free from care';[1] 'it is best for a man to lead his life as cheerful and as little troubled as possible; and this would be so, if he were not to set his pleasures on mortal things'.[2] The picture is of a happy disposition, rejoicing in good things and undisturbed, yet having its basis, as will become clearer, in the things of the soul.

Diogenes[3] adds to his definition: 'he calls it also "well-being" (εὐεστώ) and by many other names'; Stobaeus[4] supplies three of these, 'harmony, symmetry, and imperturbability', and Cicero[5] gives us the fourth and very characteristic synonym, 'undismayedness' (ἀθαμβίη). It is not certain whether Democritus used these words as exact equivalents of 'cheerfulness', or rather as derivative qualities, but a consideration of them in relation to the fragments will throw some light on the main idea. 'Well-being' (εὐεστώ) might at first sight be thought to be a wider conception than 'cheerfulness' and to include bodily welfare: but the definition in one of the fragments,[6] 'happiness arising from a good state of things at home', seems to make clear that it too refers to a mental state, and this is confirmed by an aphorism[7] in

---

[1] Stob. ii. 9. 3; D.B. 174 N. 47 ὁ μὲν εὔθυμος εἰς ἔργα αἰεὶ φερόμενος δίκαια καὶ νόμιμα καὶ ὕπαρ καὶ ὄναρ χαίρει τε καὶ ἔρρωται καὶ ἀνακηδής ἐστιν.

[2] Stob. iii. 1. 47; D.B. 189; N. 7 ἄριστον ἀνθρώπῳ τὸν βίον διάγειν ὡς πλεῖστα εὐθυμηθέντι καὶ ἐλάχιστα ἀνιηθέντι. τοῦτο δ᾽ ἂν εἴη, εἴ τις μὴ ἐπὶ τοῖς θνητοῖσι τὰς ἡδονὰς ποιοῖτο.   [3] ix. 45; D.A. 1.

[4] ii. 7. 3; D.A. 167; N. 2 ἁρμονίαν συμμετρίαν τε καὶ ἀταραξίαν.

[5] de Fin. v. 29. 87; D.A. 169.

[6] Hesych.s.v. εὐεστώ; D.B. 140. εὐδαιμονία ἀπὸ τοῦ εὖ ἑστάναι τὸν οἶκον.

[7] Stob. ii. 31. 66; D.B. 182; Ns. 189 ὅτῳ μεγάλη ἐστὶ τῇ φύσι κακεστώ. This is however only Diels' correction of a corrupt passage.

which Democritus appears to use the contrary word 'ill-being' (κακεστώ): 'a man is often prevented from doing good, he argues, who has by nature much ill-being'; the idea here is clearly of mental disturbance. 'Harmony' and 'symmetry' seem to be descriptions of the nature of 'cheerfulness', which implies a balance of mind, due to the absence of fear and other disturbing elements: the conception of 'symmetry' may not be unconnected with the idea of 'the mean', which will be seen to play a considerable part in Democritus' idea of the means by which 'cheerfulness' is to be attained. 'Imperturbability' (ἀταραξία) is an admirable description of the negative side of Democritus' idea, but does not seem to convey the positive conception of happiness and strength which is suggested by the fragment already quoted. If the word was actually used by Democritus, which is perhaps doubtful, it is a remarkable anticipation of Epicurus. For 'undismayedness' (ἀθαμβίη) we have the authority of two extant fragments: 'the glory of righteousness is a courageous and undismayed judgement',[1] 'wisdom undismayed is worth all, for it is most precious'.[2] It is 'imperturbability' in its strongest form and suggests the *nil admirari* of Horace.[3]

The general character of the Democritean 'cheerfulness' is then clear and the question arises how is it to be attained? Democritus appears to make certain distinctions and to apply certain tests. In the first place it arises naturally from pleasure or enjoyment: his maxim that 'enjoyment and its absence are the limit of the advantageous and disadvantageous'[4] has already been considered and to it may be added the statement that 'pain is the limit of evil'.[5] These aphorisms need not be regarded, as has been seen, as throwing back the conception of 'cheerfulness' on to a wider base of pleasure, but merely as supplying a practical test: we shall be conducing to 'cheerfulness', if we choose what gives us

---

[1] Stob. iii. 7. 31; D.B. 215; N. 46 δίκης κῦδος γνώμης θάρσος καὶ ἀθαμβίη.
[2] Stob. iii. 7. 74; D.B. 216; N. 34 σοφίη ἄθαμβος ἀξίη πάντων τιμιωτάτη οὖσα.   [3] Ep. i. vi. 1.   [4] D.B. 4: see p. 189, n. 2.
[5] Epiphan. *adv. Haer.* iii. 2. 9; D.A. 166; N. p. 5.

pleasure, we shall be thwarting it if we choose what gives us pain. But not all pleasures are to be chosen, and discrimination must be shown: 'ill-timed pleasures produce unpleasantness';[1] 'of all things indulgence is the worst thing for educating youth: for this it is which produces those pleasures from which an evil disposition arises'.[2] These are vague and general precepts, but the idea becomes explicit in another larger and more important fragment:[3] 'Those who take their pleasures from the stomach, passing the due measure (τὸν καιρόν) in eating or drinking or love, for all of them their pleasures are short and endure but a little while, as long as they are eating and drinking, but their pains are many and long. For first the desire of the same things is ever with them . . . and there is no good in them, but only brief enjoyment and then again they need the same things.' Here, in marked contrast to Epicurus, the pleasures of the body are definitely rejected as such, though the reason is the same which Epicurus gives against their indulgence beyond the point where natural desire is relieved, namely that they involve the great pain of desire for their renewal. On this superiority of soul to body Democritus insists with no uncertain voice: 'he who chooses the goods of the soul, chooses the more divine: he who chooses those of the body, chooses human goods'[4]—or more clearly still: 'it is fitting for men to pay attention to the soul rather than the body; for perfection in the soul corrects the faults of the body, but strength of body without reasoning makes the soul no whit better.'[5] Soul can help body, but body cannot help soul. An extension of the idea of the inferiority of pleasures of the

---

[1] Dem. 36; D.B. 71; N. 54 ἡδοναὶ ἄκαιροι τίκτουσιν ἀηδίας.

[2] Stob. ii. 31. 56; D.B. 178; N. 198 πάντων κάκιστον ἡ εὐπετείη παιδεῦσαι τὴν νεότητα· αὕτη γάρ ἐστιν ἣ τίκτει τὰς ἡδονὰς ταύτας, ἐξ ὧν ἡ κακότης γίνεται. [3] Stob. iii. 18. 35; D.B. 235; N.53.

[4] Dem. 3; D.B. 37 N. 8. ὁ τὰ ψυχῆς ἀγαθὰ αἱρεόμενος τὰ θειότερα αἱρέεται· ὁ δὲ τὰ σκήνεος τὰ ἀνθρωπήια.

[5] Stob. Flor. i. 39; D.B. 187; N. 18 ἀνθρώποις ἁρμόδιον ψυχῆς μᾶλλον ἢ σώματος λόγον ποιεῖσθαι· ψυχῆς μὲν γὰρ τελεότης σκήνεος μοχθηρίην ὀρθοῖ, σκήνεος δὲ ἰσχὺς ἄνευ λογισμοῦ ψυχὴν οὐδέν τι ἀμείνω τίθησιν.

body is found in the saying:¹ 'happiness dwells not in herds nor in gold; the soul is the dwelling of happiness'. Worldly possessions are 'human goods' and so to be ranked with the goods of the body. Akin to this insistence on the superiority of soul to body is a marked aesthetic element in his ethics, which is a foreshadowing of Plato and a notable contrast with Epicurus.² 'We must not choose every pleasure but that which is concerned with the beautiful.'³ Here the idea of 'the beautiful' is perhaps mainly moral, 'the noble', as it became afterwards in Plato, but the completely aesthetic side is seen in another fragment:⁴ 'the great pleasures are derived from the contemplation of beautiful works'. One more dictum⁵ links this on closely with the idea of the precedence of soul over body: 'the beauty of the body is but animal, unless there be mind beneath'. These two quotations certainly place one in the atmosphere of the *Republic*.

Equally notable is an anticipation in several aphorisms of the Aristotelian theory of 'the mean': true pleasure, which produces 'cheerfulness', is regarded as consisting in moderation and lying between excess and defect: 'cheerfulness comes to man through moderation in enjoyment and harmony of life: excess and defect are apt to change and to produce great movements in the soul'.⁶ Here the idea is in close connexion with the main theory: 'cheerfulness' depends on the right selection of pleasures: the true pleasures are those which come from moderation; for excess and defect disturb the soul and destroy its 'symmetry' and 'im-

---

¹ Stob. ii. 7. 3; D.B. 171; N. 10, 11 εὐδαιμονίη οὐκ ἐν βοσκήμασιν οἰκεῖ οὐδὲ ἐν χρυσῷ· ψυχὴ οἰκητήριον δαίμονος.

² See p. 508, n. 4.

³ Stob. iii. 5. 22; D.B. 207; N. 4 ἡδονὴν οὐ πᾶσαν ἀλλὰ τὴν ἐπὶ τῷ καλῷ αἱρεῖσθαι χρεών.

⁴ Stob. iii. 3. 46; D.B. 194; N. 36 αἱ μεγάλαι τέρψεις ἀπὸ τοῦ θεᾶσθαι τὰ καλὰ τῶν ἔργων γίνονται.

⁵ Dem. 71; D.B. 105; N. 16 σώματος κάλλος ζωῶδες. ἢν μὴ νοῦς ὑπῇ.

⁶ Stob. iii. 1. 210; D.B. 191; N. 52 ἀνθρώποισι γὰρ εὐθυμίη γίνεται μετριότητι τέρψιος καὶ βίου συμμετρίῃ· τὰ δ' ἐλλείποντα καὶ ὑπερβάλλοντα μεταπίπτειν τε φιλεῖ καὶ μεγάλας κινήσιας ἐμποιεῖν τῇ ψυχῇ.

perturbability'. The same idea appears more succinctly in another saying: 'equality is beautiful in all things; I like not excess or defect':[1] 'equality' here is moderation regarded from a mathematical point of view. Similar in tone are the sayings: 'if one were to exceed moderation, the most pleasant things would become most unpleasant';[2] 'to desire immoderately is the mark of a child, not of a man'.[3] Finally the notion is seen again in its special application to worldly goods in the quotation:[4] 'fortunate is the man who is cheerful with moderate possessions, and unfortunate he who is unhappy with many'.

A more precise idea can now be formed of the means by which 'cheerfulness' may be attained; pleasures which involve the pain of desire must be avoided, the pleasures of the soul preferred to those of the body, the beautiful must be the object of contemplation and enjoyment, and the mean observed between excess and defect. How then can a man make a right choice? Democritus, like Epicurus after him, laid great stress on 'prudence' or 'practical wisdom' (φρόνησις). One of his works had the title of *Tritogeneia* or *Athena*; in it he identified the goddess with Prudence and making a pun on the name said '*Three* things come from Prudence, good counsel, unerring speech, and right action'.[5] In several of the fragments the value of prudence in various spheres is clearly brought out: 'The hopes of those who think aright are attainable, but those of the unwise are beyond their power',[6] 'men are happy not through strength

---

[1] Dem. 68; D.B. 102; N. 51 καλὸν ἐν παντὶ τὸ ἴσον· ὑπερβολὴ δὲ καὶ ἔλλειψις οὔ μοι δοκέει.
[2] Stob. iii. 17. 38; D.B. 233; N. 55 εἴ τις ὑπερβάλλοι τὸ μέτριον, τὰ ἐπιτερπέστατα ἀτερπέστατα ἂν γίγνοιτο.
[3] Dem. 35; D.B. 70; N. 62 παιδὸς οὐκ ἀνδρὸς τὸ ἀμέτρως ἐπιθυμεῖν.
[4] Stob. iv. 103. 17; D.B. 286; N. 71 εὐτυχὴς ὁ ἐπὶ μετρίοισι χρήμασιν εὐθυμεόμενος, δυστυχὴς δὲ ὁ ἐπὶ πολλοῖσι δυσθυμεόμενος : cf. also D.B. 285.
[5] *Etym. Orion.*, pp. 153, 5; D.B. 2 γίνεται δὲ ἐκ τοῦ φρονεῖν τρία ταῦτα, βουλεύεσθαι καλῶς, λέγειν ἀναμαρτήτως καὶ πράττειν ἃ δεῖ.
[6] Dem. 23 a; Stob. iv. 110. 18; D.B. 58; N. 102 ἐλπίδες αἱ τῶν ὀρθὰ φρονεόντων ἐφικταί, αἱ δὲ τῶν ἀξυνέτων ἀδύνατοι.

of body or through possessions, but through righteousness and wide thoughts',[1] 'it is a great thing in misfortune to think aright',[2] 'reputation and wealth without understanding are not safe possessions';[3] a particularly interesting fragment brings prudence into relation with chance:[4] 'men have fashioned an image of chance as a cloak for their own ill-counsel. For chance rarely fights against prudence, and most things in life keen sight with understanding guides aright'. A series of sayings[5] on 'the foolish' bring out the same idea from a negative point of view: two may be quoted: 'fools live without enjoying life',[6] the absence of prudence, that is, causes men to miss the true pleasures; 'fools long for what is not there, and despise what is at hand even though it is more profitable than what has passed away'.[7]

Prudence is thus the guide to life for it enables a man to choose the pleasures which will produce 'cheerfulness'. Is it an innate gift or can it be acquired? Democritus was a strong believer in the value of education. In an aphorism[8] which has almost a Socratic ring he says, 'the cause of wrong-doing is ignorance of the better', and in many places he insists on the value of teaching. In two of them he brings it into relation with nature: 'more men become good by training than by nature'.[9] 'Nature and teaching are alike.

---

[1] Dem. 6; D.B. 40; N. 15 οὔτε σώμασιν οὔτε χρήμασιν εὐδαιμονοῦσιν ἄνθρωποι, ἀλλ' ὀρθοσύνῃ καὶ πολυφροσύνῃ.

[2] Dem. 8; D.B. 42; N. 90 μέγα τὸ ἐν ξυμφορῇσι φρονεῖν ἃ δεῖ.

[3] Dem. 42; D.B. 77; N. 78 δόξα καὶ πλοῦτος ἄνευ ξυνέσιος οὐκ ἀσφαλέα κτήματα.

[4] Stob. ii. 8. 16; D.B. 119; N. 29, 30 ἄνθρωποι τύχης εἴδωλον ἐπλάσαντο πρόφασιν ἰδίης ἀβουλίης. βαιὰ γὰρ φρονήσει τύχη μάχεται, τὰ δὲ πλεῖστα ἐν βίῳ εὐξύνετος ὀξυδερκείῃ κατιθύνει.

[5] D.B. 199–206.

[6] Stob. iii. 4. 74; D.B. 200; N. 93 ἀνοήμονες βιοῦσιν οὐ τερπόμενοι βιοτῇ.

[7] Stob. iii. 4. 76; D.B. 202; N. 60 ἀνοήμονες τῶν ἀπεόντων ὀρέγονται, τὰ δὲ παρεόντα καί⟨περ τῶν⟩ παρῳχημένων κερδαλεώτερα ἐόντα ἀμαλδύνουσιν.

[8] Dem. 49; D.B. 83; N. 28 ἁμαρτίης αἰτίη ἡ ἀμαθίη τοῦ κρέσσονος.

[9] Stob. iii. 29. 66; D.B. 242; N. 193 πλέονες ἐξ ἀσκήσιος ἀγαθοὶ γίνονται ἢ ἀπὸ φύσιος.

For teaching re-forms a man, and in re-forming him makes his nature.'[1] The contradiction in the latter saying is more apparent than real; man is born with a certain nature, education can remodel it into a 'second' nature and that is more often the cause of goodness than the original instinct. Nature and education are grouped together again and brought into immediate connexion with prudence in another saying: 'There may be understanding in the young, and lack of understanding in the old; for it is not time that teaches prudence, but nurture in due season and nature.'[2] Another quotation[3] shows clearly the connexion of education and virtue, and emphasizes in an interesting way the various departments of the normal training of the Athenian boy at the time: 'If boys are slack and fail to work, they would never learn reading or music or games, nor, what is best safe-guard of virtue, reverence; for it is from these pursuits that reverence most loves to grow.' One more quotation may be made, for though it concerns education more on the in-tellectual side, it is characteristic of its author and a striking anticipation of the thoughts of a later age: 'culture is an ornament to the prosperous and a refuge to those in adversity'.[3]

It is possible then to form a fairly clear idea of what Democritus meant by 'cheerfulness' and what he held to be the means of attaining it. It remains to be seen if any notion can be put together of the kind of life which the 'cheerful' man will lead. A reconstruction from fragments

---

[1] D.B. 33; N. 187; Clem. *Strom.* iv. 151; Stob. ii. 31. 65 ἡ φύσις καὶ ἡ διδαχὴ παραπλήσιόν ἐστι. καὶ γὰρ ἡ διδαχὴ μεταρυσμοῖ τὸν ἄνθρωπον, μεταρυσμοῦσα δὲ φυσιοποιεῖ.

[2] Stob. ii. 31. 72; D.B. 183; N. 185 ἔστι που νέων ξύνεσις καὶ γερόν-των ἀξυνεσίη· χρόνος γὰρ οὐ διδάσκει φρονεῖν, ἀλλ' ὡραίη τροφὴ καὶ φύσις.

[3] Stob. ii. 31. 57; D.B. 179; N. 197 ἔξω τί κως ἢ πονεῖν παῖδες ἀνιέν-τες οὔτε γράμματ' ἂν μάθοιεν οὔτε μουσικὴν οὔτε ἀγωνίην οὐδ' ὅπερ μάλιστα τὴν ἀρετὴν συνέχει, τὸ αἰδεῖσθαι· μάλα γὰρ ἐκ τούτων φιλεῖ γίγνεσθαι ἡ αἰδώς.

[4] Stob. ii. 31.58; D.B.180; N.183 ἡ παιδεία εὐτυχοῦσι μέν ἐστι κόσμος, ἀτυχοῦσι δὲ καταφύγιον. Cf. Cic. *pro Arch.* 7. 16.

is necessarily incomplete, but there is a considerable amount of material to draw on. A long extract[1] may first be considered which gives a clear picture and suggests lines of inquiry.

A cheerful spirit comes to men through moderation in enjoyment and harmony of life. . . . Therefore you must fix your mind on things within your power (ἐπὶ τοῖς δυνατοῖς) and be content with what you have, taking little thought of those who are envied and admired and not associating yourself with them in mind: rather you must contemplate the lives of those who have a hard time and mark their sore suffering, so that what you have and possess already may appear great and enviable to you, and you may not desire more and so come to suffer in mind. For the man who admires the rich and those whom the world blesses and associates himself with them in his thoughts at every hour of the day, is forced ever to seek some new thing and to set his desire upon doing some deed irremediable such as the laws forbid. Therefore, a man should not seek these things, but be cheerful with the others, comparing his own life with the life of the less fortunate and holding himself blessed, when he thinks of what they suffer and considers how much better is his own life and fortune. If you cling to this state of mind, you will live more cheerfully and will be rid of many evil spirits (κῆρας) in your life, envy, jealousy, and ill-will.

Here there is a strong emphasis on the ideas of moderation in practice and contentment in spirit, the whole gathered up in a self-centred view of life in which the less fortunate have their function in helping to secure one's own satisfaction. The idea is repeated in another striking saying:[2] 'the man who intends to be cheerful must not be overactive either in private or in public,[3] and whatever he does must not choose what is beyond his capacity and nature. But he must so be on his guard that even when chance falls in his way and seems to lead him to advancement, he can lay it aside and not engage in what is more than he can do. For plenty in moderation is safer than great plenty'. This gives the picture of self-centred and cautious inactivity in an extreme form

---

[1] Stob. iii. 1. 210; D. 191; N. 52, already referred to on p. 195.
[2] Stob. iv. 103. 25; D.B. 3; N. 163.
[3] πολλὰ πρήσσειν here has clearly the associations of πολυπραγμοσύνη.

and when it came to details it is not surprising that Democritus did not quite succeed in carrying it out.

In a philosophy in which moderation plays so large a part it is to be expected that much stress will be laid on the characteristic Greek virtue of 'self-control' (σωφροσύνη). The contrast between self-control and chance[1] has already been quoted and in a similar spirit Democritus says: 'self-control increases enjoyment and makes pleasure greater'.[2] The idea is exactly that of moderation: its pleasures are really greater, because they are stable and do not involve unfulfilled desire. Self-control is more than once regarded as the peculiar virtue of the old: 'strength and beauty are the blessings of youth, self-control is the flower of old age':[3] 'the self-control of a father is the greatest exhortation to the children'[4]—the latter a peculiarly shrewd observation. The character of this self-control is clearly expressed in the saying that 'to endure poverty nobly is the mark of a man of self-control',[5] and its direct relation to bodily health is emphasized in another striking aphorism: 'Men ask for health from the gods in their prayers, but do not know that they have the power over it in themselves. In their wantonness they do contrary things and themselves by their desires become traitors to their health.'[6] The same idea of the responsibility of the soul, as director, for the misuse of the body is brought out in a longer and very interesting fragment: If the body were to lay a suit against the soul for the pains and ill-treatment it has suffered during all its life, and were itself appointed

[1] pp. 187, 197.

[2] Stob. iii. 5. 27; D.B. 211; N. 56 σωφροσύνη τὰ τερπνὰ ἀέξει καὶ ἡδονὴν ἐπιμείζονα ποιεῖ.

[3] Stob. iv. 115. 19; D.B. 294; N. 205 ἰσχὺς καὶ εὐμορφίη νεότητος ἀγαθά, γήραος δὲ σωφροσύνη ἄνθος.

[4] Stob. iii. 5. 24; D.B. 208; N. 199 πατρὸς σωφροσύνη μέγιστον τέκνοις παράγγελμα.

[5] Stob. iv. 108. 70; D.B. 291; N. 83 πενίην ἐπιεικέως φέρειν σωφρονέοντος.

[6] Stob. iii. 18. 30; D.B. 234; N. 21 ὑγιείην εὐχῇσι παρὰ θεῶν αἰτέονται ἄνθρωποι, τὴν δὲ ταύτης δύναμιν ἐν ἑαυτοῖς ἔχοντες οὐκ ἴσασιν· ἀκρασίη δὲ τἀναντία πρήσσοντες αὐτοὶ προδόται τῆς ὑγιείης τῆσιν ἐπιθυμίῃσιν γίνονται.

judge in the case, it would gladly condemn the soul on the
ground that parts of the body it has ruined by carelessness
or weakened by intoxication, other parts it has destroyed
and dissipated by love of pleasure: it would be just as if,
when some instrument or vessel was spoilt, a man might
blame another for his reckless use of it.'[1] The insistence[2] in
both these quotations on the supremacy of soul over body
is characteristic.

Similar thoughts appear in passages where Democritus
deals with desire: 'immoderate desire is the mark of a child,
not of a man':[3] 'excessive craving for any one thing blinds
the soul to everything else':[4] 'the desire for more loses what
is in hand; it is like the dog in Aesop'.[5] And the lesson of
moderation is again enforced: 'if you do not desire many
things, the few will seem many; for small cravings make
poverty equivalent to wealth'.[6] Several of these aphorisms
and especially the last anticipate the principles of Epicurus.[7]

The secret of attaining this self-control and the capacity
to endure hardship lies in the practice of work: 'toils under-
taken willingly make lighter the endurance of those that
come against the will':[8] 'all toils are sweeter than idleness,
when men gain what they toil for or know that they will
win it'.[9] Work in this spirit becomes easier as it goes:
'continuous toil becomes lighter by custom',[10] and in the
end this self-training is a stronger power for good than

---

[1] Plut. *fr. de Libid. et Aegr.* 2; D.B. 159; N. 22.   [2] See p. 194.
[3] Dem. 35; D.B. 70; N. 62 παιδὸς οὐκ ἀνδρὸς τὸ ἀμέτρως ἐπιθυμεῖν.
[4] Dem. 37; D.B. 72; N. 58 αἱ περί τι σφοδραὶ ὀρέξεις τυφλοῦσιν εἰς
τἆλλα τὴν ψυχήν.
[5] Stob. iii. 10. 68; D.B. 224; N. 59 ἡ τοῦ πλέονος ἐπιθυμίη τὸ παρεὸν
ἀπόλλυσι τῇ Αἰσωπείῃ κυνὶ ἰκέλη γινομένη.
[6] Stob. iv. 24. 25; D.B. 284; N. 69 ἢν μὴ πολλῶν ἐπιθυμέῃς, τὰ ὀλίγα
τοι πολλὰ δόξει· σμικρὰ γὰρ ὄρεξις πενίην ἰσοσθενέα πλούτῳ ποιέει.
[7] See Part II, Chap. X, p. 496.
[8] Stob. iii. 29. 63; D.B. 240; N. 131 οἱ ἑκούσιοι πόνοι τὴν τῶν ἀκουσίων
ὑπομονὴν ἐλαφροτέρην παρασκευάζουσι.
[9] Stob. iii. 29. 88; D.B. 243; N. 130 τῆς ἡσυχίης πάντες οἱ πόνοι
ἡδίονες, ὅταν ὧν εἵνεκεν πονέουσι τυγχάνωσιν ἢ εἰδέωσι κύρσοντες.
[10] Stob. iii. 29. 64; D.B. 241; N. 132 πόνος συνεχὴς ἐλαφρότερος ἑαυτοῦ
συνηθείῃ γίνεται.

natural instinct: 'more men become good by training than by nature'.[1] We are back again at the importance of education,[2] though in a more practical sphere.

Besides self-control the other cardinal virtues in Greek thought are duly recognized by Democritus. Wisdom receives its tribute in the saying: 'the doctor's art heals the diseases of the body, but wisdom releases the soul from suffering',[3] but it too is only to be won by education: 'neither art nor wisdom is attainable, unless one learns'.[4] Courage is said to help in the endurance of hardship: 'courage makes calamities small',[5] but it is more than physical courage that is needed: 'the courageous man is he who vanquishes not only his enemies, but his desires. Some men are masters of cities, but the slaves of women'.[6] The popular conception is once again subordinated to Democritus' own insistence on self-control. Of justice it will be necessary to speak later when Democritus' attitude to the state is considered, but here it may be well to collect certain sayings which regard justice primarily as a virtue of the individual. His conception of justice is positive and active: 'justice is doing what should be done and injustice not doing what should be done but setting it aside',[7] and with a remarkable anticipation of later thought he sees that not only action but the will to action is what matters: 'it is good not merely to refrain from injustice but not even to wish to do it'.[8] Love of riches is a great obstacle to justice: 'a man who is altogether the slave

---

[1] Stob. iii. 29. 66; D.B. 242; N. 193 πλέονες ἐξ ἀσκήσιος ἀγαθοὶ γίνονται ἢ ἀπὸ φύσιος.   [2] See p. 197.

[3] Clem. Paed. 1. 6; D.B. 31; N. 50 ἰατρικὴ μὲν σώματος νόσους ἀκέεται, σοφίη δὲ ψυχὴν παθῶν ἀφαιρεῖται.

[4] Dem. 24; Stob. ii. 31. 71; D.B. 59; N. 188 οὔτε τέχνη οὔτε σοφίη ἐφικτόν, ἢν μὴ μάθῃ τις.

[5] Stob. iii. 7. 21; D.B. 213; N. 127 ἀνδρείη τὰς ἄτας μικρὰς ἔρδει.

[6] Stob. iii. 7. 25; D.B. 214; N. 63. 169 ἀνδρεῖος οὐχ ὁ τῶν πολεμίων μόνον, ἀλλὰ καὶ ὁ τῶν ἡδονῶν κρέσσων. ἔνιοι δὲ πολίων μὲν δεσπόζουσι, γυναιξὶ δὲ δουλεύουσιν.

[7] Stob. iv. 44, 15; D.B. 256; N. 156 δίκη μέν ἐστιν ἔρδειν τὰ χρὴ ἐόντα, ἀδικίη δὲ μὴ ἔρδειν τὰ χρὴ ἐόντα, ἀλλὰ παρατρέπεσθαι.

[8] Dem. 27; Stob. iii. 9. 29; D.B. 62; N. 38 ἀγαθὸν οὐ τὸ μὴ ἀδικεῖν ἀλλὰ τὸ μηδὲ ἐθέλειν.

to possessions could never be just',¹ and its motive should be higher than the fear of punishment: 'refrain from sinning not through fear but through duty'.² Self-respect is similarly urged as a motive in a larger fragment:³ 'do not respect other men more than yourself and do not be readier to do evil if no one will know it than if all the world will know it. Respect yourself most of all and let this law be set in your heart, to do nothing disadvantageous'. In the same lofty spirit he says: 'he who does wrong is more unhappy than he who is wronged'.⁴ Not less notable are two sayings about repentance: 'it is better to take council before acting than to repent',⁵ yet after action there is room for repentance and it brings its own blessing: 'repentance over shameful deeds is the salvation of life'.⁶ All these sayings about justice are conceived on a high plane and some of them have an almost Christian ring about them. They seem a little remote from the main conception of 'cheerfulness' and it is hard to believe that they are inspired by no loftier motive than the desire to protect oneself from depression. Democritus seems sometimes to get outside his self-centred philosophy. We may trace a similar nobility in the aphorism: 'it shows a high soul to bear an offence meekly'.⁷

A few more detached aphorisms on the individual life may serve to complete the picture. Frugality is a virtue often commended, it is of course a form of moderation:

¹ Dem. 16; D.B. 50; N. 73 ὁ χρημάτων παντελῶς ἥσσων οὐκ ἄν ποτε εἴη δίκαιος.

² Dem. 7; Stob. iii. 1. 95; D.B. 41; N. 45 μὴ διὰ φόβον ἀλλὰ διὰ τὸ δέον ἀπέχεσθαι ἁμαρτημάτων.

³ Stob. iv. 46. 46; D.B. 264; N. 43 μηδέν τι μᾶλλον τοὺς ἀνθρώπους αἰδεῖσθαι ἑωυτοῦ μηδέ τι μᾶλλον ἐξεργάζεσθαι κακόν, εἰ μέλλει μηδεὶς εἰδήσειν ἢ εἰ οἱ πάντες ἄνθρωποι· ἀλλ' ἑωυτὸν μάλιστα αἰδεῖσθαι, καὶ τοῦτον νόμον τῇ ψυχῇ καθεστάναι ὥστε μηδὲν ποιεῖν ἀνεπιτήδειον.

⁴ Dem. 11; D.B. 45; N. 48 ὁ ἀδικῶν τοῦ ἀδικουμένου κακοδαιμονέστερος.

⁵ Dem. 31; D.B. 66; N. 101 προβουλεύεσθαι κρεῖσσον πρὸ τῶν πραξέων ἢ μετανοεῖν.

⁶ Dem. 9; D.B. 43; N. 99 μεταμέλεια ἐπ' αἰσχροῖσιν ἔργμασι βίου σωτηρίη.

⁷ Dem. 12; D.B. 46; N. 218 μεγαλοψυχίη τὸ φέρειν πραέως πλημμέλειαν.

'the frugal tread in the path of the bee, for they work as if they were to live for ever'.¹ It is emphasized again and its difficulty pointed out in a very remarkable fragment which shows conspicuously Democritus' power of simile: 'the children of frugal parents, if they grow up ignorant, are like dancers leaping on swords: if as they descend they miss the one place where they ought to plant their feet, there is an end of them. But it is hard to hit this one spot; for there is only just room for their feet left. So they too if they miss the print of their father's thrift and frugality are led to destruction'.² But frugality, though good in itself, must not be carried to excess: 'frugality and hunger are good, but there is a time to be lavish too: it takes a good man to recognize it':³ 'a life without feasting is a long journey without an inn'.⁴ Here the lover of 'cheerfulness' seems for a moment to emerge above the moralist. Avarice at any rate is strongly condemned on fundamental grounds: 'a craving for possessions, if it is not limited by satiety, is far worse than the utmost poverty; for the greater the craving, the greater the feeling of want'.⁵ Jealousy is no less shrewdly condemned: 'the envious man harms himself as he would an enemy';⁶ he is only creating for himself new unsatisfied desires. Contentiousness likewise recoils upon itself: 'all contentiousness

¹ Stob. iii. 16. 17; D.B. 227; N. 80 οἱ φειδωλοὶ τὸν τῆς μελίσσης οἶτον ἔχουσιν ἐργαζόμενοι ὡς ἀεὶ βιωσόμενοι.
² Stob. iii. 16. 18; D.B. 228; N. 202 οἱ τῶν φειδωλῶν παῖδες ἀμαθέες γινόμενοι ὥσπερ οἱ ὀρχησταὶ οἱ ἐς τὰς μαχαίρας ὀρούοντες, ἢν ἑνὸς μούνου ⟨μὴ⟩ τύχωσι καταφερόμενοι, ἔνθα δεῖ τοὺς πόδας ἐρεῖσαι, ἀπόλλυνται· χαλεπὸν δὲ τυχεῖν ἑνός· τὸ γὰρ ἴχνιον μοῦνον λέλειπται τῶν ποδῶν· οὕτω δὲ καὶ οὗτοι, ἢν ἁμάρτωσι τοῦ πατρικοῦ τύπου τοῦ ἐπιμελέος καὶ φειδωλοῦ, φιλέουσι διαφθείρεσθαι.
³ Stob. iii. 16. 19; D.B. 229; N. 81 φειδώ τοι καὶ λιμὸς χρηστή· ἐν καιρῷ δὲ καὶ δαπάνη· γινώσκειν δὲ ἀγαθοῦ.
⁴ Stob. iii. 16. 22; D.B. 230; N. 229 βίος ἀνεόρταστος μακρὴ ὁδὸς ἀπανδόκευτος.
⁵ Stob. iii. 10. 43; D.B. 219; N. 70 χρημάτων ὄρεξις, ἢν μὴ ὁρίζηται κόρῳ, πενίης ἐσχάτης πολλὸν χαλεπωτέρη· μέζονες γὰρ ὀρέξεις μέζονας ἐνδείας ποιεῦσιν.
⁶ Dem. 54; Stob. iii. 38. 47; D.B. 88; N. 82 ὁ φθονέων ἑωυτὸν ὡς ἐχθρὸν λυπέει.

is folly: for while it gazes on the harm wreaked on its opponent, it does not see its own advantage'.[1] Among his miscellaneous sayings there are two which seem to arise directly out of Democritus' own experience as a 'travelled man': 'Sojourning abroad teaches self-sufficiency; for a crust of bread and a wisp of straw are the sweetest medicines for hunger and weariness.'[2] Those are the hardships of travel; this is its high spirit: 'For the wise man the whole earth is open: for the entire world is the native land of a good soul.'[3] The portrait of Democritus' 'cheerful' man is on the whole a pleasant one: in spite of the self-centredness of the motives there is much that is fine and noble in the result. We may quote lastly some characteristic reflexions on old age and death. A completed life he thinks of as a good thing: 'the old man was once young, but it is uncertain whether the young man will attain to old age; therefore the completed good is superior to that which is still to come and is uncertain.'[4] Yet for old age itself he has scanty praise: 'old age is a wholesale crippling: it has all its limbs, but all lack something',[5] and he warns his disciples more than once not to strive for old age rather than death: 'it is the foolish who through fear of death wish to grow old':[6] 'it is the foolish who crave for life fearing death instead of old age'.[7] The 'cheerful' life must remain cheerful to its close and that cannot well be if it is prolonged into old age.

[1] Stob. iii. 20. 62; D.B. 237; N. 221 φιλονικίη πᾶσα ἀνόητος· τὸ γὰρ κατὰ τοῦ δυσμένεος βλαβερὸν θεωρεῦσα τὸ ἴδιον συμφέρον οὐ βλέπει.

[2] Stob. iii. 40. 6; D.B. 246; N. 66 ξενιτείη βίου αὐτάρκειαν διδάσκει· μᾶζα γὰρ καὶ στιβὰς λιμοῦ καὶ κόπου γλυκύτατα ἰάματα.

[3] Stob. iii. 40. 7; D.B. 247; N. 168 ἀνδρὶ σοφῷ πᾶσα γῆ βατή· ψυχῆς γὰρ ἀγαθῆς πατρὶς ὁ ξύμπας κόσμος.

[4] Stob. iv. 115. 21; D.B. 295; N. 204 ὁ γέρων νέος ἐγένετο, ὁ δὲ νέος ἄδηλον εἰ ἐς γῆρας ἀφίξεται· τὸ τέλειον οὖν ἀγαθὸν τοῦ μέλλοντος ἔτι καὶ ἀδήλου κρέσσον.

[5] Stob. iv. 116. 41; D.B. 296; N. 207 γῆρας ὁλόκληρός ἐστι πήρωσις· πάντ' ἔχει καὶ πᾶσιν ἐνδεῖ.

[6] Stob. iii. 4. 80; D.B. 206; N. 95 ἀνοήμονες θάνατον δεδοικότες γηράσκειν ἐθέλουσιν.

[7] Stob. iii. 4. 79; D.B. 205; N. 95 n. ἀνοήμονες ζωῆς ὀρέγονται ⟨ἀντὶ⟩ γήραος θάνατον δεδοικότες.

Besides such aphorisms about the individual Democritus speaks often of the relation of the 'cheerful' man both to domestic and to public life. In regard to domestic life he takes up a marked attitude. Of slaves he holds the orthodox Greek view: 'Use slaves as parts of the body, each for his own purpose.'[1] His opinion of women and their position is no less emphatic: 'A woman is far quicker than a man to make intrigues':[2] 'let not a woman practice speaking; for it is dangerous':[3] 'few words are women's adornment: and simplicity in adornment is good too'[4]—a Periclean sentiment with an added sly touch of humour. He has a horror of submission to a woman: 'to be ruled by a woman would be the last disgrace to a man',[5] and in this anticipates Epicurus' aversion to the love of the sexes. Equally clearly he would dissuade his disciples from having children and bringing up a family: 'the rearing of children is unsafe; for if it succeeds it involves much struggle and anxiety, and if it fails, it is worse than any other form of pain':[6] 'I do not think one ought to have children; for I see in the possession of children many great dangers and many griefs; the blessings are rare, and such as they are, only weak and feeble.'[7] In similar passages[8] he enlarges on the difficulties of bringing up a family, and in one remarkable utterance[9] recommends, if one needs the presence of children, the adoption of those of one's friends, adding the cynical reason

[1] Stob. iv. 62. 45; D.B. 270; N. 177 οἰκέταισιν ὡς μέρεσι τοῦ σκήνεος χρῶ ἄλλῳ πρὸς ἄλλο.

[2] Stob. iv. 73. 62; D.B. 273; N. 174 γυνὴ πολλὰ ἀνδρὸς ὀξυτέρη πρὸς κακοφραδμοσύνην.

[3] Dem. 77; D.B. 110; N. 173 γυνὴ μὴ ἀσκείτω λόγον· δεινὸν γάρ.

[4] Stob. iv. 74. 38; D.B. 274; N. 171 κόσμος ὀλιγομυθίη γυναικί· καλὸν δὲ καὶ κόσμου λιτότης.

[5] Dem. 78; D.B. 111; N. 170 ὑπὸ γυναικὸς ἄρχεσθαι ὕβρις ἂν ἀνδρὶ εἴη ἐσχάτη.

[6] Stob. iv. 76. 13; D.B. 275; N. 182 τεκνοτροφίη σφαλερόν· τὴν μὲν γὰρ ἐπιτυχίην ἀγῶνος μεστὴν καὶ φροντίδος κέκτηται, τὴν δὲ ἀποτυχίην ἀνυπέρθετον ἑτέρῃ ὀδύνῃ.

[7] Stob. iv. 76. 15; D.B. 276; N. 180.

[8] Stob. iv. 76. 17, 83. 25; D.B. 278. 279; N. 178, 203.

[9] Stob. iv. 76. 16; D.B. 277; N. 181.

that 'this plan is so much the better because one can choose
out of many the child that suits one's mind. But if you beget
them for yourself there are many dangers; for you must put
up with the child who is born'. Yet once unexpectedly[1] his
cynicism seems to break down, and he admits that 'it is
possible without spending much of one's possessions to bring
up children and so set a wall of defence round one's property
and person'—still an egoistic motive, but with a touch of
humanity. Of a piece with all this is a more kindly saying:
'he who gets a good son-in-law finds a son, but he who gets
a bad one loses a daughter'.[2]

It might well be asked where this cynical old bachelor
is going to find 'cheerfulness' in his relations to others, and
the answer is, as it was with Epicurus after him, in his
friends. A series of aphorisms shows the high value which
Democritus set on friendship and the importance he attributed
to efforts to acquire and maintain it. 'The man who has not
one good friend, does not deserve to live':[3] 'the friendship of
one sensible man is worth all the fools'.[4] But a friend is not
to be acquired without giving something in return: 'the
man who loves no one cannot, I think, be loved by any
one'.[5]

Friendship must be based on common thoughts and
interests: 'it is agreement that makes friendship':[6] 'not all
one's kin are friends, but those who agree in their interests',[7]
and requires the right sort of character: 'faultfinders are not

---

[1] Stob. iv. 83. 26: D.B. 280; N. 184 ἔξεστιν οὐ πολλὰ τῶν σφετέρων
ἀναλώσαντας παιδεῦσαί τε τούς παῖδας καὶ τεῖχός τε καὶ σωτηρίην περι-
βαλέσθαι τοῖς τε χρήμασι καὶ τοῖς σώμασιν αὐτῶν.

[2] Stob. iv. 70. 18; D.B. 272 ὁ γαμβροῦ μὲν ἐπιτυχὼν εὗρεν υἱόν, ὁ δὲ
ἀποτυχὼν ἀπώλεσε καὶ θυγατέρα.

[3] Dem. 65; D.B. 99; N. 209 ζῆν οὐκ ἄξιος ὅτῳ μηδὲ εἷς ἐστι χρηστὸς
φίλος.

[4] Dem. 64; D.B. 98; N. 211 ἑνὸς φιλίη ξυνετοῦ κρέσσων ἀξυνέτων
πάντων.

[5] Dem. 69; D.B. 103; N. 208 οὐδ' ὑφ' ἑνὸς φιλέεσθαι δοκέει μοι ὁ
φιλέων μηδένα.

[6] Stob. ii. 33. 9; D.B. 186; N. 212 ὁμοφροσύνη φιλίην ποιεῖ.

[7] Dem. 73; D.B. 107; N. 213 φίλοι οὐ πάντες οἱ ξυγγενέες. ἀλλ' οἱ
ξυμφωνέοντες περὶ τοῦ ξυμφέροντος.

made for friendship':[1] 'the man with whom tested friends do not remain long, is ill-tempered'.[2] But there can be deception in friendship: 'many who seem to be friends are not; others are who seem not',[3] and a change of fortune may end friendship: 'many shun their friends, when they fall from prosperity to poverty';[4] 'in good fortune it is easy to find a friend, in bad fortune the most difficult of all things'.[5] Democritus' conception of friendship has no doubt a selfish basis, but it is at least more pleasing to contemplate than his notion of family life. That it has a generous side may be seen in certain aphorisms concerning kindnesses and gratitude: 'one should receive acts of kindness with the intention of making greater returns',[6] 'small acts of kindness at the right moment are the greatest for those who receive them',[7] 'the really kind man is not the man who looks for a return, but he who chooses to do good'.[8] In these selfishness seems at least to be mitigated by a truer feeling.

There is a good deal of information as to Democritus' attitude to the State and its functions. From his conception[9] of justice as a positive and active virtue, it follows naturally that he insists on the punishment of offenders: ' we must avenge those who are wronged to the best of our powers and not let it be; for this is just and good, and the contrary is unjust and evil'.[10] There is an interesting series of

---

[1] Dem. 76; D.B. 109; N. 217 οἱ φιλομεμφέες εἰς φιλίην οὐκ εὐφυέες.

[2] Dem. 66; D.B. 100; N. 216 ὅτεῳ μὴ διαμένουσιν ἐπὶ πολλὸν οἱ πειραθέντες φίλοι δύστροπος.

[3] Dem. 63; D.B. 97; N. 210 πολλοὶ δοκέοντες εἶναι φίλοι οὐκ εἰσὶ καὶ οὐ δοκέοντες εἰσίν.

[4] Dem. 67; D.B. 101; N. 215 ἐκτρέπονται πολλοὶ τοὺς φίλους, ἐπὴν ἐξ εὐπορίης εἰς πενίην μεταπέσωσιν.

[5] Dem. 72; D.B. 106; N. 214 ἐν εὐτυχίῃ φίλον εὑρεῖν εὔπορον, ἐν δὲ δυστυχίῃ πάντων ἀπορώτατον.

[6] Dem. 58; D.B. 92; N. 228 χάριτας δέχεσθαι χρεὼν προσκοπευόμενον κρέσσονας αὐτῶν ἀμοιβὰς ἀποδοῦναι.

[7] Dem. 60; D.B. 94; N. 225 μικραὶ χάριτες ἐν καιρῷ μέγισται τοῖς λαμβάνουσι.

[8] Dem. 62; D.B. 96; N. 226 χαριστικὸς οὐχ ὁ βλέπων πρὸς τὴν ἀμοιβὴν ἀλλ' ὁ εὖ δρᾶν προῃρημένος.　　　[9] See p. 202.

[10] Stob. iv. 46. 43; D.B. 261; N. 155 ἀδικουμένοισι τιμωρεῖν κατὰ δύναμιν

aphorisms[1] in Stobaeus' collection in which Democritus appears to approach the question of the punishment of citizens through the slaughter of harmful animals and the killing of enemies, and relates his precepts directly to his root-notions of ethics. He tells us that the man who kills harmful wild beasts is guiltless (ἀθῷος) and contributes to 'well-being' (πρὸς εὐεστοῦν), and again that the man who kills 'things that do harm contrary to justice' will have in every constitution a greater share of 'cheerfulness' and justice and courage and possessions. Advancing the next stage he says that as hostile beasts should be killed, so should hostile men, and specifies in particular the highwaymen and the pirate. Finally coming within the State itself he pronounces that 'those who do deeds worthy of exile or deserve imprisonment or fine, must be condemned and not let off; whosoever lets a man off, giving judgement for gain or affection, is a wrongdoer, and this must eat into his heart'.[2] There is a Draconian sternness about this, but the motive is clear: if the citizens are to live the 'cheerful' life, they must be freed from all forms of molestation external and internal and the principle must be rigidly applied. And this is the purpose of the existence of laws: 'the laws would never have forbidden every man to live as a law unto himself, if one man did not do harm to another. For envy lays the foundation of civil strife'.[3] But even this stern advocate for the execution of the law knows that there is something better than law in the persuasion which carries conviction: 'a man will be a greater power for virtue if he uses encouragement and persuasive speech rather than law and force. For he who is kept from injustice by law is likely to do wrong secretly, but he who is led to the right by persuasion is not likely either

χρὴ καὶ μὴ παριέναι· τὸ μὲν γὰρ τοιοῦτον δίκαιον καὶ ἀγαθόν, τὸ δὲ μὴ τοιοῦτον ἄδικον καὶ κακόν. [1] Stob. iv. 44. 16–18; D.B. 257–9.

[2] Stob. iv. 46. 44; D.B. 262; N. 157 καὶ οἳ φυγῆς ἄξια ἔρδουσιν ἢ δεσμῶν ἢ θωῆς ἄξιοι, καταψηφιστέον καὶ μὴ ἀπολύειν· ὃς δ᾽ ἂν παρὰ νόμον ἀπολύῃ κέρδει ὁρίζων ἢ ἡδονῇ ἀδικεῖ καὶ οἱ τοῦτο ἐγκάρδιον ἀνάγκη εἶναι.

[3] Stob. iii. 38. 53; D.B. 245; N. 140 οὐκ ἂν ἐκώλυον οἱ νόμοι ζῆν ἕκαστον κατ᾽ ἰδίην ἐξουσίην, εἰ μὴ ἕτερος ἕτερον ἐλυμαίνετο. φθόνος γὰρ στάσιος ἀρχὴν ἀπεργάζεται.

openly or secretly to commit a sin'.¹ For 'the purpose of law is to benefit the life of men; and this it can do, when they themselves are willing to be benefitted. For to those who are persuaded the law shows its own virtue'.² Once again the rigidity of Democritus is lightened by a shrewd human touch. Democritus' precepts on public life and the function of the State are something of a surprise. The saying already quoted,³ 'the man who intends to be cheerful must not be overactive either in private or in public', prepares us for a quietist attitude, and we should have expected him to recommend his philosopher to abstain from politics and take no part in the government of the State, but devote himself to philosophy. In fact his advice is precisely the reverse: 'learn the statesman's art as the greatest of all and pursue those toils from which great and brilliant results accrue to men,'⁴ and again he gives similar advice and expresses the highest admiration for the State and its functions: 'a man should consider state affairs more important than all else, and see to it that they are well managed. He must not be contentious beyond what is fair or clothe himself in power beyond the common good. For a well-managed State is the greatest of all successes and everything is included in it. If it is preserved, so is all besides; if it is lost, all is lost'.⁵ A man then must be prepared to play his part in the life of the

¹ Stob. ii. 31. 59; D.B. 181; N. 44 κρείσσων ἐπ' ἀρετὴν φανεῖται προτροπῇ χρώμενος καὶ λόγου πειθοῖ ἤπερ νόμῳ καὶ ἀνάγκῃ. λάθρῃ μὲν γὰρ ἁμαρτέειν εἰκὸς τὸν εἰργμένον ἀδικίης ὑπὸ νόμου, τὸν δὲ ἐς τὸ δέον ἠγμένον πειθοῖ οὐκ εἰκὸς οὔτε φανερῶς ἔρδειν τι πλημμελές.
² Stob. iv. 43. 33; D.B. 248; N. 139 ὁ νόμος βούλεται μὲν εὐεργετεῖν βίον ἀνθρώπων· δύναται δὲ ὅταν βούλωνται πάσχειν εὖ· τοῖσι γὰρ πειθομένοισι τὴν ἰδίην ἀρετὴν ἐνδείκνυται. ³ D.B. 3 : see p. 199.
⁴ Plut. adv. Colot. 32, p. 1126 a; D.B. 157; N. 133 τήν τε πολιτικὴν τέχνην μεγίστην οὖσαν ἐκδιδάσκεσθαι καὶ τοὺς πόνους διώκειν ἀφ' ὧν τὰ μεγάλα καὶ λαμπρὰ γίνονται τοῖς ἀνθρώποις.
⁵ Stob. iv. 43. 43; D.B. 252; N. 134 τὰ κατὰ τὴν πόλιν χρεὼν τῶν λοιπῶν μέγιστα ἡγεῖσθαι, ὅκως ἄξεται εὖ, μήτε φιλονικέοντα παρὰ τὸ ἐπιεικὲς μήτε ἰσχὺν ἑαυτῷ περιτιθέμενον παρὰ τὸ χρηστὸν τὸ τοῦ ξυνοῦ. πόλις γὰρ εὖ ἀγομένη μεγίστη ὄρθωσίς ἐστι καὶ ἐν τούτῳ πάντα ἔνι, καὶ τούτου σῳζομένου πάντα σῴζεται καὶ τούτου διαφθειρομένου τὰ πάντα διαφθείρεται.

State, and if need be to hold office, for, as Democritus says in a strangely Platonic aphorism: 'it is hard to be ruled by an inferior'.[1] This suggests that Democritus did not think that public office was in itself the best thing for his philosopher, but that occasionally the philosopher must be king for fear of a worse ruler. The complement of this proposition is put emphatically: 'it is better for fools to be ruled than to rule',[2] and 'when bad men come into places of honour, the more unworthy they are, the more careless they show themselves and the more are they swollen with folly and rashness'.[3] But a bad ruler, as he tells us elsewhere,[4] must be punished just like a man who has betrayed his trust. The good conduct of the State is all important for the 'cheerfulness' of its citizens: therefore the best men should undertake office, and those who rule must suffer for it. A closer connexion of thought can be traced here than in many parts of Democritus' ethics.

Among the different types of constitution Democritus undoubtedly preferred a democracy: 'poverty in a democracy is as much to be preferred to what is called prosperity under despots as freedom is to slavery'.[5] But it must be a firm and united democracy, not one torn by strife and faction: 'civil strife is an evil on both sides; for it means ruin alike to victors and vanquished',[6] and on the other hand 'by union great deeds can be done and wars accomplished for States, but not otherwise'.[7] And—once more with a strangely real

---

[1] Dem. 15; Stob. iv. 45. 27; D.B. 49; N. 143 χαλεπὸν ἄρχεσθαι ὑπὸ χερείονος.

[2] Dem. 40; D.B. 75; N. 144 κρέσσον ἄρχεσθαι τοῖς ἀνοήτοισιν ἢ ἄρχειν.

[3] Stob. iv. 43. 45; D.B. 254: N. 151 οἱ κακοὶ ἰόντες ἐς τὰς τιμὰς ὁκόσῳ ἂν μᾶλλον ἀνάξιοι ἐόντες ἴωσι, τοσούτῳ μᾶλλον ἀνακηδέες γίγνονται καὶ ἀφροσύνης καὶ θράσεος πίμπλανται.

[4] Stob. iv. 46. 47; D.B. 265; N. 166.

[5] Stob. iv. 43. 42; D.B. 251; N. 147 ἡ ἐν δημοκρατίῃ πενίη τῆς παρὰ τοῖς δυνάστῃσι καλεομένης εὐδαιμονίης τοσοῦτόν ἐστι αἱρετωτέρη ὁκόσον ἐλευθερίη δουλείης.

[6] Stob. iv. 43. 34; D.B. 249; N. 138 στάσις ἐμφύλιος ἐς ἑκάτερα κακόν· καὶ γὰρ νικέουσι καὶ ἡσσωμένοις ὁμοίη φθορή.

[7] Stob. iv. 43. 40; D.B. 250; N. 136 ἀπὸ ὁμονοίης τὰ μεγάλα ἔργα καὶ ταῖς πόλεσι τοὺς πολέμους δυνατὸν κατεργάζεσθαι, ἄλλως δ' οὔ.

touch of humanity—he considers that it is the part of the wealthy to bring about this unity by something of what we might now call practical philanthropy: 'when the powerful bring themselves to champion the poor and serve them and do kindness to them, then there is true pity: men are not left desolate, but become comrades and defend one another: the citizens are of one mind and other blessings follow greater than one could tell'.[1] Considering the general state of class feeling in most of the Greek cities, this is perhaps the most remarkable of all Democritus' sayings.

The moral teaching of Democritus is not based on any profound metaphysical or ethical basis, nor is it, as far as we can judge from detached fragments, in any sense a complete system: it does not attempt to grip together the whole of life in any reasoned deductions from a single principle. The gospel of 'cheerfulness' was, it would appear, enunciated by its author as a good practical guide to life, and the many maxims and aphorisms which have survived were designed to show in what ways a man could best become and remain 'cheerful'. The teaching rests no doubt on a selfish basis and, in so far as it remains conscious of that basis, it is self-centred in its attitude to life. The advice of Democritus seems therefore at times cynical, especially in his dealing with family life; but there is no narrowness of outlook. The precepts are wide in their application and embrace many interests and many parts of life, both private and public. At times too they rise to a real nobility, in which for the moment the egoistic foundation seems almost to be forgotten.

If it is remembered that Democritus was a 'pre-Socratic', that he taught before the sense of moral problems was felt and the need of a moral system realized, his teaching may be regarded as an interesting attempt by a man of wide

---

[1] Stob. iv. 43. 46; D.B. 255; N. 146 ὅταν οἱ δυνάμενοι τοῖς μὴ ἔχουσι καὶ προτελεῖν τολμέωσι καὶ ὑπουργεῖν καὶ χαρίζεσθαι, ἐν τούτῳ ἤδη καὶ τὸ οἰκτίρειν ἔνεστι καὶ μὴ ἐρήμους εἶναι καὶ τὸ ἑταίρους γίνεσθαι, καὶ τὸ ἀμύνειν ἀλλήλοισι καὶ τοὺς πολιήτας ὁμονόους εἶναι καὶ ἄλλα ἀγαθά, ὅσσα οὐδεὶς ἂν δύναιτο καταλέξαι.

experience to give advice to his disciples. If we look rather to the future, it will be seen that he set the tone of much in later moral theory, that he shows remarkable anticipation of the teaching of Plato, and in particular that he expresses many of the most characteristic ideas of Epicurus, and it is hard to believe that the later philosopher, for all his denials, was not indebted to him for some of them.

§ 10. *Conclusion*

The detailed review of Democritus' philosophy leaves perhaps a somewhat piecemeal and incoherent impression. This is without doubt due to a large extent to the sporadic and fragmentary way in which his teaching has come down to us. If we possessed in full, for example, one of the tetralogies on the physical theory, we should be in a very different position for judging of the consistency of his views. But even so it would probably be found that the very width of his interests and the far-reaching range of his speculations had made it impossible for him to embrace all in a coherent system: he was no doubt also more greatly interested in some parts of his inquiry than others and worked them out with disproportionate minuteness.

Yet it is impossible not to be struck with the great value and importance of his contribution to the atomic theory. He received it, as far as we can judge, from Leucippus as a rather crude and tentative speculation: he left it, if not a consistent system, yet a correlated attempt to put together on an atomic basis some account of the world and of man's knowledge of it. All parts of the theory have been greatly strengthened and developed by Democritus. He cleared and defined the conceptions of the atoms and of space: he arrived at a working theory of atomic motion and the causes that underlie it; he thought out the method by which the atoms united in compound bodies, he analysed the properties of compounds and attempted to distinguish between them and the subjective elements in sense-perception; he laid the foundations of a materialist psychology and attempted to follow out with great elaboration the metaphysical implications of his view. Finally he added, if only in loose connexion, a moral theory to the physical. In all these ways the atomic theory was immensely improved and may be said to have passed from being a mere reconciliation of opposing views into a constructive theory of the nature of the world.

Nor was he apparently blind to the problems which such a view might rouse. His subtle developments of the theory of perception were an attempt to get over some of the difficulties which a purely material system must entail: his elaborations of the ideas of atomic motion were an effort to establish the supremacy of 'natural law', and his strange and precarious metaphysic was due to a fearless logic which led him to follow out his psychology to its conclusions.

It must be owned that he left a rather uncouth and unsafe edifice to his successors: it was disproportionately developed in many of its parts and it rested on a shifting sand. In order to grip it together and import stability to it Epicurus was in many parts of it compelled to simplify and even to blind himself to difficulties. But just for that reason Democritus in many ways had the superior mind, and in not a few respects it may be said that with him Atomism as such reached its highest development in Greece.

PART II
EPICURUS

I
LIFE AND WRITINGS

THE exposition of the atomic theory by Democritus seems to have made no very deep impression on his contemporaries or on his immediate successors; nor is the cause of its failure to attract attention far to seek. The visits of the Sicilian sophists with their new ethical and rhetorical teaching were turning men's minds away from the old cosmogonical speculations to the new and more fascinating pursuits of moral and political philosophy. Socrates himself may be taken as typical of his generation: even if in his early years he may have speculated, like thinkers of the previous generation, on physics and 'the things of the sky', in later life his chief study was man, and his disciples were at pains to conceal any earlier interests, as though they were a slightly discreditable episode of youth. Plato, carrying on his master's tradition, spoke slightingly of the studies of astronomy and physics, and would relegate them to the early training of young men, who were being prepared for the higher pursuit of dialectic. Thus the older tradition of philosophy as the inquiry into nature (φυσιολογία) was obscured by the newer discussion of ethics, politics, and metaphysics, and was not prominently revived again until physics found its place in the encyclopaedic system of Aristotle. Of Aristotle's interest in Democritus' theories sufficient proof may be found in his constant criticisms, but Atomism carried no conviction to him: so far from being the logical outcome of previous speculations, it appeared to him rather as an aberration. Nevertheless the Democritean tradition did not wholly die out,[1] and in the second half of the fourth century B.C. it was maintained by Epicurus' slightly senior contemporary, Nausiphanes[2] of Teos. It is

---

[1] D.L. i. 15 implies that he had many followers, though none were famous.
[2] D.L. ibid.: cf. Suid. s.v. Ἐπίκουρος (Diels, *Nausiphanes*, A. 4), Cic. *de Nat. Deor.* 1. 26. 73; D.A. 5; and D.L. x. 13.

unfortunate that of Nausiphanes we know but little, except through Epicurean channels, vitiated by Epicurus' desire to maintain his own philosophic independence which took the form of violent abuse of those to whom he owed most. We gather however that Nausiphanes, professing himself a pupil of Democritus, was also considerably influenced by Pyrrho.[1] If he adopted something of Pyrrho's scepticism, this need have been no eclectic combination, for Democritus himself had shown very clear traces of a sceptical tendency and Nausiphanes may have done little more than push his master's doubts a little farther. Of his writings very little is known, except that he published a work called 'The Tripod'[2] which was said to have been the basis of Epicurus' Canon. In the fragments of Philodemus'[3] book on Rhetoric are certain references to 'The Tripod', from which it appears that Nausiphanes supported the position that the physical scientist (ὁ φυσικός) was well adapted for the study of rhetoric: it is reasonable to conjecture that Philodemus wishing to introduce into Epicureanism a study which his master had excluded was glad to appeal to Epicurus' own teacher. A more interesting reference[4] tells us that Nausiphanes selected as the end of conduct 'undauntedness' (ἀκαταπληξία), which seems a kind of half-way house between Democritus' 'undismayedness' (ἀθαμβίη) and Epicurus' 'imperturbability' (ἀταραξία).

Philosophy is perhaps less influenced by outward circumstances than most branches of human thought and literature, but it was inevitable that the changed conditions of life in Greece, and especially in Athens, towards the end of the fourth century should affect both the sphere of its activity and the direction of its teaching. The interest in ethical and political problems had been the natural outcome of the vigorous existence of the Athenian democracy in the fifth century, when the identification of the good man and the good citizen and even the dream of the philosopher king

[1] D.L. ix. 64, 69; cf. Seneca, *Ep.* 88. 43 ; D. B. 4.
[2] D.L. x. 14.   [3] ii. 48 and iv. 10.   See Diels, B. 1 and 2.
[4] Clem. Alex. *Strom.* ii. 130; Diels, B. 3.

were but an idealization of the life of the normal Athenian citizen. The temporary recovery of Athens after the Peloponnesian War and the subsequent struggle against the incursion of Philip of Macedon kept the same ideal before men's eyes and made possible the philosophy of Plato. The domination of Alexander and the submersion of the Greek city-states in the new and ever-extending kingdom has its reflection in the works of Aristotle: a greater individualism in Ethics and the revival of the earlier scientific interests are natural in the teacher at the king's court, but enough of the old spirit remained to preserve the political ideal almost unchanged. But in the last quarter of the century,[1] when Alexander was dead, and the civilized world had become the battlefield for his 'Successors', when Athens herself fell into the hands of one conqueror after another and retained only sufficient freedom to greet each new master with more fulsome flattery than his predecessor, civic life had become little better than a formality and the old ideal of the good citizen but a mockery. Athens was no longer a state but a municipality: statecraft had given way to commerce, politics to society, and—a small but very significant change —the Old Comedy to the New. With the change of life and manners went also a change of thought: the aspirations and hopes of the free democracy had generated idealism in speculation, the commercial common sense of the new régime turned to the sensible and material. The effect on philosophic thought was bound to be twofold: on the one hand political philosophy must disappear, for it was almost meaningless, and its place was likely to be filled, in order to answer the demand for common sense materialism, by a revival of the interest in physics: on the other moral philosophy must take an individualist turn, and men be taught to live, if not as isolated units, at least as private members of a community. And so about the same time there naturally arose the two rival creeds of Stoicism and Epicureanism. Differing widely in some of their underlying tenets—princi-

---

[1] A fuller and interesting account of the fortunes and conditions of Athens will be found in Wallace's *Epicureanism*, Chap. II.

pally in their theology, for the Stoic believed in the divine government of the world and of the life of man, while to the Epicurean the very idea was abhorrent—they both equally answered to the demand; their explanation of the physical world was material, their morality was individual. Further, they approach curiously near to one another in their practical ethical ideals: the 'self-sufficiency' (αὐτάρκεια) of the Stoic was not far removed from the 'imperturbability' (ἀταραξία) of the Epicurean. For four centuries the two creeds were to do battle with one another, first in Greece and then in Rome, and time and controversy drew them gradually farther apart: but both were alike in origin the natural product of circumstances, answers, differing mainly in tone, to the same requirements. And it was just these requirements which made impossible that they should be developed from the Socratic tradition passing through Plato and Aristotle: the physical philosophy now needed must be something nearer akin to the earlier speculation of the pre-Socratics and the root-ideas of moral teaching must be sought elsewhere than among Academics or Peripatetics. Although in Epicurus there are traces of the influence of Aristotle[1] and a keen critic[2] has even seen an approach to the doctrines of Plato, there is never a word of polemic against either: Epicurus' controversy is with the pre-Socratics, and his debt, unacknowledged and even violently denied, is to Leucippus and Democritus. It is not indeed true to say that Epicurus borrowed his physical theory wholesale from Democritus, for in many fundamental points he differed from him, most notably in the rejection both of scepticism and of determinism, but not only are the root-ideas of Atomism derived immediately from the older school, but at every point in the theory broad conceptions and details alike may be traced back to their source. Epicurus' great distinction as a philosopher lies in part no doubt in the clearness of his thought—though unfortunately not of its expression—in part in the perspicacity with which he saw how the material he needed lay ready to hand in the

---

[1] See e.g. Chap. ix, p. 450.
[2] Giussani, *Stud. Lucr.*, p. 257, n. 1.

work of Democritus, and the ingenuity with which he was able to mould and adapt it to suit new requirements.

A patch-work 'life' of Epicurus is given by Diogenes Laertius,[1] compiled apparently from various sources without any thought of consecutiveness or even consistency, from which however it is possible to put together a fair picture of a not very eventful career. His father Neocles, who was an Athenian of the deme of Gargettus, a village a few miles north-east of Athens, had been one of many who after the conquest of Samos began to go out to the island as colonists in 352 or 351 B.C. in the hope of improving their fortunes. There he apparently followed the profession of school-master,[2] while his wife, Chaerestrata, is said to have been a kind of quack priestess, who went from house to house performing superstitious rites of purification. Epicurus was born in 342 or 341 B.C., whether in Attica or after the removal to Samos is unknown, but it is certain that he passed his childhood and boyhood in the island, assisting his parents, as the legend says, in their vocations: if there is any truth in the story that he went about with his mother as an acolyte, reciting the formulae of her incantations, he may well have been inspired in quite early years with the hatred of super-stition, which was afterwards so prominent a feature in his teaching. He took to the study of philosophy, as he used to tell himself, at the age of fourteen, impelled to it, as the story goes, because his schoolmasters were unable to explain to him what Hesiod meant by the primeval 'chaos': another story, not inconsistent with this, states that about this time he came across the works of Democritus and eagerly de-voured them. However this may be, at the age of eighteen Epicurus went to Athens, no doubt in order to pass his 'examination' (δοκιμασία) and be enrolled among the Ephebi of his native deme. His visit occurred at a critical moment,

---

[1] x. 1–27. References will only be given for Epicurus' life to authorities other than Diogenes.

[2] The suspicious resemblance of this story to the charges made against Aeschines' parents by Demosthenes, de Cor. 313, has caused its truth to be doubted.

for on the death of Alexander in 323 B.C. Athens fell into the hands of Perdiccas, the guardian of his sons, who on the advice of Antipater, regent of Macedonia, practically drove out the democracy, leaving the city to the management of the richer commercial classes, who were likely to be disposed for peace at all costs. As a part of the same movement of suppression Perdiccas expelled the Athenian settlers from Samos, and, while Epicurus was still at Athens, Neocles was obliged to settle in Asia Minor. There Epicurus returned to his family and for some ten years was with them in various Asiatic towns, and principally at Colophon and Teos. Here he undoubtedly pursued his philosophic studies, and it was at this period that he must have met Nausiphanes, who was then teaching at Teos. Though he always professed the greatest contempt for 'the Mollusc'[1] (πλεύμων) and maintained that he owed nothing to him, he yet admits that he did attend his lectures 'in the company of certain bibulous youngsters', and he was doubtless still further attracted by his teaching to the Atomism of Democritus. To the same period may be assigned his study of the pre-Socratic philosophers, among whom he owned to a favourable appreciation of Anaxagoras and Archelaus, Socrates' teacher: by Pamphilus, a disciple of Plato, he is said to have been already influenced before he left Samos, but it was probably an early enthusiasm and seems to have left little mark on his thought.

In his thirtieth year (311 B.C.) he settled in Mitylene, gathered round him certain disciples—including no doubt his three brothers, whose devotion to him continued throughout life[2]—and was now recognized as a philosophical teacher. Later on in Lampsacus his school grew and he made many devoted adherents, including Metrodorus, subsequently the most important of the Epicurean writers, Colotes, the object long afterwards of Plutarch's attack, Polyaenus, Idomeneus, and Leonteus, with his wife Themista. Inspired, as it appears, by this success, he determined to return to Athens, and there form a kind of permanent brotherhood, to live

<hr />

[1] Sext. Emp. *adv. Math.* 1. 3; C.B. *fr.* 22; U. 114: cf. D.L. x. 7, 8.
[2] Plutarch, *de Frat. Amor.*, 16. 487; U. 178.

together in the practice of his principles. Athens was now (307 B.C.) under the domination of Demetrius Poliorcetes, to whom the citizens devoted themselves with such servile flattery as to make civic or political life in any real sense of the term a hopeless impossibility: their very reverence too for the new master was charged with the grossest superstition. In Athens Epicurus purchased a house in the quarter of Melita, between the city and the Peiraeus, and also, though probably not attached to the house, the famous Garden. There withdrawn from the world and taking no part in political or even social life, Epicurus remained with his little community, except for an occasional voyage to see his friends in Lampsacus, for about thirty-seven years. Besides his brothers and the disciples who had arrived with him at first, or came from time to time to visit him from Lampsacus, he was joined also by Hermarchus of Mitylene, who subsequently succeeded Epicurus in the headship of the community. We hear too of Pythocles,[1] a young man greatly beloved and admired by Epicurus, and Timocrates, the brother of Metrodorus, who subsequently separated from the brotherhood and became one of its most virulent opponents. Women also had their place in the community, and among them not only women of position such as Leonteus' wife Themista, but several also of the class of hetaerae. The most prominent of these was Leontion, who showed considerable philosophic ability and married Metrodorus, by whom she had a son and a daughter. Even slaves were admitted, and one Mys, whom Epicurus subsequently freed in his will, attained to some distinction in the brotherhood.

Epicurus lived with his disciples in the 'Garden' on terms of the greatest friendship and affection. He himself wrote much and encouraged the more able of his followers to write too: the others were recommended to get the main principles of the system by heart. We do not gather that Epicurus gave lectures or even formal instruction to his pupils, as did the leaders of the other schools, but there was much friendly discussion, master and disciples together working out and

[1] See C.B. *fr.* 33, 34; U. 161–5 : to him the second letter is addressed.

discussing new details and aspects of the system. It was inevitable that the close intimacy of the community, especially seeing the presence of women among them, should provoke scandal, and both Diotimus, the Stoic, and Timocrates, the renegade, published violent attacks on Epicurus, representing the life of the brotherhood as one of sensual debauchery. There is no reason to suppose that there was any truth in these charges, though on the other hand, as Epicurus' moral philosophy shows, the ideal of the community was not one of an absolute or ascetic purity. That they certainly did not indulge in gluttony is clear from many indications of the simplicity of their life. They used to spend a mina a day for the needs of the table: half a pint of wine now and then would satisfy them, but their ordinary drink was water. The food was on a par—nothing but bread as a rule with the occasional addition of a relish:[1] 'send me some preserved cheese,' Epicurus wrote to a friend, 'that when I like, I may have a feast'. Luxury was indeed forbidden by the principles of Epicureanism, as it did not really contribute to the true pleasure even of the body: 'I am thrilled with pleasure in the body',[2] the master wrote, 'when I live on bread and water, and I spit upon luxurious pleasures, not for their own sake, but because of the inconveniences that follow them.' This is far enough removed from the living of an 'epicure'. From time to time a feast day was observed, in particular on Epicurus' birthday, and at any rate after his death, on the 20th of each month in memory of himself and Metrodorus. Though this frugal living did not involve much expenditure, yet funds for the community were required. Epicurus would not have a common stock formed, for he thought that savoured of distrust, but accepted and even asked for voluntary contributions: 'send us', he writes to Idomeneus, 'offerings for the sustenance of our holy body on behalf of yourself and your children'.[3]

---

[1] C.B. *fr.* 39; D.L. x. 11.

[2] Stob. *Flor.* xvii. 34; C.B. *fr.* 37; U. 181.

[3] Plut. *adv. Colot.* 18. 1117; C.B. *fr.* 26; U. 130: cf. Philodem. V. H.² 1. 127; C.B. *fr.* 41; U. 184.

The picture of the community may be supplemented by certain details of Epicurus' own personal character. Not merely did he withdraw from public life, and ask for no recognition from the State or its rulers, but he expressly disclaimed any desire for popularity: 'I was never anxious to please the mob. For what pleased them, I did not know, and what I did know was far removed from their comprehension;'[1] 'I write this not for the many,'[2] he says to one of his disciples, 'but for you: we are audience enough to one another.' On the other hand his affection and personal kindness to his friends and followers knew no bounds. This is sufficiently illustrated by the numerous extant fragments of letters to absent friends, which contain not only, like the letters preserved in full by Diogenes, epitomes of different parts of his philosophy, but many personal touches of friendship and intimacy. He speaks of himself applauding in a tumult of excitement on receipt of a letter from his 'dear little Leontion',[3] he tells Pythocles that he will 'Sit down and wait for his lovely and godlike appearance',[4] and thanks[5] his friends for their care of him and the proofs 'heaven-high' of their good will. Particularly characteristic is the often-quoted letter to a child, possibly the daughter of Metrodorus and Leontion, written during one of his absences from Athens: 'We have arrived at Lampsacus safe and sound, Pythocles and Hermarchus and Ctesippus and I, and there we found Themista and our other friends all well. I hope you too are well and your mamma, and that you are always obedient to papa and Matro, as you used to be. Let me tell you that the reason that I and all the rest of us love you is that you are always obedient to them.'[6] The same deep affection was shown by Epicurus to his parents and his brothers, and attention is called more than once to his gentle-

---

[1] Gnomolog. cod. Par. 1168, f. 115ʳ; C.B. *fr.* 43; U. 187.
[2] Seneca, *Ep.* 7. 11; U. 208.
[3] C.B. *fr.* 32; D.L. x. 5.
[4] C.B. *fr.* 34; D.L. x. 5.
[5] Plut. *contr. Ep. beat.* 15, 1097 e; C.B. *fr.* 40; U. 183.
[6] Pap. Herc. 176, col. 18; C.B. *fr.* 35; U. 176.

ness and generosity to his slaves. In religious matters in spite of his hatred of superstition and his own theological doctrines, he was devout in his attendance at the state-festivals, and it was in no mocking spirit that he wrote a treatise on 'Holiness'.

Almost the only feature, which reveals to us an unpleasant side in Epicurus' nature, is his violent opposition to other philosophers, which takes a very peculiar form. He claimed complete independence of them all and maintained that he was entirely self-taught. In consequence when in the course of his extant works he has occasion to refute their doctrines, he always does so without mentioning their names: when, on the other hand, he does name another philosopher, it is only to cover him with abuse, which increases in violence, the more Epicurus was really in his debt. Nausiphanes he not only referred to as 'The Mollusc', but called him 'Illiterate', 'Cheat', and even worse names. Democritus he nicknamed Lerocritus ('Nonsense'), while as for Leucippus, he denied that there ever was such a philosopher, a statement which modern critics have quaintly enough been inclined to take quite seriously.[1] Other great men fared no better at his hands: Aristotle was 'the Profligate', Heraclitus 'the Muddler' (there seems some justification in this case), Pyrrho 'ignorant' and 'uneducated'. It is certainly a serious weakness in a great man, but methods of controversy were perhaps not so delicate in the days of Athenian degeneracy, and it may have appeared to Epicurus necessary for his own dignity to preserve his independence even by these very undignified means. His pupils[2] were willing enough to admit his indebtedness at any rate to Democritus, but to Epicurus himself the suggestion seems to have been unbearable.

At the age of seventy he was seized with a painful disease, and after a fortnight's agony, borne with the greatest fortitude, he died urging his friends to remember the doctrines. In his will he bequeathed the house and garden to Hermarchus and his successors in the headship for the use of the faithful, made

---

[1] See Part I, Chap. II, p. 66.   [2] Plut. *adv Colot.* 3. 1108; U. 234 n.

provision for the celebration of the Epicurean festivals, and commended to the care of his trustees the son and daughter of Metrodorus, who had died before him. It is difficult to imagine anything but a gentle and noble influence upon the disciples, resulting from the character of such a master.

Epicurus is said to have been the most voluminous writer among the philosophers of antiquity and the rolls of his books amounted to three hundred. Of these books the titles have come down to us, and some of the many fragments which have remained embedded in later Greek and Latin authors may be assigned with certainty to definite works. The most important of his writings was undoubtedly the treatise on Nature (περὶ φύσεως), which extended to no less than thirty-seven books. Other titles which suggest works of importance are On Atoms and Void, On Choice and Avoidance, On the End (i.e. the moral purpose of life), The Canon (i.e. the principles of procedure: it is this work which is said to have been based on Nausiphanes' *Tripod*), On the Gods, On Holiness, On Lives (i.e. the different types of life which men choose or may choose for themselves), The Symposium, On Sight, On Touch, On Destiny (no doubt, an attack on Democritus' determinism), On 'Idols' (i.e. the images of vision), On Music, On Justice and the other Virtues, On Kingship. His biographer tells us that he used 'ordinary language' to set out his theories and that his style was 'clear'. Any one who has attempted to study the *Letter to Herodotus* or the *Principal Doctrines* will be inclined to dispute this statement, and to join rather in the censure of Aristophanes the Alexandrian critic, who complained that there was too much 'peculiarity' in Epicurus' style.[1] The fact is probably that Epicurus in endeavouring to carry out his own precept[2] that each word must convey a clear idea corresponding exactly to the thing spoken of, did not realize how technical his diction had in consequence become: the ideas were no doubt clear to himself, but the phraseology is very obscure to the uninitiated. The *Letter to Menoeceus*,

---

[1] D.L. x. 13 ἰδιωτάτη ἐστίν. [2] Ep. i. § 38.

which makes a more general appeal, is far clearer in style, and perhaps we should recognize an exoteric and an esoteric style in Epicurus' writings.

Of the extant sources of our knowledge of Epicureanism the most important are the three letters preserved by Diogenes Laertius purporting to be written by Epicurus himself to his three disciples Herodotus, Pythocles, and Menoeceus. The first deals with the main principles of the physical theory, the second with celestial phenomena, and the third with the moral theory. Of the authenticity of the first letter practically no suspicion has been entertained, and the third, though it is in a very different and far less crabbed style, is now generally admitted to be the work of Epicurus: the letter to Pythocles, which bears traces of compilation, was probably not written by Epicurus himself, but undoubtedly embodies correct Epicurean tradition. To these are added in Diogenes a collection of forty 'Principal Doctrines' (Κύριαι Δόξαι), whose genuineness is generally admitted. Of the other works of Epicurus himself scraps are of course preserved in quotation in many of the Greek and Latin writers: the indefatigable energy of Hermann Usener[1] has collected a vast quantity of these into a beautifully arranged and invaluable volume. To this collection must be added a series of eighty aphorisms[2] discovered in a Vatican MS. dealing almost entirely with the moral theory. Besides the work of Epicurus himself certain other writings of Epicureans have survived. The few fragments[3] which remain of Metrodorus do not afford any great assistance to the understanding of Epicurean doctrine. More useful material can be found in the great stone inscription[4] which was discovered at Oenoanda in Lycia in 1884, on which a certain Diogenes, an Epicurean, had set forth the main tenets of his creed in the hope of the conversion of the

---

[1] *Epicurea*: Leipzig, 1887.

[2] Published by C. Wotke in *Wiener Studien*, 1888, pp. 191 ff., with observations by Usener and Gomperz.

[3] These have been gathered together by A. Koerte (Teubner, 1890).

[4] Published in the Teubner series, ed. I. William (1907).

passer-by. The exploration of Herculaneum too at the end of the eighteenth century produced valuable Epicurean treasure in a large number of papyrus rolls, the greater part of which proved to be works by Philodemus, the Epicurean contemporary of Cicero and tutor of Piso, the consul of 58 B.C. The rolls have of course been badly charred and mutilated and the process of opening them was so difficult that more damage was done. It has however been possible to publish[1] many of them in a fragmentary state. Of Philodemus' works the most important are treatises on Rhetoric and on Signs, the latter a kind of Epicurean Logic, both of which show new interests in the school developed after the Master's death, and an essay on Piety,[2] which in spite of its very mutilated condition is of considerable use in helping us to reconstruct the Epicurean theology. But by far the most valuable Epicurean document is of course the great poem of Lucretius. That for all his poetic imagination and anti-religious fervour, which at times carry him away from the immediate exposition of the system, he yet was faithful to the main doctrines of his master, has always been believed; but it has been left to modern scholarship,[3] by careful comparison and continuous research, to reveal the extraordinary accuracy and insight with which he has expressed even in minutest detail the ideas and even the phraseology of Epicurus. It may be taken as certain that he had always before him a text of one of his master's works (probably the 'Greater Epitome'[4]), and although there may be places where

[1] *Volumina Herculanensia*: published from 1861 onwards in Naples. Gomperz in his *Herculanische Studien* (1865) edited the treatises on Signs and on Piety, and treated of others in magazine articles. W. Scott (*Fragmenta Herculanensia*, 1885) has edited considerable portions of the pencil tracings made at the time of the discoveries and deposited in the Bodleian Library.

[2] ed. Gomperz, 1866. The remains of several of the works of Philodemus have been published in the Teubner texts: περὶ οἰκονομίας, ed. C. Jensen, 1906; περὶ κακιῶν, lib. x, ed. C. Jonson, 1911; περὶ μουσικῆς, ed. I. Kemke, 1884; περὶ τοῦ καθ᾿ Ὅμηρον ἀγαθοῦ βασιλέως, ed. A. Olivieri, 1909; περὶ παρρησίας, ed. A. Olivieri, 1914; *Volumina Rhetorica*, ed. S. Sudhaus, 1892, 1895, 1896; περὶ ὀργῆς ed. C. Wilke, 1914.

[3] The greatest debt is due to Munro, Woltjer, Tohte, Brieger, and above all to Giussani.   [4] See Giussani, *Studii Lucreziani*, pp. 1–20.

he has not fully comprehended its meaning, it is exceedingly improbable that he has at any point introduced notions or developments of his own.

Besides the writings of Epicureans, we gain also much useful information from their critics. Cicero in the *de Finibus* criticizes the moral theory and in the *de Natura Deorum* the theology of Epicurus. His manifest ·contempt for Epicureanism and his haste in writing led him often to be content with a careless paraphrase of his original, and in difficult places, where he was apparently unable to understand it, he was satisfied with a verbal reproduction. He is therefore most useful as giving confirmatory evidence of what we otherwise know, but in the few crucial places on which we have to rely on his unsupported authority, especially in regard to certain obscure problems in Epicurus' theology, he proves a very uncertain guide. Plutarch attacked Epicureanism in two works, 'Against Colotes', a criticism of an essay in which the disciple of Epicurus had attempted to show that life was impossible under any other philosophical theory, and a dialogue intended to prove 'that a Happy Life is not possible according to Epicurus' doctrine'. Both these are of value for the consideration of the moral theory, especially as Plutarch is careful, wherever it is possible, to quote Epicurus' own words. Seneca in many of his writings, especially in the Moral Letters, frequently cites Epicurus' doctrines and often with approval: he is more accurate in his translations than Cicero, but his citations are almost entirely confined to the ethical side of the system. Of the other authors who help us at all considerably the principal are Sextus Empiricus, who described Epicurean doctrines at some length in his work *Adversus Mathematicos*, Stobaeus, a Byzantine scholar of the sixth century A.D., who besides compiling a Florilegium containing many of Epicurus' sayings, was the original author of the 'Dogmas of the Philosophers' popularly attributed to Plutarch, and Athenaeus, whose 'Deipnosophistae' has many occasional citations and allusions. No other author contains anything like a continuous account of Epicureanism or any part of it, but allusions and references have been collected by Usener from many other sources.

The modern critic of Epicurus must use as the basis of his work the three letters and the *Principal Doctrines* in Diogenes and the *de Rerum Natura*: these he must compare and use to supplement one another, filling in gaps and obtaining support or criticism from the other sources. The work has usually been done, especially in England, in a rather eclectic spirit, striking ideas being taken from different places and put together without much thought of the underlying connexion. The result is a confirmation of the popular idea that Epicurus was a loose thinker and his philosophy a patchwork. It is the object of the following account of his system to attempt to knit together its various parts more closely. This may be done without any violent distortion or forced interpretation of our authorities, and the more carefully Epicurus is examined with this intention, the more clear will it become that the different portions of his theory are not merely in themselves consistent pieces of work, but are all alike founded directly on the one fundamental principle, from which he started, of the infallibility of sensation.

II

CANONICE

IN dealing with Democritus and the earlier philosophers it was convenient to treat last of their metaphysic or theory of knowledge and to regard it as a deduction from their psychology and theory of sensation, by which it is inevitably in great measure conditioned. For the discussion of the system of Epicurus it will be better to reverse the order of procedure; not that his Canonice, as he called it, is any less dependent on his theory of sensation or his account of the soul, but partly because he has himself[1] placed it at the outset of the extant summary of his physical system, and still more because it supplies the one central principle of his philosophy on which all the rest hangs. It is indeed this single principle which gives to Epicurus' system, with all its weaknesses and blemishes, a far greater organic unity than the theories of his Atomic predecessors, and the failure to recognize its importance as the keystone of the whole has led many of his critics, both ancient and modern, to underestimate the philosophic value of Epicureanism. In order to discuss this principle and its consequences at this stage, it will be necessary, since the whole system is very closely interrelated in its parts, to anticipate to some extent the conclusions of later sections, especially those dealing with the Soul, the Gods, and the Moral Theory: similarly in those sections the ground of the Canonice will in part have to be trodden again. But it is fortunately possible to examine it now without discussing disputed points of the psychology, though the later details will throw fresh light upon it.[2]

[1] Ep. i, §§ 37, 38.

[2] A recent writer (F. Merbach, *De Epicuri Canonica,* 1909) has indeed maintained that the Canonice is quite independent of the Epicurean psychology and that it is expressed and thought out in language and ideas, which are non-materialistic: so also Joyau, *Épicure,* p. 78. This would, if true, be a serious charge of inconsistency against Epicurus, but (1) there is no real difficulty, except such as must inevitably attach to a materialist system, in reconciling the

Epicurus' own primary interest lay in his moral theory. The decay of political life, the general decline of activity in thought and literature, the weakening of the moral and intellectual value of the old religious ideas all pointed in the same direction: a moral guide for the individual life was the first demand made of a new philosophy. He therefore came forward not as a teacher of science, the successor of the Ionian philosophers, nor as a great abstract thinker with an idealist system such as that of Plato, but primarily as a preacher with a Gospel of life—the Gospel of peace both of body and mind. 'Philosophy', he proclaimed,[1] 'was a practical activity intended by means of speech and reasoning to secure a happy life.' Yet even for the purpose of that 'happy life' some knowledge both of external nature and of the workings of man's mind and the relations between them was essential, such knowledge at any rate of the nature and laws of the physical world as would save men from the two great terrors which might disturb their lives,[2] the dread of the arbitrary interference of divine beings in the world and the fear of the punishment of the soul after death. Moreover he believed that the investigation of the phenomena of the physical world itself constituted the natural pleasure of the intellect ($\delta\iota\acute{\alpha}\nu o\iota\alpha$),[3] and, since it brought with it little or no attendant pain, it was characteristically a 'pure' pleasure: he was therefore led himself to make such inquiry his supreme mental interest and to recommend the more advanced of his pupils to imitate him.

But of what nature was this inquiry to be? On what basis was it to rest and how should it be conducted? Epicurus desired above all things to be the teacher of the 'plain man'. His moral ideal was to be one attainable by all, and his

Canonice with the psychology, (2) all other serious modern critics have taken the opposite view, (3) Merbach's only proof (p. 11) appears to be that Epicurus treats of it before dealing with psychology—which only shows that in a closely woven system, wherever you begin, you must assume something to be proved hereafter.

[1] Sext. adv. Math. xi. 169; U. 219.
[2] Ep. i, §§ 78–82; Ep. iii, §§ 123–7; K. Δ. i, ii, &c.: see Chap. X, p. 502.
[3] Ep. i, § 78: see Chap. X, p. 504.

physical system similarly must be grounded on the common-sense of the average man: it should be intelligible to any one who would take the trouble to learn its principles. From this followed immediately two important consequences: firstly a disbelief in the necessity or value of education external or preliminary to philosophy and in the second place a profound distrust of Logic, or abstract rules of thought, which tended to lead the mind away from the real world to remote and unsubstantial abstractions.

In both these respects Epicurus found himself in opposition to the current schools of thought. Plato had demanded from his disciples a long course of training in the ancillary sciences before they might enter upon 'dialectic': Aristotle had given his followers a comprehensive survey of human knowledge and thought: Democritus himself had ranged freely over a vast field of intellectual interests. But Epicurus would have none of this: 'Blest youth,'[1] he said, addressing his pupil Pythocles, 'set sail in your bark and flee from every form of culture'. His anathema extended to almost all recognized branches of education. For the older training in literature he had a profound contempt: 'for literary problems and the linguistic researches of critics he would not even allow occasion over the wine'.[2] Nor did he believe in the rhetorical training of the sophists either as a useful education in itself or as a preparation for philosophical thought:[3] it produces a certain 'gracefulness of diction'[4] (εὐμορφία), but is a 'base artifice',[5] and only of value for that public life, which the true disciple will avoid. Mathematics[6] fared no better at his hands: it was not likely that one who held that area and matter were alike a succession of discrete *minima*[7] should have sympathy with the abstract conceptions of the mathematicians. For Epicurus it was enough that

[1] D.L. x. 6; *fr.* 33.   [2] Plut. *contr. Ep. beat.* 13, 1095; U. 5.

[3] It is interesting to find Philodemus, Cicero's contemporary, trying to introduce Rhetoric into Epicureanism.

[4] Philodemus, *de Rhet.*; V.H.² iv. 93; U. 50.

[5] κακοτεχνία, *Amm. Marc.* xxx. 4. 3; U. 51.

[6] Plut., op. cit., 11, and other references in U. 229 a.

[7] Ep. i, §§ 57, 58.

a disciple should come to him knowing his letters.[1] His contempt for Logic is equally marked: he despised 'dialectic as misleading',[2] and later critics are fond of making this contempt a charge against him. Plutarch[3] complained that Epicurus did not even know that the syllogism consists of three propositions, and Cicero[4] laments in the same strain, 'he abolishes definitions, he has no teaching about division and distribution, he does not tell how reasoning is conducted or brought to conclusions, he does not show by what means sophisms may be exposed, and ambiguities resolved'. That Cicero's charge is somewhat exaggerated will become clear from the examination of the Canonice; for though Epicurus was precluded by his fundamental point of view from any belief in the rules of abstract thought, he yet laid down rules of procedure, which played in his system the part which Logic holds in others.[5] But there can be no doubt as to his general attitude, and for it there are two strong causes. In the first place all operations of the mind were to Epicurus mere physical movements of the atoms: there could then be no separate department of inquiry into the laws of these movements, at the best such inquiry could only be a subordinate part of physics. And in the second, his fundamental and universal materialism made Logic a meaningless pursuit: the 'real' in the sense of the material was the sole existence: thought divorced from the content of reality was an object not of philosophical interest, but of the deepest suspicion. The only purpose which he could have in view in establishing rules of procedure was to keep thought always in the closest and most immediate relation with reality. The sole method of investigation was organized observation and inference from analogy.

It was such practical rules for investigation that Epicurus

---

[1] Sext. *adv. Math.* i. 49; U. 22.   [2] D.L. x. 31.
[3] Aul. Gell. ii. 8.   [4] *de Fin.* i. 7. 22; U. 243.
[5] F. Thomas (*de Epicuri Canonica*, 1889) is at pains to show that Epicurus in practice recognized the procedure of other Logical systems and had ideas corresponding to all the leading notions of Logic: but such an attempt is really contrary to the whole genius of Epicureanism.

set out to establish in his 'Canon'.[1] That work has unfortunately perished and the extant references to it are scanty. But enough has survived in the introductory section of the letter to Herodotus,[2] in a discussion later on of truth and error,[3] and in certain of the *Principal Doctrines*[4] to make it possible to recover its general content. The 'Canonice' or 'Canonicon', as this body of rules was called, dealt primarily with the criteria of truth and laid down principles of observation and inference, which are tacitly assumed throughout the system. Epicurus again and again warns his disciples of the practical necessity for such observation, and it is a fine testimony to the permanence of the Epicurean tradition that Lucretius, even though his explicit references to the Canonice are but few and casual, yet observes it in practice as scrupulously as his Master.

The primary necessity for a philosophical system is obviously an understanding as to the sources of our knowledge. The ancient world recognized always on the one hand a cognizant mind, on the other a real world of things: the question raised was as to the relation or communication between them. 'No one (in antiquity) ever challenged the existence of a real world of things lying behind the phenomena of which we are conscious:'[5] but philosophers asked how we obtain our knowledge of this world. Is it by the evidence of the senses or by reason or by both? Epicurus' predecessors[6] in physical speculation had raised this question and given varying answers; more or less sceptical according as their theories were related to ordinary experience. Democritus,[7] as has been seen, had reached a semi-sceptical position: thought about the ultimate realities, the atoms and space, was alone true, and sense-perception could be regarded as containing truth in so far as it supplied information as to

---

[1] 'The Canonicon', says Diogenes, x. 30, 'gives the method of approach to the system' ἐφόδους ἐπὶ τὴν πραγματείαν ἔχει. The title was no doubt suggested by Democritus' work περὶ λογικῶν Κανών.

[2] §§ 37, 38.   [3] §§ 50–2.   [4] Especially xxii–xxiv.

[5] R. D. Hicks, *Stoic and Epicurean*, p. 312.

[6] See Part I, Chap. I, § 4, pp. 58 ff.

[7] See Part I, Chap. III, § 8, pp. 177–86.

these and their primary qualities of size and shape: the 'secondary qualities' of compound things were merely 'experiences of sensation' and therefore 'conventional'. Epicurus made an emphatic return to the view of common sense: if his system was to be intelligible to the ordinary mind, he must start from its normal presumptions. As the root-axiom of all inquiry he affirms the truth or reality—for to him they are identical—of the external world as known to perception: 'Epicurus said that all objects of perception are true and real: for it was the same thing to call a thing true and to call it existing. True then means that which is as it is said to be, and false that which is not as it is said to be.'[1] This is clearly enough a statement of the common-sense attitude of the normal man; but it has several implications which must be distinguished. In the first place there is an external world of things which has existence, our perceptions are not self-created or subjective. In the second this world of external things is truly perceptible by us: things are as we perceive them: in other words truth and reality are identical: the world as communicated to us by perception is the world as it exists. But we express our sensations in words and in relation to such expression truth acquires a new meaning: truth in words is the exposition of what actually exists, that is, of what is actually perceived, falsehood in words is the expression of what does not actually exist, what is not perceived. Here in brief is the essential teaching of the whole Canonice with regard to the reality of the external world, our relation to it, and the use of language, and it is not difficult now to answer the question 'how is our knowledge of the external world acquired?' For the immediate corollary of the belief in the reality and truth of the perceptible world is the assertion that the one method of cognition of truth is sense-perception: sensation is the ultimate and only guarantee or criterion of truth. This is indeed the

---

[1] Sext. *adv. Math.* viii. 9; U. 244 ὁ δὲ Ἐπίκουρος τὰ μὲν αἰσθητὰ πάντα ἔλεγεν ἀληθῆ καὶ ὄντα· οὐ διήνεγκε γὰρ ἀληθές εἶναί τι λέγειν ἢ ὑπάρχον. . . . ἔστι, φησίν, ἀληθὲς τὸ οὕτως ἔχον ὡς λέγεται ἔχειν. καὶ ψεῦδός ἐστι, φησί, τὸ οὐχ οὕτως ἔχον ὡς λέγεται ἔχειν.

one fundamental principle of Epicurus' whole system and the Canon is only the exposition of its consequences and necessary deductions. That it involves considerable difficulties was clear to Epicurus himself and still clearer to some of his followers, but it will be best to follow out his own exposition of his principles: certain problems will arise incidentally and general criticism may be reserved.

It is at first sight surprising to find that Epicurus[1] stated in the Canon that there was not one but three 'criteria' of truth, the sensations, 'anticipations' (προλήψεις), and feelings.[2] But this is no contradiction of the fundamental principle, for it will be seen that of the other two criteria the one owes its validity to its immediate derivation from sensation, the other to the fact that it is in itself a special kind of sensation. It was therefore essential at first to establish the main position that sensation is the immediate and ultimately the sole guarantee of truth. For this position Epicurus does not for the most part consent to argue: it is the root-axiom of his whole philosophy. The Canons, as Plutarch[3] says ironically, 'fell from heaven', like the sacred shield of Mars, and their fundamental principle must be accepted as an inspiration or an irrefutable axiom. But Diogenes[4] in his abstract of the Canon suggests that Epicurus did not wholly refrain from argument and that he rested his contention mainly on two grounds. In the first place sensation, which is 'irrational'

---

[1] D.L. x. 31 ἐν τοίνυν τῷ Κανόνι λέγων ἐστὶν ὁ Ἐπίκουρος, κριτήρια τῆς ἀληθείας εἶναι τὰς αἰσθήσεις καὶ προλήψεις καὶ τὰ πάθη.

[2] It must be noted that αἴσθησις in the singular and plural is used in several slightly different, but closely allied, senses in Epicurus, (1) the act of sense-perception or sensation in general, (2) as here, the acts of sense-perception of the different sense-organs and the sensation of other parts of the body, (3) individual acts of sense-perception or sensation, (4) as Aetius notes, iv. 8. 2, p. 394D; U. 249, passively of the sense-impression so made (τὸ ἐπαίσθημα, ὅπερ ἐστὶ τὸ ἐνέργημα). A similar looseness will be noticed in the use of πρόληψις, but the context always makes the particular meaning clear.

[3] adv. Colot. 19, 1118; U. 34 οἱ διοπετεῖς κανόνες: cf. Cic. de Fin. i. 19. 63; U. 34 'quasi delapsa de coelo est ad cognitionem omnium regula'. In spite of the ironical tone of both passages there can be little doubt that Epicurus himself applied the epithet διοπετής to the Κανών.   [4] x. 31.

(ἄλογος), is therefore immediate and does not admit of question: it is its own guarantee. Secondly, there is no other criterion by which sensation could be checked. 'Every sensation is irrational and does not admit of memory: it is not set in motion by itself nor, when it is set in motion by something else, can it add to it or take from it. Nor is there anything which can refute the sensations. For a similar sensation cannot refute a similar because it is equivalent in validity: nor a dissimilar a dissimilar, for the objects of which they are the criteria are not the same. Nor again can reason, for all reason is dependent upon sensations: nor can one sensation refute another, for we attend to them all alike.' The two arguments are in reality complementary. If we analyse the fact of sensation, we see that it stands absolutely by itself: it is not connected with any other mental or bodily process.[1] It cannot spontaneously set itself in motion: we cannot see or hear without seeing or hearing something. It is wholly detached as an occurrence from any previous facts of the same nature; a fresh sensation involves no recollection of previous sensations. Nor has it a content which is due to other activities of the mind; thought may of course be subsequently concerned with it and must indeed be concerned, if it is to become in any sense an act of cognition, but it has no part in the mere sensation. It must then be accepted without question as a guarantee of its own truth. Conversely, if we ask from the outside, whether there is any means by which we can check the veracity of the sensation, the answer must be that it stands entirely alone. Another sensation of the same organ cannot contradict it: what we have seen one moment cannot be altered by what we see the next, for each sensation is of equal validity. Nor can it be checked by another sense: what we see cannot be affected by what we hear, for the two sensations are not *in pari materia*. Nor can reason act as a check, for reason in the Epicurean system, as will be seen more clearly later on, is but a combination of the results of sensations: it owes its own validity to sensations and cannot therefore be used as

[1] See Sext. Emp. *adv. Math.* vii. 203; U. 247.

a standard by which to correct them. It might be held that these arguments[1] only show that we have no means of proving sensations false: not that they are necessarily true. To this an Epicurean might reply that to Epicurus non-contradiction is equivalent to truth:[2] but the common-sense philosopher prefers to reply that sensation is a primary fact of our nature and our only means of relation with the external world, and we must therefore accept it. If we do not, the whole possibility of knowledge is overthrown. This is brought out clearly in the *Principal Doctrines*: 'if you fight against all sensations, you will have no standard by which to judge even those of them which you say are false':[3] nay more, 'if you reject any single sensation . . . you will confound all other sensations as well . . . so that you will reject every standard of judgement'.[4] In other words, scepticism of the validity of sensation destroys its own right of sceptical judgement. This position is well put in a famous passage of Lucretius:[5]

if any one thinks that nothing is known, he knows not whether that can be known either, since he admits that he knows nothing. . . . And were I to grant that he knows this too, yet would I ask this one question: since he has never before seen any truth in things, whence does he know what is knowing and not knowing each in turn, what thing has begotten the concept of the true and the false, what thing has proved that the doubtful differs from the certain? You will find that the concept of the true is begotten first from the senses, and that the senses cannot be gainsaid.

Unless we accept the truth of sensation, all knowledge is impossible and we live in an unknown world. For the apostle of common sense, such a belief is inconceivable, and we are driven from sheer lack of alternative to the assumption of the truth of sensation. That this root-principle involves great difficulties will become abundantly evident, but to it Epicurus clings with unswerving loyalty, and without it every part of his system must fall.[6]

[1] See Tohte, *Epikurs Kriterien der Wahrheit*, p. 8 *fin*.
[2] See below, p. 259.
[3] xxiii.   [4] xxiv.   [5] iv. 469–79.
[6] Diogenes (l.c.) adds a third argument, which is not of such cardinal

Sensation is thus the ultimate and only guarantee of reality, and on it all knowledge must depend: 'sensation is true' is the first and fundamental principle of the Canonice, and 'we must keep all our investigations in accord with the sensations'.[1] It is necessary then before proceeding farther to examine a little more closely what Epicurus meant by sensation and how he conceived its process.[2] In a material system it is clear that the only possible relation between one thing and another is that of contact: if one body is to affect another it must touch it. All sensation then, in its physical analysis, is an atomic movement[3] due to the touch resulting from the contact of material bodies. Hence the simplest form of sensation is the feeling of contact which we may experience in any portion of our body, when an external body impinges upon it, and to such contact all sensation must ultimately be reduced. But when we pass from the

importance as the other two and is more technical, implying an analysis of the process of sensation: καὶ τὸ τὰ ἐπαισθήματα δ' ὑφεστάναι πιστοῦται τὴν τῶν αἰσθήσεων ἀλήθειαν: ' the fact of apperception confirms the truth of the sensations'. Besides the mere sensation (in sight) of colour and form, we have also a superadded perception (ἐπαίσθημα) of what they represent, of the content of the sensation: now this perception is brought about on the Epicurean theory by the incidence into the eye of a series of similar ' idols ' (see Chap. VIII, pp. 418–421), no one of which owing to its fineness of texture is individually perceptible. But the net result of the series is an impression (φαντασία) of the external object. The argument then is that the fact of a continued series of similar ' idols', combining into one single impression, is evidence of the truth of the sensation—for it must mean the continued correspondence of the individual 'idols' to the object from which they come. If they changed and no single impression was produced, then there might reasonably be doubt of their truth: but what could not be guaranteed by a single 'idol' is guaranteed by the series of similar 'idols' (see Tohte, op. cit., p. 9). The argument is too technically Epicurean to have weight outside the system, and I strongly suspect that it was used primarily to support the truth of the images of the gods seen in sleep, &c. (see Chap. VIII, 414 ff.).

[1] Ep. i, § 38 κατὰ τὰς αἰσθήσεις δεῖ πάντα τηρεῖν.

[2] The full examination of the process and its implications from the physical point of view must be reserved till the discussion of Epicurus' psychology (see Chap. VIII, where references will be found), but we can at this point form a general notion sufficient to explain the Canonice, which cannot be rightly understood without at least the main outlines of the sensational theory.

[3] See Lucr. ii. 434 ff.

simple sensation of touch to the sensations of the other four senses, this contact assumes more complex and less immediate forms. In the case of taste we have indeed the immediate contact of the food or drink and the tongue and palate, and the special quality of the sensation is due to the relation between the atomic formation of the external object and the palate of the recipient. But in smell, hearing, and sight it is clear that there is no such immediate contact, and to secure contact at all, Epicurus was driven, like Democritus before him, to postulate 'effluences' passing from the object to the percipient. Smell is caused by the impact on the nostrils of an effluence of particles coming from 'deep within' the object and again causing a difference of sensational quality by difference of atomic formation. Sound similarly is due to the impact on the ear of material particles varying in shape and size emitted by the speaking person or the sounding object. Most complex of all—and most important, because it is at once the source of the majority of our knowledge of the external world and therefore the assumed ground of the greater part of Epicurus' discussion—is the sensation of sight. This is not the place for a full examination of the famous theory of 'idols',[1] but certain points in it are essential for the understanding of the Canonice. All bodies are constantly throwing off a succession of thin films or 'idols', exactly like in form and colour to themselves, and these by impinging upon the eye form the same indirect contact between object and percipient as is established in the case of smell and hearing. But there is this important difference: whereas each individual smell- or sound-particle can be directly perceived by nostril or ear, so subtle are the 'idols' in texture that they cannot be individually perceived, but only in the mass of their quick succession. What we actually perceive is not the single 'idols', but the image (φαντασία) produced by their agglomeration in the eye. Now when this image is of an object close at hand, it is perfectly 'clear' (ἐναργής): there is no blurring of outline, no uncertainty as to shape or colour. 'A thing is clear, when we perceive all

[1] See Chap. VIII, pp. 406–411.

its marks and qualities at once, or at least it is within our power to do so.'[1] And it is this 'clear image' which it is the object of all scientific inquiry to obtain. How can this be done? In some cases, that, for instance, of a very close sight or sound, it is, as it were, forced upon us. Yet even so, it never has its true value, unless we direct (ἐπιβάλλειν) our senses upon it. Sights and sounds and scents may be presented clearly to us, but if our senses are not 'attending', the clear impression will not be made: we must not merely 'see' but 'look'. It is the 'clear image' obtained by the 'attention of the senses' (ἐπιβολή τῶν αἰσθητηρίων)[2] which alone is of scientific value. When we are dealing with distant objects, still more with things imperceptible to the senses, this 'clear image' may be difficult to obtain, and the lack of it may often, as will be seen later, lead us into error, but it alone is finally satisfactory and certain. All 'images' perceived by the sight are true, because they correspond to an external reality, but it is only the 'clear image' obtained by 'apprehension of the senses' which can be used as the basis of scientific knowledge.[3] This point in the Epicurean Canon has not, I think, been sufficiently emphasized, and its importance in the later developments is very great.

But what is the content of this sensation? Is it of itself

---

[1] Merbach, op. cit., p. 18, who has done much to bring out the importance of the ἐνάργημα in Epicurus' theory: for ἐναργής, see Ep. iii. 123; D.L. x. 33, ἐνάργεια, Ep. i, §§ 48, 52, 71, 82; K. Δ. xxii.; and ἐνάργημα, Ep. i, § 72; ii. 91, 93, 96.

[2] This 'apprehension of the senses' is referred to in Ep. i, § 50 (ἐπιβλητικῶς . . . τοῖς αἰσθητηρίοις), and implied in §§ 38, 51, 62. For a fuller discussion, see Chap.VIII, and Appendix III on ἐπιβολὴ τῆς διανοίας. Also Tohte, op. cit., p. 21, and Merbach, op. cit., pp. 31 ff. The idea undoubtedly came to Epicurus from Empedocles.

[3] Ep. i, § 50 ἦν ἂν λάβωμεν φαντασίαν ἐπιβλητικῶς τῇ διανοίᾳ ἢ τοῖς αἰσθητηρίοις . . . μορφή ἐστιν αὕτη τοῦ στερεμνίου, γινομένη κατὰ τὸ ἑξῆς πύκνωμα ἢ ἐγκατάλειμμα τοῦ εἰδώλου. Epicurus appears to have said that 'no one image or sensation was clearer (ἐναργεστέρα) than another ' (Plut. adv. Colot. 25; U. 252). This is true of the passive sensation itself, but the right interpretation of it all depends on the attention of the senses and the nearness of the object (τὸ παρὸν ἤδη κατὰ τὴν αἴσθησιν, K.Δ. xxiv), see pp. 253–7.

significant, and can even the 'clear image' alone be self-sufficing for the purposes of science? Clearly not, for the sensation itself (it is convenient still to take the complex case of sight as the type) is only an isolated vision of a certain shape and colour.[1] Such an isolated sensation is meaningless and can have no value for philosophy, the ordered knowledge of the world, or even for the purposes of practical life, unless it can be correlated with other sensations. A mere coloured shape is nothing to us, unless we can know 'what it is': we must be able to compare the new image with previous experience and to identify it with or distinguish it from other things which we already know. In other words the process of sensation, if it is to be a perception, must be completed by cognition: the act of the sense-organs must be followed by an act of the mind. How can this be? what is it that enables the mind on the occurrence of a sense-perception to say this is, or is not, such and such a thing, and what guarantee of truth have we in this new process? According to Epicurean psychology[2] the act of perception in the sense-organ stirs the particles of 'soul' in its neighbourhood and they communicate the movement to other soul-particles and so on till the movement reaches the mind (which is situated in the breast), and there creates a representation of the sense-image. The mind then by a spontaneous movement (δόξα), akin to the act of attention on the part of the senses, compares the new image with previously existing general conceptions and pronounces that 'this is, or is not, so-and-so'. Just as without cognition mere sensation is valueless, so the individual image is without significance apart from the general concept:[3] 'apart from the

---

[1] Sext. adv. Math. vii. 207; U. 247 οὐ γὰρ ὅλον ὁρᾶται τὸ στερέμνιον . . . ἀλλὰ τὸ χρῶμα τοῦ στερεμνίου.

[2] See Chap. VIII, p. 418. Some critics have thought that Epicurus supposed that the actual 'image', or the series of 'idols', passed into the mind, but this is unlikely: see p. 417.

[3] For the close connexion of image and opinion, or, as we should rather say, sensation and cognition, which are almost simultaneous and often hard to separate, see Sext. adv. Math. vii. 203; U. 247 δυοῖν ὄντων τῶν συζυγούντων ἀλλήλοις πραγμάτων, φαντασίας καὶ τῆς δόξης.

general concept no one can inquire or feel doubt or even hold an opinion, no, nor refute one'.[1] So far Epicurus' position does not seem to be peculiar: the acceptance of cognition as a necessary element in perception, and the admission of the impossibility of classification or even recognition without general conceptions are practically universal. It is necessary to ask how Epicurus conceived his general concepts, what was their origin and what their validity.

To return for a moment to psychology, the 'mind-image' aroused by the movements of the soul-particles started in their turn by the sensational motions of the sense-organs, does not immediately perish, but remains stored up in the mind, and may be, as it were, 'called up' for subsequent contemplation. Thus an act of memory is the momentary attention of the mind to an 'image' so preserved in itself, and a mental comparison is the apprehension by the mind of two or more such images side by side. But this is not all, for when as the result of many individual perceptions of objects of the same class, a series of similar images, is, as it were, heaped one upon another in the mind, the result is a kind of 'composite photograph' of the genus or species: the dissimilarities of the individual images have disappeared, and that which is common to all is retained in what is in fact a 'general concept'. The combined 'images' of many horses, seen in sense-perception, has created in the mind the 'general concept' of 'horse'. To this 'general concept' Epicurus gives the name of 'anticipation' (πρόληψις): it is that which we have permanently in our mind to enable us to anticipate the general appearance of anything for which we are looking or wish to create, and to identify and distinguish the individual images of sense-perception when they are presented to us. 'Anticipations' then take their place as the second criterion of truth. They owe their validity to the fact that, although they are not themselves directly sensations, they are immediately built up of sensations: our 'anticipation' of horse is simply the aggregate—or perhaps one should rather say the average—of a number of individual sensations of

[1] Epicurus apud Clem. Alex. *Strom.* ii. 4. 157, 44; U. 255.

horses. The 'anticipation' is not itself 'true' for it does not correspond to or issue from any one external existence, but it is a 'clear vision' and as such a test of truth:[1] that which is the common element in a number of 'images' of 'horse' must itself constitute a clear general 'image' of 'horse', and to it may be referred as a certain test the subsequent 'images' presented to us in sense-perception.

This account of the 'anticipations' is not to be found explicitly stated in any Epicurean source, but it is generally adopted by modern writers[2] and is strongly supported by such testimony as is available. Three pieces of evidence may be cited which all tend to the same conclusion from different points of view. Diogenes' discussion[3] of 'anticipation' looks as if it were compiled from several different sources, but there is nothing in it inconsistent either with itself or with the explanation given above. It is worth quoting at length because of the strong support afforded by his illustrations:

the 'anticipation' they speak of as an apprehension or right opinion or thought or a general idea stored within the mind, that is to say a recollection of what has often been presented from without, as for instance, 'such and such a thing is a man'; for the moment the word 'man' is spoken, by means of the 'anticipation' his form (τύπος) too is thought of (νοεῖται), as the senses give us the information (προηγουμένων). Therefore the first signification of every name is immediate and clear evidence (ἐναργές). And we could not look for the object of our search, unless we have first known it; for instance we ask 'is that standing yonder a horse or a cow?': to do this we must know by means of an 'anticipation' the shape of horse and of cow. Otherwise we could not have named them, unless we previously knew their appearance by means of an 'anticipation'. So the 'anticipations' are clear and immediate evidence.

---

[1] Merbach (p. 51) notices that Epicurus never speaks of προλήψεις as ἀληθεῖς, but as ἐναργεῖς.

[2] e.g. Tohte (op. cit.), pp. 15 sq.; Brieger, *Epikurs Lehre von der Seele*, p. 11; Giussani, *Stud. Lucr.*, p. 174. For other views of πρόληψις see Appendix II.

[3] x. 33. The definition runs: τὴν δὲ πρόληψιν λέγουσιν οἱονεὶ κατάληψιν ἢ δόξαν ὀρθὴν ἢ ἔννοιαν ἢ καθολικὴν νόησιν ἐναποκειμένην, τουτέστι μνήμην τοῦ πολλάκις ἔξωθεν φανέντος, οἷον τὸ Τοιοῦτόν ἐστιν ἄνθρωπος.

Here we have the main points clearly put. The 'anticipation' is the general concept, it is derived from frequently repeated sense-perceptions and it is 'clear'. It is the fundamental necessity for all inquiry and it is intimately connected with the naming of things: the name must represent the clear concept to which it is attached. Equally significant is a notable quotation from Epicurus himself preserved in a late writer:[1] 'anticipation he defines as an act of attention to something clear or to the clear concept of the thing'. Here, with a slight shift of the point of view, the general concept in the mind is a clear image, which the mind grasps in the act of anticipation: we have the active process instead of the more usual passive notion, but once more the general concept is 'clear' and therefore a test of truth. Finally, to bring out another side of the idea of 'anticipation', we have two passages in Lucretius, where he argues that it is impossible to set to work to make a thing unless you have already in your mind an 'anticipation' (*notities*) of it, derived from previous experience. 'How could the gods have made a world, he asks, unless they had already an anticipation of it due to a previous pattern?'[2] 'how could any man have deliberately invented speech, unless he had a pattern in the speech of men around him?'[3] Here we have the general concept as the condition of action as well as of knowledge.

Thanks then to the concepts or 'anticipations' the act of sense-perception is completed by cognition: we are not left with a series of detached unmeaning sensations, but are enabled to correlate them, to identify and distinguish. Our

---

[1] Clem. Alex. *Strom*. ii. 4. 157; U. 255 πρόληψιν δὲ ἀποδίδωσιν ἐπιβολὴν ἐπί τι ἐναργὲς καὶ ἐπὶ τὴν ἐναργῆ τοῦ πράγματος ἐπίνοιαν. It must be noted that πρόληψις is here used definitely in the active sense of the mental operation of 'anticipation'. It has a similar active force in the first two instances in the previously quoted passage of Diogenes, but normally (as in the third instance above) it has especially in the plural the passive meaning of the general concept which is the means of anticipation. The same variation of meaning in the use of αἴσθησις has already been noted, and it is also latent in ἐπιβολὴ τῆς διανοίας (see Appendix III). Note, too, that πρόληψις itself is here an ἐπιβολή, which as usual is connected with an ἐναργές.

[2] v. 181–6. [3] v. 1046–9.

experience becomes a connected whole and on it we can
base an ordered world built up by scientific inquiry. The
concepts are themselves infallible as tests of truth, just as are
the individual sensations: error arises, as will be seen later,
not through any want of 'clearness' in the concepts, but
through the mental operation of opinion (δόξα) which may
make false comparisons, wrongly assigning sensations to
concepts, and so producing false identifications and distinctions. It is clear then that the concept has a large part
to play in the whole realm of thought (ἐπίνοια): for not only is
it concerned in the identification of individual sensations,
but in those combinations of ideas which constitute abstract
thought—or, as Epicurus would rather have put it, thought
about the invisible (ἄδηλα). Moreover it is also closely connected with the whole problem of language: a concept is not
fully known until it is named, until it has a label by which it
may be at once called into prominence in the mind. Thus the
growth of language consists in the application of names to
concepts, and the first requisite of philosophical thought is to
be sure that names represent clear concepts. Both these
questions of thought and language in their relation to concepts will become prominent later on in the Canonice: for
the present the 'anticipations' must be regarded primarily
as the infallible means, if only opinion makes no false combinations, of interpreting sensations in the act of cognition.
The second criterion of truth completes the work of the first,
and owes its validity to its derivation from it.

The third criterion of truth is feeling (πάθος).[1] Its understanding is happily less beset with difficulties than that of
the second, but its nature must be clearly defined, for, as
will be seen, one whole branch of Epicurus' philosophy, and
that not the least important, rests on it. 'Feeling' is an
immediate sensation, but it acts in its own special field and
is a test of its own peculiar truth. In a wide sense[2] of course
all sensation is 'feeling' (πάθος), for in every case of sensation,
in the higher sense-perceptions as well as in the most

---

[1] D.L. x. 31.

[2] Tohte (op. cit., p. 18) drew attention to this wider meaning.

rudimentary cases of touch, we are 'acted upon' (πάσχειν) and 'feel' the sensation. So in the letter to Herodotus Epicurus speaks of the 'feeling of hearing'[1] and similarly of the 'feeling'[2] which smell produces. But 'feeling' as a 'criterion' of truth is used in a narrower and restricted sense, not of sensation itself, but of its invariable accompaniment. For in intimate and necessary connexion with every sensation we have also a 'feeling' of something 'akin' or 'alien' to us,[3] a sensation of the agreeable or disagreeable, in other words of pleasure or pain. This is true of all sensations from the most elementary sense of touch due to the impingement of an external body on our body up to the most complicated perception of sight: in all cases our sensation not merely informs us of the presence of something external to ourselves (αἴσθησις) but brings with it the sense of pleasure or pain (πάθος): 'the feelings are two, pleasure and pain, which occur to every living creature'.[4] It might be objected by a critic of Epicureanism that feelings are really three, for in a large number of our sensations we are not conscious of either positive pleasure or positive pain, but of a negative or indifferent state. But for Epicurus there were only two 'feelings', for absence of pain[5] is in itself pleasure, indeed in his ultimate analysis the truest pleasure: every sensation must in this sense either be accompanied by pleasure or by pain, for it is either associated or not associated with pain. The validity then of 'feeling' as a criterion cannot be questioned nor need any difficulty be raised as to its origin: for it has not a derivative value, like the 'anticipation', but is itself, like sensation, immediate and therefore a guarantee of its own certainty. But of what kind of truth is it a test? Is it a test of the reality of an external object or of its nature? No doubt

[1] Ep. i, § 52 ἀκουστικὸν πάθος.
[2] § 53. In the same way Sext. adv. Math. vii. 203; U. 247, speaks of τῶν φαντασιῶν, παθῶν περὶ ἡμᾶς οὐσῶν, which is perhaps going farther than Epicurus would himself have gone.
[3] D.L. x. 34 τὴν μὲν οἰκεῖον τὴν δὲ ἀλλότριον.
[4] D.L. l.c. πάθη δὲ λέγουσιν εἶναι δύο, ἡδονὴν καὶ ἀλγηδόνα, ἱστάμενα περὶ πᾶν ζῷον.
[5] Cf. K.Δ. iii, &c.

in part it is: our feeling of pain, if we touch a burning coal, is in part evidence of the existence of the coal and of its present condition. But so far it is merely a form of 'sensation' [1] and is no independent criterion of truth. 'Feeling', as such, is not concerned with knowledge but with morals: it does not inform us of the existence of things or their physical nature, but whether they are good or bad: for that which is pleasurable to us is invariably that which we seek, in other words, good, that which is painful to us we avoid, it is bad. In short, 'feeling' plays the same part in Epicurean Ethics, which sensation does in his physical theory: it is the basis from which everything must start and the standard to which all must be referred. It is the test of rightness in morals, that is, of rightness in action, just as sensation is the test of truth in knowledge, that is, of the rightness of apprehension. With the difficulties which are involved in this theory at its root, and the modifications which Epicurus found necessary in its working out, we are not now concerned.[2] The third criterion of truth takes its place beside sensation; it is of equal validity, for it is a part of sensation, and is the test of its own peculiar truth, of the goodness or badness which is to be judged immediately by pleasure or pain. Thus the ethical theory of Epicurus does not stand by itself as an independent or detached adjunct to the physical theory, but rests upon the same fundamental principle, the immediate and necessary validity of sensation.

Sensation then together with its derivative 'anticipation' and its necessary accompaniment, feeling, acting in the special field of conduct, are the three criteria of truth which, as Diogenes [3] informs us, Epicurus admitted in 'the Canon'. But in at least one passage [4] of the letter to Herodotus and in the *Principal Doctrines* there is apparently associated with them a fourth test of truth, which was explicitly raised by

---

[1] Merbach (op. cit., p. 16), who deals very summarily with πάθος, has fallen into the error of supposing that the truth which πάθος attests is the existence of external things: the passage which he quotes in support (Sext. *adv. Math.* vii. 203) ought in itself to have shown him his mistake.

[2] See Chap. X, pp. 485–7.   [3] x. 31.   [4] § 38; K. Δ. xxiv.

subsequent Epicureans [1] to the position of a criterion. A full discussion of the great difficulties which surround the understanding of the 'apprehension of the mind' (ἐπιβολή τῆς διανοίας) must be reserved till the Epicurean psychology [2] has been examined in detail. But it is possible here to indicate what was its probable function as a criterion. Epicurus held —and the idea is very characteristic of his thought—that there are certain concrete existences which throw off 'idols' like all other material things, but 'idols' so subtle that they cannot be perceived, even when accumulated as 'images', by the comparatively coarse mechanism of the senses. Nevertheless they can penetrate through the pores of the body to the mind and there cause a disturbance of the mind-atoms which produces an immediate mental apprehension of the image. Yet even then, so fine is the texture of the 'idols' that the mind itself cannot apprehend them without an active 'attention' or 'act of apprehension', comparable to that with which the senses 'look' instead of passively seeing (ἐπιβολή): it is for this reason that such images are most frequently seen in sleep,[3] when the mind is not disturbed by other appearances or thoughts. Of such objects the most conspicuous examples are the divine persons of the gods: [4] their bodies are constantly throwing off a succession of such fine images which come to us and immediately move the atoms of the mind. Here then we have a kind of direct mental sensation, analogous to sense-perception, and produced in the same manner by means of 'idols': the sole difference being that the perception is made immediately by the mind without the intervention of the senses. The fourth criterion [5] would thus owe its validity to the fact that it is in itself a very

---

[1] D.L. x. 31. [2] See Chap. VIII and Appendix III.

[3] Cf. Lucr. v. 1171.

[4] Lucr. v. 1175–6; Cic. de Nat. Deorum. i. 19. 49: see Chap. IX.

[5] In one passage of the Letter to Herodotus (§ 62) we have apparently an instance in which ἐπιβολὴ τῆς διανοίας is not concerned with such immediate perception by the mind, but with a reasoned conclusion as to the ultimate realities of the atomic world. Its importance is discussed in Chap. VIII, pp. 422–5, and in Appendix III. Here it may for the time be neglected.

specialized form of sensation. Why Epicurus omitted reference to the fourth criterion in the Canon, but assumed its
existence in the First Letter and the *Principal Doctrines*,
while even then it was left to 'the Epicureans' to include it
with the other criteria, it is hard to say. It may be that to
Epicurus when he wrote 'the Canon' 'mental apprehension'
presented itself merely as a form of sensation, not explicitly
to be distinguished from it, that he made the distinction in
other places when he was thinking specially of these particular cases which could not fairly be classed with normal
sensations, and that the Epicureans, whose religious orthodoxy was much called in question, were forced in self-defence
to exalt the basis of their theology into a criterion of truth.
However this may be,[1] it is not hard to see how it could be
connected directly with the fundamental truth of sensation.

The examination of the subordinate criteria of truth has
shown that they are all in one way or another restatements
of the fundamental infallibility of sensation; 'feeling' and
(if it be a criterion) 'mental apprehension', because they are
but forms of sensation, 'anticipation', because it is in each
case an accumulation of or abstraction from sensations. The
whole Epicurean philosophy is thus based, as its founder
intended it to be, on the common-sense point of view that
'sensation is true': there is a world of existing external things
and our senses report to us truly about them. It is time to
go back a little and inquire into some of the difficulties which
this thesis involves: some of these were perceived by Epicurus himself and dealt with in the secondary principles
of the Canonice, some were raised by critics of the system
and attempts were made to meet them by the later Epicureans. It will be convenient to deal with them in connexion
with the various branches of inquiry which Epicurus saw
were necessary for a system of physical science.

All true experience, and in particular all scientific observation, must be built on the 'clear view' of the object near at
hand:[2] 'the clear view is the foundation and the first step in

---

[1] For another suggestion see Appendix III.

[2] *Κ.Δ.* xxiv τὸ παρὸν ἤδη κατὰ τὴν αἴσθησιν.

everything'.[1] But we are not always dealing with objects close at hand or indeed perceptible by the senses at all, and accordingly various difficulties arise, with which Epicurus has dealt in the subordinate principles of the Canonice. He groups the objects of inquiry under two heads, 'perceptible things' (πρόδηλα) of which we can obtain a clear view, and 'imperceptible things' (ἄδηλα) which he subdivides into celestial phenomena (μετέωρα), of which, though they are perceptible to the senses, a close view can never be obtained, and things wholly imperceptible in the strict sense, the ultimate facts of reality, the atoms and space, which can never be perceived by the senses but only apprehended by the operation of thought. It will be convenient to follow these divisions and to deal with the various problems as they arise.

The 'plain man', whose philosophy Epicurus wished to embody in his system, while maintaining in general the truth of his sensations, would probably be the first to argue that even in matters of everyday terrestrial experience, some of his sensations are, or at least seem to be, false, for they are not a correct report of the external realities from which they are derived. A square tower seen at a distance seems small and round,[2] an oar half in the water appears to be bent, I see so-and-so coming towards me and, when he comes nearer, he 'turns out' to be some one else: in all these instances the first sensation appears to be false. It was of course difficulties of this kind which had led earlier philosophers to their distrust of the senses. Now Epicurus saw clearly enough [3] that to admit the falsity of a single sensation would overthrow his whole system: for if one sensation is false, there is no reason that any should be true, for all have equal validity. How then can he meet these objections?

[1] Sext. *adv. Math.* vii. 216; U. 247 πάντων δὲ κρηπὶς καὶ θεμέλιος ἡ ἐνάργεια.

[2] These are instances quoted by Sext. Emp. (l.c.) and are undoubtedly the commonplaces of Epicurean tradition. The whole passage, which Usener gives in full, is of great value for this portion of the Canonice. Compare also D.L. x. 34 and Lucr. iv. 379–468, where other similar examples are given.

[3] *K.Δ.* xxiv.

His answer lies in the distinction already observed between the two elements in the process of sense-perception, the mere passive sensation in the sense-organs, and the act of cognition performed by the mind. The mental faculty of 'opinion' (δόξα), which performs the cognition by the assignment of the passive sensation to an 'anticipation' or general concept, is indeed allied to the infallible 'mental apprehension',[1] because it is in itself a kind of apprehension or mental attention, but it differs from it in that it is liable to error: it may make a false combination of sensation and 'anticipation'. Indeed it is a 'movement' which is, so to speak, ever on the alert, and eager to make its additions (προσδοξαζόμενα) to the data of sense, to put its interpretation on them before sufficient material has been supplied. The apparent falsity of our sense-perceptions is then due not to any falsity in the sensation, which is always true, but to the 'additions of opinion',[2] and it is the function of the philosopher to distinguish carefully on all occasions between these two elements: the additions of opinion must, as it were, be separated off and the pure sensation, the only criterion of truth, left, at any rate for the time, without interpretation. Take the case of the approaching man: all that we really saw was a man walking, indeed to be absolutely strict, we saw a certain shape with certain colouring moving in a certain direction: it was 'opinion' making a comparison of the sensation with the 'anticipation' already in the mind, which assigned it at once to the concept of 'so-and-so'. There was nothing false in the sensation, for it was 'irrational', it did not imply any interpretation of itself: the error lay in the false identifications made by opinion. In the case then of such distant views of external objects, we must regard our sensation as a 'thing awaiting confirmation' (προσμένον ἐπιμαρτυρήσεσθαι).[3] Opinion will indeed pronounce on it, for

---

[1] Ep. i, § 51 τὸ δὲ διημαρτημένον οὐκ ἂν ὑπῆρχεν, εἰ μὴ ἐλαμβάνομεν καὶ ἄλλην τινὰ κίνησιν ἐν ἡμῖν αὐτοῖς συνημμένην μὲν ⟨τῇ φανταστικῇ ἐπιβολῇ⟩, διάληψιν δὲ ἔχουσαν.

[2] Ep. i, § 50 τὸ διημαρτημένον ἐν τῷ προσδοξαζομένῳ ἀεί ἐστιν.

[3] προσμένον is used absolutely by Epicurus and his followers as a technical

it is irrepressible and will not leave an insignificant sensation as such and nothing more, but we must not accept the pronouncement of opinion until we have had the close view of the object near at hand: then 'if it is confirmed, it is true, if it is not confirmed, it is false'.[1] So far there seems no serious difficulty and a simple rule of the Canonice deals with the first set of problems—distant terrestrial objects. The first sensation no less than the second is true, 'for it stirs our senses',[2] but only the near view gives us the full information as to the nature of the external object, which is requisite for complete or scientific knowledge. 'Confirmation is the comprehension by means of the clear vision that the object of opinion is such as it was supposed to be.'[3] But the other instances mentioned above are not so easily disposed of: in the case of the distant tower and the oar seen through the water it is by no means so easy to say that the error lay in the 'additions of opinion'. The first sensations were of a round object and a bent object: the near view showed that the realities were square and straight respectively. In what sense can it be said that these first sensations are 'true': 'for that is true which is as it is said (or seen) to be?'[4] With this difficulty Epicurus himself—wisely enough perhaps—never deals very explicitly, but his answer may be extracted from the very interesting and curious passage in which he speaks of the size of the sun

term, e.g. Ep. i, § 38; Κ.Δ. xxiv. It is falsely interpreted by D.L. x. 34 as 'an act of waiting on our part', τὸ προσμεῖναι καὶ ἐγγὺς γενέσθαι τῷ πύργῳ καὶ μαθεῖν ὁποῖος ἐγγὺς φαίνεται. Steinhart was misled by this passage: see Tohte, op. cit., p. 14, n. 1. There can be no doubt of its real meaning and implied construction: see Ep. i, § 50 ⟨ἐπὶ τοῦ προσμένοντος⟩ ἐπιμαρτυρήσεσθαι—the addition being certain—and Κ.Δ. xxiv τὸ προσμένον ... τὴν ἐπιμαρτύρησιν.

[1] D.L. x. 34. It at first sight seems strange that Epicurus speaks always of οὐκ ἐπιμαρτύρησις in this context, and not ἀντιμαρτύρησις—but the latter word is reserved, as will be seen, for connexion with the ἄδηλα.

[2] D.L. x. 32 κινεῖ γάρ· τὸ δὲ μὴ ὂν οὐ κινεῖ in reference to the analogous case of dream visions: see Chap. VIII, p. 415.

[3] Sext. Emp. adv. Math. vii. 212 ἔστι δὲ ἐπιμαρτύρησις μὲν κατάληψις δι' ἐναργείας τοῦ τὸ δοξαζόμενον τοιοῦτον εἶναι ὁποῖόν ποτε ἐδοξάζετο.

[4] Sext. Emp. adv. Math. viii. 9; U. 244: see p. 237, n. 1.

and moon:[1] 'the size of sun and moon, he says, is for us
(κατὰ μὲν τὸ πρὸς ἡμᾶς) what it appears to be; and in reality it
is either ⟨slightly⟩ greater than what we see or slightly less
or the same size'. 'For us', can only imply, 'this is what the
sun and moon look like as seen from the distance which we
are from them.' Similarly then in the case of the tower: the
first sensation was true 'for us', it told us, that is, what a
square tower looks like at a distance, and it was a false
addition of the mind to infer that the tower is itself round.
So with the oar: the bent oar is what an oar in the water looks
like 'for us': we have no right to infer that it really is bent.
This is a poor way of saving the situation: for the 'truth' of
a sensation can mean nothing else than its correspondence
with the object which it represents. Either then the first
perception was false and did not truly represent the object,
or else the tower and the oar changed in the interval between
the two sensations and the objective permanence of the
external world is destroyed—which, as Epicurus would
himself say, is 'unthinkable' (ἀδιανόητον). However Epicurus
himself does not seem to have been conscious of the difficulty, and was not perhaps sufficiently attacked with regard
to it to cause him to elaborate a reply. But his followers did
not escape from the pressure of criticism, and, as Sextus
shows,[2] they took up two lines of defence. In the first place,
they argued that their opponents were demanding greater
accuracy in the sphere of sight than they would require in
the other senses. No one would say that hearing was false,
because what was really a loud noise appeared at a distance
soft. To this plea it might easily be replied that though
diminution in size by distance was not falsification, it was
another matter with apparent alteration of shape. The
second line of defence[3] put forward by the Epicureans is
more serious and far more important in its consequences.
The image of sensation, they argued, is true, because it
corresponds always to the 'idols' which reach the eye; but

---

[1] Ep. ii, § 91.   [2] adv. Math. vii. 206–9; U. 247.
[3] Ibid., § 209: cf. Plutarch, adv. Colot. 25, 1121; U. 252, who pushes
up the advantage gained by this admission with great effect.

these 'idols' in their transit from an object at a distance may be altered. The square 'idols' of the tower when they have a long interval to traverse have their corners knocked off and so create in our eye the sensation of a round object: the image we see is 'true' to them, but not necessarily to the object from which they come. This theory is of course a fatal admission and cuts at the very roots of the whole Epicurean system. For by the truth of a sensation Epicurus meant and could only mean its truth to the external object which it represented. If we have no guarantee of such correspondence, but are at the mercy of the accidents which may befall individual 'idols' in their transit, then the 'truth' of sensation is valueless not merely for scientific inquiry, but even for the most rudimentary requirements of practical life: 'there is an end to your "all sensations are true, and none are untrustworthy and false"'; [1] we shall indeed be 'moving about in worlds not realized'. But Epicurus must not be made responsible for the sins of his children. A modern critic cannot disguise the great difficulty which besets his fundamental principle even in the simplest of conditions, but Epicurus rested in the belief that he had fully disposed of it in the distinction between the 'clear vision' of near sensation and the possibly false additions of opinion. The first then of the subordinate principles of the Canonice will take shape thus: 'in the case of distant objects perceptible to the senses, suspend judgement, till you have examined them in the nearer view'. Epicurus' own interest lies not in the problem but in the process of verification on whose truth he insists emphatically: 'every image which we obtain by an act of apprehension (ἐπιβλητικῶς) on the part of the mind or of the sense-organs, whether of shape or of properties, this image is the shape ⟨or the properties⟩ of the concrete object (τοῦ στερεμνίου)'.[2]

The second department of inquiry—or perhaps more correctly the first subdivision of the department of the 'imperceptible' (ἄδηλα)—is concerned with things perceptible

---

[1] Plut. l.c. σοὶ δὲ οἴχεται τὸ πάσας ὑπάρχειν ἀληθεῖς, ἄπιστον δὲ καὶ ψευδῆ μηδεμίαν.

[2] Ep. i, § 50.

indeed themselves to the senses, yet so remote from them that it is impossible to approach them and obtain the 'clear view' which would tell us their true nature and the causes of their behaviour. These are summed up by Epicurus under the general title of the 'things of the sky' (μετέωρα): they include the heavenly bodies and their workings and all such phenomena as rain, thunder, lightning, hail, snow, &c., which we more strictly class as meteorological, and form the subject of the Second Letter,[1] whether it be by Epicurus himself or a follower scrupulously preserving his tradition, addressed to Pythocles. Even here there are certain data given us by immediate sense-perception, and when this is so, we must make no attempt to get behind them: for they must be true. We have,[2] for instance, a perfectly 'clear vision' of sun and moon as bodies of a certain size: this 'clear vision' cannot be called in question and we know therefore with certainty that such is the size of sun and moon. But on most occasions, when, for instance we are investigating the occurrence of solstices or eclipses, or the nature of thunder and lightning, and in particular, whenever we are attempting to discover the causes of 'celestial things', no such direct information can be obtained. How then are we to proceed? How is the supremacy of the senses to be maintained in a region where the data of sense are insufficient? Epicurus' answer [3] is characteristic and ingenious. In the first place we must start here too from sensation. If sensation will not give us a direct answer to our problems, yet it will frequently supply 'signs' (σημεῖα) or 'indications' (τεκμήρια), which will help us to a conclusion. Sometimes the celestial phenomena themselves in this way suggest their own explanation: more often 'we can obtain indications of what

[1] Cf. Lucr. v. 509–770; vi.

[2] Ep. ii, § 91; Lucr. v. 564–91. This seems inconsistent with the admission that the size of the tower is apparently diminished by distance, but Epicurus (as Lucretius carefully shows in a very interesting argument) had special theories about distant lights, connected closely with the theory of 'idols' and that of the clear vision. See a fuller discussion in Chap. VII, pp. 371–3.

[3] It is put most clearly in the opening sections (85–8) of the letter to Pythocles: but implied also in §§ 38 and 51 of the first letter.

happens above from some of the phenomena on earth'.[1] On the basis of these indications we may by thought [2] (ἐπίνοια), comparing phenomena with general concepts, or combining concepts one with another, frame hypotheses to explain what we see. But if thought were allowed thus to work at random, it is clear that its action might be even wilder than that of 'opinion' in the interpretation of sensation. Under what check then must it work? Still, obviously, under the control of the senses: 'all our investigations must be kept in accord with our sensations'.[3] But since it is clear that we cannot hope in such instances to have the confirmation (ἐπιμαρτύρησις) of the nearer view (ἐνάργεια, τὸ παρόν), how can this be? The check in the case of celestial phenomena—and indeed of all 'imperceptible things'—is no longer positive, but negative. We must bring the hypotheses we frame to the test of the senses [4] and see if they are inconsistent with anything which sense-perception observes: if they are contradicted (ἀντιμαρτυρεῖται) they must at once be rejected, but if not contradicted, they must be accepted as true. The test of scientific certainty is no longer 'confirmation' (ἐπιμαρτύρησις), but only the negative condition of non-contradiction (οὐκ ἀντιμαρτύρησις), which is defined as 'the agreement of the hypothesis or opinion about an imperceptible thing with the phenomenon'.[5] As the senses are the starting-point, so are they the touchstone of investigation. The general idea may best be brought out by

[1] Ep. ii, § 87. The later Epicureans, who showed an illicit tendency to develop a logic of Epicureanism, were greatly interested in the doctrine of 'signs', and remains of a treatise of Philodemus on this subject were found at Herculaneum.

[2] For the psychological analysis of thought on the atomic basis see Chap. VIII, pp. 422–30. Thought (ἐπίνοια) and opinion (δόξα) are closely allied and not always carefully distinguished, but Epicurus' usual practice seems to be to speak of 'opinion' in relation to the interpretation of the sensations of sense-perception, 'thought' in the operations of reason with reference to all classes of the 'imperceptible' (ἄδηλα).

[3] Ep. i, § 38.

[4] Ep. i, § 51; Ep. ii, § 88. The process of testing conclusions by phenomena is expressed by Epicurus by the verb ἐπικρίνειν: see Ep. i, § 37.

[5] Sext. Emp. adv. Math. vii. 213 ἀκολουθία τοῦ ὑποσταθέντος καὶ δοξασθέντος ἀδήλου τῷ φαινομένῳ.

an example taken from the other class of the 'imperceptible'
—those never perceptible by the senses—which are, as will
be seen, under precisely the same control: it has the advantage of being Epicurus' own instance. 'Epicurus [1] says that
there is empty space, which is an imperceptible thing, and
this is borne out (πιστοῦται) by the clear (ἐναργοῦς) fact of
motion, for if there were no empty space, there ought not
either to be motion, as the moving body would have no
place to which to shift because everything would be a solid
mass: therefore, since motion exists, the phenomenon does
not contradict the opinion about the imperceptible.' Similar
examples [2] might be found in plenty in Epicurus' astronomy
and meteorology.

So far then the rule of the Canonice might be framed
thus: 'explanations of things celestial must be based on the
indications given by phenomena and when framed submitted
to the test of phenomena'. Now it is obvious that this
requirement is by no means so exacting as that in the case
of terrestrial sense-perceptions: and indeed in many cases
it might be that several explanations would satisfy the merely
negative test that they are not contradicted by phenomena.
Are we then to accept them all as true or distinguish between
them, and if so, on what principle? Epicurus' answer is
startling, but unhesitating: all explanations which satisfy the
required conditions are to be accepted as equally true.
Celestial phenomena 'admit of more than one account of
their nature, which harmonizes with our sensations'.[3] What
then has become of truth? How will these 'several explanations' accord with the real world of celestial things? Can it
be supposed that all uncontradicted explanations really
correspond to actual facts? Again Epicurus does not flinch
from the consequences of his position. 'Several explanations' are true, because celestial phenomena happen in
several ways:[4] there is no one certain account of them,

---

[1] Sext. Emp. *adv. Math.* vii. 213.

[2] e.g. Ep. ii, § 90, a case of contradiction, §§ 92, 93, &c.   [3] Ep. ii, § 86.

[4] Ibid.: cf. Ep. ii, §§ 87, 88, 113, and many particular instances throughout
the letter: also Ep. i, §§ 78–80.

because the ways of their occurrence vary. The conclusion is surprising, but perfectly consistent, and Epicurus bore it out by another characteristic doctrine. Even if in our world there should be only one true explanation of a given phenomenon, yet thanks to the 'equal distribution'[1] (*ἰσονομία*) of things in the whole universe, the other explanations[2] will hold good in other worlds. They must then all be accepted equally, and the attempt[3] to tie down a celestial phenomenon to a single explanation savours of 'myth'; it is an arrogance unworthy of the spirit of true physical inquiry. In this astonishing but wholly consistent conclusion lies the reason of the many curious passages in Epicurus' astronomy and meteorology which must strike any reader of the Letter to Pythocles[4] or of the fifth and sixth books of Lucretius' poem, where again and again what we know to be the true explanation of a phenomenon is classed side by side with the most puerile hypotheses. It is impossible for a modern critic of Epicureanism—accustomed to the accurate methods of modern scientific inquiry—not to regard Epicurus' method as extremely unsatisfactory and slovenly. Indeed there is some evidence that even his disciples were unwilling to follow their master whole-heartedly at this point: Lucretius is occasionally more dogmatic than the Letter to Pythocles, and omits alternative explanations suggested there, or else, as in the instance already noticed, relegates their operation to other worlds. There was indeed good reason why Epicurus should insist less on exactness of results in this department of inquiry than in the discussion of the ultimate constitution of the world: for the phenomena of the sky had in themselves but little intrinsic interest for him, provided he could once establish the great principle that they were regulated by natural law, and so free men from the terrors of belief in the

---

[1] For a fuller discussion of *ἰσονομία* see Chap. IX, pp. 461–7.

[2] A characteristic instance of this idea will be found in Lucr. v. 526–33.

[3] Ep. ii, § 87 ὅταν δέ τις τὸ μὲν ἀπολίπῃ, τὸ δὲ ἐκβάλῃ ὁμοίως σύμφωνον ὂν τῷ φαινομένῳ, δῆλον ὅτι καὶ ἐκ παντὸς ἐκπίπτει φυσιο-λογήματος, ἐπὶ δὲ τὸν μῦθον καταρρεῖ.

[4] 'Unica illa in omnium temporum physica epistula Pythoclea', as Merbach (p. 27) aptly calls it.

divine agency: 'first of all, says the Letter to Pythocles,[1] we must not suppose that any other object is to be gained from the knowledge of the phenomena of the sky . . . than peace of mind (ἀταραξία) and a sure confidence'. But a truer motive for his conclusions than such comparative intellectual slackness must surely be found in the rigid acceptance of consequences, which is the clear mark of all his work. In reaching his conclusions he was only following 'where the argument led', and as usual was perfectly fearless of contempt or ridicule, when he was himself persuaded of their truth. Be this as it may, the rule of the Canonice concerning the investigation of celestial phenomena must now be amplified: 'Explanations of things celestial must be based on the indications given by phenomena and when framed submitted to the test of phenomena, but all explanations are true and correspond to existing facts, which are not contradicted by phenomena.'

There remains the other department of the 'imperceptible', far more important for scientific and philosophical inquiry, things namely, which are in the strictest sense imperceptible, for from their very nature they never can be perceived by the senses. A certain class of these has already been touched on,[2] objects which like the bodies of the divine beings cannot be perceived by the sense-organs, yet send off images which are directly apprehensible by the mind: but seeing that this 'mental apprehension' is more nearly akin to sense-perception than to thought, it is most in accordance with Epicurean principles to regard it as a species of direct sensation. At any rate discussion now must turn rather upon those 'imperceptible' things, which lie at the foundation of the physical constitution of the world, the ultimate realities of existence, on which the whole universe is built up. How is it possible, in a system which rests wholly on the basis of sensation to obtain knowledge of them? It must be remembered, in the first place, that to Epicurus these ultimate realities were always material and concrete. An inquiry into ultimate realities does not mean, as it might with some

[1] § 85 : see Tohte, op. cit., p. 15.　　　　[2] See p. 251.

philosophers, a discussion of abstract principles or immaterial 'ideas', but an investigation of the nature and behaviour of atoms and space, separately and in combination. The objects then of such an inquiry do not differ in kind from the things of sensation or the celestial phenomena, for they are always material and physical. If our sight were only strong enough to perceive the extremely minute, we should be able to examine the behaviour of atoms and atomic compounds just as we can that of any of the perceptible realities: it is only the limitation of our senses which relegates the inquiry in this case to the realm of thought instead of the realm of sensation. Further, it must always be borne in mind that to Epicurus the processes of thought and perception were in no way different in kind: thought,[1] like sensation, is a 'movement' of soul-atoms, situated in the mind, not in the sense-centres: this 'movement' is aroused by 'images' in just the same way and is undoubtedly conceived by Epicurus as a process of 'visualization': its most remote speculations are only in reality the result of such movement combining the images of concepts, built up ultimately out of sensations, into a new image. In short the mental processes are nothing but a subtler reproduction of the processes of sensation. If this is so, and neither the objects nor the instrument nor the process of inquiry differ in essence from those in use in other departments, we should expect to find that the principles regulating such inquiry were also the same. And this is indeed the case. Nowhere does Epicurus make any distinction as regards procedure between the investigation of the imperceptible, in the strict sense, and that of celestial phenomena: they are always grouped together. Procedure[2] in both cases must start from phenomena, and opinions formed must be checked by phenomena: 'contradiction' and 'non-contradiction' are for both departments alike the test of falsehood and truth: the example quoted above—Epicurus' proof of the existence of the void from the acknowledged

---

[1] For a fuller discussion of the process of thought see Chap. VIII, pp. 422–30.

[2] See the passages quoted above with reference to τὰ μετέωρα.

fact of motion—is a typical case of procedure in dealing with ultimate realities: if an hypothesis be shown to be inconsistent with the evidence of phenomena it must be rejected. Here then we have the origin of two features of Epicurean argument in the exposition of the physical system, which became more prominent in the more expanded work of Lucretius than in the brief *résumés* of his master's teaching which have come down to us. In the first place the refutation of opponents or rival philosophers takes the form of showing that their theories are inconsistent with the facts of experience:[1] they do not admit the existence of a void, which would make motion impossible, or they allow infinite division, which would destroy the permanence of the material world and so on. Secondly, the positive proof of Epicurean theories again and again takes the form of an appeal to the facts of sensational experience, either as demonstrating the truth of the underlying suppositions or as illustrating them by analogy: thus the many glorious passages of description which constitute in no small degree the poetic beauty of Lucretius' work are ultimately but the strict carrying out of the precepts of the Master's Canonice.

In procedure then it is neither possible nor necessary to distinguish between the two departments of the imperceptible. But when the results come to be examined, a notable difference is at once obvious. The main characteristic of the investigation of celestial phenomena is the acceptance as equally true of several explanations of the same phenomenon: this was seen to be a consequence of the purely negative test of 'non-contradiction', and also to correspond, as Epicurus held, to a real multiplicity of causes of the production of such phenomena. But when the theory of Epicurus as to the ultimate physical constitution of the world is examined, it is seen at once that this multiplicity of causes and explanations has passed away. There is no hesitation as to the true

---

[1] See especially Lucr. i. 635–920, in which he deals with the predecessors of the Atomists. The same tendency in Epicurus himself may be seen in Ep. i, § 49, where he states very briefly that other theories of vision will not explain the facts as well as his own.

explanation, and in no single instance is there a suggestion of a possible alternative: Atomism is not one among several possible theories of the universe, nor with regard to any of its details is there a hint that any other view than that expounded by Epicurus himself could be true. Indeed the Letter to Pythocles[1] draws the distinction clearly and unmistakably: 'we must not in the case of celestial phenomena', says the writer, 'expect our investigation to be in all respects like the principles concerning ethics or the solution of the other physical problems, as for example, that the universe is matter and space or that the elements are indivisible, or any other such statements in circumstances where there is only one explanation which harmonizes with phenomena (τοιαῦτα ὅσα μοναχὴν ἔχει τοῖς φαινομένοις συμφωνίαν)'. If procedure in the two departments is identical, how is it that results can be so different? How can Epicurus claim, as he apparently does, a higher—or more single—certainty in the realms of inquiry most remote from the evidence of the senses? The full discussion of this difficulty, which belongs rather to the consideration of processes of thought than procedure, must be postponed till the examination of the Epicurean psychology is reached,[2] but the conclusion there reached may be shortly stated. Thought—or reasoning—about the ultimate realities of the world is conducted by the comparison and combination of 'clear' concepts, each stage in the process being a new concept recognized as self-evident. These concepts are grasped by 'an act of apprehension on the part of the mind' (ἐπιβολὴ τῆς διανοίας) exactly similar to that by which the senses apprehend the 'clear vision' of the near object, or the mind the subtle images which penetrate to it. Thus, although the data are now most remote from immediate sensation, and the process by which they are reached and developed is purely mental, that process is yet exactly similar to—and even in the wholly materialistic conception of Epicurus—identical with the simplest of all forms of the apprehension of truth, the act of observation in which the senses grasp the image immediately presented to them. It

[1] Ep. ii, § 86.　　　　[2] See Chap. VIII, pp. 425–30.

is thus no arbitrary assumption on Epicurus' part that the concepts of science have a 'single' certainty, but once again, just as surely as the plurality of explanations in the case of celestial phenomena, a strict deduction from the psychological analysis of the process. It will be seen, when the question is fully discussed, that this account is not explicitly given in any Epicurean source, but it is strongly supported by more than one piece of evidence, nor can the strange divergence in results between the two processes of investigation be otherwise explained. We may then formulate the rule of the Canonice thus: 'Explanation of the ultimate realities must be based on the indications of phenomena and when framed submitted to the test of phenomena: truth is attained by the "mental apprehension" of the "clear" vision of concepts.'

Just then as the various criteria of truth were seen to be based on the one fundamental principle of the infallibility of sensation, so now the rules of the Canonice turn out to be only a reassertion of that infallibility and a statement of the manner in which it must be used in all departments of inquiry. In each case the start must be made from sense-experience, the hypotheses of opinion and thought must be referred back to experience and tested by it, and the supremely important moment in each process is the 'clear vision', whether sensible or mental, viewed with deliberate observation (ἐπιβολή). We are now in a position to give its full force to the brief summary of this part of the Canonice in the opening section of the letter to Herodotus:[1] 'we must keep all our investigations in accord with our sensations and in particular with the immediate apprehensions whether of the mind or of any one of the instruments of judgement, and likewise (in the field of morals) in accord with the feelings existing in us, in order that we may have indications whereby we may judge both the problem of sense-perception and the

---

[1] § 38 ἔτι τε κατὰ τὰς αἰσθήσεις δεῖ πάντα τηρεῖν καὶ ἁπλῶς ⟨κατὰ⟩ τὰς παρούσας ἐπιβολὰς εἴτε διανοίας εἴθ' ὅτου δήποτε τῶν κριτηρίων (here =sense-organs, αἰσθητηρίων, see my note ad loc.) ὁμοίως δὲ καὶ κατὰ τὰ ὑπάρχοντα πάθη, ὅπως ἂν καὶ τὸ προσμένον καὶ τὸ ἄδηλον ἔχωμεν οἷς σημειωσόμεθα.

unseen'. It is in fact, when we fully understand its terms, a singularly terse and complete summing up of the whole principles of Epicurean investigation.

So far the rules of the Canonice have been concerned with the processes of observation and thought. But the philosopher must not merely think and observe: he must, especially if he is to be a teacher, express his thoughts in language. And so in the same short introductory section,[1] which represents the Canonice in the letter to Herodotus, there is a discussion of language and terminology which at first sight appears almost disproportionate. But the reasons for this emphasis are not far to seek. In the first place it is no doubt part of Epicurus' protest on behalf of the 'plain man' against the 'professionalism' of other philosophic schools. As he distrusts their dialectic,[2] so also he distrusts their dialect:[3] the obscure and technical are to have no place in his system. Since it is to be addressed to the 'commonsense' man, it shall be couched in clear and ordinary phraseology. But apart from this polemical motive, there is a deeper reason underlying his precepts, which has its origin directly in the theory of the criteria of truth. The importance of the 'name' attached to concepts has already been noticed:[4] the 'anticipation', owing its validity to the series of perceptions of which it is composed, is of no value for philosophy, or even for practical reflection and the act of cognition itself, unless it be labelled with a name: we cannot convey our ideas to others, or even formulate them to ourselves, unless we can put them into words. When in a later section of the letter[5] Epicurus discusses the origin of language, he throws much light on the psychology of naming. It was, he holds, at first a natural process (φύσει): men impelled by a desire to express their feelings and impressions, 'emitted air formed into shape' to express them in different ways, as it came

---

[1] §§ 37, 38.   [2] D.L. x. 31 : see p. 235.
[3] Ep. i, § 72 καὶ οὔτε διαλέκτους ('dialectical expressions') ὡς βελτίους μεταληπτέον. ἀλλ' αὐταῖς ταῖς ὑπαρχούσαις κατ' αὐτοῦ χρηστέον.
[4] See p. 248.
[5] §§ 75, 76.

naturally to them, each in his own tribe. Later on,[1] when the convention of language was consciously understood, men in each nation by common agreement (θέσει) invented names for things, to prevent the confusion which would result if every man 'spoke in his own tongue'. Finally, as new things were brought from foreign tribes either their foreign name was introduced with them or one chosen by reasoning (λογισμῷ) was assigned to them. Concepts then must be reflected in names: and, as the necessary converse, names must reflect concepts. What philosophy requires in excess of the demands of ordinary life is that, just as its concepts must be clear, so its terms must clearly reflect them. 'First of all we must grasp the ideas attached to words (τοῖς φθόγγοις), in order that we may be able to refer to them and so to judge (ἐπικρίνειν) the inferences of opinion (τὰ δοξαζόμενα) or problems of investigation (ζητούμενα) or reflection (ἀπορούμενα), so that we may not either leave everything uncertain and go on explaining to infinity or use words devoid of meaning.'[2] The philosophic vocabulary is to be the immediate and certain record of accumulated perceptions, and therefore, as it were, the coinage for the interchange of philosophic thought: only the coinage must not belie its face value. As such it will facilitate, and indeed render possible, the process of testing the inferences of the mind by the evidence of sensation, which is the keystone of all true thought and investigation alike in ordinary life and in the various departments of scientific and philosophic inquiry. But how can this be carried out? For one of our most common experiences in ordinary life is that names by no means always represent clear concepts: words are apt to have a most confusing number of different meanings, and it is by no means always the case that 'the moment a word is spoken, immediately by means of the "anticipation" the form of the thing is thought

---

[1] Giussani, *Stud. Lucr.* 267–84, called attention to the importance of this later stage: Epicurus dealt with the old controversy whether language arose φύσει or θέσει by arguing that both processes had their place but in different stages of the growth of speech.

[2] Ep. i, § 37.

of'.[1] Epicurus is prepared to meet this difficulty: 'It is essential that the first mental image (ἐννόημα) associated with each word should be regarded and that there should be no need of explanation (ἀποδείξεως), if we are really to have a standard to which to refer a problem of investigation or reflection or a mental inference:'[2] for as Epicurus said elsewhere,[3] 'the first signification of every name is immediate and clear evidence'. We come back again to simplicity and common sense: the 'first' or most obvious meaning of words is to be taken and preserved. Not merely is philosophy itself to be within the reach of the ordinary man's observation, but its exposition must be in language within his immediate comprehension.

The rule of the Canonice then with regard to the use of words is the direct outcome and counterpart of his principles of investigation, and there is no need to attempt a formulation of it, for it could not be more clearly or tersely expressed than in Epicurus' own words. Unfortunately it is an ideal which in practice it is very difficult—almost impossible—to carry out, nor could there be a more convincing illustration of its difficulty than Epicurus' own writings. Although Diogenes[4] tells us that 'he uses current diction (λέξει κυρίᾳ) to expound his theory' and the Epicurean in Cicero's[5] dialogue maintains that 'Epicurus expresses in words what he wishes to say and states clearly what I can understand', critics both ancient and modern have alike complained of the obscurity of his style, and it would certainly be hard to find any piece of philosophic writing more crabbed than the letter to Herodotus. It abounds in highly specialized terms—the 'clear vision' (ἐνάργεια), the 'image awaiting confirmation' (προσμένον), the 'apprehension of the mind' (ἐπιβολὴ τῆς διανοίας) are some whose difficulty has already been noticed—and in spite of his professions, he is by no means free from the crime of employing words in more than one meaning, 'Sensation'[6] (αἴσθησις) and 'anticipation' (πρόληψις) are used

---

[1] D.L. x. 33.   [2] Ep. i, § 38.
[3] D.L. x. 33 παντὶ οὖν ὀνόματι τὸ πρώτως ὑποτεταγμένον ἐναργές ἐστι.
[4] x. 13.   [5] de Fin. i. 5. 15.   [6] See notes on pp. 238, 247.

both for the act and for its result, 'feeling'[1] (πάθος) has both
a wider and a narrower sense. The fact is that Epicurus was
attempting to combine two almost incompatible ideals, the
use of common words in their ordinarily accepted sense, and
great precision in meaning and expression. The ordinary
words of common language are not precise and exact, any
more than the general concepts which they represent, nor
is the language of everyday life adapted for the accuracy of
philosophic expression. In effect Epicurus paid more attention to accuracy than to lucidity, and in many cases where
he found ordinary words ambiguous or had already used
them in their 'first meaning', he was driven to invent new
terms. The consequence is that he practically created a new
and highly specialized vocabulary, intelligible indeed to himself and conveying definite notions, but travelling very far
from common language—all the farther, indeed, the more
clear-cut and circumscribed the significance of his terms
became to himself. Nor, on the other hand, has he altogether
avoided the pitfall of ambiguity; words must necessarily take
so much of their meaning from their context that to establish
for a single word a single definite meaning and never to
depart from it or modify it is an ideal that even the most
accurate thinker would find it well-nigh impossible to satisfy.
As a natural result, though Epicurus' exposition of his
system would be understood by the trained Epicurean,
drilled in the exact sense of the Epicurean terminology and
the shades of its variations, it appeared obscure to those who
stood outside the tradition, and is peculiarly difficult to us
who have lost the clue to many of the technicalities and can
only recover it very tentatively by the careful comparison of
passage with passage. Nevertheless not only was his ideal
in harmony with the general trend of his philosophy and the
rule he laid down a consistent completion of the Canonice,
but his avowed purpose deserves much greater attention in
the interpretation of his writings than many modern critics
have given it. To know that Epicurus intended always to
use the same word in the same sense, and that sense the

[1] See pp. 248–50.

'first' and most natural, is an extremely valuable guide to the understanding of many dark places, and those who neglect this principle are most likely to go astray. Though his terminology was not always consistent, any more than his philosophy, both alike were intended to be so, and to create a rigidly consistent whole.

The detailed consideration of the Canonice shows then that alike the criteria of truth and the rules of procedure depend for their validity on the fundamental principle of the infallibility of sensation. Although a critical examination has from time to time revealed difficulties and deficiencies in the theory, these have not been found due to faults in logical sequence or connexion, but are rather inherent in the main principle itself. The Canonice is a connected whole and in more than one point Epicurus' fearless consistency in carrying out his principles and his inferences from them has given occasion for remark. Criticism must then fall, as it always has with both in ancient and modern commentaries, on the bare principle itself. Some of the difficulties,[1] and in particular those connected with the sense of sight, have already been discussed, and it has been seen how the attempts made by Epicurus and his followers to escape from the admission of the falsity of any sensation or class of sensation, only cut more deeply at the root of the main position. Criticism of a similar kind were early made with regard to his treatment of other forms of sensation, and no account of his system can fairly pass them over. Take, for example, the senses of taste and touch:

'if,' argues Plutarch,[2] 'when one man says that a wine is rough and another that it is sweet, neither of them is deceived in his sensation, how can the wine be in itself rough any more than sweet? Again, one often sees the same bath regarded by some people as hot, by others as cold: for these order more cold water to be added and those more hot. . . . If then, neither sensation is truer than the other, it seems to follow that the water is in itself not hot any more than cold. For if it is argued that it appears different to different people, that is equivalent (if all sensations are true) to saying that it is both hot and cold.'

---

[1] See pp. 253–7.   [2] *adv. Colot.* 4, 1109; U. 250.

Epicurus [1] attempted to explain these differences by diversity in the atomic conformation of the sense-organs of the percipient: the palate of the man who thinks the wine rough is differently formed from that of his friend, and accordingly, though the atomic structure of the wine remains the same in both cases, it may produce a difference of effect. But though no doubt such a theory may help to explain the diverse judgements of taste, yet, as Plutarch points out, the theory that all sensations are true, does, when sensations are contradictory, annul the reality of quality in the object and leave us with a purely subjective standard of judgement: [2] contradictory sensations cannot both give us true information about the external reality. The same difficulty appears more serious in the field of ethics. There the one standard for the judgement of right conduct is the 'feeling of pleasure and pain': that which gives us pleasure is good, that which gives us pain is bad. But once again, men's feelings may differ: what is pleasant to me may be painful to another. There is then no objective standard of good and bad, and every man must be a law to himself. We seem once again to be brought back to the semi-scepticism of Democritus. Atoms and space are the only full realities and thought concerning them and their conduct alone true: qualities and the phenomena which are known by them have but a secondary kind of reality, and sensation which gives us that knowledge is liable to be fallacious.

But though Epicurus had no doubt more of Democritus' philosophy in his bones than he was aware of, certainly more than he would ever have consented to acknowledge, so that he admits, for instance, that the 'secondary qualities' are merely the possession of atomic compounds (συγκρίσεις) and have no place in the world of ultimate realities, yet he will have none of Democritus' scepticism. The compound is no less a real existence than the atoms and the void which form it, its qualities are no less real than the primal properties of the atoms, and the sensation which gives us our knowledge of

[1] See Chap. VIII, p. 404.
[2] Plut. l. c. μηδὲν μᾶλλον εἶναι τοῖον ἢ τοῖον.

it is not only true, but the sole instrument of certain knowledge. However near his system scepticism may be hovering, if its principles be logically carried out, Epicurus will have no truck with it: he is satisfied that he has sufficiently dealt with such difficulties as are involved in the doctrine of the infallibility of sensation. Yet even if we shut our eyes to the incidental difficulties of the theory there remains the one weakness which haunts the system of Epicurus, as it must necessarily any sensationalist philosophy—the supreme difficulty both in the field of knowledge and in the field of ethics of obtaining objective truth and an objective standard. Truth and goodness must be universal, yet the sensations by which they are to be known are the sensations of the individual. What guarantee is there that his sensations are identical with his neighbour's or even with his own on some previous or future occasion? That Epicurus and his followers were conscious of this weak spot we may infer from their eagerness, when occasion offered, to appeal to the universality of sensations and beliefs, as, for instance, in support of the existence of matter[1] or the existence of divine beings.[2] But in reality the Gospel of sensation, for all its attractive simplicity and apparent certainty must lead to an individualism, such as that of Protagoras: the individual man must become 'the measure of all things'. He is left isolated with his own sensations and his own criteria, and it is a mere chance whether his neighbour will be given similar data and therefore reach similar conclusions. The Epicurean consciously shut himself off from public life and took no part in the common activities of the state; but he did not realize that the very foundation of his system in reality cut him off in thought and conduct from his fellow-men and left him a philosopher stranded to all intents and purposes on a desert island.

But it is not the object of the present work to criticize Epicureanism from the outside or to estimate its value in comparison with other philosophies. It is indeed necessary at the outset to point out the difficulties involved in its

[1] Ep. i, § 39. [2] Lucr. v. 1169 ff.

fundamental position, but a more correct, because more sympathetic, estimate of its worth will be obtained, if we attempt to regard it rather from within, to trace its genesis, and to see how it coheres in a consistent unity, which makes it worthy of attention as a serious philosophy. With this view I have endeavoured to show in this chapter how the axioms and rules of the Canonice are one and all built up on the single fundamental principle. The following chapters, which deal with the physical and ethical sides of the system, will be treated from the same point of view. The Canonice is the necessary starting-point of Epicureanism, however much it may involve what can only be clear after the examination of other departments, because on it depends the whole of the rest of the system. It may indeed be said without exaggeration that Epicurean physics and ethics are but the elaboration in many different fields of the supreme principle of the infallibility of sensation.[1]

[1] It may be interesting to compare with the principles of the Canonice a recent and strangely similar statement of the attitude and method of modern science written by Dr. A. S. Russell in his chapter on *The Dynamic of Science* in *Adventure*, p. 6: 'The reality of the scientist embraces two broad classes of concepts. First, those things, such as ourselves, the stars, the table, and so on, which are ordinarily described as being directly observed by the senses, the reality of which is accepted uncritically by common sense. Secondly, hypothetical entities like atoms, electrons, wireless waves, and ether, which cannot be directly observed. These hypothetical entities are regarded as real, firstly, if an analogy can be found to make them correspond with things which are judged to be real, and, secondly, if they give a satisfactory account of the experimental facts for the explanation of which they have been invoked.'

III

ATOMS AND SPACE

IN passing from Leucippus to Democritus the atomic theory has been seen to grow in consistency and harmony: with Epicurus the change is even more marked. It is now felt to be a system of interrelated parts: the connexion of one proposition with another has been thought out and the various conceptions involved in Atomism ordered and organized on fundamental principles. This impression is due in some degree, no doubt, to the form in which our information has reached us: the theories of the earlier Atomists have to be pieced together from scattered fragments, the accounts of the doxographers and the detached criticisms of later philosophers; for Epicurus we have the compressed and rather confused, though far better ordered, account in his own letter to Herodotus, and the continuous commentary of the poem of Lucretius. But there is much more than this: Epicurus had the master mind, which would not rest content with a mere 'adoption' of Democritus' Atomism, as hasty critics have been too ready to suppose, but insisted on development, modification, and improvement, and above all on the correlation of the whole system under the central principle of the infallibility of sense-perception. No account can do justice to Epicurus' physics which does not attempt to grasp it as a whole, to emphasize the interdependence of its parts and the constant control of the principles of the Canonice. It is from this point of view that I shall attempt in the following pages to describe it.

Epicurus makes his start, like Democritus, from the principle of causality and permanence: 'nothing is created out of the non-existent', but unlike his predecessor [1] he does not leave the principle as an *ex cathedra* assumption, but supports it by argument. Here we are dealing with perceptible and imperceptible alike; the problem is universal and

[1] Ep. i, § 38

cannot be solved directly by the senses: we must ask whether the senses give us any 'indication' to support the principle or whether they in any way contradict it. Such an 'indication' Epicurus finds in the ordered generation of things in the perceptible world: 'nothing is created out of the non-existent; for, if it were, everything would be created out of everything with no need of seeds'. Lucretius[1] follows the same argument and brings it out with a wealth of illustration. The proof is tersely put, but is clearly on the lines demanded by the Canon. Critics have proclaimed it unsatisfactory on the ground that Epicurus, to put it in modern phraseology, is arguing against 'spontaneous generation' by denying 'sporadic creation'. The truth is surely that he proves more than he need: all it was necessary for him to show was that every created thing was sprung from an antecedent something, was created of substance which already existed. Epicurus has gone beyond this and pointed out that not merely is there always pre-existing substance, but in each case substance in a particular form, a 'seed', which can only produce one particular thing and nothing else. Suppose for a moment that the opposite were true, that things could suddenly come into existence without being formed from pre-existing substance? What is the evidence of phenomena? That things require definite 'seeds' for their creation. The evidence of sensation interposes its, veto (ἀντιμαρτύρησις), and the supposition is untenable: it must be true that 'nothing is created out of the non-existent'. There is no confusion in the argument: it is, if anything, gratuitously specific.[2] It may be noticed that it has a double application: (1) the sum total of things is never increased by new additions, (2) every material thing has a material cause.

The second principle—the complement of the first—is next stated and proved. 'If that which disappears were destroyed into the non-existent, all things would have perished, since that into which they were dissolved would not exist.' The statement here is less lucid, principle and proof

[1] Lucr. i. 149–214.
[2] Cf. also Woltjer, *de Epicuri Philosophia cum fontibus comparata*, p. 13.

being run into one: Lucretius puts the principle more clearly: 'nature breaks up each thing again into its own first-bodies, nor does she destroy ought into nothing',[1] nothing, in other words, ceases entirely to exist: as nothing is added to the sum of things, so nothing is entirely taken from it. The proof again is from phenomena: if things were utterly destroyed, and by the first principle nothing new could be added, the sum total of the universe must gradually be diminished, and ultimately would pass out of existence altogether. But this is not the evidence of the senses: we do indeed see things perish, cease, that is, to be what they were before, but this perishing means only the assumption of another form. Change we see all around us, but not the absolute cessation of existence. Lucretius is fond of using this principle as an axiom in the converse form, 'whatever changes and departs from its own limits is straightway the death of that which was before'.[2] Once again there is a double implication in the principle: (1) the sum of matter is never decreased by absolute loss—this is the modern idea of the 'permanence of matter', (2) no individual thing is utterly destroyed, but only resolved into its component atoms.

There follows a third principle: 'the sum of things always was such as it is now and always will be the same'. This is in part a direct deduction from the other two: if nothing is added, the universe cannot increase; if nothing perishes, it cannot decrease. But Epicurus adds other arguments: 'there is nothing into which it changes: for outside the universe there is nothing which could come into it and bring about the change'. This is the reference to sense-experience. Among phenomena two conditions are always required for change, (1) something for the original 'thing' to change into, something which it may become, (2) some external agent to effect the change—by means, as Epicurus held, of a blow. But by 'mental apprehension', by 'looking at' the concept

[1] I. 215, 6.
[2]   nam quodcumque suis mutatum finibus exit,
         continuo hoc mors est illius quod fuit ante, i. 670, &c.

we have already formed of the universe, we can see that neither of these conditions can in its case be fulfilled: the universe cannot change into something else, for there is nothing else which it could become, nor is there anything external to it, which could effect the change. The argument is put in a more elaborate form by Lucretius in a passage probably based on the Greater Epitome.[1] He seems to imply three possibilities by which the universe might change, (1) if there were anything outside it into which any part of it might escape, (2) if there were anywhere from which a new force might come into the universe and alter it, (3) if change could be caused by internal rearrangement. Epicurus in the letter to Herodotus[2] seems to have the first two of these causes most prominently in his mind. The third[3] might at first sight seem to be at work in the universe in the constant dissolution and recomposition of the atomic compounds, but Epicurus' answer would lie in his conception of equilibrium ($\mathit{i}\sigma o\nu o\mu\mathit{i}a$): the atoms have long ago entered into all possible combinations and cannot create anything new which could alter the sum total. The universe then cannot change for there is nothing for it to change into and no external or internal force to change it. It is birthless, deathless, and immutable.

In these three primary principles themselves there is nothing new: they were practically implied in the Parmenidean conception, they were enunciated by Empedocles and Anaxagoras and explicitly stated by Democritus. But Epicurus has done more than 'adopt' them: he has adduced proof for them, and in doing so has linked them directly to the base principles of his whole system. The proofs from phenomena and the trust in sensation which they involve are the new and characteristic addition.

In what form then does this eternal universe exist? 'In the form of body (or matter) and space (or, as Epicurus here

---

[1] Lucr. ii. 304 ff.   [2] § 39.

[3] Bignone, *Epicuro*, Appendix III, p. 253, sees a reference to this third notion in the words $o\mathit{v}\theta\grave{\epsilon}\nu$ $\gamma\grave{a}\rho$ $\check{\epsilon}\sigma\tau\iota\nu$ $\epsilon\mathit{i}s$ $\mathring{o}$ $\mu\epsilon\tau a\beta\acute{a}\lambda\lambda\epsilon\iota$ (or as he reads, following Usener, $\mu\epsilon\tau a\beta a\lambda\epsilon\hat{\iota}$). I think it more probable that this clause refers to the first possibility and that the third is passed over here by Epicurus.

says, "place").'¹ That body exists is testified by universal sensation:² all men through all their senses are made conscious of matter. That space exists is shown by the existence and motion of matter: 'if there were not that which we term void and place and intangible existence (ἀναφὴς φύσις), bodies would have nowhere to exist and nothing through which to move, as they are seen to move.'

At this point certain difficulties arise, though rather from a modern than an ancient point of view. In the first place it is true that the sensation of matter is universal, but that has not hindered philosophers from calling in question the objective reality of the external world, or asking what meaning, if any, can be attached to the statement of its existence as apart from a percipient intelligence. But, if we are inclined to raise this objection, we must bear in mind that it is essentially a modern difficulty, unknown to the ancient world, and secondly that Epicurus spoke here, as always, as the average man of common sense. To him, as to the modern man of science, the existence of matter is sufficiently testified and its properties sufficiently made known by the senses. Once again he is content to take as his starting-point what 'common sense' would say, without any attempt to get behind it.

The difficulty connected with the syllogistic argument by which Epicurus inferred space from the fact of motion is more serious, for it was a problem which antiquity had very fully discussed. Parmenides and the Eleatics had, as has been seen,³ in order to preserve the unity of the world, denied both space and motion: the world was a single corporeal *plenum*, compact 'body' without space, and the appearance of motion was merely a delusion of the senses. As against this theory Epicurus was justified, indeed impelled, by his own first principles to reassert the evidence of the senses: we perceive motion, therefore motion is a reality. But is it

¹ § 39 ἀλλὰ μὴν καὶ τὸ πᾶν ἐστι ‹σώματα καὶ τόπος›. The missing words can be supplied with certainty from other passages. See especially περὶ Φύσεως, i; C.B. *fr.* 14.

² Cf. Lucr. i. 422 ' communis sensus'.   ³ Part I, Chap. I, p. 26.

necessary to infer from this the existence of void? Some modern scientists, holding the hypothesis of ether, would answer in the negative, and a very similar solution was put forward by Epicurus' contemporaries, the Stoics. They, under the stress of their desire to assert the divine unity of the world, maintained that the whole world was but one primary substance, which however was elastic and capable of existing in various degrees of tension;[1] under the greatest strain it appeared as fire, with less tension as air, with less again as water, and with least of all as earth. Motion, on this view, then is but an interchange of parts, much as one might move about the various portions of a piece of putty without causing a break, or as one sees changes of position in a kaleidoscope. With this possibility Epicurus does not concern himself, though it must have been current at the time of the writing of his letter, but that it did become a real question to the later Epicureans, we may infer from the fact that Lucretius[2] consents to deal with it. His main answer is, in effect, simply the restatement of the common-sense view: there must be empty space in order that there may be a beginning of motion; a thing cannot begin to move unless there is 'room' for it to move into. His second argument[3] is an illustration from experience—if you clash two broad bodies, e.g. boards, together and then quickly draw them apart, the air rushes round to fill up the space between them: but there must be an interval of time in which that space is empty or 'void'. That Epicurus' own answer would have been on these lines may safely be inferred from the fact that in the controversial passages[4] about the Epicurean view of space the examples are drawn from such illustrations as the interior of a cask or a vessel—not of course that Epicurus would have denied that they were filled with air; but would have argued rather that they afforded an 'indication' of that real empty space which lay between atom and atom. More cogent is Lucretius'[5] third argument that the

---

[1] See Hicks, pp. 24 ff.   [2] Lucr. i. 370–97.   [3] 384 ff.
[4] Especially Themistius paraphr. Arist. *Phys.* Δ. 4, 214; U. 273.
[5] i. 396, 7.

'elasticity' of the primary substance, its power to condense and rarify, must itself imply the existence of void. The Stoic view, Epicurus would have maintained, is not that immediately suggested by sensation: it is an 'addition of the mind' which the 'clear facts' of sensation refute. Once again 'common sense' is good enough. Matter then and space are the sole independent existences: 'and besides these two nothing can be thought of . . . such as could be grasped as whole existences and not spoken of as the accidents or properties of such existences'.[1]

We must ask then next how are we to conceive these two existences, 'body' and space? 'Among bodies', Epicurus proceeds, 'some are compounds (συγκρίσεις) and others those of which compounds are formed'.[2] This is little more than a verbal explanation: the term 'body' is in itself ambiguous, for it may be applied alike to the 'bodies' or 'things' which we perceive by sensation or to the ultimate bodies of which they are composed. But the confusion is only momentary and does not produce any serious difficulty either in Epicurus or in Lucretius,[3] who follows him in making the distinction: for as soon as the character of these ultimate bodies has been determined, there will be other descriptive names to apply to them in order to distinguish them from the bodies of sensation. What then are they? 'These latter',[4] says Epicurus, 'are indivisible (ἄτομα) and unalterable (ἀμετάβλητα) (if, that is, all things are not to be destroyed into the non-existent, but something permanent (ἰσχῦόν τι) is to remain behind at the dissolution of compounds): they are completely solid (πλήρη) in nature and can by no means be dissolved in any part. So it must needs be that the first-beginnings are indivisible corporeal existences (ἀτόμους σωμάτων φύσεις).' Here then is the first statement of the atomic position. The argument by which it is supported is put very briefly in the parenthesis and requires examination. It rests on the Atomic contention that there must be a limit to the divisibility of

---

[1] Ep. i, § 40. For the Epicurean view of 'accidents and properties' see Chap. IV.

[2] Ep. i, § 40.   [3] i. 483–4.   [4] Ep. i, § 41.

matter, but this is put both negatively and positively. In the first place Epicurus appears to maintain that, unless there were such a limit, things would pass out of existence altogether, which would be a contradiction of the principle that 'nothing is destroyed into the non-existent'. The idea is that if it were possible to go on dividing and dividing you would ultimately find that matter had disappeared and you had reached 'nothing'. Strictly this is of course a fallacy: it is theoretically possible, apart from such a physical barrier as Epicurus supposes, to go on dividing and subdividing to infinity and yet to reach only smaller and smaller particles of matter. And it is improbable that Epicurus would seriously have maintained the point: it is rather a popular way of putting what he meant. For the stress of the argument lies on the other, the positive, side: 'something permanent (or "strong") must remain'.[1] Here the argument is independent of the fallacy of ultimate resolution into nothing. For if infinite division were possible, all particles of matter however small would be compound bodies, for they could always be separated into smaller particles. But the compound body on Epicurus' view is always a mixture of matter and void, and the presence of void is a source of weakness: for it means the possibility of destruction by external blows. If, then, however low one may go in the scale of minuteness, nothing indestructible is ever reached, matter as we know it in external things could not exist; for there could be no solid and permanent substratum—'nothing strong'—to hold it together and to resist the shocks of collision.

The argument recurs in two other contexts in the letter, which will throw some light upon it. In the first Epicurus[2] is arguing that the atoms have none of the 'secondary qualities', which we associate with things: 'for every quality changes; but the atoms do not change at all, since there must

---

[1] The words ἰσχῦόν τι are an emendation of my own, which was made independently by Bignone (*Epicuro*, p. 76, n. 1) for the manuscript reading ἰσχύοντα. But the point does not rest on the emendation, for it is confirmed by other passages, especially Ep. i, § 54 and § 56 and Lucr. i. 628 ff.: see below.

[2] § 54.

needs be something which remains solid and indissoluble at the dissolution of compounds, which can cause changes'. Just then as there must be indestructible particles to explain the creation and the destruction of phenomena, so to explain their changes, there must be something unchanging: and this can be nothing else than the atom, the hard body without the admixture of void, which alone can resist the attacks of external blows. The second passage [1] is more directly connected with our argument, for Epicurus is there proving that the atoms must have a definite size, they cannot be 'infinitely small'. 'We must', he says, 'do away with division into smaller and smaller parts to infinity in order that we may not make all things weak and so in the composition of aggregate bodies be compelled to crush and squander the things that exist into the non-existent.' Again the idea is the same: if there is no limit to the smallness of particles, there is no permanent strength in the substratum; things become weak and can be whittled away past the limits of material existence. A more striking and interesting form of the same proof occurs in a difficult passage of Lucretius,[2] which has been clearly explained by Giussani.[3] If there were no *minimum*, the poet maintains, but the infinite division of matter were possible, then, because the process of dissolution is quicker than that of creation, all things, i.e. perceptible things, must long ago have ceased to exist. Let us suppose, for instance, that the process of dissolution is twice as quick as that of creation, and that it takes ten years to create a living creature and bring it to its maturity: then in five years it can be dissolved into particles of the size from which it started, and in ten, if there is no limit to division, the particles will be as much smaller again. If out of these particles a similar creature is now to be formed, it will require twenty years, and on the next occasion forty and so on. In all the ages which have passed since the creation of the world, the powers of destruction would have so got the upper hand that by now no perceptible things would be left. Again, division cannot go on to infinity:

[1] § 56. [2] i. 551–64. [3] *Stud. Lucr.* 48–52.

there must be some permanent *minimum* 'with strength' to resist the influences of destruction. The passage is unusually interesting and throws considerable light on the general Epicurean argument.

This, as I understand it, is the contention of Epicurus for the existence of indivisible particles as the permanent substratum of matter: not that, without them, matter would cease altogether to exist—for however minutely divided, it must still continue to be matter—but that without a limit to division, it is impossible to arrive at anything completely solid, and so sufficiently strong to resist the attacks of destruction, in other words, the blows of other particles. The result would be continuous destruction and no formation: in this sense 'all things would be dissolved into the non-existent', for there would be no power to keep existing things as they were, or to create similar new ones.

The atom then is a necessary postulate for the existence of the world as we know it. How is it to be conceived? Certain characteristics follow immediately from its definition as an 'indivisible existence'. It must be completely solid,[1] completely compact,[2] and entirely without void:[3] it is, that is to say, pure body without any intervals. From this it immediately follows that it is 'unchangeable':[4] for change is due to the alteration of the position of parts and that can only be brought about in compound bodies, in which there is an admixture of void. What then are the properties of this indissoluble, unalterable body? They are according to Epicurus,[5] three in number, size, shape, and weight.

The question of the size of the atom was already, as we have seen, a problem with a history in the Atomic theory. Leucippus[6] wishing to insist on their extreme minuteness had stated that they were 'without parts' (ἀμερῆ): Democritus,[7] seeing that it might then also be said that they were

---

[1] στερεόν, § 54.   [2] πλήρη τὴν φύσιν ὄντα, § 41.

[3] ἀμέτοχα κενοῦ, Aet. i. 3. 18; U. 267.

[4] ἀμετάβλητα, § 41.

[5] § 54 τὰς ἀτόμους νομιστέον μηδεμίαν ποιότητα τῶν φαινομένων προσφέρεσθαι πλὴν σχήματος καὶ βάρους καὶ μεγέθους.

[6] See p. 78.   [7] See pp. 125, 126.

without magnitude, i.e. without material existence, had denied this and gone so far as to maintain that some of them were even 'very large'. Epicurus [1] dealt with the question in a more systematic and philosophic manner.

'We must not suppose', he says, 'that every size exists among the atoms, in order that the evidence of phenomena may not contradict us, but we must suppose that there are some variations of size. . . . The existence of atoms of every size is not required to explain the differences of qualities in things, and at the same time some atoms would be bound to come within our ken and be visible: but this is never seen to be the case, nor is it possible to imagine how an atom could become visible.'

Here then is the answer to Democritus: sense-perception is against his theory: there must be an upward limit of magnitude, otherwise atoms could be seen. What of the downward limit? It follows of course from the very definition of an atom, as a limit of division, that it cannot be of infinite smallness, but Epicurus proceeds to treat the question in a subtle and very characteristic argument. This argument must be studied in the original and compared with the rather more lucid, but less far-reaching version of Lucretius.[2] I shall here attempt to give the gist of it in as simple a form as possible.[3] Epicurus appeals as usual to the facts of sensation: and the appeal involves the expression of strong controversial views with regard to area and extension. 'Not merely can we not admit infinite division, but we cannot suppose an 'infinite progression from less to less (μετάβασις εἰς ἄπειρον ἐπὶ τοὔλαττον).' His contention here is directed primarily against the geometrical view of surface or area, which held that surface was perfectly continuous, and that it was possible, in considering for instance a line to pass continually to smaller and smaller sections to infinity: the idea is clearly expressed in the well-known story of Achilles and the tortoise. As against this theory Epicurus upholds the view of common sense based upon the experience of sensation. If we take any object and try by looking

[1] §§ 55–9.　　　　[2] i. 599–634.
[3] See Giussani, *Stud. Lucr.* 64–72; Hicks, op. cit., pp. 242–50, C.B. notes *ad loc.*

at it to analyse its surface, we find that we may indeed proceed from smaller to smaller parts for a long distance: but
ultimately we come to a point—not a geometrical but a
material point (ἄκρον)—which is the smallest visible thing.[1]
If we attempted to see any smaller part, we should pass out
of the range of the perceptible altogether. Indeed, this point
itself is only visible as a part of a larger whole: it is 'distinguishable, but not perceptible by itself' (διαληπτὸν εἰ μὴ
καθ' ἑαυτὸ θεωρητόν), and if we try to look at its 'right-hand
or left-hand part', we shall find that our eye has in reality
wandered to the next similar point. We have then in this
point reached something from which further progression to
anything smaller is impossible (ἀμετάβατον): in other words,
surface is not continuous and does not permit of infinite
progression, but is a series of discrete *minima*. Further, these
'least parts' (*minimae partes*) afford a standard of measure: as
we pass from one of them to another, we can—or could,
if we had patience—go on till we reached the last point,
then count them up and so from their number reckon the
size of the object. This, Epicurus holds, is the only view
of surface which is warranted by the 'clear vision of perception', and the opposite view is due to the contamination
of the sense-perception by the false addition of opinion.
Yet, if we pass from the world of sensation to the world of
thought, we know that even these 'points', the 'least parts'
for perception, are themselves aggregates (ὄγκοι) of infinitely
smaller particles: in thought division may still be carried
on. But in the world of thought the analogy still holds:
ultimately we come to the 'least possible' (ἐλάχιστα), the *minima*
of extension. They similarly are not separable: they can
only exist as parts of the atom. They never come together
to form it, they are not parted in it by void, they could
themselves have no 'powers',[2] but they may in thought be
distinguished. They too are 'boundary marks' (πέρατα) and
by their number the size of the atom which they compose

---

[1] We can perhaps illustrate the idea best to ourselves by the example of
the extreme point of a needle.

[2] Lucr. i. 628–34.

may in thought be calculated. The world of thought corresponds exactly (ἀναλογίᾳ κέχρηται) to the world of sense: in the world of sense we have the visible body composed of 'distinguishable' points, in the world of thought the atom composed of 'inseparable' parts. This imaginative analogy has then given us the answer to Leucippus and his critics and to Democritus: the atoms are not 'without parts' (ἀμερῆ) in the sense that they have magnitude and parts 'distinguishable' by thought; they are on the other hand without parts in the sense that they are not formed of parts which could be separated. In other words the atom has size, i.e. measurable extension, but it remains an 'indivisible existence'. The size of the atom then is neither 'very great' nor infinitely small: it is extremely minute but with a lower as well as an upper limit.

Furthermore there are some variations in the sizes of atoms: 'for if this be the case, we can give a better account of what occurs in our feelings and sensations'.[1] As will be seen later,[2] difference in the size of the component atoms is a large factor in producing difference of qualities in things. That the atoms will have shape is manifest from the fact that they have size, but now that we have the theory of the least parts, we can go farther: for it is obvious that the shape of the atom varies according to the number and disposition of the 'least parts'. An ingenious critic[3] has worked out some of these differences. If, for instance, we suppose the *minimae partes* to be cubes of exactly the same size, then, if an atom contains two only, it can have but one shape ▦; if it contains three, two shapes ⊟ and ⊞; if four, five shapes on one plane,

⊟ ⊞ ⊞ ⊞ ⊞, and two more in two planes, according as one of the parts in the last figure be placed on top either of one of its neighbours, or of that at the opposite corner: with five or six parts the possibilities are very

---

[1] Ep. i, § 55.   [2] See p. 354.

[3] Brieger, *Jahrbuch Fleck.*, 1875, p. 630, quoted by Giussani on *Lucr.* ii. 483.

largely increased. Are we to suppose then that this process of variation may be infinitely continued, or is there a limit to the possible varieties? Epicurus' answer is again carefully thought out: the number of different atomic shapes [1] is indefinitely great (ἀπερίληπτον), but not infinite. It must be 'inconceivably great': 'for it is not possible that such great varieties of things should arise from the same (atomic) shapes, if they are limited in number'. Phenomena, as usual, give the 'indication': the varieties of compound bodies are very largely due to the difference of shape in the component atoms, and it would not be possible to account for these varieties, if we conceived of any comparatively small number of atomic shapes. Why then is there a limit to the number? Epicurus does not himself give us any reason, but Lucretius [2] suggests two proofs, so characteristically Epicurean that they must represent the regular tradition of the school. The first is an argument suggested by 'mental apprehension': variety of shape, as we have seen, can only be obtained by supposing an increase in the number of least parts: or, in other words, an increase of size. If this process were infinitely continued, we should again arrive at atoms so large as to be perceptible to the senses: we should be guilty of the fallacy of Democritus.[3] The second is based on the 'indications' of phenomena: varieties of quality in things are caused by varieties of atomic shape: yet even the varieties of things are limited; there is an extreme of beauty and ugliness, just as there is of hot and cold. But if there were infinite varieties of atomic shape, there could be no such limitation of qualities: all that we find most beautiful and most hideous would long ago have been surpassed. We must conclude then that these varieties of shape in the atoms are indefinitely great, yet not infinite. On the other hand the number of atoms of each particular shape is infinite,[4] for if it were not so (the reason is again given by Lucretius[5]), the sum total of atoms would itself be limited—which is not the

---

[1] Ep. i, § 42.   [2] ii. 481–521.   [3] See p. 285.
[4] καθ᾽ ἑκάστην δὲ σχημάτισιν ἁπλῶς ἄπειροί εἰσιν αἱ ὅμοιαι, § 42.
[5] ii. 522–68.

case. The ideas connected with the shape of the atoms are not so penetrating as those relating to their size, but are particularly well thought out and form an interesting example of the application of the principles of the Canon.

Thirdly, the atoms have weight.[1] The question whether weight is a property of the atoms has, as has already been seen, a very perplexing history in the Atomic theory. Leucippus makes no mention of weight and it may be taken for certain that he did not assign weight to the atoms. Over the attitude of Democritus controversy still rages, but we have seen reason to think that he did not regard it as an absolute property of the atoms,[2] but only as a derivative from their size which comes into action in the cosmic 'whirl'. We might therefore naturally suppose that the idea was introduced into the system by Epicurus himself in order to account for the 'downward' motion of the atoms in space. This conclusion is however made improbable by a passage in Lucretius[3] in which, evidently following Epicurus, he argues against the idea that variation in weight was the cause which enabled the atoms to meet in the downward fall, on the ground that in the void, which offers no resistance, all bodies, whatever their weight, must fall at an equal 'atomic' pace. It is true that Lucretius puts this idea as a supposition,[4] but it is hard to believe that he is not arguing against some definite suggestion on these lines, and if so, the idea of weight as the absolute property of the atoms and the cause of downward motion must have been introduced by some one into the atomic theory before Epicurus— possibly by Nausiphanes. In view of the history of the discussion it is certainly strange that we find no argument on the question in Epicurus. He is content with the mere mention of weight[5] together with size and shape as one of the properties of the atoms. Lucretius assumes it all through, and it is only in a passage of the *Placita*[6] that we find any kind

---

[1] Ep. i, § 54.   [2] See Part I, Chap. III, § 3, pp. 128 ff.   [3] ii. 225 ff.

[4] ii. 225, 'quod si forte aliquis credit'.   [5] Ep. i, § 54.

[6] [Plut.] *Plac. Philos.* 1. 3. 26; U. 275 ὁ δὲ Ἐπίκουρος τούτοις καὶ τρίτον βάρος προσέθηκεν· ἀνάγκη γὰρ, φησί, κινεῖσθαι τὰ σώματα τῇ τοῦ βάρους

of proof recorded, a proof, as might be expected, from the fact of motion: 'it must needs be, says Epicurus, that the bodies (i.e. the atoms) are moved by the blow of their weight: for otherwise they will not move'. That this was Epicurus' own argument is clear, apart from the testimony of Plutarch, from the passages in which he speaks of the 'natural downward motion of the atoms owing to their weight'.[1] There are reasons too which may be suggested for the absence of explicit argument on the subject. On the one hand the weight of the atoms is an immediate deduction from their size: solid matter, having size, must also have weight: demonstration is hardly needed as soon as the idea of 'weight' had become explicit. On the other hand—a more subtle consideration—though differences of size and shape in the atoms were productive of important results, difference of weight is not effective. For to the atoms, always moving in the void at an equal rate, difference of weight[2] does not produce difference of motion, and in compound bodies where difference of weight first begins to tell, it is not the weight of individual atoms that matters, but the weight of the aggregate of matter compared with the aggregate of void.[3] The atoms then have weight, and since they are solid matter with no admixture of void, their weight varies directly with their size: their weight is moreover the cause of their natural 'downward' motion, but difference of weight has no effect so far as rate of motion is concerned.

Size, shape, and weight are thus proved to be properties of the atoms, but beyond these they have no other qualities.[4] Here it might seem that the evidence of sensation was against such a conclusion: all things that we can perceive have other qualities, colour, smell, sound, cold, heat, and so on: we

πληγῇ. I have no doubt that the manuscript reading πληγῇ is here right as against Usener's emendation ὁλκῇ. That Epicurus could speak of the 'blow' of weight is proved by the similar quotation in Aet. 1. 3. 18; D. (Democritus) A. 47 ἀνάγκη κινεῖσθαι τὰ σώματα τῇ τοῦ βάρους πληγῇ: cf. Cic. de Fato, 20. 46; D. ibid.

[1] § 61 ἡ κάτω διὰ τῶν ἰδίων βαρῶν: ἢ ἔξωθεν ἢ ἐκ τοῦ ἰδίου βάρους: cf. the more direct statements in Lucr. ii. 84 and 215–16.

[2] See p. 313.　　[3] Cf. Lucr. i. 358–69.　　[4] Ep. i, § 54.

might reasonably conclude that the atoms too were similarly endowed,[1] that white things were made of white atoms, black of black, and so forth. But this would be a false assumption. For all qualities are susceptible of change:[2] the wave which was green one moment becomes white the next;[3] the colours on the peacock's tail are always shifting, as the light strikes it:[4] but the atoms cannot change. They are, as has been proved, unalterable and we must not attribute to them qualities which imply alteration. How then can we account on an atomic basis for the changing qualities of things? The unchangeable atoms are themselves the cause of change: 'there must be something which remains solid and indissoluble . . . which can cause changes: not changes into the non-existent or from the non-existent, but changes effected by the shifting of position of some particles, and by the addition or departure of others'.[5] All the qualities of things are thus due to their atomic conformation: their original qualities are given them by the size and shape and arrangement of the atoms which compose them, the change in their qualities is caused by the mutual change of position and order among the atoms, and in some cases because some of the original atoms break off or new ones are added. Nor is this difficult to conceive, when we remember that the atoms inside compound bodies are continually in motion,[6] ever clashing against one another and starting off in new directions, so that in every perceptible moment of time their position and arrangement is altered: the marvel is rather on Epicurus' view that the qualities of things should remain as constant as they do. Here we are once more on the lines of atomic tradition: the differences of quality are due to the three 'differences' of the atoms originally postulated by Leucippus, the differences of shape, position, and arrangement. Epicurus of course is not contented with mere tradition, but as usual appeals to phenomena: even in things

---

[1] Lucr. ii. 731 ff.
[2] Ep. i. 54 ποιότης γὰρ πᾶσα μεταβάλλει· αἱ δὲ ἄτομοι οὐδὲν μεταβάλλουσιν.   [3] Lucr. ii. 766 ff.
[4] 806 ff.   [5] Ep. i. 54.   [6] See pp. 330–7.

perceptible which change their shape by a mutual rearrangement of their parts, we see that other qualities are altered,
but the shape of the parts remains the same. So then in all
changes; the atoms with their unchangeable shapes cause
the differences and alterations in the qualities of things. The
idea is greatly elaborated by Lucretius,[1] who adduces a
series of proofs to show that the atoms are without colour
and then conscientiously applies the same notion to the
qualities perceptible by the other senses. We need not consider his arguments in detail, but we must here notice a
very important addition, which is not suggested in Epicurus'
more summary treatment. Not merely are the atoms without
qualities, but they are also without sensation:[2] here again
analogy might lead us astray and we might suppose that
those atoms which compose our 'soul' are themselves endowed with sensation. But this is not the case: all atoms are
completely without sensation and sensation and consciousness in us are due merely to particular movements on the
part of a particular combination of atoms: as arrangement
results in qualities, so movement may produce sensation.
It is manifest that this position will prove of great importance, when we come to consider the Epicurean psychology.

This denial of qualities to the atoms by Epicurus was
the subject of considerable criticism in antiquity.[3] In the
first place the critics asked how could atoms without qualities
merely by 'coming together' create things with qualities.
In the second they argued that Epicurus' theory was in
effect a denial of the reality of quality: if quality did not
belong to the atoms—the only real material existences—it
was in things a delusion: Democritus was right when he
said that qualities existed only in appearance (νόμῳ): the
senses were mistaken in attributing them to things, and
were not therefore infallible. Both criticisms are discerning
and important, but both rest on a failure to appreciate
Epicurus' true view of the nature of a compound body. If
a compound body were a mere aggregate of atoms—a

---

[1] ii. 730–864.   [2] ii. 865–990.
[3] See Plut. *adv. Colot.* 8, p. 1111 a, and other authorities quoted in U. 288.

collection of atoms, as it were, arbitrarily separated off from the hosts of surrounding atoms (much as the old astronomers separated off a 'constellation' from the surrounding stars), then these criticisms would hold true: the atoms could acquire no new powers in the compound body and must remain as they ever were. But this was by no means Epicurus' view: the compound body to him was not a mere aggregate, but a new entity, an 'organism' almost (σύστημα), or, as Lucretius calls it again and again, a *concilium*. In the organism of the whole the atoms did collectively acquire new properties and characteristics which as detached individuals they could never possess: no number of independent atoms could have colour, but unite them in the new entity of the whole, and it acquired colour. The idea is important and fruitful and we shall meet it again in the Epicurean kinetics and psychology. Moreover this whole is a reality, not a delusion: its reality for sense is as great as the reality of the atoms for thought: it is directly grasped by sense-perception, as the atoms are by 'mental apprehension'. And this carries with it the reality of its qualities: indeed, it is by the perception of its qualities that a thing's existence is known. To argue then that no quality which is not possessed by the individual atoms is 'real' in the compound, is to misunderstand fundamentally the Epicurean position. There are two worlds, or rather two departments of the same world, the one known by sense, the other by 'mental apprehension'; both are equally real, and in passing from the one to the other, matter acquires new qualities. The notion is in reality, as we have seen, underlying the Canonice,[1] and to lose sight of it in the physical theory is to misconstrue Epicurus all through.

We must turn now to Epicurus' conception of space, for, although from the nature of the case it is not so complicated as that of the atoms, it involves certain difficulties which cannot be disguised. The syllogistic argument by which he inferred the existence of space from the fact of motion has

---

[1] An interesting illustration of this idea is shown in Epicurus' argument in Ep. i, § 62, that the motion of a compound body is more than the aggregate motions of its compound atoms.

been discussed already:[1] we must now inquire more closely what it was that he meant by space. The mathematical conception of space as extension may be put out of court: it is impossible that Epicurus should have meant that for several reasons; (1) it would have been inconsistent with his whole attitude to the mathematical point of view, (2) it would have clashed with his theory of area as a succession of discrete *minima*,[2] (3) it is sufficiently contradicted by the many synonyms which he employs to describe it, and particularly with its definition as 'intangible existence'.[3] Space is an 'existence' just as much as body, it is not mere measurement or extension: it is a 'thing', but a thing whose sole property is that it cannot touch or be touched, it can offer no sort of resistance to body. Here then is his answer to the difficulties of the earlier Atomists: he does not trouble himself with their subtle discussions as to whether space is 'nothing'[4] (οὐκ ὄν), or 'non-existent' (μὴ ὄν); he simply affirms, with the same meaning but much closer precision, that it is an 'intangible existence'. The conception is not abstract but concrete: it is derived from that of body by a negation of its properties.

Yet considerable difficulty remains. Are we to conceive space as absolutely continuous and universal, coextensive with the universe itself, or as discrete and consisting only of the intervals between bodies? In other words, is there space in a place which is occupied by body, or is there not? does he mean 'place' or 'empty space'? The question is a very difficult one to decide and there seem many indications on either side. If we consider the synonyms[5] which Epicurus uses, we see that two of them, 'place' (τόπος) and 'room', (χώρα) are in favour of the former view, that by space he means occupied as well as empty space—a continuous whole: the same conclusion may be drawn from the definition of space as that 'in which things exist and through which they move',[6] and possibly (though I think it need not be inter-

---

[1] See p. 260.   [2] See p. 285.   [3] ἀναφὴς φύσις, Ep. i, § 40.
[4] See p. 279.   [5] §§ 39, 40.
[6] § 40: cf. Lucr. i. 442 'erit ut possint in eo res esse gerique'.

preted in this sense) the contention that space is infinite in extent: for if there is no space, where bodies are, then there is a limit to space. On the other side, we have the fourth synonym, 'the empty' (κενὸν),[1] which clearly suggests only unoccupied space, and the frequent reference to the void in compound bodies as 'intervals' (διαστήματα) between the component atoms. Most of the ancient commentators too seem to interpret Epicurus in this sense,[2] and among their comments is the express statement [3] of Simplicius that the Epicureans regarded space as 'the interval between the boundaries of that which surrounds it'. A consideration of the main passages in Epicurus and Lucretius, where space is mentioned, seems to show that they both oscillate between the two conceptions. Are we then to leave this difficulty—so fundamental in the system—as a point which Epicurus never really thought out? I believe that it arises largely from the fact that we are not easily able to approach Epicurus with a sufficiently concrete conception. Giussani,[4] in one of the most interesting of his Essays, has very largely cleared the matter up. He points out that we must think of Epicurus' notion primarily in relation to the ideas which he was combating. The Parmenideans, for instance, would readily admit the conception of space in the sense of 'extension', but they would maintain that there is matter everywhere, there is no such thing as empty space. In strong opposition to this view Epicurus wished to maintain not merely that there was empty space between portions of matter, but that empty space was a necessary presupposition to that of matter: there must be empty space in order that things may exist at all; otherwise there would be 'nowhere for them to be and nothing through which they might move'. 'Void' then is the fundamental notion always in the mind of Epicurus and his disciple, and therefore he is most often apt to think of it as completely empty space, or the intervals between matter.

[1] Lucretius' 'inane'.   [2] See U. 273, 274.

[3] Simpl. in Arist. *Phys.* Δ. 4, 211 b; U. 273 τὸ διάστημα τὸ μεταξὺ τῶν ἐσχάτων τοῦ περιέχοντος.

[4] *Stud. Lucr.*, i. 21–6.

Yet even where matter is present, he can still speak of
'place' or 'room', and think not of something which has
ceased to be void, but rather of potential void: it is indeed
empty space which happens temporarily to be occupied.
Space then does mean to Epicurus primarily 'empty space',
but he is not inconsistent when at times he includes in it
the 'place' which matter is for the moment filling. The two
ideas are significantly combined in another passage of
Simplicius,[1] where he says that the Atomists say that 'empty
space is infinite, and exceeds bodies in infinity (i.e. of extension), and for this reason can admit different things in its
different parts'. Here the conception works outwards, as
it were, from the notion of 'interval' to that of omnipresence.
But the unity of the two conceptions is made very much more
intelligible, if we remember that in Epicurus' idea[2] matter is
in perpetual motion: the atoms even in compound bodies
are never still. Consequently the occupation of empty space
by matter is never more than instantaneous: for no two consecutive instants is the same space occupied by the same atom.
The idea then of occupied space becomes almost an abstraction: it is an attempt to take a static view of what is always
kinetic. Our difficulty thus arises in great part from the
fact of our approaching the question with the presupposition
of a world of (mostly) stationary objects: if we can put ourselves back in thought to Epicurus' world of ever-moving
atoms, the contradiction between the two views of space very
largely disappears. Space thus means 'void', any portion of
which may momentarily, but not more, be occupied by an
atom.

We come back then to the original conception of the
Universe as atoms moving in space and we must ask finally
whether this universe and its two constituents are or are not
infinite. Epicurus gives the traditional answer of the atomic
school, but once again supports it with argument.[3] 'The
universe is boundless. For that which is bounded has an
extreme point: and the extreme point is seen against some-

---

[1] In Arist. *Phys. Δ*. 5, 213 a; U. 273.
[2] Ep. i, § 62: see p. 311.   [3] Ep. i, § 41.

thing else. So that as it has no extreme point, it has no limit; and as it has no limit it must be boundless and not bounded.' Lucretius[1] puts the proof rather more lucidly: 'it is seen that nothing can have an extreme point, unless there is something beyond to bound it, so that there is seen to be a spot farther than which the nature of our sense cannot follow it. As it is, since we must admit that there is nothing outside the whole sum, it has not an extreme point, it lacks therefore bound and limit.' The appeal is then once again to phenomena: the condition of limitation there, the existence of something else beyond, is one which cannot be applied to our mental conception of the universe. Lucretius brings out his point by the famous illustration of the hurling of the spear. 'Go, if you can, he challenges the doubter, to the extreme limit of the universe and hurl a spear: either it will be stopped or it will go on: if it is stopped, there will be matter beyond, if it goes on there will be empty space: in either case you did not start from the end of the universe. The same will happen wherever you take your stand.' The universe then cannot have a limit.

Moreover the two constituents are also infinite, though in different senses, the atoms in number and the void in extent.[2] For, as Lucretius argues,[3] in order that the sum total, the universe, may be unlimited, either both or one or other of its constituents must be infinite. Epicurus then deals with the two questions separately. 'If the void were boundless, and the bodies limited in number, the bodies could not stay anywhere, but would be carried about and scattered through the infinite void, not having other bodies to support them and keep them in place by means of collisions.' The statement is careful and precise: the condition of the creation of things is the constant collision of atoms and their crowding together in such numbers as to be able to enter into the combined existence of a compound, which in its turn is kept together and held in its place by the

[1] i. 960–7.
[2] Ep. i, § 41: τῷ πλήθει τῶν σωμάτων ἄπειρόν ἐστι τὸ πᾶν καὶ τῷ μεγέθει τοῦ κενοῦ.   [3] i. 1008–13.

external blows of other countless atoms. That this may occur in an infinite universe, it is necessary that there should be an infinite supply of matter: otherwise the comparatively few collisions which would take place would just send individual atoms wandering far out into space, where they would have no chance of meeting their fellows. Lucretius[1] elaborates the idea with a fine imaginative description of the chaos which must ensue.

Similarly, space is infinite in extent: for 'if the void were limited, the infinite bodies would have no room wherein to take their place'.[2] Lucretius'[3] argument here is rather different and perhaps less satisfactory: 'if space were limited, the atoms through the downward motion due to weight would all have sunk to the bottom and there remained in an inert mass: it is because there is no bottom that they are still kept in eternal restlessness'. The limitation of space would in fact preclude the ceaseless motion of the atoms which is an essential part of the atomic conception. The argument is more esoteric and less likely than Epicurus' own to convince a non-Epicurean. It is simpler and more cogent to maintain that unless space were infinite, there would not be room for infinite atoms.

The idea of the infinity of space raises again the question of the conception of space and presents the same difficulty. One is inclined to ask: does not the existence of the infinite number of atoms really preclude the infinity of space: for each atom, inasmuch as it is not itself empty space, is really a limitation to it? This question requires a careful answer. It is tempting to argue that the instantaneous occupation of any 'piece' of space by an atom does not interfere with the conception of space as continuous and infinite 'place', in which the atoms have their momentary station. But there is a good reason against this: if this were the Epicurean conception, then space would itself be coextensive with the universe, whereas Epicurus always speaks of the universe as 'body plus void':[4] the sum total of matter, divided though it

---

[1] i. 1014–51. [2] § 42. [3] i. 988–1007.
[4] § 39: τὸ πᾶν ἐστι σώματα καὶ τόπος: cf. Lucr. i. 1008–113.

is into infinite particles in ceaseless motion has to be added to infinite void to make the sum total of the infinite universe. Similarly it is significant that in this section space is spoken of throughout as 'the void' (κενὸν) and not 'place' (τόπος) as before. It would probably be a more correct solution of the difficulty to say that this 'internal' limitation of space, if it may be so described, was not here present to Epicurus' mind. He was thinking rather, as he clearly was when speaking of the infinity of the universe, of an 'external' limit (πέρας). In extension outward space is unlimited (ἄπειρον), even though internally it might be thought of as limited by the presence of atomic matter. Once again the notion of 'empty space' seems to be uppermost and that from which Epicurus started: the kinetic view of matter helps to an understanding of his point of view, but the particular difficulty would not have troubled him.

We have then at last reached the traditional atomic conception of an infinite universe, consisting of atoms infinite in number moving in space infinite in extent. The conception has not varied since Democritus, but in its gradual unfolding in Epicurus it seems almost to have changed its nature. Each step in the argument has now been thought out under the definite rules of the Canonice: the detached notions about the character of the atoms have been correlated into a self-dependent whole: a universe seems not to have been assumed but created in thought. There has been occasion here and there to point out weak points in the argument or possibly hazy and ill-defined conceptions. But the result is one worthy of a great thinker: it is no mere wholesale adoption of the theory of Democritus—in certain places it has been seen to differ conspicuously from it: nor is it the work of a preacher, who hastily patched together some kind of physical theory to act as a basis for his moral teaching. With all its limitations, it is the construction of a master-mind, working on definite lines and with a deep and penetrating interest in his subject for its own sake. Nor will these characteristics be missed, as the further development of the system is traced in detail.

IV

PROPERTIES AND ACCIDENTS

THE title of this section might seem to suggest that Epicurus' profession of disbelief in the value of Logic was something of a pretence and that he was after all driven back on the current terminology of the schools. But, as will be seen, nothing could be farther from the truth: if Epicurus was led to make a distinction corresponding roughly to that between properties and accidents, he was not influenced by any considerations of Logic, nor does the distinction take a Logical form. His problem is essentially material and his answer is on strictly material lines and perfectly consistent with the rest of his theory—indeed he is at pains to refute more intellectual and idealistic views.

To recall the position hitherto reached, the only absolute, i.e. independent, existences are the atoms and the void: the atoms corporeal, body or matter and nothing else, the void incorporeal, simply that which separates the atoms or that in which the atoms 'move and have their being'. Now, if we turn to the language and experience of ordinary life, it is clear that this dualism does not exhaust the whole of existence. It does indeed account for the whole material world, since things as we know them, things perceptible to the senses, are but aggregates of atoms with greater or smaller interstices of void. But there is a residue: we attribute to things properties and qualities: even to the atoms are assigned size, shape, and weight, and to compound bodies qualities expressive of their relation to the senses, colour, scent, taste, and sound, or of their character, goodness and badness, virtue and vice: we speak also of their doings and sufferings and of events which concern one or many things and persons: we have further the conception of time, in which such events occur. What is to be said of all these from the atomic point of view? It is clear that they cannot be classed under either of the heads of being which have hitherto been established: they are not independent existences, either corporeal like the atoms, or incorporeal like the void—for they cannot be thought of apart from the things to which they are attributed; nor again are they independent corporeal compounds of atoms and void. How then can their existence be described? They are, says Epicurus,[1] either 'something which always accompanies things'[2] (συμβεβηκότα) or roughly speaking 'inseparable properties', or 'something which from time to time happens to things' (συμπτώματα), or 'separable accidents'. These two notions must be examined more closely.

In introducing his conception of the 'accompaniments' (συμβεβηκότα) Epicurus[3] in his usual manner briefly dismisses without any mention of names the theories of rival schools. Plato in the theory of ideas had imagined qualities as independent existences, and supposed the reality of phenomena to depend on their 'participation' in such 'ideas': this conception Epicurus dismisses by the test of 'visualization': 'we must not suppose that they are independent existences, for it is impossible to imagine that', we cannot, that is, form any mental picture of a quality apart from the thing which possesses it. Aristotle had conceived qualities as 'incorporeal existences accompanying body': Epicurus meets him with a mere negative, but his reason would doubtless be that they cannot be incorporeal, for they are perceptible by the senses. Similarly he rejects the notion of his predecessor Democritus that 'they absolutely do not exist'—for immediate experience contradicts it—and that of the Stoics[4] that they are material parts (μόρια) of things. None of these theories are consistent with the Epicurean canons, or, as he

---

[1] Ep. i, § 68.

[2] We must notice that Epicurus uses the word in a different sense to that in which it had been employed by Aristotle: to him it meant 'an occasional accident', to Epicurus 'a permanent property', a meaning more naturally associated with the perfect participle: 'that which has come to be permanently with' a thing.   [3] See Hicks, op. cit., p. 272.

[4] The Stoics spoke of properties, accidents, qualities and emotions, and even of time itself as 'bodies' (ζῷα or σώματα): see Giussani, *Stud. Lucr.* p. 28; Zeller, *Gesch. der Phil. der Griechen*, iii. 1 (3rd ed.), pp. 118 ff. and passages there quoted, esp. Plut. *Comm. Not.* 45, 2 and 5, and Sen. *Ep.* 106, 5.

would have said himself, correspond with the ordinary experience of perception.

Epicurus' own explanation [1] of the 'accompaniments' is careful and, in spite of certain textual difficulties in the passage, easily intelligible.

We must suppose that the whole body in its totality owes its own permanent existence (τὴν ἑαυτοῦ φύσιν ἀΐδιον) to all these, yet not in the sense that it is composed of properties brought together to form it (as when, for instance, a larger structure is put together out of the parts which compose it . . .), but only that it owes its own permanent existence to all of them. All these properties have their own peculiar means of being perceived and distinguished (ἐπιβολὰς . . . ἰδίας . . . καὶ διαλήψεις), provided always that the aggregate body (τὸ ἄθροον) goes along with them and is never wrested from them, but in virtue of its comprehension as an aggregate of qualities acquires the predicate of body.

The property, that is, is perceptible by the senses: shape, size, weight, colour, &c., are all known to us by sensational evidence and therefore are real, are in that sense material existences. Further they are distinguishable one from another and make each their own peculiar appeal to the senses: we cannot tell weight by the sense of smell, nor colour by touch, &c. But this existence is not an independent one: it is wholly dependent upon the presence of the body to which they are attributed: we cannot perceive or even conceive properties existing apart from body. Conversely, the matter may be considered from the point of view of the body as a whole. The body is in the purely material sense an aggregate of particles, which came together to form it: but it is also an aggregate of qualities existing in it always and together making up its 'permanent' existence.[2] It is just the sum of its shape, size, weight, colour, smell, &c., which make a thing what it is: and no one of them could be removed without destroying the existence of the thing as such.

[1] § 69.

[2] By 'permanent' (ἀΐδιον) Epicurus does not of course intend to imply the eternity of compound bodies, which is contrary to all his teaching, but only that the aggregate of qualities makes the thing what it is as long as it lasts.

Lucretius[1] in his definition lays emphasis on this aspect of the conception: 'a property is that which in no case can be sundered or separated without the fatal dissolution of the thing': if we tried to remove a property from a compound thing there would follow an atomic or material dissolution (*discidium*).[2] The 'accompaniment' is then inseparable from the thing in the sense that its removal, possible only in thought, would at once destroy both its own nature and that of the thing. Epicurus nowhere gives us a concise definition, but we may extract it from his discussion: 'properties (or "accompaniments") are existences perceptible by the senses, but inseparably associated with things, whose permanent nature in their aggregate they constitute'.

It may serve to bring out the idea and to prepare the way for further criticism, if we attempt in a few instances, as Lucretius[3] has done, to apply this notion. What are the properties of the two primary existences, atoms, and the void? The void has but the one negative property of intangibility:[4] it is, by definition, an 'intangible existence' (ἀναφὴς φύσις). If it lost this property, if it could at any point or under any circumstances be touched, it would cease to be void and become matter. The properties of the atoms are, as has been seen,[5] size, shape, and weight: to remove in thought any one of these is to destroy the conception of the atom as a material existence—it would pass out of the range of matter altogether.[6] When we pass to compound things, it is clear that they still retain the three properties of

---

[1] i. 451. Note that Lucretius, following the principle of the Canonice, does not attempt to translate συμβεβηκός, but uses the normal Latin *coniunctum*, which will convey the clearest idea to his countrymen.

[2] *discidium* in Lucretius is the opposite of *concilium*, the union of atoms in a 'thing', which is more than a mere aggregate.

[3] i. 453, 4.

[4] Lucr. i. 454, *intactus inani*: Munro in excising this line removes an absolutely essential point from the argument: cf. Sext. Emp. *adv. Math.* x. 221 ἀντιτυπία μὲν τοῦ σώματος, εἶξις δὲ τοῦ κενοῦ.

[5] p. 290: to these might be added hardness or solidity or, as Sextus has it, ἀντιτυπία, the 'power of returning a blow', i.e. of colliding with other atoms and knocking them away as it rebounds itself.

[6] Cf. the discussion of the πέρατα on p. 286.

the atoms: an aggregate of atoms must have all the properties which the component parts possess and we can conceive of no material body apart from size, shape, and weight. But this is not now all: for the compounds acquire also new properties: fire for instance must have heat and water wetness.[1] If either of them was to be deprived of these respective qualities, it would cease to be what it is: if water, for instance, is frozen so hard that it is no longer wet, it is not now water but ice, and as such acquires new 'accompaniments', because its physical constitution is changed. There is then no difference in the conception of the 'accompaniments' of compound bodies and the atoms: but when it comes to the enumeration of the 'accompaniments' there is a difference. Of the atoms it may be said finally that their permanent and only 'accompaniments' are size, shape, and weight: but the 'accompaniments' of compound bodies differ with all the variety of things which they constitute: each one of them is the sum of those 'accompaniments', those properties and qualities, the removal of any one of which would alter the physical constitution of the thing.

The notion of the 'things which happen' (συμπτώματα), which we may roughly translate 'accidents',[2] follows almost directly from that of the 'accompaniments'. They are similarly neither imperceptible, nor incorporeal, nor independent corporeal existences like the whole body:[3] nor yet are they, as are the properties, the invariable and 'permanent' accompaniments of the whole. Rather they are occasional accompaniments, which may come and go, and are perceptible not in all acts of apprehension of the senses, but only in some. We cannot, for instance, have any perception of a man which does not tell us of his size and shape, but we may have many which do not tell us whether he is rich or poor, free or slave, asleep or awake. Lucretius[4] again puts it well for us from the atomic point of view. Accidents are such things

---

[1] Lucr. i. 453.

[2] So Lucr. i. 458, explaining his use of the current term, renders:
'haec soliti sumus, ut par est, eventa vocare'.

[3] Ep. i, § 70.   [4] i. 456, 7.

'by whose going and coming the nature of things abides untouched', that is, their presence or absence involves no atomic dissolution (though it may involve atomic rearrangement), and does not alter the nature of things as such. The main difficulty in the idea is that the term is extremely wide: Epicurus wishes it to cover not merely what we might call 'secondary qualities', but also states of action and suffering, and the whole field of occurrences. It may be well again to illustrate from the three kinds of existing things: it is an 'accident' of the void that a certain atom is moving in it in a certain direction, it is an 'accident' of an atom to have a certain 'position'[1] (θέσις) or 'place' (τάξις) or to enter into the formation of a certain compound body. These are simple cases, but when we come to compound things the idea is more far-reaching. All kinds of qualities, colour, heat, cold, goodness, badness, hardness, softness, and so on, may be the 'accidents' of bodies, and so is everything that they do and everything that happens to them: 'slavery and liberty, poverty and wealth, war and peace' are Lucretius' examples, and later on[2] he explains that all the events of history are the accidents of the persons concerned in them or of the places where they occur.[3]

Under the head of 'accidents' Epicurus deals with Time.[4] To us who are accustomed to class Time, whether as a condition of perception or in any other category, always with space, this treatment may seem strange. But it must be remembered that Epicurus' conception of space was essentially concrete, and so conceived it had taken its place for him as one of the two ultimate realities. To it Time offered no apparent analogy: it did not, like space, enter into the physical composition of things, nor could it, he held, be at all conceived, as space could, as existing apart from things

---

[1] See p. 80.   [2] i. 464 ff.

[3] It is not necessary here to discuss the curious problem relating to past events which is treated by Lucretius in i. 464–82: it arises from a Stoic objection to the conception of events as the 'accidents' of persons or things themselves no longer existing, and Lucretius rightly replies that the events *were* their accidents, for without the persons or things the events could not have occurred.   [4] §§ 72, 73.

happening in it. He must then search for an explanation of
time in accordance with ordinary experience and in strict
conformity with atomic principles. Now all other things,
concrete existences and their attributes, are recognized by
means of reference to a general concept or 'anticipation'[1]
(πρόληψις): we know a horse because of the general image of
'horse' which is stored in our mind, we know hardness or
wetness by similar reference to a concept built up out of a
number of individual experiences. But this is not so with
time: we do not recognize a 'time' by reference to a general
notion of 'times' resulting from many experiences. On the
contrary it is a continuous experience, incapable of general
conception, but always with us, and always an immediate
'clear perception' (ἐνάργημα). Moreover it cannot be explained by means of any description,[2] or by any reference to
anything analogous to it:[3] it is in our experience *sui generis*.
Is it then impossible to analyse further this perception?
Epicurus thinks not except in relation to the ordinary
associations of everyday life. Time is something that we
connect with other things, yet not directly, as attributes and
qualities are associated with things: time is not thought of
as immediately dependent on things or persons. Rather it is
associated with the actions of persons and things,[4] with what
happens to them, with their movements or cessations from
movement, with the succession of light and darkness which
we call day and night. Now all these things are themselves
the accidents of things, and time stands to them in the same
relation as they themselves occupy to things: it is then, in
other words, as Sextus Empiricus[5] tells us that Epicurus
himself defined it, 'an accident of accidents, accompanying
days and nights and seasons, and states of suffering and
quiescence and movement and rest.' Lucretius[6] again assists
us with a clear statement free from technicalities: 'Time

---

[1] See pp. 245 ff.　　　[2] οὔτε διαλέκτους ὡς βελτίους μεταληπτέον.
[3] οὔτε ἄλλο τι κατ᾽ αὐτοῦ κατηγορητέον.　　　　　　　　[4] § 73.
[5] *adv. Math.* x. 219; U. 294 σύμπτωμα συμπτωμάτων ... παρεπόμενον
ἡμέραις τε καὶ νυξὶ καὶ ὥραις καὶ πάθεσι καὶ ἀπαθείαις καὶ κινήσεσι καὶ
μοναῖς.　　　　　　　　　　　　　　　　　　　[6] i. 459–61.

exists not by itself, but from actual things comes a feeling, what was brought to a close in time past, then what is present now, and further what is going to be hereafter.' This is not perhaps a profound investigation into the problems which surround the conception of time—problems more apparent to the modern than the ancient world—but it is at least a more satisfactory account than that of Epicurus' Stoic opponents, who regarded time as an independent concrete entity (σῶμα) superadded to things, and it is reached by the consistent analysis of the 'clear intuition' of everyday experience.

The main notions then which Epicurus attaches to the words συμβεβηκότα and συμπτώματα are clear enough, but they are not without difficulty in their application, and critics who have been perhaps too ready to assume the identity of Epicurus' ideas with those expressed by the accepted translations 'properties' and 'accidents' have accused him of indefiniteness and inconsistency. Thus Munro [1] complains that the two notions are not clearly distinguished and in particular that Epicurus [2] speaks of 'doing' and 'suffering' as 'accidents' of the soul, whereas, seeing that they are invariable experiences they must be 'accompaniments'. Brieger [3] similarly charges him with inconsistency in putting colour among 'accompaniments', whereas the mere fact that the atoms are colourless is sufficient proof that it is not an invariable accompaniment of body. The only answer to such criticism is, as Giussani [4] has admirably pointed out, that the critics themselves have not accurately grasped Epicurus' conception. Two points in it must be emphasized. In the first place, the whole notion is essentially material and directly related to the main ideas of the atomic theory: the 'accompaniment' is not merely invariably present, but an essential element in the physical constitution of things. Time is inseparably connected with all material existence, but so far from being an 'accompaniment' of anything, it is, as has been seen, an 'accident of accidents': weight on the other hand, a physical constituent of body as such, is an 'accom-

---

[1] On Lucr. i. 449.   [2] § 67.
[3] *Epikurs Brief an Herodot*, p. 7.   [4] *Stud. Lucr.*, pp. 33 seq.

paniment'. Here is the answer to Munro: though the soul
is always acting and suffering, yet these states are not a
direct characteristic of the atomic constitution of the soul:
they are therefore 'accidents'.

In the second place the terms in Epicurus' usage are not
absolute but relative. It is not Epicurus' intention to divide
all qualities rigidly and permanently into the two categories,
nor would he have said absolutely of any quality 'this is
always an 'accompaniment', or 'this is always an accident'.
Rather any quality might stand in the relation of 'accompaniment' to one thing and 'accident' to another. It is
because they have not grasped this relativity in Epicurus'
idea and the consequent interchangeability of the two terms
in their application to individual qualities and have looked
rather for a rigid division such as that of 'primary' and
'secondary qualities', that critics have complained of Epicurus' vagueness or inconsistency. But a closer examination of his words makes the point quite clear. The
section opens thus:[1] 'as regards shape and colour and size
and weight and all other things which are predicated of body
as though they were "accompaniments" either of all things
or of things visible or recognizable through the sensation of
these qualities'.[2] Brieger accuses Epicurus of inconsistency
in having here included colour in the list of 'accompaniments',
though it is not always an 'accompaniment' of body. In
relation to the atoms colour is clearly neither 'accompaniment' nor 'accident', for under no circumstances whatever can the atoms have colour. In the case of compound
bodies in general, colour is an 'accident', for in the dark
they have no colour and it requires the blows of light
falling upon them so to arrange the configuration of their
surface that they have colour. Of what then is it an 'accompaniment'? Clearly of *visible* things: it is impossible for us

---

[1] § 68 ὡσανεὶ συμβεβηκότα ἢ πᾶσιν ἢ τοῖς ὁρατοῖς καὶ κατὰ τὴν
αἴσθησιν αὐτῶν γνωστοῖς. The text at the end of the clause is uncertain.
αὐτῶν, the reading of P3, is preferable to αὐτοῖς of the manuscripts; but
there is no need for more drastic emendation, such as was proposed by Usener:
see my note on the passage.   [2] See Lucr. ii. 795 ff.

to see anything, except it has colour: things can only be visible when the atomic formation of their surface is such as to produce colour: alter it, so that they could have colour no longer, and they would pass out of the range of the visible. Colour is the 'accompaniment' not of all things, but of visible things. And it is clearly for this reason that Epicurus having included colour amongst the 'accompaniments' has added in direct reference to it the words 'or of visible things'. Similarly amplifying the idea in reference to the other senses he adds: 'or of things recognizable through the sensation of these qualities': this will include, for instance, things capable of being tasted and smelt: their taste and their smell is in these categories 'an accompaniment', but it will not be if they are thought of simply as 'compound bodies' or as 'visible things'. Similarly 'slavery', to take one of Lucretius' examples, is an 'accident' if thought of in relation say to Epictetus, but an 'accompaniment', if in relation to 'a slave'. If the essentially atomic character of the whole idea and the consequent relativity of the terms be borne in mind, there is no ground for charging Epicurus either with indefiniteness or inconsistency.

Having thus enunciated his doctrine of 'accompaniments' and 'accidents' Epicurus has from the Atomic point of view covered the whole field of possible existence. All things which can be the objects of perception or of thought must be either one of the two ultimate realities, atoms and space, or concrete bodies, formed by their combination, or the 'accompaniments' or 'accidents' of these, or, in the single instance of Time, an 'accident' of 'accidents'. It may be that his theory is lacking in philosophic penetration and that he had not fully considered the difficulties which it involves, but it is entirely consistent with his general position and arises directly from his conception of the constitution of things and the nature of perception and thought. The base-conception of the universe has thus been established and it remains to consider next the more strictly physical part of the theory, to see what are the motions of the atoms in the void and how they combine to form things.

V

MOTION OF THE ATOMS

NO part of Epicurus' physical theory was worked out with greater elaboration than his conception of atomic motion. Nor merely does he devote a quite disproportionate part of his Letter to Herodotus to this subject,[1] but he there deals with it with a minuteness which shows the importance he attached to its right understanding. His pupil Lucretius too, though he does not enter into some of the refinements of his master, gives a large section of the Second Book to its special consideration and alludes to the topic again in other places.[2] Nor indeed is this surprising: for it is in this portion of his work that Epicurus most conspicuously broke away from Democritus and produced in the doctrine of the atomic 'swerve' the most characteristic notion in his system: moreover his treatment of the motion of the atoms in compounds reveals the subtlety of his thought at its best and throws considerable light on his whole conception of matter and space. Though the subject is not free from difficulty—the sections on motion in the first Letter are among the most obscure—it is possible to put together a fairly clear account of his views.

§ 1. *The 'free' atoms*

The first matter to be considered is the motion of the 'free' atoms, that is to say, those not as yet entangled in compound bodies or atomic nuclei. Though, as will appear later, this is for the most part but a theoretical condition, yet some atoms are always in this state,[3] and their unimpeded motion is always a necessary logical antecedent to the

---

[1] § 43, parts of §§ 46 and 47, §§ 61 and 62, all of which (except the one sentence in § 43) should probably, as was suggested by Giussani (*Stud. Lucr.* 14), be rearranged so as to be consecutive. They form about one-tenth of the whole letter and it is probable that at least one section has been lost which belonged to the same topic: see p. 316.

[2] ii. 62–293.

[3] Lucr. ii. 109–11.

movements of atoms in compounds and of compound bodies as a whole. The atom is situated in empty space: is it at rest or in motion? and if in motion, what is the ultimate cause of its motion and what is the character of the motion? These were the questions which the Atomists had to answer. Some uncertainty prevails, as has been seen,[1] with regard to Democritus' solution of these problems, but it is most probable that he held that in the void the atoms were 'naturally' always in motion in all directions. Of Epicurus' answer there can be no doubt—whether the idea was his own or had already been introduced into the Atomic theory by Nausiphanes or some one else:[2] 'the atoms move continuously for all time',[3] their motion is 'downwards',[4] and the primary cause of motion is their weight.[5] Epicurus[6] having insisted as against Democritus that weight was a primary and absolute property of the atoms was free to use it as a cause of motion, and he argued doubtless on the direct analogy of phenomena. Every material body perceptible to the senses is caused to fall downwards by its own weight: therefore it must be the same with the imperceptible material bodies, the atoms.

But here a difficulty immediately arises: what can be

---

[1] See Part I, Chap. III, § 3, pp. 128 ff.   [2] See p. 129.

[3] Ep. i, § 43 κινοῦνταί τε συνεχῶς αἱ ἄτομοι τὸν αἰῶνα. It is unfortunate that there is a lacuna after these words, but statements elsewhere make it possible to fill in the sense with some certainty: see C.B. notes ad loc.

[4] Lucr. ii. 217:
>corpora cum deorsum rectum per inane feruntur
>ponderibus propriis.

Simplicius (in Arist. *de Caelo*, A. 8, p. 121 a 18, and again p. 121 b 25; U. 276) attributes to Epicurus the theory that weight caused the atoms to move towards the centre. This is inconsistent with everything else in Epicurus' theory of motion and is expressly refuted as a Stoic doctrine by Lucr. i. 1052ff. It must be due to confusion with the account of the motion of particles in the cosmic 'whirl'.

[5] § 61 ἡ κάτω (φορὰ) διὰ τῶν ἰδίων βαρῶν, ibid. ἐκ τοῦ ἰδίου βάρους, cf. Lucr. ii. 83:
>cuncta necessest
>aut gravitate sua ferri primordia rerum
>aut ictu forte alterius.

[6] See § 2, p. 289.

meant by motion 'downwards' in reference to infinite space? Plato [1] had already argued that to speak of 'up' and 'down' in relation to infinite space is an absurdity, and it is possible that if the idea had been introduced into Atomism before Epicurus, some direct criticism had been made on it. At any rate Epicurus himself seems acutely conscious of the difficulty and argues about it at some length in a misplaced and obscure paragraph in the Letter to Herodotus.[2] It is true, he says in effect, that in infinite space we cannot speak of an 'up' and 'down' with reference to a highest or lowest point in space itself, for such there cannot be. But we can say that motion is in a certain direction, 'up' or 'down' in reference to objects situated in space: for instance, we may call motion in the direction from our own head to our feet motion 'down' and that in the reverse direction motion 'up', 'even though that which passes from us into the regions above our heads arrives countless times at the feet of beings above and that which passes downwards from us at the heads of beings below; for none the less the whole motions are thought of as opposed, the one to the other, to infinity.'[3]

This reply has provoked the scorn of modern critics[4] as a puerile evasion of a serious difficulty, and indeed such criticism would be justified if Epicurus' conception of space were that of the modern mathematician. To him motion in a certain direction in infinite space is unthinkable, because the relative position of two points—even the absolute position of a single point—in infinite space is itself unthinkable: if infinite space is infinite extension in the abstract, no terms involving relation can be used with regard to it.[5] But it

---

[1] *Timaeus,* 62 d.   [2] § 60.

[3] The argument seems lame, for if motion upwards from us went on arriving at the feet of persons in the worlds above us, it would still be motion upwards to them and our idea would be confirmed. I suspect that the words 'at the feet' (ἐπὶ τοὺς πόδας) and 'at the heads' (ἐπὶ τὴν κεφαλήν) ought to be interchanged: see C.B. notes ad loc.

[4] e.g. Brieger, *de atomorum motu principali* (*Philosoph. Abhand. zu Martin Herz*), p. 217 'quae quam inepte excogitata sint nemo est quin videat'.

[5] Giussani, *Stud. Lucr.* 133, n. 1, replied to Brieger's objection by a *reductio ad absurdum* on his own assumption. If relative position and determinate

cannot too often be repeated that Epicurus' notion of space was physical [1]—one might almost say concrete—and geocentric. To him space was a void, every part of which was capable of being filled or actually filled with matter: and its infinity [2] he would have pictured to himself as extending outwards in every direction from the earth to the limits of our world and then on beyond to other worlds and beyond them again without limit: space extends in all directions *away from us*. In such a conception there is a possibility of the determination of relative position, relative direction, and relative motion: we can, as he says, take a point in our world and speak of motion as 'up' and 'down' in relation to it. The weight of the atoms, as he conceived it, must always produce motion in one determinate direction and that direction may be described as 'downward' in reference to ourselves. The reply no doubt to some extent shirks the difficulty, but Epicurus never felt himself bound to think out his views in reference to other systems, but only to make them consistent with his own. His idea may perhaps be regarded as a first essay in Relativity.

The atoms in the void are thus carried 'downwards' by their own weight, falling in perpendicular straight lines [3] 'like drops of rain'.[4] How can they ever meet and form things? Lucretius [5] is here our sole authority for a view which, one may reasonably suppose, had been put forward at some stage in the Atomic theory, after weight had been recognized as the cause of motion. It might be inferred on the analogy of the sensible world, that differences of weight in the atoms are the cause of their meeting; that the heavier atoms in their downward course catch up the lighter and so come into collision and form atomic nuclei which afterwards

motion in infinite space are unthinkable, the phenomenal world becomes a delusion. But such an argument would not have been present to Epicurus, and it seems possible and more satisfactory to discover a positive reply in Epicurus' own main conceptions. [1] See § 2, pp. 293 ff.

[2] Compare the argument with regard to the infinity of the universe in §§ 41, 42, and Lucr. i. 958 ff.

[3] κατὰ στάθμην is the Epicurean description of this straight fall: Aet. i. 12. 5; U. 280, &c. [4] Lucr. ii. 222. [5] ii. 225 ff.

unite to produce sensible things. But here the subtlety of Epicurus' mind came into play and he saw that the analogy would not hold: in the sensible world the cause of the diminution of speed was a check given to the moving body either by the opposition of some external body or in the case of a compound by the internal vibration of its component atoms.[1] Thus when bodies are falling through air or water,[2] the comparatively loose texture of the medium is not able to stop them altogether, but it does oppose a check, and the lighter the falling body, the more effective is the check and the slower its progress. Or again the motion of a compound body started by an external blow may be impeded and ultimately stopped by the internal movements of its constituent atoms in all directions. But in the case of atoms falling through space neither of these conditions can come into play. The void can offer no resistance and the constitution of the atom itself is perfectly solid; the 'least parts' have no separate existence and cannot move internally apart from the atom as a whole. Difference of weight then cannot be the cause of atomic collision, for all the atoms,[3] heavier and lighter alike, will move downwards through the void at an equal rate. Epicurus has thus arrived by a 'mental apprehension' at the result which modern science has confirmed by experiment that in a vacuum all bodies irrespective of their weight will fall at an equal speed.

This motion of the atoms through the void, being absolutely unimpeded, will be of incomprehensible velocity: 'their passage through the void, when it takes place without meeting any bodies which might collide, accomplishes every comprehensible distance in an inconceivably short time'.[4] The

---

[1] Ep. i, § 46 βράδους γὰρ καὶ τάχους ἀντικοπὴ καὶ οὐκ ἀντικοπὴ ὁμοίωμα λαμβάνει. For the fuller treatment of the characteristic idea of ἀντικοπή see pp. 329 ff.   [2] Lucr. ii. 230–4.

[3] § 61 ἰσοταχεῖς ἀναγκαῖον τὰς ἀτόμους εἶναι: cf. Lucr. ii. 238–9 f.
omnia quapropter debent per inane quietum
aeque ponderibus non aequis concita ferri.

[4] § 46b ἡ διὰ τοῦ κενοῦ φορὰ κατὰ μηδεμίαν ἀπάντησιν τῶν ἀντικοψόντων (U. ἀντικοψάντων MSS.) γινομένη πᾶν μῆκος περιληπτὸν ἐν ἀπερινοήτῳ χρόνῳ συντελεῖ.

atom, that is, can traverse any distance of which we are capable of conceiving in a space of time so small that we cannot visualize it: the speed of the atoms may therefore well be described in the expressive phrase of Giussani as 'absolute motion'.[1] Lucretius' illustration is peculiarly apt and gives occasion for one of his finest pieces of brief description.[2] At sunrise we see the whole world suddenly bathed in light: the sun's light travels with incredible velocity: yet it is impeded both externally and internally; how much greater must be the speed of the unimpeded atom? Once again modern science gives confirmatory evidence in statistics of velocity.[3] The later commentators give us more precise ideas of Epicurus' conception of atomic motion. Pursuing his usual line of argument against the Eleatics and their successors,[4] Epicurus[5] apparently held that there was not merely a minimum of extension (the πέρας or *minima pars*) and a minimum of physical existence (the atom), but also a minimum of movement (κίνησις) and a minimum of time (χρόνος). He held that the unimpeded atom accomplishes a minimum of movement in the minimum of time, and there would thus be a basis for the calculation of speed, just as the 'least part' gives the basis of calculation of size. This conception seems to be borne out in an important passage in the Letter to Herodotus, which must subsequently be considered, in which he speaks of the atoms in the compound body moving in different directions 'in moments of time perceptible only by thought',[6] the minimum that is of time. The whole notion of the incredible swiftness of this minimum of atomic movement was apparently expressed by Epicurus

---

[1] *Stud. Lucr.* 107.   [2] ii. 142–64.

[3] We are told, for instance, that the molecule of hydrogen moves at the rate of 1859 metres per second: see Masson, *Lucretius*, p. 124.

[4] On this point, see von Arnim, *Epikurs Lehre von Minimum*, and Bignone, *Epicuro*, Appendix V, pp. 228 ff.

[5] Simpl. in Arist. *Phys.* Z. 1. 232 a 1–17; U. 278 ἐξ ἀμερῶν γὰρ τὴν κίνησιν καὶ τὸ μέγεθος καὶ τὸν χρόνον εἶναι, idem in Arist. *Phys.* Z. 2. 232 a 23; U. 277 τοῖς περὶ Ἐπίκουρον ἀρέσκει ἰσοταχῶς πάντα διὰ τῶν ἀμερῶν κινεῖσθαι.

[6] § 62 κατὰ τοὺς λόγῳ θεωρητοὺς χρόνους.

by saying not that the atom 'moves' (κινεῖται) over the minimum of distance in the minimum of time, but that it 'has been moved' (κεκίνηται):[1] the action is instantaneous and complete as soon as begun. This idea exposed him to much criticism on the ground that it was impossible to conceive of a continuous motion composed of these instantaneous 'jerks', but on a more sympathetic view it is easy to see what Epicurus was trying to express by it. The idea is important as showing once again the penetration of Epicurus' kinetics, and because it becomes of value in explaining his conception of the relation of the movements of the atoms to that of the whole body in a compound.

§ 2. The 'swerve'

The atoms then, if this were a complete account of their motion, would fall for ever in the void at 'atomic speed' in parallel straight lines, 'nor could collision come to be, nor a blow be brought to pass for the first-beginnings; so nature would never have brought aught to being'.[2] By his stern refusal to avail himself of a false analogy in the sensible world Epicurus seems to have brought his system to a standstill. But he had his own characteristic solution, which though it has brought a storm of criticism on his head as a childish blunder, was yet not only meant in all seriousness, but designed as one of the crucial points in his system. It is curious that there is no mention of the 'swerve' of the atoms in the Letter to Herodotus: it must have been there either at the beginning of § 43, where some words have been lost, or in another section which has perished. But we have evidence enough for it elsewhere. Diogenes of Oenoanda [3] refers to it in a rhetorical passage in which he is

---

[1] Them. paraphr. Arist. *Phys.* Z. 1. 232 a; U. 278 ἐφ᾽ ἑκάστου δὲ τῶν ἀμερῶν ἐξ ὧν συγκεῖται (*sc.* the whole distance travelled) οὐ κινεῖται ἀλλὰ κεκίνηται: cf. Simpl. ad eundem locum; U. 278 ἐπάγει δὲ καὶ ἄλλο ἄτοπον ἀκολουθοῦν ταύτῃ τῇ ὑποθέσει, τὸ κεκινῆσθαί τι μὴ πρότερον κινούμενον.

[2] Lucr. ii. 223, 4.

[3] *fr.* xxxiii, William, col. ii, *fin.*, William [οὔκουν] οἶδας, ὅστις ποτὲ εἶ, καὶ ἐλευθέραν τινὰ ἐν ταῖς ἀτόμοις κίνησιν εἶναι, ἥ[ν] Δημόκριτος μὲν οὐχ εὗρεν Ἐπίκουρος δὲ εἰς φῶ[ς] ἤγαγεν, παρεγκλιτικὴν ὑπάρχουσαν,

arguing against an imaginary supporter of Democritus: 'do you not know, whoever you are, that there is also a free motion in the atoms, which Democritus did not discover, but Epicurus brought to light, a "swerving" motion, as he proves from phenomena'. Lucretius [1] too has dealt fully with the subject and the ironical criticisms of Plutarch [2] and Cicero [3] help further to an understanding of the nature of the 'swerve' and the manner in which it suggested itself to Epicurus' mind. The root-notion is clear enough: as the atoms are falling in the void, 'at times quite undetermined and at undetermined spots they push a little from their path; yet only just so much as you could call a change of trend'.[4] This swerving causes collision with other atoms: as the result of such collisions direction is changed again, and there results at once the ferment of atoms moving in every direction, which gives rise to their union in compounds and causes the world of sensible things.

The most scathing criticism has been directed against this notion of the 'tiny swerve'[5] both by ancient and by modern writers. Thus Cicero speaks of it as a 'puerile invention',[6] and with more penetration complains elsewhere that such a notion is really a disgraceful abandonment by Epicurus of his main position.[7] This is indeed the line of attack which has been most usually adopted: this 'swerve' of the atoms is a contradiction of the 'laws of nature' (*foedera naturai*) on which Epicurus' system is based: it is a breach of his own first principle that 'nothing is created out of nothing', for it is a force absolutely without a cause. The laws of atomic

---

ὡς ἐκ τῶν φαινομένων δείκνυσιν ; παρέγκλισις must have been Epicurus' technical term for the 'swerve': cf. Aet. I. 12. 5 κινεῖσθαι δὲ τὰ ἄτομα τότε μὲν κατὰ στάθμην, τότε δὲ κατὰ παρέγκλισιν: cf. idem, i. 23. 4; U. 280: Lucretius' translation is *clinamen*.   [1] ii. 216–93.

[2] *de Sollertia Anim.* 7, p. 964 e; U. (Spic.) 281 ἄτομον παρεγκλῖναι μίαν ἐπὶ τοὔλαχιστον, ὅπως ἄστρα καὶ ζῷα καὶ τύχη παρεισέλθῃ καὶ τὸ ἐφ᾽ ἡμῖν μὴ ἀπόληται.   [3] *de Fin.* i. 6. 19; *de Fato*, 10. 22. U. 281.

[4] Lucr. ii. 218–20.   [5] 'exiguum clinamen', Lucr. ii. 292.

[6] *de Fin.* i. 6. 19 'res ficta pueriliter'.

[7] *de Nat. Deor.* i. 25. 70 'hoc dicere turpius est quam illud quod volt non posse defendere.'

being require that the atoms should fall eternally without meeting: here is an occasional causeless interruption of that universal principle—almost a self-assertion of the atom against the whole realm of nature. From an outside point of view no doubt such criticism is justifiable. But the matter did not so present itself to Epicurus: it is clear from Lucretius' treatment that he did not regard the 'swerve' as a weakness which must be glossed over and disguised, but as a strong point of cardinal importance in the system, which must be brought out into the prominence which it deserved. Criticism will be more effective, if an attempt is first made to discover how Epicurus arrived at the idea and what was its importance for him.

It is a commonplace to state that Epicurus, like his follower Lucretius, intended primarily to combat the 'myths' of the orthodox religion, to show by his demonstration of the unfailing laws of nature the falseness of the old notions of the arbitrary action of the gods and so to relieve humanity from the terrors of superstition. But it is sometimes forgotten that Epicurus viewed with almost greater horror the conception of irresistible 'destiny' or 'necessity', which is the logical outcome of the notion of natural law pressed to its conclusion. This conclusion had been accepted in its fulness by Democritus, but Epicurus conspicuously broke away from him: 'it were better to follow the myths about the gods than to become a slave to the "destiny" of the natural philosophers: for the former suggests a hope of placating the gods by worship, whereas the latter involves a necessity which knows no placation'.[1] Diogenes of Oenoanda[2] brings out the close connexion with moral teaching: 'if destiny be believed in, then all advice and rebuke is annihilated'. If any ethical system is to be effective it must postulate the freedom of the will. If in the sphere of human action too

---

[1] Ep. iii, § 134 κρεῖττον ἦν τῷ περὶ θεῶν μύθῳ κατακολουθεῖν ἢ τῇ τῶν φυσικῶν εἱμαρμένῃ δουλεύειν· ὁ μὲν γὰρ ἐλπίδα παραιτήσεως ὑπογράφει θεῶν διὰ τιμῆς, ἡ δὲ ἀπαραίτητον ἔχει τὴν ἀνάγκην.

[2] fr. xxxiii, col. iii (William) πιστευθείσης γὰρ εἱμαρμένης αἴρεται πᾶσα νουθεσ[ί]α καὶ ἐπιτίμησις.

'destiny' is master, if every action is the direct and inevitable outcome of all preceding conditions and man's belief in his own freedom of choice is a mere delusion, then a moral system is useless: it is futile to tell a man what he ought or ought not to do, if he is not at liberty to do it. Here at all events 'destiny' must be eliminated. It is a more fatal enemy than superstition, for it means complete paralysis: spontaneity—*voluntas*—must be at all costs maintained.

But why, in order to secure this very remote object, should a protest against 'inexorable necessity' be made at this point in the physical system? It would have been easy, one might think, to accomplish the immediate purpose of securing the meeting of the atoms in their fall through space by some device, such as the Stoic notion that all things tend to the centre,[1] which should not be a breach of the funda-mental law of causality, instead of this sporadic spontaneous deviation. And in what sense can this 'swerve' be said to be vital for the freedom of the will, with which Lucretius[2] so emphatically connects it? The answer must be looked for in the very material notions of Epicurus'[3] psychology, which may be briefly anticipated here. The mind ($\nu o \hat{u}s$) is a con-centration in the breast of an aggregate of very fine atoms, the same in character as those which, distributed all over the body and intermingling with the body atoms, form the vital principle ($\psi v \chi \acute{\eta}$). This aggregation of atoms may be set in motion by images, whether coming directly from external things or stored up as an 'anticipation' ($\pi \rho \acute{o} \lambda \eta \psi \iota s$) in the mind itself. Suppose, for instance, that in this way there comes before my mind the image of myself walking: ultimately the atoms of the mind being themselves stirred, will set in motion the atoms of the vital principle: they in turn will stir the atoms of body, the limbs will be moved and I shall walk. But before this can happen another process must take place, the process of volitional choice. When the image is presented to the mind it does not of itself imme-diately and inevitably start the chain of motions which results in the physical movement; I can at will either accept or reject

<hr>

[1] See Lucr. i. 1052 ff.   [2] ii. 251–93.   [3] See Chap. VIII.

the idea which it suggests, I can decide either to walk or not to walk. This is a matter of universal experience and it must not be denied or rejected. But how is this process of choice to be explained on purely material lines? It is due, said Epicurus, to the spontaneous swerving of the atoms: the act of volition is neither more nor less than the 'swerve' of the fine atoms which compose the mind. The fortuitous indeterminate movement of the individual atoms [1] in the void is in the conscious complex (*concilium*) of the mind transformed into an act of deliberate will. The vital connexion, indeed the identity of the two processes is clearly brought out by Lucretius at the close of his exposition of the theory: 'but that the very mind feels not some necessity within in doing all things, and is not constrained like a conquered thing to bear and suffer, this is brought about by the tiny swerve of the first-beginnings in no determined direction of place and at no determined time'.[2] It is not merely, as has been suggested, that Epicurus decided to get over two difficult problems in his system economically by adopting a single solution, but that he perceived an essential connexion between them: if freedom is to be preserved, it must be asserted at the very basis of the physical world.

The 'swerve' of the atoms is, no doubt, as the critics have always pointed out, a breach of the fundamental laws of cause and effect, for it is the assertion of a force for which no cause can be given and no explanation offered. For if it be said that the atom swerves because it is its nature to do so, that is merely to put 'nature' as a *deus ex machina* on a level

---

[1] For a further discussion of this point see Chap. VIII, p. 435.
[2] ii. 289–293.

sed ne mens ipsa necessum
intestinum habeat cunctis in rebus agendis
et devicta quasi cogatur ferre patique,
id facit exiguum clinamen principiorum
nec regione loci certa nec tempore certo.

Brieger, *de motu atomorum principali*, regards the two processes as parallel but not causally connected exhibitions of the same spontaneity. His view has been successfully combatted by Giussani (*Stud. Lucr.* i. 125 ff.; *Clinamen e Voluntas*).

with 'necessity' as it was conceived by some of the early physicists, a force which came in to do what could not otherwise be explained. But it was no slip or oversight on Epicurus' part which a more careful consideration of his principles might have rectified. On the contrary it was a very deliberate breach in the creed of 'necessity' and is in a sense the hinge on which the whole of his system turns. He wished to secure 'freedom' as an occasional breach of 'natural law'. If criticism is to be brought against him, it must not be on the technical ground of inconsistency in this detail, but on the broader ground that in his system as a whole he was attempting the impossible. To escape from the old notion of the divine guidance of the world, the Atomists had set up a materialist philosophy directed solely by uniform laws of cause and effect. Democritus saw that this, if pursued to its logical conclusion, must lead to an unflinching determinism, which with more scientific insight perhaps, but less care for his ethical precepts, he had wholly accepted. Epicurus, unwilling in this way to risk his moral system, tried to escape from the *impasse* without abandoning a materialist position. Such a compromise is in reality impossible: a wholly materialist view of the world, which excludes altogether the spiritual and the supernatural, must lead to determinism, and there is no real path of escape, except in the acknowledgement of other than material conditions and causes. From the point of view of ultimate consistency, the 'swerve' is a flaw in Epicureanism, but it is not to be treated as a petty expedient to get over a temporary difficulty, or an unintelligent mistake which betrays the superficial thinker.

It may not be uninteresting to notice that a parallel difficulty arises for modern thinkers [1] and that a solution not unlike that of Epicurus' atomic swerve has sometimes been propounded. The modern scientist is not indeed concerned with the question of free will, which he usually regards as outside his province, but he is concerned with the origin

---

[1] See a very interesting account in Masson, *Lucretius, Epicurean and Poet*, chap. x.

of consciousness, and as he pursues it lower and lower in
the scale of being he asks whether there is a point at which
it can be said that consciousness begins or whether it must
be traced back into inorganic matter. There has recently
been a series of thinkers who have been prepared to state
that consciousness must be pushed back right to the very
atoms themselves. Thus W. K. Clifford[1] argues that 'in
order to save continuity in our belief, we are obliged to
assume that along with every motion of matter, whether
organic or inorganic, there is some fact which corresponds
to the mental fact in ourselves', 'a moving molecule of inorganic matter does not possess mind or consciousness, but
it possesses a small piece of *mind-stuff*'. Similarly Haeckel[2]
was led to postulate that in the most elementary form of
matter there is what he calls a 'psycho-plasm', and even to
speak of 'atoms with souls'. In a recent work one of the
younger English biologists states[3] in the same spirit that
'we must . . . believe that not only living matter, but all
matter, is associated with something of the same general
description as mind in higher animals' and argues that a new
word is wanted to describe the 'world-stuff' which is both
matter and mind. But the most striking parallel not only
to the ideas but even to the phraseology of Lucretius is found
in the *Note-Books*[4] of Samuel Butler: the passage is worth
quoting almost in full.

When people talk of atoms obeying fixed laws, they are either ascribing
some kind of intelligence and free will to atoms or they are talking
nonsense. There is no obedience unless there is at any rate a potentiality of disobeying. No objection can lie to our supposing potential or
elementary volition or consciousness to exist in atoms, on the score that
their action would be less regular or uniform if they had free will than
if they had not. By giving them free will we do no more than those
who make them bound to obey fixed laws. They will be as certain to
use their freedom of will only in particular ways as to be driven into
these ways by obedience to fixed laws. The little element of individual
caprice (supposing we start with free will), or (supposing we start with

[1] *Essays and Remains*, vol. ii, pp. 61, 85.
[2] *The Riddle of the Universe.*
[3] J. S. Huxley, *Essays of a Biologist*, 1923, p. 243.   [4] pp. 72, 73.

neccessity) the little element of stiff-neckedness, both of which elements we find everywhere in nature, these are the things that prevent
even the most reliable things from being absolutely reliable. . . . Atoms
have a mind as much smaller and less complex than ours as their bodies
are smaller or less complex.[1]

These theories are no doubt still unorthodox and do not
represent the normal view of the modern man of science,
but they show unmistakably a tendency towards a solution
closely parallel to that of Epicurus, and may serve to make
his problem intelligible to us in modern phraseology.

Before leaving the doctrine of the 'atomic swerve', whose
psychological implications will have to be dealt with later,[2]
there are certain other points and problems concerning it
which must be noticed. The first is of the nature of a
caution. Though in the aggregate of the soul-atoms the
'swerve' is productive of conscious volition, it must not be
supposed that Epicurus represented the swerving of any
individual atom as in any sense conscious or volitional. Such
an idea would be contrary to the very root-principles of his
materialism, for it would be introducing a supra-natural
element into the action of the lowest and most rudimentary
forms of matter, or, as he would have put it in his own terms
—assigning to the individual atoms a power that could only
belong to the subtlest aggregate of the very finest and
minutest among them under very special conditions. The
atom, so far from having conscious volition, has not even
sensation:[3] the 'swerve' of the individual atoms is in no
sense conscious; it could at most be described as a mechanical
freedom corresponding to the psychical freedom of the will.

A second point is of less importance. It has been maintained by one modern critic [4] that Epicurus meant that any
individual atom could only swerve once and no more. Such

---

[1] It may be noticed that Butler here attacks not only the problem of consciousness, but that of free will which was raised by Epicurus and Lucretius,
and incidentally touches the question of spontaneity in nature, which Guyau
associates with Epicurus' παρέγκλισις.

[2] See Chap. VIII, p. 435. [3] Lucr. ii. 886 ff.

[4] Brieger, de atom. mot. princ., p. 224: see Giussani, Stud. Lucr. p. 138, n. 1.

an idea would be so arbitrary as to be very unlike Epicurus'
usual modes of thought, there is no evidence for it in the
authorities and it would immensely complicate the psychological explanation of free-will. Moreover the main argument on which this contention rests, that the atom having
once swerved from the line of the perpendicular fall could
not return to it again and so be in a position to swerve once
more is valueless; for on the one hand, there is nothing to
show that Epicurus did not conceive of a 'swerve' from some
other line of motion, on the other it will be seen later that it
is highly probable that he did conceive of the return of the
swerving atom to its perpendicular line.

A far more interesting problem is raised by the notion of
the working of the 'swerve' as a principle of contingency
in inorganic nature, which was put forward in the brilliant
essay of M. Guyau.[1] His contention is briefly this. At the
lowest point of material existence—in the individual atoms—
there is that power of spontaneous movement; at the highest
point of the scale—in the subtle complex of fine atoms which
constitutes the mind of men—the same power appears again
in the act of volition. What has happened to it meanwhile?
Is it to be supposed that in the whole realm of inorganic
nature this power lies dormant? It cannot be that the atoms
cease to swerve: is it possible that their 'swerve' is without
perceptible or appreciable effect? Epicurus, answers Guyau,
cannot so have conceived it: the chain must be continuous
from the individual atoms up to their finest complex. The
'swerve' then will show itself in inorganic nature as a certain
element of chance or contingency, which contravenes the
iron despotism of the law of necessity in the inanimate just
as much as in the animate world. Occasionally things happen
'by chance', apart from the working of the laws of nature,
and these chance events are just a fresh manifestation of the
atomic 'swerve'. Guyau is himself at some pains to show
that such an idea would not be, as it might be thought, a
re-introduction into the scheme of the element of 'miracle',
which it was Epicurus' main object to exclude. The argu-

[1] *La Morale d'Épicure*, chap. ii, § ii, pp. 85–91.

ment is unnecessary, for 'miracle' implies the action of some external power interrupting and altering natural law. A contingency due to the 'swerve' would be an internal force, itself the direct outcome of the one element of spontaneity which Epicurus admitted into his system. As Guyau has himself summed up the conception of the 'swerve' and its action, 'spontaneity precedes, follows, and completes nature, and prevents it from being a mere mechanism incapable of improvement and subject to an inexorable fatalism: it is for this reason that Epicurus maintains it'.[1]

The idea is very attractive and would give a completeness and consistency to Epicurus' whole system, but it is very doubtful whether it can safely be ascribed to him. It is true that Epicurus' conception of 'chance' is less scientific than that of Democritus[2] and that he does appear to regard it not as an unpredictable result of the working of natural law, but as the intervention of an unaccountable force which to some extent thwarts natural law. It appears in this sense several times in connexion with the moral theory: simple diet 'fits us to be fearless of fortune',[3] 'in but few things chance hinders a wise man',[4] the prudent man recognizes that 'some things happen by necessity, some by chance',[5] and 'sees that chance is inconstant',[6] 'nature teaches us to pay little heed to what fortune brings'.[7] A more explicit passage[8] in the third letter states that the prudent man 'does not regard chance as a god (for in a god's acts there is no disorder), nor as an uncertain cause of all things': chance is an uncertain cause, but it only controls certain things in the

---

[1] Op. cit., p. 91.   [2] See Part I, Chap. III, § 3, p. 142.

[3] Ep. iii. 131 πρὸς τὴν τύχην ἀφόβους παρασκευάζει.

[4] Κ.Δ. xvi βραχέα σοφῷ τύχη παρεμπίπτει.

[5] Ep. iii, § 133 <ἃ μὲν κατ' ἀνάγκην γίνεται>, ἃ δὲ ἀπὸ τύχης.

[6] Ibid. τὴν δὲ τύχην ἄστατον ὁρᾶν.

[7] C.B. fr. 77; τὰ παρὰ τῆς τύχης μικρότερα (ἡ φύσις) διδάσκει νομίζειν.

[8] § 134, τὴν δὲ τύχην οὔτε θεόν . . . ὑπολαμβάνων (οὐθὲν γὰρ ἀτάκτως θεῷ πράττεται) οὔτε <πάντων> ἀβέβαιον αἰτίαν. The manuscript text οὔτε ἀβέβαιον αἰτίαν cannot be right, as that is exactly what Epicurus did think chance to be: the insertion of πάντων seems the easiest way to mend the clause: see my note, ad loc.

world and those sporadically. It might perhaps be held that the language in these passages on the moral theory is loose and untechnical and that 'chance' is used in a popular sense. But it is possible to find parallels in the physical theory too. In a careful description of the formation of worlds in the second Letter[1] Epicurus says that 'seeds of the right kind make junctions and articulations and cause changes of position to another place, *as it may happen*', and in the same context Lucretius tells us that 'the seeds of things themselves of their own accord, jostling from time to time *by chance*, were driven together in many ways, rashly, idly, and in vain, and at last those united which could produce a world'.[2] Similarly in speaking of the end of the world Lucretius prays: 'may fortune at the helm (*fortuna gubernans*) steer this far away from us'.[3] Equally significant is a later passage[4] in which speaking of the services of Epicurus to mankind Lucretius says 'he showed what there is of ill in the affairs of mortals everywhere, coming to being and flying abroad in diverse forms, *be it by the chance or by the force of nature*, because nature had so brought it to pass'. Here 'chance' and 'force' are as definitely opposed as were chance and necessity in the Letter to Menoeceus and both are described as 'natural'.

There can then hardly be any doubt that Epicurus admitted the existence of a real contingency in nature, an element of 'chance' which at times worked in contravention of necessity. This is what might be expected from his general attitude in desiring to circumscribe the working of a universal

---

[1] Ep. ii, § 89 προσθέσεις τε καὶ διαρθρώσεις καὶ μεταστάσεις ποιούντων ἐπ' ἄλλον τόπον, ἐὰν οὕτω τύχῃ.

[2] ii. 1059–62:

> sponte sua forte offensando semina rerum
> multimodis temere incassum frustraque coacta
> tandem coluerunt ea quae coniecta repente
> magnarum rerum fierent exordia semper.

[3] v. 107.

[4] Lucr. vi. 29 ff.:

> quidve mali foret in rebus mortalibu' passim,
> quod fieret naturali varieque volaret
> *seu casu seu vi*, quod sic natura parasset.

necessity. So far Guyau is justified, but is it possible to take the further step of assigning this contingency to the working of the atomic swerve? The one passage which seems to give support to this idea is the brief and strange statement of Plutarch already quoted: 'An atom swerves the very least so that heavenly bodies and living beings *and chance* may come into existence and our free will may not be lost.'[1] This certainly seems to suggest chance as an effect of the swerve intermediate between the formation of compound bodies, animate and inanimate, and the establishment of free will in man. But it stands absolutely alone. It is not of course remarkable that no notion of the kind emerges in the Letter to Herodotus, for the section dealing with the 'swerve', if there was one, has been lost. But it is remarkable that there should be no hint of the idea in Lucretius' full and careful treatment of the subject: his transition [2] is direct from the 'swerve' of the atoms to the act of volition in the soul. On the whole it seems safest to conclude that Epicurus did admit the element of contingency in the world, and may possibly have attributed it to the atomic 'swerve': most probably the brilliant idea devised by Guyau did not occur to him, but he would gladly have adopted it if it had.

§ 3. The 'blow'

The results of the 'swerve' must now be considered as it affects the motion of the 'free' atoms and their behaviour in compound bodies. It was said earlier[3] that the perpendicular fall of the atoms in parallel lines was a 'theoretical condition' and the reason is now clear: for the moment that a single atom had swerved and thus came into collision with another atom, the result of the blow must be that the two start off again in new directions. They then impinge upon others, which in their turn are deflected at an angle from their straight course, and thus is started the infinite series of motions in all directions which leads directly to the attachment of atoms to one another and then by the gradual

[1] Plut. *de Sollertia Anim.* 7, p. 964 e; U. Spic. 281, quoted on p. 317, n. 2.
[2] See especially ii. 256, and again 284–6.   [3] p. 310.

accretion round nuclei to the creation of 'things'. And so it comes about that in what is logically the second stage, but in fact is the eternal condition of things, the direction of motion is mainly determined by the blow ($\pi\lambda\eta\gamma\dot{\eta}$) of atom on atom. Thus Lucretius [1] can speak of the primary and secondary causes of motion as practically on an equality: 'it must needs be that all the first-beginnings of things move on either by their own weight or sometimes by the blow of another'. What Democritus conceived as the original state of things due to a 'natural' movement of atoms in all directions is indeed historically original, but it is due to the action of the 'swerve' modifying the 'downward' fall due to weight. Weight still remains the ultimate cause of motion and in the absence of a blow determines its direction, but the blows are so frequent that practically they are the determinants of the character of atomic movement.

Thus conceived the motion of the atoms is infinitely complex and, as Lucretius says,[2] it would not be possible 'to follow up such of the first-beginnings severally to see by what means each one is carried on'. But certain principles can be safely established. First of all it is at this point at last that difference of weight begins to tell: when two heavy atoms clash together and a light one at the same moment falls between them, the result is that the light atom is 'squeezed out' and driven in an upward direction.[3] Lucretius,[4] though he does not explain the process clearly, is careful to point out that upward motion is not the natural motion either of atoms or of things. It is in fact a secondary outcome of the 'swerve', but it is clear that upward motion is henceforth established as surely as the original downward motion and the sideways motions due to blows. The idea is of course the Democritean notion of the 'rush' ($\sigma o\hat{v}s$) [5] in the new and more elaborate form in which the more scientific and detailed treatment of Epicurus is able to present it.

---

[1] ii. 83–5, quoted above, p. 311, n. 5.   [2] ii. 165–6.

[3] Simplicius in Arist. *de Caelo*, Γ 1. 299 a; U. 276 ἐξωθούμενα τὰ κουφότερα ὑπ' αὐτῶν ὑφιζανόντων ἐπὶ τὸ ἄνω φέρεσθαι.

[4] ii. 184 ff.   [5] See Part I, Chap. III, § 3, p. 94, n. 4.

A more important principle is that, though a blow means the change of direction in the atom's motion, it never causes any diminution in its speed: as it meets another atom, its course is instantaneously deflected, but the original 'absolute' velocity is always maintained. This principle is stated clearly enough by Epicurus[1] himself: no atomic motion, he says, is quicker or slower than another, 'neither the motion upwards or sideways owing to blows, nor again that downwards owing to their own weight'. The blow is instantaneous and as soon as the change of direction has occurred, the atom starts off again through the void: and since it is still in the void, there is no check or opposition and it therefore moves at 'atomic' speed, 'quick as thought'. This notion[2] becomes of supreme importance for the understanding of the behaviour of atoms in compounds.

It is now possible to form a clearer idea of the external 'check' (ἀντικοπή) resulting from the collision of one atom with another and its subsequent affects. Such collision is the only thing which can affect the movement of a 'free' atom— indeed of any atoms—and it affects it only by changing its direction. There is an instant in which the two colliding atoms are in contact and then each flies off at 'atomic' speed in a direction determined by the angle of their original incidence. An ingenious modern critic[3] has indeed maintained that the duration of the instant of contact is just that of the 'minimum of time',[4] so that, if it were desired to compare the time in which a given distance could be travelled by an unimpeded atom A, and another atom B which met with many collisions, it would be possible to answer that the time occupied by B will be that taken by $A + 1$ 'minimum

---

[1] Ep. i, § 61 οὔθ' ἡ ἄνω οὔθ' ἡ εἰς τὸ πλάγιον διὰ τῶν κρούσεων φορά, οὔθ' ἡ κάτω διὰ τῶν ἰδίων βαρῶν: see on this point Bignone, Appendix I, pp. 226 ff.

[2] It is curious that this principle is never clearly stated by Lucretius; but his treatment of kinetics is altogether slight and allusive. Perhaps the whole subject was too abstruse for him; more probably it was only slightly dealt with in the Μεγάλη Ἐπιτομή and this may be the reason for the disproportionate length of its treatment in the Letter to Herodotus.

[3] Bignone, l.c., p. 230.   [4] See above, p. 315.

of time' for every collision suffered. But there seems to be no authority for the equation of the duration of the collision with the 'minimum of time' and the idea must be regarded as an ingenious but uncertain inference. Anyhow the atom after its collision proceeds at once at 'atomic' speed in the direction given it by its last blow until it is deflected again or—and this is a new idea of importance—in a long transit through the void the original downward tendency will assert itself. This must be the meaning of Epicurus when he says in continuation of the passage last quoted:[1] 'for as long as either of the two motions (that due to weight and that due to a blow) prevails, so long will it (the atom) have a course as quick as thought, until something checks it either from outside or from its own weight counteracting the force of that which dealt the blow'. The downward tendency then still survives even in the atom buffeted by collisions and may come into play in a sufficiently long unimpeded course, but it may be noted that whereas the change of direction due to collision is immediate, the downward motion would only reassert itself gradually. The idea was probably suggested to Epicurus by the trajectory of a missile, in which the force of the throw gradually expends itself and the weapon falls to earth. He does not himself make much use of the conception in the working out of his kinetics, but it must be borne carefully in mind.

§ 4. *Motion in compound bodies*

So far inquiry has been limited to the motion of the 'free' atoms, which continue to move independently in the void and have not been brought by their collisions and clashings into the closer and more permanent connexion with other atoms, which forms the compound body. But this 'implication' of atoms with atoms is of course the all-important result

---

[1] § 61 ἐφ' ὅποσον γὰρ ἂν κατίσχῃ ἑκατέρ⟨α αὐτ⟩ῶν, ἐπὶ τοσοῦτον ἅμα νοήματι τὴν φορὰν σχήσει, ἕως ⟨ἄν τι⟩ ἀντικόψῃ, ἢ ἔξωθεν ἢ ἐκ τοῦ ἰδίου βάρους τὴν τοῦ πλήξαντος δύναμιν. There is no reason to follow Usener in excluding the words πρὸς τὴν τοῦ πλήξαντος δύναμιν as a gloss: see Giussani, *Stud. Lucr.* i. 104, and C.B. note ad loc. The influence of the downward tendency is rather loosely spoken of as an ἀντικοπή.

of the swerve and is the ultimate fate of by far the greater part of the atoms.[1] It may be explained briefly thus.[2] When the atoms meet one another, some become locked in a close and strong bond of union; these form bodies of great mass and density, such as stone, iron, &c.; others 'leap back', but nevertheless remain in a loose union; these form thin and fine substances, such as liquids or air. Between these extremes there is every possible variety of looseness and closeness of texture, producing substances of corresponding degrees of density.

What then becomes of the motions of the atoms thus imprisoned in compounds? Is it checked, slackened, or lost? does the atom come to rest and only regain its motion, if ever, when it is once again liberated by the dissolution of the compound? It is one of the most striking of Epicurus' acts of 'mental apprehension' that he saw that this was not the case. The motion of the atom through the void at 'atomic' speed is not in any way diminished or altered by its entry into the compound body. In no compound—even that of the hardest rock—is the density so great, the texture so close, that the atoms in any sense coalesce: there is always between them a greater or lesser 'interval' of void. The only result of density of formation is that the atom, as it moves at absolute speed, more immediately comes into conflict with other atoms and is again changed in direction: its 'trajects' —if this term may be applied to its infinitely minute journeyings to and fro—are made shorter and its collisions more frequent: 'the atoms move continuously for all time . . . some are borne on separating to a long distance from one another, while others again recoil and recoil, whenever they chance to be checked by the interlacing with others, or else shut in by atoms interlaced around them'.[3] An atom

---

[1] The combination of atoms in compounds is more fully treated in Chap. V.

[2] Ep. i, § 43: cf. the much more detailed description in Lucr. ii. 95–111, and its subsequent elaboration in 381–477, and see Chap. VI, pp. 339–41.

[3] Ep. i, § 43 κινοῦνταί τε συνεχῶς αἱ ἄτομοι τὸν αἰῶνα καὶ αἱ μὲν . . . εἰς μακρὰν ἀπ' ἀλλήλων διιστάμεναι, αἱ δὲ αὖ τὸν παλμὸν ἴσχουσιν, ὅταν τύχωσι τῇ περιπλοκῇ κεκλιμέναι ἢ στεγαζόμεναι παρὰ τῶν πλεκτικῶν.

then must never be supposed to be more than instantaneously at rest at the moment of collision: in the compound, no less than in its free state, it is for ever in motion: 'if you think that the first-beginnings can stay still, and by staying still beget new movements in things, you stray very far from the true reasoning'.[1] Thus the compound body, the aggregate of atoms ever in ceaseless movement, is always in a condition of feverish vibration (παλμός), even when the whole is at rest. Lucretius [2] in a striking passage brings out the notion clearly:

herein we need not wonder why it is that when all the first-beginnings of things are in motion, yet the whole seems to stand wholly at rest, except when anything starts moving with its entire body. For all the nature of the first-bodies lies far away from our senses, below their purview: wherefore, since you cannot reach to look upon them, they must needs steal away their motions from you too; above all, since such things as we can look upon, yet often hide their motions, when withdrawn from us on some distant spot.

Lucretius clinches his argument with two beautiful illustrations from experience, the distant flock of sheep, which looks like 'a white mass on a green hill', and the distant army manœuvring which appears 'to be at rest and to lie like a glimmering mass upon the plains'.

It is not difficult thus to conceive of the internal but wholly imperceptible atomic vibration in a thing at rest—modern science teaches the same idea—but what of a compound body in motion? what is the effect of this vibration on its motion, and what is in general the relation of the motion of the individual atoms to the motion of the whole body which they compose? These are much more difficult questions to which Epicurus [3] has devoted an obscure section in the Letter to Herodotus, which has however been considerably elucidated by modern scholars.[4]

[1] Lucr. ii. 80–2.　　　　　　　　　　　　　　　[2] ii. 308–32.

[3] § 61 to which, in my opinion, must be added a portion of § 47, which occurs in the text in the section devoted to the εἴδωλα of vision, but must refer to atomic motion in compounds generally: see my notes, ad loc.

[4] Especially by Giussani, Cinetica Epicurea; Stud. Lucr. pp. 97–124; and Bignone, Epicuro, Appendix, § 1.

In the first place it is clear that this internal movement of the atoms, vast numbers of them hastening in directions different to—and even directly contrary to—that of the whole, must act as a retardation on the motion of the whole body. In other words the effect of the collisions (ἀντικοπή) of atom with atom and their subsequent 'trajects' in all directions is that of a 'check'. 'Anticope' thus comes to have the secondary sense of an internal 'check' or 'drag' on the whole body, but the internal 'anticope' is in no sense a different thing from the external 'anticope' of the atoms; it is only its inevitable outcome. Lucretius [1] in a famous passage traces the upward growth of this retardation. The individual independent atom moves at 'absolute' speed: when two or three atoms join in a nucleus, that nucleus is retarded by their contrary motions within it: it joins with other nuclei in a body whose pace is still slower till at last there is formed a body sufficiently large and sufficiently slow in movement to be perceptible to the senses—such as the mote in the sunbeam, by whose behaviour the poet illustrates the movement of the atoms. The notion is one of the most penetrating and—from the point of view of modern science— one of the most interesting in the whole Epicurean system.

With this conception of the internal motion of the compound body it might then be said roughly that the motion of the whole body is the aggregate motion of its component atoms. When it is at rest, that must mean that the internal movements of the atoms counteract one another and produce an equilibrium;[2] when it is in motion, the direction and pace of that motion is determined by the resultant of the sum of the movements of the atoms. This account is in the main true, but Epicurus raises certain points about it, a consideration of which will serve to make the idea clearer. In the first place [3] it must not be forgotten that the body as

---

[1] ii. 132–41.

[2] It is also possible that the condition of rest is produced when the majority of the atoms have returned to the original 'downward' tendency.

[3] Ep. i, § 62. The passage is obscure, the text not certain, and critics have differed considerably as to interpretation. I have therefore contented myself

a whole may move at different speeds and in various directions, whether as the result of a blow or of its natural tendency to fall. Suppose two bodies *A* and *B* are so moved in the same direction, but that *A* is travelling twice as fast as *B*: even if we take the least possible period of continuous perceptible time (κατὰ τὸν ἐλάχιστον συνεχῆ χρόνον), *A* still covers twice the distance covered by *B*. We are inclined to infer that the atoms which compose *A* are moving twice as fast as those of *B*. But if we try to pass beyond the region of sense-perception to 'atomic' time,[1] to an instant of time only perceptible in thought (κατὰ τὸν λόγῳ θεωρητὸν χρόνον), we perceive that at this instant the atoms are not, like the compound bodies, all moving in the same direction, those of *A* twice as fast as those of *B*, but on the contrary the individual atoms are all moving at an equal 'absolute' rate, colliding and clashing momentarily and striking off on their 'trajects' in all directions. 'Mental apprehension' has here corrected a false inference from sensation: 'for the addition of opinion with regard to the unseen, that the moments perceptible only by thought will also contain continuity of motion, is not true in such cases; for we must remember that it is what we observe with the senses or grasp with the mind by an apprehension that is true'.[2] The 'opinion' then that the atoms of *A* are moving twice as fast as those of *B* in the same direction is false: what is true is (*a*) 'what is observed' by the senses that the whole body *A* is travelling twice as fast as *B*, and (*b*) 'what is apprehended by the mind' that the atoms inside both *A* and *B* are still moving at atomic speed in all directions. The motion of the whole is to be reckoned in continuous time as observed by the senses, that of the

with paraphrasing what I believe to be its meaning. Bignone agrees almost entirely with me, Giussani and Usener both postulate what I believe to be unnecessary corrections of the text.

[1] Notice that the ideas here are based on the conceptions of the 'minimum' of movement and the 'minimum' of time: see p. 315.

[2] τὸ γὰρ προσδοξαζόμενον περὶ τοῦ ἀοράτου, ὡς ἄρα καὶ οἱ διὰ λόγου θεωρητοὶ χρόνοι τὸ συνεχὲς τῆς φορᾶς ἕξουσιν, οὐκ ἀληθές ἐστιν ἐπὶ τῶν τοιούτων· ἐπεὶ τό γε θεωρούμενον πᾶν ἢ κατ' ἐπιβολὴν λαμβανόμενον τῇ διανοίᾳ ἀληθές ἐστιν.

atoms by the discrete minima of movement in the minima of time as apprehended by the mind.

So far Epicurus has a caution against possible misunderstanding, but it is difficult to refrain from pursuing the matter farther and asking what then is the relation between the motion of the whole and the motion of the atoms, which enables the one body to move twice as fast as the other, although the rate of the internal atomic motion is always the same? The answer which Epicurus would surely have given is that in the body *A* twice as many atoms are moving in the direction of the whole as in the body *B*, whose pace is slackened by greater internal 'anticope'. Imagine that each body consists of 24 atoms: if in *A* 16 are moving from east to west and 8 in other directions more or less impeding, whereas in *B* 8 only are moving from east to west and 16 in other directions, *A* travels from east to west twice as fast as *B*. In other words, 'anticope' is the inverse determinant of speed. For this conclusion at least there is the authority of Epicurus himself:[1] it is true of the motion of compounds just as much as of 'free' atoms that 'it is "anticope" and its absence which take the outward appearance of slowness and quickness'.[2]

We must not then interpret the motions of the component atoms by the motion of the whole body, even though it is itself the resultant of the sum of their motions. Epicurus'[3] second caution is the converse of this: we must not suppose the motion of the whole body to be that of each or any of the

---

[1] § 46 βράδους γὰρ καὶ τάχους ἀντικοπὴ καὶ οὐκ ἀντικοπὴ ὁμοίωμα λαμβάνει.

[2] Giussani (l.c.) has attempted to follow up the question farther and inquire precisely what is the atomic effect on a body propelled by an external blow. The inquiry is fascinating, especially as I think Giussani is mistaken in some of his conclusions, but as there is no warrant for a decision in any Epicurean text, it is better left alone. Giussani's main weakness is a desire to pursue his inquiries too far and to read his own ideas into Epicurus' mind.

[3] § 47 b. This is the passage attached in the manuscripts to the account of the εἴδωλα: it is almost impossible to make sense of it there: here it is exactly in point. Again I am using the text and interpretation adopted in my edition.

component atoms. This 'first principle' (στοιχεῖον, as Epicurus calls it) is again couched in rather obscure language due no doubt to criticisms levelled at Epicurus' theory:

nor must it either be supposed that in moments perceptible only by thought the moving body too passes to the several places to which its component atoms move (for this too is unthinkable, and in that case, when it arrives all together in a sensible period of time from any point in the infinite void, it would not be taking its departure from the place from which we apprehend its motion): for the motion of the whole body will be the outward expression of its internal collisions, even though [1] up to the limits of perception we suppose the speed of the motion not to be retarded by collision.

If the component atoms are in the atomic minima of time performing tiny trajects in all directions, it might be supposed that in the same imperceptible minima of time the whole body performs this series of motions and reaches the end of its journey after having followed a devious course in all directions. Such an idea, says Epicurus, is unthinkable, as can be seen from its implications: for if it were true, a body which we see to be moving from east to west may in reality in an imperceptible minimum of time have been moving along the course of some of its component atoms from north to south.[2] The problem and its solution, as here stated by Epicurus, seem crude and almost puerile. It is hard to suppose that any one could have the idea which he is at pains to refute. But behind it lies an important question. If the movement of the whole body is the sum of the motion of its component atoms, and these motions are the tiny trajects in all directions in imperceptible moments of time, are not those motions alone real and is not the motion of the compound body a delusion? To this question Epicurus would

---

[1] There is no reason to suppose, with Giussani, that Epicurus' reference is to the points from which the individual atoms started in the void before they entered the compound body. The idea is very far-fetched and, as Bignone points out, there could be no possible reason for identifying the motion of the whole body with the *previous* motions of its atoms.

[2] This is my interpretation of the vague expression μέχρι τοσούτου: see notes, ad loc.

reply unhesitatingly, No. The motion of the whole body is the outward expression in continuous time perceptible to the senses of the invisible motions of the atoms. Both are realities, the one for thought and the other for the senses, and the latter is the sensible exhibition of the former. As he remarks in the conclusion of the previous section,[1] 'what we observe with the senses or grasp with the mind by an apprehension is true'.

This paradox rests in fact on one of the most important of Epicurus' physical conceptions, which will be dealt with more fully in the next chapter, that of the compound body as a new unity (ἄθροισμα, concilium). The compound is, in his view, not a mere aggregate, it is an entity which acquires new powers and faculties. This becomes clear in his theory of the secondary qualities: the atoms themselves are, for instance, colourless, but by their differences of shape and arrangement they produce colour in the compound, and that colour is no delusion, but a new reality. So here in the case of movement: as separate identities the atoms perform tiny trajects at imperceptible speed, but as parts of the new unity they combine to make up a new motion. This underlying idea lies at the very root of Epicurus' physical conceptions: both the world of phenomena, perceived by the senses and the imperceptible world conceived by thought are real and the former is the outward manifestation of the latter. The notion of the compound body is then the aggregate resultant of the motions of its atoms, but it is also a new reality of itself. In the light of this conception of the 'organism' of the compound body, both the main theory becomes more intelligible and also the questions raised by Epicurus and his answers to them. At the same time the theory of motion in the compound body aids considerably the understanding of the conception of the 'organism'.

If there were no other part of Epicurus' system which could be adduced to refute the charge that he was a loose and superficial thinker, the atomic kinetics would in itself

[1] § 61, fin.

suffice. It was a department of Atomism which had hardly
been touched by Leucippus and Democritus and Epicurus'
development of it was all his own. The minuteness of detail
with which he followed out the movements of the atoms in
the compound body is almost worthy of the careful investigation of a modern physicist, and indeed in its notion of internal vibration comes very near to his conclusions. And if the
idea of the 'swerve' is in a strict material sense a weakness, it
was at least a daring attempt to meet on material grounds the
supreme difficulty of the issue of materialism in determinism.
Epicurus' kinetics are indeed as profound an attempt to
think below the surface of phenomena as any in the ancient
world—even in Aristotle.

VI

COMPOUND BODIES AND THEIR QUALITIES

A CURIOUS chance has brought it about that there is
comparatively little first-hand information extant about
the process by which Epicurus supposed that the atoms
were formed into compounds and about the nature of the
resultant bodies. In the chapter of the Letter to Herodotus [1]
in which this immediate result of the motion of the atoms
is most likely to have been discussed there is almost certainly
a lacuna, which besides treating of the 'swerve' may very
likely have given more detailed information on the process
of combination: similarly in the second Book of Lucretius [2]
a long passage must have been lost in which he dealt at
greater length with the subject than in the brief summary
which still exists.[3] The loss is the less serious in that it is
clear from the information available and from the references
of later critics that Epicurus in the main followed the lead
of Democritus in this part of his theory: but there are several
questions of great interest—raised in part by the criticism
of antiquity—on which more authoritative statement than
can now be given would have been welcome.

The general notion is simple and straightforward and may
be summed up in Epicurus' words in the chapter cited. He
is dealing with the motion of the atoms and (in the lacuna)
has spoken of the motions of the 'free' atoms and their
collisions: he now goes on to speak of the formation of compounds as the result of collisions: 'some of them separate
to a long distance from one another, while others again keep
up vibration (παλμός, the traditional atomic word), whenever
they chance to be checked by the interlacing with others
(περιπλοκή) or else shut in (στεγαζόμεναι) by atoms interlaced
around them (παρὰ τῶν πλεκτικῶν)'. With this brief account
may be compared the rather more explicit statement of Lucre-

---

[1] § 43 : see above, Chap. V, p. 316.

[2] Before line 165 : 165 and 166 appear to be the conclusion of such a
section.   [3] ii. 85–111.

tius:[1] 'some when they have dashed together, leap back at great space apart, others too are thrust but a short way from the blow. And all those which are driven together in more close-packed union and leap back but a little space apart, entangled by their own close-locking shapes, these make the strong roots of rock and the brute bulk of iron and all other things of their kind. Of the rest [2] which wander through the great void, a few leap far apart, and recoil afar with great spaces between: these supply for us thin air and the bright light of the sun'. In both these descriptions there is an obvious distinction between 'rare' and 'dense' compounds [3] and Lucretius gives us the help of examples. In the former the atoms leap apart at great distances, though they still remain united in a compound: these produce what we might now call 'gaseous' bodies, such as the air and sunlight (which the Atomists always conceived as a corporeal 'thing'). In the latter the atoms remain in a much closer and more definite union and produce, as Lucretius says taking the extreme examples, hard solids like rock and iron. But a closer examination of Epicurus' statement reveals a further sub-division among these denser formations. Some of them are 'checked by the interlacing with others': all the component atoms, that is, are in close connexion with one another: these are the solids. Others are shut in by atoms interlaced around them: their own combination, that is, is comparatively loose, and they could not be kept together unless they were enclosed in an outer case, composed of interlaced atoms, to which Epicurus [4] elsewhere gives the name of the 'shell' or 'covering' (στεγάζον). This rather strange conception is in fact Epicurus' notion of the structure of such bodies as liquids, and it becomes of great importance when he subsequently applies it to the constitution of the 'soul'. It would seem then

[1] ii. 98–108.

[2] The text is here uncertain, but I have followed Merrill in transposing *paucula* and *cetera* at the beginning of ll. 105, 106.

[3] Brieger, *de Atom. mot. Princ.*, has suggested the convenient names *texturae* and *mixturae* to distinguish the dense and rare compounds.

[4] § 65 τοῦ στεγάζοντος λυθέντος εἴθ᾽ ὅλου εἴτε καὶ μέρους τινός. § 66 τὰ στεγάζοντα καὶ περιέχοντα.

that Epicurus in fact distinguished between three kinds of compound bodies, each with its own form of structure, (1) those in which the atoms are at considerable distances from one another and the texture is very loose, roughly the 'gases' covering the elements 'air' and 'fire'; (2) those in which the atoms are in a closer union, but require to be kept together by a 'shell', roughly, the liquids ('water'); (3) those in which the atoms are held together by their own close interlocking, roughly, the solids ('earth'). The new theory is thus brought into relation with the old division of the 'elements'.

As regards at any rate the second and third classes of compound, two points of importance may be noted at this stage. Firstly, the essential condition for their formation is the 'entanglement' (περιπλοκή): it is not enough that a certain number of atoms should be congregated in a certain limit of space; there must be such interlacement either among all the atoms or among those which compose the outer 'shell', as will serve at once to imprison the enclosed atoms and to mark off the resultant compound body as an entity independent of other compounds and of the surrounding atoms moving in space. Secondly, in all such compounds, even in the most compact, there must always be empty space, forming intervals (διαστήματα) between the component atoms, or rather, since they are in eternal motion and the intervals between them are consequently ever changing, a field in which they can perform their 'trajects' from collision to collision. Of these two conditions the former is the essential for the production of things (γένεσις, σύγκρισις), the latter for their destruction (φθορά), or, more strictly speaking, for their dissolution (διάλυσις, διάκρισις).

It has been seen that Epicurus regards the formation of a perceptible 'thing' as a gradual process.[1] He does not suppose that on any occasion a sufficient aggregate of atoms gathers together suddenly to form a complex large enough to be perceptible to our senses; rather they form at first small nuclei or clusters, which move about in union, growing gradually by the accretion of fresh independent atoms or of

[1] Chap. V, p. 327.

other nuclei like themselves, until at last they are large enough for our sense to become aware of them. Is there any stage in this process of greater significance than the rest, any point at which the aggregate acquires properties or powers which mark it off from smaller nuclei and qualify it particularly for the further union which constitutes 'things'? A recent writer [1] claims to detect such a conception—which he compares to that of the molecule of modern chemistry—and believes that it was expressed by Epicurus in the technical term 'mass' or 'particle' (ὄγκος), which is translated by Lucretius *cacumen*: this is the term used to express the *minimum visibile* in the concrete 'thing'.[2] 'These *cacumina*,' he says, 'which when regarded as extension are the least points in the field of the sensible, when regarded as substance are the molecules of a body, that is to say, the *partes minimae* which have the character of that body or substance.' The least visible part, that is, of a piece of iron is also the smallest part which has the character and properties of iron: any thing smaller than that is either individual atoms or atomic nuclei which have not yet attained to the properties of substance. For this notion there is no evidence either in Epicurus or in Lucretius; nor is there any reason to suppose that Epicurus would not have imagined that far below the range of perception a particle might still retain the character of the substance which it helps to compose. If he at all consciously approached the question at what point an atomic nucleus becomes one of the substances of perception, he certainly did not express his view in the word 'mass' (ὄγκος) which apart from its technical use[3] to denote the *minimum visibile*, means simply a chance nucleus of atoms, or from the other point of view, a particle of matter, which is indeed a stage in the formation of things, but is in no wise marked

[1] Giussani, *Stud. Lucr.*, p. 58. The idea is rightly rejected by Masson, op. cit., p. 129.

[2] Ep. i, § 56: see Chap. III, p. 286. In his note on ii. 454, Giussani further suggests that *glomeramina* is used by Lucretius to mean 'the molecule of liquids'; it means nothing more there than 'drops'.

[3] See Appendix IV for a fuller discussion of the meaning of ὄγκος, *cacumen* and *glomeramen*.

out by peculiar characteristics from other stages earlier or later. The whole attempt at a parallelism between Epicurus' atomism and modern chemistry is in fact misleading and has done mischief both here and at other points in the exposition of the theory.

If there is any trace of a technical idea in the early stages of the creation of things, before the formation of the compound body, it will be found rather in the notion of the 'seed' (σπέρμα, *semen*). Epicurus seems to think of the 'seed' as a nucleus of atoms of such shapes and relative arrangement that it is specially adapted for the creation of some particular thing. Thus at the outset of the physical theory[1] he supports his main principle that 'nothing is created out of the non-existent' by the argument that 'if it were, everything would be created out of everything with no need of seeds', and the elaborate development of the theme in Lucretius[2] shows that the idea is not that of minute particles, such as the atoms or 'molecules', but rather of complexes of atoms which are fit to become the germs of living things. Again in a curious passage,[3] where he is arguing that there are other worlds than ours with similar plants and living creatures, Epicurus says that 'no one could prove that in a world of one kind there might or might not have been included the kinds of seeds, of which living things and plants and all the rest of the things we see are composed, and that in a world of another kind they could not have been'. Here again the seed is the 'germ' primarily of organic existence. In the parallel passage[4] of the second letter he states that a new world is created 'when seeds of the right kind have rushed in from a single world or interworld (μετακόσμιον) or from several'. Here by 'seeds' he might conceivably mean individual atoms, but it seems more natural in view of the earlier passage to suppose that the word again denotes the already formed nuclei, specially adapted for the making of 'things'. Lucretius' use of *semen* is far more frequent and he seems to oscillate between two meanings for it. At the beginning of the poem[5] he mentions

[1] § 38.   [2] i. 159–214.   [3] § 74.   [4] § 89.   [5] i. 59.

the word among the synonyms which he intends to employ for the atoms or first particles and in a certain number of places he does undoubtedly so use it. In the passage [1] in the Second Book for instance, where he is arguing that the atoms themselves are colourless, he constantly speaks of them as *semina*,[2] as he does later in the similar proof that the atoms are without sensation.[3] So again of the 'smooth and round' atoms which constitute the light of the heavenly bodies [4] and the texture of the human soul.[5] But in the vast majority of instances he too seems to have in mind rather the complex germ, which is the source of the creation of things. Often it is used in reference to living organisms: so in the argument already referred to at the beginning of the First Book, and again throughout the long passage [6] at the end of Book IV, where it is used consistently of the germ of the living human being. But almost more striking are the instances where he employs it to denote the 'germ' of inanimate things: so in the refutation of Anaxagoras,[7] change is caused because there are mingled in things 'the seeds of many things', and again and again in the explanations of curious phenomena in Book VI we have such phrases as 'the seeds of fire',[8] 'the seeds of heat',[9] 'the seeds of light',[10] 'the seeds of water'.[11] It is true that in these last cases it would be possible to take *semina* in its other sense and to suppose that he means 'the atoms which when they enter into combinations are capable of forming fire, water, &c.', but both grammatically and philosophically the more natural meaning is better. It may then be maintained that Epicurus denoted by the 'seed' or 'germ' a definite conception of a stage in the process of creation, a complex of atoms of such shape and placed in such arrangements that they are now ready to create particular living or inorganic things.

[1] ii. 730–841.   [2] e.g. 760, 773, 833.
[3] 988.   [4] v. 456.   [5] iii. 187.
[6] iv. 1036–1277, where the word occurs some fifteen times.
[7] i. 895: cf. 902: here Lucretius is no doubt intentionally using Anaxagoras' own word (σπέρμα).
[8] vi. 160, 200, 206, 213, 217, 863, 867, 876.
[9] 271, 275, 883.   [10] 316.   [11] 497, 507, 520.

The internal construction of the compound body must now be considered more closely. Roughly, as has been seen, three classes of compound may be distinguished according to the density or rarity of their texture, but these distinctions are not rigid, and in fact there may be all possible varieties of union from the very loose mesh of atoms, which produces air or light, to the tightly packed formations with very little admixture of void, which produces the hard solids. But the one essential is that there must be cohesion, the atoms must be in some way 'entangled' (περιπλεκόμενοι, *impedita*). Now if the compound were a static body, this would be easy enough to understand: the excrescences of one atom might be pictured as catching in the cavities of another, so that their motions were checked and a solid body formed by the juxtaposition of atoms at rest. And indeed some of the language employed to describe the atomic compounds does suggest a static structure rather than internal motion. The word 'entanglement' [1] (περιπλοκή) itself is really more appropriate to such a conception, and a late Latin writer [2] renders it by the verb to 'cohere' (*cohaerere*) which is certainly a static word. Simplicius [3] too in describing the theory of Democritus says that he 'assigns as the reason that the compounds remain together for a time the interconnexions and graspings of the atoms'. Many of the expressions too used by Lucretius in describing the differences between the shape and combination of the atoms composing different classes of things seem more appropriate to atoms at rest. Thus 'hard things',[4] he says, 'are made of particles more hooked one to another, and are held together close-fastened at their

---

[1] Ep. i, § 43.

[2] Lactantius, *Divin. Instit.* iii. 17. 22; U. 287 'si levia sunt et hamis indigent, cohaerere non possunt'.

[3] In Ar. *de Caelo*, A. 10. 279 τοῦ δὲ συμμένειν τὰς οὐσίας μετ' ἀλλήλων μέχρι τινὸς αἰτιᾶται τὰς ἐπαλλαγὰς καὶ τὰς ἀντιλήψεις τῶν σωμάτων D. (Democritus) A. 37

[4] ii. 444–6:

> denique quae nobis durata ac spissa videntur,
> haec magis hamatis inter sese esse necessest
> et quasi ramosis alte compacta teneri.   cf. 468.

roots, as it were by branching particles'; olive oil [1] as contrasted with wine 'is composed of particles either larger or more hooked and entangled one with the other'. It is tempting to suppose that the earlier Atomists did in fact hold that in compounds the atoms come to rest, and that some of the language that they used was taken over by Epicurus without the full sense of its implications. But it has been seen [2] that the doctrine of the movement of atoms in compounds was held by Leucippus and Democritus. One or two passages seem to give evidence of a subtler doctrine, which would explain this apparently static phraseology, if allowance be made for a certain inexactness of expression. Simplicius [3] in the same account of Democritus' theories uses a careful phrase: 'they are entangled in such a way that they touch and are near one another, yet never make in truth any single existence': the entanglement that is to say produces contact but never leaves the atoms absolutely fixed to one another. A passage in Lucretius [4] seems to go a step farther: 'all those which are driven together in more close-packed union and leap back but a little space apart, entangled by their own close-locking shapes'. They 'leap back' but are yet 'entangled'. This seems to suggest that in very closely packed compounds of 'hooked' atoms, the atoms while they retain their movement yet for a time at least are literally entangled with one another, so that instead of actually performing 'trajects', they would oscillate until the chance blow set them free from one another. This is perhaps over-subtle, but there seems no other way to account for the close

---

[1] ii. 393–4:
> aut quia nimirum maioribus est elementis
> aut magis hamatis inter se perque plicatis.   cf. 405.

[2] Part I, Chap. II, § 3, p. 88; Chap. III, § 3, p. 137.

[3] l.c.

[4] ii. 101–2:
> exiguis intervallis convecta resultant
> indupedita suis perplexis ipsa figuris.

With this may be compared the phrase in l. 98 'confulta resultant': this is the manuscript text and if it is right the participle may be predicative and the meaning 'they leap back still in contact'.

entanglement of the atoms and yet to retain their ceaseless motion. There can in any case be no doubt that the doctrine of 'vibration' is true Epicureanism and therefore we may regard some of the 'static' expressions of Lucretius and other commentators as slightly loose ways of describing a condition of things which it was curiously difficult to depict accurately.

How then are union and unity to be conceived in a body of which each single atom is in constant motion at 'absolute' atomic speed? This is the difficulty expressed in one of the many acute criticisms of the atomic theory made by Plutarch:[1]

'this interlacing,' he says, 'which prevents dissolution only increases the occasions of collision, so that this process which they call creation (γένεσις) is not even a mixture (μῖξις) or a cohesion (κόλλησις), but only a confusion and a battle (ταραχὴ καὶ μάχη): and if the atoms at one moment move apart instantaneously owing to collision, and at another approach each other when the blow is spent (his cinetics are not quite right at this point), they spend the greater part, perhaps even double their time apart from each other, never touching or coming near, so that nothing could be created out of them, not even an inanimate body.'

The difficulty is a serious one and in reality involves a double problem: externally, what line of demarcation can there be between a compound 'thing' and other 'things' or the mass of free atoms moving all round it and striking on it? internally, what unity can there be between these ever-moving and colliding particles? Formally the answer lies in the fact that the compound body is more than an aggregate of atoms —it is an 'organism' (σύστημα) or, as Lucretius so constantly and expressively calls it, a *concilium*: there is about it a real cohesion, which gives it a unity of its own and marks it off from other atoms and atomic compounds. But of what nature is this cohesion? what really constitutes a *concilium*? Once again a modern theorist[2] has attempted to answer this difficult problem by introducing the analogy of chemistry: a *concilium*, he suggests, is in fact a 'chemical combination', a complex, that is, in which the component atoms so lose their

---

[1] *adv. Colot.* 10, p. 1112 b; U. 286.
[2] Masson, op. cit., p. 129.

identity that they are merged in a new substance, different
in kind from that of any of them, as hydrogen and oxygen
combining in certain proportions make water. This comparison is surely misleading: for a chemical combination
must mean that the atoms change their nature, and such
change is fundamentally inconsistent with their eternity: if
they so change, they must perish.[1] Whatever Epicurus' conception of combination may be, it is of a purely mechanical
union, in which each atom throughout retains its own
individuality and may at any moment, by means of the
appropriate blow, be set free from the compound.

A perusal of Epicurus' own writings might suggest that
he had left unanswered this all-important question of unity
and identity. But Lucretius, as so often, seems to give the
clue, doubtless preserving as usual the true Epicurean tradition. After explaining the different kinds of texture formed
by the atoms in union he continues:[2] 'and many (atoms)
besides wander on through the great void, which have been
cast back from the unions (*conciliis*) of things, nor have they
anywhere else availed to be taken into them and to *link on
their movements (consociare motus)*.[3] This 'linking of movements' seems to supply the required answer. All the atoms
are in constant movement, even inside the *concilium*, but the
essential of the *concilium* is that its internal movements are,
so to say, 'sympathetic'. The individual atoms are moving
in all directions, but there is a harmony in their diversity,
which enables them in all their differences to form one body
with one motion; and it is just this harmony of movement
which constitutes the unity of the 'thing' and distinguishes
it from external things and independent atoms. A new atom
colliding with a formed 'thing' may join with it, if its movements will 'fit': if not, it is driven off at a tangent and, as

[1]   nam quodcumque suis mutatum finibis exit
                continuo hoc mors est illius quod fuit ante.
                                        Lucr. i. 670–1, &c.

[2] ii. 109–11.

[3] There seems to be a hint of this idea in Epicurus in the expression which
occurs twice in the Letter to Herodotus (§§ 47 and 61) πάντα πόρον σύμμε-
τρον ἔχοντα: see my notes ad loc.

it were, lost again in space till a new collision gives it a new chance of union. Two illustrations from different parts of the system will serve to bring out the idea.

Consider first a reason given for the tremendous velocity of the thunderbolt. Lucretius assigns for it several causes and among them one which is not at first sight easy to understand: [1] 'once again, because it comes with a long-lasting impulse, it is bound to gather speed ever more and more, which grows as it moves, and increases its strong might and strengthens its blow. *For* it brings it about that all the seeds of the thunderbolt are one and all carried in a straight line, as it were towards one spot, driving them all as they fly into the same course'. How does this happen, for of course there is no idea of gravity or the attraction of the earth to increase the speed of the thunderbolt as it approaches the ground?

The idea must be analysed on the strict lines of Epicurean cinetics. The thunderbolt is a *concilium* of very loose texture and, as Lucretius says,[2] formed of small and smooth atoms: but the peculiarity of this *concilium* is that it can only admit atoms all moving in practically the same direction: others will either be driven back from it or, it may be supposed, pass transversely through its loose meshes. Now since it is a *concilium* and its atoms are, however slightly, linked, and since there must be minute differences of direction, there will be 'anticope'; the velocity of the bolt therefore will be something less than 'absolute'. And now a new atom moving at 'absolute' speed in the same direction, catches up the bolt: it joins it, 'links its motion' and at the same time delivers a blow to the whole which increases its speed. This operation is repeated again and again: the thunderbolt is augmented by new atoms and at the same time its speed grows ever faster and faster. Here then is a case where 'cohesion of motion' is of the very essence of the 'thing': to this it owes its chief characteristic, a speed, which contrary to the conditions which hold with most compound bodies, is increased as it acquires new atoms.

[1] vi. 340–5.   [2] vi. 330.

Turn from the loose texture of the thunderbolt to the closer and much closer formation of the 'soul'. Why is it that the soul cannot remain in union after it has left the body? Not merely because the body is its proper shell (στεγάζον) but because [1] 'in close mingling throughout veins and flesh, throughout sinews and bones, the first-beginnings of mind and soul are held close by all the body, nor can they freely leap asunder with great spaces between: and so shut in they make those sense-giving motions, which outside the body, cast out into the breezes of air after death, they cannot make, because they are not in the same way held together. For indeed air will be body, yea a living thing, if the soul can hold itself together and confine itself to those motions which before it made in the sinews and right within the body'. Once again the cause of identity is not merely local contiguity or imprisonment in a 'shell', but harmony of motion. Harmony then, though not necessarily identity of motion seems to be the condition of individuality in 'things': the *concilium* is kept together by it and atoms which cannot effect this cohesion of motion cannot become part of the particular compound. It is at once the cause of internal unity and external identity. It is not surprising to find that Lucretius' striking list [2] of the necessary properties and capacities which must be possessed by 'matter which can be creative' (*genitalis materies*) ends with 'meetings and motions'.

It must not however be supposed that the identity of the compound body implies absolute permanent identity in the component atoms, or that the atoms which originally unite to compose it remain in union until the final blow which once again dissolves it and sets them free. On the contrary there is a constant process of gain and loss—a kind of 'give and take' with the surrounding universe. On the one hand there is a continual accretion of new atoms and particles, which as they collide with the 'thing' are able to be taken into it and 'link on their motions'; on the other, as the result of the internal 'anticope', atoms previously caught in the

[1] Lucr. iii. 566–75.　　　　　　　　　[2] i. 632.

compound are now deflected at new tangents and driven out from it into the surrounding void. In particular there is the constant—though very slight—loss to things due to the efflux of the films which are the cause of their perception by sight, and of the particles which produce sound and smell. The whole notion has been clearly summed up in a passage of severe criticism: [1]

all compound bodies are liable to flux and change, they are always in process of being created or destroyed, since countless 'idols' are for ever coming off from them and flowing away, and countless others, we must suppose, flowing into them from their surroundings and filling up the compound which is for ever being varied by this process of exchange and mixed afresh.

We must indeed imagine a continual renewal of substance in the compound by means of the counterplay of loss and gain, and it would almost be true to say that in the Epicurean complex form is the element of permanence rather than matter. There is a supreme example of this conception in Epicurus' explanation of the physical structure of the gods,[2] but those who scoff at the absurdity of the notion there, will do well to remember that the same principle is true on Epicurus' view, though in a less degree, of every compound body.

It is this interaction of the 'thing' and its surroundings which gave Epicurus his explanation of the phenomena of growth and decay. In a notable passage at the end of the Second Book [3] Lucretius has described the whole process, arguing from the history of the living organism to that of the world itself. At first, while a body is young and 'climbing the steps to its full growth, it takes in more bodies than it gives off from itself, 'while the food easily makes its way into all the veins, and while the limbs are not so wide spread that they give out much and cause more waste than the life takes in as food. For in truth we must confess that many bodies flow off and depart from things; but it must needs be that more come to join them, until they have touched the

---

[1] Plutarch, *adv. Colot.* 16, p. 1116 c; U. 282.
[2] See Chap. IX, pp. 449 ff.   [3] Lucr. ii. 1105–74.

topmost point of growth. Then little by little age breaks their powers and their full-grown strength and life melts away on the downward path. For indeed the vaster a thing is, when its growth is once lost, and the wider it is, the more bodies it scatters abroad now and casts off from itself'. And thus, alike in the small bodies of 'things' and in the vast body of our world itself, the process of decay continues by reason of the excess of matter given off over that taken in: each part is thus gradually weakened and more exposed to the effect of the external blows which 'cease not to rain upon it'.[1] And so comes the final dissolution, due, in most cases, not merely to the gradual wasting of decay but to the ultimate advent of the appropriate external blow. The void between the atoms is now more extensive than it was when gain outweighed loss, and when a blow of the right strength comes it can break up the 'interlacings' and at last dissolve the compound and set the individual atoms free.

The conception of dissolution is thus no less exact than that of creation. During the whole existence of the compound there is a constant raining of atoms upon it from the outside: some of these may be taken in to increase it and cause its growth: some fly away after dealing it blows, which, at any rate in the stage of growth, may act as a strengthening influence, for they will, as it were, keep the shell in shape and drive back the atoms, which threaten to escape.[2] But occasionally there will come a blow so strong that it causes the internal structure of the body to reel and sway and come near to dissolution, as when, for instance, a sudden shock[3] to the human body wounds it and causes the soul within it to lose its senses in a swoon. But in such a case the 'interlacing' is not shattered and after a time of weakness the body is able to recover and continue its existence. At last, when the loss from decay has for some time gone on, comes the blow 'found strong enough to overcome the texture of each thing':[4] the 'interlacings' are undone, the 'shell' breaks up,

---

[1] 1142.
[2] See the remarkable idea expressed only, I think, in Lucr. i. 1042–5.
[3] Lucr. iii. 170.   [4] Lucr. i. 247.

and the imprisoned atoms are freed. The thing is destroyed, not because one jot of matter has perished, but because the structure is dissolved, the form is lost, and the eternal atoms wander again in independence to re-form themselves once more in a new compound.

One other point of great importance with regard to the character of compound bodies must be considered here, even though it involves to some extent the anticipation of the theory of perception, which will be discussed later,[1] namely, the nature of the qualities of things and the phenomena of qualitative change. Here the fundamental ideas of Epicurus are in strong opposition to Democritus, but his working out of the details is largely followed. For Democritus, it will be remembered,[2] the only absolute properties of things, as of the ultimate atoms in the cosmos, are size, shape, and weight: all other qualities, sound, colour, smell, taste, &c., are 'experiences of sensation' caused in us by differences of atomic arrangement. For Epicurus, whose root-principle is the infallibility of sensation from which follows immediately the insistence on the reality of the phenomenal world, such a view was impossible. We perceive qualities in things, therefore they are *their* qualities and not merely subjective changes in our sensations. Colour, taste, &c.,[3] may be either the 'permanent accompaniments' (συμβεβηκότα) of things or their 'accidents' (συμπτώματα), according as they are regarded as an essential part of their physical character or a quality which they may acquire and lose without essential change. Thus colour is a 'permanent accompaniment' of visible things, but an 'accident' of every solid body—for it has not colour in the dark, but in both cases it is the real quality of the 'things'.

In spite of this fundamental difference of conception Epicurus was free to adopt Democritus' elaborate working out of the differences of shape and arrangement of the atoms to produce not now differences of sensation in us, but differences of quality in things which we perceive by sensation.

[1] Chap. VIII.   [2] See Part I, Chap. III, § 6, p. 168.
[3] See above, Chap. IV.

Once again it is not dealt with in the extant writings of Epicurus, but Lucretius has a detailed exposition in the Second Book,[1] which may be summarized. Differences of taste in compound bodies are due to differences of shape in the component atoms:[2] things which taste sweet are composed of smooth and round atoms, things which taste bitter and sharp are 'held bound together with particles more hooked and for this cause they are wont to tear a way into our senses and at their entering in to break through the body'. Difference of atomic shape accounts likewise for differences in sound[3] and smell:[4] in each case pleasantness results from smoothness in the atom, unpleasantness from roughness.[5] All this is traditional and comes with but little alteration from Democritus.[6] In regard to colour the notion is more elaborate. Lucretius[7] argues at length that the atoms themselves are colourless and that the difference of colour in things is due not merely, as in the case of other qualities, to the shape of the component atoms but to their arrangement relatively to one another: 'it is of great matter with what others all the seeds are bound up, and in what position'.[8] He argues that if the atoms had colour, changes of colour would be impossible to account for, whereas with colourless atoms, they can be easily explained:

the sea, when mighty waves have stirred its level waters, is turned into white waves of shining marble. For you might say that when the substance of that which we often see black has been mingled up, and the order of its first-beginnings changed and certain things added and taken away, straightway it comes to pass that it is seen shining and white. But if the level waters of the ocean were made of sky-blue seeds, they could in no wise grow white. For in whatever way you were to jostle together seeds which are sky-blue, never can they pass into a marble colour.[9]

The appeal to sense-experience is characteristic and shows an advance on the *ex cathedra* decisions of Democritus. The consideration of colour, which most conspicuously among

[1] ii. 381–477. [2] ii. 388–407. [3] 410–13.
[4] 414–17. [5] 422–5. [6] See Part I, Chap. III, § 6 (b).
[7] ii. 730–841. [8] 760–1. [9] ii. 766–75.

secondary qualities undergoes alteration, leads immediately to the consideration of change: the peacock's tail,[1] for instance, assumes different colouring according as the light strikes upon it. This change is due to nothing but the movement and consequent alteration in position of the atoms. For the constant internal movement of the component atoms must always be remembered. At times, especially in dense bodies, this may be more like oscillation, and lead to little alteration of order and relative position. But when, especially owing to an external blow, such as the impact of light, the reciprocal change of position is great, the object colourless before in the dark may receive colour, or change it, when it receives the light at a different angle, as is the case with the breaking wave[2] or the 'iris on the burnished dove'.[3] The same is true of heat and cold and all other changes of quality: they are due to rearrangement in the atoms. All the qualities of things then are due to the shape and position of the atoms which go to form them, and all change of quality is due to change in that position ($\mu\epsilon\tau\acute{a}\theta\epsilon\sigma\iota\varsigma$).[4]

The difficulties involved in this position [5] have already to some extent been dealt with in discussing the properties of the atom, but they must be considered now from the point of view of the compound body. The atoms themselves are without qualities: how can they by mere juxtaposition or by mere 'harmony of motion' produce things which possess qualities? how is it conceivable that a number of colourless particles can create not merely a coloured object, but an object whose colour may change with the motion and rearrangement of those particles? Plutarch[6] once again put the criticism acutely and with point: 'it is incumbent on you to show how bodies without quality can produce qualities of all kinds by merely coming together. For instance whence comes what we call heat? how does it supervene on the atoms? For they neither possess heat before they meet nor do they become hot after they have met: the former would be the mark of something which had quality, the latter of

---

[1] ii. 806–7.   [2] 766–71.   [3] 801–5.   [4] Cf. Ep. i, § 54.
[5] Chap. III, p. 291.   [6] *adv. Colot.* 8, p. 1111; U. 288.

something which could suffer change: but you argue that neither of these two can be assigned to the atom owing to its indestructibility'. The example of heat brings out the difficulty clearly: the whole body is hot, yet none of its component atoms are hot: *ex hypothesi* they can neither be so nor become so. It might be answered that the position which Epicurus takes up is in fact the only position consistent with his general theory of the nature of the atom: for, as Lucretius points out,[1] to endow the atoms with qualities is to suppose them susceptible to change, in other words to destruction. But this only puts the difficulty a stage farther back. The true reply must be found in the conception of the *concilium*. As has already been noticed more than once, the complex body is more than an aggregate of atoms: the close relation between them, which is established by the 'interlacing' and the 'harmony of motion' constitutes it a new entity. And as such it acquires new characteristics and faculties: the motion of the whole body is different from the sum of the motions of its atoms, the spontaneous unconscious 'swerve' of the individual atom becomes in the complex of the soul the conscious act of volition. And so it is with qualities; the new entity of the compound has in fact the colour, taste, sound, smell, and heat, no one of which can belong to the atoms as individual particles. Nor are these qualities a delusion, or in any sense unreal or less real than the properties of the atoms. For the complex body perceived by sense is as real as the atom. Indeed the whole form of the argument as presented by Plutarch is to the Epicurean perverse. Epicurus starts, as has been pointed out often, from the reality of sense-perceptions: the most certain thing in the world is their reality and truth. They tell us of bodies with these qualities: the qualities therefore are real and true. This is the starting-point and it is only from this that it is possible to go on and ask about the realities for thought (the atoms): are they like the bodies of sense-perception or does the 'apprehension of the mind' cause us to deny them the attributes which we know are true of the bodies of sense?

[1] ii. 749–56.

This is the form in which the question is put throughout by
Lucretius and the only form in which an Epicurean could
propound it. There might be doubt about the absence of
quality in the atoms, but could be none about its presence as
a full reality in compound things. Epicurus in fact conceives, as it were, of two interrelated worlds, the world of
sense-objects known immediately in perception and the
world of atoms, known by thought, inferred from the world
of sense, but not always on direct analogy. There is truth
and reality in both worlds, and the world of sense is the
'outward expression' (ὁμοίωμα) of the unseen world of atoms.
The transition from the atoms without quality to things with
quality, so far from being unthinkable, is a necessary conclusion from the data of sense-perception and the inference
of the mind acting on the principles of the Canonice.

There is one more 'accident' (σύμπτωμα) which may attach
to the compound body and is of very great importance for
the Epicurean system in general. If the atoms of the right
shape are in the right arrangement and perform the appropriate motions, the *concilium* of insensible atoms may itself
obtain sensation: this is the origin of the soul of living
creatures and the mind of man. Sensation is after all only
another quality, like colour or heat, dependent no doubt on
infinitely subtler dispositions and motions, but yet just
another 'accident', which supervenes on the particular complex body under particular circumstances, just as do colour
and smell and taste. Again there is no information to be
gained from the Letters, but Lucretius[1] discusses the question at considerable length at the end of the Second Book
with a full sense of the importance of his conclusions for
the account of the soul which is to be given in Book III.
The argument is in the main parallel to that in reference
to the qualities. There is no question of the reality of the
existence of sentient bodies: that is itself an immediate
sensation and cannot be other than true. The only problem
raised is with regard to the world of thought: are the atoms
which compose this sentient whole themselves sentient? The

[1] ii. 865 990.

main portion of the discussion is occupied in negative argument against the opposite view that the soul-atoms have
sensation or in refuting other views, such as that sensation is
produced by a change in the component atoms which takes
place at the moment of birth.[1] The positive arguments
adduced seem rather puerile, first that we often see living
worms created out of insensate mud,[2] and secondly that we
see water and grass turning into the bodies of domestic
animals:[3] these in their turn we feed on and so sensation is
produced in our bodies out of our food! 'do you not then see
now that it is of great matter in what order all the first-
beginnings of things are placed and with what others
mingled they give and receive motions?'[4]

Lucretius' arguments may seem weak and the position
reached that sensation is nothing but the motions of certain
atoms in certain positions, arrangements, and motions is not
one which would commend itself to most modern minds.
A fuller discussion of this paradox must be reserved till
Epicurus' psychology[5] has been examined, but it may be
said here that Epicurus was at this point face to face with
the fundamental difficulty of any purely material system. If
there is no form of existence save particles of matter moving
in space, then everything of which we are conscious, sensation, thought, will, all that is mental and spiritual, must be
expressed in terms of the motion of material bodies, for there
is no other plane or sphere of reality to which it can be
referred. And if the resulting explanation appears unsatisfactory, the weakness is fundamental and inherent in the
whole system. Epicurus is at least consistent: he reached
a conclusion which was inevitable from his premises and
which was of immense value to him when he came to give
an account of the soul and its fate.

---

[1] ii. 931–43.   [2] 871–3.   [3] 874–85.
[4] 883–5.   [5] Chap. VIII.

VII

WORLDS AND OUR WORLD

THE cosmogony of Epicurus does not show any very great originality. He is content for the most part to adopt the theories of the Atomists, modifying and expanding here and there, and protesting occasionally against an idea which he regards as arbitrary or in conflict with the evidence of the senses. An exception must be made in the department of astronomy, where the rigid application of the principles of the Canonice leads either to surprising conclusions or to a curious suspension of judgement, which does more credit to Epicurus' capacity for consistency than to his faculty of criticism. For the rest there is not much that is new to chronicle, but certainly a greater unity of conception than can be extracted from the scattered testimonies to the theories of Leucippus and Democritus.

Epicurus starts with the conception of an infinite universe,[1] that is, space stretching for ever in every direction, and in every part of it atoms moving and colliding. From time to time, after many fruitless meetings and combinations, the atoms will in some part of space form a world ($\kappa\acute{o}\sigma\mu os$): 'for in very truth not by design did the first-beginnings of things place themselves each in its order with foreseeing mind, nor indeed did they make compact what motions each should start, but because many of them shifting in many ways throughout the world are harried and buffeted by blows from limitless time, by trying movements and unions of every kind, at last they fall into such dispositions as those whereby our world of things is created and holds together'.[2] Teleology is from the first excluded: there is no design, no assignment of parts and functions, no conscious organization: merely the long sequence of events, due to motions and blows, which inevitably results on occasions in the formation of a world like that we know.

[1] See Chap. III, pp. 296 ff. [2] Lucr. i. 1021–8.

What then in this sense is a world? Roughly, we know that for Epicurus, as for all the older cosmologists it means a system containing earth, and heavenly bodies with definite boundaries and definite shape. But fortunately there is preserved a definition of[1] Epicurus' own which contains several points of interest:

A world is a circumscribed portion of sky, containing heavenly bodies and an earth and all the heavenly phenomena, whose dissolution will cause all within it to fall into confusion; it is a piece cut off from the infinite and ends in a boundary either rare or dense, either revolving or stationary: its outline may be spherical or three-cornered or any kind of shape.

Notice first the general resemblance of this definition to the description of any ordinary atomic complex.[2] A world is not any more than any smaller 'thing' a mere aggregation of atoms: it is an 'enclosure ($\pi\epsilon\rho\iota o\chi\acute{\eta}$) of sky' with a definite boundary or 'shell', which may be of very varied shapes and of varying density of texture—in other words, there must, as always, be the 'interlacing' of atoms on the outside, which can hold the complex together and imprison the myriad atoms within, which by their various shapes, arrangements, and motions constitute the component parts of the world. Further, it must be a *concilium*, an organism of interdependent parts: 'its dissolution will cause' the atomic dislocation of every part of it: when through the process of decay and the blow 'strong enough' it has broken up, it must, like every other thing, resolve its constituent parts into their original atoms. The conception is gigantic, but it is made easier to the imagination if it is remembered that Epicurus had no notion at all of the vast expanse of the heavens and the distance between one heavenly body and another, and conceived of 'our world' as a comparatively small thing.

The latter half of the definition makes it clear that Epi-

---

[1] Ep. ii, § 88. I am inclined to regard the definition as a conflation from several Epicurean sources, but there seems no reason to believe that it was put together by any one other than the compiler of the Second Letter and therefore no cause to follow Usener in rejecting portions of it as glosses: see my notes on the passage. [2] See p. 341.

curus did not conceive of 'our world' as unique, but merely as one of a species, which might show many varieties of shape and arrangement. And indeed there is ample evidence that he held the traditional atomic view that worlds are infinite in number. The Letter to Herodotus [1] is explicit in its statement and reasons:

There are infinite worlds both like and unlike this world of ours. For the atoms being infinite in number . . . are borne on far out into space. For those atoms which are of such nature that a world could be created out of them or made by them, have not been used up either on one world or a limited number of worlds, nor again on worlds which are alike, or on those which are different from these. So that there nowhere exists an obstacle to the infinite number of the worlds.

Thus the infinity of worlds is practically a direct deduction from the infinity of the universe. There is a countless number of atoms suited for the formation of worlds and an infinite extent of space for them to gather together in:[2] it is unreasonable then to suppose that they do not at certain times and in certain places gather together and form other worlds as they have formed ours. The argument is characteristically Epicurean: there is nothing in phenomena to contradict the hypothesis, it may then be assumed to be true. These proofs Lucretius repeats and elaborates and adds the strange argument that nothing we know of is unique, but always one of a species;[3] there is about an equal number of things of every kind: it is therefore probable that there are countless other worlds in infinite space, and not only our own. Among these infinite worlds there may be considerable varieties of structure. Their outer 'shell' may differ in density and may be either rare, like the *flammantia moenia*[4] of our own world, or of denser and more solid formation. They may revolve, as that of our world was imagined as doing, or remain

---

[1] § 45.

[2] This point is added by Lucr. ii. 1053–5: it is a necessary step in the argument and may have fallen out accidentally in the Letter to Herodotus.

[3] ii. 1077–89. For this curious idea of the equal distribution of things (ἰσονομία) which appears from time to time in Lucretius see Chap. IX, pp. 461–7, and Giussani, *Stud. Lucr.* pp. 245 ff.

[4] Lucr. i. 73.

stationary. There may too be great varieties of shape among worlds.[1] They may be 'round' (στρογγύλοι),[2] or rather 'spherical (σφαιροειδεῖς),[3] or elliptical—'egg-shaped'—(ᾠοειδεῖς),[4] or even 'triangular' (τρίγωνοι),[5] by which Epicurus presumably means 'pyramidal'. Whether any shape whatever was considered possible is doubtful: the text of the second letter seems to assert it,[6] but it is contradicted by the scholium on the first,[7] which is probably of almost equal value. The question is not important, for in any case it is only the elaboration of an idea inherited from the atomists. Finally in between the various worlds which have their position in infinite space, are 'interworlds' (μετακόσμια) of greater or less size, which are of importance partly because they afford fields for the creation of new worlds,[8] partly because they were selected by Epicurus as the seat of the undisturbed abodes of the gods.[9]

More interesting problems are connected with the actual process of the creation of a world, for here Epicurus seems definitely to break with his predecessors. Leucippus,[10] it will be remembered, had the idea of a solid *plenum* of matter placed in an infinite void, the creation of a world being brought about when from time to time a mass of atoms of all kinds fell off from the *plenum* into 'a great void', where it was caught up in a whirl and gradually evolved itself into a world. This notion Epicurus[11] scornfully dismisses: a world will be created 'in a place with much void (ἐν πολυκένῳ τόπῳ) and not in a large empty space quite void, as some say'. The difference in the two accounts arises naturally from the fundamental discrepancy in the two conceptions of the uni-

---

[1] See Ep. i, § 74 ἔτι δὲ καὶ τοὺς κόσμους οὔτε ἐξ ἀνάγκης δεῖ νομίζειν ἕνα σχηματισμὸν ἔχοντας.

[2] Ep. ii, § 88.　　　　[3] Schol. on Ep. i, § 74.　　　　[4] Ibid.

[5] Ep. ii, § 88.　　　[6] § 88 ἢ οἵαν δή ποτε ⟨ἔχουσα⟩ περιγραφήν.

[7] οὐ μέντοι πᾶν σχῆμα ἔχειν, Schol. on i, § 74.

[8] Ep. ii, § 89 ⟨ἐν⟩ μετακοσμίῳ, ὃ λέγομεν, μεταξὺ κόσμων διάστημα.

[9] Hipp. *Philosoph.* 22. 3; U. 359 καθῆσθαι γὰρ τὸν θεὸν ἐν τοῖς μετακοσμίοις οὕτω καλουμένοις ὑπ' αὐτοῦ: cf. Cic. *de Nat. Deor.* i. 8. 18 ex Epicuri intermundiis, and see Chap. IX, p. 467.

[10] See Part I, Chap. II, § 3, p. 92.　　　　[11] Ep. ii, § 89.

verse: for Leucippus all that was not occupied either by existing worlds or by the original *plenum* was of necessity 'quite void', whereas to Epicurus, who thought of individual atoms moving all over infinite space, there was no such thing: but a world would naturally form itself in a place where there was not already a great conglomeration of atoms, in a place of 'much void'. His scorn is perhaps more justifiable than usual, for his own theory is indeed less arbitrary and improbable. Soon afterwards he turns to Democritus,[1] who believed like Epicurus himself in scattered atoms in infinite space, but held that they were gathered in a whirl by necessity and so formed into a world, which, as it continued to revolve, was constantly growing by accretions from without, until it got so large that it collided with another world and then was destroyed. Against these notions Epicurus once more rebels;[2] they are at once fantastic and unwarranted by the evidence of phenomena:

it is not merely necessary for a gathering of atoms to take place, nor indeed for a whirl and nothing more to be set in motion, as is supposed, by necessity, in an empty space in which it is possible for a world to come into being, nor can the world go on increasing until it collides with another world, as one of the so-called physical philosophers says. For this is a contradiction of phenomena.

The points are clear: the mere conglomeration of atoms (ἀθροισμός) is not enough, they must be atoms of the appropriate shapes, meeting in appropriate ways and able to fall into the requisite motions.[3] The whirl set in motion by 'necessity' is a mere subterfuge: unless it arose naturally out of previous motions it was not created by 'necessity', or else 'necessity' is a very arbitrary power.[4] Lastly, phenomena give no support at all to the notion of the gradual 'inflation' of worlds and their collisions with other worlds: the process of destruction, as we see it in other things, is indeed evidence against such a belief.[5]

---

[1] See Part I, Chap. III, § 4.   [2] § 90.
[3] Lucr. v. 442 motus inter sese dare convenientis.
[4] See Part I, Chap. III, § 4, pp. 138 ff.
[5] Cf. Lucr. ii. 1105–74, and see p. 352.

Epicurus' own account,[1] which he opposes to these rejected theories, is set out very briefly, and would be obscure, if we were not able to explain it by the much amplified and splendidly picturesque description of Lucretius.[2] 'A world may come into being both inside another world [3] and in an interworld, by which we mean a space between worlds . . . this occurs when seeds of the right kind have rushed in from a single world or interworld or from several: little by little they make junctures ($\pi\rho\sigma\theta\acute{\epsilon}\sigma\epsilon\iota s$) and articulations ($\delta\iota\alpha\rho\theta\rho\acute{\omega}\sigma\epsilon\iota s$), and cause changes of position ($\mu\epsilon\tau\alpha\sigma\tau\acute{\alpha}\sigma\epsilon\iota s$) to another place, as it may happen, and produce irrigations ($\acute{\epsilon}\pi\alpha\rho\delta\epsilon\acute{\upsilon}\sigma\epsilon\iota s$) of the appropriate matter until the period of completion and stability, which lasts as long as the underlying foundations are capable of receiving additions.' The idea then is of the gathering not of a mere chance collection of atoms, but, what must happen much more rarely, of the appropriate 'seeds'[4] either in the space occupied by a decaying world or in some space hitherto unoccupied by any world. At first all is chaos[5] and confusion, and then a triple process takes place represented in Epicurus' account by the three rather obscure words 'junctures, articulations, and changes of position', but fully explained by the parallel passage in Lucretius: 'from this mass[6] parts began to fly off hither and thither and like things to unite with like ($\pi\rho\sigma\theta\acute{\epsilon}\sigma\epsilon\iota s$) and so to unfold a world and to sunder its members (*membraque dividere*, clearly a translation of $\delta\iota\alpha\rho\theta\rho\acute{\omega}\sigma\epsilon\iota s$) and dispose its great parts, that is, to mark off the high heaven from the earth, and the sea by itself, so that it might spread out with its moisture kept apart, and likewise the fires of the sky by themselves, unmixed and kept apart.' It is the old cosmological idea of the 'separation out of opposites' and the union of like with like, which in its atomic setting produces the transition of the atomic nuclei into the compound formation of the 'elements'. And then follows

---

[1] Ep. ii, § 89. [2] v. 416–508: cf. also ii. 1105–74.
[3] A very curious notion: see my note on the passage.
[4] See p. 363, and cf. Ep. i, § 73 $\acute{\epsilon}\kappa$ $\sigma\upsilon\sigma\tau\rho\sigma\phi\hat{\omega}\nu$ $\acute{\iota}\delta\acute{\iota}\omega\nu$.
[5] Lucr. v. 432–42. [6] 443–8.

the third stage (μεταστάσεις): the heavier matter of earth 'meets together in the middle and takes up the lowest places':[1] the light seeds[2] are squeezed out and rise to form sky and heavenly bodies; and between them the seeds of intermediate weight form the sea which rests upon the earth.[3] More and more the elements become distinct from one another; sun, moon, and stars are created in the heavens,[4] the land sinks in valleys or rises in mountains,[5] and the sea shapes itself over the low-lying parts of earth. At last the world has assumed the appearance that we know.[6] The general idea follows the traditional lines, but it has been more carefully thought out and is expressed with magnificent dramatic force by the great Roman poet.

One difficulty seems to have been felt by Epicurus in adapting this traditional account to his own conceptions. The heavy matter of earth is said to 'meet together in the middle and take up the lowest place'. This is the traditional language of 'the whirl'[7] in which the larger and denser bodies meet in the centre, where there is more resistance to the rotation: from the point of view of the rotating sphere the centre can naturally be referred to as the 'lowest place'. Epicurus had in general accepted the conception of 'the whirl', and might well have been contented to follow it in this point. And in his own writings there is no trace of hesitation, but a strange passage in Lucretius suggests a difficulty.[8] It may reasonably be supposed that Epicurus, having adopted weight as one of the essential properties both of the atoms and of things, now felt some hesitation in stating that the heavier bodies gathered together in the centre of the world and remained there. At any rate Lucretius is concerned to explain how this can be. If, he argues, the earth were directly imposed upon air underneath, the

---

[1] 449–51.
[2] 453–70. *expressa* in Lucretius represents the ἔκθλιψις of the Atomists.
[3] 480–91.   [4] 471–9.   [5] 492–4.
[6] The whole description may be compared with Virgil's intentionally Epicurean account of the creation of the world in Eclogue VI.
[7] See Part I, Chap. III, § 4.   [8] v. 534–63.

air would undoubtedly be unable to support its weight and it would sink: but the fact is that the earth gradually 'thins out' [1] underneath into a 'second nature', which acts as a link between earth and air and forms, as it were, a kind of spring which supports the earth: 'so then the earth is not suddenly brought in as some alien body, nor cast from elsewhere on alien air, but it has been begotten with it from the first beginning of the world, a determined part of it, as our limbs are seen to be of us'.[2] The idea at first sight seems to be fantastic, another weak subterfuge from a difficulty. But if it is looked at more carefully in the light of Lucretius' phraseology and illustrations, there is nothing inconsistent with the main principles of the system. It is wrong from the Epicurean point of view to think of earth and air and the 'second nature' as wholly independent existences (*aliena*): they are all in reality parts of the great *concilium* of the world, interrelated as parts of the same body and growing up together. In the same way, Lucretius argues,[3] head and limbs are not felt to be a weight by the individual man, though in themselves they are weighty things, and 'the force of the soul, though exceeding fine',[4] can, owing to this intimate connexion, lift the whole weight of our body when we jump. Just as above[5] the earth is gradually connected with the sky by the intermediate link of the atmosphere, so it is with the air beneath by means of this intermediate matter. Epicurus had to some extent created his own difficulty, but he solved it ingeniously on his own lines.

A world once created, its history as a whole is not far different from that of any other *concilium*. It is surrounded from the first by space in which countless atoms are always moving towards it from all directions. Many of these will enter the world and become merged in it. This happens specially in the early stages of its growth: there are 'irriga-

[1] 535-8:

> evanescere paulatim et decrescere pondus
> convenit, atque aliam naturam subter habere
> ex ineunte aevo coniunctam atque uniter aptam
> partibus aeriis mundi quibus insita vivit.

[2] 546-9.   [3] 540-5.   [4] 556-63.   [5] 550-3.

tions'[1] of the 'appropriate matter' which feed the world in its various members 'until its full completion', that is, as Lucretius[2] explains, for all the time that the world is taking in more than it gives out and is therefore growing. During this period even atoms which cannot enter the *concilium*, may yet play their part in holding the world together; for they may batter on its outer shell,[3] checking the atoms which tend to be driven off from it and holding the whole in shape. But meanwhile even from the first there is a tendency for atoms to escape from the *concilium* and pass out into the void, driven off at a tangent by their collisions. And gradually the proportion of atoms entering lessens in comparison with those driven out, until at last loss begins to get the upper hand over gain, and decay sets in. Then the atoms battering from without can no longer check the flow, and their blows[4] from being a source of strength, become an attack on the 'interlacings' of the world. And so little by little the world begins to perish: its 'underlying foundations' are no longer capable of receiving additions, loss becomes greater and greater, external blows have a more and more destructive effect. At last the great organism is broken up and the atoms are once again set at liberty to wander in the void or to unite perhaps again in the formation of some fresh world. Lucretius[5] insists at great length on the ultimate destruction of worlds, and, holding, as he does,[6] that our world is already on the path of decay, prays that the final end may not come in his time.[7] This tremendous thought of the final dissolution of the world was already present in the atomic tradition,[8] but here it may be regarded as a further proof of Epicurus' consistent conception of even a world as in every respect a perfect, however gigantic, example of an atomic *concilium*.

With the detailed mechanism of our world, thus created, with the motions and phases of the heavenly bodies, with the phenomena of the sky (μετέωρα), clouds, rain, lighting, &c.,

---

[1] Ep. ii. 89 ἐπαρδεύσεις.   [2] ii. 1105–30.   [3] Lucr. i. 1042–4.
[4] ii. 1144, 5.   [5] v. 64–109, 235–415.
[6] ii. 1150–74.   [7] v. 107.   [8] See p. 148.

and with certain curiosities among earthly phenomena, Epicurean tradition dealt in great detail. The Second Letter, that to Pythocles, attributed to Epicurus himself, but more probably an authoritative compilation, is entirely devoted to these topics, and Lucretius in his fifth and sixth books has resumed the greater number of them with a wealth of poetic amplification. The great majority of the explanations advanced are derived from the hypotheses of previous philosophers,[1] not only from the Atomists, but from the Ionians, Pythagoras, Empedocles, and Anaxagoras, and there is little which is characteristically Epicurean, except the occasional working out of an idea such as that of the genesis of lightning or the atomic mechanism of the action of the magnet. It is not therefore profitable to review this part of the Epicurean system in detail—though its study contains much that is in itself of interest—but it must be briefly considered in so far as it suggests or illustrates principles, which are very closely concerned with Epicurus' theory of knowledge and his conception of philosophic procedure. For it is in this portion of his work more than any other that the practical weakness of the absolute trust in sense-perception is revealed. When a 'sensational' theory has to deal with facts, which are in themselves obvious but depend on remote and imperceptible causes, it is apt to be at its worst; for it is not permissible to fall back wholly on reason, yet sensation itself is apt to be but a poor guide. It does Epicurus great credit that even here he remained true to his principles and resisted the temptation to dogmatize.

In the first place what is Epicurus' attitude towards this whole department of inquiry? Had he a real interest in it for its own sake and does he demand in it such accuracy as he required in the fundamental propositions of the atomic theory? These questions are answered clearly enough in the exordium of the Letter to Pythocles:[2]

we must not suppose that any other object is to be gained from the knowledge of the phenomena of the sky than peace of mind and a sure confidence. We must not try to force an impossible explanation,

[1] See notes on Ep. ii.   [2] §§ 85, 86.

nor employ a method of inquiry like our reasoning either about the modes of life or with respect to the solution of other physical problems: witness such propositions as that 'the universe consists of bodies and the intangible', or that 'the elements are indivisible', and all such statements in circumstances where there is only one explanation which harmonizes with phenomena. For this is not so with the things above us: they admit of more than one cause of their coming into being and more than one account of their nature which harmonizes with our sensations.

This passage is of the greatest importance for the understanding of Epicurus' treatment of astronomical and meteorological phenomena, for it not merely shows the attitude of mind in which he approached them, but the connexion between this part of his inquiry and the rest of his system. He was primarily an ethical teacher: his first object was to secure for man's life pleasure, which he interpreted to be freedom from disturbance (ἀταραξία); for this purpose it was essential that a man should have an exact comprehension with regard to his mode of life, and with regard to the fundamental nature of the universe. He must know that the world is ultimately of purely material constitution, and that its workings are governed in general by the operation of natural law. And in detail too these principles must be maintained: the great enemy to be faced here, as always, is religion: enough must be known about the nature and movements of the heavenly bodies, &c., to be sure that the beliefs of theology are baseless. 'Such phenomena[1] must not be thought to be due to any being who controls and ordains or has ordained them[2] . . . nor again must we believe that the heavenly bodies, which are but fire agglomerated in a mass, possess blessedness and voluntarily take upon themselves these movements.' We must reject, that is, both of the current theological explanations, the more popular view that the heavenly bodies are themselves divine, and the more philosophic belief that they are indeed themselves material bodies, but are fashioned and controlled by a divine being

[1] Ep. i, §§ 76, 77.
[2] For the text, see my notes on the passage.

or obey laws once ordained by a Creator. But for this purpose it is enough that we can establish in each case the general truth that the actions of the heavenly bodies are regulated by purely natural causes: it is not necessary to be able to point to some one cause and say that it and it alone is operative. Indeed to attempt to do so, is in itself almost theological dogmatism:[1] for it is pretending to a certainty of knowledge about uncertain material, which is like the theologian's postulate of a supernatural revelation. In cases then where several explanations may be suggested,[2] all of which are equally consistent with phenomena, we must not attempt to choose between them, but rest content with the knowledge that in any case the operation is purely natural and due to nothing but material causes. All the way through the Second Letter and the corresponding Books of Lucretius these two notes are struck again and again: on the one hand the violent rejection of 'myth' or of any teleological explanation, which may approach a theological view, on the other the constant warning that a given phenomenon 'may happen in several ways' and that it is not for us to state which is the true cause in the particular case.

Before proceeding to illustrate this attitude of mind, it is necessary to return for a moment to the principles of the Canonice and see what they demand with regard to procedure in this kind of inquiry. Are the workings of the heavenly bodies matters of immediate perception or are they rather to be classed with the 'unseen'? What rules must be formulated to regulate our investigations? The circumstances are peculiar: the *facts* with regard to such phenomena are matters of immediate sense-perception, and concerning them there can be no dispute; they *are* as we see them. But with the *causes* it is different: they are unseen and we must pursue the methods of investigation which in such cases the Canonice

---

[1] See a very remarkable passage in Ep. ii, § 87 ὅταν δέ τις τὸ μὲν ἀπολίπῃ, τὸ δὲ ἐκβάλῃ ὁμοίως σύμφωνον ὂν τῷ φαινομένῳ, δῆλον ὅτι καὶ ἐκ παντὸς ἐκπίπτει φυσιολογήματος, ἐπὶ δὲ τὸν μῦθον καταρρεῖ.

[2] For the connexion of this principle with the Epicurean theory of knowledge see Chap. I, pp. 260–2.

demands. In the first place we must use the analogy of phenomena on earth whose causes we can trace: 'we can obtain indications (σημεῖα) of what happens above from some of the phenomena on earth: for we can observe how they come to pass, though we cannot observe the phenomena in the sky'.[1] Secondly,[2] we can work by the 'apprehension of the mind' (ἐπιβολὴ τῆς διανοίας), combining concepts. In these ways many explanations may be reached, and to them the test of phenomena must at once be applied: any explanations[3] may be accepted which are not contradicted (ἀντιμαρτυρεῖται) by phenomena. Of such explanations there may in many cases be several: if none of them are contradicted by phenomena, then none can be rejected, and all must be accepted as possible. Thus by the rules of the Canonice, no less than by the requirements of the ethical theory we are driven back into acquiescence in the 'plurality of causes': for the primary moral purposes of our life we do not require knowledge so accurate as to enable us to decide between several possible explanations, and our accepted rules of procedure show us that such decision is in these cases impossible.

These two considerations, of the ultimate purpose of the inquiry and of the application of the rules of the Canonice, explain much in Epicurus' astronomical theories which has seemed to commentators foolish and almost childish: it will be worth while to consider one or two instances in order to see the principles at work. Take first of all the famous statement that the size of the sun and moon is just what we see it to be, and examine carefully Epicurus' argument.[4] 'The size of sun ⟨and moon⟩ and the other stars is for us what it appears to be; and in reality it is either ⟨slightly⟩ greater than what we see or slightly less or the same size: for so too fires on earth when looked at from a distance seem to the senses. And every objection at this point will easily be dissipated, if we pay attention to the clear vision (τοῖς ἐναργήμασι).' The conclusion seems merely puerile, but it is

---

[1] Ep. ii. 87: cf. Ep. i. 80. [2] See Chap. I, p. 265.
[3] See Ep. ii. 88. [4] Ep. ii, § 91.

due to a rigid and accurate application of the Canons. The size of the sun and moon is a matter of immediate sense-perception: we see it immediately and therefore we must accept the truth of our perception without question. But this is a case of a distant vision: therefore what we see is the truth 'for us', i.e. this is the size that sun and moon look at a distance, just as the square tower looks round. Is it then their real size? This must be regarded as a 'problem awaiting solution' (προσμένον), and above all our perception must not be contaminated with any inference of opinion (προσδοξαζόμενον) as to probabilities. In the case of a terrestrial object, we can solve our problem by going near to the object and obtaining the 'clear vision' of the close view: we learn, for instance, that the tower was in reality square. It is not possible to do this with the heavenly bodies and we must therefore have recourse to the use of analogy. The very brief statement of the letter at this point would be unintelligible, if we were not assisted by a reference of the scholiast to the eleventh book 'On Nature'[1] and the fuller treatment of Lucretius.[2] The latter treats the sun and moon separately, but in both cases uses the analogy of earthly fires, which the author of the Letter clearly had in mind. 'Earthly fires, he argues, at a distance lose their heat before they appear to diminish in size, but the sun's heat is as great as it can be: therefore he is not far enough away for his size to have diminished. Again earthly fires become blurred in outline by distance before they diminish in size; but the moon's outline is clear-cut: therefore it is not diminished in size.' The analogy is complete and there is nothing in the 'clear vision' of sun and moon, which tells against it. Therefore the conclusion must be accepted, and, if to us it seems ridiculous, we must again remember that Epicurus' whole conception of the world was of something very much smaller than modern science has taught us to have in mind. Finally notice the conclusion: the size of sun and moon is either what we see or 'a little greater or smaller': analogy, unsupported by

---

[1] εἰ γὰρ τὸ μέγεθος διὰ τὸ διάστημα ἀπεβεβλήκει, πολλῷ μᾶλλον ἂν τὴν χρόαν.   [2] v. 564–91.

the near vision, does not permit us to reach absolute certainty or accuracy, but the knowledge which we can so obtain is sufficient at least to enable us to put any theological explanation out of court.

An example of a somewhat different method of procedure may be found in the discussion of the phases of the moon.[1] 'The wanings of the moon and its subsequent waxings might be due to the revolution of its own body, or equally well to successive conformations of the atmosphere, or again to the interposition of other bodies; they may be accounted for in all the ways in which phenomena on earth invite us to such explanations of these phases; provided only one does not become enamoured of the method of the single cause and groundlessly put the others out of court, without having considered what it is possible for a man to observe and what is not, and desiring therefore to observe what is impossible.' This problem clearly belongs to the second class: the fact of the moon's phases is a matter of immediate perception, but its cause is not: accordingly the analogy of terrestrial phenomena must be used and any explanations may be put forward as probable against which the evidence of phenomena is not contradictory: but there is no criterion by which any one of them may be selected as true to the exclusion of others. The compiler of the Letter then states the conjectures of the earlier philosophers and ranks them all as of equal authority—the view of Heraclitus that the moon was a body light on one side and dark on the other, which gradually turned round, the notion of Xenophanes that it travelled through tracts of air which were not equally well supplied with the necessary fuel, and the belief of Anaximenes that there was another opaque body—or bodies—which intervened and screened the moon from us. It is perhaps remarkable that the true explanation of the phenomenon, which is placed first by Lucretius,[2] is omitted altogether by the author of the letter: Lucretius seems at times to have had a rather un-Epicurean eye for probabilities in the matter of astronomy. Here then is a good instance of the suspense

---

[1] Ep. ii, § 94.   [2] v. 705–14.

of judgement: analogy does not warrant any decision between rival theories, for with earthly bodies, any of them
might produce the required effect. We must therefore be
content with a 'plurality of causes', but they are again sufficient to show that the phenomenon has natural causes and
to exclude the explanations of 'myth'.

In these two instances, and indeed, throughout the astronomical section, there is nothing distinctively atomic, and
Epicurus is willing to look with an impartial eye on the views
of any previous philosopher provided they are not contradicted by phenomena. But it must not be thought that in the
details of his cosmology he in any sense abandoned atomism
or was not at pains to think out his explanations on atomic
lines. An instance or two to show this may be taken from his
treatment of celestial phenomena and terrestrial curiosities.
The discussion of the causes of lightning is a good case in
point.[1]

Lightnings are produced in several ways: for both owing to the friction
and collision of clouds a conformation of atoms which produces fire
(note the notion of the 'seed' again) slips out and gives birth to the
lightning, and owing to wind bodies which give rise to this flash are
dashed from the clouds: or compression may be the cause, when clouds
are squeezed either by one another or by the wind. Or again it may
be that the light scattered abroad from the heavenly bodies is taken in
by the clouds, and then is driven together by the movement of the
clouds and wind, and falls out through the clouds; or else light composed of most subtle particles may filter through the clouds, whereby
the clouds may be set on fire by the flame and thunder produced by the
movement of the fire. Or the wind may be fired owing to the strain
of motion and its violent rotation: or clouds may be rent by wind and
atoms fall out which produce fire and cause the appearance of lightning.
And several other methods may easily be observed, if one clings always
to phenomena and can compare what is akin to these things.

The method is here the same: sense-perception gives no
immediate knowledge of causes, and the analogy of phenomena in which the cause can be traced, suggests this almost
bewildering array of alternative possibilities, between which

[1] Ep. ii, §§ 101, 102.

there is no ground for choosing. But it is not here a mere recapitulation of the views of other thinkers with very different fundamental principles, but a careful thinking out of possibilities on strictly atomic lines: the 'formation of atoms which produces fire', 'bodies which give rise to the flash', the taking in of light from the heavenly bodies into the clouds, the 'light composed of most subtle particles', the falling out of 'atoms which produce fire'—all these are essentially atomic notions, which would be meaningless on any other view of physical phenomena. Lucretius'[1] elaborate treatment of the same topic reveals almost clearer evidence of the same consistent habit of thought, and his discussion of the cause of the pace of the thunderbolt[2] is a notable addition to our understanding of the nature of the atomic *concilium*. Lucretius[3] concludes characteristically with an emphatic protest against the theological view that the lightnings and thunders are the weapons of divine beings.

The curiosities of terrestrial phenomena are not fully dealt with in any extant portion of Epicurus' writings, but they were part of the atomic tradition handed down by Democritus,[4] and Lucretius has dealt very fully with some of them in the latter half of the Sixth Book. A simple case may be selected to illustrate the careful investigation on strictly atomic lines, the problem of the well of Jupiter Ammon,[5] which was cold by day and hot by night. The popular explanation of the phenomena, in so far as it was not regarded merely as a miracle, was, as Lucretius explains, that the sun in his nightly journey under the earth warmed the fountain from below. To this view he very naturally objects that if the sun could not warm the water in the day-time, when it was fully exposed to its heat, it is not likely that it could do so at night when it would have to act through 'the dense body of earth'. The true cause is to be sought in an atomic view. The earth round the well is naturally of loose texture and contains many 'seeds of fire': at night the cold contracts

---

[1] vi. 160–378.   [2] See Chap. V, p. 349.
[3] 379–422.   [4] See Part I, Chap. III, § 5, pp. 152–4.
[5] vi. 848–78.

the earth and the seeds of fire are naturally 'squeezed out' into the well: in the day-time the earth is again rarefied by the sun's heat and the 'seeds of fire' return to it from the well. The modern man of science would probably apply the brutal test of the thermometer and discover that the well remained always at much the same temperature, but that it seems cold in the heat of day and hot in the frosty night. Nevertheless the Epicurean thinkers may once again be allowed credit for an ingenious explanation thought out in accordance with the principles of their general physical theory. A still more distinctively 'atomic' explanation is that given immediately after of a well,[1] over which sticks of wood would ignite—but for the best example of this treatment, both in its great elaboration and the extreme subtlety of its realization of atomic conditions is Lucretius'[2] singular explanation of the action of the magnet.

To Lucretius[3] again we are indebted for the only full account of the Epicurean view of the early history of the earth and the gradual development of plant, animal, and human life: at one crucial stage the Letter to Herodotus comes in to help and critics and commentators have preserved some details of interest. But there is no doubt that here again, though the marvellous vigour and picturesqueness of description is his own, Lucretius has strictly preserved Epicurean tradition. Though there is nothing which affects our view of fundamental principles, there are many points of considerable interest in themselves, and a brief account must be given of the main notions which he embodies in the poem. When the elements had finally separated themselves, and the earth was formed in hill and valley with the waters here and there 'covering its face', it first began to be covered with vegetable life. Trees and plants and grass grew out from it 'as do feathers and hair and bristles'[4] from the bodies of birds and animals (plants to the

---

[1] vi. 879–905.

[2] vi. 906–1089: cf. Galen. *de Facultat. Natur.*, i. 14, t. ii, p. 45 κ; U. 293: we know that Democritus wrote on this subject.

[3] v. 772–1457.

[4] 783–9.

Epicurean[1] were not 'living things' (ἔμψυχα), and their growth and movement was mechanical and not vital). And then 'the races of living things'[2] (*mortalia saecla*) began to spring up from the earth, their mother, even as now under the influence of rain and sun, worms and other vermin may be created.[3] Finally from 'wombs rooted in the ground'[4] came forth the race of men, whom the earth, like a human mother, fed with milk through her pores, until they were strong enough to seek food for themselves. These curious notions, which have of course been much ridiculed, are not a mere extravagance of fancy, but are undoubtedly intended to show the perfect continuity of creation, from the inorganic, through the vegetable to the animal kingdom and so to the race of men. Nor need Lucretius' account present any real difficulty in a system for which sensation is a mere mechanical accident of atomic arrangements and motions: once again the difficulty of transition from the inanimate to the animate and conscious is glossed over, or rather totally ignored.

A striking passage[5] follows in which Lucretius describes the early development of the animal kingdom: nature made many experiments, producing creatures without arms or legs, or blind or eyeless, or sexless or with limbs indistinctly formed. But all such, since they could not help themselves or propagate their species, gradually perished. Indeed, he says, in a passage[6] which to many readers has recalled the modern hypothesis of natural selection, only those species survived which by strength or craft or swiftness could prove their worth, or by their usefulness to man insure his protection. Those who had none of these resources, 'fell a prey and spoil to others, all entangled in the fateful trammels of their own being, until nature brought their kind to destruction'.[7] On the other hand Lucretius[8] stoutly denies the creation of such monsters as are told of in myth and legend,

---

[1] Aet. v. 26. 3, p. 438 D.; U. 309 τὰ δὲ φυτὰ αὐτομάτως πως κινεῖσθαι, οὐ διὰ ψυχῆς.　　　[2] 791–804.

[3] This curious belief plays a large part in Lucretius' argument for the creation of a sensible soul out of insensible atoms.　　　[4] 805–20.

[5] 821–54.　　　[6] 855–77.　　　[7] 875–7.　　　[8] 878–924.

Centaurs and Scyllas and Chimaeras, composed of elements
from different races: for the period of growth of the various
tribes of animals is so different that they could not possibly
combine in such a complex formation, 'when three years
have come round the horse is in the prime of vigour, but
the child by no means so. . . . Later when the stout strength
and limbs of horses fail through old age and droop, as his
life flees from them, then at last youth sets in in the prime of
boyish years and clothes the cheeks with soft down'.[1] The
observation is acute and serves as yet another weapon of
attack on the 'myths' of religion.

Not less acute from the point of view of the modern study
of anthropology is Lucretius'[2] account of the life of primitive
man and the beginnings of civilization. Here again he runs
counter to the accepted traditions. Greeks and Romans alike
looked back to an imaginary Golden Age, in which man
was greater and stronger and happier and better than at
present, when through a long series of degeneration he had
reached the Age of Iron. Lucretius will have none of this:
man's life was then far harder.[3] He lived like the beast of
the field,[4] feeding on acorns and wild fruits and drinking
from mountain-torrents.[5] He hid in caves or groves or
thickets for shelter and every man fought for his own hand;[6]
at night he lay down to rest, but had no special fear for its
terrors:[7] rather his supreme care was to protect himself from
the attacks of wild animals. Not more men perished then
than now:[8] they were killed by wild beasts or accidental
poisoning, but warfare and navigation were unknown. All
this is largely confirmed by modern investigations into the
life of savage tribes, and the anthropologist would find little
with which to quarrel: but it shows a singular penetration
for one who had but very few recorded data on which
to work and the whole force of popular tradition against
him.

Then began the slow process of civilization. Men devised

---

[1] 883–9.	[2] v. 925–1457.	[3] 925 ff.
[4] 931–44.	[5] 945–52.	[6] 955–61.
[7] 973–87.	[8] 988–1010.	

for themselves huts to dwell in and skin-clothes to wear[1] and above all learned the use of fire.[2] Family life began to be recognized[3] and even the union of families in communities under a compact 'not to harm or be harmed'[4]. This idea of the 'Social Contract' plays a large part in Epicurus' early history of man and is very closely connected with his ethical theory: a considerable series of his *Principal Doctrines* are concerned with it.[5] Justice in itself is not a virtue, it is neither good nor bad. The only moral ideal of man is pleasure: but in order to secure his own pleasure it is necessary for a man to make himself safe from the attacks of other men. The best way to secure this result is to make a compact with them 'neither to harm nor to be harmed', to surrender something of one's own pleasure in hurting others in order to secure immunity as its reward. 'The justice which arises from nature is a pledge of mutual advantage to restrain men from harming one another and save them from being harmed':[6] 'justice never is anything in itself, but in the dealings of men with one another in any place whatever and at any time it is a kind of compact not to harm or be harmed'.[7] The ethical aspect of this theory must be considered later:[8] here it may be noticed that Epicurus would regard the first beginnings of common life and the recognition of the rights of others as a gradual and somewhat cynical realization of the selfish advantages which it procured.

When the start was once given to common life, matters, as Lucretius conceived, moved fast. The strongest men in communities became kings and settled the distribution of property.[9] Then the discovery of gold brought a new and sinister motive into life:[10] wealth, not strength and prowess, became the touchstone of power, and political ambition brought social catastrophe. Kings were driven out, popular rule ensued, and magistrates were created:[11] the poet's account is obviously influenced by the traditional history of Rome.

---

[1] 1011. [2] 1091–1104. [3] 1012–14.
[4] 1019–27. [5] xxxi–xxxviii. [6] *K.Δ.* xxxi.
[7] *K.Δ.* xxxiii. [8] See Chap. X, pp. 510–15. [9] v. 1105–12.
[10] 1113–35. [11] 1136–60.

Later on Lucretius returns to a more primitive period and shows how the use of metals[1] was learnt from the processes of nature, of bronze first and then of iron,[2] which drove out bronze because of its superior usefulness, especially in the processes of war. Then, after a digression on the use of animals in warfare,[3] he shows how nature again taught men the operations of agriculture,[4] and the songs of birds suggested imitation, which was the origin of music.[5] Then came the knowledge of astronomy,[6] and private property[7] and the science of navigation,[8] and lastly the finer arts of poetry and painting and sculpture:[9] 'for they saw one thing after another grow clear in their mind, until by their arts they reached the topmost pinnacle'.[10] All this is of great interest and is described with a brilliancy and irony as great as anything in the poem; but there are two points of greater importance than the rest, the discussions of the origin of religion and the origin of language. With the former it will be more convenient to deal in speaking of the Epicurean theology, but the latter question must be briefly discussed here, as it has considerable prominence in the Letter to Herodotus[11] and Epicurus' position is slightly obscured in Lucretius and has not always been rightly understood. His theory of the origin and development of language throws considerable light on his general ideas of the development of the arts.

Epicurus plunges rather abruptly, after discussing the creation of worlds, into the general problems of civilization, and he appears to recognize, far more clearly than Lucretius, two stages in the development of the arts, the first in which nature constrained men to do things by sheer force of circumstances, the second in which reason deliberately developed and elaborated what had been introduced by nature and made further inventions for itself. He then proceeds to apply this general theory to the particular case of language.[12]

---

[1] 1241–80.	[2] 1281–1307.	[3] 1308–49.
[4] 1361–78.	[5] 1379–1415.	[6] 1436–9.
[7] 1441.	[8] 1442.	[9] 1450–3.
[10] 1456–7.	[11] §§ 75, 76.	[12] § 75.

And so names too were not at first deliberately given to things, but men's natures according to their different nationalities had their own peculiar feelings and received their peculiar impressions, and so each in their own way emitted air formed into shape (note the peculiar atomic form of speech)[1] by each of these feelings and impressions, according to the differences made in the different nations by the places of their abode as well. And then later on by common consent in each nationality special names were deliberately given in order to make their meanings less ambiguous to one another and more briefly demonstrated. And sometimes those who were acquainted with them brought in things hitherto unknown and introduced sounds for them, on some occasions being naturally constrained to utter them, and on others choosing them by reasoning in accordance with the prevailing mode of formation, and thus making their meaning clear.

It has been usual to compare this discussion with that of Plato in the *Cratylus*, but Giussani,[2] who was the first to realize the full import of this passage in the Letter to Herodotus, has pointed out the considerable difference in the point of view of the two philosophers. Plato is considering the relation of language to thought and asks whether there is a natural and inevitable relation (φύσει) between words and their objects, or whether the relation is deliberate and conventional (κατὰ συνθήκην): he is in other words discussing the psychology of fully developed language. Epicurus on the other hand approaches the question as a problem of the actual history of primitive man. He believes then that there were two stages in the development of language. In the first it was made wholly 'by nature': men's internal emotions (πάθη) or impressions received from phenomena (φαντάσματα) constrained them to utter certain sounds, which then reproduced similar emotions and impressions in other men and so conveyed ideas. These sounds differed according to the racial conformation of different tribes (καθ' ἕκαστα ἔθνη) and even geographical position (ἡ παρὰ τοὺς τόπους διαφορά) had its influence. In the second stage man, having now become aware of the possibilities of language, proceeded deliberately (θέσει) to make distinctions accurate and invent new expressions for new things. These new

---

[1] See Chap. VIII, p. 405.   [2] *Stud. Lucr.* 267–84.

expressions again sometimes occurred as the natural result of a new impression, sometimes arose from reasoned choice acting on the lines of natural cause. The account of the whole process is carefully and minutely thought out, and it is possible to recognize clearly, though in a complex form, the two stages of 'nature' and 'deliberation' which Epicurus had postulated for the development of the arts in general: it is once again singularly near to what would now be said of the historical origin of language. Two rather remarkable points may however be noticed. In the first place Epicurus seems to conceive of the entire process as comparatively rapid and shows little understanding of the gradual growth of language or of the survival of the first 'natural' stage even after the second has been reached. Secondly, he seems to imagine that each nation evolved its language independently. Both these peculiarities are in fact due to his conception of our world as a comparatively shortlived thing: just as to him it was comparatively small in size, so was the length of its existence brief: there had been no time for the slow development of ages.

In the Epicurean tradition, the polemical desire to maintain the origin of language as 'natural' seems to have obscured the recollection of Epicurus' second stage, in which words were invented deliberately. Thus Diogenes of Oenoanda[1] in his famous inscription expressly denies deliberate invention, and in Lucretius'[2] long and vivid description of the first stage, which he admirably illustrates by the efforts of children and animals to make themselves understood, the second stage is represented by a single verbal hint.[3] The master was here greater than his pupils and the penetration and subtleness of the theory forms an admirable example of his care in the outlying parts of his system, where fundamental ideas were not immediately concerned.

---

[1] *fr.* x, col. iii (William) μήτε τῶν φιλοσόφων πιστεύωμεν τοῖς λέγουσι κατὰ θέσιν καὶ διδαχὴν ἐπιτεθῆναι τὰ ὀνόματα τοῖς πράγ[μα]σιν.

[2] v. 1028–90.

[3]   at varios linguae sonitus natura subegit
       mittere et *utilitas expressit nomina rerum.* 1028, 9.

The subjects of this section have lain perhaps off the beaten track of Atomism and Epicureanism, which are as a rule concerned rather with the infinitely small than the infinitely great. But it is important to realize the capacity of the School for wide and far-reaching speculation as well as for minute and subtle reasoning. The cosmology of Epicurus, though weakened perhaps by the logical insistence on the principles of the Canonice, was the stronger and more vigorous for being based on an atomic foundation.

VIII

THE SOUL, SENSATION, THOUGHT, AND WILL

IT has several times been necessary, and especially in treating of the Canonice,[1] to anticipate Epicurus' theory of the soul of man and its action; an attempt must now be made to examine it in fuller detail. It is an interesting department of his system not merely because his conclusion that the soul perishes at the dissolution of the body was of such vast importance for his ethical theory, but also because in the purely materialistic account which he gives of its nature he was pushing his fundamental assumptions to their utmost limit and from time to time seems almost conscious of failure—certainly of difficulty. This is no doubt also in a great measure the reason why this portion of the Epicurean theory has seemed so obscure to modern commentators and given rise in certain parts of it to such a strange divergence of opinion: it is almost impossible for us to approach the whole question in a sufficiently materialistic mood, and we are inclined to apply our own psychological notions to the explanation of difficulties without bearing in mind throughout the consistently material basis on which Epicurus is working: to do so is always to court failure. It is true that Epicurus had probably not thought out—certainly he has not recorded in extant documents—a complete psychology of sensation and thought, but all that he has left us is on strictly and consistently materialist lines which we must never desert in our attempts to understand him.

For Greek thinkers in general the conception of the soul (ψυχή) was wide and comprehensive, and included on the one hand an irrational element (ἄλογον), the spirit or 'vital principle', as it might be called, which gave life to the body and was the seat of the passive and irrational feelings which are classed together as sensation (αἴσθησις), and on the other

[1] Chap. II.

a rational part (λόγον ἔχον), the mind, which was the seat of the active movements of thought and will. Most philosophers made a distinction between these two parts of the soul and treated of them, if not separately, at least as separable in thought. Of such a distinction there is no trace in the Letter to Herodotus; there is little doubt that Epicurus himself made it, as his followers certainly did, but the lack of fuller explanation has given rise to considerable difficulties and has led to some highly improbable explanations. For the present however 'the soul' must be thought of in a wide general sense covering both these elements.

Epicurus, after a preliminary caution that in forming a theory everything must be referred to the test of our sensations and feelings, opens his account[1] of the soul with the startling but unmistakable statement 'the soul is a body' (σῶμα). This is to the 'plain man' perhaps the most paradoxical utterance in the whole letter, but the paradox is at once explained if the fundamental principles of the system are borne in mind. The whole universe and all that is in it consists solely of the two constituents, atoms and the void: all other existing things are a compound of the two. It is impossible to doubt the real existence of the soul, when we are constantly aware of its workings in ourselves and others, and therefore it must be, like all other existences, an atomic compound, in other words a body. So obvious does this conclusion seem to Epicurus himself that he makes little attempt at the moment to defend his position except by the usual appeal to experience. 'All this,' he says after adding a description of this 'body', which will be considered immediately, 'all this is made manifest by the activities of the soul and its feelings . . . and by what we lose at the moment of death.' This rather obscure contention is made clearer by Lucretius:[2] the soul can set the limbs in motion: this cannot be done without contact, and contact implies body. Again the soul suffers with the body: it must then have a bodily nature. Once more, whole limbs may be removed from the body and it will still live,[3] but if a few

[1] Ep. i, § 63.   [2] iii. 161–76.   [3] 119–29.

particles of breath and heat desert the body, it dies.[1]
Experience then, as interpreted on a materialistic basis,
demands the conclusion that the soul is corporeal. Epicurus
returns again to his main position[2] at the end of his section
on the soul, and with his eye on rival theories, he gives a
fuller and more satisfactory argument in favour of his own
view. The two notions of the soul which would be most
likely to come into competition with it were firstly, that of
ordinary belief, which found its expression in the philosophy
of Plato and Aristotle, that the soul was a non-material or
spiritual existence, and secondly that of certain members of
the school of Aristotle, and in particular[3] of the musical
theorist Aristoxenus, that the soul was a condition or 'harmony' of the whole body. It is against the first of these
theories that Epicurus' argument is primarily directed and
it is founded on the base-notions of his system. The only
incorporeal thing which has independent existence, that is,
is not a 'property' or 'accident' of some corporeal existence,
is the void: the soul then cannot be incorporeal, unless it is
void. But void can neither act or be acted upon, for such
interaction implies touch, which in its turn implies body.
Yet these two capacities for acting (in thought and will) and
being acted upon (in sensation) are just those which are
most closely associated with the soul. The soul then cannot
be void: it must be corporeal or material and popular belief
is mistaken. Here we are on familiar atomic ground: touch
is the pre-requisite of interaction and nothing can touch
except body: if Epicurus' theory of the soul is to be attacked,
it must be here, at the ultimate basis of materialism.

But the second notion, that the soul is a 'harmony' of the
body, would not be open to the same *a priori* objection, for
the soul would then be, not indeed an independent im-

---

[1] 'Heat' (*calor, vapor*) is of course to Lucretius, as to Epicurus, a corporeal
substance.   [2] § 67.

[3] It seems probable that the idea of the soul as a 'harmony' was originally
a medical, not a musical, notion, and Burnet (E. G. P.3, p. 295) is inclined
to connect it with the Pythagorean Philolaus. This does not of course affect
Lucretius' main contention, but makes his irony less effective.

material existence, but an 'accident' (σύμπτωμα)[1] of the body, an occurrence, not inseparable—for the body can exist without it—but occasional under certain conditions. With this theory Epicurus does not deal in the Letter, but that he assailed it elsewhere is clear from Lucretius'[2] explicit attack on it. He argues that it cannot be true either of the mind (*animus*) or of the spirit (*anima*): not of the mind, because it often feels pleasure, even when the body is in pain and vice versa, and moreover it is active, when the body is at rest in sleep; nor again of the spirit, for it often remains intact when whole limbs of the body are removed, and on the other hand, if a few particles of heat and air are lost, the body loses its life. So far then from being an 'accident' of the body, the soul, though conjoined with body, is seen to be independent in action: sensation and consciousness are 'accidents' of the soul, but it is not itself an 'accident' of the body: 'let these Greek musicians confine their theories of harmony to their own subjects'. The soul then is a wholly corporeal and concrete being. This relentlessly material conception may be more profitably examined when the deductions which follow from it have been reviewed. At this point it is more important to notice its perfect consistency with the main ideas of the system. Here, if ever, the apostle of common sense found popular opinion against him: but with a courage, which was almost desperate, he was ready to fly in the teeth of prejudice and in maintaining his materialism at all costs, to forge another weapon against the terrors of superstition.

The soul being thus, like any other body, an atomic compound, it is possible to inquire into its composition and analyse its constituents, and this Epicurus proceeds to do. Democritus[3] had been content to say that the soul-atoms were 'fiery' (πυρώδεῖς), for the reason that the atoms composing fire were spherical and therefore most mobile. Epicurus preserves this idea, but it is not by itself sufficiently subtle for him. Rather the soul is 'a body of fine particles . . . most resembling breath with a certain admixture of heat and in

---

[1] See Chap. IV.   [2] iii. 98–135.   [3] See Part I, Chap. III, § 7.

some parts like to one of these and in some to the other'.
Heat is thus retained as a constituent element, but to it is
now added the element of breath or wind (πνεῦμα). The reason
for this addition is not far to seek: it is once again due to
empirical observation. 'This is made manifest ... by what we
lose at the moment of death.'[1] The dead body appears to contain all that it had in life except breath and heat: 'the seeds of
wind and burning heat', says Lucretius,[2] 'are the cause that
life lingers in the limbs: there is then heat and a life-giving
wind in the very body, which abandons our dying frame'.
The assumption of Democritus was made on *a priori* grounds
in order to assign to the soul the kind of atoms which would
be most likely to account for its quick movements: his conjecture is confirmed and amplified by Epicurus' observation.

Breath and heat then, or rather, as Epicurus states it,
with a scrupulous accuracy not imitated by his follower,
'particles resembling those of breath and heat', are the first
constituents of the soul; here it may be noticed that heat
is an addition to the 'breath' of Democritus—an addition
due to observation—and that the scrupulous description of
the particles suggests already a consciousness that the soul
is something finer than the bodies we know in experience.
Besides these two other elements are mentioned, which
require consideration. In the first place Lucretius, who in
the earlier passages quoted above contents himself with the
mention of particles of heat and wind and may be following
the Letter or a corresponding source,[3] yet when he comes
later to a fuller account of the structure of the soul,[4] adds to
these two elements a third constituent 'air', giving the
rather cryptic explanation, 'nor indeed is there any heat,
that has not air too mixed with it'. Two questions suggest
themselves: is this a spontaneous addition to Epicurus'
theory made by Lucretius on his own authority and, whether
this is so or not, what is the significance of the addition?
The first question is the more easily answered. It is highly
improbable that Lucretius, who in all parts of the poem is so

---

[1] § 63.   [2] iii. 128–9: cf. 214–15, and 232–3.
[3] See Brieger, *Epikurs Lehre von der Seele*, p. 10.   [4] 231–6.

scrupulous in following his master's lead in every detail, has here gratuitously amplified him, and indeed there is other evidence that the element of 'air' was included by Epicurus himself. Aetius[1] states that Epicurus held the soul to be a compound of four constituents, an element like fire, one like air, one like breath or wind (πνευματικοῦ), and a fourth nameless element (which will have to be considered immediately), and his testimony is confirmed by Plutarch.[2] It is therefore safe to assume that Lucretius was here following a fuller Epicurean source than the Letter (probably, as usual, the Greater Epitome), and that Epicurus himself, writing to a disciple already initiated in the system, gives merely a rough summary: possibly, the mention of the element of 'air' has accidentally dropped out in our text of the Letter.

The second question is more important and requires closer consideration: how does the element of 'air' differ from that of 'wind' and what is the significance of its presence as an element in the soul? Giussani[3] has offered a most ingenious answer. He reminds us that to Epicurus 'heat', 'wind', and 'air' are all substances: 'heat', or 'vapour', as Lucretius[4] often calls it, is composed of specific heat-forming particles,[5] 'wind'[6] of particles which similarly produce cold, and 'air' or 'atmosphere', as we might call it, of particles of various kinds, which are squeezed out from the earth and sea[7] or enter from the outer sky and in combination form a substance of middle or tepid temperature.[8] 'Wind' is thus distinct in substance from 'air' and is composed of colder particles, just as 'vapour' is of particles warmer than 'air'. The three elements in the soul then represent, as Giussani thinks, three distinct temperatures, 'air', the normal temperature of the atmosphere, 'heat' a temperature above normal, and 'wind' below normal. The soul has thus, according to

---

[1] iv. 3. 11; U. 315.

[2] adv. Colot. 20, 1118; U. 314 ἔκ τινος θερμοῦ καὶ πνευματικοῦ καὶ ἀερώδους.

[3] Stud. Lucr. pp. 184–6.   [4] e.g. iii. 233.   [5] Lucr. ii. 456 ff.

[6] Lucr. vi. 319 vis frigida venti.   [7] Lucr. v. 273 ff.

[8] For the general idea, cf. Lucr. ii. 517 'calor ac frigus mediique tepores'.

the prominence of one or other element,[1] the capacity for change of temperature. There is nothing in this explanation which is inconsistent with Epicurean notions and it is to some extent borne out by Lucretius'[2] subsequent demonstration of the effect on character of the predominance of one or other of the elements in the soul, 'heat' causing a tendency to anger, 'wind' to fear, while 'air', if it prevails, produces a generally equable temperament. But it is doubtful whether the idea of temperature was the primary notion in Epicurus' mind and the consideration of the historical development of the theory from the Atomists points rather to the simpler explanation suggested by Aetius,[3] that of the three elements 'wind' is the cause of motion,[4] 'air' of rest, and 'heat' of the perceptible warmth of the body. It is more likely that Epicurus in this way took the traditional notion of the Atomists and amplified it to account for other elements which experience led him to think were present in the soul, than that he was led to his conclusion by a psychological analysis of character. The theory once formed, however, there is no doubt that the three elements were used by Epicureans, as by Lucretius, to explain differences of character and moods of feeling both in human beings and in animals.

But for all his materialism Epicurus is not satisfied with an analysis of the soul into elements 'like that of' recognizable concrete things, even things as fine in nature as fire, wind, and air. To account for sensation and thought and will there must be something else in its composition more subtle still, and indeed as near as possible to the borders of the immaterial. 'There is also', he says, 'the part which is many degrees more advanced than these in fineness of com-

---

[1] Cf. Lucr. iii. 282-4

> consimili ratione necessest ventus et aer
> et calor inter se vigeant commixta per artus
> atque aliis aliud subsit magis emineatque.

[2] iii. 288-313.   [3] iv. 3. 11; U. 315.

[4] We may notice too that Epicurus himself (§ 63) in adducing the psychical phenomena which prove the truth of his theory includes 'the mobility (αἱ εὐκινησίαι) of the soul'—probably with similar reference to the presence of the element of 'wind'.

position, and for this reason is more capable of feeling in harmony with the rest of the structure as well.'[1] Much turns upon the understanding of this 'fourth nature'[2] in the soul and it will be well to begin by collecting such additional evidence as can be gathered. Plutarch[3] gives his testimony: 'that with which the soul judges and remembers and loves and hates and generally speaking the practical and rational intelligence arises, as Epicurus says, out of a nameless element (ἔκ τινος ἀκατονομάστου ποιότητος)', and Aetius[4] adds 'the nameless element produces sensation in us: for sensation does not lie in any of the named elements'. Lucretius[5] has two considerable passages of description of the 'fourth nature', the main points of which may be resumed: it is entirely nameless: it is subtler and more mobile than anything else in the world, and composed of smaller and smoother particles: it starts all the movements of sensation in the limbs: if severe pain penetrates to it, the result is likely to be fatal to the whole body. And again in the second passage he states that all the four elements combine to form a single nature, but that the 'fourth nature' starts the movements of sensation and passes them on to the other elements: that it lies deep hidden and is farther from the surface than anything in our bodies, and is moreover to the rest of the soul as the soul itself is to the body: it is indeed the soul of the soul and is supreme (dominatur) in the whole body.

These accounts sound at first mysterious and rather far removed from the normal terminology of materialism. Indeed there can be little doubt that, as Giussani[6] has pointed out, the idea of the 'fourth nature' is derived from Aristotle's 'fifth element' in the soul (πέμπτη οὐσία, ἐνδέλεχεια), which was

---

[1] § 63. I retain the manuscript text ἔστι δὲ τὸ μέρος ... συμπαθὲς δὲ τούτῳ μᾶλλον καὶ τῷ λοιπῷ ἀθροίσματι as against Usener's corrections and interpret it as suggested by Giussani: see my text and notes.

[2] 'quarta natura', Lucr. iii. 241, &c.: to him it is a fourth element owing to the inclusion of 'air', but in Epicurus' own account it is of course the third.

[3] adv. Colot. 20; U. 314.

[4] iv. 3. 11; U. 315.   [5] iii. 241–57, and again 262–81.

[6] Stud. Lucr., p. 187: see especially Cic. Tusc. Disp. i. 10. 22, where, speaking of Aristotle, he says quintum genus adhibet vacans nomine.

of course wholly spiritual and non-material. One is tempted to suppose that these extravagant phrases, the 'nameless' element, the 'soul of the soul', are but a thin disguise for the abandonment of the materialist position and conceal the confession that it is impossible to account for sensation and thought except by the admission of some force which is not material. It is indeed abundantly clear that Epicurus is pushing his materialism to the utmost limit, as he did at the other crucial point in his system, the 'swerve' of the atoms. But here, as there, a closer examination reveals that the limit is not passed and that each of these extravagant expressions has a very clear and definite material sense. The 'fourth nature' is to be the subtlest existence in creation: it must therefore be composed of very small and very smooth particles: for largeness of size means coarseness of structure and roughness means a possibility of cohesion, which again makes for a coarser structure than one in which all the atoms are perfectly free. It is for this reason that the 'fourth nature' is 'nameless' or rather 'unpredicable' (ἀκατονόμαστον), so absolutely unique, that is, that it is impossible to predicate of it any quality: for to do so would be to imply its likeness to something else, as in the case of the other elements of the soul, which are coarse enough to be said to be 'like' familiar concrete existences. The fourth element[1] is present in all parts of the soul with the other three elements, but whereas any one of the other elements[2] may come to the surface or retire beneath the others, the 'fourth nature' is always hidden deep beneath them: the other three form, as it were, a case to contain it. It is in this sense primarily that it is the 'soul of the soul'; as the soul is contained in the body, so the 'fourth nature' is contained in the other three. But much more is it so, because it communicates to the other three

---

[1] My account of the *quarta natura* and its functions agrees throughout with that of Giussani: there is however a prevailing opinion among German critics that the *quarta natura* is confined to the mind (*animus*). This very important divergence involves considerable differences in the understanding of the process of sensation and I have thought it best to deal with the whole question in Appendix V.

[2] Lucr. iii. 282–7.

elements the capacity of sensation, just as the soul as a whole does to the body. For the 'fourth nature' alone has in itself the power of sensation and is the cause of it first in the other elements and then through them in the body. By what steps this comes to be will be considered more conveniently when the process of sensation is examined: at the present moment the previous question must be put, how does the 'fourth nature' itself possess or acquire the power of sensation? Here, if anywhere, a difficulty will be found in the materialist account. The 'fourth nature' is, as has been seen, an aggregate of exceedingly fine and smooth atoms: the individual atoms have not of course themselves sensation, either apart or when combined in the aggregate, but the compound which they form has sensation. How can this come to pass? It has already been observed[1] that Epicurus believed that under certain circumstances the insensible could produce sensation:[2] worms are produced, as he thought, out of the dead body, inanimate food could be transformed into animate flesh: all depended on the kind of atoms present, their positions and arrangement. So here the insensible smooth atoms, combining in particular ways, may produce sensation in the bulk: the creation of sensation from the insensible was to him no miracle. But a nearer parallel to his idea of sensation in the 'quarta natura' may be found in his account of the genesis of colour in things.[3] Atoms themselves colourless may by the appropriate position, arrangement, and movements create a body which has colour: the organism (*concilium*) acquires a new quality, not possessed by any of the individuals which compose it. This analogy gives two important clues to the understanding of the creation of sensation in the 'fourth nature': in the first place there is the idea of the *concilium*: sensation is an 'accident' which supervenes on the *concilium* of the insensible atoms of the 'fourth nature', just as colour does on the *concilium* of the colourless atoms. And secondly there is the all-important idea of movement. Again and again Lucretius insists that sensation is

---

[1] Chap. VII, p. 377. [2] Lucr. ii. 865 ff.
[3] See Chap. VI, p. 356. Lucr. ii. 730 ff.

produced when the soul-atoms are forced into the 'appro-priate movements': the body enclosing the soul constrains it into the movements which create sense;[1] it is the 'fourth nature'[2] which disseminates the 'sense-bearing' movements through the other elements of soul and so through the body. And indeed it is just this appropriate movement in a *con-cilium* of the right kind of atoms in the right positions and arrangements which for Epicurus *is* sensation. This may not to a critic who approaches the theory from the supra-material point of view seem a satisfactory answer: the move-ment whether of Epicurean atoms or of the modern scien-tists' 'brain-matter' is not for him itself sensation, although it is its invariable accompaniment. But it is the only answer which a purely materialist thinker can give: the modern materialist will state in much the same terms as Epicurus that sensation is a movement, which is 'superinduced' as an 'accident' in certain forms of corporeal formation. At least the theory is consistent with itself and with the materialism of the rest of the Epicurean system.

Certain other statements with regard to the 'fourth nature' can now be explained. It is through the subtlety of its composition 'more capable of feeling in harmony with the rest of the structure as well',[3] because owing to its intense mobility it can, as it were, both adapt its movements to those around it and communicate its own movements to its neigh-bours; whereas the particles of the other three coarser ele-ments might remain unmoved. Secondly,[4] if a severe pain (*acre malum*) were to penetrate to the 'fourth nature' hidden not only below the atoms of body, but also beneath the other elements of soul, it would mean the destruction of life, because it would cause the disruption of that which is the very seat of life and the source of every vital sensation, emotion, and thought.[5] Finally, to go back to Epicurus'[6]

---

[1] iii. 570, 574: cf. 335.   [2] 245, 271–2.
[3] Ep. i, § 63.   [4] Lucr. iii. 252–7.
[5] This passage is of considerable importance in the discussion of Brieger's theory of the 'fourth nature' and I think Giussani has not fully understood its meaning: see Appendix V.   [6] Ep. i, § 63.

proof from experience that the nature of the soul is as he has described it, it is now clear that it is 'the powers of the soul and its feelings and its readiness of movement [1] and its processes of thought' which prove the existence of the 'fourth nature' as the seat of conscious life, while 'what we lose at the moment of death' is the other elements of 'wind', 'heat', and 'air'.

In order to keep the material notion firmly before our eyes, it will be well at this point to attempt to visualize more clearly Epicurus' conception of the soul: [2] in this way too a better notion can be formed of its relation to the body. The soul is composed of the four elements: of what character will its component atoms be? They are 'very minute',[3] that is to say, they consist of very few 'least parts', and will therefore only combine into nuclei which in their turn are very small and thus very mobile. A scholium [4] on the Letter to Herodotus adds that Epicurus said elsewhere that the component atoms are 'very smooth and very round, far surpassing the atoms which compose fire'. Lucretius confirms these additions, stating that the soul-atoms in general are 'very round' [5] and that those of the 'fourth nature'[6] are very smooth. Of the smoothness of all the component atoms there can be no doubt, but that they are all round may be regarded as a rough generalization. For since the element of 'air' [7] was composed of an effluence from all manner of things in earth and sea, it would naturally consist of atoms of many shapes, but all of them such as were unable to join in the more stable structures of solid and liquid bodies, that is to say,

---

[1] The 'readiness of movement' may also be in part referred to the element of wind: see above, p. 390.

[2] Brieger has some very suggestive remarks at this point: op. cit., pp. 10, 11.

[3] Lucr. iii. 179, 187.

[4] § 67 ἐξ ἀτόμων αὐτὴν συγκεῖσθαι λειοτάτων καὶ στρογγυλωτάτων, πολλῷ τινι διαφερουσῶν τῶν τοῦ πυρός.

[5] iii. 186.   [6] iii. 244.

[7] v. 273. Brieger is, I think, mistaken (p. 10) in stating that the atoms of air were all very small and round, nor do the passages which he adduces from Lucretius seem to prove more than that they were mobile, which implies the presence of round atoms, but does not preclude a mixture of others.

smooth atoms without 'hooks'. Of the shape of the atoms of wind there is no information, but it may be supposed that they resembled those of air: those of heat were, according to the regular tradition of the Atomists, round.[1] The soul then is an aggregation of atoms, all small and smooth, the vast majority also round, that is to say, spherical. It is obvious that there is no possibility in them of close coherence: they cannot unite in the fibrous structure which forms the body of a solid: in other words, they can only form a 'mixture' and not a 'texture'.[2] Now it is the characteristic of a 'mixture', of which liquids are the main example in nature, that they cannot hold together of themselves, but only when contained in some other structure, which is itself solid. Just then as a vase holds together water[3] and prevents it straying and breaking up into small drops, so the body holds together the soul, which without its protection would break up and dissolve: the body is to the soul, in the first place, a protecting and enclosing vessel.[4]

This connexion of soul and body must be more clearly realized. The soul, says Epicurus,[5] is 'distributed throughout the whole structure (of the body)', not, as Democritus[6] had crudely conceived it 'alternately', first an atom of soul and then an atom of body and so on, but in far finer and rarer particles than those of body, preserving intervals between them 'as great as are the smallest bodies which, when cast upon us, can first start the motions of sensation in the body'. That is to say, as Lucretius explains,[7] that some things

---

[1] Brieger (l.c.) on the authority of Lucr. ii. 456–63, argues that the heat-atoms were 'pointed but not hooked', but a careful reading of the passage shows that he is speaking not of mere heat, but of pungent things like flame, smoke, and mist (*nebulas*, perhaps 'steam'): these even if they are not made entirely of smooth and round particles, yet are not 'hampered by particles closely linked', i.e. the heat in them is due to round particles, their pungency to others which even so are smooth.

[2] The technical terms are Brieger's: see Chap. VI, p. 340.

[3] Lucretius' frequent comparison (iii. 434 ff., 440, 555) is thus more than a metaphor.

[4] τὸ στέγαζον, § 65: cf. § 64 εἰ μὴ ὑπὸ τοῦ λοιποῦ ἀθροίσματος ἐστεγάζετό πως.

[5] § 63, init.   [6] Lucr. iii. 370–95.   [7] 381 ff.

which fall upon us, such as spider's web, down, and very small animals, do not arouse any sensation: such things cannot have been in contact with any soul-atoms at all: or in other words, the intervals between the soul-atoms must be greater than objects not felt, and their distance may be measured by the size of the smallest things which we do actually feel. The picture may be completed by thinking also of the nature of the body, as Epicurus conceived it. Our body is a structure of different parts of varying degrees of atomic compactness: in some parts, such as the bones, the component atoms are closely interlaced, hooking into one another and grasping each other with many different kinds of entanglement, so that the structure is firm and solid; in others, such as the flesh, sinews, and nerves, the formation is much looser and the component atoms smoother. But in all parts, hard and soft, compact and loose alike, there are intervals of space, pores [1] in between portions of even the most closely hooked atoms and in all parts the atoms are in everlasting motion at atomic speed. [2] In these pores between the atoms of body are enclosed the fine and subtle atoms of soul, penetrating into every part, yet constantly shifting with their own atomic motion [3] and the changes of the surrounding structure caused by the movement of the body atoms. [4] The general idea may be illustrated by the parallel of a rising tide penetrating alike into the hollows of rocky caverns, into the interspaces of the shingle on the beach and the tiny crevices between the grains of sand upon the shore, only the rocks, stones, and sand must be conceived of as

---

[1] 'caulae corporis', Lucr. iii. 255, 702.

[2] For the grounds of this description see the discussion of compound bodies in Chap. VI.

[3] Lucr. iii. 262:

> inter enim cursant primordia principiorum
> motibus inter se.

[4] Brieger (op. cit., p. 9) rightly points out that Lucretius misconceives the relation of body and soul when he says, iii. 557, '*conexu* corpus adhaeret, and again, 691, 'ita *conexa* est per venas viscera nervos', for *conexus* implies the close interlacing of a 'texture', which the soul has neither in itself, nor in relation to the body.

themselves also in constant and changeful notion, varying at each instant the shape and position of their hollows, cracks, and crevices. If we cannot but feel dissatisfied at the materialism of Epicurus' idea, we must yet admire the ingenuity which has produced so subtle and fascinating a conception of the possible differences of corporeal structure and the variety of their relations to one another.

The insistence both of Epicurus himself and of Lucretius on the close relation of soul and body is now more intelligible, for their collocation, at any rate, is by now more fully grasped. The soul owes its own coherence, its very existence as an aggregate 'body', to its confinement within the pores of the body-atoms, and in its turn it penetrates the body even to its inmost recesses. Yet this connexion is not in itself enough to account for our experience, and Epicurus conceived the relation as something closer and more important than a mere juxtaposition even of this intricate nature. The enclosure of the soul in the body has all-important results: for as its atoms, confined in the narrow pores of the body-structure, are ever moving at incredible speed, they are forced by the very minuteness of their field of movement, into the 'appropriate motions' of sensation. This occurs primarily only to the 'fourth nature'; when an external body comes into contact with soul-atoms, the 'fourth nature' is moved and by its movement awakes into feeling and becomes 'sensible' (αἰσθητικόν); but it then communicates the 'sense-bearing' movements to the other elements in the soul and first to the fiery particles, for they are most subtle. These pass it on to the particles of 'wind', and those in their turn to the less easily moved particles of 'air'.[1] The whole soul is now in motion with the movement of sensation and jostling constantly against the surrounding particles of body stirs them too with the same movement until the body itself, thanks to the presence of soul, can feel. In the body too there is a fixed succession in the spread of sensation from the looser to the more compact structures:

[1] For this succession of sensation in the three other soul-elements see Lucr. iii. 246–7.

first 'the blood receives the shock, then all the flesh feels
the thrill: last of all it passes to the bones and marrow, be
it pleasure or the heat of opposite kind'.[1] Here then is a new
mutual relation between soul and body. From the protection
of the body the soul has acquired sensation: in return, as it
were, for this gift it communicates the capacity for sensation
to the body.

Epicurus explains this point at length in the first Letter,
as a matter of great importance:[2]

the soul possesses the chief cause of sensation: yet it could not have
acquired sensation, unless it were in some way enclosed by the rest of
the structure. And this in its turn, having afforded the soul this cause
of sensation, acquires itself too a share in this contingent capacity
(σύμπτωμα) from the soul. Yet it does not acquire all the capacities
which the soul possesses: and therefore, when the soul is released from
the body, the body no longer has sensation. For it never possessed this
power in itself, but used to afford opportunity for it to another existence,[3] brought into being at the same time with itself: and this
existence, owing to the power now consummated within itself as a
result of motion, used spontaneously to produce for itself the capacity
of sensation and then to communicate it to the body as well, in virtue
of its contact and correspondence of movement.

The passage is clearer and more emphatic than many in the
Letter and its importance is borne out by Lucretius'[4] insistence on the same ideas in a more poetical mood:

with first-beginnings so closely interlaced from their very birth are
they (sc. body and soul) begotten, endowed with a life shared in common, nor, as is clear to see, can the power of body or mind feel apart,
either for itself without the force of the other, but by the common
motions of the two on this side and on that is sensation kindled and
fanned throughout our flesh. . . . So from the beginning of existence
body and soul, in mutual union, learn the motions that give life, yea,
even when hidden in the mother's limbs and womb, so that separation
cannot come to pass without hurt and ruin.

The connexion of body and soul is thus vital: it is owing to
their close local relation that they are able to form a living

---

[1] Lucr. iii. 249–51. [2] § 64.
[3] For the text here see my notes ad loc. [4] iii. 331–47.

being. Neither can be itself without the other: the body
without the soul could not live or grow or move: the soul
without the protection of the body could not hold together
or make the movements requisite for that sensation, which is
the essential characteristic of the living being, the 'formation',[1] as Epicurus calls it, 'which has life'.

But in this partnership the sharers are by no means equal
in their contribution: the soul has by far the greater function
in the creation and sustinence of life, for in the 'fourth
nature' it possesses that which alone can initiate sensation:
whereas the body does but provide the requisite conditions
and receive, as it were, a reflected capacity for sensation,
when once it has come into existence. 'Therefore,' continues Epicurus,[2] 'so long as the soul remains in the body,
even though some other part of the body be lost, it will never
lose sensation: nay more, whatever portions of the soul may
perish too, when that which enclosed it is removed either
in whole or in part, if the soul continues to exist at all, it
will retain sensation. On the other hand, the rest of the
structure, though it continues to exist either as a whole or
in part, does not retain sensation, if it has once lost that
sum of atoms, however small it be, which together goes to
produce the nature of the soul.' This is a clear deduction
from the main position and is elaborated by Lucretius[3] with
copious illustrations from the loss of arms and legs in battle
and other cases where limbs and even a portion of the vital
spirit enclosed in them are removed, but life still persists.
A much more important conclusion follows: 'moreover, if
the whole structure is dissolved, the soul is dispersed and no
longer has the same powers nor performs its movements, so
that it does not possess sensation either. For it is impossible
to imagine it with sensation, if it is not in this organism and
cannot effect these movements, when what encloses and surrounds it is no longer the same as the surroundings in which
it now exists and performs these motions'.[4] The soul that is,
is dispersed when the body perishes and there can be no

---

[1] μόρφωμα μετ' ἐμψυχίας, Sext. Emp. *adv. Math.* vii. 267; U. 310.
[2] § 65.   [3] iii. 403–16: cf. 634–69.   [4] § 65, *ad fin.*

question of its survival after death, not so much because being like the body a material existence, it must come to an end, but because in no other circumstances could it find the requisite conditions for sensation. Even if it could find something else to hold it together and enclose it, it could not be so constrained as to be forced into the movements required to produce sensation or consciousness: there can be no life either for body or soul after death. This conclusion Lucretius reinforces with a series of twenty-eight arguments occupying the greater part of the Third Book[1] and drawn in the main from the general ideas of the structure of the soul and its relation to the body:[2] he then bursts out into that great paean on the mortality of the soul, which is from the poetical point of view the most justly famous portion of his poem. The certainty that the soul perishes with the body is indeed, together with the assurance that the gods are not concerned with the affairs of the world, the ultimate condition of Epicurean happiness and is so put forward in the second of the *Principal Doctrines*: 'Death is nothing to us; for that which is dissolved, is without sensation, and that which lacks sensation is nothing to us.' The moral import of the conclusion cannot here be examined, but it is well to emphasize at this point that the conclusion itself is once again the fearless deduction from main principles. If it is to be disputed, the attack must turn upon the fundamental materialism of Epicurus' conception of the soul: if sensation can be atomic movement and nothing more, it is impossible to refuse to accept the conclusion that the soul perishes.

Hitherto mere passive sensations have been considered resulting from contact with external objects, sensations which may be felt at and, as Epicurus strongly holds, *by* any portion of our bodies. It is time to pass to the more complex form of sensation, which is known as sense-perception, which takes place only through the medium of the sense-organs and gives us not mere passive feeling, but information concerning the external world. But before this can be examined, it is essential to return to the distinction between

[1] iii. 416–829. [2] iii. 830 ff.

'spirit' and 'mind' (*anima* and *animus*).[1] Oddly enough, though this distinction is so universal in Greek philosophers and was made by Democritus,[2] it is not explicitly stated in the Letter to Herodotus, which speaks throughout simply of 'the soul'. That the distinction was made by Epicurus there can be no doubt: it is implied in the passages[3] which speaks of the act of apprehension by the mind (ἐπιβολὴ τῆς διανοίας), and the scholiast[4] on the Letter says in so many words: 'part of the soul is irrational and is distributed through the rest of the body, but the rational part is in the breast, as is clear from the feelings of fear and joy'. This statement is confirmed by Aetius,[5] and is strongly emphasized by Lucretius,[6] who makes use of the distinction throughout the Third Book. It may be again that some words dropped out in the text of the Letter, it is less probable that Epicurus omitted to notice the distinction by inadvertence, and most probable that he left it out because, for a reason that will be seen, it was not of sufficient importance to be mentioned in a summary, which dealt only with very essential or difficult points in the theory. However this may be, the division between the irrational and rational parts of the soul may confidently be accepted as part of the true doctrine of Epicurus. What then does it come to? In spite of the view of certain German critics[7] that the 'fourth nature' was confined to the mind and was not present at all in the 'spirit' distributed through the body, the very explicit testimony of Lucretius, apart from many other considerations, makes it certain that such was not Epicurus' doctrine. In material composition there is no difference at all between spirit and mind; both are alike composed of the same four elements and each of them contains them all. The difference lies in the surrounding conditions of the two and a conse-

---

[1] The English words are not satisfactory, for the irrational element is hardly as much as 'spirit' and the rational includes more than we generally understand by 'mind': but they are perhaps the nearest equivalents.

[2] See Part I, Chap. III, § 6, p. 160. [3] §§ 38, 50, 51, 62.
[4] § 67. [5] iv. 4. 6, p. 390 D; U. 312.
[6] iii. 94–8, 117–18, 136–60. [7] See Appendix V.

quent divergence of powers and functions. The spirit is, as
has been shown, distributed throughout the whole body and
intermingled at all points with the body-atoms: it is the
cause of the passive sensations of contact, and it is also, as
will be seen immediately, the cause in the sense-organs of
the act of sense-perception. The mind on the other hand is
an aggregation of pure soul-atoms, unmixed with those of
body, in a far larger cluster than can gather at any other
point in the body. In consequence its movements are far
less impeded and it is therefore able to develop more subtle
motions and so a fuller power of sensation and a greater
degree of consciousness. Its functions are thus higher and
more complex: it takes its part in sense-perception, not in
the act of sensation, but in the subsequent process of cognition; it is the seat of emotion as distinct from feeling and it
alone has the powers of recollection, of generalization, of
thought, and of will. It is, therefore, as Lucretius[1] says,
'more the keeper of the fastnesses of life, more the monarch
of life than the power of the spirit. For without the mind
and understanding no part of the soul can hold out in the
frame for a tiny moment of time, but follows in its train
without demur, and scatters into air, and deserts the chill
frame in the frost of death. Yet one, whose mind and understanding have abode firm, abides in life. . . . In such a compact are spirit and mind ever bound together'. In other
words the spirit is, roughly speaking, the passive element,
the mind the active element in the soul: the one means life
and feeling, the other consciousness and will; the mind is,
in fact, the governing or ruling part (τὸ ἡγεμονικόν).[2] Though
most philosophers agreed in this distinction, they were
divided as to the place of the mind in the body, some locating
it in the brain, others in the breast. Epicurus decided for
the breast on the characteristic ground of experience: for
it is in the breast that we experience the feelings of fear
and joy.[3] The distinction then of mind from spirit is of

---

[1] iii. 396–416.
[2] Lucretius translates by 'consilium regimenque', iii. 95.
[3] Schol. on § 67: Lucr. iii. 140–2.

importance in the consideration of psychological functions, but not in dealing with physical structure. This is probably the cause of its omission in the Letter to Herodotus. With this preface it is possible to proceed to consider sense-perception: the powers and functions of the mind will become clearer in the process.[1]

In its essence sense-perception does not differ, according to Epicurus, from the passive sensation of touch: it is brought under the same inclusive term (αἴσθησις) and rests in all cases on the primary condition of contact between the object and the organ of sense. This idea is of course essentially inherent in a material system: without contact any kind of interaction, either active or passive, is impossible: 'for touch, yea touch,' says Lucretius in an unusual outburst of emphasis, 'by the holy powers of the gods, is the sense of the body'.[2] But when this general idea is applied to the several senses, it is attended with varying degrees of difficulty. In the case of taste the function of touch is clear enough:[3] as we bite our food, the juice is squeezed out into the mouth and so passes into the pores of tongue and palate and affects them either pleasantly or otherwise according to the atomic conformation of the thing eaten and sometimes also of the recipient's palate. Smell and hearing are more difficult to explain, for in their case there is no perceptible contact between the object and percipient. Epicurus, however, following in the steps of Democritus, solves the difficulty by the assumption of an effluence or emanation from things. In the sensation of smell the process is comparatively simple: 'certain particles[4] are carried off from the object of suitable size to stir this sense-organ, some of them in a manner disorderly and alien to it, others in a regular manner and akin in nature', this difference in the particles

---

[1] In the following sections it will be necessary to some extent to traverse the same ground as was considered in the chapter on the Canonice: but whereas there the emphasis was on principles, here it is rather on psychological processes.

[2] Lucr. ii. 434–5.

[3] Epicurus does not himself deal with taste, but Lucretius, iv. 615–72, treats of it explicitly and is no doubt, as usual, following closely a good Epicurean source.   [4] Ep. i, § 53.

causing the distinction between pleasant and unpleasant smells. Lucretius [1] in his elaboration adds certain interesting details: the effluence of smell comes from 'deep down in things', as can be seen from the fact that things smell more when broken open: consequently it is liable to fail in its struggle to issue, or to perish after it has won its way out, and in any case comes slowly from the object and cannot be carried very far. Moreover [2] it is composed of rather large elements, as is seen from its inability to penetrate through solid obstacles, such as walls, in the way that sound can. Finally he notices that different smells are better adapted to the perception of different animals, the smell of honey to bees, of beasts of the chase to dogs, &c. The case of hearing is rather more complicated. There is no difficulty here about emanation: 'particles of sound',[3] conceived of as entirely corporeal,[4] 'are emitted' by the living thing when it utters or by the inanimate object when it makes a noise, but how can we explain the fact that many persons [5] at once, situated in very different positions with regard to the object, can all hear equally well? This difficulty Epicurus overcomes by supposing that the current ($\dot{\rho}\epsilon\hat{v}\sigma\iota s$) [6] of sound emitted by the object 'is split up into particles ($\ddot{o}\gamma\kappa o\iota$) each like the whole, which at the same time preserve a correspondence of qualities ($\sigma\nu\mu\pi\acute{a}\theta\epsilon\iota\alpha\nu$) with one another and a unity of character ($\dot{\epsilon}\nu\acute{o}\tau\eta\tau\alpha$ $\dot{\iota}\delta\iota\acute{o}\tau\rho\sigma\pi\sigma\nu$) which stretches right back to the object which emitted the sound'. This of course was not the theory of Democritus,[7] which Epicurus [8] explicitly denounces: 'we must not suppose that the actual air is moulded into shape by the voice which is emitted or by other similar sounds—for it will be very far from being so acted upon'. As in other cases,[9] he rejects what he considers the over-subtlety of Democritus in favour of a more

[1] iv. 673–705.　　　　[2] 698 ff.
[3] ἔκθλιψις ὄγκων τινῶν Ep. ad Hdt., § 53.
[4] Lucretius argues for this at some length (iv. 526–48), adducing the physical effect of speaking on the throat of the speaker.
[5] Lucr. iv. 563–4.　　　　[6] § 52.
[7] See Part I, Chap. III, § 6, p. 171.　　　　[8] § 53.
[9] Especially that of sight, as will be seen immediately.

directly materialistic explanation, but it must be confessed that his own theory is a very crude solution of the difficulty, and supposes a very improbable and artificial contrivance on the part of nature. However by the theory of effluences Epicurus has established both in the case of smell and hearing the requisite contact, not now immediate, but secondary, between the object perceived and the percipient.

The problem of sight is much more intricate and difficult, and since sight is also of far more importance for our knowledge of the external world than any of the other senses, it is necessary to consider it in detail and to examine not only the preliminary means by which contact is established between object and sense-organ, but the subsequent act of sensation, with regard to which sight will act as a type of all the other senses. Epicurus[1] consents to mention, though only to condemn off-hand, two rival theories as to the means of contact, firstly that of Democritus,[2] which was also adopted in a subtler form by Aristotle,[3] that the object made an impression ($\dot{a}\pi o\tau \dot{v}\pi\omega\sigma\iota s$) of itself in the air, just as a seal does in wax, which then travelled to the eye and entered it, secondly that of Plato,[4] which in a cruder form may have been used by Empedocles,[5] that sight was due to the meeting of rays ($\dot{a}\kappa\tau\hat{\iota}\nu\epsilon s$) both from the object and from the eye. Of these two views Epicurus says no more than that the effect could not be produced nearly so well by either of them, as by the process which he himself describes, but the fact of his mentioning rival theories at all shows that he was considerably impressed by them. His own view he apparently considered, as usual, the only possible interpretation of experience, and he started, it seems,[6] from the observation of

---

[1] § 49.   [2] See Part I, Chap. III, § 6, p. 171.

[3] *de Sensu*, 2. 438 b 3, and 3. 439 a 21.

[4] *Timaeus*, 45 c, 46 a, 67 c.

[5] According to Plut. *Epit.* iv. 13, but there is some doubt whether he is not attributing a Platonic doctrine to Empedocles: see Beare, *Greek theories of Elementary Cognition*, p. 17.

[6] Alex. Aphrod. in Arist. *de Sensu*, B. 438 a; U. 319 τεκμήριον παρατίθεται τὸ ἀεὶ τῶν ὁρώντων ἐν τῇ κόρῃ εἶναι τὴν τοῦ ὁρωμένου ἔμφασιν καὶ εἴδωλον, ὃ δὴ καὶ τὸ ὁρᾶν εἶναι.

the image in the pupil of the eye: this was clearly the means by which sight was effected and the only question to be asked is how did it get there? Epicurus'[1] reply was simple and direct: that all objects were constantly giving off from their surface fine films[2] which were exact replicas of their shape and colour: that these passed through the intervening air and fell into the eye, where they awoke the sensation of sight. The general idea of this theory of 'idols' (εἴδωλα, simulacra) has already been discussed, but the detailed working out of the notion by Epicurus is so ingenious as to justify a full restatement.

In the first place the giving off of the films from the surface of the body must be considered: the idea is of course closely akin to that of the effluence of smell and the emission of sound-particles, but Lucretius[3] supports the possibility of such an occurrence with more homely examples from ordinary life; the giving off of smoke by wood, of heat by flames, the shedding of its slough by the snake and its skin by the grasshopper, &c.: such examples show that there is nothing repugnant to nature in the idea of the emission of films. But that Epicurus' notion was not a merely arbitrary assumption will be more clearly realized from a reconsideration of the structure of the compound body. However firm and compact such a body might be, its component atoms[4] were nevertheless always moving and the whole body alive with internal vibration (πάλσις): the atoms were always jostling one another and starting each other off in new directions, so that the whole body is only kept together because the atoms driven outwards meet others nearer the surface of the body and are driven back again. But on the surface itself there is nothing to drive back the atoms in the same way: there are, it is true, the atoms of the surrounding atmosphere (τὸ περιέχον),[5] but this is much rarer in texture than the loosest solid or liquid body, and offers much less resistance. Every object is in this way constantly losing individual atoms, and

---

[1] §§ 46–50.
[2] So Lucr. iv. 50 'quae quasi membranae vel cortex nominitandast'.
[3] iv. 53 ff.   [4] See Chap. V, pp. 330 ff.   [5] § 46.

in the same way complete films [1] may be loosed from its surface, and the films coming simultaneously from the various side surfaces of the object form the 'idol' which is an exact representation of the thing. It might be objected that in that case the object would be gradually lessened by the loss of successive films and so dwindle away. But Epicurus [2] has forestalled this objection by observing that the contrary process is also always at work: atoms from the surrounding air are constantly joining the compound body and filling up the gaps: 'the flow from the surface cannot be detected by any lessening in the size of the object because of the filling up of what is lost'. These films are being given off from the surface of every object in a constant succession 'as quick as thought'.[3] They far surpass perceptible things 'in the subtlety of their texture',[4] for however delicate the structure they leave, they are merely its surface atoms, 'skimmed', as it were, from the whole: further, though the 'idols' are combined from the films of different surfaces (e.g. front and sides), they are hollow inside,[5] and thus in every way incredibly light and fine. Further, when they leave the object they 'preserve the respective position and order, which they had before in the solid bodies'; they are, that is, a faithful reproduction of the surface of the body, simply because the atoms composing them were, in fact, themselves that surface. This 'position and order' they will retain 'for a long time, though it is occasionally confused', which accounts for the blurred appearance of a distant object: the 'idol' in such cases has been a little knocked out of shape and frayed round the edges in transit. Having left the body the

---

[1] Neither Epicurus nor any of his followers deals with the problem how a film could come off a body of three dimensions without a break at some point: possibly their answer would have been that we never see all the sides of a body at once, and the image is only that of the surfaces exposed to our view. But there are many such *minutiae* in which the theory was not satisfactorily worked out.

[2] § 48 ῥεῦσις . . . οὐκ ἐπίδηλος τῇ μειώσει διὰ τὴν ἀνταναπλήρωσιν.

[3] ἅμα νοήματι, § 48.

[4] § 46.

[5] τῶν κοιλωμάτων, ibid: see my notes ad loc.

'idols' travel with 'an unsurpassable speed of motion,[1] since they have a capacity for movement in any direction proportionate to the fact that 'nothing or at least very few things hinder (ἀντικόπτειν) their emission by collisions';[2] owing, that is, to the extreme fineness of their structure, they collide but rarely with other objects, and, what is more important, there is extremely little internal atomic vibration to delay them.[3] Lucretius, in a passage of unusual interest and insight,[4] has elaborated and supported this notion of the incredible speed of transit of the 'idols'. He attributes it not merely to the rarity of their texture,[5] which enables them easily to pass through opposing objects, but also to their original impulsions by a 'tiny cause';[6] the force which is impelling them from within the compound body is that of the movement of individual atoms, and as they themselves are in motion at 'absolute' speed, they can communicate to the light texture of the films a speed which is in its turn only just short of 'absolute'. The idea is penetrating and is in complete accordance with Epicurean kinetics.[7]

How then can these 'idols' cause the sensation of sight? The answer for Epicurus is simple enough. From the surface of every object the 'idols' are flying off in every direction in everlasting quick succession, and when the eye is turned towards an object, a succession of 'idols' beats upon it. The process is then exactly similar to that of the passive sensation: the soul-atoms are touched, the 'fourth nature' is set in 'sense-bearing' motion, it communicates with the three other soul-elements, and they in their turn with the body-atoms and then the eyes see: the sole difference here is that by a special peculiarity of their structure, sensation in the sense-organs is not, as it is in the rest of the body, a mere passive feeling of contact, but a 'perception'; the eyes do not merely feel, but see. Two points of importance should be noted.

---

[1] § 47 τάχη ἀνυπέρβλητα ἔχει.
[2] The text here is uncertain: see critical and explanatory notes on the passage.
[3] See Chap. V, p. 333.   [4] iv. 183–98.   [5] 196–8.
[6] 193–5.   [7] See Chap. V, p. 333.

The first is hinted at by Epicurus[1] and stated explicitly by Lucretius:[2] no single 'idol' can, owing to the extreme slightness of its structure, awake sensation and be perceived by the eyes, but only the incredibly quick succession of images crowding one upon the other: yet, although the 'image'[3] thus seen (φαντασία) is in reality 'cinematographic', if we may use a modern term, so quick is the succession that the eye is not conscious of any break, but perceives only a single object: the succession of 'idols' 'reproduces the image of a single continuous thing and preserves the corresponding sequence of qualities and movements from the original object'.[4] This is again a subtle observation and it becomes of great importance for the understanding of the 'mental apprehension' of 'idols'. Secondly, the process of sensation may be not merely passive but active: the 'idols' may not merely impinge upon the eye and automatically start the movement of sensation, but the eye may, as it were, make an effort to grasp or apprehend the image (ἐπιβολή). This is always the case when we 'look' (θεωρεῖν) as opposed to mere 'seeing' (ὁρᾶν). At any moment there are crowding round the eye 'idols' from any number of objects lying in the direction to which the eye is turned, and in order to apprehend the image produced by any one series of them, the eye must, as it were, definitely attend to it. It makes a kind of choice among the images presented to it and fixes its attention upon it. One case of such attention is particularly noteworthy: it sometimes happens, especially in the case of distant objects, that the 'idols' reach the eye in a blurred or indistinct form: we can be certain that the image (φαντασία) seen by the eye corresponds to the 'idols', but we have not sufficiently certain information as to the nature of the object from which the 'idols' proceeded. In that case the eye must look again, and it is only when it has grasped by an act of attention the 'clear view' (ἐνάργημα) of the object that we

[1] § 50 τοῦ ἑνὸς καὶ συνεχοῦς τὴν φαντασίαν ἀποδιδόντων.
[2] iv. 89 'nec singillatim possunt secreta videri'.
[3] I think it is clear from Epicurus' use that φαντασία is the technical term for the 'image' resulting from a succession of individual 'idols'. [4] § 50.

can be certain of the complete correspondence of object, 'idols', and image. This is the process of 'confirmation' (ἐπιμαρτύρησις) which plays so large a part in the Canonice;[1] the 'clear vision' of the 'near view' is obtained by an act of attention or apprehension on the part of the sense-organs (ἐπιβολὴ τῶν αἰσθητηρίων). To this act Epicurus alludes several times in the Letter in conjunction with the parallel act on the part of the mind,[2] and Lucretius[3] has in an interesting passage underlined his master's meaning and brought it into relief. Finally, it should be noticed that the theory raises once again the fundamental difficulty of materialism, but this time in an even more acute form; the mere movement of atoms is now not only a passive sensation of contact or feeling, but an active perception of external things.

That the theory of the 'idols' is open to a large number of obvious objections and involves many mechanical difficulties, which the opponents of the atomic system were quick to raise, may be seen from the criticism of Theophrastus on Democritus,[4] which has already been noticed. Epicurus has escaped several of them by substituting for Democritus' 'air-impressions' the theory of 'idols' with a texture so fine that they could collide and pass through one another without causing any effective damage. There is, however, one mechanical difficulty which must be taken into consideration. The 'idol', as it left the concrete object, would be of course of the same size as the object itself: how then, if the object were a large one, could it enter the tiny pupil of the eye, or if it could not, how did it produce the image of the whole thing and not merely of such a small part as would come into contact with the pupil? Epicurus may have intended to deal with this difficulty when he stated that the 'idol' enters the eye 'in the appropriate size',[5] but he never

---

[1] See Chap. II, pp. 254-7.   [2] §§ 38, 50, 51 : see Appendix III.
[3] iv. 802 ff.

[4] de Sensu, §§ 52, 53; D. (Democritus) 135 : see Part I, Chap. III, § 6, p. 166.

[5] § 49 κατὰ τὸ ἐναρμόττον μέγεθος. I believe, however, that this means merely that the 'idols' gross enough to be seen stay in the eye, others pass on inward to the mind : see notes, ad loc.

speaks of it explicitly, nor does Lucretius. So far as I know, Giussani[1] is the only critic who has attempted to tackle this difficult question. He believes that an actual diminution in the size of the 'idols' in transit is wholly inconsistent with Epicurean theory, and that Epicurus must mean that the 'idols' are so 'adapted' to the eye, as to be able to give an image of the whole object while yet indicating its real size. Comparing a fragment in the Herculanean rolls,[2] where it is said that the 'idols' in transit preserve 'extension (τάσιν)[3] and unity and fineness of structure and smallness of parts by means of concentration (διὰ τῶν συνιζήσεων)', he has invented the subtle theory that, as the eye confronts a large object, 'idols' flow towards it from all parts of the opposite surface preserving their original size: a fragment of each of these will strike the eye and the eye piecing together these fragments will grasp an image of the whole, yet of the right size. But, even granting that the eye has, as Giussani suggests, a power of determining the 'provenance' of each of these fragments, the result would surely be a hopelessly confused vision, from which the eye could not obtain an orderly image of the whole. A simpler solution would be that the image in transit from the object to the eye is actually reduced in size, so that it can enter the eye as a whole: this is not merely perfectly consistent with Epicurean theory generally, but in fact supported by such information as is extant. The 'idols' in passing through the air, slight as they are, would yet be beaten upon on all sides by a large number of atoms and loose compound bodies. This constant succession of blows the solid compound can resist because of its internal structure:[4] but the effect upon the 'hollow' 'idol'[5] would surely be to cause it to collapse,[6] or be squashed inwards and so gradually diminished in size. The longer the transit, the

[1] vol. iii. Excursus I to Book IV, p. 285, and especially note (1).
[2] From Book II of the περὶ φύσεως.
[3] This should possibly be τάξιν or βάσιν: cf. Ep. i., § 46.
[4] See Chap. VI, p. 352.   [5] § 46.
[6] This is the exact meaning of συνίζησις: it is so used of the collapse of the earth ἐς τὰ κοῖλα, Arist. de Mundo, 4. 395, and of the collapse of houses, Plut. Crass. 2.

further would the process of diminution be carried: hence it results that we do actually 'see' a distant tower the same size as a small stone close at hand: the rate of diminution would be uniform, and the amount proportionate to the distance. Giussani objects that in that case the eye can have no perception of the real size of objects. It surely has not, either on Epicurus' theory or any modern theory of vision: what it does perceive is the diminished image caused by the succession of diminished 'idols' together with a sense of distance derived, as Lucretius[1] has most carefully explained, from the length of the current of air which enters the eye before the arrival of the 'idols'. It is the function of the mind to combine these two pieces of information and to infer from them the original size of the object, a process in which it is very frequently liable to error, which must be corrected by subsequent 'confirmation' (ἐπιμαρτύρησις). This seems at least a consistent theory, and will explain incidentally several of the difficulties connected with the vision of the distant object, but it must be admitted that the evidence for it is slight. It is strange that there should be no information on so cardinal a point.

But the discussion of such mechanical difficulties[2] is not perhaps profitable, as Epicurus' theory of vision could not in any case be now supported as even a plausible explanation. It is more worthy of observation that he has once again secured indirect contact between the object and the eye and that the general idea, though crude, is not after all so very far removed from the 'sight-wave' theory of modern science: the same difficulty of contact has to be surmounted by a more subtle and scientific, but not wholly dissimilar, hypothesis. It is necessary now to proceed to the consideration of the function of the mind (νοῦς) in sense-perception and thought.

---

[1] iv. 244–55.

[2] Giussani, for instance (l.c., p. 283), has raised the question how the 'idols', being of almost 'atomic' texture, can preserve the colour of the original object, which is due to the internal movement of atoms in a *concilium*, and asks again (285 n. fin.), how it is that with two eyes we do not see two images. As he says himself *satis hariolati sumus*.

In the first place there is a series of instances in which the mind plays, as it were, the part of a sense-organ, and itself directly apprehends 'idols',[1] which are imperceptible to the normal sense-organs. The eye can never perceive single 'idols', but only the image (φαντασία) created by a succession of 'idols': but it may be sometimes that the single 'idol'[2] will penetrate through the pores of the body to the mind itself and there be perceived by an act of 'apprehension'. This occurs in several different instances. The first is that of the curious class of 'idols' known as 'compounds' (συστάσεις),[3] which, since 'it is not necessary for their substance to be filled in deep inside', since, that is, the 'idol' is a mere skin without any solid substance, may easily be formed in the air either by a chance union of atoms[4] or by a casual conjunction of 'idols' thrown off by two or more real objects.[5] In the latter case we may receive the mental impression of strange compound animals like Centaurs, and Scylla and the Chimaera, parts of the 'idols' of existing things being accidentally united, in the former the image presented to the mind may be merely grotesque and assume any fantastic form. But in each instance[6] the single 'idol' is so slight that it requires an act of attention on the part of the mind to grasp it.

The second instance of mind-perception[7] is that of images seen in sleep. Here a succession of 'idols' is perceived, but

[1] By ἐπιβολὴ τῆς διανοίας. For a discussion of this most disputed phrase see Appendix III. I have assumed in the text the conclusion there formed.

[2] See Lucr. iv. 746–8:

> facile uno commovet ictu
> quaelibet una animum nobis subtilis imago;
> tenvis enim mens est et mire mobilis ipsa.

[3] Ep. i, § 48.

[4] Lucr. iv. 131:

> sunt etiam quae sponte sua gignuntur et ipsa
> constituuntur in hoc caelo qui dicitur aer.

[5] Lucr. iv. 738: et quae confiunt ex horum facta figuris.

[6] See Lucr. iv. 802:

> et quia tenvia sunt, nisi quae contendit acute
> cernere non potis est animus.

[7] καθ' ὕπνους γινομένων, Ep. i, § 51: cf. Lucr. iv. 757–776.

they do not, as in the case of sense-perception, unite to form a single image, but are grouped separately so as to form a series, often representing bodies¹ moving and gesticulating (the 'cinematograph' here helps us to understand Epicurus' meaning). Such images may either be due to 'idols' which penetrate,² now that the sense-organs are dormant, to the mind or are called up from the memory-store in the mind, or again they may be accidental and fantastic creations corresponding to no reality. Akin to the visions of sleep are the visions of the madman: these must arise in the majority of cases from a combination of the 'idols' of real things. In both these cases³ the vision is 'true', because it corresponds to real 'idols': the delusion is not due to the mind's perception, but to its subsequent inference that the image seen is directly derived from a real object. So, as Sextus⁴ explains, 'in the case of Orestes, when he thought he saw the Erinyes, the perception which was stirred up by 'idols' was true, for the 'idols' were really there, but the mind, when it thought that these were solid realities (στερέμνιοι), was forming a false opinion (ἐψευδόξει). Very like to these two is the vision of dead persons,⁵ but that the originating cause is slightly different. Here the 'idols' did indeed spring from the living body, but have continued to float about in the air 'unused', so to speak, even after their original is dead: these also are usually perceived by the mind in sleep. Once more the image is 'true', now in a fuller sense, for it corresponds to 'idols' produced by realities, but the inference that the persons are still living is false.

But by far the most important instance of 'mind-perception' is the vision of the gods. This must be treated more

---

¹ Lucr. iv. 768 ff., and especially 771-2:

  quippe ubi prima perit alioque est altera nata
  inde statu, prior hic gestum mutasse videtur.

² Ibid. 758-9.

        simulacra lacessunt
  haec eadem nostros animos quae cum vigilamus.

³ D.L. x. 32 τά τε τῶν μαινομένων φαντάσματα καὶ ⟨τὰ⟩ κατ' ὄναρ ἀληθῆ· κινεῖ γάρ.

⁴ adv. Math. viii. 63; U. 253.   ⁵ Lucr. iv. 733-4, 760-1.

fully in the next chapter, but here it may be noticed that the bodies of the gods send off a succession of idols, just as do all other concrete existences, but owing to the great subtlety of the structure of their bodies,[1] their 'idols' are so fine that they cannot be perceived by the sense-organs at all, but only by the finer and purer soul-compound of the mind. Here 'mental perception' is not merely 'true' because it corresponds to 'idols', but true in the fullest sense because it is evidence—the only direct evidence—of the existence of a corresponding reality.

In all these instances alike the 'idols' and successions of 'idols' are directly conveyed to the mind, but just as the senses, surrounded by crowding 'idols', need actively to 'apprehend' the particular image, so these single 'idols', much finer and more fleeting than the normal images of sense-perception, must be grasped by the act of attention on the part of the recipient mind.[2] All such 'images', as has been seen, are 'true' in the sense of corresponding to 'idols', and Epicurus[3] in several passages asserts their truth. He himself, however, remembering probably that some such images grasped by the mind did not correspond to external objects,

---

[1] Cf. Lucr. v. 154.

[2] ἐπιβολὴ τῆς διανοίας: R. Philippson, *Zur Epikureischen Götterlehre* (*Hermes*, li, 1916, pp. 568–608), who is anxious to establish a strict terminology in the Epicurean psychology, states that διάνοια is Epicurus' word for the special faculty of the mind which apprehends single images. It is true that it is so used (Ep. i. 38, 49, 50, 51; *K.Δ.* xxiv), but it is also used by Epicurus himself (1) of an ἐπιβολὴ τῆς διανοίας as part of the process of reasoning about ἄδηλα (Ep. i, § 62), (2) of mental grasp of reasoning or of a principle (Ep. i, § 78; *K.Δ.* xx), (3) as the seat of fear and pleasure (*K.Δ.* x, xviii). Still less is it the case, as he states, that Lucretius' translation of διάνοια in this sense is always *mens*. *Mens* and *animus* in Lucretius are interchangeable terms for 'the mind' in general, and in the passages in the Fourth Book which deal with the mental apprehension of *simulacra*, *mens* is used seven times as the equivalent of διάνοια (iv. 748, 750, 754, 767, 780, 976, 1011), *animus* six times (iv. 731, 747, 787, 803, 812, 814), and *mens animi* once (758). In his discussion of psychology Philippson appears to me not to have sufficiently before his mind the essentially material character of Epicurus' idea of thought, all of which is occasioned by a mental visualization: its different processes were not therefore for him so rigidly distinguished.

[3] Ep. i, §§ 50, 62 : cf. *K.Δ.* xxiv.

was content to leave the matter here: his followers, anxious perhaps to establish their orthodoxy by asserting their certain knowledge of the existence of the gods, took the further step of exalting 'mental apprehension' into a criterion of truth.[1]

But besides this special function of 'mind-perception', the mind has its necessary share in all normal sense-perception: it must distinguish and interpret the data of the sense-organs. It is necessary to return once more to the examination of normal sense-perception and consider what follows on the original sensation in the eye. Our authorities are not very explicit at this point, but with a little filling in of gaps, it is possible to put together an account which will not greatly misrepresent Epicurean orthodoxy. The 'idols'[2] are 'like in colour and form' to the object from which they come; but though their shifting succession may represent 'accidents'[3] happening to the object, change of posture, movement, &c., they cannot in themselves convey to us any other of its qualities. What is it then that the eye actually sees, what is the image (φαντασία) which the eye grasps as the result of the incidence of successive 'idols'? Nothing, clearly, but a certain mass of colour or colours of a certain size and shape: the interpretation of this image, the recognition of the general nature or individuality of the object which it represents, is not a matter of mere perception, nor is it the function of the sense-organ: it must be performed by the mind. How then can this be? how in the first place does the mind receive the image and how in the second has it the capacity for distinguishing and classifying images, so that it can pronounce the judgement 'this is so and so'? The answer to the first question is not easy to give. Certain passages in Lucretius[4] might lead us to suppose that the 'idols' themselves actually passed on through the pores of

[1] D.L. x. 31. This question is discussed in Appendix III: there were probably other reasons as well which actuated both Epicurus and his followers: see also Chap. II, pp. 250-2.

[2] § 49 ὁμοχρόων καὶ ὁμοιομόρφων.

[3] Cf. Lucr. iv. 788–801.

[4] Especially iv. 749 ff. Zeller (iii. 1. 389) has gone astray on this point, as Tohte notes (*Epikurs Kriterien der Wahrheit*, p. 4 fin.).

the body into the mind, but a closer examination of his illustrations shows clearly that he is thinking not of normal sensation, but of the images directly apprehended by the mind: further the very careful distinction of such subtle images from those of normal sense-perception in itself makes it clear that the latter do not come into direct contact with the mind. It has been supposed [1] that Epicurus meant that 'the atomic images only penetrate to the sense-organs or the pores' (in the passive sensation of contact), 'but that the image of the object reaches the mind in an immaterial form'. This is a contradiction of the most elementary principles of Epicurus' system: even if an 'immaterial image' could ever exist, which it could not, it could have no effect on the mind, for contact would be impossible. It will be much nearer Epicurus' mode of thought, even though he may never himself have elaborated this part of his theory, to suppose that the movement of sensation in the eye [2] causes a movement to pass along the chain of soul-atoms to the mind, and so by sympathetic movement (συμπάθεια) there is reproduced in the mind the image of sense-perception. It is strange and perhaps significant that modern scientific inventions should help us so much to understand Epicurus' physical theories: here it is clear that the analogy we want is that of the sympathetic movement of the needle in the receiver of the telegraph.

The image being thus apprehended by the mind, how does it perform its function of interpretation? Epicurus' answer is characteristic and its main outlines have already been sketched in discussing the Canonice. The individual image, being created in the mind, does not perish, but is stored up and may at any moment be 'called up' by the mind, or more correctly, be apprehended by an act of attention, which selects it out of the infinite number of similar images always present in the mind.[3] This is the act of memory.

[1] Tohte, *Epikurs Kriterien der Wahrheit,* p. 5.

[2] See Giussani, *Stud. Lucr.,* p. 190.

[3] Lucr. iv. 777–87, 802–17, really a consecutive argument, the intervening lines being an interruption and apparently an alternative version of 768–76.

But this is not all. Individual images of the same class of objects (e.g. horse, cow, &c.) collect and accumulate in the mind and by a kind of superposition form the 'general concept', or, as Epicurus prefers to call it, the 'anticipation' (πρόληψις) of the class:[1] here the analogy to help us is that of the 'composite photograph'. This 'recollection of that which has frequently been imaged from without', as Epicurus[2] defined it, can similarly be called up or attended to on demand.[3] When then the mind has received the new image, it can, as it were, look at various 'general concepts' and compare them with the new vision, and so pronounce the judgement 'this is a horse or a cow'.[4] The 'anticipation' is like sense-perception itself an infallible criterion of truth[5] (i.e. we cannot be misled by its images), because it is itself built up of sense-perceptions, which are immediately true. By means of it the mind is enabled not only to interpret individual sensations, but also, when it wishes to create,[6] to know how to set about the work, because it has a vision of the thing which it wishes to produce: it is in this latter sense that Epicurus' name 'anticipation' is most easily intelligible. What then is the result of this process of comparison? Clearly that what was before a mere irrational sensation has been given content and transformed into a piece of informa-

---

[1] See Chap. II, p. 245. It is not worth while discussing mistaken ideas of the πρόληψις, such as Schömann's that it is an 'innate idea', or Steinhart's that it includes the individual recollection. D.L. x. 33 is very explicit about it, and Tohte (op. cit., pp. 15–18) has explained the whole notion clearly enough.   [2] D.L. x. 33 μνήμη τοῦ πολλάκις ἔξωθεν φανέντος.

[3] Clemens Alex. Strom. ii. 4, p. 157, 44; U. 255; quotes a striking passage from Epicurus in which πρόληψις is defined as ἐπιβολὴν ἐπί τι ἐναργὲς καὶ ἐπὶ τὴν ἐναργῆ τοῦ πράγματος ἐπίνοιαν.

[4] D.L. x. 33 τὸ πόρρω ἑστὼς ἵππος ἐστὶν ἢ βοῦς· δεῖ γὰρ κατὰ πρόληψιν ἐγνωκέναι ποτὲ ἵππου καὶ βοὸς μορφήν.

[5] D.L. x. 31.

[6] It is in this sense that Lucretius in several passages uses notities, his rendering of πρόληψις: e.g. v. 181 ff.: how could the gods have created man, when they had no 'anticipation' of men in their minds? v. 1046, no man could have created language, unless he had heard other men speaking before: cf. iv. 475–7; v. 124 (where the sense is nearer to the ordinary notion of 'general concept').

tion with regard to the external world. The mind has inferred
from what was previously an image of shape and colour, that
this image is an indication of the presence within the range
of vision of e.g. a man: more than this, by means of the
indication of distance,[1] it will have decided how far the man
is from us, according to the sameness or alteration of successive images it will know whether he is at rest or moving
towards or away from us, or engaged in any particular action:
it may even by comparison with certain special and particular
'anticipations' (still of course built of many separate images)
be in a position to determine who the man is. It has, in
fact, performed an act of 'comprehension' (ἐπαίσθησις),[2] and
so given meaning to the simple 'perception' (αἴσθησις). The
sensation of hearing affords perhaps an even clearer notion
of this function of the mind than that of sight. The 'sound-
particles'[3] emitted from the throat of our friend reach the
ears, and there awake the sensation of mere noise: the act
of perception takes place in the ear, but it is the perception
of a succession of irrational sounds. The sensation is 'telegraphed' to the mind, and the mind by comparison with the
'anticipations' built of previous sounds, is able, very literally
in this case, to interpret the sounds: for it can assign to
them the content of meaning and translate them into speech.
Thus in all sense-perception there are two parts:[4] the receipt
of the sensation, as mere irrational shape and colour, or
sound, &c., which is performed by the sense-organ and is,
like the passive contact-sensation, purely local, and its interpretation and understanding, by comparison and classification, which is performed by the mind, acting by means of
the 'anticipation'. The notion is perhaps complicated, but
perfectly in accordance with Epicurus' general psychology,
and, allowing for the materialistic form in which it is put,

[1] See above, p. 413.   [2] Ep. i, § 52 : cf. D.L. x. 32.
[3] Cf. p. 405.
[4] Cf. an interesting passage in Aet. iv. 8. 2, p. 394 D; U. 249 τό ⟨τε⟩
μόριόν ἐστιν ἡ αἴσθησις, ἥ τις ἐστὶν ἡ δύναμις, καὶ τὸ ἐπαίσθημα, ὅ περ
ἐστὶ τὸ ἐνέργημα. ὥστε διχῶς παρ' αὐτῷ λέγεσθαι αἴσθησιν μὲν τὴν
δύναμιν, αἴσθησιν δὲ τὸ ἐνέργημα.

not very divergent from the account which would be given by other philosophers, ancient or modern.

During the whole of the above explanation an active capacity of the mind to attend, compare, and form judgements has been assumed, and it may well be thought that we have moved some way from the purely materialistic and atomic conception from which we started. It is necessary then to return to it and ask what is this power which the mind possesses, and how, speaking in atomic terms, it comes to possess it. Happily Epicurus has not at this point left us in the lurch: there is, he tells us in a passage of curious interest [1] in the Letter to Herodotus, 'another kind of movement produced inside ourselves closely linked to the apprehension of images, but differing from it'. This is an unmistakable return on the underlying materialism of the whole theory. The capacity of the mind to apprehend images (φανταστικὴ ἐπιβολὴ τῆς διανοίας), which was being considered just now, is, like the perception of the sense-organs and the passive sensation of the rest of the body, neither more nor less in ultimate analysis than a movement of atoms: but as the atoms in question are now undiluted soul-atoms, they are capable of finer apprehensions. Side by side with this movement there is another, closely akin to it, because it too deals with images,[2] but to be distinguished from it, because it does not now 'apprehend' the special fine images which visit the mind from without, but by a process of selection chooses out a 'general concept' to which it will assign the newly received image. This secondary movement is in fact that of 'opinion' (δόξα), which is the characteristic function of the mind not only in the interpretation of sense-perception, but in all forms of thought. Its primary difference then from the 'apprehension of images' lies in its object, but there is a second distinction which is of far greater importance. The former activity is always 'true' in the sense that it must apprehend an image which corresponds to an 'idol'

[1] § 51.
[2] I am here assuming the results of the discussion of ἐπιβολὴ τῆς διανοίας in Appendix III.

or a succession of 'idols', even though these do not always in their turn originate from a concrete reality. But opinion has no such guarantee of truth: it selects, as it will, the 'general concept' to which it will assign the new image. In most cases, no doubt, where the image is clear (ἐναργής) and the object easily recognizable, it will make no mistake; but it is always liable to error, especially in dealing with the images of distant objects. This then is the origin of the apparent errors of the senses: there is no error in the sense-perception, for it is the immediate outcome of the contact of the 'idol' with the sense-organ; the error [1] lies in the 'addition of opinion', the selection by this secondary movement of the mind of the general concept with which it will identify the image. Hence arises the rule of the Canonice,[2] that any vision other than the 'clear sight' (ἐνάργημα) of the near view must be regarded as a 'problem awaiting solution' (προσμένον). The mind should withhold its judgement until the inference it is inclined to make is either confirmed (ἐπιμαρτυρεῖται) or not by the clear vision.[3] It is unnecessary to refer again to the stock instances of the square tower at a distance or the approaching man: what must be emphasized here is that the uncertainty of the results of cognition are due to the independent character of the mental movement of opinion. There is no uncertainty about the individual image, there is no uncertainty about the 'general concept', but the 'movement' of opinion is liable to error in connecting the two: the apparently almost arbitrary rule of the Canonice turns out to be the necessary deduction from the atomic analysis of the operation of sense-perception in its various parts.

So far the operations of the mind have been considered only in relation to sense-perception. But besides being called upon to interpret and classify the reports of sensation about the perceptible external world (φαινόμενα, πρόδηλα), the mind has another and almost more important function to perform. For it has similarly to form conclusions about matters 'im-

---

[1] § 50 τὸ δὲ ψεῦδος καὶ τὸ διημαρτημένον ἐν τῷ προσδοξαζομένῳ ἀεί ἐστιν.   [2] See Chap. II, p. 254, and Ep. i, §§ 50, 51.

[3] See Chap. II, p. 255.

perceptible' (ἄδηλα). These, as the Canonice has shown,[1] may be of various kinds. First of all there is a class, which is almost on the borderline, of things perceptible indeed to the senses, but so remote that their inner workings cannot be directly perceived and are a matter for the investigation of the mind: these are the heavenly bodies and generally what Epicurus following the Atomists sums up as the 'things of the sky' (τὰ μετέωρα). More important than these are things which from their very nature must always remain imperceptible, and of this class the principal example is of course the atoms themselves and their movements in space. Here no direct assistance can be obtained from sense-perception, but sense-perception can give us a start in our investigations, for it can provide us with signs (σημεῖα)[2] or indications (τεκμήρια) in the visible world which may suggest inferences to the invisible. The work then must be done by thought (λογισμός)[3] alone and hypothesis must be framed on the basis of phenomena.

What then is the process of its work? It is not easy to conceive how a purely materialistic system can represent in a concrete form the processes of thought, and there are not many indications left in the authorities, but an account can be given which will at least not go far from what Epicurus imagined. In the first place it is clear that all thought must

---

[1] See Chap. II, pp. 257, 262. [2] See Ep. ii, § 87.

[3] λογισμός is the most general word in Epicurus for the process of reasoning about the unseen (Ep. i. 39 τὸ ἄδηλον τῷ λογισμῷ τεκμαίρεσθαι, see also Ep. i, §§ 75, 76; Ep. iii. 132; K.Δ. xvi, xix, fr. 74 (C.B.); D.L. x. 32, 117, 120): he also uses ἐπιλογισμός (i, § 73, and K.Δ. xx), διαλογισμός (ii, § 84; Sent. Vat. x), and διαλόγισμα (i, § 68; ii, § 85). The result of this process is a 'thought-image' (ἐπίνοια, i, § 45; D.L. x. 32), and ἐπινοεῖσθαι (i, § 40), διανοεῖσθαι (i, § 49), νόησις (Aet. iv. 8. 10), and διανόησις (i, § 63) are used in a corresponding sense. The equivalent in Latin of λογισμός is ratio (Cic. de Fin. i. 9. 30, and Lucretius, passim). δόξα in Epicurus is mainly concerned with the interpretation of sense-impressions, λογισμός with the more wholly mental processes of thought and reasoning, but there is some overlapping. R. Philippson (l.c., p. 571) states that λόγος is the faculty of νοῦς which deals with ἄδηλα, but in Epicurus' usage it is a quite vague word found in such expressions as λόγῳ θεωρητός: Philippson has pressed a theoretical view beyond the facts.

be a process of the combination of images: nothing but images [1] can stir the sensory movements in the mind, nor can the mind apprehend anything but images: all thought is to Epicurus, as we might say in modern phraseology, 'visualization'. Further, just as in the interpretation of sense-perceptions, the faculty of opinion has the capacity to put together images already existing and compare them for identification, so here the faculty of thought about the imperceptible world can combine previously existing images or concepts and by such combinations create new images which are in fact its hypotheses (δοξαζόμενα). This account is borne out by Diogenes' [2] résumé of the processes of thought: 'all thought-images (ἐπίνοιαι) have their origin in sensations by means of coincidence (περίπτωσις) and analogy and similarity and combination (σύνθεσις), reasoning (λογισμός) too contributing something'. The account is condensed and not wholly clear, but its meaning must be something like this: if we wish to reach any conclusion about the imperceptible world, we must start from sense-perceptions which seem to us akin to the object of our pursuit, either because we think they are produced by the underlying causes which we are seeking or because they seem to resemble the workings of such causes. From this basis we must try to 'work by signs' (σημειοῦσθαι).[3] Occasionally a merely accidental combination of concepts, made, as it were, by chance without any definite effort of search or inquiry on our part, will lead us to a fruitful conclusion, or, in strictly Epicurean phraseology, create a new image. Sometimes again an apparent likeness or even similarity between perceptible phenomena and the unseen will set us on the track of our conclusion: such a case would be Epicurus' own argument[4] for the

---

[1] Cf. Aet. iv. 8. 10; U. 317 Λεύκιππος Δημόκριτος Ἐπίκουρος τὴν αἴσθησιν καὶ τὴν νόησιν γίνεσθαι εἰδώλων ἔξωθεν προσιόντων· μηδενὶ γὰρ ἐπιβάλλειν μηδετέραν χωρὶς τοῦ προσπίπτοντος εἰδώλου. ἔξωθεν is not of course strictly true of images or concepts already in the mind, but it is of their origin.

[2] D.L. x. 32. Some useful comment on this passage is made by Tohte, Kriterien der Wahrheit, p. 12.   [3] Cf. Ep. i, § 38: cf. Ep. ii, § 104.

[4] §§ 55–9: see Chap. III, pp. 285–7.

existence of the *minimae partes* in the atom. In other instances again we may form our new image by the intentional juxtaposition of previously existing images, however derived: as, for example, when we reach the notion [1] of the infinity of the void by the mental combination of many images of 'empty space'. In all these cases then thought is working, just as in sense-interpretation, by comparing and combining images: the whole process is purely visual. But, it might be objected, Epicurus [2] is reported as saying that 'reason' makes some contribution to the process of thought. The phrase is vague and without support in the Letter to Herodotus, but there is no question even here of any process of non-visual thought, and certainly nothing non-material is implied. Reasoning to Epicurus is nothing more than, as we might say, 'putting two and two together',[3] and this for him must necessarily be a process of the combination of images: in other words 'reasoning' is itself an 'intentional combination' (σύνθεσις) and the phrase of Diogenes is loose.

Thought then proves to be a movement in the mind, which by the combination and comparison of previously existing images creates new images by a kind of 'visualization'. Its subject-matter is different from that of 'opinion', for it is no longer concerned with the interpretation of the data of sense, but has to create,[4] as it were, its own data. Does it differ from opinion in its results? Is it similarly liable to error or has it, in its scientific use at any rate, any guarantee of greater certainty? The Canonice [5] gives us the principles by which it can be controlled: just as the inferences of 'opinion' must be referred back to the 'clear vision' of the 'nearer view', and only accepted if they are confirmed, so the hypotheses of thought must be tested by being referred back to sensation. Confirmation (ἐπιμαρτύρησις) is no longer

---

[1] See Giussani, *Stud. Lucr.*, p. 176.   [2] D.L. x. 31, cited above.

[3] So συλλογίζεσθαι is used in the Second Letter about inferences to μετέωρα from perceptible phenomena: § 112 ἐάν τις δύνηται τὸ σύμφωνον τοῖς φαινομένοις συλλογίζεσθαι.

[4] This is true even with regard to celestial phenomena: for thought is engaged in investigating the imperceptible causes of phenomena.

[5] See Chap. II, pp. 263, 264.

possible, because the 'clear view' of sensation is no longer possible, but phenomena may contradict (ἀντιμαρτυρεῖν), and if so the hypothesis must be rejected as untrue. At each stage then in the process of scientific reasoning thought must be checked by sensation. In the chapter on the Canonice attention was also drawn to the singular difference in results between thought as regards celestial phenomena and thought dealing with the ultimate realities of existence—the atoms and the void. In the former case, all explanations which are not contradicted by sensation are to be accepted as equally true, for they correspond to a real diversity of occurrence in celestial phenomena: in the latter there is a one and only truth.

What are the psychological grounds of this conclusion and what process of thought can there be which will justify this assumption of the one and only truth in the realm of ultimate realities—the realm most remote from the immediate and certain data of sense? No explicit solution of this difficulty is to be found in the works either of Epicurus himself or of his followers, and it has been too lightly passed over by his critics, who have been content to group both classes of 'the imperceptible' together and to apply the idea of the multiplicity of causes to both alike, without perceiving the startling divergence in the results. Yet nothing could be more marked than the difference in this respect between the Letters to Herodotus and to Pythocles: the reader seems to be almost in a different atmosphere of argumentation. It would of course be easy to accept this difference and to condemn Epicurus as a loose or dishonest thinker: to point out that whereas he had no intrinsic interest in astronomy and meteorology, he could admit diversity of explanation and of truth in that field, but that the ultimate principles of atomism were vital to him and in defiance of logic he would stoutly resist any incursion of multiplicity. But before such a condemnation is passed, it is well to see if some defence cannot be made.

Historically it is not very difficult to see how Epicurus was led to claim this higher certainty, or singleness of truth,

for his ultimate physical speculations. Despite all his pro-
testations of originality, it is obvious that his system as a
whole is based on that of Democritus, and though in the
Canonice in particular he seems to break away from his
predecessor in his emphatic reassertion of the supremacy of
sensation and of the reality of the phenomenal world, he is
yet even here more influenced than he imagined by Democritus' metaphysics.[1] He consequently still felt something
of a superior reality[2] in the existence of the too fundamental
constituents, and was led therefore to claim almost unconsciously a dogmatic certainty for his thought about their
nature and conduct.

Yet such an explanation of his position, if it stood alone,
would still leave Epicurus open to the charge of unconscious
intellectual dishonesty, and it is necessary to inquire whether
even on his own assumptions his attitude cannot be justified.
For this purpose the analysis[3] of the process of thought about
the imperceptible must be carried a little farther: how are
these hypotheses framed for which this unique certainty is
claimed. Consider first the data: in the case of terrestrial
problems sensation can supply alike the problems and their
solution, in the case of celestial phenomena sensation can
supply the problems, but thought must suggest the solution,
but in the case of the ultimate truths of science both problems and their solution must come from thought. Sensation, though it can give us indications and must be used as
the test of reference, cannot directly supply the data, for
the ultimate realities, the atoms and space, cannot from their
very nature throw off 'idols'. In other words the mind is
dealing no longer with the images of sense-perception, but
wholly with mental concepts. By what process then must
the work be done? Clearly by 'combination' (σύνθεσις).[4] The
mind by putting together previously existing concepts, each

---

[1] This point was insisted on by Natorp, *Forschungen*, chap. v.

[2] A trace of the same feeling may be seen in his denial of the secondary
qualities to the atoms, which carries with it a faint sense of their unreality
in compound things: see Chaps. III and VI.

[3] See Chap. II, pp. 265, 266.   [4] D.L. x. 32, see above, p. 424.

tested as they were formed by the reference to the senses, forms a new concept. But so far this is equally the process in the case of the celestial phenomena and may lead to a plurality of conclusions: what is the difference in the case of the ultimate realities? There are, I conceive, two differences, one in the nature of the concept, and the other in the nature of the process. The concept of science is not only tested by reference to the senses, but it is 'clear' in the very special sense of being 'self-evident': it is not formed arbitrarily by the loose and erratic operation of 'opinion', but is immediately grasped by the kindred 'act of mental apprehension' ($\epsilon\pi\iota\beta o\lambda\dot{\eta}$ $\tau\hat{\eta}s$ $\delta\iota\alpha\nuo\acute{\iota}\alpha s$).[1] In other words the operation of the formation of a new scientific concept is for Epicurus, what we might call in modern phraseology, the 'immediate intuition of a self-evident proposition': the mind 'looks' and sees a new picture that is perfectly 'clear' and could not be otherwise than it is. An illustration may make the idea clearer. Suppose, for instance, that we are inquiring into the nature of the motion of the atoms. We have as our data, first the concept of the atom, reached by the combination[2] of the sensational concept (if we may use the term to mean a concept built immediately of sensations) of the *minimum visibile*, together with that of further division and that of a similar limit. All these concepts are 'clear' and their combination must form one new concept and one only, that of the atom as conceived by thought. Secondly, we have the concept of bodies moving downwards owing to their own weight, and thirdly that of bodies moving sideways in a slight 'swerve'. These concepts are put in juxtaposition in the mind. The mind 'looks' and by an immediate 'act of apprehension' or intuition it sees the new picture or image of the infinite infinitesimal movements of the atoms in all directions,[3] colliding at every moment and leaping apart in new directions only to meet with new collisions. There is no question of alternative solutions here: the previous concepts are placed together and the mind has only to 'look'

[1] Ep. i, § 51.　　　　　　[2] See Giussani, *Lucretius*, i. 176.
[3] See Chap. V, pp. 327 ff.

and see the new concept, which is the self-evident image resulting from those just before it in the series. The whole of scientific thought[1] is then to Epicurus a chain of such self-evident or 'clear' concepts, grasped by the act of 'mental apprehension' each in their due order: its 'uniqueness' of truth is as inevitable as is that of the science of mathematics. At each step we directly apprehend an image that is itself a precise and certain reproduction of the imperceptible realities.

Such, I believe, is Epicurus' notion of the process of thought about the 'imperceptible' things of ultimate reality, and the justification of his claim for it that it leads in each case to a 'one and only' (μοναχόν) truth. But it would of course be rash to assume this, if it were wholly unsupported. Happily it is not, for not only does it fully accord, as has been seen, with Epicurus' account of thought as reported by Diogenes, but in a curious and very valuable passage[2] in the Letter to Herodotus we have an unexpected confirmation. Epicurus there warns us that we must not always argue directly from the analogy of the senses to the conduct of the atoms, for sometimes such an analogy is entirely misleading. We have, he argues in effect, two parallel modes of obtaining certainty: in the region of sensation we obtain truth from observation (τὸ θεωρούμενον ἀληθές), that is, from the 'clear vision' obtained in the near view by an apprehension of the senses (ἐπιβολὴ τῶν αἰσθητηρίων): but in the region of the imperceptible truth must be obtained by 'mental apprehension' (ἐπιβολὴ τῆς διανοίας). Now in the passage in question, which deals with the atomic motion which takes place in a moving compound body, the conclusion which Epicurus

---

[1] A quotation from Professor Clement Webb's *Problems in the Relations of God and Man* (p. 79) will express exactly what I conceive to have been Epicurus' idea of his own scientific system: 'The highest conceivable form of religious knowledge, as of all knowledge, would, I suppose, be intuitive throughout, in the sense that the whole result would be present to consciousness in the parts or moments, and all the parts or moments explicit in the whole or result.'

[2] Ep. i, § 62: for the fuller discussion of this passage and its consequences see Appendix III.

reaches is made precisely in the manner which we have described: the previously formed concepts of the behaviour of the atoms are examined in a new situation, and it is found that the picture thus formed and grasped by 'mental apprehension' is different from that which a mere analogy of phenomena would suggest. The analogy of phenomena then must in this instance be abandoned and the intuitive apprehension is the one and only truth. Here is the practical confirmation of the view advanced above.

The process of scientific reasoning then, conducted by the 'mental apprehension' of clear concepts, is at once the highest intellectual function of the mind and also that most remote from immediate sensation. Yet Epicurus can claim for it a certainty unknown in the operations of 'opinion' dealing directly with sensations, and a capacity to reach the single truth unknown to thought itself when dealing with the remoter sensations of celestial phenomena. The paradox is striking, yet its solution is clear. It is that this 'act of apprehension' of the 'clear view' of the scientific concept is a process exactly parallel to the 'act of apprehension by the senses' of the 'clear view' of the near object, which is the guarantee of full and absolute truth in sensation. Nor is it indeed merely a parallel: for thanks to the wholehearted materialism of the Epicurean psychology, there is no essential difference between the structure of the sense-organs and that of the mind, between the atomic composition of the image of sensation and the mental image of the concept, between the movement of the two 'acts of apprehension'. The simplest process of the acquisition of truth and the most complex meet in an identity which is not fully shared by the intermediate processes of opinion and thought about celestial phenomena. The mind at the moment of its greatest remoteness from sensation shares the certainty of sensation, for its nature and the circumstances of its action are identical. Such I believe to have been the conception of Epicurus, even though the evidence for it may be slight, and it forms a fitting crown to his carefully worked-out account of psychological processes.

The mind then has the function of interpretation and judgement in all fields, in sense-perception, in the explanation of physical phenomena, in the discovery of the ultimate realities of the world. Yet thought unaided can only form opinion and is always liable to error. In any department truth may be reached, but only by keeping thought constantly checked by reference to sensation: 'we must keep all under the control of the senses'.[1]

The mind has, however, functions in other fields than that of thought. It is firstly the seat of the emotions: joy and fear, love and hatred, &c., all originate from the mind situated in the breast. The authorities[2] do little more than tell us that this is so, but a closer analysis may be attempted. To begin with it is important to distinguish these more complex emotions from the more passive feelings ($\pi \acute{a} \theta \eta$) of pleasure and pain. The latter are matters of immediate sensation, they are perceived locally and immediately in the parts of the body where the contact or movement which causes them occurs, and take their origin in the movement of the 'fourth nature' in the 'spirit', which is then communicated to the other soul-elements and so to the atoms of body. But though they are distinct, there is a connexion between these simple sensations of the body and the complex emotions of the mind, and this connexion is exactly parallel to that between the sense-organs and the mind in sense-perception. The body has a simple sensation of pleasure or pain ($\pi \acute{a} \theta o s$): this is 'telegraphed' to the soul, which then by its own peculiar movement translates the simple sensation into an emotion, by an inference as to the external body which

[1] Ep. i, § 38.
[2] Schol. on Ep. i, § 67; Lucr. iii. 136–60; Plut. adv. Colot. 20, p. 1118 d; U. 314. The last is an important passage. Epicurus, as quoted there, ascribes the emotions of love and hatred to the 'nameless element', and Brieger has used this as an argument for its identification with the animus. This is quite unnecessary: these emotions do of course originate from the 'fourth nature' in the mind and Epicurus was here thinking of the activities of the mind only and not those of pure sensation: see Appendix V.

caused the sensation, and a mental attitude towards that body. At times the emotion is so strong, as Lucretius tells us,[1] that it is transferred back again to the spirit-particles and through them to the body, so that all the frame seems to take its part in the emotion which started in the breast: 'when the understanding is stirred by some stronger fear, we see that the whole soul feels with it throughout the limbs, and then sweat and pallor break out over all the body, and the tongue is crippled and the voice is choked, the eyes grow misty, the ears ring, the limbs give way beneath us, and indeed we often see men fall down through the terror in their mind'. Nor need the original stimulus always come from the bodily sensations: the cause of fear or joy, hatred or love, may equally well lie in a sense-perception, or even in an inference of thought based on sense-perception. The important point is that these emotions of the mind are not merely arbitrary or spontaneous; but, just as in all its other activities, the original motive cause is derived in one form or another from sensation: we do not rejoice or grieve or fear or love or hate without an ultimate external cause.[2] Once again the mental activity is dependent on the sensory stimulus.

Closely analogous to the genesis of emotion is a still more important function of the mind, the act of will: here again the movement of the mind is the determining factor and the motive power, but it acts on the sensory stimulus. The process is admirably described by Lucretius,[3] who takes the example of a determination on our part to walk:

First of all idols of walking[4] fall upon our mind, and strike the mind. Then comes the will; for indeed no one begins to do anything, ere the mind has seen beforehand what it will do, and inasmuch as it sees this beforehand, an image of the thing is formed. And so, when the mind

---

[1] iii. 152–8.

[2] There is, I admit, no authority for this account of the stimulation of the emotions, but it is surely demanded both, as Epicurus would argue, by our experience, and by the analogy of the other mental functions of which we have an explicit account.   [3] iv. 877–906.

[4] 881 'simulacra meandi': he should more strictly have said 'images of us walking' or 'of one walking', *meantis*.

stirs itself so that it wishes to start and step forward, it straightway strikes the force of the soul which is spread abroad in the whole body throughout limbs and frame. . . . Then the soul goes on and strikes the body, and so little by little the whole mass is thrust forward and set in movement.

The parallelism is clear: the sensory stimulus is followed by the movement of the mind; the mind communicates with the spirit, and the spirit with the body: the only difference is that in this case the result is not thought or emotion but action. But one caution is necessary: the act of the mind must not be thought of as a purely mechanical reaction: it is not inevitably and immediately set moving by the sensible image. For when the image has been perceived, 'then comes the act of will': the mind is free and it may choose either to act or not to act in answer to the stimulus of sense. How then can this be? It has been already seen [1] that the freedom of the will is due ultimately to the 'slight swerve' of individual atoms, but the process must be considered again in the light of the analysis now made of the soul and its workings: for it leads at once to the central question of all Epicurus' psychology.

In an earlier chapter [2] it was seen that the nature of the atomic 'swerve', as the physical cause which led to the union of atoms to form things, must be regarded as an exception to the physical law of necessity (*foedera naturai*), a spontaneous but purely mechanical movement, which may be made by any atom 'at any moment and in any place'. It was there also concluded that not only did Epicurus believe that this atomic 'swerve' was the cause of free-will in man, but that it was largely his strong desire to save the freedom of the will in a world governed by the inevitable sequence of cause and effect, which led him to place this element of spontaneity at the basis of his physical system. Our present business then is to discover on the lines of the preceding analysis of the mind and its workings what is the effect of the 'swerve' in the act of will. The act of will, no less than the acts of sense-interpretation or of thought or of emotion,

[1] Chap. V, p. 319.   [2] Chap. V, p. 320.

is an atomic motion, initiated, as always, in the particles of the 'fourth nature' and communicated to the other elements of the mind. Now, setting aside the 'swerve', there are only two causes which can start movement, weight, and an external blow due to the contact with another body. This is as true of the mind as of any other body, except that from the circumstances of its nature and position in the body, weight is not an effective cause of motion. It is the blow from the atomic movements communicating the sense-perception which start in the mind the movements of sense-interpretation, it is the blow of the image or 'general concept' which initiates the movements of thought, and the blow of the movement communicating the passive sensation of the body which sets going the movements of emotion: in every case the mental movement is the inevitable reaction to the stimulus of an external blow.[1] But what is it in the case of an act of will? Is the act of will a purely mechanical reaction to the blow of the image of an action? No, for in that case there would be no question of choice, the mind would always react and we could never refuse to accept the prompting of the image. Lucretius'[2] account makes this clear. The image is presented to the mind and 'beats upon the mind': but then follows a break in the mechanical chain: 'then comes the act of will'; the mind chooses whether it will act or no, and 'moves itself'.[3] Its movement which results in action (or the refusal of action) is not the result of the external blow, but of this internal power of movement, which is due to the 'swerve': so Lucretius[4] unmistakably sums up his earlier argument: 'that the very mind feels not some necessity within in doing all things, and is not constrained like a conquered thing to bear and suffer, this is brought about by the tiny swerve of the first-beginnings in no determined direction of place and at no determined time'. The movement of will is wholly initiated within the mind and the mind in starting it is wholly self-determined.

[1] Except possibly that of the ἐπιβολὴ τῆς διανοίας, but though that is an active movement, it is not initiated without stimulus.

[2] iv. 881 ff.   [3] 'sese commovet,' 886.   [4] ii. 289–93.

Of what nature then is this self-initiated movement? In the individual atom it is automatic, spontaneous, and wholly undetermined in occasion or direction. Is the movement of the mind in will merely the result of such a movement in one of its component atoms, or even the sum of many such movements? If so it too must be automatic and undetermined. When the image of action is presented to the mind, it is impossible to foretell in what way the movement will occur, or even whether it will occur at all. In other words the mind is not really self-determined, but is at the mercy of wholly undetermined movements inside itself, and free-will after all its careful preservation turns out to be nothing better than chance. This is indeed the conclusion reached by one modern critic,[1] and it is not to be wondered at that he is unwilling to believe that Epicurus himself can have rested the claim for freewill on the atomic 'swerve'. But the solution of this difficulty[2] lies once again to the Epicurean conception of a compound body (*concilium, conciliatus*). The compound is more than a mere aggregate of independent atoms: it is their union in a complex, which has a new individuality of its own in which it may acquire qualities and even powers which are not possessed by the individual component atoms. The soul or mind[3] is a compound body of such peculiar constitution in the nature of its component atoms and their motions among themselves, that it acquires the power of sensation or consciousness. The automatic swerve of the individual atoms then is translated in the complex of the mind into a consciously spontaneous movement, in other words into a movement of volition. 'The complete conception of the will according to Epicurus', Giussani argues in an admirable summary of his position, 'comprises two elements, a complex atomic movement which has the characteristic of spontaneity, that is, is withdrawn from the necessity of mechanical causation: and then the *sensus*, or self-consciousness in virtue of which the will, illuminated by previous movements of sensation, thought, and emotion,

[1] Brieger, op. cit., p. 21.
[2] See Giussani, *Stud. Lucr.* p. 140.   [3] See p. 398.

profits by the peculiar liberty or spontaneity of the atomic motions, to direct or not to direct these in a direction seen or selected.' In other words the blind primitive 'swerve' of the atom has become the conscious psychic act. It may be that this account presses the Epicurean doctrine slightly beyond the point to which the master had thought it out for himself, but it is a direct deduction from undoubted Epicurean conceptions and is a satisfactory explanation of what Epicurus meant: that he should have thought that the freedom of the will was chance, and fought hard to maintain it as chance and no more, is inconceivable.

And if the further question is asked how can a complex of blind spontaneous movements of atoms become the conscious act of volition of the mind, we are only thrown back once more on the ultimate difficulty, which has made itself felt all through this account of the soul. For indeed, if we look back over it, we find that here and there crudities of thought or incoherences in the connexion of ideas have been noted,[1] yet as a whole the general theory is self-consistent and complete; but at the back of it always lies the difficulty which must beset Epicureanism or any other form of materialism: can the movement of insensible particles produce or account for consciousness? That all forms of consciousness have their physical counterpart, that sensation, thought, will are accompanied by material movements of parts of the physical organism is credible, and indeed scientific investigation seems to be revealing this parallelism more and more clearly to us. The more material thinkers of our own time are content to say that consciousness 'supervenes' as an 'epiphenomenon' on the movements of matter: Epicurus went the step farther and was prepared to say that consciousness, sensation, thought, and will *are* the movements of the soul-atoms. Such an idea is to most modern minds, as it was to the majority of philosophers in Epicurus' day, unthinkable: between the one set of facts and the other there is a great gulf fixed: nothing can bridge the gulf that lies between the most elementary sensation and the

[1] Especially with regard to the theory of 'idols'.

atomic vibrations which accompany and condition it. If we accept a purely materialistic system in any form, its conclusions will have to be *mutatis mutandis* something like those of Epicurus: but he has done nothing to bridge over the abyss or to make the gulf seem less wide. *Consequitur sensus, inde voluntas fit*, his pupil says glibly, but each time rouses in us the same feeling that this is just what can never be understood.

And if it is impossible to accept his account of the nature of the soul and its workings, so the inference from it cannot be admitted. If the soul is a mere atomic complex, a 'body', then no doubt like the body it perishes and cannot have any sort of existence after death. But if that account be unsatisfactory, then the problem of survival remains open: the soul may or may not survive bodily death, but the question cannot be decided on the basis of a purely material analysis.

It is impossible in dealing with a material system to refrain from pointing out its fundamental weakness, but in an attempt to estimate Epicurus as a thinker, it is less profitable to quarrel with his base-principles than to think of the superstructure he has built upon them. And once again in examining the account of the soul, for all its weaknesses, we are conscious of the workings of a great mind, capable of grasping alike broad ideas and minute details of elaboration. We are certainly not left with the picture of a moral teacher, who merely patched together any kind of physics and metaphysics to back up his ethical preaching.

IX

THE GODS—THEOLOGY AND RELIGION

ONE of the earliest and most constant accusations against the Epicureans was that of atheism. Plutarch,[1] though he knows the Epicurean doctrine, yet charges its followers with overthrowing religion, 'which is the first ordinance of any civilized state': Cicero,[2] though to him we owe the most explicit exposition we possess of the Epicurean theology, takes up a similar position, and his Epicurean contemporary Philodemus had to devote a treatise,[3] of which we possess valuable fragments, to the refutation of the charge. The tradition was continuous through the Middle Ages and even after the Renaissance it brought Gassendi, who revived Epicurus' physical doctrines, into disrepute and danger; it is glibly repeated against the Atomists and Epicurus in a well-known passage of Bacon.[4] Its foundation is of course obvious enough: as the very first condition of the moral life Epicurus insists on the belief that the gods have no part in the government of the world: 'the blessed and immortal nature knows no trouble itself nor causes trouble to any other, so that it is never constrained by anger or favour'.[5] For him, as for Democritus before him, the traditional theology was but 'myth',[6] and the whole ceremonial of prayer and worship valueless,[7] in so far as it was a definite attempt to influence divine beings to alter the course of mundane events. Yet Epicurus was very far from denying either the existence of the gods or the value of religion as he himself conceived it: 'for gods there are, since the knowledge of them is by clear vision (ἐναργής).[8] But they are not such as the many believe them to be. And the

---

[1] *adv. Colot.* 31.

[2] *de Nat. Deor.* i, especially cc. 43, 44.

[3] περὶ εὐσεβείας, for the fragments see Gomperz, *Herculanische Studien*, part ii.　　　　[4] *Essays*, xvi.　　　　[5] *K.Δ.* i.

[6] ὁ περὶ θεῶν μῦθος, Ep. iii, § 134, and elsewhere.

[7] Lucr. v. 1198 ff.　　　　[8] Ep. iii, § 123.

impious man is not he who denies the gods of the many, but he who attaches to the gods the beliefs of the many'. It is probable that Epicurus was at pains to think out with great care his conception of the nature of the divine beings and the mode of their existence, and both practised himself and urged upon his followers a reasoned 'piety' which he believed to have the highest value in human life. But it unfortunately happens that at this most important point in the system our normal sources of information fail: none of the Letters give any real help towards the reconstruction of the Epicurean theology, and Lucretius after promising to deal fully with the whole subject has failed to do so except in very brief references.[1] We are thrown back on less trustworthy authorities, whose statements are obscure and in some cases corrupt, so that it is very difficult to put together anything like a certain account of the nature of the gods. Modern critics have in consequence supported very different hypotheses, and it will therefore be necessary later on to discuss the evidence at some length. Meanwhile in the earlier stages there is comparatively safe ground.

Epicurus started from the universal belief of mankind in the existence of gods: 'for he saw in the first place that gods exist, because nature herself had implanted a conception of them in the minds of all men . . . and that on which all men are by nature agreed, must of necessity be true. We must therefore acknowledge that there are gods'.[2] To what then is this universal consensus due? It is due to two causes, one of which is a valid proof of the truth of the belief, the other a false and valueless inference. In the first place[3] men's minds are constantly visited, especially when they are undis-

---

[1] v. 155.

[2] Cic. de Nat. Deor. i. 16. 43, 44; U. 352; cf. Lucr. v. 1161 ff.

[3] Lucr. v. 1169–82: cf. Sext. Emp. adv. Math. ix. 25; U. 353 Ἐπίκουρος ἐκ τῶν κατὰ ὕπνους φαντασιῶν οἴεται τοὺς ἀνθρώπους ἔννοιαν ἐσπακέναι θεοῦ, and similarly, ix. 42. So also Cic. de Nat. Deor. i. 19. 49 'eam esse vim et naturam deorum ut . . . non sensu sed mente cernatur', with which we may compare Aet. i. 7. 34; U. 355 Ἐπίκουρος ἀνθρωποειδεῖς μὲν τοὺς θεούς, λόγῳ δὲ πάντας θεωρητοὺς διὰ τὴν λεπτομέρειαν τῆς τῶν εἰδώλων φύσεως.

tracted in sleep, by images of beautiful and powerful beings, and these images the mind grasps by an 'act of apprehension' (ἐπιβολὴ τῆς διανοίας). Now such images, though necessarily true to the 'idols' which produce them, are not always a guarantee of the existence of a corresponding external object: for the 'idols' themselves may be produced by the mere chance combination of other single 'idols' or even of independent atoms (συστάσεις). And so in Cicero's dialogue, Cotta the Academic, who appears as the critic of Epicureanism, asks pertinently enough:[1] 'what difference is there whether we have a vision of a god or of a hippocentaur?' Epicurus' answer would have been that the frequency and universality of the visions of the gods was cogent proof of an objective reality corresponding to them: the sporadic vision of an individual may be due to a spontaneously formed 'idol', but a vision that comes constantly to all men cannot be produced by chance on separate occasions, but must be caused by 'idols' flowing from a concrete reality.[2] The images in fact constituted, as Epicurus[3] himself says, 'knowledge by clear vision' (ἐναργὴς γνῶσις), or as Cicero[4] puts the case even more strongly, the 'idols' came so frequently to the minds of all men that they had formed an 'anticipation' or 'general concept' (πρόληψις) of divine beings. For a double reason then, in accordance with the Epicurean principles, these images of the gods are true, firstly because they are grasped by an 'apprehension of the mind', and secondly because they constitute an 'anticipation', which is itself a criterion of truth: or to put it in untechnical language, the

[1] i. 38. 105.
[2] Cf. D.L. x. 32 καὶ τὸ τὰ ἐπαισθήματα δ' ὑφεστάναι πιστοῦται τὴν τῶν αἰσθήσεων ἀλήθειαν, and see Chap. II, p. 240, n. 6.
[3] Ep. iii. § 123.
[4] de Nat. Deor. i. 16. 43 'quae est enim gens aut quod genus hominum, quod non habeat sine doctrina anticipationem quandam deorum? quam appellat πρόληψιν Epicurus—and similarly later, 17. 44 'intellegi necesse est esse deos, quoniam insitas eorum vel potius innatas cognitiones habemus', where he does not mean what we should call an 'innate' conception, but one which nature by successive visions has implanted in us: see Giussani, Stud. Lucr. p. 229, and Mayor's note on the passage.

clearness and the universality of the visions attest a reality to which they correspond. It is certain then that gods exist.

But besides these direct visions, there is another reason which leads the majority of mankind to a belief in the existence of the gods, which so far from being accepted, must at all costs be fought against, for it is the greatest enemy of that peace of mind (ἀταραξία) which is at once the aim and the condition of the moral life. Men when they see the marvels of earth and sky and come to know the majesty of the heavenly bodies and the orderliness of their movements, are apt either to suppose that sun, moon, and stars are themselves divine beings,[1] or that the world was created and is governed by the will of the gods.[2] For neither of these beliefs is there any foundation: the heavenly bodies are in fact 'so far sundered from divine power . . . that they are thought rather to be able to afford us the concept of what is far removed from vital motion and sense',[3] and the world, as the whole of Epicurus' physical theory proves, is governed by the laws of nature, the natural processes of change which arise directly from the atomic motions of its component parts. These popular ideas are indeed merely the false inferences of opinion, making the unjustifiable combination of the true images of the gods which we receive in our mind with the workings of the external world. They are 'not conceptions derived from sensation (προλήψεις), but false suppositions (ὑπολήψεις ψευδεῖς)',[4] and it is the business of the philosopher to root them out of life altogether.[5] We do indeed know with certainty of the existence of the gods, but not through this false inference from phenomena.

Thus far all accounts of the Epicurean theology agree, but the difficulties begin when the inevitable question is asked, whence come these subtle images into the mind, and of what nature are the bodies which throw them off, if such there be? Singularly divergent answers have been given to this question, the difference turning for the most

---

[1] Lucr. v. 114 ff.: cf. Plut. *adv. Colot.* 27. 1123 a.
[2] Lucr. v. 1183 ff. [3] Lucr. v. 122–5. [4] Ep. iii. § 124.
[5] Epicurus is here opposing Stoic doctrine quite as much as popular belief.

part on the interpretation of the famous passage in Cicero[1] taken in conjunction with a statement of a scholiast[2] on the Tenth Book of Diogenes Laertius, and illustrated by certain fragments of Philodemus.[3] It will be necessary to examine this evidence in some detail, but first it will be well to consider what was Epicurus' starting-point and what was required of his theology by the general principles of his system.

The first question one naturally asks in examining a difficult problem in Epicurus' system is what was his inheritance from Democritus. Though many places[4]—often fundamental places—in his system have been noticed where Epicurus broke away from Democritus, yet it is clear that in general the Atomists supplied his starting-point. The views of Democritus about the gods are unfortunately, as has been seen, not easy to recover,[5] but it may safely be stated that besides a general vague theism which caused him to recognize 'elements of mind' in the universe, he held that the whole air was full of 'images' or 'idols', derived apparently from a 'divine essence' or 'existence'. These images, which visited man and animals, Democritus appears to have regarded as themselves living beings—gods or daemons— with human form, but very large and capable of doing men good or harm: further, though they were not immortal, they were 'hard to destroy' and therefore lived long.

Some features in this account we should expect to find reproduced by Epicurus, and if he made deviations from it there should be reasons in other parts of his system. And there are indeed certain undisputed points of resemblance in Epicurus' account, enough at least to give us reason to think that Democritus' theory was, as usual, his basis. Thus, it is obvious both from Cicero and from Lucretius that the 'images' played a large part in Epicurus' conception.

[1] Cic. de Nat. Deor. i. 19. 49, 50.   [2] Schol. to K.Δ. i.
[3] See Gomperz, Herculanische Studien, pp. 93–151.
[4] Such, for instance, as the introduction of the 'swerve' to account for the meeting of the atoms, or the simplification of the processes of hearing and sight by the omission of the ἀποτύπωσις in the air.
[5] See Part I, Chap. III, § 7, where the authority for the views here stated is given in the foot-notes.

Further, there can be no doubt that he conceived of the gods in human form, for this is expressly stated by the scholiast[1] on Diogenes and repeated by Aetius:[2] Lucretius[3] adds that they were, as Democritus had conceived them, 'of wondrous bulk of body'. But there were also points in Democritus' account which Epicurus could not accept. His view[4] that the gods were wholly unconcerned with the affairs of this world made it impossible for him to admit that they existed within the limits of the world or that they could directly affect men for good or evil: for the same reason the pantheistic notion of the 'elements of mind' in the universe must be excluded. Similarly his desire[5] that the gods should be the perfect example of happiness—the ethical ideal for men—made it necessary that they should be immortal: for perfect happiness is precluded by a fear or expectation of death. Lastly, the idea of 'images' or 'idols' which were themselves living beings would be inconsistent with the conceptions of the theory of vision.[6] In these respects changes would be expected in Epicurus' view. He must place his gods somewhere outside the world and let them have no communication with it, except that they must be cognizable by men: they must be immortal and they must have an existence more real than that of mere 'idols'. It will be seen that Epicurus' account satisfied these conditions, but the crux of his problem lay in the necessity for conceiving of the gods as a concrete reality of atomic construction, capable of sending off perceptible 'idols', and yet not subject to dissolution.

The passage in Cicero must now be considered in detail.[7] It is very obscure and there is good reason to suppose, as most commentators agree, that though he is clearly following

[1] l.c., see p. 446, n. 1.
[2] i. 7. 34; U. 355 Ἐπίκουρος ἀνθρωποειδεῖς μὲν πάντας τοὺς θεούς.
[3] v. 1171.
[4] See W. Scott, *Journal of Philology*, xii. 230; and Giussani, *Stud. Lucr.*, p. 229.   [5] See below, p. 469.
[6] Hirzel does not apparently think so: see Appendix VI.
[7] A long technical discussion seems inevitable at this point, but a reader who wishes only to know its upshot may pass to p. 466.

an Epicurean text, he did not fully understand it and has contented himself with a rather unintelligent word-for-word translation. It must be worked out by comparison first with some very valuable repetitions in the scornful criticisms made later on in Cicero's dialogue by the Academic opponent Cotta, then with the scholium in Diogenes Laertius, and lastly with various fragments of Philodemus which have been recovered from the Herculanean rolls, and especially with those of the Third Book 'On the Gods'.[1] It is, however, necessary to be cautious, for there is reason to believe that Philodemus—from whom Cicero probably derived his information—had gone beyond the tradition of Epicurus himself and worked out the notion of the constitution of the gods on his own lines. It would indeed be possible to regard the whole Ciceronian doctrine as due to later Epicurean writers, but that the scholiast appears to attribute a similar idea to Epicurus himself.

After the general statements [2] already noticed of the universality of the 'anticipation' of the gods in the minds of men and of their eternal happiness and their anthropomorphic form the Epicurean Velleius in Cicero's dialogue proceeds to expound their physical constitution (*forma*). His first statement is quite general: 'the form (*species*) of the gods is not body, but a kind of body (*quasi corpus*), it has not blood, but a kind of blood'. This rather mysterious utterance is important as it prepares us for the description of some form of existence which is akin to that of the normal atomic com-

---

[1] These have been edited by H. Diels in *Abhandlungen der Kön. Preuss. Akad.*, 1916, Parts 4 and 6.

[2] The interpretation here given follows in the main the solution originally put forward by Lachelier (*Revue de Philologie*, 1877, pp. 264 ff.), and independently elaborated by W. Scott (*Journal of Philology*, xii. 212 ff.) and Giussani (*Stud. Lucr.*, p. 229), but with some modifications due to the theory of Schömann (*Opuscula*, iv. 336–59) and of R. Philippson (*Hermes*, li, 1916, pp. 568–608). I have also derived much assistance from Diels's edition of the περὶ τῆς τῶν θεῶν ἀγωγῆς fragments mentioned in the previous note. Philippson's theory stands apart from the others in his whole conception of the passages in the Scholiast and in Cicero, and I have therefore thought it better to deal with it independently in Appendix VI.

pound, yet different from it, something which may apparently be more easily described as 'form' than as 'body'. Then follows the detailed description[1] which must provisionally be translated as literally as may be: 'Epicurus teaches that the power and nature of the gods is of such a kind that in the first place it is perceived not by the senses but by the mind: it has not solidity,[2] so to speak, or numerical identity, like those things which on account of their compactness he calls "solids";[3] it is perceived rather by images apprehended by similarity and "passing",[4] since infinite forms (or possibly with Brieger, "an infinite series") of most similar images arise from innumerable atoms and stream to the gods: our mind and intelligence straining fixedly with the highest pleasure towards those images comes to understand what is the blessed and eternal nature.' With this may be set in comparison at once the statement of the scholiast on the first of the *Principal Doctrines*, which purports to record a saying of Epicurus himself and therefore, if correct, would represent an older tradition than Cicero's account: 'Epicurus says elsewhere that the gods are perceptible by thought, some

[1] Cic. *N. D.* i. 19. 49 'Epicurus ... docet eam esse vim et naturam deorum ut primum non sensu sed mente cernatur (cernantur *Schömann*), nec soliditate quadam nec ad numerum, ut ea quae ille propter firmitatem στερέμνια appellat, sed imaginibus similitudine et transitione perceptis, cum infinita simillimarum imaginum species (series *Brieger*) ex innumerabilibus individuis exsistat et ad deos (eos *codd.* nonnulli: nos *Lambinus*) adfluat, cum (tum *codd. duo*) maximis voluptatibus in eas imagines mentem intentam infixamque nostram intelligentiam capere quae sit et beata natura et aeterna'. The punctuation is uncertain and is varied by the editors according to their general view of the meaning.

[2] That *soliditate quadam* is not to be construed with *cernatur*, but regarded as a descriptive ablative with *eam esse vim et naturam* is proved by the parallel passage, i. 37, 105 'sic enim dicebas speciem dei percipi cogitatione non sensu, nec esse in ea ullam soliditatem, neque eandem ad numerum permanere, eamque esse eius visionem ut similitudine et transitione cernatur, neque deficiat unquam ex infinitis corporibus similium accessio'.

[3] Again the parallel passage quoted in the previous note shows that the ablative *imaginibus ... perceptis* is to be construed with *cernatur*, and not as a substantive description of the form of the gods.

[4] The word *transitione* must be translated literally if unintelligently for the moment: see below, p. 447.

of them existing in numerical identity, some in likeness of
form owing to the constant streaming up of similar "idols"
which are perfected at the same spot: they are of human form.'[1]

The preliminary statement that the nature of the gods is
perceived not by the senses but by the mind accords with
what has already been seen;[2] the gods are never seen by the
eyes as the result of an 'image' formed by a succession of
'idols', but by the mind which is visited by a series of single
'idols' which owing to its own subtlety it is able to apprehend.

The same idea is conveyed by the scholiast's statement that
the gods are 'perceptible by thought': it is a vague phrase,
traditional in the philosophers, and used by Epicurus[3] in
reference to the *minima* of time in which the atoms perform
their tiny trajects: its implication is that the gods are to be
ranked among the 'unseen things' ($\mathring{a}\delta\eta\lambda a$). The same idea
is brought out by Lucretius[4] in one of the few passages where
he has dealt with the nature of the gods: 'the fine nature of
the gods, far sundered from our senses, is scarcely seen by
the understanding of the mind'. The gods then cannot be
known by sense, but only by 'mental apprehension' ($\grave{\epsilon}\pi\iota\beta o\lambda\grave{\eta}$
$\tau\hat{\eta}s$ $\delta\iota avoias$), and it is worth noticing how strongly this idea
is emphasized by the phrase at the end, 'our mind and
intelligence straining fixedly': this is exactly the notion of
the 'attention of the mind', and it will be remembered that

---

[1] Ad *K.Δ.* i, D.L. x, § 139 ἐν ἄλλοις δέ φησι τοὺς θεοὺς λόγῳ θεωρητούς,
οὓς μὲν κατ' ἀριθμὸν ὑφεστῶτας, οὓς δὲ κατὰ ὁμοείδειαν ἐκ τῆς συνεχοῦς
ἐπιρρύσεως τῶν ὁμοίων εἰδώλων ἐπὶ τὸ αὐτὸ ἀποτετελεσμένων, ἀνθρωποειδεῖς.
οὓς μὲν ... οὓς δέ] οὐ μὲν ... ὡς δὲ Gassendi: οὐ μὲν ... γνωστοὺς δὲ
Schömann: οὐ μὲν ... οἴους δὲ Bignone ἀποτετελεσμένων] ἀποτετελε-
σμένους Kühn.
[2] See Chap. VIII, pp. 414–17.
[3] Ep. i, § 62 κατὰ τοὺς λόγῳ θεωρητοὺς χρόνους, cf. § 47 b: see Chap. V,
p. 329. R. Philippson (*Hermes*, 1916), who lays great stress on the inferences of
reason as to the gods, and holds the view that λόγος in Epicurus means 'reason'
in the strict sense (see Chap. VIII, p. 423, n. 3), takes the phrase to mean 'cognizable by reason'. But θεωρητούς would be strange in this sense: see Appendix VI.
[4] v. 148–9 tenvis enim natura deum longeque remota
sensibus ab nostris animi vix mente videtur.

it was largely to secure the reality of this direct cognizance of the gods that Epicurus' followers[1] raised the act of 'mental apprehension' to the level of a criterion of truth.

It will be convenient for the moment to pass over the next clause and come to that in which Cicero continues the explanation of the means by which the 'power and nature of the gods' is perceived by 'images apprehended by similarity and by passing'.[2] This is clearly a further description of the process of cognition. The 'images' will be the single 'idols' which enter the mind: these are apprehended according to Cicero 'by similarity and passing': what is the meaning of this strange phrase? The intention, no doubt, is to distinguish the mode by which direct knowledge of the gods is obtained on the one hand from normal sense-perception, on the other from other cases of 'mind-perception'. In sense-perception there is a succession of 'idols' which forms an 'image', no one 'idol' being perceived by itself, in 'mind-perception'[3] sometimes, as in the vision of a centaur or Scylla, a single 'idol' is perceived and nothing more, sometimes, as in the visions of sleep, a succession of single 'idols' separately perceived gives a shifting picture of a moving body. In the apprehension of the gods by the mind it is again a succession of single 'idols' which is perceived, but by their 'similarity' they give the impression not of a moving and changing object, but of a permanent 'form': as Lucretius[4] puts it with accuracy and brevity, 'their images came in constant stream and the form remained unchanged'. What of the other word (*transitione*) which for the moment has been translated 'by passing'? There are two possibilities

[1] D.L. x. 31 : see Chap. II, p. 251; Chap. VIII, p. 417.

[2] Philippson (l.c.) has shown the importance of trying to retranslate Cicero's phrases into the Greek from which he borrowed them. I take it that this phrase ran ἀλλὰ εἰδώλοις ὁμοιότητι καὶ . . . κατειλημμένοις, the missing word being either μεταβάσει or ὑπερβάσει: see the subsequent discussion. For Philippson's own view that the phrase was μεταβάσει καθ' ὁμοιότητα see Appendix VI.

[3] See Chap. VIII, p. 414.

[4] v. 1175–6   semper eorum
        suppeditabatur facies et forma manebat.

as to its meaning. It may, as Scott[1] and Giussani[2] interpret it, represent the 'flux' or 'succession' in which the single 'idols' come to the mind: the Greek word in Cicero's original would then probably be μετάβασις,[3] which is used by Epicurus[4] in the section concerning the *minimae partes* of the atom for the process of 'passing' or 'progression' from one part of a thing to another, a sense quite consonant with that required here. In that case the whole phrase may be translated 'by images apprehended by their similarity and succession', or if we may suppose a hendiadys, 'apprehended by the succession of similars'.[5] The meaning then will be that the nature of the gods is perceived by means of 'images', i.e. forms apprehended by the similarity of the successive single 'idols'.[6] The process is not unlike both that of normal sense-perception, except that the 'idols' perceived separately are consciously put together into an 'image' by the mind, and that of the formation of a 'concept' (πρόληψις), except that there the 'images' combined are not all exactly alike, here the 'idols' are, so that they naturally fall into a single image. But it is also possible that *transitio* has a quite different sense. In Philodemus'[7] treatise 'On the gods' there is a passage in which he is apparently discussing the means by

---

[1] Op. cit., p. 219.   [2] l.c., p. 232.

[3] Scott suggests πόρεια, which is less probable.

[4] Ep. i, § 56 τὴν μετάβασιν . . . εἰς ἄπειρον: cf. § 58 τὸ τὰς μεταβάσεις ἔχον: and see Chap. III, pp. 285–7.

[5] Scott and Giussani, following Mayor, would like to take the meaning to be 'by the perception of a train of similar images'. Philippson rightly objects that this is not grammatically possible; Scott himself perceives this and supposes that Cicero not understanding his original purposely used a vague phrase. But it is surely possible to construe the words as they stand. Philippson agrees that *transitione* stands for μεταβάσει, but interprets it quite differently.

[6] This is exactly expressed in Cic. *N. D.* i. 39. 109 'fluentium frequenter transitio fit visionum, ut e multis una videatur'.

[7] col. 9. 20: see Diels, l.c., Part 6, p. 28 καὶ κατὰ [τὴ]ν ὑπ[έρ]βα[σιν οὐ]δὲ τῇ μεταξὺ <διασ>τάσει [πρ<οσ>αποδοτέον τὰς σ[υ]μπλοκάς, which Diels translates 'und bei dem Überspringen (der göttlichen Bilder von den Intermundien zu uns) darf man nicht auch noch dem Zwischenraum die Verflechtung (der Bilder) zuschreiben'. Cf. also, f. 118 (Gomperz, p. 134; Diels, l.c., p. 30 ἐξ ὑπερβά[σεως] τῶν μεταξύ.

which the 'idols' of the gods can pass from their remote abodes[1] in the *intermundia* to the human mind: if they have to pass first through great tracts of empty space and then through the clash and turmoil of the atomic world, they would be particularly liable to destruction or distortion. He therefore supposes that they have the power of 'passing over' (ὑπέρβασις) intervening space. It is just possible that *transitio* here may represent this idea, but less probable because the notion combines far less well with *similitudine* and there being no trace of it elsewhere, it looks as if both the problem and the solution were not traditional but had been raised by Philodemus himself; it would involve a certain arbitrariness, which is not likely to be due to Epicurus.

Having thus completed provisionally the account of the way in which the mind's cognition of the gods is accomplished, it is possible to go back to the intervening clause: the nature of the gods 'has not solidity, so to speak, or numerical identity, like those things which on account of their compactness he calls "solids"'.[2] The general sense is clear: the constitution of the bodies of the gods is not that of the ordinary objects of sense-perception, which are solid and have each of them a permanent material individuality. Just as the method of their cognition is different, so also is their physical constitution. But the detail of the description requires further consideration. In the first place 'there is not in it any solidity',[3] as Cotta says more explicitly in his reply; the body of the gods has not the 'compactness' (*firmitas*) of the solid bodies of sense-perception. So Lucretius[4] in speaking of the abodes of the gods says that they are 'fine in texture (*tenues*) even as are their bodies'. But a more definite conception of the Epicurean idea may be obtained from Cicero's sarcastic comments: 'the gods',[5] he

---

[1] See below, p. 467.

[2] This clause might tentatively be reconstructed in Greek οὐ στερεότητά τινα ἔχουσαν οὐδὲ κατ' ἀριθμὸν ὑφεστῶσαν, καθάπερ ἐκεῖνα ἃ διὰ τὴν πυκνότητα στερέμνια ὀνομάζει.

[3] 'nec esse in ea ullam soliditatem', Cic. *N. D.* i. 37. 105.

[4] v. 154.

[5] *N. D.* ii. 23. 59 'Epicurus monogrammos deos et nihil agentes commen-

says in ridicule, are 'mere outlines', they are 'like men at least in their outer lines'.[1] This appears to mean that the gods exist as an outline or form without the depth or solidity which characterizes solid objects: the nearest parallel would perhaps be that of the 'hollow forms'[2] of the 'idols', the mere external films of things, which possess no interior structure or solidness. Secondly, the gods do not exist as 'numerical identities'. What is the meaning of this phrase and to what is it opposed? It may safely be assumed that the words *nec ad numerum* are a translation of οὐδὲ κατ᾽ ἀριθμόν (the recurrence of the expression in the Diogenes scholiast guarantees this in spite of the difficulties which it raises), and that Epicurus was here following Aristotle who distinguished between things[3] which have a unity by way of numerical identity (κατ᾽ ἀριθμόν) and those which are one 'by way of identity of form' (κατ᾽ εἶδος). On the one hand there are things whose matter is permanent, e.g. a rock or any solid body (στερέμνιον), and on the other things whose component matter is always changing, but whose form remains constant, e.g. a flame, or a river, or a waterfall. The water composing the fall is shifting from instant to instant, but the whole retains an identity of form and by virtue of that identity remains the same fall. This seems exactly the idea

tus est', which is borne out by Dionysius Eus. *Praep. Ev.* xiv. 27, p. 783 κενὰς ἀνυποστάτων θεῶν τερατευσάμενος ἐζωγράφησε σκίας, U., p. 234 n.; R. Philippson (l.c., p. 596, n. 1) would take *monogrammos* in the sense which it bears in Lucilius (Nom. 37. 11) of 'a thin man', a 'skeleton', as we might say. But the parallel passages in *N. D.* quoted below seem to show unmistakably that Cicero was using the literal meaning.

[1] Cic. *N.D.* i. 44. 123 'neque enim tam desipiens fuisset ut homunculi similem deum fingeret, liniamentis dumtaxat extremis, non habitu solido'; cf. 27, 75 'cedo mihi istorum adumbratorum deorum liniamenta atque formas'; and 35, 98 'deum tamen nosse te dicis, modo liniamenta maneant'. U., p. 234 n.   [2] Cf. Chap. VIII, p. 408.

[3] *Metaphys.* Δ. 6. 1016b 32 τὰ μὲν κατ᾽ ἀριθμόν ἐστιν ἕν, τὰ δὲ κατ᾽ εἶδος ... ἀριθμῷ μὲν ὧν ἡ ὕλη μία, εἴδει δ᾽ ὧν ὁ λόγος εἷς: cf. ibid. *I.* 2. 1054 a 34, and other passages collected by Scott, p. 216. It is true that this distinction is not so marked in the atomic physics, for there even the hardest στερέμνιον is continually changing its matter by accretion and loss, but comparatively speaking the difference still holds good.

which the scholiast expresses when he says that (some of) the gods exist 'in likeness of form' (κατὰ ὁμοείδειαν). The gods are not like the solids of sense-perception which have a more or less permanent material identity, but their identity is secured, like that of the waterfall, by permanence of form though with a shifting material. This idea corresponds very well with that of the absence of solidity in the body of the gods: the permanent element in them is their form.

Why, if this account be true, did Epicurus adopt so singular a conception of the nature of the gods? It is obvious that his purpose was to find a solution of the main difficulty of combining atomic structure with immortality. No normal atomic compound can be imperishable, for sooner or later either a blow will cause its disruption or it will gradually cease to take in as much atomic material as it gives off and so decay. But it is possible to conceive of an imperishable form, provided that there is an everlasting supply of matter constantly flowing in to take the place of that which passes away. This appears to be exactly the conception which has now been reached: the gods, says Scott,[1] 'have not numerical or material but only formal identity; in other words, the matter of which they are composed, instead of remaining fixed and identically the same through a finite space of time, as is the case with visible and tangible objects, is perpetually passing away to be replaced by fresh matter, the *form* or *arrangement* of the matter alone remaining unchanged'. Now this description might be applied to the waterfall: but the waterfall, though its identity is 'formal', yet ultimately comes to an end, when the supply of water gives out. How then does Epicurus secure his gods from a similar failure of material? This can only be done if it can be made certain that the supply of appropriate material is inexhaustible. This Epicurus believed that he had assured by placing the abode of the gods in the *intermundia*,[2] the interspaces between the

---

[1] l.c., p. 214.

[2] Hipp. *Philos.* 22. 3, p. 572; U. 359; Cic. *de Div.* ii. 17. 40: see below, p. 467.

worlds. Within any one of the worlds the amount of material is limited: there is only a certain number of atoms of any given kind able to form and maintain any particular object or class of objects. But in the 'interspaces' there is no such limitation, but atoms of all shapes are everlastingly streaming and moving in all directions throughout the universe and the matter requisite for the constitution of the divine form will for ever be at hand, coming from 'innumerable atoms'[1] (*ex innumerabilibus individuis*). This contention Epicurus supports,[2] as will be seen later by the application of his principle of 'equilibrium' (ἰσονομία): if within the worlds the forces of destruction prevail, then in the *intermundia* the forces of creation and preservation must prevail. In short, the gods are immortal because they are 'identities in form' with the certainty of an everlasting supply of matter to constitute that form.

Lucretius in an interesting passage which is twice repeated in the poem,[3] enumerates various conditions which may secure eternity. Though he is not thinking of the gods, but is testing the claims first of the human soul and secondly of our world to immortality, it is a useful experiment to apply his test to the present conception of the gods. Things are immortal, he says, either because their body is absolutely solid and can repel all blows, like the atoms, or because it cannot suffer at all from blows, like the void, or because there is no space outside it into which matter can recede from it, as is the case with the universe, the sum total of atoms and void. If the immortality of the gods is to be accounted for under any of these heads, it is clear that it must be the second: it resembles the void in not feeling blows, not because blows do not come to it, but because the continual arrival of external atoms which cause the blows is itself the very condition of the permanence of existence: the atoms of the right kind are taken up to form the momentary image, those of other kinds pass through the fine texture without hurt. The divine being would thus be immortal

[1] l.c., Cic. *N. D.* i. 19. 49.   [2] pp. 461 ff.
[3] iii. 806–18; v. 351–63.

for the very reasons for which Lucretius[1] denies immortality to the soul, 'because things harmful to its life come not at all, or because such as come in some way depart defeated before it can feel what harm they do'.

But this is not a very satisfactory result and there is some evidence to show that Epicurus conceived of a fourth class of immortal beings, which he described as 'similarities' (ὁμοιότητες). In a remarkable passage of Aetius,[2] after stating Epicurus' view that the gods were immortal and perceptible by the mind, the writer continues: 'the same philosopher says elsewhere that there are four existences immortal in their kinds, namely, the atoms, the void, the universe, the "similarities"'. Now, if, as seems clear, the bodies of the gods are indicated under the last head, there is here a new reason for supposing their indestructibility. The notion is supported by a passage in Philodemus,[3] which undoubtedly refers to the gods: 'It is possible for beings constituted by a "similarity" to have perfect happiness for ever, since bodies with permanent identity (ἑνότητες) may be produced by

[1] iii. 821–3.
[2] Aet. i. 7. 34 (=Plut. *Plac.* i. 7. 15; Stob. *Ecl.* ii. 29) Ἐπίκουρος ἀνθρωποειδεῖς μὲν πάντας τοὺς θεούς, λόγῳ δὲ πάντας θεωρητοὺς διὰ τὴν λεπτομέρειαν τῆς τῶν εἰδώλων φύσεως. ὁ δ' αὐτὸς ἄλλας (ἄλλως, Gassendi, Scott, Giussani, after some manuscripts) τέσσαρας φύσεις κατὰ γένος ἀφθάρτους τάσδε, τὰ ἄτομα, τὸ κενόν, τὸ ἄπειρον, τὰς ὁμοιότητας· αὗται δὲ λέγονται ὁμοιομέρειαι καὶ στοιχεῖα. Bignone (*Bollettino di Fil. Class.* xvii, 1910–11, pp. 135 ff.) argues for the retention of the reading ἄλλας and maintains that the ὁμοιότητες are 'species', which are 'uguaglianze formali degli atomi delle diverse forme', under which the gods might be subsumed. But this contention seems to me forced and I prefer to follow most recent critics in reading ἄλλως. In either case the general argument will not be affected, as the gods will be an example of ὁμοιότητες, if not the only example.
[3] περὶ εὐσεβ, col. 83 (Gomperz, *Herc. Stud.*, p. 110) δύναται γὰρ ἐκ τῆς ὁμοιότητος ὑπάρχουσι (ὑπάρχουσα, Gomperz) διαιώνιον ἔχειν τὴν τελείαν εὐδαιμονίαν, ἐπειδήπερ οὐχ ἧττον ἐκ τῶν αὐτῶν ἢ τῶν ὁμοίων στοιχείων ἑνότητες ἀποτελεῖσθαι (Gomperz ὑποτελεῖσθαι pap.) δύνανται. Bignone (l.c., p. 136, n.2) has shown that it is unnecessary to read ὑπάρχουσα. It is unnecessary to transpose αὐτῶν and ὁμοίων (Scott, p. 232) or to read μᾶλλον for ἧττον (R. Philippson, op. cit., p. 592, n. 1): the emphasis of a comparison often falls on the second member.

elements which are alike just as much as by those which are the same.' Endeavours[1] have been made to find support for this idea in other passages of Philodemus, but the text is so corrupt that it is hardly safe to rely on possible restorations. Still less, as will be seen,[2] can support be derived from the Diogenes scholiast or the main passage in the *de Natura Deorum*. But it is clear that Epicurus had the notion of a 'unity of similars' and that he almost certainly so regarded the gods. A 'unity of similars' is set in opposition to a 'unity of the same', of which the sole example is the atom, composed of inseparable parts which can never be removed or altered, and therefore immortal. All the normal objects of sense-perception are unities of shifting material of many kinds, and it is just the existence of alien matter in them which causes decay and ultimate destruction. The gods too are constituted of shifting matter, but the matter is always 'similar' and there never enters into their composition the alien and fatal elements. If it be asked what exactly is meant by 'similar', it is not possible to give a definite answer. Schömann[3] boldly states that the meaning is 'round atoms', of which the gods, like fire and the soul, are entirely composed: but there is no evidence for this, and it is better to leave the idea vague: the bodies of the gods are composed wholly of one kind of material and that entirely akin to them: they are therefore exempt from internal disruption, just as they are secured externally by the infinite supply of appropriate matter. The argument is not perhaps a very strong one, but there seems little doubt that it was used by Epicureans, if not by Epicurus himself.

The conception so far reached of the constitution of the bodies of the gods is that they are permanent in form, but not in matter: the matter which from time to time makes the form is always 'similar' in character and therefore not liable to internal decay or disruption, and the supply of this

---

[1] By R. Philippson (l.c., pp. 589 ff.), e.g. περὶ εὐσεβ, col. 83 (Gomperz, p. 113), col. 118.

[2] See below, p. 456.

[3] Opusc. iv, p. 357, but see Appendix VI.

matter in the *intermundia*, where there is no limit to the
number of atoms of all sorts and the forces of creation prevail
over those of destruction, is unlimited. Can this conception
be brought into relation with the notion already formed of
the means of cognition of the gods? We have our 'mental
apprehension' of the gods by means of a succession of
similar 'idols' entering our mind and there building up an
'image', much as the 'images' of normal sense-perception
build up a concept. But what in effect are these 'idols'?
A normal solid body sends off as its 'idol' the outer atomic
'film' or 'skin': but the body of a god is *ex hypothesi* not solid
but mere 'form'. The successive 'idols' then which come
to our minds are in effect the successive atomic constituents
of the 'form': the 'like' atoms rush in from all parts of the
universe, constitute for a moment the body of the god, and
then pass away as the 'idol ': their place is instantaneously
taken by a fresh supply of atoms from the *intermundia* and
the process continues for ever. This is in effect the Scott-
Giussani theory,[1] and though it has been greatly ridiculed,[2]
it is hard to find any other view consistent with the evidence
—certainly no satisfactory explanation has yet been propounded.

But before this theory can be accepted there remain two
serious difficulties which must be carefully considered.
Firstly there is the following clause in the Cicero passage
provisionally translated: 'since infinite forms of most similar
images arise from innumerable atoms and stream to the
gods',[3] which must be compared with the parallel expression
in the Diogenes' scholiast 'owing to the constant streaming
up of similar "idols", which are perfected at the same spot'.[4]

---

[1] I have purposely endeavoured to use a different line of investigation from
theirs, but find myself forced to the same general conclusion.

[2] e.g. by Masson (op. cit.), pp. 279 ff.; and *Class. Rev.* xvi, p. 277.
R. Philippson also rejects it in certain details and Diels (op. cit., p. 29, n. 3)
in one particular: see below, p. 458, n. 1.

[3] 'cum infinita simillorum imaginum species (series *Brieger*) ex innumerabilibus individuis exsistat et ad deos (eos *codd. nonnulli* : nos *Lambinus*) adfluat.

[4] ἐκ τῆς συνεχοῦς ἐπιρρύσεως τῶν ὁμοίων εἰδώλων ἐπὶ τὸ αὐτὸ ἀποτετελεσμένων.

These clauses raise a problem of which three main solutions might be offered.[1]

Firstly it might be supposed that the clauses are intended to describe not the formation of the body of the gods, but the passing of the 'idols' from their bodies into our minds. This at first sight seems the most natural interpretation on account of the occurrence of the words 'idols' and 'images' in both the passages, and it might be supposed that Cicero is referring to this clause when later on he says 'a passing of a flux of images frequently takes place'.[2] A good general sense can thus be obtained: 'there is a constant flow of similar images from the bodies of the gods to our minds'. But in order to get this sense the Cicero passage[3] must be emended and an unnatural interpretation given to the scholium.[4]

Secondly, the Cicero clause might be taken to refer to the constitution of the gods 'out of similars'.[5] This might seem to be supported by the later statement[6] which does undoubtedly refer to this clause: 'there never fails an accession of similars from an infinite number of bodies (sc. atoms)'.

[1] The weakness of Scott's exposition—and in some respects of Giussani's—is that he does not perceive the difficulties and is apt to confuse the process of the formation of the bodies of the gods with that of the progress of the 'idols' to the mind. Thus here, though he takes the Cicero clause to refer to the former, he quotes as parallel to it N. D. i. 39. 109 'fluentium frequenter transitio fit visionum, ut e multis una videatur', which clearly describes the creation of the image in the mind, and 'finds no difficulty in it'. Philippson takes the Diogenes clause to refer to the process of cognition, the Cicero passage to the formation of the gods: but they cannot be separated.

[2] N. D. i. 39. 109, quoted in the previous note.

[3] ad nos must be read for ad deos and probably series for species: the latter is in any case to my mind almost necessary.

[4] Unless with Philippson ὁμοείδειαν is taken to refer not to the constitution of the gods, but to the similarity of the 'idols', it would be necessary to bracket οὓς μὲν to ὁμοείδειαν and take ἐκ τῆς συνεχοῦς ἐπιρρύσεως with θεωρητέον. But (a) ἐκ is not then the natural preposition, and (b) it is almost impossible to make sense of ἐπὶ τὸ αὐτὸ ἀποτετελεσμένων. Neither of Philippson's proposed renderings (p. 581), 'die zu demselben Ergebnis führen' and 'die in derselben Weise gestalten sind', seem to me possible.

[5] See p. 453, above.

[6] i. 37. 105 'Neque deficiat unquam ex infinitis corporibus similium accessio'.

But it involves still greater tampering with the text of Cicero [1] in order to get rid of the idea of the flux of 'images', and against it is the corresponding reference to 'idols' by the scholiast.

Thirdly, the plain meaning of the Cicero passage as it stands is this: 'infinite forms (or if we may accept the emendation *series*, which though not absolutely necessary, is a great improvement, "an infinite succession") of similar images arise from innumerable atoms [2] and stream to the gods',[3] and the scholiast says correspondingly 'owing to the constant streaming up of similar "idols" which are perfected at the same spot'. Now if the account given of the constitution of the body of the gods is correct, the 'form' of which it at any moment consists is in fact what will subsequently become an 'idol', and it is not impossible that the successive atomic formations which constitute the 'form' from moment to moment should be spoken of proleptically as 'images' or 'idols'. But the Cicero clause seems to go beyond this and to suggest that the 'images' come to the gods, so to speak, 'ready-made', that they are formed in space before they enter the divine form. This conclusion was accepted by Scott[4] who says: 'they (the gods) are formed by perpetual successions of "images" or material films, of precisely similar form, which having arisen (in some unexplained way) out of the infinite atoms dispersed throughout the universe, stream to a sort of focus, and there, by their meeting, constitute for a moment the being of the gods'. The words in brackets suggest a sense of difficulty and the extreme

---

[1] Philippson (p. 604) supposes that *imaginum* is a gloss and would substitute *rerum*; Diels (p. 29, n. 3) applauds the suggestion and seeing no reason for the superlative *simillimarum* would prefer to read *similium rerum*. In any case *rerum* is a very strange word and Cicero would naturally have expressed what Philippson and Diels wish him to mean by *similium corporum* or *similis materiae*.

[2] *individuis* is Cicero's regular word for 'atoms'; Zeller's translation (*Stoics and Epicureans*, p. 466 n.) 'from innumerable (divine) individuals' is an amusing mistake, which has been corrected by all subsequent critics.

[3] The manuscripts vary between *ad deos* and *ad eos* which would have the same sense: there is no authority for Lambinus' *ad nos*.   [4] l.c., p. 214.

arbitrariness of this notion has been seized on as an absurdity by the critics of his theory.[1] Dr. Masson asks pertinently, 'if the divine images arise in some "unexplained way" from the atoms, why should they not flow directly into our minds? why assume at all that they first meet together and form divine bodies? On this theory the images cease to be a proof that gods exist'. And indeed if this 'pre-formation' of the images must be accepted as a necessary part of the theory, it would certainly constitute a serious weakness in the whole conception.

One is loth to suggest, as is done so recklessly by those who support other views,[2] that Cicero has reported Epicurus wrongly, and the suggestion should not be made unless there is good authority by which to correct him. This authority seems to be supplied here by the scholiast, if his words are rightly interpreted: the gods, he says, have likeness of form 'owing to the constant streaming up of similar idols *which are perfected at the same spot*'.[3] The images, that is to say, are not images until they are perfected as such, as the atoms converge on one place. Infinite atoms of the right kind (ὅμοια) are always streaming together from all quarters of the universe to the spot in which the gods have their 'formal' existence. At every moment a sufficient number of them to constitute a material film unites within the 'form' and for that moment constitutes it: they instantaneously leave it, not now in the independence in which they arrived, but united as an 'idol'; and the 'idol', not now living but inanimate, flies off to become in the mind of men an 'image' of the divine form. The instant that one image has fled, another is formed to take its place out of the confluent atoms. This is the natural interpretation of the scholiast's text and it gives an exact parallel to terrestrial things which have an

---

[1] Masson, *Lucretius*, p. 279; Philippson, l.c., p. 604; Diels, l.c., p. 29, n. 3.

[2] See Appendix VI.

[3] This seems to me the natural meaning of the words ἐπὶ τὸ αὐτὸ ἀποτε-τελεσμένων. Scott (p. 219) translates 'the continual streaming up of like images wrought into one and the same object', and explains 'streams or trains of like images directed to a common point', viz. the point where the gods are.

identity of form: the innumerable atoms are as the innumerable drops of water flowing together from many sources to constitute momentarily the being of the waterfall. Moreover this interpretation is strongly confirmed by a later passage[1] in Cicero's dialogue, where Cotta asks critically: 'why is an Epicurean god not in fear of destruction, seeing that he is beaten upon without a moment's cessation and harried by the everlasting inrush of atoms, and "images", are for ever streaming from him?' This is exactly the thought: it is the *atoms* which rush in to the form of the god, but they leave unified as an *image*: on the other hand this passage is quite inconsistent with the idea of 'pre-formed' images. On the strength then of his own later statement and that of the scholiast on Diogenes Cicero may fairly be convicted of an inaccuracy due to brevity of expression: he ought rather to have said: 'an infinite succession of similar images is formed out of innumerable atoms, which flow together to make in successive instants the forms of the gods'. If this assumption may be made—and there seems good reason for making it—the most serious obstacle to the whole theory disappears. It remains, no doubt, improbable and fantastic, but it is, as with many of Epicurus' strangest notions, the result of a logical following out of his ideas in the pursuit of an end—here the explanation of the existence of gods, immortal but of atomic construction.

The second problem arises out of a notable contradiction in our two main authorities, which cannot be passed over. Cicero states in effect that the gods have not 'numerical', but only 'formal' identity; the scholiast on Diogenes asserts more definitely that Epicurus said that there were two classes of gods, some with 'numerical', others with 'formal' identity. How can these statements be reconciled? Two eminent critics,[2] taking the scholiast at his word, have supposed that Epicurus had two doctrines, one esoteric, one popular

---

[1] *N. D.* i. 41. 114; U., p. 235 n. 'nec video quo modo non vereatur iste deus beatus ne intereat, cum sine ulla intermissione pulsetur agiteturque atomorum incursione sempiterna, cumque ex ipso imagines semper afluant'.

[2] Hirzel and Mayor: see Appendix VI.

(incidentally they disagree as to which was which), and that Cicero has become confused between the two. But the majority of recent writers agree in thinking it impossible that Epicurus can have admitted a class of gods with 'numerical' identity, or that he ever taught that doctrine either popularly or to his own disciples. Some have in consequence attempted to get rid of the contradiction by emendation,[1] Scott[2] and Giussani suppose that the statement of the compiler was due to some misunderstanding of the passage which he was reporting, while Philippson[3] working the passage out on his own theory would assign a strange and unusual meaning to the contrast. It is however doubtful whether the statement can be so easily explained away: it is singularly explicit and the introduction of the words with the formula 'he says elsewhere' looks as if the commentator were making an actual quotation from Epicurus. Diels[4] too has pointed out that there are passages in Philodemus which seem to lend support to the view that Epicurus did in fact conceive of a class of gods who existed 'by numerical identity'. A passage[5] for instance in the treatise 'On Piety' would run, if it has been correctly emended: 'he says that the constitution of the gods, at least of those who have numerical identity, is not only deathless but everlasting'. Diels himself is inclined to

---

[1] οὐ μὲν κατ' ἀριθμὸν ὑφεστῶτας, ὡς δὲ κατὰ ὁμοείδειαν was the original suggestion of Gassendi: Schömann (l.c., p. 356) accepting οὐ μὲν proposed γνωστοὺς δέ, a most improbable correction, which would change the second clause into an account of the perception of the 'idols', Bignone (p. 55, n. 2) would prefer the more modest change οἵους δέ. But οὐ μὲν is very unusual Greek and the opposition οὖς μὲν . . . οὖς δέ does not look like the result of a corruption. In a note on K. Δ. 1, in my edition of Epicurus, I was inclined to accept emendation, but now regard it as unsatisfactory.

[2] Scott, p. 221; Giussani, p. 234.

[3] 'partly . . . partly', p. 580: see Appendix VI.

[4] Op. cit., pp. 29 ff.

[5] See Körte, Metrodori Epicurei Fragmenta, p. 543, where he reads φησὶν θεῶν σύγκρισιν τῶν γε κατ' ἀριθμὸν οὐ μόνον ἄφθαρτον ἀλλὰ καὶ ἀΐδιαν, but the text as given by Gomperz (Herc. Stud. 132, p. 138) runs φησὶν [. . . . σύγ]κρίσιν τῶν [. κατ' ἀ]ριθμὸν οὐ μόν[ον ἄφ]θαρτον ἀλλὰ [. . .]αν shows that the restoration is at best doubtful. Scott (p. 237) would read τῶν μὴ κατ' ἀριθμόν.

believe that the gods which existed in 'numerical identity' were in fact the 'star-gods' (Gestirngötter), Helios, Selene, &c., of popular belief, which were admitted by the Epicurean alongside the more philosophically conceived gods of their own system. This may have been good doctrine in the Herculanean villa of Philodemus, but it certainly was not in Epicurus' garden. On the whole the question must be left in doubt, but if Epicurus did in fact admit gods with 'numerical identity', we have no information at all how he conceived them nor how he reconciled the idea of a 'solid' god with the requirement of immortality. All that our information enables us to do is to reconstruct with pain and difficulty, as has been seen, the conception of the gods who existed 'by likeness of form'.

To complete this account of the Epicurean view of the nature of the gods one more argument adduced by Cicero for their existence and immortality must be considered.

To the *a posteriori* evidence of the universal concept in the mind of man, Cicero's Epicurean Velleius adds with regrettable brevity an *a priori* argument. 'Mighty [1] is the power of infinity and most worthy of long and earnest consideration, for we must realize that its nature is such that all things are equal in number and correspond among themselves. This principle Epicurus calls "isonomia", that is to say, "equal distribution". From it follow the results that if there is so great a number of mortal things, there must be no less a number of immortal, and if the forces which destroy are innumerable, the forces which preserve ought also to be infinite.' The critics [2] who all through think lightly of the

---

[1] Cic. *N. D.* i. 19. 50 'Summa vero vis infinitatis et magna ac diligenti contemplatione dignissima est, in qua intelligi necesse est eam esse naturam, ut omnia omnibus paribus paria respondeant. Hanc ἰσονομίαν appellat Epicurus, id est aequabilem tributionem. Ex hac igitur illud efficitur, si mortalium tanta multitudo sit, esse immortalium non minorem, et si quae interimant innumerabilia sint, etiam ea quae conservent infinita esse debere'.

[2] So Mayor (ad loc.) speaks of ἰσονομία as 'the card-castle of the Epicurean philosophy', and Masson (op. cit., p. 277) exclaims contemptuously, 'An infinite number of Gods is, no doubt, a doctrine repellent to reason, but what is reason compared with logic, or even with the semblance of logic?'

value of this passage of Cicero and are content to regard Epicurus as a shallow thinker, take this to be a merely arbitrary puerility intended to back up the previous unsatisfactory explanation of the nature of the gods. On the other hand Scott[1] and Giussani,[2] who are prepared to regard Velleius' argument as a serious, if somewhat confused, account of a subtle piece of reasoning on the part of a penetrating thinker, have, in attempting to work out the Epicurean argument at length, ascribed to it a profundity and ingenuity greater than there is any warrant for assuming. An attempt may be made with such help as can be obtained from other sources to see at least how Cicero—or his Epicurean authority—intended the argument to hang together without yielding to the temptation of introducing over-refined speculations. Unfortunately, there is no other explicit reference to the doctrine in connexion with the gods, except in Cotta's[3] criticism later on in the dialogue which only repeats the argument, but there are at least three—and probably more—passages in Lucretius,[4] where the idea of 'isonomia' is prominent in other contexts, and these throw much light on the missing links in Velleius' summary.

The nexus of the argument is clear enough: 'isonomia' is the direct result of infinity: from 'isonomia' follow two results, the equality of the numbers of things in opposite classes and the equality of the forces of disintegration and conservation; and both these deductions point in their turn to the existence of immortal beings. Can this argument be reduced to terms of Epicurean atomism? Infinity for Epicurus means the existence of a boundless universe, which consists of an infinite number of atoms moving in space infinite in extent. Now in the first place, these atoms[5] are of a limited number of different shapes, but there is an infinite number of atoms of each shape. Thus any given combination

---

[1] pp. 222–5.   [2] pp. 245–58, 262–3.   [3] i. 39. 109.

[4] Giussani (p. 246) is right in excluding from Reisacker's list (*Quaestiones Lucretianae*), ii. 1112 ff., and v. 392 ff. He would himself add ii. 1084–9, where the argument, though in a different context, resembles that of ii. 532 ff.

[5] See Chap. III, p. 288.

of shapes will occur an equal number of times: for there is nothing to cause the more frequent production of one combination rather than another. But any particular combination of atomic shapes produces a particular species of thing. Two results follow: firstly, there will at any given time be equal numbers of things of each different species. This is Lucretius' argument in the passage[1] in the Second Book, where he maintains that there is this 'equal distribution' of animals of different species: though the elephant, for example, is rare with us, he is plentiful in India. Secondly, it also follows that any given species of things will be produced in equal numbers at all times: so Lucretius argues earlier in the same Book[2] that 'such things as have been wont to come to being will be brought to birth under the same law, will exist and grow and be strong and lusty, inasmuch as is granted to each by the ordinances of nature'. It is moreover this same idea, as Giussani[3] points out, which is really at the bottom of Epicurus' principle[4] with regard to celestial phenomena that any cause which can produce the phenomenon must be a real cause and be at work somewhere,[5] even though it is not active in our world. But there is further an 'equal distribution' not only of atomic shapes but also of atomic movements: from this follows that the movements which tend to atomic combination, the movements of creation, will be equally balanced by those which lead to atomic dissolution, the movements of destruction. On this principle again Lucretius[6] insists in a short, but impressive passage: 'And so, neither can the motions of destruction prevail for ever, and bury life in an eternal tomb, nor yet can the motions of creation and increase for ever bring things to birth and preserve them. So war waged from time everlasting is carried on by the balanced strife of the first-beginnings. Now here, now there, the vital forces of things conquer and are conquered alike.'

These principles must now be applied to the problem of

[1] 532–40.
[2] 300–2.
[3] p. 249.
[4] See Chap. II, p. 261.
[5] See especially Lucr. v. 526–33.
[6] ii. 569–76.

the existence of immortal gods. From the equality of the numbers of things of *different* species, it is an easy—indeed, for the mind of antiquity,[1] almost an inevitable—step to the equality of numbers in *opposite* species. It may then be argued directly that if there is created a vast number of beings liable to death, there must be an equally large number of beings exempt from death. In other words the number of mortal beings in the world must be balanced by the number of immortal gods outside it. Velleius' second argument is less satisfactory. It will be noticed that his principle differs from that of Lucretius in that, while Lucretius speaks of the forces of creation, which is the natural contrast to the forces of destruction, Velleius speaks of the forces of preservation. This is not a legitimate opposition and seems like a slight distortion of the natural deduction from the infinity of atomic movements made to suit the purposes of the particular case.[2] There is a further difficulty in the argument in that in fact both the forces of increase and the forces of decay are alike at work *in the mortal world*, for things are produced and brought to maturity before the work of destruction begins.[3] It is therefore false to oppose the two forces as Velleius does, as though the movements of destruction alone worked in our world and therefore it must be supposed that elsewhere there are movements of preservation. But, though this difficulty[4] may be got over by a more subtle analysis of

---

[1] See Giussani, l.c., p. 251.

[2] It may be observed however that Lucretius in ii. 571–2 seems to make a similar confusion between increase and preservation: 'nec porro rerum genitales auctificique motus perpetuo possunt *servare* creata', and indeed preservation is of course a continued increase compensating loss.

[3] Cf. Lucr. ii. 1105 ff.

[4] This difficulty is perceived by Mayor (notes on Cic. *N. D.* 19. 50), who, as I think, rightly interprets the argument of Velleius, but in his sarcastic criticism does injustice to the Epicurean system as a whole, and greatly misunderstands the idea of the *intermundia*, which are certainly not places 'sacred from the intrusion of atoms'. Scott and Giussani are naturally troubled by the insufficiency of the contention as it stands and attempt to fill it in more subtly. Scott's argument (p. 223) is very ingenious and completely in accord with Epicurean principles: 'The processes of growth and decay, of combination and dissolution, may either prevail *alternately* in each individual

Epicurean possibilities, there is surely little doubt that Cicero—and probably his Epicurean authority—intended object, so that the result on the whole will be a perpetual decay of existing things, accompanied by a perpetual growth of fresh things in their place: or the two processes may go on *simultaneously* in a given object, so as to produce an equilibrium, the result of which will be *eternal duration*. Consequently (to apply the principle of ἰσονομία once more) if we take an infinite number of cases (that is, if we consider the whole universe) the *alternate* and the *simultaneous* action of the two processes must go on *to an equal extent*. Now in our world (and, by analogy, in *all* the worlds) the *first* alternative is that which universally prevails; that is, the motions of growth and of decay operate *alternately*, both on the world as a whole, and (at shorter intervals) on each individual within it, thus producing universal death and universal birth. Hence, *outside* the worlds, or in the *intermundia*, room must be found for the *other* alternative; that is, the 'motus auctifici' and the 'motus exitiales' must there work *simultaneously*, and instead of producing successions of different beings must result in the immortality of such beings as exist.' The contention is admirable and might well have been used by an Epicurean who had learnt ταῖς ἐπιβολαῖς ὀξέως δύνασθαι χρῆσθαι, but there is no trace that either Epicurus or his followers employed it, certainly not in the text of Cicero, where the argument is clearly cruder and less complete.

Giussani's explanation (pp. 252–8) is still more subtle, and (if I apprehend it rightly) runs as follows: 'Epicurus regards ἰσονομία as a balance of opposites. It was not invented to support his theology, but if the conditions for the creation of immortal beings are possible, it applies automatically. How then did Epicurus come to think out the physical existence of gods as described? (a) By ἰσονομία all species are eternal, but not all individuals, owing to lack of the persistence of matter. But there are grades in such persistence: for there is also the substitution of new matter. Reintegration thus occurs to some extent in all bodies, but especially in organic and particularly in animal bodies. Why then must animals die? Because after their period of growth they cannot assimilate enough new matter to repair their losses (Lucr. ii. 1105 ff.). Epicurus then conceived the gods as beings in whom there was a continuous change of matter and always assimilation of exactly as much as was lost. (b) Moreover animals, &c., apart from natural decay, are liable to death from external causes, such as disease or blows, and even if the balance of loss and accretion were perfect, must in time so perish. This liability is due to the temporary persistence of matter in their bodies. The gods then must have absolute non-persistence of matter, which incidentally also secures them against the first danger from overgrowth. Again we have the analogy of flames, rivers, waterfalls, and the sun: yet even the sun must one day be extinguished from loss of matter. There are thus innumerable grades in the persistence of matter between the two extremes which are the two forms of eternity, (1) absolute persistence of matter—the atoms, (2) absolute non-persistence of matter, but only persistence of form—the gods. Granted in this way the possibility of the argument to run as it stands: in our world the forces of destruction prevail and beings are mortal, therefore elsewhere the forces of conservation must prevail and beings must be immortal. No greater subtlety than this is warranted by the text and the same *naïveté* in the application of the principle of 'isonomia' is again seen in Cotta's [1] criticism, which is thrown into the form of an imaginary dialogue between himself and Velleius: ' "How do you prove that the succession of images is continuous? or if it is, how are they eternal?" "There is, you answer, an infinite supply of atoms." "Will not that same cause make all things eternal?" At this point you take refuge in your "equilibrium"—for so we will call your "isonomia", if you like—and you say, since there is a mortal nature, there must also be an immortal.' The thought here is simple: one might expect from the infinity of atoms and therefore from the limitless supply of material that all things would be immortal, but this cannot be the case because there must be this balance between things mortal and immortal, between the forces of destruction and conservation. The principle of 'isonomia' then, acting in

conditions in which the forces of conservation prevail over those of destruction, then by ἰσονομία, i.e. the equilibrium of the forces of conservation and destruction, which is secured by the infinity of atomic movements, the number of mortals and immortals must be equal.' This argument, in spite of its excessive subtlety, seems to me to have more warrant in Epicurean theory than that of Scott: but, though it may be accepted as representing more or less the process by which Epicurus reached—or might have reached—his conception of divine beings, all it proves is that, granted the existence of such immortal beings, then by ἰσονομία they will be equal in number to mortal beings. Velleius surely intended ἰσονομία to prove also the *existence* of the gods.

Masson, in a review (*Class. Rev.* xvi. 453–9) of the essays of Scott and Giussani, rebukes them for over-refinement and ridicules their theories, but makes no attempt to explain the idea of ἰσονομία and its application here, except as an arbitrary assumption (see also *Lucretius, Epicurean and Poet*, p. 277). I hope I have shown in the text that a middle course is possible, that, though there are gaps and flaws in Velleius' exposition of the argument, the principle of ἰσονομία is a direct outcome, as he maintains, of Epicurus' conception of infinity, and may be used in the two distinct ways he suggests without unreasonable distortion, to prove the existence and countless number, of the gods.   [1] *N. D.* i. 39. 109.

two ways, through the infinite number of atoms and their infinite movements, forces the conclusion that there do exist immortal beings, or in other words, gods.

The result of this long discussion may be summed up as follows: There do exist divine beings or gods: they are innumerable as are the created things which perish and immortal even as created things are mortal. They are, as is proved by their 'idols' which visit us, like in figure to men. In constitution they are eternal in form but composed of transient matter: this matter, which is all 'alike' and contains no alien elements, comes from the innumerable atoms moving in the void between the worlds: in everlasting succession the atoms stream into the 'forms' of the divine beings and unite there for the moment to constitute their body. Then they fly off again in the union in which they have now joined, thus forming the continuous succession of like 'idols', which are perceived by the mind and are our direct source of knowledge of the existence of the gods.

It remains to inquire how the life of the gods may be conceived and what is its place in the Epicurean system. The inquiry is not without its own difficulties, but the ground is firmer than in the previous discussion as to the nature of the gods. Epicurus placed the abode of the gods in the 'interspaces between the words'.[1] The worlds, it must be remembered, were to Epicurus portions, as it were, of infinite space in which atoms gathering together had fallen 'into such dispositions as those whereby our world of things is created and holds together'.[2] Although such worlds are innumerable,[3] yet space is infinite and between the worlds are left large tracts where the atoms have not developed those motions which cause mundane phenomena, 'peaceful abodes, which neither the winds shake nor clouds soak with showers, nor does the snow congealed with biting frost besmirch them with its white fall, but an ever cloudless sky

---

[1] Hipp. *Philos.* 22, 3; U. 359 καθῆσθαι γὰρ τὸν θεὸν ἐν τοῖς μετακοσμίοις οὕτω καλουμένοις ὑπ' αὐτοῦ; for *intermundia* see Cic. *N. D.* i. 8. 18; *de Fin.* ii. 23. 75; *de Div.* ii. 17. 40; and Lucr. iii. 18–24.

[2] Lucr. i. 1027, 8.   [3] Ep. i, § 45.

vaults them over, and smiles with light bounteously spread abroad'.[1] There the gods dwelt in peace in 'abodes, fine even as are their bodies'.[2] The reasons for this apparently strange belief were numerous. The moral theory was not without influence: for the gods in the *intermundia* could live the life of perfect happiness, which was to be man's example, without being troubled by mundane affairs, and man might strive to imitate them on earth with the security that there was no divine power in terrestrial phenomena which might wreck his plans. But there was also a strong reason for the belief on the side of the physical theory as well. The gods lived in the *intermundia* 'through fear of destruction', as Cicero[3] says ironically, and this may be interpreted seriously to mean not merely that they were there safe from the shocks of mundane occurrences[4] and above all from the occasional catastrophe of the breaking up of a world, but also that they could have no fear of decay for lack of the supply of material: in a world this supply is limited, but 'between the worlds' the flow of the infinite atoms is ceaseless.[5]

That the gods were of human form was directly guaranteed by the images[6] which so presented them to man, but Velleius also advances reasons for the belief: since the gods are happy and eternal, they must also have the most beautiful form, and it is impossible that there should be 'a disposition of limbs,[7] a configuration of outlines, a general shape or appearance more beautiful than that of man'. The anthropomorphic idea being once accepted, it was impossible, even

---

[1] Lucr. iii. 18–22.   [2] Lucr. v. 154.

[3] *de Div.* ii. 17. 40.

[4] For this primary idea see Seneca, *de Beneficiis*, iv. 4. 19; U. 364 'ruinas mundorum supra se circaque se cadentium evitat' (*sc. deus*).

[5] A serious mistake is made sometimes about the *intermundia* in supposing that they were places entirely free from the incursion of atoms (see Mayor's note on Cic. *N. D.* i. 19. 50). Such a place it is wholly impossible for Epicurus to conceive and it would be fatal to the existence of the gods, which depends on the countless stream of atoms towards them.

[6] Cic. *N. D.* i. 18. 46 'quae enim forma alia occurrit unquam aut vigilanti cuiquam aut dormienti ?'

[7] Ibid. 47 'quae compositio membrorum, quae conformatio lineamentorum, quae figura, quae species humana potest esse pulcrior ?'

though the cruder notions of the popular mythology were sternly excluded, that it should not to some extent be carried out in detail, but we are hardly prepared for what we find. Philodemus in his work on the mode of life of the gods appears to have discussed in full how far the ordinary habits of men could be attributed to them. He decides that they need both food and drink,[1] that even if they do not sleep [2]—for sleep, being akin to death, is the attribute of mortality—they yet have periods of repose resembling sleep, that they hold converse with each other and employ speech; [3] for 'we shall not be considering them any happier or less destructible, if we think of them as not speaking nor conversing with one another, but resembling dumb men'.[4] Indeed it appears that the language they use is Greek [5] or something 'not far from it'. On the other hand he seems to decide that the gods probably do not use furniture![6] All this seems rather remote from the 'transient matter in the permanent form' and the ever-constant succession of images, and it must surely be supposed that though there was no definite distinction between esoteric and popular doctrines in the theology of Epicurus, Philodemus was in concession to popular prejudice working out the anthropomorphic idea with a greater elaboration than his master would have approved: for, in spite of the argumentative and philosophical appearance of Philodemus' exposition, the result is not very far from the anthropomorphism of Homer or the ordinary popular belief. It is at least noticeable that in Epicurus himself and the earlier authorities we have no hint of this popular aspect of theology.

But there is one attribute of the gods which is of supreme importance in the theory, and for which there is the fullest authority—and that is their eternal happiness. Here again

---

[1] *Vol. Herc.* i. vi. 13–17.   [2] *Frag. Herc.* (W. Scott), pp. 167–73.
[3] *Vol. Herc.* i. vi. 13; U. 356.
[4] Philodem. *de Vict. Deor.*; *Vol. Herc.* i. vi. 13; C.B. *fr.* 56; U. 356.
[5] Ibid. 14 καὶ νὴ Δία γε τὴν Ἑλληνίδα νομιστέον ἔχειν αὐτοὺς διάλεκτον ἢ μὴ πόρρω.
[6] See Scott, *Frag. Herc.*, p. 198.

it is stated that the images which we perceive give us immediate certainty that this is so. Velleius [1] puts it directly enough: 'our mind and intelligence straining fixedly towards these images comes to understand what is the blessed and eternal nature', and Cotta [2] in his criticism twice repeats the idea. That the everlasting succession of images should give us the idea of the eternity of the gods can well be understood: the ordinary succession of the 'idols' of sense-perception, which produce one 'cinematographic' image, could not do this, but it is the special property of the 'idols' of the gods that they do not produce the effect of a single image, but of a continuous series.[3] This continuous series then gives us directly the conception of an eternal existence. But how does it also inform us of the happiness or 'blessedness' of the gods' life? Lucretius'[4] account is here valuable:

Men assigned them everlasting life because their images came in constant stream and their forms remained unchanged, and indeed above all because they thought that those endowed with such great strength [5] could not readily be vanquished by any force. They thought that they far excelled in happiness, because the fear of death never harassed any of them, and at the same time because in sleep they saw them accomplish many marvels, yet themselves not undergo any toil.

[1] N. D. i. 19. 49, quoted above, p. 445, n. 1.

[2] Ibid. 37. 105 'ex eoque fieri ut in haec intenta mens nostra beatam illam naturam et sempiternam putet'; 38. 106 'hoc idem fieri in deo, cuius crebra facie pellantur animi, ex quo esse beati atque aeterni intellegantur'.

[3] Of course they do give the effect of a single image in the sense that any given series conveys to us the idea of a single continuous personality: cf. N. D. i. 39. 109; U., p. 234 n. 'fluentium frequenter transitio fit visionum, ut e multis una videatur'.

[4] v. 1175–82.

[5] Giussani explains (p. 238) that the 'great strength' of the gods 'consists just in the *semper faciem suppeditari*, guaranteed by the infinite provision of atomic material and guaranteeing the *formam manere*, or the eternity of personal existence'. I doubt whether Lucretius, even if he completely understood the Epicurean theology, had such an elaborate idea in his mind: it was surely rather the direct impression of strength conveyed by the visions, just like the accomplishment of the 'many marvels' below. Giussani is so intent on the theoretical significance of the existence of the images of the gods that he sometimes seems to forget that the visions must have had content: the gods must have had a definite appearance and seemed to be acting.

If the last sentence be compared with Epicurus' conception of human life, Lucretius' meaning is seen at once. The two great causes in human life which produced sorrow and prevented happiness were the fear of the gods and the fear of death:[1] in a less degree too the inevitable accompaniment of all activity with a sense of weariness. That the gods were free from the first fear is obvious: they were also free owing to their constitution from the fear of death, either by process of natural decay or through external blows: thirdly the visions showed them performing mighty feats without sense of toil; for the sense of toil or weariness comes to men from the loss of tissue in the course of labour, and such loss the eternal body of the gods cannot suffer. The happiness of the gods then is the immediate deduction from their eternity: indeed so impossible is it to separate happiness from eternity that the two ideas are said by Velleius to be immediately conveyed together. And so 'the blessed and immortal'[2] becomes the regular Epicurean periphrasis for the divine existence. Indeed the blessedness of the gods might well be called the central point of the Epicurean theology, for it at once makes their life the moral ideal towards which man must strive and to which he may assimilate himself by contemplation of the divine being, and also secures to him one of the two primary conditions of 'pleasure', since it is the guarantee that the gods do not interfere in the affairs of the world, for 'the blessed and immortal nature knows no trouble itself nor causes trouble to any other'.[3]

Is it possible to analyse at all the content of the divine happiness? In the moral theory of Epicurus the conception of pleasure tends to resolve itself into an absence of pain in the body (ἀπονία) and trouble in the mind (ἀταραξία): in the same way the blessed life of the gods is almost always

[1] Note especially the striking passage (iii. 59–86), where Lucretius attributes all human crime to the fear of death.

[2] τὸ μακάριον καὶ ἄφθαρτον K.Δ. i. τὸν θεὸν ζῷον ἄφθαρτον καὶ μακάριον Ep. iii. 123: cf. Lactantius, de Ira Dei, 17. 1; U. 360 'incorruptus est ac beatus', and many other Epicurean passages.

[3] K.Δ. i.

expressed by Epicureans in negative terms and ideas, and
the prominent note in its descriptions is supreme peace and
tranquillity. The famous description in Lucretius [1] may be
taken as a typical summary: 'it must needs be that all the
nature of the gods enjoys life everlasting in perfect peace,
sundered and separated far away from our world. For free
from all grief, free from danger, mighty in its own resources,
never lacking aught of us, it is not won by virtuous service
nor touched by wrath'. Almost the only positive note, apart
from Philodemus' very concretely anthropomorphic notions,
which can hardly be taken seriously, is the statement of an
Epicurean writer,[2] apparently quoting in part from Epicurus
himself: 'the blessed and deathless being, filled with all good
things and impervious to every ill, is wholly concerned with
the continuance of its own happiness and immortality'. The
divine being cannot be concerned with the 'continuance of
its own happiness and immortality' in the sense that it felt
any anxiety about them or that it could itself or need do
anything to secure them, so that it must be supposed that
its concern is rather that of contemplation and enjoyment.
The gods, that is, not merely live the life of perfect peace and
tranquillity but are conscious of it and this consciousness is
their happiness. The idea does not seem at first sight profoundly inspiring, but when taken in connexion with the
Epicurean Ethics its significance is clear enough: for man
too has pleasure in so far as he attains the consciousness of
tranquillity. Meanwhile the examination of the negative
conception of happiness is of real value for Epicurean
theology because it establishes at once the relation—or rather
the absence of relation—between the gods and the world.
The main ideas are summed up in Lucretius' description,
and indeed even more briefly in the first aphorism of the
Principal Doctrines: 'The blessed and immortal nature knows
no trouble itself nor causes trouble to any other, so that it

---

[1] ii. 646–51.

[2] [Plut.] *Plac. Philos.* 1. 7. 7; U. 361: Usener takes the last words ὅλον
ὂν περὶ τὴν συνοχὴν τῆς ἰδίας εὐδαιμονίας τε καὶ ἀφθαρσίας to be a quotation from Epicurus himself.

is never constrained by anger or favour. For all such things exist only in the weak.'[1] These are in fact just the two new ideas which Lucretius' description adds to the notion of freedom from danger and pain, which is the immediate outcome of eternity of existence. They might almost be said to be the inward and outward aspects of the same fact. The gods know no anger or favour, no hatred or love: for these are signs of dependence upon others and influence by others, signs of weakness which can have no place in the perfect power of divine beings. The gods 'give not nor take any share in any good thing':[2] therefore the offerings of men are doubly vain, for neither will the gods receive them nor will they give blessings in return. Nor yet on the other hand is it possible to rouse their wrath by neglect or crime: the old superstitions of the avenging thunderbolt of heaven[3] and even more philosophical notions of divine indignation are false, and man may lead his life without fear of divine punishment. And indeed the gods are wholly devoid of all emotion: 'if there is in God an emotion of joy which leads to gratitude, or an emotion of hate which leads to anger, it must be that he has also fear and lust and covetousness and all other emotions, which belong to human weakness'.[4] Internally then the peace of the gods is perfect: and this is due to external tranquillity. He has no trouble himself and causes it not to others: neither can the affairs of the world reach the gods nor do they for a moment influence them. Here we must pause for a moment, for it was at this point that the Epicurean theology came most markedly into conflict with other philosophies as well as with popular religion, and much assistance may be obtained from considering the lines on which it opposed them.

Velleius at the outset of his statement[5] of the case for the

---

[1] τὸ μακάριον καὶ ἄφθαρτον οὔτε αὐτὸ πράγματα ἔχει οὔτε ἄλλῳ παρέχει, ὥστε οὔτε ὀργαῖς οὔτε χάρισι συνέχεται· ἐν ἀσθενεῖ γὰρ πᾶν τὸ τοιοῦτον.

[2] Euseb. *Praep. Ev.* xiv. 27, 8; U. 364 θεοὶ πάντων ἀγαθῶν ἀδώρητοί τε καὶ ἀμέτοχοι.   [3] See Lucr. vi. 379–422.

[4] Lactantius, *de Ira Dei*, 15. 5; U. 366.   [5] Cic. *N. D.* i. 8. 18.

Epicurean theology strikes the note of opposition: 'Listen', he says, 'to no baseless or imaginary opinions about a fashioner and builder of the world, a god according to Plato's Timaeus, nor again about a prophetic witch, the "forethought" (πρόνοια) of the Stoics.' And if the Epicurean polemics are examined, it appears that it is these two ideas which they were almost always combatting, the Platonic notion of the creator of the world (Δημιουργός), and the Stoic conception of the continued divine care for the progress of events in the world. The divine creation of the world and in particular of man is refuted on two main grounds, both of which are prominent in Lucretius. In the first place the world [1] cannot have been created by perfect and all-powerful divine beings, because it is made so badly: 'so great are the flaws with which it stands beset'. Great tracts of earth are useless, occupied by mountains and forests and rocks and huge lakes and the sea: two-thirds of it are either too hot or too cold to support life, and even in the better parts the cultivation of the earth is a constant struggle against the depredations of nature. Man's life again is at the mercy of the wild beasts and the human infant is a miserable helpless creature as compared with the young of animals. In all this there are no signs of divine creation or care for man: 'there is no ordering of things, for many things are made otherwise than they should have been'.[2] Secondly,[3] why should the gods in their perfect happiness have wished to create a world and human beings?' Our worship can add nothing to their blessedness,[4] nor can it be that weary of their own blessedness[5] they craved some new excitement. But, adds Lucretius,[6] with a characteristically Epicurean conclusion, even if they had wished to create a world, they could not have done so, unless nature had previously made a world and so given them an 'anticipation' (*notities* =

---

[1] v. 195–234: cf. ii. 167–81.
[2] Lactantius (quoting Epicurus), *Divin. Instit.* iii. 17. 16; U. 370.
[3] Lucr. v. 165–86.
[4] Compare also Lactantius, op. cit., vii. 5. 3 and 7; U. 371.
[5] So too Velleius in Cic. *N. D.* i. 9. 22.   [6] v. 181–6.

πρόληψις) to act as an example for their work. The world is no divine creation, but only the fortuitous result of the movements of the infinite atoms in infinite space. The argument is crude and it is not fanciful to see in Lucretius' personifications[1] of 'nature the creatress' and 'nature the perfecter' the germs of a higher religious notion in which creation is not the arbitrary act of divine beings, but the natural expression of a divine power present in the world: if he answered Plato crudely, it was because, as the apostle of common sense, he apprehended him crudely. So eager was he to establish the principle of natural law as against the idea of the arbitrary workings of divine beings in the world that he did not stop to ask whether it was not itself reconcilable with a less naïve conception of divinity.

More eager still were Epicurus and his followers in their opposition to the Stoic view of the continued presence of the divine will in the world and the idea of the government of its affairs by 'forethought' (πρόνοια, providentia, prudentia); for even supposing the divine being had created the world, if he had then stepped aside and left it to its own workings, like Plato's Demiurgus, man would still have some chance of exercising his free will, but if the gods may interfere at any moment, then man's moral freedom is gone. Epicurean authorities [2] are full of this combat against the idea of 'providence', and the school apparently went the length of attributing 'non-providence' (ἀπρονοησία)[3] to their gods as a special characteristic. No special arguments on the subject are found apart from those directed against the divine creation, for indeed the whole physical theory of Epicurus is one long indictment of the Stoic and popular belief. The great sequence of events, in which each is the inevitable outcome of its predecessors, and every gradation of growth and preservation and decay—even the immortality of the gods themselves—is determined by the blind movement of atoms, is in itself an all-sufficient answer to religions or philosophies

[1] *Natura creatrix*, i. 629; *perfica natura*, ii. 1116.
[2] See quotations in Usener, pp. 246 ff.
[3] Alex. Aphrod. *de fato*, c. 31, p. 100; U. 368.

which believe the world and its government to be divine. The hand of God is not in the world, for God himself was never and never will be within the limits of a world. Of peculiar interest to modern readers is the closely allied attack on the teleological view of physiology which crops up from time to time in Epicureanism. Lucretius'[1] exposition has so modern a ring that it is worth quoting in full:

Herein you must eagerly desire to shun this fault, and with fore-sighted fear to avoid this error; do not think that the bright light of the eyes was created in order that we may be able to look before us, or that, in order that we may have power to plant long paces, therefore the tops of shanks and thighs, based upon the feet, are able to bend; or again, that the forearms are jointed to the strong upper arms and hands given us to serve us on either side, in order that we might be able to do what was needful for life. All other ideas of this sort, which men proclaim, by distorted reasoning set effect for cause, since nothing at all was born in the body that we might be able to use it, but what is born creates its own use. Nor did sight exist before the light of the eyes was born, nor pleading in words before the tongue was created, but rather the birth of the tongue came long before discourse, and the ears were created much before sound was heard, and in short all the limbs, I trow, existed before their use came about: they cannot then have grown for the purpose of using them.

Epicurus wished not merely to exclude the gods from the world, but even any notion of the unconscious forethought of nature itself, which might seem to give colour to a theological view of phenomena. If this argument is a striking instance of his anticipation of the attitude of modern science, it is also a conclusive proof of the thoroughness of his desire to leave the world a wholly mechanical structure and to exclude even the faintest suspicion of divine working. The gods exist indeed, but the popular notions of their powers and functions are wholly erroneous.

The question naturally arises whether there is any conceivable relation possible between men and such gods as Epicurus imagines, whether in fact there is room left for

---

[1] iv. 823–42. The same argument may be found in Lactantius, loc. cit.; U. 370: cf. also the quotation from Galen in U. 381, 382.

anything approaching to religion. Certainly there is no place for the ordinary religious notion of prayer as an appeal to divine beings who can hear the appeal and grant the blessings which are asked: if the Epicurean had nothing to fear from his gods, he also had nothing to hope. 'And so', says Seneca[1] in an ironical summary of the Epicurean position, 'God gives no blessings, but without care or thought for us turning away from the world He does other things or else —for this seems the greatest happiness of all to Epicurus— He does nothing at all, and is touched no more by service than He is by injury. One who says this, does not listen to the voice of prayer.' Epicurus[2] himself is said to have remarked with bitter contempt, 'If God listened to the prayers of men, all men would quickly have perished: for they are for ever praying for evil against one another.' In a quieter mood Lucretius[3] reaches the same general conclusion, though we seem to see in his words an almost pathetic affection for the ceremonies of the religion he has abandoned: 'nor is it piety at all to be seen often with veiled head turning towards a stone, and to draw near to every altar, no, nor to lie prostrate on the ground with outstretched palms before the shrines of the gods, nor to sprinkle the altars with the streaming blood of beasts, nor to link vow to vow'. In short, prayer and vow and sacrifice can have no meaning at all for the believer in the gods of the 'interworlds'. Still less had Epicurus any belief in the popular practice of divination or the validity of oracles: 'prophecy', he says himself, 'does not exist, and even if it did exist, things that come to pass must be counted nothing to us'.[4] Cicero[5] bears this out: 'there is nothing which Epicurus derides so much as the prediction of future events'. If the gods had no part in the ordering of events, much less would they foretell their course to men.

[1] *de Beneficiis*, iv. 4. 1; U. 364.
[2] Gnomolog. cod. Par. 1168, f.115; U. 388; C.B. *fr*. 58.
[3] v. 1198–1202.
[4] D.L. x. 135; C.B. *fr*. 3. The remark is obscure: see my notes, ad loc.
[5] Cic. *N. D.* ii. 65. 162; U. 395.

And yet it is stated more than once that Epicurus was a devout attendant at religious ceremonies and in his own writings recommended a similar conformity to his disciples. 'Of his reverence towards the gods',[1] says his biographer, 'it would be impossible to speak adequately', and Philodemus insists on this point again and again: 'it will be found that Epicurus both observed them all (sc. religious ceremonies) and recommended others to do the same':[2] 'not only did he teach this doctrine,[3] but he is found in his practice to have observed all the fasts and sacrifices of his own land': 'he took part in the festival of "the Pitchers" and the Attic mysteries and other rites'.[4] 'Let us at least sacrifice piously and rightly,'[5] Epicurus wrote in a passage of the Physics, 'where it is customary, and let us do all things rightly according to the laws, not troubling ourselves with common beliefs in what concerns the noblest and holiest of beings.' He even carried his piety into ordinary life and wrote to his friends, as any orthodox Athenian might, that he would come and stay with them 'if the gods were propitious'.[6] Moreover, just as Philodemus wrote his work, On Piety, so Epicurus himself had before him written On Holiness.[7] It can hardly be supposed that Lucretius similarly observed the festivals at Rome, but that the Epicurean tradition of conformity was alive in his time is clear from Philodemus' treatise. How then can this apparent inconsistency be explained? The opponents of Epicureanism were not slow to make a charge of hypocrisy: it is brought against Epicurus by Cotta[8] at the end of his speech in Cicero's dialogue and, as he quotes Posidonius as his authority, it is clear that the accusation was no new one: 'the truth is no doubt that Epicurus thought that there were no gods, and what he said about immortal gods was only put forward to

---

[1] D.L. x. 10. [2] Gomperz, Herc. Stud. 110, p. 128.
[3] Ibid. 109, p. 127. [4] Ibid.
[5] Philodem. περὶ εὐσ.; V. H.² ii. 108; C.B. fr. 57; U. 387.
[6] Θεῶν εἴλεων ὄντων, Philodem. περὶ εὐσ. V. H.² ii. 107; U. 99; C.B. fr. 19.
[7] Περὶ Ὁσιότητος, D.L. x. 27. [8] N. D. i. 44. 123.

deprecate unpopularity'. But if there is one point that seems clear in the character of Epicurus it is his absolute sincerity, nor indeed at the time when he lived would a philosopher who refused to conform to the outward observances of religion have found himself in invidious isolation. He must have believed that his own observance was justified and that it had for him a real meaning, and though the evidence is scanty, there is enough to make clear what this was. Epicurus himself used apparently to claim that 'though he destroyed providence, he left a place for piety'.[1] If one could not ask the gods for benefits or feel a gratitude towards them, it was yet possible to experience true religious feeling towards them, which might properly express itself in the orthodox ceremonies of worship.

If one looks in the Epicurean writers for signs of this 'piety', it is possible to find at least three distinct aspects of it. In the first place it is a right attitude of man towards the gods: the knowledge that he has nothing to fear from them should enable him to look on life with an untroubled mind, and this peace of mind is itself an act of worship towards the gods: 'the summing up of his whole argument about the gods was this, says Plutarch,[2] not to fear god but to cease from being troubled', and Lucretius[3] puts it with a strangely strong feeling of peacefulness: the true piety is not to pray and sacrifice, 'but rather to be able to contemplate all things with a mind at rest'. Secondly, as has already been hinted, the tranquil being of the gods was to the Epicurean the realized ideal of his moral life: in contemplating their happiness and peace he might hope to come nearer himself to perfect pleasure and complete freedom from disturbance. Just as the old anthropomorphic deities of mythology represented human life glorified—and oddly enough glorified at times—so were the gods of the 'interworlds' the pattern to which the Epicurean might look and aspire.

---

[1] Plut. adv. Colot. 8. 1111 b; U. 368 καὶ γὰρ τὴν πρόνοιαν ἀναιρῶν εὐσέβειαν ἀπολιπεῖν λέγει.

[2] Contra Epic. Beat. 8. 1092 b; U. 384 τὸ μὴ φοβεῖσθαι θεὸν ἀλλὰ παύσασθαι ταραττομένους. [3] v. 1203.

'Those who believe in the oracles we have given about the gods', says Philodemus,[1] 'will wish, as far as mortals may, to imitate their happiness.' The life of the gods becomes a moral ideal in the life of man. And lastly, strange though it may seem, Epicurus and his followers seem to have felt that an even closer and more valuable relation was possible than this, a relation which approached singularly near to the higher feelings of a true religion. It is said that the Epicurean was conscious even of 'a blessing coming to man from the gods'.[2] The idea seems almost that of a kind of mystical communion with the gods: 'he admires their nature and their state',[3] says Philodemus presumably of the Master, 'and endeavours to draw near to it and as it were yearns to touch it and be with it, and he calls the wise the friends of the gods and the gods the friends of the wise'. Lucretius in a strange passage[4] makes the idea clearer to us: you must get rid, he argues, of the old superstitions about the gods, for otherwise 'the holy powers of the gods, degraded by your thought, will often do you harm; not that the high majesty of the gods can be polluted by you, so that in wrath they should yearn to seek sharp retribution, but because you yourself will imagine that those tranquil beings in their placid peace set tossing the great billows of wrath, nor with quiet breast will you approach the shrines of the gods, nor have strength to drink in with tranquil peace of mind the images which are borne from their holy body to herald their divine form to the minds of men'. The contemplation with placid mind of the perfect peace of the gods becomes in this way a 'blessing' to the worshipper, for it enables him to assimilate himself more closely to them and to allow the images which tell him of their form to bring with them into his mind something of the tranquillity which they represent.

---

[1] Philodem. περὶ εὐσ. 28, Gomperz, *Herc. Stud.* p. 148.

[2] Atticus Eusebii, *Praep. Ev.* xv. 5; U. 385 ὄνησις τοῖς ἀνθρώποις ἀπὸ θεῶν γίνεται.

[3] Philodem. *de Deor. Vict.*; *V. H.*[1] vi, col. 1; U. 386.

[4] vi. 68–78. The thought is echoed in an unfortunately broken fragment of Philodem. περὶ εὐσ. 110, Gomperz, p. 128.

It is a fine and really living conception and is certainly very far removed from the abnegation of religion: there were probably few of those who stood at Epicurus' side in the Athenian festivals who had so high an ideal of what their religion meant to them and what real benefit might come to them in their lives from the worship of the gods.

The theology of Epicurus then is not lightly to be put aside as though it were either trivial in itself or unimportant in its place in his system. Once again it shows the subtle mind, which could think out the intricacies of the atomic movements and express in material terms the workings of the soul, occupying itself in a problem which his whole system had made to him intensely difficult. His theology is correlated alike with his physical theories and his moral system: it is indeed in some sort the link between them. If its main ideas seem at first to be fantastic subtleties, and its deductions arbitrary, a closer examination reveals their intimate connexion both among themselves and with the whole body of Epicurean doctrine.

X

ETHICS

THE primary interest of this work is in the physical theory of Epicurus regarded as the last stage in the development of Greek Atomism: his ethical teaching from the atomic point of view is of comparatively little importance. Moreover, since Epicurus has usually been regarded as a moral teacher, and his moral doctrine, largely through misconception of its true character, has become notorious, attention has most often been focussed on this side of his system, and it has in consequence been more fully described and discussed than his physics.[1] But it is clear that any account of Epicurus which should omit the moral theory would be lamentably one-sided, and the very fact that it has frequently been dealt with in detachment from the physical theory, makes it worth while to attempt a restatement: for the connexion between the two sides of his system is far closer than is usually realized, certainly by those who believe that Epicurus was a poor thinker who laid hands at random on the first physical theory that presented itself to act as a basis for his morals. For in fact his ethical doctrine arose directly by a parallel growth with the physical system out of the primary belief in sensation, and it is only by keeping the physical system in mind that its drift and intention can be fully understood: at all the critical points of its development the underlying physical ideas are the key to the moral doctrine. A certain difficulty attaches to the inquiry in that our authorities for the moral theory, although far more numerous than those for the physical theory, are also less profound: Epicurus' own letter[2] on the subject is more of

---

[1] The most brilliant modern account of the moral theory is that of M. Guyau (*La Morale d'Épicure*). He did for the Ethics of Epicurus something of the work which Giussani has done for the Physics: unfortunately he was even more liable to read into Epicurus modern modes of thought and his own ingenious subtleties. A good brief account of the moral theory, which perhaps lays too much stress on the social aspect, will be found in R. D. Hicks, *Stoic and Epicurean*. [2] Ep. iii to Menoeceus. Diog. Laert. x. 122–35.

a popular exposition than the letter to Herodotus, and his critics in antiquity were in the habit of isolating the moral theory and attacking it in relation to rival philosophies rather than in its connexion with his own general system. The traditional method of Greek moral theory demanded the selection of some general 'end' to which all conduct should be subordinated, and by which all action should be judged. Epicurus is decisive and unhesitating in his statement that pleasure is the end: 'pleasure',[1] he says in a passage whose full meaning cannot be completely realized till after a closer investigation, 'we call the beginning and end of the blessed life'. The choice of pleasure as the moral end has in itself been sufficient to bring upon him in all ages the obloquy which has attached to the name 'Epicurean'. His critics seizing upon the word, and not troubling to investigate the idea underlying it, have accused him of opening the door to every kind of luxury, debauchery, and sensual enjoyment. The deductions which Epicurus made from this primary conception must be closely investigated before passing judgement on the theory as a whole. But first it is necessary to inquire into the causes which led him to make this choice.

Epicureans were in the habit of resting their defence of the selection of pleasure as the end on the grounds of experience: 'as proof that pleasure is the end he points out that all living creatures as soon as they are born take delight in pleasure, but resist pain by a natural impulse apart from reason'.[2] There are several characteristic points in this argument. In the first place it must be observed that Epicurus' moral theory is not based on any abstract ideal of human nature, or any conception of obligation, but merely on the fact of experience. He is not concerned with what 'ought' to be or what is 'fitting', but simply with what is: pleasure *is* the end. In other words, just as in the physical

---

[1] Ep. iii, § 128 τὴν ἡδονὴν ἀρχὴν καὶ τέλος λέγομεν εἶναι τοῦ μακαρίως ζῆν.

[2] D.L. x. 137 ἀποδείξει δὲ χρῆται τοῦ τέλος εἶναι τὴν ἡδονὴν τῷ τὰ ζῷα ἅμα τῷ γεννηθῆναι τῇ μὲν εὐαρεστεῖσθαι, τῷ δὲ πόνῳ προσκρούειν φυσικῶς καὶ χωρὶς λόγου.

theory it is impossible to go behind sense-perception, for sensation is true, so in the field of morals the universal fact about conduct conveyed by sense-perception is final: 'pleasure *is* the end'. When sensation can give an answer, it is unnecessary and futile to apply to any other court of inquiry,[1] and even if an appeal were made to reason, it could not,[2] based as it is on sense-perceptions, suggest any other end without involving the fallacious aid of opinion: for the general concept produced in the mind by experience will be identical with those of the repeated sense-perceptions. And in fact Epicurus in his argument is at pains to exclude reason: the experience on which he bases his conclusion is not that of the grown man, but that of children and animals at the first moment of their birth. He wishes to get back to experience when it is most irrational, for it is then that the animal 'soul' is most completely under the control of sensation and free from the false inferences of thought. And in this condition we see, he argues, that it always chooses pleasure and avoids pain 'by a natural impulse apart from reason', or as is said elsewhere, 'untaught'.[3] Ethics then, like physics, is to be concerned with what is, not with what ought to be, and its source of information is precisely the same as in the physical field, the experience which consists of the impressions received from the continued series of sense-perceptions.

But, although he rejected the aid of reason, Epicurus was not content to rest his choice of pleasure as the moral end merely on the observation of the behaviour of others: for he regarded the relation of pleasure and good as an immediate

[1] Torquatus, the Epicurean in Cicero's dialogue, *de Finibus*, admits (i. 9. 31) that some Epicureans are not content with this demonstration from experience of the fact of the pursuit of pleasure and would argue that reason too tells us that pleasure *ought to be* the end, and that we have an 'innate concept' (πρόληψις) to that effect. But he rightly rejects this line of support as alien to the true doctrine: there is, I believe, no trace of it in Epicurean literature. Guyau (pp. 22 ff.) has built too much on this unorthodox argument.

[2] See Chaps. II and VIII.

[3] Sext. Emp. *adv. Math.* xi. 96; U. 398 φυσικῶς καὶ ἀδιδάκτως τὸ ζῷον φεύγει μὲν τὴν ἀλγηδόνα διώκει δὲ τὴν ἡδονήν.

subjective experience. 'There is no need of reasoning and argument to show that pleasure is to be sought and pain avoided: this we perceive at once, just as we do that fire is hot, that snow is white, that honey is sweet: there is no necessity to establish any of these things by abstruse reasoning, it is enough merely to call attention to them ("tantum esse satis admonere").'[1] The conclusion is immediate, it is indeed itself a part of the direct sensation: 'it is enough to have sensation and to be a creature of flesh, and pleasure will be seen to be a good'.[2] To understand this it is necessary to go back for a moment to the Epicurean psychology.[3] In the simplest bodily sensations the contact of an external body large enough to touch the atoms of soul distributed among the body-atoms, stirs the 'fourth nature' at once to the movements of sensation, which are then communicated to the other soul-atoms and so to the atoms of body, with the result that the body then feels. The same process occurs not merely in other bodily sensations caused by internal movements, such as those of nerves or stomach, but also in the sense-organs, with the difference that there the result is not a mere passive sensation, but the more active sensation of perception. In one and all of these sensations, there is a certain atomic dislocation and readjustment due to movement. In the vast majority of instances this dislocation causes not only the sensation of contact or perception, but also an added feeling (πάθος) of pleasure or pain, and this, not as a consequence, but as an inherent part of the sensation. Just as by the sense of touch we know that fire is not only fire but hot, by the sense of sight that snow is not only snow but white, and by taste that honey is sweet, so also by all the senses we know equally directly that the touch, taste, smell, sound, or sight is pleasant or painful. And in Epicurus' analysis just as the atomic movement *is* perception, so also the atomic dislocation or readjustment *is* pain or

---

[1] Cic. *de Fin.* i. 9. 30; U. 397.
[2] Plut. *adv. Colot.* 27. 1122 d; U. p. 279 n. αἴσθησιν ἔχειν δεῖ καὶ σάρκινον εἶναι, καὶ φανεῖται ἡδονὴ ἀγαθόν.
[3] See Chap. VIII, pp. 398 ff.

pleasure.[1] By pleasure or pain then is meant simply that which is good or bad to the senses: 'there are two feelings, pleasure and pain, which occur to every living creature, and of these pleasure is the feeling akin to us (οἰκεῖον) and pain alien (ἀλλότριον)'.[2] This feeling superadded to the mere perception is a direct indication, a test in its pleasantness or painfulness of the good and the bad. It is for this reason that feeling[3] (πάθος) takes its place along with sensation (αἴσθησις) and the concept (πρόληψις) as a criterion of truth. Feeling is as immediate a test of goodness and badness as sensation is of truth: to the senses pain is always bad and pleasure always good. The criterion is direct and is the direct experience of all living creatures.

The weak point in the Epicurean position might seem to be the identification of that which is good for the senses with the morally good, and many cogent arguments against it might be and were adduced by the upholders of other philosophies. Two answers might at once be given to such an objection. That in the first place it is perhaps a misnomer to speak of Epicurus' 'moral theory': for a 'moral theory' necessarily implies a conception of obligation, whereas Epicurus had no such conception and only wished to base a practical method of life on the universal fact of experience, that pleasure is in itself desirable or good and pain undesirable or bad. Secondly, what is more important and more to the present purpose, a system which rests on the infallibility of sense-perception and on that alone, could give no other answer: for the only good and bad which the senses know is pleasure and pain. The supreme interest to the student of Epicureanism is the perfect correlation of this idea which lies at the root of the ethical theory with the whole of the rest of the system. The choice of pleasure as the end of life is not to Epicurus an arbitrary selection detached from his

---

[1] For pain as atomic dislocation see Lucr. ii. 963–6: in such cases readjustment is pleasure. For pleasure as atomic movement (ἡδονὴ κινηματική) see Plut. *adv. Colot.* 27. 1122 e λεῖα καὶ προσηνῆ κινήματα τῆς σαρκός and other passages in U. 411–14. [2] D.L. x. 34.

[3] D.L. x. 31: cf. Ep. iii, § 129 ὡς κανόνι τῷ πάθει πᾶν ἀγαθὸν κρίνοντες.

physical explanation of the world, but the immediate and necessary outcome of the fundamental trust in sensation on which the physical theory was likewise built. Just as in the physical world we trust sensation because it is true, so in the world of action we must trust the feelings of pleasure and pain: for they are the sole and infallible criterion of good and bad. The 'loose patchwork' of two independent theories, with which Epicurus is sometimes reproached, turns out after all to be a very closely woven texture.

That all pleasure then is good and all pain bad is the primary principle which must lie at the base of all conduct, and the ethical problem is simply to tell men how the maximum of pleasure can best be attained. Now since there is no other standard of judgement beyond the simple feeling of pleasure and pain, it is obvious that any qualitative distinction of pleasures is impossible: one pleasure can only be said to be better or worse than another, if there lies behind pleasure some more fundamental criterion, such as virtue, self-development, and so on, which may be applied as a test. Pleasure itself being the final court of appeal, no distinction can be made except that of quantity: the aim of conduct must be to secure the maximum amount of pleasure.[1] We must ask then in the first place what kind of pleasures produce the most evident feeling, and the answer is clear— the pleasures of the body (σάρξ), its sense-perceptions, and sensations of movement. These then must have the first place in the life of pleasure, and Epicurus and his followers never hesitate to assert their claim: 'I know not how I can conceive the good, if I withdraw the pleasures of taste and sexual passion and hearing, and the pleasurable emotions caused to sight by beautiful form.'[2] But among these pleasures of the flesh[3] it is possible by purely quantitative

[1] Aristocles Eusebii, *Praep. Ev.* xiv. 21. 3; U. 442 μετρεῖσθαι γὰρ αὐτὰ τῷ ποσῷ καὶ οὐ τῷ ποιῷ.
[2] Epicurus περὶ τέλους quoted by Athenaeus, xii. 546 e; U. 67; D.L. x. 6; C.B. *fr.* 10; Cic. *Tusc.* iii. 18. 41; *de Fin.* ii. 3. 7; U. 67.
[3] Epicurus in these contexts always uses the word 'flesh' (σάρξ), the σῶμα being for him the whole atomic body. The word forms one of several signs

measurement to distinguish grades:[1] the pleasures of the eye and ear, which are partly aesthetic and even intellectual, even the pleasures of taste, which have a certain refinement, are less strong, because less truly corporeal, then the sensual pleasures of the body. The greatest quantitative pleasure, the most completely bodily, is the pleasure of the stomach, and Epicurus with relentless pursuit of his principles to their logical conclusion assigns to it the first place: 'the beginning and the root of all good is the pleasure of the stomach: even wisdom and culture must be referred to this'.[2] The primary application then of the 'hedonistic calculus' leads to the ranging of pleasures in precisely the opposite order to that in which they would be placed in an idealist system such as that of Plato, which ranks pleasures according to an extraneous standard of better and worse. The weakest pleasures are those of the mind, then stronger the pleasures of sense-perception, sight and hearing at the bottom of the scale, then smell and taste, and finally the strongest of all are the gross sensual pleasures of the stomach. In the graphic phrase of Plutarch[3] 'the Epicureans measure the amount of pleasures as with compasses from the stomach as centre'. It is of course this audacious reliance on the cardinal test of the amount of sensation and the conclusion to which it leads, which brought Epicureanism into disrepute: the life which had its 'roots' in the pleasure of the stomach seemed little better than the life of pigs.[4] And indeed if the philosophy of Epicurus stopped here and recommended, as its opponents pretended to believe it did, the momentary enjoyment of the maximum of sensual pleasure, not merely

in his Letters of the approximation of the language to the Hellenistic Greek of the New Testament.

[1] See Guyau, p. 31.

[2] Quoted by Athenaeus, ibid.; U. 409; C.B. *fr.* 59 ἀρχὴ καὶ ῥίζα παντὸς ἀγαθοῦ ἡ τῆς γαστρὸς ἡδονή· καὶ τὰ σοφὰ καὶ τὰ περιττὰ ἐπὶ ταύτην ἔχει τὴν ἀναφοράν.

[3] *contra Ep. beat.* 17, p. 1098d.; U. 409 οἱ ἄνθρωποι τῆς ἡδονῆς τὸ μέγεθος καθά περ κέντρῳ καὶ διαστήματι τῇ γαστρὶ περιγράφουσι.

[4] Horace, *Ep.* 1. 4. 16 'Epicuri de grege porcum'; Cic. *in Pis.* 16. 37 'Epicure noster, ex hara producte, non ex schola'.

would it have deserved all the censure and ridicule which has ever been heaped upon it, but it could not possibly have attained the position it held among the practical philosophies of Greece and Rome. But it was a total misconception of the Master's meaning to take this as his final judgement on the life of man. He had reached here by unswerving faithfulness to his principle the lowest ebb, as it were, of his doctrine: it is necessary to inquire now how the tide could rise again, and to suspend judgement until it has been seen at its height.

The philosophy of Aristippus and the Cyrenaics, which superficial critics have sometimes accused Epicurus of borrowing wholesale, did indeed recommend this momentary pursuit of the highest pleasure: each moment,[1] regarded as a detached instant, was to be filled with the maximum of pleasure and the happiness of life was the aggregate of such individual experiences. But to Epicurus' mind the 'blessed life', as he called it, was not a succession of independent instants, but a continuous whole, no one moment of which could properly be regarded as detached from the time preceding or following: life must be regarded as a unity. Now the moment this notion of continuity is introduced, it is obvious that the most important effects follow with regard to the doctrine of pleasure. For it is seen that certain pleasures are followed by attendant pains, which may be so great as to counterbalance the original pleasure: conversely, certain pains may produce as a consequence so much pleasure that it is worth while to endure them. The first principle then that the maximum amount of pleasure must be attained may lead, if this continuous view of life be taken, to a choice which will be the exact reverse of that which the Cyrenaics would recommend. Epicurus has put this strongly and clearly in the Letter to Menoeceus:[2] 'And since pleasure is the first good and natural to us (σύμφυτον), for this very reason we do not choose every pleasure, but sometimes we pass over many pleasures, when greater discomfort (δυσχερές) accrues to us as the result of them: and similarly we think

[1] Clem. Alex. *Strom*. ii. 417: see Guyau, pp. 37 ff.
[2] § 129: cf. *K.Δ.* viii, and *fr.* 62 C.B.; U. 442.

many pains better than pleasures, since a greater pleasure comes to us when we have endured pains for a long time. Every pleasure then because of its natural kinship to us (διὰ τὸ φύσιν ἔχειν οἰκείαν) is good, yet not every pleasure is to be chosen (αἱρετή): even as every pain also is evil, yet not all are always of a nature to be avoided (φευκτή).' This consideration of consequences once established, the 'hedonistic calculus' assumes another form. It becomes a balancing of pleasures and pains alike, not now regarded merely in themselves but in company wíth their consequences. Pleasures must indeed be estimated by quantity, as before, but after deducting, as it were, the quantity of attendant pain; and similarly with pain: 'by a scale of comparison (συμμέτρησις) and by the consideration of advantages and disadvantages we must form judgement on all these matters'.[1] It is manifest that the conclusions will now be very different. Is there any test by which it is possible to recognize the pure (ἀκέραιοι)[2] pleasures, unattended by pain, or by which pleasures may be graduated in a scale? Is there again any rule of life by which in the long run, when all the calculation and balancing is done, we may hope to have attained the maximum of pleasure?

Epicurus gives several answers to these questions, which it is easy to state, but it is less easy to follow out the process by which he arrived at them or the connexion that he saw between several slightly different avenues of approach to his ultimate conception of the 'blessed life'. One critic thinks that Epicurus' doctrines can only be understood in the light of the theories to which they were opposed,[3] another regards the process as one of continual modification of his system in answer to the objections or possible objections of critics:[4] others have been content to leave the various notions independent, as they are found scattered up and down in our authorities without attempting to discover any close nexus between them. The clue is almost certainly to be found in the physical theory, if it can be applied rightly. A rather

---

[1] Ep. iii, § 130.
[2] K.Δ. xii.
[3] Wallace, *Epicureanism*, p. 134.
[4] Guyau, Livre I, cap. iv.

closer analysis then must be attempted of the psychology of pleasure, as Epicurus understood it. Pleasure is the fulfilment of desire (ἐπιθυμία): what does this mean? Desire may arise in two ways: it may in the first place have a purely corporeal origin: the waste caused by bodily effort or merely by the natural processes of life results in a loss of material:[1] consequent upon this comes a movement of pain due to want (τὸ ἀλγοῦν κατ' ἔνδειαν):[2] this pain calls up the image of its satisfaction and that in turn produces the painful movement of desire.[3] Then, if the means of satisfying the desire is within our attainment, there follows another movement accompanying the process of satisfaction: this movement (κίνησις) is a kind of pleasure.[4] As the result of the completion of the process there ensues a second kind of pleasure (ἡδονὴ καταστηματική),[5] the static pleasure of the equilibrium (εὐστάθεια)[6] or freedom from pain (ἀπονία) which the body now enjoys. But the image of desire may also be presented to the mind without the antecedent process of loss and pain due to want, as in the case of gluttony or the social desires of ambition and so on; the desire is in this case also in itself painful and satisfaction is attended with the pleasure of movement, but, as it was not originally caused by the pain of want due to loss, it was a gratuitous upsetting of the pleasure of equilibrium. What then is to be our attitude to these different kinds of pleasures and desires? It is clear that of the two kinds of pleasure that of equilibrium is superior, for it is pure and in itself entirely free from pain, antecedent, accompanying, or resultant. Indeed if the body

[1] Lucr. ii. 1128–9.

[2] Ep. iii. § 130; K.Δ. xviii, xxi.

[3] Lucr. iv. 858–76, gives the outline of the process which may be filled in from the parallel account of the act of will in the following paragraph.

[4] Plut. *An seni sit gerenda res publica* 5: compare other quotations in U. 411.

[5] Olympiodorus in Plat. *Phileb.* 274; U. 416 καὶ ὁ' Ἐπίκουρος λέγει τὴν κατὰ φύσιν ἡδονήν, καταστηματικὴν αὐτὴν λέγων.

[6] Plut. *contr. Ep. beat.* 4, p. 1089d αὐτοί μοι δοκοῦσι ... εἰς τὴν ἀπονίαν καὶ τὴν εὐστάθειαν ὑποφεύγειν τῆς σαρκός : and below τὸ εὐσταθὲς σαρκὸς κατάστημα fr. 11 C.B.; U. 68.

could be kept in this perfect equilibrium, it would, apart from the incursion of pain from without in the shape of disease or accident (which must be considered later), be wholly free from pain: and it is because of the perfect and instantaneous adjustment of supply and loss that the bodies of the gods are wholly without pain and their life continuously and perfectly happy. But with the human body the adjustment can never be either perfect or instantaneous: there must always be the pain due to want and the pleasure of the movement of satisfaction. Now this kinetic pleasure, merely because it is pleasure, is good, but it is always counterbalanced by the antecedent pain. It is therefore inferior as an object of choice to the pleasure of rest: it is indeed a necessary element in human life owing to the inevitable process of physical loss and repair, but it is not in itself a pure pleasure. Hence we find that on the one hand Epicurus[1] admits the pleasure of movement as a necessary constituent in bodily pleasure, but on the other speaks of it contemptuously: the 'ticklings' of the flesh[2] is a favourite name and elsewhere he speaks of the 'smooth and gentle movements in the flesh'.[3] Can any practical conclusion be formed? It must be that in order to secure the maximum amount of pleasure and the least amount of pain, we must aim as much as possible at the pleasure of equilibrium, and, what is the converse of this proposition, as little as may be at the pleasures of movement. Or in other words, the satisfaction of the bodily wants, hunger, thirst, &c., is in itself a necessity and conduces to the true pleasure of equilibrium: the satisfaction of other wants is unnecessary and, even if it added to the total of pleasure, would counteract itself by adding also to the aggregate of pain. And here is exactly the difference between Epicurus and the Cyrenaics: 'they do not admit static pleasure, but only that which consists in motion. But Epicurus admits both kinds in the soul and

---

[1] Athenaeus, xii. 546 e; U. 413.

[2] γαργαλισμοί, Athenaeus, ibid.: cf. Plut. *de Occulte Vivendo*, 4, 1129; Seneca, *Ep.* 92. 6 'beatum facit titillatio corporis'; U. 412.

[3] Plut. *adv. Colot.* 27, 1122; U. 411.

in the body.'[1] And of the two kinds the static is the purer, because it does not involve antecedent or consequent pain. With this problem of the different kinds of desire Epicurus has dealt himself and his attitude can now be better understood. Of desires, he holds,[2] some are natural and necessary, some natural but not necessary, and others neither natural nor necessary but 'idle' (κεναί) or 'due to idle imaginings' (παρὰ κενὴν δόξαν γινόμεναι). And of the necessary some are necessary for happiness (εὐδαιμονία), others for the repose (ἀοχλησία) of the body, and others for very life. A scholium further explains the distinction with illustrations:[3] 'the desire for food and clothing is necessary: the desire for sexual pleasures is natural but not necessary, the desire for particular food or particular clothing is neither natural nor necessary'. This account may be completed by the distinction, which can be fairly certainly made, between the three kinds of necessary desires: those necessary for very life will be the desire of breath, food, &c., those necessary for the repose of the body will be those of warmth, shelter, clothing, &c., and those necessary for happiness will be freedom from fear, &c.; the last class will be considered again when pleasures of the mind come to be discussed. What then is the right attitude towards these various kinds of desires? The natural and necessary desires must of course and can easily be fulfilled:[4] without the satisfaction of some we cannot live at all, others if satisfied produce equilibrium of body and others equilibrium of mind. At the other end of the scale the 'idle' desires, which result merely from vain imaginings of pleasures greater than we at present possess, and will contribute nothing to the equilibrium of body and mind but may well destroy it, must be got rid of at all costs. The

[1] D.L. x. 136.
[2] See Ep. iii. § 127, and K.Δ. xxix: the general idea was anticipated by the division of 'goods' in Plat. Rep. 357b.
[3] On Arist. Eth. Nic. iii. 13; U. 456. The scholium on K.Δ. xxix makes the mistake of classing the desire for ποικίλματα (special kinds of food, &c.) among the natural but not necessary desires, but enlarges the idea of the third class by the example of the desire for 'crowns and statues'.
[4] Cic. Tusc. Disp. v. 33. 93; U. 456.

middle class of the natural but not necessary desires causes slightly more difficulty: 'it is not difficult either to obtain them or to forego them'.[1] On the whole the wise man will make a just and moderate use of them and his practical wisdom (φρόνησις) must be his guide in every case. Going back now to the psychical account of desire, it is not hard to see that Epicurus' decision here is completely in accord with his attitude to the two kinds of pleasure. The natural and necessary desires are those which spring from the pain of want (τὸ ἀλγοῦν κατ' ἔνδειαν) and their satisfaction is productive not only of the pleasure of movement, but of the pleasure of equilibrium: they must then be gratified. The natural but not necessary desires are typically the 'ticklings of the flesh': they cannot arise without certain painful bodily movements and therefore their satisfaction does to some degree produce the pleasure of equilibrium, but much more does it arouse the pleasure of movement: they must therefore be indulged sparingly. The desires which are neither necessary nor natural produce pleasures which are wholly kinetic: so far from contributing to static pleasure they are the cause of those 'storms and gusts'[2] which are most inimical to the 'calm' of the body: they must be wholly suppressed. Once again we are brought back to the satisfaction of the primary needs of the stomach.

These two avenues of thought lead then to the same conclusion: but the whole idea is brought out more clearly by a third line of approach, which was a favourite with Epicurus and his disciples. The great mistake,[3] they thought, which men make about the pleasures of the body is that they suppose them unlimited: it is always possible, men suppose, to go on adding new pleasures and so piling up the aggregate amount: if this is true we can never reach the maximum of

---

[1] Ibid. 'nec ad potiendum difficile esse censet nec vero ad carendum'.

[2] Plut. contr. Ep. beat. 5, 1090 χειμῶνας . . . καὶ καταιγισμούς: cf. Athenaeus, xii. 456 e; U. 413.

[3] Κ.Δ. xx ἡ μὲν σὰρξ ἀπέλαβε τὰ πέρατα τῆς ἡδονῆς ἄπειρα καὶ ἄπειρος αὐτὴν χρόνος παρεσκεύασεν (the last word is uncertain, but the sense clear, see my notes).

pleasure, and for its full enjoyment infinite time is necessary. Epicurus' analysis of the process of pleasure shows that this is not so: there is a limit to the amount and the maximum is easily attained at any moment. For the perfect pleasure, that in which there is no pain, is reached as soon as the 'pain due to want' is removed: we then enjoy the pleasure of equilibrium, and any attempt to go beyond this may indeed create the inferior pleasure of movement with its attendant pain, but it cannot increase the true static pleasure, for that knows no increase. 'The pleasure in the flesh is not increased, when once the pain due to want is removed, but is only varied (ποικίλλεται):'[1] 'the limit of quantity in pleasures is the removal of all that is painful'.[2] A later critic explains this more clearly:[3] 'nature increases the pleasure up to the point when pain is stopped, but beyond that point it does not permit any increase in amount, but only admits of unnecessary diversifications (ποικιλμούς), if pleasure occurs when there is no pain; the advance to this point which is made with the accompaniment of longing (ὄρεξις) is the measure of pleasure: it is short and brief'. The new conception of the limit thus leads once again to the same practical conclusion, that the satisfaction of the primary needs brings with it the maximum pleasure, beyond which no real increase is possible. And if so, this maximum pleasure is not a matter of infinite time, but is accessible at any moment, and the pleasure of the single moment is as great as could be obtained in any length of time: 'infinite time contains no greater pleasure than limited time, if one measures by reasoning the limits of pleasure'.[4] Again, the existence of this natural limit affords a basis for distinguishing between pleasures: 'if every pleasure could be intensified (κατεπυκνοῦτο) so that it lasted and influenced the whole organism or the most essential parts (τὰ κυριώτατα μέρη) of our nature, pleasures would never differ from one another':[5] as it is the limit enables us to

---

[1] *K.Δ.* xviii.   [2] *K.Δ.* iii.

[3] Plut. *contr. Ep. beat.* 3, p. 1088 c; U. 417.

[4] *K.Δ.* xix ὁ ἄπειρος χρόνος ἴσην ἔχει τὴν ἡδονὴν καὶ ὁ πεπερασμένος, ἐάν τις αὐτῆς τὰ πέρατα καταμετρήσῃ τῷ λογισμῷ.   [5] *K.Δ.* ix.

separate the perfect pleasure of equilibrium from the less perfect, because less pure, pleasure of movement or diversification. Lastly, it is now possible to make a very important practical deduction, namely that this maximum of pleasure is within the reach of any man at any time: for 'the wealth demanded by nature is both limited and easily procured, but that demanded by idle imaginings stretches on to infinity',[1] or, as Lucretius[2] has put it sagely and picturesquely, 'if a man would but steer his life by true reasoning, it is great riches to a man to live thriftily with calm mind: for never can he lack for a little'. The highest pleasure then for Epicurus is no far-off ideal attainable only by the rich and powerful or by the trained philosopher, but simple and easily reached even by the poorest and humblest: 'thanks be to blessed Nature, because she has made what is necessary easy to supply and what is not easy unnecessary'.[3]

So far, from the examination of bodily pleasure the position has been reached that the static pleasure resulting from the satisfaction of necessary wants is pure and complete: in the human body it cannot be absolutely continuous, because there must always be the process of loss and supply, the pain of want and its satisfaction, but the means required for its restoration, when momentarily upset, are accessible to all and the process is short and easy. The abjuration of all unnecessary pleasures of movement in the variation of enjoyments and the control of the unnecessary physical pleasures by practical wisdom prevents any attempt to go beyond the limit and so introduce gratuitous disturbance. The life of perfect bodily rest (ἀοχλησία) and health (ὑγίεια) is thus the true pleasure and easily attainable by any man. But it must not be forgotten that there are other pains besides those of physical desire: for disease or accident may bring upon us greater sufferings, and sufferings too which are not, or at any rate only to a small extent, within our control. Such pains will necessarily upset the balance and

---

[1] *Κ.Δ.* xv ὁ τῆς φύσεως πλοῦτος καὶ ὥρισται καὶ εὐπόριστός ἐστιν, ὁ δὲ τῶν κενῶν δοξῶν εἰς ἄπειρον ἐκπίπτει.   [2] v. 1117–19.
[3] Ioannes Stob. *Floril.* xvii. 23; C.B. *fr.* 67; U. 469.

materially interfere with the 'blessed' life of continuous happiness: what is to be our attitude towards them? They are of course bad: 'all pain is bad', nor can the pain of disease be placed among those which we 'think better than pleasures, since a greater pleasure comes to us when we have endured pains for a long time'.[1] Epicurus' answer is at first sight[2] unexpected in view of the fundamental principle of the moral system and has an almost Stoic ring: we must accept pain, he says in effect, and we shall find that it does not really interfere with the pleasure of our lifetime, for [3] if it is severe, it is short: if long, it is not severe: 'Pain does not last continuously in the flesh, but acute pain is there for a very short time, and even that which just exceeds the pleasure in the flesh does not continue for many days. But chronic illnesses permit a predominance of pleasure over pain in the flesh.'[4] There is here no real inconsistency with his main position. Pain must be endured if it comes, but in the calculation of happiness, there will always be a balance on the side of pleasure: if pain lasts long, its comparative mildness will give pleasure a continuous advantage, and if it is very severe so that it does for the time outweigh pleasure, then either it cannot last long and the moments of its duration will be as nothing to the time in which we are free from it, or else if it does last,[5] it will bring death, and our 'hedonistic calculus' is over. This balance of pain against pleasure in the confidence that the account will end to the advantage of pleasure may seem to those who have suffered much bodily pain a hard saying, but it was made by one who, suffering agonies of bodily torment in his last hours, could yet speak of 'this blessed day'[6] and write to a friend that though he was enduring 'suffering which could not be

---

[1] Ep. iii, § 129.
[2] See Cic. de Officiis, iii. 33. 117; U. 446 'non id spectandum est quid dicat, sed quid consentaneum sit ei dicere, qui bona voluptate terminaverit, mala dolore.'
[3] Ep. iii, § 133.
[4] K.Δ. iv: compare other quotations in U. 446–8.
[5] Plut. contr. Ep. beat. 23, 1103; C.B. fr. 65; U. 448 ὁ γὰρ πόνος ὁ ὑπερβάλλων συνάψει θανάτῳ.   [6] D.L. x. 22; C.B. fr. 30; U. 138.

more intense, yet against it all is set the joy in my heart at the recollection of my conversations with you'. It is a noble idea and certainly involves no departure from the principles of the moral theory.

It has been inevitable now and then in speaking of the pleasures of the body to imply a participation of the mind, but its special pleasures must now be considered more carefully: what are they in themselves and what is their relation to the pleasures of the body? To go back once again to the Epicurean psychology; the mind does not differ materially from the rest of the body, but is an accumulation of atoms of particular shapes and in particular combinations situated in the breast. Sensations (both αἰσθήσεις and πάθη) are felt by the body in the places where the contact or movement giving rise to them takes place: the mind itself does not directly feel pleasure and pain, but these feelings are, just like the passive sensations and sense-perceptions, 'telegraphed' to it by the movements of the soul-particles in the body, and are reproduced in the mind not exactly as feelings of pleasure and pain, but rather as the 'emotions' of joy and grief: 'all pleasurable movement through the flesh is sent up to form a kind of pleasure or joy for the mind'.[1] The pleasure of the mind then is primarily at any rate a kind of reflex of the pleasure of the body: 'the soul' as a contemptuous critic[2] puts it scornfully, 'receives the memory of the pleasure, and preserves it as a kind of fragrance (ὥσπερ ὀσμήν) and nothing more'. Similarly the soul shares the body's pains: 'think it not unnatural that when the flesh cries aloud, the soul cries too. The flesh cries out to be saved from hunger, thirst, and cold. It is hard for the soul to repress these cries and dangerous for her to disregard nature's appeal to her'.[3] The opponents indeed of Epicureanism were wont to attribute to him[4] the doctrine that all

---

[1] Plut. contr. Ep.beat. 2 p. 1087b.; U. 433 πᾶσα διὰ σαρκὸς ἐπιτερπὴς κίνησις ἐφ᾽ ἡδονήν τινα καὶ χαρὰν ψυχῆς ἀναπεμπομένη.

[2] Ibid. 4.   [3] Porph. ad Marc. 30, p. 209; C.B. fr. 44; U. 200.

[4] Cic. de Fin. ii. 30. 98 'negas animi ullum esse gaudium quod non referatur ad corpus'; U. 430.

the pleasures of the soul were simply the reflexion of pleasures of the body, and though this is not really a fair account of his teaching, it is yet true that he held that all the pleasures of the soul were either derived thus directly from the pleasures of the body or had reference to the body's welfare: 'the mind does not naturally take joy or find peace (γαληνίζειν) in anything but the pleasures of the body, present or expected'.[1] This is of course again a relentless application of the root-principle that all pleasure originates in the flesh; but though at first sight it seems to allow but a limited field of action for the mind, if the thought is followed out, it develops very considerably.

In the first place the mind can rejoice not merely or even principally in the individual movements of pleasure in the flesh, but also in its more complete and permanent pleasure of equilibrium.[2] This in itself is no slight extension, for it at once gives the mind an opportunity not merely for transient emotions of rejoicing, but for a permanent condition of peaceful happiness (ἀταραξία) corresponding to the freedom from pain (ἀπονία) in the body. But a far more important extension of the mind's activity is opened out by its own peculiar capacities. The body is conscious of its pleasure—whether of movement or rest—only at the moment of its occurrence, and though the whole purpose of the attainment of equilibrium is the prolongation and constant re-creation of these moments, yet the succession must be interrupted, as well by natural processes as by the occasional incursion of disease or accident. But it is the peculiar property of the mind, thanks to its own special movements of sensation, that it can 'look before and after': it has memory and anticipation. It is not therefore confined to the contemplation of such pleasures and pains as the flesh may 'send up' to it at any given moment, but can return upon the experience of the past: 'the recollection of good things in the past is the greatest contribution to the pleasant life'.[3]

---

[1] Plut. *contr. Ep. beat.* 4. 1088 e; U. 429.
[2] Ibid. 5. 1089 d; U. 431.
[3] Plut., op. cit., 18. 1099 d; U. 436.

For even though the body may at any given moment be sending news of pain, yet the mind by choosing to dwell on the memory of past pleasures may overwhelm, or at any rate lessen, its present distress: 'by the recollection of past blessings present evils are mitigated'.[1] Nor is this all, for the mind may look into the future and, confident in the result which will ensue from the carrying out of the moral doctrine, may rejoice by anticipation in the pleasure of the body which is to come. It is indeed noticeable that Epicurus[2] in indicating the sources of the 'highest and most certain joy' combines with the 'stable condition of rest in the flesh' not the recollection of past pleasure, but 'the sure and certain hope' of pleasure to come. No doubt it is conversely true that the pains of the mind,[3] embracing past, present, and future, are also worse than those of the body, but the mind, thanks to this power of projection away from the present, has more control over its emotions than the body has over its feelings, and the philosopher can train himself to contemplate pleasures rather than pains. Diogenes notes that in this view that both the pleasures and the pains of the soul were greater than those of the body, Epicurus again differed from the Cyrenaics.

The positive pleasure then of the mind is the joy of the contemplation of the pleasures of the body in past, present, and future, and its concentration upon this contemplation leads to a condition of tranquillity (ἀταραξία) corresponding to the equilibrium of the body. But this tranquillity of the mind may again be interrupted, like the tranquillity of the body, by the invasion of pain, and the mind has special pains of its own. The pains of the mind are primarily, like its pleasures, derived from the body: present pain in the body may cause mental grief, and so also may the recollection

---

[1] Hieronymus, *Comm. in Isaiam*, xi. 38; U. 437. A practical example of this may be seen in the saying of Epicurus on his deathbed, quoted on p. 497.

[2] Quoted by Plut., ibid. 4; C.B. *fr.* 11; U. 68 τὸ γὰρ εὐσταθὲς σαρκὸς κατάστημα καὶ τὸ περὶ ταύτης πιστὸν ἔλπισμα τὴν ἀκροτάτην χαρὰν καὶ βεβαιοτάτην ἔχει τοῖς ἐπιλογίζεσθαι δυναμένοις.

[3] D.L. x. 137.

of past pain. But the mind has its own 'unnecessary desires', whose indulgence may bring pain. The first of these is avarice, the desire for wealth, which only produces gratuitous disturbance in the mind: 'many men when they have ac- quired riches have not found the escape from their ills but only a change to greater ills',[1] 'by means of occupations worthy of a beast abundance of riches is heaped up, but a miserable life results'.[2] Far better is the life of poverty which produces contentment: 'poverty, when measured by the natural purpose of life, is great wealth, but unlimited wealth is great poverty'.[3] Another of the mind's unlimited desires is for honour and position, for 'crowns and statues',[4] as the scholiast puts it. A striking aphorism sums up the futility of all these desires: 'the disturbance of the soul cannot be ended nor true joy created either by the possession of the greatest wealth or by honour and respect in the eyes of the mob or by anything else that is associated with causes of unlimited desire'.[5] It is however the capacity of the mind to project itself into the future which gives it its most characteristic and peculiar pains: for mental pain for the future is of course fear.[6] Fear is from the nature of the case unknown to the body, yet even this peculiar pain of the mind is in a sense derived from the body, for mental fear is primarily at least concerned with the fate of the body. Now this fear may be of many kinds, for it may be excited by many causes. It may be a fear lest the body should be unable to maintain the pleasure of equilibrium, but it should not be, for of that we have a 'sure hope': it may be a fear of disease or accident, but again it should not be, for we know that even if pain comes, pleasure will in the long run have the upper hand. It may again be fear of the interference[7] of other men in our

---

[1] Porph. *ad Marc.* 28, p. 208; C.B. *fr.* 72; U. 479.
[2] Ibid., p. 209; C.B. *fr.* 73; U. 480.   [3] *Sent. Vat.* C.B. *fr.* xxv.
[4] Schol. ad *K.Δ.* xxx.   [5] *Sent. Vat.* C.B. lxxxi.
[6] See e.g. Ep. iii, § 128 τούτου γὰρ χάριν πάντα πράττομεν ὅπως μήτε ἀλγῶμεν μήτε ταρβῶμεν.
[7] D.L. x. 117 βλάβας ἐξ ἀνθρώπων ἢ διὰ μῖσος ἢ διὰ φθόνον ἢ διὰ καταφρόνησιν γίνεσθαι: see also *K.Δ.* vi, xl, and pp. 511–13.

life of happiness, but it is possible in several ways to guard against this.[1] There are however two great and overwhelming fears which may attack the mind, and if they are not dissipated, may swallow up all pleasure in a continual and abiding dread. The fear of the interference of the gods in the affairs of the world wrecks the tranquillity of the mind, because it destroys the 'sure hope' of the future, which rests upon a belief in the perfect regularity of the process of cause and effect: if miracles may happen, there is no possibility of a sure calculation of future happiness for the rest of this life. And the fear of death, if it is combined with a belief in survival, is an almost stronger provocative of constant dread: for even if we can so order this life as to secure the pleasure of tranquillity, there may be awaiting us in an after life punishments and tortures so horrible that the anticipation of them will absolutely destroy that tranquillity. So terrible indeed is this dread that Epicurus sometimes believed it to be the motive of almost all crimes in life;[2] at times man will even commit suicide to escape from fear of death![3] It is therefore a primary condition of mental tranquillity that man should be freed from these fears. And so Epicurus at the outset of his Letter to Menoeceus[4] sets out as the 'first principles' (στοιχεῖα) of the good life the two beliefs that god is an immortal and blessed being, who does not help the good or harm the bad, and that death is nothing to us. The same two principles stand similarly at the head of the *Principal Doctrines*,[5] and are indeed the very foundation and prime condition of the blessed life. We must learn that the gods do indeed exist, but know no trouble themselves, nor cause it to others: we must learn that death means the complete extinction of consciousness,[6] that is, the end of all good and evil, for it is the end of pleasure and pain. It cannot hurt us when it comes, nor can its anticipation cause us distress: 'for that which gives no trouble when it comes, is

---

[1] See p. 511. [2] See Lucr. iii. 59 ff.
[3] Ibid. 79–81; Seneca, *Ep.* 24. 23; U. 497, 498.
[4] § 123. [5] *K.Δ.* i, ii.
[6] Ep. iii, § 124 στέρησις δέ ἐστιν αἰσθήσεως ὁ θάνατος.

but an empty pain in anticipation'.[1] The loss of consciousness and personality in death is complete: 'the state after death is the same as that before our birth';[2] 'even as in the time gone by we felt no ill . . . so, when we shall be no more, when there shall have come the parting of body and soul, by whose union we are made one, you may know that nothing at all will be able to happen to us, who will then be no more, or stir our feeling; no, not if earth shall be mingled with sea, and sea with sky'.[3] Even if, as Lucretius suggests in a curious speculation which seems to have good Epicurean authority, 'time should gather together our substance after our decease and bring it back again as it is now placed, if once more the light of life should be vouchsafed to us, yet, even were that done, it would not concern us at all, when once the remembrance of our former selves were snapped in twain'.

Now these 'first principles' may be accepted on authority as a matter of faith, and as such Epicurus commends them to Menoeceus: 'become accustomed,' he says, 'to the belief that death is nothing to us'.[4] But for the initiated this faith is not sufficient: if he is to have a sure grasp of the principles, he must be able to prove both the unconcern of the gods and the mortality of the soul. How Epicurus effected these proofs has been seen in previous chapters, but a new link may be noticed here between the moral and the physical sides of Epicureanism. For just as the moral idea is an essential part in and an immediate consequence of the physical theory, so now the physical theory becomes a necessity for the full realization of the moral ideal. 'If we were not troubled by our suspicions of the phenomena of the sky and about death, fearing that it concerns us, and also by our failure to grasp the limits of pains and desires, we should have no need of natural science ($\phi \upsilon \sigma \iota o \lambda o \gamma \iota a$):'[5] 'a man cannot dispel his fear about the most important matters if he does not know what is the nature of the universe, but

---

[1] Ibid., § 125.
[2] Pseudo-Plut. *Consol. ad Apollonium*, 15. 109 e; U. 495.
[3] Lucr. iii. 832–42. [4] Ep. iii, § 124. [5] *K.Δ.* xi.

suspects the truth of some mythical story. So that without natural science it is not possible to attain our pleasures unalloyed'.[1] In this sense indeed it is true that Epicurus' physical theory, though his interest in it for its own sake led him far beyond the immediate necessity of establishing the 'first principle', does exist for the sake of the moral life: it is in a sense its handmaid: 'to discover accurately the cause of the most essential facts is the function of the science of nature, and a blessed life for us lies in this'.[2] It is true that the blessed life is in its practice open to the most humble and least gifted, yet for its complete realization it requires the co-operation of thought (διάνοια)[3] penetrating into the inmost workings of the imperceptible. And thought, which is of course a special activity of the mind, in this research finds in its turn its own peculiar pleasure, which is simultaneous with its effort and unlike that of the body, is almost unlimited: 'in all other occupations the fruit comes painfully after completion, but in philosophy pleasure goes hand in hand with knowledge'.[4] In other words, the intellect has practically the whole range of physical science as its pleasure-ground, and in the pursuit of its own pleasure is incidentally securing the conditions of the pleasure of the mind as a whole. It is with reason that Epicurus urges on Menoeceus the practice of philosophy at all ages of life: 'both when young and old a man must study philosophy, that as he grows old he may be young in blessings through the grateful recollection of what has been, and that in youth he may be old as well, since he will know no fear of what is to come'.[5] Nor does the study of his philosophy require any previous education or training; indeed it is a positive disadvantage: 'I congratulate you, Apelles,' says Epicurus to a disciple, 'in that you have approached philosophy free from all blemish',[6] and to another he exclaims with vehemence: 'Blest youth, set sail in your bark and flee from every form

---

[1] K.Δ. xii.   [2] Ep. i, § 78.
[3] Ep. i, § 78 καὶ τοῦτο καταλαβεῖν τῇ διανοίᾳ ἔστιν ἁπλῶς εἶναι.
[4] Sent. Vat. C.B. fr. xxvii.   [5] Ep. iii, § 122.
[6] Athen. xiii, p. 588 a; C.B. fr. 24; U. 117.

of culture.'[1] By the study of physical science alone can the
tranquillity of the mind be fully and permanently secured:
freed from the possibility of the great fears for the future,
and pleasurably occupied in the search for scientific truth,
which will confirm its freedom, it may peacefully rest in the
contemplation of the pleasures of the body, past, present,
and future, and so attain its own characteristic 'imperturbability' (ἀταραξία). There will then be but little room left,
even as there is little inclination, for vain desires: 'through
love of true philosophy every disturbing and troublesome
desire is ended'.[2] And the result is a happy and useful life:
'we must laugh and philosophize at the same time and do
our household duties and employ our other faculties, and
never cease proclaiming the sayings of the true philosophy'.[3]

Thus by a series of logical deductions the original simple
notion of the pursuit of pleasure has broadened out into a
wide conception of the 'blessed' life, whose 'end is the health
of the body and tranquillity of the mind',[4] the latter being
the direct outcome of the former. Pleasure and pain, though
always the final tests of good and bad, are modified through
the application of the calculus of pleasure, into a practical
choice and avoidance, and as a guide for choice and avoidance
certain definite principles have been laid down. But in
practical life there must always remain a residuum of borderline cases, where the Epicurean will have to make up his
mind as to the right course. In such cases there is but one
guiding principle: 'if on each occasion instead of referring
your actions to the end ordained by nature, you turn to some
other nearer standard when you are making a choice or an
avoidance, your actions will not be consistent with your
principles'.[5] We must never be content to judge a problem
of action by any intermediate or derivative test, such as that
of any one of the virtues, but always have before us the
ultimate standard, the 'end of nature', pleasure, which is

[1] D.L. x. 6.   [2] Porph. *ad Marc.* 31, p. 209; C.B.*fr.* 66; U. 457.
[3] *Sent. Vat.* C.B. *fr.* xli.
[4] Ep. iii, § 128 τὴν τοῦ σώματος ὑγίειαν καὶ τὴν <τῆς ψυχῆς> ἀταραξίαν, ἐπεὶ τοῦτο τοῦ μακαρίως ζῆν ἐστι τέλος.   [5] *K.Δ.* xxv.

the restful equilibrium of body and mind: no other standard of judgement is safe. But the application of this principle is by no means always easy, and for this reason Epicurus regards as the supreme possession of life the faculty of practical prudence or right judgement (φρόνησις), which partly relying on experience and partly on a kind of intuition —it is like the faculty for the right use of 'apprehensions' on the intellectual side—enables a man to make a right choice. 'The beginning of all this and the greatest good of all is prudence: it is a more precious thing even than philosophy.'[1] Philosophy is not within the grasp of all, nor does it so greatly matter if a man were to go astray in the intellectual apprehension of the principles of the system: but to be mistaken in the practical distinction of good and evil and so to make a wrong choice might mean the wrecking of a life. Such practical prudence is within the reach of all and it alone can help a man to the right application of the principles he has learnt.

The wise man thus instructed and provided is well prepared to meet life, its changes and chances and its end in death. 'He neither seeks to escape life nor fears the cessation of life: for neither does life offend him, nor does the absence of life seem to be any evil. And just as with food he does not seek simply the larger share and nothing else, but rather the most pleasant, so he seeks to enjoy not the longest period of time, but the most pleasant.'[2] His normal life, thanks to the tranquillity which he has attained both in body and mind, is one of pure, if not uninterrupted, pleasure, and when pain comes he bears it in the certainty of the ultimate preponderance of pleasure: 'the wise man',[3] cried Epicurus in a moment of enthusiasm which has given much merriment to his critics, 'is happy, even if he be on the rack'. Chance, that unpredictable element of spontaneity in nature, he will not regard as itself a bestower of good and evil,[4] but as affording 'opportunities for great good and evil: and he will

---

[1] Ep. iii, § 132.　　　　　　　　　　　　　[2] § 126.
[3] D.L. x. 118 κἂν στρεβλωθῇ δ' ὁ σοφός, εἶναι αὐτὸν εὐδαίμονα.
[4] Ep. iii, § 134: cf. K.Δ. xvi.

think it better to be unfortunate in reasonable action than
to prosper in unreason:' he would rather let chance spoil his
well-chosen plans, than be successful in an ill-chosen course
by its aid. And so, indifferent as far as possible, to events
and occurrences over which he has no control, he will live
his peaceful life of happiness, and 'when circumstances bring
about his departure from life, he will not approach his end
as though he were falling short in any way of the best life'.[1]
For the old age of the philosopher Epicurus had a peculiar
sympathy:[2] 'it is not the young man who should be thought
happy, but an old man who has lived a good life . . . the old
man has come to anchor in old age as though in port, and
the good things for which before he hardly hoped he has
brought into safe anchorage in his grateful recollections'.
And to the last his effort must be prolonged: 'we must try
to make the end of the journey better than the beginning, as
long as we are journeying: but when we come to the end,
we must be happy and content'.[3] And so 'when it is time
for us to go, spitting contempt on life and those who have
vainly clung to it, we will leave life crying aloud in a glorious
triumph-song that we have lived well'.[4]

It is a noble structure which Epicurus has raised on the
foundation of pleasure, and it is not in a mere enthusiasm
that he compares the life of the truly wise man to the happiness of the gods: 'You shall live',[5] he tells Menoeceus, 'like
a god among men': 'if you take away his eternity,'[6] says
Cicero in scorn, but with a singularly true statement of the
Epicurean position, 'Jupiter is no more blessed than Epicurus: for both alike enjoy the highest good, that is pleasure'.
With greater exactness Epicurus has himself expressed the
comparison in a brief phrase which well sums up the blessed
life of the wise: 'there are two ideas of happiness: complete

---

[1] *K.Δ.* xx.
[2] *Sent. Vat.* C.B. *fr.* xvii.
[3] *Sent. Vat.* C.B. *fr.* xlviii.
[4] *Sent. Vat.* C.B. *fr.* xlvii.
[5] Ep. iii, § 135.
[6] *de Fin.* ii. 27. 88; U. 602: cf. *Sent. Vat.* C.B. *fr.* xxxiii. 'The flesh cries
out to be saved from hunger, thirst, and cold. For if a man keep this safety
and hope to keep it, he might rival even Zeus in happiness.'

happiness, such as belongs to a god, which admits of no increase, and the happiness which is concerned with the addition and subtraction of pleasures'.[1] The wise man's happiness is not absolutely continuous owing to the necessary wants of life and the inevitable disturbances of pain and grief, but all the happiness he has is in itself as perfect as that of the gods.

It would be natural to pause at this point and attempt some estimate of the Epicurean moral theory in general, but that it is necessary first to deal with the philosopher's attitude to virtue, and in particular to those virtues which involve dealings with other men: 'egoistic hedonism' will not then perhaps shine so brightly. Virtue is of course not in itself an end to Epicurus, it is not even in itself desirable: indeed it is only 'an empty name'.[2] Pleasure is the only end and the practical prudence of the wise man has to decide in each case whether a given course of action will ultimately produce greater pleasure than its opposite. What is commonly known as virtue, and is made itself the end of action by other thinkers, can only be chosen by the Epicurean, if at all, as a means to an end: it is in itself nothing, but it may usefully contribute to the real end of pleasure. The position is succinctly summed up by Diogenes: 'for the sake of pleasure the virtues are preferred, but not for their own sake, just as the doctor's art is employed for the sake of health'.[3] We wish to attain the true end, and the application of the 'hedonistic calculus' shows us that the 'virtuous' course of action is on the whole a useful means towards it, though in itself it may well be laborious and painful and therefore even hateful: 'I spit upon the honourable' (προσπτύω τῷ καλῷ), Epicurus exclaimed, 'and upon those who vainly admire it, when it does not produce any pleasure.'[4] It is not therefore possible

---

[1] D.L. x. 121a.

[2] See Cic. *Tusc. Disp.* v. 26. 73, and other quotations in U. 511.

[3] x. 138.

[4] Quoted by Athenaeus, xii. 547 a; C.B. *fr.* 79; U. 512. τὸ καλὸν here probably includes both 'the beautiful', the aim of aesthetic culture, and 'the honourable' as a moral end, e.g. in Plato.

to discuss virtue as such with an Epicurean: even to speak of 'the virtues' is a kind of brachylogy, for the real question for him is the course of action on each occasion which will produce the most pleasure: 'virtue, according to Epicurus, is concerned with the selection of pleasant things'.[1] This selection is the province of practical prudence exercising its choice unfettered as occasions arise. Yet the experience of the wise man may make generalizations, and experience shows that prudence does choose the virtues,[2] for its calculations show that they are conducive to pleasure: 'the virtues', Diogenes of Oenoanda[3] wrote on his great inscription to the passer-by, 'are never an end, but they are productive of the end'. Indeed not only are they productive of the end, they are actually inseparable from pleasure: 'virtue alone is inseparable from pleasure',[4] for prudence itself 'teaches us that it is not possible to live pleasantly without living prudently and honourably and justly, nor again to live a life of prudence, honour, and justice without living pleasantly'.[5] In practice then the pendulum seems to have swung round again: virtue is nought in itself, yet as a practical means to pleasure it is indispensable. We should expect then to find that the Epicurean, however widely his motives of action might differ, lived a life not very different from that of other men, and in practice followed the ordinary lines of virtuous conduct. Yet even this conclusion is not fully justified, for Epicurus' logic in the moral field is relentless, and his eye is always on the main end of the pleasure of tranquillity. There are then striking differences in practice as well as motive from the ordinary code, and these will be seen most clearly by a consideration of his attitude towards some of the individual virtues: it will be convenient to take the three cardinal moral virtues of temperance, courage, and justice: wisdom has in effect been discussed already.

Temperance is 'not to be chosen for itself, but because it brings peace to our minds and calms and assuages them

---

[1] Alexander Aphr. *de Anima*, ii. 22, p. 156; U. 515.
[2] See Ep. iii, § 132.   [3] Diog. Oen. *fr.* xxv, col. iii (William).
[4] D.L. x. 138.   [5] Ep. iii, § 132: cf. *K.Δ.* v.

in a kind of concord'.[1] It has no value in itself, it is even painful and therefore bad, but it is derivatively worthy of choice, because it contributes to the highest pleasure of body and mind. For temperance is just the rule of conduct which avoids the mere kinetic pleasures, the unnecessary desires, and the 'diversification' of pleasure, and chooses rather the conduct which conduces to the perfect pleasure of tranquillity. The conclusion is here straightforward: the Epicurean will choose temperance and cling to it as strictly as any philosopher who made it an end in itself. For the practice of courage the Epicurean has even stronger arguments: for here it is not a question of avoiding pleasures, which apart from their consequences are in themselves good, but of choosing pains 'in order to avoid greater pains'.[2] The man who cannot show courage submits himself to pains of the body, to the tyranny of other men, and to the fears of the mind which are one and all far greater pains than the effort which is required to resist them. Moreover the Epicurean has a better equipment for courage than other philosophers: for he 'despises death . . . and is prepared to meet pains with the assurance that the greatest pains are ended by death, and that lesser pains have many intervals of rest'.[3] He can estimate rightly what it is that he has to endure and so can go to meet pain and even death with 'a strong and lofty spirit free from all care and anguish'.[4] For courage he has both a stronger motive and a greater capacity than others: for the sake of his own peace it is infinitely worth while, and he knows that the demand on it is not so great as it might seem.

The problem of justice is at once more complicated and more interesting, for it involves the whole question of relations to other men. In other philosophies, such as those of Plato and Aristotle, justice was represented as the natural outcome of man's capacity and desire to live in society with his fellow men: it exists by nature (φύσει) and not by con-

---

[1] Cic. *de Fin.* i. 14. 47.
[2] Origenes, *contra Celsum*, v. 47; U. 516.
[3] Cic. *de Fin.* i. 15. 49.   [4] Ibid.

vention (νόμῳ). Such a position was of course impossible for
Epicurus: the individual is concerned with his own maximum pleasure and cannot consider other men, except as they
affect that pleasure: 'there is no such thing as human society:
every man is concerned for himself'.[1] But this very concern
for himself makes it necessary for the philosopher to determine his attitude to other men: for they may either be a very
serious hindrance to his pleasure or possibly be made to
subserve it. The motive of fear is in this case stronger than
the motive of hope. Indeed the fear of other men, though
not nearly so great or so serious as the fear of the gods or
the fear of death, was yet one of the chief disturbing causes
of the peace of the mind. It must then be the main object
of the individual in his intercourse with others to secure
freedom from the fear of men (θαρρεῖν ἐξ ἀνθρώπων).[2] There
were several possible means which might be employed for
this purpose, but the principal was undoubtedly the line of
action known to the world as the virtue of justice. Justice,
just like temperance and courage, is in itself of no intrinsic
value, but is useful as a means of securing one's own happiness. What then is its nature from the Epicurean point of
view? It would clearly be most to the advantage of the individual to have perfect freedom of action, which in life among
other men means complete disregard for them, their property and their interests. But if this is to be the universal
course of action, it is obvious that any one individual, having
every man's hand against him, is likely to suffer very much
more than he can gain. It therefore becomes to his advantage to forego the pleasures of aggression, on condition that
he is guaranteed freedom from attack: justice is in other
words a kind of compact between members of a community
to refrain from harming one another. 'Justice never is anything in itself, but in the dealings of men with one another
in any place whatever and at any time, it is a kind of compact
not to harm or be harmed'[3]—or as Epicurus again puts it
with obviously controversial intention, 'The justice which

---

[1] Quoted by Lactantius, *Divin. Instit.* iii. 17. 42; U. 523.
[2] *K.Δ.* vi, xl.   [3] Ibid. xxxiii.

arises from nature'[1]—as opposed, for instance to Plato's idea of 'natural' (φύσει) justice—'is a pledge of mutual advantage (σύμβολον τοῦ συμφέροντος) to restrain men from harming one another and save them from being harmed'. This is of course practically the seventeenth-century idea of the 'Social Contract', and indeed Lucretius,[2] like the modern philosophers, represents the making of this contract as an actual historical event in the history of primitive man. More conspicuously then than either of the two former virtues is justice a *pis aller*, a painful thing in itself and only to be tolerated because it contributes to tranquillity of the mind, which it relieves from fear of worse pains. The ideal from the individual's point of view is really injustice: if only he could commit injustice consistently without ever being discovered, that would be best, but unfortunately not only is there the danger of detection, but what is still worse, because it is a permanent disturbance of mental peace, there is always the dread of detection. This extreme position Epicurus takes up unhesitatingly: 'injustice is not an evil in itself, but only in consequence of the fear which attaches to the apprehension of being unable to escape those appointed to punish such actions'.[3] And this dread will never leave one, for 'it is not possible for one who acts in secret contravention of the terms of the compact not to harm or be harmed, to be confident that he will escape detection, even if at present he escapes a thousand times. For up to the time of death it cannot be certain if he will indeed escape'.[4] In his book of 'Problems'[5] (Διαπορίαι) Epicurus actually posed the question: 'will the wise man do things that the laws forbid, if he knows that he will not be found out?'; both his consistency and his humanity are revealed in his reply that

[1] K.Δ. xxxi. Bignone following Philippson (*Arch. f. Gesch. der Philosoph.*, 1910, pp. 291 ff.) would translate σύμβολον 'symbol', 'expression', holding that Epicurus believed that there is a 'natural justice' of which just conduct is the outward sign. But elsewhere the 'contract' idea is most prominent: e.g. in συνθήκας in K.Δ. xxxii. [2] v. 1019–20.

[3] K.Δ. xxxiv: cf. Plut. *contr. Ep. beat.* 6, p. 1090 c; C.B. *fr.* 82; U. 532.

[4] K.Δ. xxxv.

[5] Plut. *adv. Colot.* 34, p. 1127 a; C.B. *fr.* 2; U. 18.

'a simple answer is not easy to find'. Lucretius has finely brought out the magnitude of this dread in a curious passage[1] in which he states that the stories of punishment in the next world are but allegories of men's mental sufferings here: Tartarus and Cerberus and the Furies are only legends, but the real terror is the 'fear of punishment for misdeeds in life and the atonement for crime, the dungeon, and the terrible hurling down from the rock, scourgings, executioners, the rack, pitch, the metal plate, torches; for although they are not with us, yet the guilty mind, fearing for its misdeeds, sets goads to itself, and scars itself with lashings, nor does it see meanwhile what end there can be to its ills or what limit at last to punishment, yea, and it fears that these same things may grow worse after death. Here after all on earth the life of fools becomes a hell'. To save himself from this hell the wise man accepts the trifling inconvenience of the compact: for it is clear that 'the just man is most free from trouble, the unjust most full of trouble'.[2] The life of justice so conceived is a disagreeable necessity, but it saves a man in every way from great pains and it helps to the supreme end of true pleasure, for 'the greatest fruit of justice is freedom from trouble (ἀταραξία)'.[3] Therefore the wise man is content that there should be laws on the understanding that 'the laws exist for the sake of the wise, not that they may not do wrong, but that they may not suffer it'.[4]

Epicurus is at pains to emphasize this idea of justice in several other ways, all tending to show that justice is nothing in itself, but has only a derivative value. Its very existence he holds is dependent on the existence of the compact: 'for all living things which have not been able to make compacts not to harm one another or be harmed, nothing ever is either just or unjust: and likewise too for all tribes which have been unable or unwilling to make compacts not to harm or be harmed'.[5] Unless there is the deliberate understanding there is no obligation to refrain from acts of aggression

---

[1] iii. 1011–23.
[2] *K.Δ.* xvii.
[3] Clem. Alex. *Strom.* vi. 2, p. 266; C.B. *fr.* 80; U. 519.
[4] Stob. *Floril.* 43. 139; C.B. *fr.* 81; U. 530.
[5] *K.Δ.* xxxii.

and no security against them: it is incidentally interesting to see this doctrine applied to nations, for the modern attitude to weaker and less civilized races has often been based on much the same principle: if a nation is not strong enough to enforce justice, it has no international rights. Still more significant are the aphorisms which deal with the variability of justice: the same actions are by no means always just among different peoples or at different times. 'In its general aspect justice is the same for all, for it is a kind of mutual advantage in the dealings of men with one another; but with reference to the individual peculiarities of a country or any other circumstances, the same thing does not turn out to be just for all.'[1] The argument is that if justice had an independent existence of its own, if, as Epicurus would say, it were 'something', its content would not vary with varying circumstances, but would be the same all the world over: as it is varying circumstances naturally make a difference to what is advantageous. The same conclusion may also be reached from the point of view of time: an enactment, which was just at the time when it was made, may cease to be just: 'if a man makes a law, and it does not turn out to lead to advantage in men's dealings with each other, then it no longer has the essential nature of justice'.[2] Again the content of justice is shifting, and has no existence or value other than the advantage of the time being. In short, as Epicurus summed matters up with almost brutal directness, 'the laws exist for the sake of the wise, not that they may not do wrong, but that they may not suffer it'.[3]

There is no doubt then that justice is but of secondary value. Temperance and courage the wise Epicurean will cultivate assiduously with a strong belief in their value, because they contribute immediately and necessarily to the increase of his pleasure and the diminution of his pains. But justice is a makeshift: the 'wise man' accepts it with a view of getting what he can out of it; but he would gladly evade it, if he could only be certain that he would not be

---

[1] K.Δ. xxxvi. [2] Ibid. xxxvii.
[3] Stob. *Flor.* 43. 139; C.B. *fr.* 81; U. 530.

detected in the breaking of his tacit compact. It is not a very pleasant picture to contemplate and one does not like to think of the possible decisions of an Epicurean casuist on this basis. The weakness of the Epicurean morality begins to show itself, as that of any form of egoistic hedonism necessarily must, as soon as the individual is set in relation with his fellow men. Nor does the picture become brighter if the virtues are left and certain other means are considered which the 'wise men' will pursue to secure 'immunity' from his fellows.

Epicurus' general attitude is seen with special distinctness in the precepts which he gives his disciples with regard to public life, to friendship, and to the family: in each instance he has his eye very firmly fixed on the supreme pleasure of tranquillity of mind and is fearless in his deductions, however much they differ from those of common custom or conventional morality. The injuries which one may receive from one's fellow men arise, he holds,[1] 'from hatred, envy, or contempt', that is, from the action of those who are respectively one's equals, inferiors or superiors in station: against all these the 'wise man' must provide and it is possible for him to 'overcome them by reasoning'. Now the habit of the world, which in its own blind way does half-consciously attempt to deal with these adverse circumstances, is to try for personal power and authority. But there are considerable dangers about this course. In the first place it is by no means certain that it will secure the desired end: it may indeed leave one without superiors to hurt one by contempt and even free one from the hatred of equals; but it also increases the number of inferiors who may be prompted by jealousy to do one harm. 'Some men wished to become famous and conspicuous, thinking that they would thus win for themselves safety from other men. Wherefore if the life of such men is safe, they have obtained the good which nature craves: but if it is not safe, they do not possess that for which they strove at first by the instinct of nature.'[2] Like the guilty criminal such men may appear at times to have attained their

[1] D.L. x. 117.　　　　　　　[2] K.Δ. vii.

end and be free, but there is always the danger that vengeance may overtake them. Moreover, just as to the criminal the external danger proved to be a small thing compared with the internal dread which disturbed his mind, so here too the main objection to this striving for power is the internal effect on the mind. The peace of mind of the man in high places is constantly disturbed not only by the dread of an attack of his inferiors—'a man who causes fear cannot be free from fear' [1]—but also because power begets the craving for more power, and the mind becomes a prey to the 'idle desires' for 'crowns and statues'. 'The happy and blessed state belongs not to abundance of riches or dignity of position or any office or power, but to freedom from pain and moderation in feelings and an attitude of mind which imposes the limits ordained by nature.' [2] In short, the life of power however successful it may be is not compatible with the true ideal of happiness. What then is Epicurus' remedy? The only sure way of securing 'immunity from men' is to avoid public life altogether: the 'wise man' must 'flee public life as an injury and disturbance to blessedness'.[3] 'We must release ourselves from the prison of affairs and politics.'[4] We must 'live unnoticed':[5] so alone can a man be sure that he will avoid the attack of enemies and prevent the intrusion of care and anxiety upon his own peace of mind. And whatever may be the pleasures of rule and office and its consequent honour and glory—for Epicurus does not deny the existence of such pleasures [6]—they are as nothing compared to the glory of the tranquil mind: 'The crown of tranquillity is beyond comparison with great positions of authority.' [7] The wise man will make the choice which prudence dictates and keep himself far from the snares of ambition: for he knows that 'it is far better to obey

[1] Gnomol. *Cod. Par.* 1168; C.B. *fr.* 84; U. 537.
[2] Epicurus quoted by Plut. *de Audiendis Poetis*, 14. 37; C.B. *fr.* 85; U. 548.   [3] Plut. *vit. Pyrrhi*, 20; U. 552.
[4] *Sent. Vat.* C.B. *fr.* lviii.
[5] λάθε βιώσας, C.B. *fr.* 86; U. 551: cf. Plutarch's dialogue on the subject.
[6] Idem. *contr. Ep. beat.* 18; U. 549.
[7] Idem. *adv. Colot.* 31; U. 556.

in peace than to long to rule the world with kingly power and to sway kingdoms'.[1] There is a marked churlishness and a depressing timidity about the 'wise man's' action, but if he is to be consistent with his beliefs, this is the only course he can take.

In his attitude to friendship the 'wise man' seems at first sight to present a more human and attractive side of his nature. 'Of all the things',[2] says Epicurus himself, 'which wisdom acquires to produce the blessedness of the complete life, far the greatest is the possession of friendship', and the Epicurean[3] in Cicero's dialogue echoes and amplifies this: 'of all the means which wisdom has acquired for living the blessed life none is greater than friendship, none richer, none sweeter'. He adds that Epicurus upheld this belief not merely in words but much more in his life and actions and character. Similarly his biographer states that he was renowned for his 'unsurpassed kindness to all'.[4] The picture of the life of the philosopher with his friends in his 'Garden' is familiar, and the fragments of his letters[5] which have been preserved show clearly his deep affection and care for them: even in his death-bed agony he writes that he is consoled by the thought of his pleasant discussions with Idomeneus,[6] and his will makes provision for his friends and his friends' children.[7] The tradition lasted in the School, and Lucretius[8] can speak of 'the pleasure of sweet friendship, for which I hope' with the scarcely worthy Memmius as one of his chief inducements in undertaking his great task.

Further information as to Epicurus' view of friendship deepens this pleasant impression with the additional note of genuine trust and unselfishness and even of self-sacrifice. Epicurus did not wish, it is said,[9] that his community should throw their property into a common stock, 'for to do so implied distrust, and distrust could not go with friendship'. In the same spirit he is reported to have said that 'it is more

---

[1] Lucr. v. 1129–30.   [2] *K.Δ*. xxvii.
[3] Cic. *de Fin.* i. 20. 65; U. 539.   [4] D.L. x. 9.
[5] C.B. *frs.* 18–52.   [6] D.L. x. 32; C.B. *fr.* 30.
[7] D.L. x. 16–21.   [8] i. 140.   [9] D.L. x. 11.

pleasant to do good than to receive it',[1] and advancing to
greater heights of unselfishness to have maintained that 'for
friendship's sake we must even run risks',[2] and that the
'wise man' will be prepared to 'endure the greatest pains for
his friends'[3] and even 'to die for a friend'.[4] It seems indeed
as if there were here a higher conception of the value and
beauty of friendship than is met with elsewhere even in
Greek literature: the joys of friendship last through life and
even beyond, for though there is of course no kind of continuity after death, yet 'sweet is the memory of a dead friend',[5]
and we must 'show our feeling for our lost friends not by
lamentation, but by meditation'[6] on what their friendship
has been to us. Almost equally striking perhaps is the extension of friendship even to slaves: 'the wise man will not
punish his slaves, but will rather pity them and forgive any
that are deserving';[7] the position of the slave Mys in the
Epicurean community shows this precept in practice.
Friendship seems indeed the highest blessing in life: 'the
noble soul occupies itself with wisdom and friendship: of
these the one is a mortal good, the other immortal',[8] and in
a moment of enthusiasm, when thinking of its many links,
Epicurus even exclaimed: 'friendship goes dancing round
the world proclaiming to us all to awake to the praises of a
happy life'.[9] The 'wise man' may almost be forgiven his
refusal to take his share in the burdens of politics when the
beauty of his life with his friends is realized.

But, though friendship is without doubt the brightest
spot in Epicurean life, there is another side to the picture.
For when its motives are examined, it is found that this
suggestion of self-forgetfulness and devotion is something
of a delusion, and that friendship like every other interest
and action in the 'wise man's' life is based on the primary
consideration of personal pleasure: 'friendship has practical

---

[1] Plut. *contr. Ep. beat.* 15, 1097 a; U. 544.   [2] *Sent. Vat.* C.B. *fr.* xxviii.
[3] Plut. *adv. Colot.* 8, p. 1111 b; U. 546.   [4] D.L. x. 121.
[5] Plut. *contr. Ep. beat.* 28, p. 1105 d; C.B. *fr.* 50; U. 213.
[6] *Sent. Vat.* C.B. *fr.* lxvi.   [7] D.L. x. 118.
[8] *Sent. Vat.* C.B. *fr.* lxxviii.   [9] Ibid. lii.

needs as its motive',[1] 'Epicurus says that there is no one
who cares for another except for his own advantage.'[2] A
more explicit aphorism brings out the two sides of this advantage:[3] 'friendship cannot be divorced from pleasure and
for that reason must be cultivated, because without it neither
can we live in safety and without fear, nor even pleasantly'.
In the first place then friendship is part of the provision
made by the 'wise man' to secure freedom from fear of other
men. For this purpose he attaches to himself those who
might otherwise be his enemies: as Epicurus[4] puts it in
a rather impersonal manner: 'the man who has best ordered
the element of disquiet arising from external circumstances,
has made those things (including persons) that he could
akin to himself and the rest at least not alien'. And friends
once secured act as a kind of bodyguard against the aggres-
sions of others: 'it is not so much our friends' help that helps
us as the confidence of their help';[5] the man with many
friends feels himself hedged round with security. Secondly
friendship is valuable because it enhances the pleasure of
one's own life without introducing a disturbing element of
desire and passion such as attaches to love, which Epicurus
wholly condemned. Once more the root-motive even of this
great blessing of friendship is self-interest and the increase
of the aggregate of pleasure in the individual life.

The contrast is strongly marked and it does not seem easy
to reconcile the two pictures of friendship derived from the
contemplation of its practice on the one hand and its motives
on the other, nor to acquit Epicurus altogether of inconsistency. A link of connexion might seem to lie in the idea
that 'it is more pleasant to give than to receive':[6] if this were
really Epicurus' belief, then it might follow that altruism
is in reality the highest egoism and the greatest joys of
friendship would be found to lie in the opportunities which

---

[1] D.L. x. 120.
[2] Lactantius, *Divin. Instit.* iii. 17. 42; U. 540.
[3] Cic. *de Fin.* ii. 26. 82; U. 541.   [4] *K.Δ.* xxxix: cf. *K.Δ.* xl.
[5] *Sent. Vat.* C.B. *fr.* xxxiv.
[6] Plut. *contr. Ep. beat.* 15; U. 544.

it affords of giving happiness to others. But the statement, as we have it, is not supported by argument or parallel and in view of the directly egoistic attitude which prevails throughout the discussion of pleasure, it does not ring quite true: it ought, for instance, to carry with it a willingness to perform public service. It is probably safer to suppose that Epicurus did, as usual, found his advocacy of friendship on the purely utilitarian motive of personal advantage in protection and the pleasures of intercourse, but that on that foundation grew a true sense of the more unselfish enjoyment of friendship for its own sake. This view is not unsupported: 'all friendship',[1] the philosopher says in a brief aphorism, 'is desirable in itself, though it starts from the need of help', and the idea [2] is elaborated by his biographer: 'friendship has practical needs as its motive: one must indeed lay its foundations (for we sow the ground too for the sake of crops), but it is formed and maintained by means of community of life among those who have reached the fullness of pleasure'. If there is inconsistency, this single relaxation of an austere and almost cynical devotion to self-interest may well be pardoned: the true-hearted man emerges for once over the stern philosopher, and the account of friendship remains as an oasis in the rather arid desert of Epicureanism on its social side.

Just as friendship is the highest blessing, so the passion of love is wholly a curse. Epicurus naturally regarded it as a supreme example of an 'idle desire', which makes true peace of mind impossible: 'it is',[3] he said, 'a vehement yearning for sexual pleasure accompanied by a goading restlessness', and his denunciation of its physical side is unmistakable: 'sexual intercourse has never done a man good and he is lucky if it has not harmed him'.[4] It is possible that Lucretius'[5] famous attack upon love may have been heightened, as the traditional story of his life suggests, by personal

---

[1] Sent. Vat. C.B. fr. xxiii.   [2] D.L. x. 120.
[3] Hermias in Plat. Phaedr. 76; U. 483 σύντονος ὄρεξις ἀφροδισιῶν μετὰ οἴστρου καὶ ἀδημονίας.
[4] D.L. x. 118: cf. Sent. Vat. C.B. fr. li.   [5] iv. 1058 ff.

experience and suffering,[1] but there can be no doubt of its virulence and deep sincerity; and even if the violence of the onslaught is his own, it is certain that he was following correct Epicurean tradition: 'the wise man will not fall in love, nor is it true that love is heaven-sent'.[2] But if the disease is fatal, it is easily possible in Epicurus' eyes to avoid it: 'remove sight, association, and contact and the passion of love is at an end'.[3]

Apart from passionate love Epicurus did not look kindly on marriage or family life. 'Epicurus discourages marriage and the begetting of children because of its many unpleasantnesses and distractions from more serious matters.'[4] The chief 'unpleasantness and distraction' in his eyes appears to have been the presence of the children who might divert the philosopher from his high thoughts. But even here Epicurus' humanity seems to peep through his cynical mask and he admits that 'if once one has a child, it is no longer in us to refrain from loving or caring for it',[5] and there are certain fragments which suggest at least a personal understanding and affection for children. In one strange extract he advises them how to behave when their parents are angry: 'if parents are justly angry with their children, it is certainly useless to fight against it and not to ask for pardon: but if their anger is unjust and irrational, it is quite ridiculous to add fuel to their irrational passion by nursing one's own indignation, and not to attempt to turn aside their wrath in other ways by gentleness'.[6] Another is a charming extract from a letter to a child telling him of his safe arrival at Lampsacus and adding, 'I hope you too are well and your mamma, and that you are always obedient to pappa and Matro, as you used to be. Let me tell you that the reason that I and all the rest of us love you is that you are always

---

[1] It is said that he was poisoned by a love-philtre, wrote his poems in the lucid intervals of the resultant madness, and finally committed suicide: see Jerome's *Fasti, Chron.* Euseb.

[2] D.L. x. 118.   [3] *Sent. Vat.* C.B. *fr.* xviii.

[4] Clem. Alex. *Strom.* ii. 23; U. 526.

[5] Arrian, *Epict. Dissert.* i. 23. 5; U. 525.

[6] *Sent. Vat.* C.B. *fr.* lxii.

obedient to them.'[1] And one more perhaps incautious outburst shows that he was at least not indifferent to the attrac-
tions of a harmonious family life: 'most beautiful is the sight
of those near and dear to us, when our original kinship makes
us of one mind'.[2] Once again it looks as if the philosopher
would not press very far the relentless requirements of
'imperturbability'.

In his attitude then to public affairs and to family life
the 'wise man' is consistently egoistic, and though in the
matter of friendship there seems to be a momentary wavering
towards altruism, it is not enough to disturb the general
idea which has been formed. The underlying conception
of the nature of justice is well borne out in other departments
of life, and it may be said generally that the contemplation
of the 'wise man' as a member of the community has done
nothing to modify the picture of his isolation. Epicurus at
least succeeded in all the ramifications of his theory in
keeping firmly in view the main principle of an egoistic
'pleasure' and in 'following wherever the argument led'.

The main points of Epicurus' moral theory have now
been reviewed, and a brief attempt must be made to survey
it as a whole. It is clear in the first place that his debt to
Democritus is here much less than in the physical theory.
Democritus' 'ethic' hardly amounts to a moral theory: there
is no effort to set the picture of the 'cheerful' man on a firm
philosophical basis or to link it up in any way with the
physical system: he is content in a discursive manner to
draw a portrait. Epicurus' theory is much deeper and broader
than this. It is made one with the physical system by its
foundation on the base of sensation, its security is provided
for by the insistence on free-will, guaranteed by the 'swerve'
of the atoms, and its main conception of 'pleasure' as the
end goes farther back than Democritus' root-idea and is
based on the empirical observation of experience. The theory
is indeed not now a picture but a structure. There is in
consequence a notable difference of tone between the two

[1] Pap. Herc. 176, col. 18; C.B. fr. 35; U. 176.
[2] Sent. Vat. C.B. fr. lxi.

philosophers: the aphorisms of Democritus leave one with
the impression of a series of comments on life made from
no very deep conviction of its ultimate purpose, but rather
with an acceptance of conventional standards and modes of
expression: the moral system of Epicurus is the work of
a preacher with a gospel to proclaim, the work too of a
scientific thinker evolving a connected system of fearless
deductions, flying often in the face of conventional ideas,
and all worked out with a consistent observation of fundamental principles. The idea of 'pleasure' is carefully
analysed through the distinction of static and kinetic pleasure
and the division of desires, and it is only when as the result
of a series of inferences he has reached the notion of 'imperturbability', that he is brought into relation with Democritus. Then there are no doubt some points of likeness.
The conception of 'imperturbability' is not greatly different
from Democritus' 'cheerfulness'—indeed it was one of the
synonyms used by Democritus himself. There are details
too in which similarity may be traced, such as the general
notions of temperance and bravery and the rejection of
family life. Yet in detail too Epicurus takes his own line,
when his argument requires it: his attitude to public life
is precisely the reverse of that of Democritus and friendship
plays a far more prominent part. It would perhaps be difficult
to assert with confidence that Epicurus' moral theory owes
nothing to his predecessor's work or that, if Democritus had
not existed, it would have taken precisely the same form,
but there is no doubt that Epicurus was here almost entirely
independent and showed himself at once a more profound
thinker and a more sincere believer in the value of his own
teaching.

The system which is thus built up cannot but affect us
strangely, for it has such strongly marked heights and depths.
At times, as for instance, in the general idea of the tranquil
mind and especially in its endurance of pain, Epicureanism
seems a broad and even noble conception: at other moments,
especially in the discussion of the 'wise man's' relation to other
men, it appears narrow and almost degrading to human

nature. It may help to clear the general idea of Epicureanism to consider briefly some of the criticisms which it suggests.

It is perhaps hardly necessary to dissipate the 'vulgar error' which regards Epicureanism as a doctrine of pure sensualism. Such an idea could only arise from the most superficial consideration of its teaching: though pleasure is to the Epicurean the only good, though the root of all pleasure lies in the flesh and even in the stomach, yet Epicurus' 'wise man' is very far removed indeed from the common notion of an 'Epicure', picking and choosing his pleasures so as to obtain the maximum of bodily titillation at the moment. The misconception is a very old one and was made even in Epicurus' own lifetime, for we find him replying to it in a passage[1] of the Letter to Menoeceus, which should in itself finally dispose of the charge: 'when therefore we maintain that pleasure is the end, we do not mean the pleasures of profligates and those that consist in sensuality, as is supposed by some who are either ignorant or disagree with us or do not understand, but freedom from pain in the body and from trouble in the mind. For it is not continuous drinkings and revellings, nor the satisfaction of lusts, nor the enjoyment of fish and other luxuries of the wealthy table, which produce a pleasant life, but sober reasoning, searching out the motives for all choice and avoidance and banishing mere opinions, to which are due the greatest disturbance of the spirit'. These vulgar charges might with more justification be brought against the doctrine of Aristippus and the Cyrenaics, but Epicurus had made them wholly inapplicable to his system, first by the introduction of the conception of the 'blessed life' as a whole with its consequent continuous balance of pleasures and pains, and secondly by the distinction of the pleasure of movement and the pleasure of rest, and the selection of the latter as the true, because the only pure, form. For all his belief in the mortality of the soul Epicurus could never say 'Let us eat, drink, and be merry, for to-morrow we die', for the simple reason that he believed that by such a course of conduct a man is

[1] §§ 131, 2.

failing to secure the maximum pleasure of life. 'Your aim is good', he might have said to Aristippus or to an 'Epicure', 'but you are totally mistaken as to the means.'

Nor again is it justifiable, as might be suggested by a consideration of the practice of Epicureanism—of the 'wise man's' withdrawal from the life of his fellows and the almost monastic limitation of his pleasures—to regard it as an ingenious and attractive apology for asceticism. It is true that in practice Epicurus' teaching has a strong ascetic flavour: the complete suppression of all 'idle desires', the rejection of all 'diversifications' of pleasure, and the confinement of bodily enjoyment to the simple satisfaction of necessary needs are indeed a surprising outcome of a system based upon the pleasures of the flesh. But however much practice may suggest an ascetic ideal, the motives of Epicureanism are dead against it. The mortification of the flesh would be in itself almost a crime to Epicurus' mind, nor even in temperance as such is there any merit: and it may be carried to excess: 'frugality too has a limit, and the man who disregards it is in like case with him who errs through excess'.[1]

The maximum of pleasure for the body and therefore for the mind is always the aim of conduct, and it is only because as the result of the balancing of pleasures against pains it is found that through temperance this pleasure is secured at its maximum height and with the least break in continuity, that a practice anything like ascetic can be recommended: 'we think highly of frugality, not that we may always keep to a cheap and simple diet, but that we may be free from desire regarding it'.[2] There is never for a moment any ulterior idea of virtue as regulating pleasure in Epicurus' mind, and that he has succeeded in eliminating it more successfully than most advocates of Hedonism, is shown in the fearless originality of his conclusions with regard to social life, which were the very reverse of the ordinary Greek notion of virtue.

There is then no disguise or reservation about Epicu-

[1] *Sent. Vat.* C.B. *fr.* lxiii.
[2] Stob. *Floril.* xvii. 14; C.B. *fr.* 29; U. 135 a.

reanism: it is a system of uncompromising egoistic hedonism. The supreme difficulty which always and necessarily attaches to a hedonistic system is the establishment of a satisfactory calculus of pleasure: if pleasure is to be the sole test of good, then the worth of actions can only be judged by the amount of pleasure which they produce: there can be no qualitative, but only a quantitative distinction of pleasures. How then is it possible to measure one pleasure against another or to decide which is quantitatively the greater? Epicurus surmounts this difficulty with greater ingenuity and success than many of the modern Utilitarians by the distinction between kinetic and static pleasure and the doctrine of the limit. Absence of pain is the only pure pleasure: the pleasure of movement is only a 'variation' and is impure because it necessarily involves accompanying pain. It is thus possible not only to establish a scale of pleasures, but, what is even more satisfactory, to point to one kind of pleasure, which alone is perfect, and which is within the reach of all men at all times. But satisfactorily as he has thus overcome his greatest difficulty, he has in so doing laid himself open to another serious criticism: for many of the ancient philosophers, Plato for example, did not admit that absence of pain was pleasure at all: it was, they held, an indifferent state lying intermediate between the two and not to be classed with either. This was, as might be expected, the ground on which the Cyrenaics criticized Epicurus' theory: 'the removal of pain produces merely the tranquillity of a corpse (νεκροῦ κατάστασις)'.[1] We do not unfortunately possess any reply of Epicurus in so many words to this criticism, but we can surely conjecture safely enough what it would be. Guyau[2] endeavours to meet the difficulty by pointing to the essentially positive and 'constitutive' notion which Epicurus had of the pleasure of rest. It is not merely absence of pain and absence of trouble, but a positive harmony of body and mind, an equilibrium (εὐστάθεια): 'the last word of Epicureanism ought not to be ἀπονία, the absence of pain, but rather the conservation of pleasure': tranquillity has a

---

[1] Clem. Alex. *Strom.* ii. 21; U. 451. [2] pp. 52 ff.

positive and not merely a negative value. This is no doubt true of Epicurus' conception, but it does not go to the root of the difficulty. For what right had Epicurus to claim as a positive pleasure, that which others regarded as a merely indifferent state? Epicurus' answer would surely be to return to the ultimate principle from which he started. We must take the evidence of sensation: there are only two feelings (πάθη), pleasure and pain: these are mutually exclusive and cover the whole ground of experience. An indifferent state between them is not conceivable: we have no such feeling: if we have not pleasure, we are in pain, and if we have not pain, we have pleasure. In the experience of life the two, though distinct, are no doubt often combined: we are conscious simultaneously of elements of pleasure and of pain. These may be in different fields, or sometimes, as in the case of certain of the kinetic pleasures, attendant on a single action. The only pure pleasure, and therefore the most completely positive pleasure, must be the entire absence of pain: these are mere synonyms for the same feeling. Once again then, if we are to quarrel with Epicurus' moral theory, we must quarrel with his psychology, and if we are to quarrel with his psychology, we must attack the root-principle of the whole system, the infallibility of sensation.

In the detailed working out of his system Epicurus from time to time makes inferences which most other philosophies, and indeed the normal outlook of the plain man, would find it hard to accept. This is especially the case with regard to man's social activities: the guiding motives which rule the 'wise man' in his conduct to others frequently revolt us, and sometimes the resultant course of action no less than the motives. Here of course is a difficulty which inevitably attaches to any system of egoistic hedonism: the man who professes it can have no care for others except for his own profit. He is thus at once brought into conflict with the social instincts of man and the normally accepted notions of justice and altruism in general. It is possible to circumvent this difficulty, and Epicurus shows an inclination to make the attempt in dealing with friendship by the paradox that altruism is after all only a higher form of egoism, but most modern hedonistic systems[1] have preferred to abandon egoism in favour of a social utilitarianism aiming at the 'greatest happiness of the greatest number'. Epicurus however is prepared to stand by his principles and take their consequences. He does not flinch from the ugly sound and evil reputation of certain forms of selfishness, which are the natural outcome of his main position. The picture of the 'wise man' who would count justice as nought, if only he could be sure of escaping detection in injustice, spurning alike the life of the family and all notion of service to the State, can have been no more pleasing to Epicurus' contemporaries than it is to the modern reader. But it is the direct result of a fearless pursuit of the main principle of his creed to whatever conclusion it may lead him.

These are some of the more obvious criticisms and problems which the examination of Epicurus' moral theory must inevitably suggest. When tried by the standard of the best moral systems, ancient or modern, it is no doubt found inferior: even taking it, as its author would most have preferred to represent it, as a practical method of conduct, based on the observation of what is, it is insufficient, as it does not account for some of the most natural impulses of the normal human being. But for us, who are examining Epicurus primarily as a thinker, the supreme interest is in its consistency, and in this respect at least it demands admiration. Starting from a principle derived as immediately from the fundamental trust in sensation as are the primary principles of the Canonice, he has worked out a system simple indeed, yet characterized by something of the same ingenious subtlety which helps him over the difficult places in the physical theory: he has pursued his system into detail, each step following closely from the last, and all knit together by an unwavering adherence to the ultimate standard of judgement. Once again as a moral teacher Epicurus is at least a serious and consistent thinker.

[1] For a very interesting account of the relation of modern Utilitarianism to the theory of Epicurus see Guyau, Livre IV.

XI

CONCLUSION

IT is not easy to put Epicurus in his due place in the succession of the Atomists because in many ways he lies so far out of the direct line. That the Atomic theory of Democritus and Leucippus was his working basis there can be no possible doubt, and the foregoing essays will have furnished abundant proof of his dependence on it both in fundamental ideas and in detail. But they will also have provided ample evidence of Epicurus' originality. He started from a base-principle, the trust in sensation, which Democritus would have rejected, but which he himself passionately embraced and applied in a far-reaching spirit to all parts of his system. In working out the detail he was rigidly faithful to it and used Democritus' ideas only in so far as they were consonant: he never hesitated to throw them over where they proved unsuited to his own sensationalism. Many of these divergencies have been noticed in the course of the review of Epicurus' system. He rejected for instance Democritus' conception of the 'very large' atoms,[1] because they would have been perceptible to the senses and sensation gives us no intimation of their existence: in its place he set up the extremely subtle doctrine of the *minimae partes*, working out the idea in a polemical spirit against the Eleatics with a minuteness and penetration which were probably beyond the capacity of his predecessor. He added weight to the primary properties of the atoms,[2] because sensation showed it to be a property of all perceptible things, and having done so thought out anew the picture of the 'free' atoms moving in space and the cause of their meetings: introducing here the idea of the atomic 'swerve', he used it to escape from the Democritean determinism. He insisted[3] on the reality of the 'secondary qualities' of compound bodies against Democritus' belief that they were subjective

---

[1] See Chap. III, pp. 284–7.
[2] See Chaps. III, pp. 289–90, and IV, p. 304.
[3] See Chap. VI, p. 353.

'experiences of sensation', because sensation presented perceptible things as possessed of colour, taste, &c.; but here he preserved Democritus' account of the differences of atomic shape and arrangement as their cause, since it could be adapted to his own view. He immensely elaborated and refined the psychology of Democritus,[1] adding the idea of the 'nameless' element to push materialism to the utmost limit; he worked out the whole atomic machinery of sensation and thought with complete originality and introduced the conceptions of the active 'apprehensions' of the senses and the mind. He invented the atomic psychology of the 'will' and as its basis insisted on its freedom.[2] Most conspicuously he showed his originality in his moral theory, based like his physics on the trust in sensation; the root-notion of 'pleasure' as the natural end was his own, and he cannot be said to have done more than take from Democritus a few general notions concerning the life of the 'wise man', and even here in details of the picture he was always prepared to desert and contradict him, when he felt that the requirements of the true doctrine of static 'pleasure' demanded it.

These are some of the ways in which Epicurus showed his independence of the Atomists and a careful study reveals many more: they should at least suffice to justify Epicurus' claim to be an original thinker and to put an end to the negligent tradition that he 'adopted Democritus' Atomism to act as a basis to his moral theory'. But after all his originality is shown mostly in his conception of the system as a whole and in the fundamental metaphysic of the Canonice. It may be that the semi-scepticism of Democritus was a truer analysis of the conditions of man's knowledge of the world around him and its ultimate constituents, but it produced an almost unworkable combination of rationalism and sensationalism, and was regarded by him rather as a deduction from his analysis of things than as a guiding principle of all his observation and thought. Epicurus returned to a crude sensationalism, believing it to be the only possible foundation of scientific thought. Its weaknesses

[1] See Chap. VIII, pp. 388 ff.   [2] See Chap. VIII, pp. 432–7.

have been obvious at many points in his system, but he never lost sight of it and pursued it relentlessly into detail. In result it binds together his theories with a uniformity and consistency which Democritus never attained and leaves them as a far wider and more audacious attempt to correlate thought and knowledge than the encyclopaedic but discursive views of Democritus. Atomism is a theory, but Epicureanism is a system.

In the ancient world it was the moral theory of Epicurus which had the greatest and most lasting influence. His atomic theory was hardly taken seriously as an explanation of the world except by a few ardent spirits such as Lucretius, and by even so conscientious a thinker as Cicero it was regarded almost as a joke. But Epicureanism as a theory of life made a deep impression and for at least four centuries it remained one of the leading philosophies of antiquity. The school [1] as an organization endured throughout that time and could reckon its heads in unbroken succession back to Epicurus himself. In Rome in the last century of the Republic and in the early Empire it practically divided the allegiance of the 'intellectuals' with Stoicism; among Cicero's contemporaries his own great friend Atticus and Cassius, Caesar's murderer, were prominent Epicureans, and in a later generation Seneca, though he professed himself a Stoic, was always ready to cull practical maxims from Epicurus. The fact is that though they started from very different bases, the two philosophies were not in practical teaching very far apart. Epicurus' austere development of the theory of pleasure as the natural moral end was not far from the ruling principles which the Stoic derived from his belief in the presence of the 'divine spark' in man. Indeed in Epicurus' precepts from time to time we stumble on the actual catchwords of the Stoics. 'Self-sufficiency' (αὐτάρκεια), the leading Stoic idea, takes its place in Epicurus' system as the means by which the 'wise man' dealing with his desires reaches 'imperturbability'. 'Self-sufficiency (or rather perhaps, as Epicurus conceived it, "independence of desires")

[1] D.L. x. 9.

we think a great good—not that we may at all times enjoy but a few things, but that, if we do not possess many, we may enjoy the few in the genuine persuasion that those have the sweetest pleasure in luxury who least need it.'[1] This is a position that the Stoic would have been prepared to accept and still nearer akin to his own beliefs would have been the two sayings: 'Self-sufficiency is the greatest of all riches,'[2] and 'the greatest fruit of self-sufficiency is freedom'.[3] In another aphorism the idea is combined with the other Stoic notion of living according to nature: 'The man who follows nature and not vain opinions is self-sufficient in all things.'[4] All these sayings are perfectly consonant with Epicurus' own teaching, but he seems almost to be claiming in them that he can satisfy the Stoic ideals too. At least he shows that in practical precept there is no great gulf fixed between the two creeds.

If one asks the reason of the great popularity of the Epicurean morality in antiquity, there are probably two main answers. In the first place there is no doubt that it found favour by its misinterpretation: a gospel of 'pleasure', hastily grasped without any attempt to follow out the master's interpretation of it, might seem to supply a cloak for a life of sensual pleasure and was no doubt so used by some unworthy followers. Cicero's invectives against his contemporary Piso, who professed himself an Epicurean, may not have been justified in the particular case, but they show that a degraded interpretation of Epicureanism was not unknown: 'as soon as he heard that pleasure was so highly praised by the philosopher, he made no distinction . . . . but thought he had found a preceptor in vice'.[5] There were 'epicures' in antiquity to give a false currency to Epicureanism. But to its more serious followers it probably appealed as against Stoicism in that, while it commended a mode of life not less noble than that of its rival, it was based on common

---

[1] Ep. iii, § 130.   [2] Clem. Alex. *Strom.* vi. 2; C.B. *fr.* 70; U. 476.
[3] *Sent. Vat.* C.B. *fr.* lxxvii.
[4] Porph. *ad Marc.* 27, p. 207; C.B. *fr.* 45; U. 202.
[5] Cic. *in Pis.* 28. 69.

sense. There is a type of mind, common at least among the practical Romans, to which the semi-mystic pantheism of the Stoic would have been revolting, and the matter-of-fact theory of Epicurus, based not on any high-flown conception of duty, but on the observation of what men do in fact aim at in life, must have made a strong appeal. And it is surely this foundation in experience which entitles Epicureanism to a high place among 'pleasure' systems: he does not, as some modern types of Utilitarian have done, set up 'pleasure' as a moral end—the common sense of mankind seems to turn instinctively away from that—but starting from the root-fact that men naturally choose pleasure and avoid pain by an immediate instinct, he asks what theory of life can be built upon that fact, and pursuing his argument fearlessly reaches a standard which at least, on the self-regarding side, is worthy of admiration and respect.

To the modern mind on the other hand it is probably the physical side of Epicurus' speculations—the Atomism whose history it has been the purpose of this book to trace—which will make the strongest appeal. The moral theory, even in the days of the Utilitarian school, would have seemed crude and possibly narrow—it made no provision for that false but popular offshoot of a 'pleasure-theory', Collective Hedonism —and to-day, as one contemplates it, apart from gleams of suggestive thought here and there, it appears 'stale and unprofitable'. But the physical theory is very much alive: its main idea is a shrewd guess which anticipated in its general conception the accepted basis of modern scientific inquiry, and if its details are reached by conjecture and inference without the verification by experiment which is the test of all scientific work to-day, yet they are worked out with a real penetration and in some particulars have startlingly anticipated modern problems and even modern discoveries. The poem of Lucretius, where Epicurus' system is most connectedly and most lucidly set out for us, is read not merely for the beauty of its poetry and the fire of its evangelistic passion, but even to-day for the interest and subtlety of the theories which it expounds.

The weaknesses of the theory as an explanation of the world and of life are obvious and spring in the main from two great flaws. In the first place Epicurus has attempted to extend what was a reasonable theory of the physical constitution of things beyond its proper sphere. By attempting to explain psychology on a material basis he exposed himself to the difficulties which must beset any materialist theory which attempts to grapple with the things of the mind and the spirit: it can point to a material counterpart to thought and sensation, but when it attempts to cross the gulf and to say that physical movement *is* thought and consciousness, it is doomed to failure. Epicurus seems to have been conscious himself of this difficulty and to have known that in the theories of the 'nameless' element in the soul and the atomic 'swerve' he was pressing his materialism almost to breaking point: but it did not break and just for this reason it is inadequate. Secondly his basic trust in sensation creates difficulties almost as great as his rigid materialism: he is hard put to it to explain the apparent errors of sensation by the intrusions of opinion, and, though he acknowledges it less, to justify on a purely sensational foundation the conclusions of the mind as to the 'ultimate realities' of the physical universe. The active 'apprehension' of the senses and still more the 'active apprehension' of the mind are frail planks on which to build a far-reaching system of the universe.

But just because he was so rigid in the application of his principles and refused ever to cross the bridge and to seek the aid which might have been given him by rationalism or a spiritual view of the world, his system attains a completeness and consistency which proves it to be the work of a great thinker. Taking his stand on a single fundamental idea he has raised on it an edifice of thought which, for its penetration sometimes, and always for its fearlessness and for its coherence, is deserving of more study and consideration than the modern histories of philosophy have often given to it.

APPENDICES

APPENDIX I

On the theory of Anaxagoras

IT has always been recognized that the central doctrine of the theory of Anaxagoras is contained in the famous fragments [1] preserved by Simplicius: 'there is a portion of everything in everything', and 'each thing is and was most manifestly those things of which it has most in it'. This is alike his statement of the ultimate constitution of things and his answer to the problem of the phenomena of change. But the difficulties which beset his theory arise the moment an attempt is made to interpret this statement. What are the 'things' of which everything has a portion and how are they combined in a manner which will account for change? Four main answers [2] have been given to this question and must be carefully considered.

1. The simplest view, which is that taken by Simplicius [3] and Lucretius [4] and most modern historians of philosophy, is that by 'things' Anaxagoras meant simply corporeal substances. A piece of bread, to take Anaxagoras' [5] own illustration from nutrition, can become flesh, blood, hair, nerves, tissues, &c., because, though by far the largest portion of the particles which compose it are particles of bread, it also contains particles of all other substances, and among them particles of flesh, blood, &c. When we eat the bread, these latter particles come away and join the flesh, blood, &c., in our bodies. To this straightforward interpretation many objections may be brought. Lucretius argues naïvely that in that case when we grind corn, we ought to come across particles of flesh, blood, &c. Burnet,[6] putting what is really the same objection with more penetration, maintains that such a view is inconsistent with Anaxagoras' own principle [7] that matter is

---

[1] In Arist. *Phys.* A. 2. 184 (27. 2); D.A. 41.

[2] I have not referred at length to the view of P. Leon, published in *Class. Quart.* xxi, pp. 133 ff., because it is founded mainly on one fragment, whose treatment is much disputed, and leads in my opinion to a fantastic theory which does not affect the main issues.

[3] In Arist. *Phys.* Γ. 4. 203 a; D.A. 45.

[4] i. 875 ff.   [5] D.B. 10.   [6] *E. G. P.*3, p. 263.

[7] See D.B. 3, 6. Incidentally I cannot agree with Burnet that in 3 Zeller's τομῇ is a convincing correction of τὸ μή. The whole expression τομῇ οὐκ εἶναι 'to cease to be by being cut' seems to me odd Greek, the construction οὐκ ἔστιν . . . οὐκ εἶναι (instead of μὴ εἶναι) is surely impossible, and the general argument of the passage—'just as you cannot pass from the greatest to the all, so you cannot pass from the least to nothing'—is spoilt by the intrusion of the idea of cutting.

infinitely divisible: 'if everything were made up of minute particles of everything else, we could certainly arrive at a point where everything was "unmixed", if only we carried division far enough'. But it is not necessary to go so far afield: if this were what Anaxagoras meant, we could convict him at once by the general principle from which he starts. Consider more closely what would happen in the case of nutrition and suppose for the sake of simplicity that there are 100 ultimate substances. The piece of bread then contains particles of all these 100, the bread-particles prevailing and giving the character to the whole. When we eat it, the particles of flesh and blood come away: we need not go farther, for then we shall have three examples, the new flesh, the new blood, and the remaining composition of 98 elements, in no one of which are there now 'portions of everything'. The notion at the very outset defeats its own object and it is impossible that Anaxagoras can have meant anything so simple.

2. Burnet,[1] following the lead of Tannery,[2] has propounded a more subtle explanation of Anaxagoras' meaning. He holds that the 'things' of which Anaxagoras says that everything has a portion are not corporeal substances, but 'qualities'—or rather, as he now states his view, the 'opposites' of Anaximander and the Milesians. He further draws attention to the fact that Anaxagoras speaks of the 'seeds'[3] (σπέρματα) of things, i.e. minute particles of which they are composed, to which the commentators obviously refer under the famous title of ὁμοιομέρειαι.[4] He rightly argues then that the theory of structure must be referred from whole objects to the 'seeds' which compose them, 'seeds' homogeneous in substance with one another and with the whole which they compose. Anaxagoras' position may then be stated thus: he[5] 'held that, however far you may divide any of these things—and they are infinitely divisible—you never come to a part so small that it does not contain portions of all the opposites. On the other hand, everything can pass into everything else just because the "seeds", as he called them, of each form of matter contain a portion of everything, that is, of all the opposites, though in different proportions'. The theory is attractive, but I cannot believe that it is more than at best a partial representation of what Anaxagoras meant.

[1] *E. G. P.*3, pp. 263 ff. The statement of his view has been somewhat modified since the first edition, but the idea remains substantially the same.

[2] *Science hellène*, pp. 283 ff.

[3] D.B. 4.

[4] e.g. Simpl. l.c., Aet. i. 3. 5; D.A. 46.

[5] *E. G. P.*3, p. 264.

Burnet supports his view mainly by three of the fragments, which run in his own translation as follows:

1. *Frag. 8.* The things that are in one world are not divided nor cut off from one another with a hatchet, neither the warm from the cold nor the cold from the warm.

2. *Frag. 15.* The dense and the moist and the cold and the dark came together where the earth is now, while the rare and the warm and the dry (and the bright) went out towards the further part of the aether.

3. *Frag. 4, § 2.* But before they were separated off, when all things were together, not even was any colour distinguishable; for the mixture of all things prevented it—of the moist and the dry, and the warm and the cold, and the light and the dark, and of much earth that was in it,[1] and of a multitude of innumerable seeds in no way like each other.

It is clear enough that in these fragments there is mention of the 'opposites' of the Milesians, but do they prove Burnet's view of the constitution of 'all things' according to Anaxagoras? In the first place it must be observed that no one of these three passages concerns the constitution of individual things, still less, as they ought to, on Burnet's theory, the constitution of the σπέρματα, of which things are composed, but the first two deal with the structure of individual worlds and the third with the state of things which prevailed in the original μεῖγμα before the separating out of the ἀποκρίνομενα. It is clear then that no one of them can be quoted as, at any rate, any direct support of the view that the 'things' of which everything has a portion are opposite qualities. But this argument must not be pressed, for, as I hope to show, there is a very exact and indeed necessary parallel between the structure of the original μεῖγμα and that of the 'seeds' of things. It is more important to observe that in the third of these fragments there is added to the list of Milesian 'opposites' 'earth and a multitude of innumerable seeds in no way like each other'. Now 'earth' has no natural 'opposite', rather it makes us think of the other Empedoclean elements; and the 'innumerable seeds' are not opposite to each other, but different: it is obvious that the idea of the 'opposites' will not cover the contents of the μεῖγμα.

But to test Burnet's view effectively, it is necessary to inquire more closely into the nature of the 'opposites' and to ask in practice how the theory would work. In his first edition he boldly followed Tannery

---

[1] The modification of Burnet's view since the first edition enables him now to construe the very straightforward genitive καὶ γῆς πολλῆς ἐνεούσης, of which previously he could 'make nothing'.

in asserting that they were qualities. He admits that Anaxagoras had not the conception of quality, but 'had Anaxagoras possessed it, all this could have been made much clearer: it is only obscure because he is obliged to call the primary opposites things'.[1] Now it seems a sufficient answer to this view that if Anaxagoras had not the conception of qualities, he could not have meant qualities, but he may have been striving after an idea he could not reach, and it will be well to test the idea in application. We may take a case which at first sight seems strongly to favour the 'quality' theory, Sextus'[2] famous instance of the way in which Anaxagoras contrasted the evidence of the senses with the inference of thought: 'Anaxagoras opposed to the impression that snow is white the consideration that snow is congealed water: now water is black: snow then must be black too'. Work this out on Burnet's view: water is composed of a large number of $\sigma\pi\acute{\epsilon}\rho\mu\alpha\tau\alpha$, in each of which all the opposites are combined, but blackness prevails: however far you divided, you could not find a particle or a 'seed' which was white. Now by no amount of rearrangement or recombination could these 'seeds' produce anything but what not only 'is' but appears black: for in each one of them and therefore in any whole which they might compose blackness must prevail. To produce snow you would need another kind of seeds in which the proportions are different and whiteness prevails and such substitution could not be accomplished by rearrangement. So far from advancing matters, the 'quality' view leads to an *impasse* as great, if not greater, than does the old view. The 'things' cannot in this sense be 'qualities'.

In the modification of his view which he has since propounded, Burnet only once[3] speaks of 'opposite qualities', but elsewhere consistently of 'the opposites', connecting Anaxagoras' theory directly with the notions of the Milesian school. Now 'the opposites' of Anaximander are simply corporeal substances, moist substance and dry substance, cold matter and hot matter, &c. If then Anaxagoras meant merely the Milesian opposites, when he spoke of things, his theory of the ultimate constitution of things was even less satisfactory than it is assumed to be on the 'old view'. For in the first place, the 'seeds', which are no ultimate particles like the atoms of Leucippus and Democritus, are themselves infinitely divisible, and in the process of division we should arrive at a point where the hot substance and the cold substance, the moist substance and the dry substance were separate, and should reach things which no longer contained everything. In

[1] *E. G. P.*[1], p. 289. [2] *Pyrrh. Hypot.* i. 33; D.A. 97.
[3] *E. G. P.*[3], p. 264, l. 2.

other words, Burnet's modification is open to exactly the same objection as he brings against the 'old view'; it will not stand the test of infinite division. Moreover if 'things' be confined to opposites, their combinations even in different proportions will not be sufficient to account for the infinite variety of things: Anaxagoras himself in Frag. 4 shows clearly enough that in the original $\mu\epsilon\hat{\iota}\gamma\mu\alpha$ there were many 'things' besides the 'opposites'—'much earth and innumerable seeds in no way like each other'.

And indeed, unless we are to reject all the evidence of the commentators and historians of philosophy, it is abundantly clear that Anaxagoras, even if he included in 'things' the Milesian 'opposites', meant also much more—an endless series of substances corresponding to each of the concrete things of normal existence. A few pieces of evidence must be quoted. The context of Simplicius'[1] famous quotation is typical: 'all the $\acute{o}\mu o\iota o\mu\epsilon\rho\hat{\eta}$[2] are uncreated and imperishable, but they appear to come into being and pass away only owing to combination and separation, since all things are in all things and each receives its character owing to that which prevails in it. For that appears as gold in which there is much gold-substance ($\chi\rho\nu\sigma\acute{\iota}o\nu$), although as a matter of fact all things are in it. At any rate Anaxagoras says, "in everything there is a portion of everything and each single thing is and was most manifestly that of which it has most in it"'. This is clear enough: 'gold-substance' is not one of the 'opposites', still less is it a quality: it is concrete matter corresponding exactly to the gold of experience. In another passage[3] Simplicius is equally explicit with regard to the process of nutrition: 'seeing that all things are separated[4] out from each of the things which are now separated from one another, as for instance, flesh and bone and so on from bread, as though these were all formerly in it and mixed together, as the result of this he surmised that all things were formerly mixed together before they were separated apart'. Here we seem to have a perfectly clear statement of exactly what Burnet denies: 'it once was usual, he says,[5] to represent the theory of Anaxagoras as if he had said that wheat, for instance, contained small particles of flesh, blood, bones, and the like'. The 'usual' view is certainly nearer to Simplicius' understanding of Anaxagoras than Burnet's theory. Many more pieces of evidence might be

---

[1] In Arist. *Phys.* A. 2. 184 (27. 2); D.A. 41.

[2] I prefer to leave this word untranslated for the present, as it will be fully discussed later.   [3] Simpl. in Arist. *Phys.* Γ. 4. 203; D.A. 45.

[4] These compounds of κρίνω and their importance in the theory will be discussed later.   [5] E. G. P.3, p. 263.

quoted,[1] but perhaps the most interesting is another fragment[2] of Anaxagoras himself, because it is one of the few extracts which deal with the 'seeds'—which is just what is required. He is talking about the constitution of other worlds on the same lines as our own: 'this being so, we are bound to suppose that there are many elements of all kinds in all the worlds[3] and seeds of all things having all kinds of shapes and colours and tastes'. Here then are qualities and so far from all the 'seeds' having all of them, each 'seed' has its own peculiar qualities distinct from others—a contradiction of Burnet's theory as direct as is Simplicius' affirmation of what Burnet denies that Anaxagoras meant.

Burnet's view then, in either of its forms, appears to be contradicted by the evidence, and in neither form can it in practice lead to a working hypothesis of the ultimate constitution of things: in trying to escape from the difficulties which beset Tannery's theory, he has now done no more than limit the range of the 'old view' and leave it exposed to the same objections. The 'things' which are in everything must be concrete substances, particles in fact corresponding to the things of sensation: so far the 'old view' is right. But in two respects at least it requires amendment and modification. In the first place, Burnet has clearly shown that it is not so much the structure of whole things on which attention must be concentrated, but rather that of the 'seeds' of which they are composed. In the second place, if Anaxagoras' theory is to be regarded as more than a very loose piece of thinking, the 'old view' must in some way be reconciled with 'infinite division'.

3. An ingenious attempt to get over the difficulties of the theory was made by Giussani.[4] He explains that according to Anaxagoras ὁμοιομέρεια is in the first place absolutely complete: division may be carried to infinity, yet however small the particles into which we might divide, for instance, a piece of gold, we should always find gold and nothing else. On the other hand the piece of gold and all its particles contain 'everything'. How can this be? Because the particles of 'things' are so infinitely small that they not merely are not perceptible but never could be: just as, in the colour grey, it would be impossible to separate the black and white of which it is composed. So far, though it is still open to the objection that if things are really divisible, we should in theory, at any rate, ultimately reach particles of pure gold,

---

[1] See especially Aet. i. 3. 5; D.A. 46; Arist. *de Caelo, Γ.* 3. 302 a; D.A. 43.
[2] D.B. 4, § 1.

[3] συγκρινόμενα, 'compound bodies', but here used specially of the compound worlds.   [4] *Lucretius*, Book I, Excursus III, pp. 147 ff.

bread, flesh, &c., Giussani's view is valuable: I think Anaxagoras certainly meant his particles to be far below the ken of the senses. But how then are we to explain the phenomena of change? Because, says Giussani, a piece of bread, for example, appears to us as bread not because it contains *more* ultimate particles of bread than a piece of flesh: there are just the same number of particles of every kind in it. It appears as bread because the bread-particles are gathered together in it into perceptible lumps, whereas the particles of all other things are scattered all in amongst each other, never more than very few of the same kind being together at a time. When we eat the bread, the effect of the blow of the teeth is to cause a separation (διάκρισις) of the bread-particles and a gathering together (σύγκρισις) of the flesh and blood-particles, so that the whole now appears as flesh and blood. The theory is immensely ingenious, but it cannot be right. It is not really consistent with the notion of infinite divisibility, σύγκρισις and διάκρισις are not used in this way by Anaxagoras, the two fragments [1] on which Giussani relies are misinterpreted by him, we have to suppose too arbitrary an incident in the process of eating, and above all Anaxagoras distinctly says, 'each thing is those things of which it has *most* in it'. Giussani's brilliance, here as elsewhere, has led him too far away from the evidence on which he is commenting.

4. A very original and penetrating explanation has recently been given by A. L. Peck.[2] His view is complicated and not easy to summarize, but its essential argument may be represented thus. Anaxagoras' specific interest was in physiological change, which the doctrine of the ὁμοιομερῆ was intended to explain: this doctrine is in close connexion with his view of the original μείγμα. In the beginning [3] all things were so small that nothing was visible: everything was ἄπειρον, 'that is, it was as yet nothing in particular, there was no order about it'. But there were in the original mixture (1) the 'opposites', (2) the 'elements' earth, air, water, fire, which always remain ἄπειρα, (3) the 'seeds', or 'parts'. μοῖρα is a technical term, 'a part or portion' of organic things (p. 70) of which σπέρμα is a synonym. ὁμοιομερές means not, as it has hitherto been translated, 'having parts like to the whole', but simply 'having like parts': the ὁμοιομερῆ are 'the things which have like parts', i.e. have a portion of everything. But the σπέρμα or μοῖρα is not merely static, but capable, under the direction of νοῦς, and nourished by the 'opposites', of development and growth, just like the seed of a plant or an animal. Thus in the piece of bread

[1] D.B. 3 and 6.
[2] *Class. Quart.* xx, no. 2, April 1926, pp. 57–71.   [3] D.B. 1.

there were seeds of all things, but 'mind decreed that the Seed or Part of Bread should develop and actually produce the Bread which it was capable of producing' (p. 62); bread is now in that thing τὸ κρατοῦν. But when the bread is eaten and passes into the constituent parts of the body, 'mind has decreed that here, in the body, at this particular place, such Parts as Flesh, Blood, and Hair shall be in control', i.e. their seeds develop and now overcome the bread-seeds.

With parts of this exposition, and especially with the attempt to link the doctrine of the ὁμοιομερῆ with the description of the original μεῖγμα I am in great sympathy, but I do not think its conclusions can be accepted as a whole. (1) Like Giussani's theory it appears to me to go considerably beyond the evidence. In particular the conception of the growth and development of the σπέρμα under the direction of νοῦς, which is the central point of Peck's explanation, has no warrant in any of the fragments or notices. The notices of the 'domination' (κρατεῖν) of one part or the other must be explained by the famous dictum 'each thing is and was most manifestly those things of which it has the most (πλεῖστα plural) in it'. This points clearly to the numerical superiority of one or other of the 'things', and is surely an impossible way of expressing the 'development' of one or other of the seeds. (2) The sense given to the word ὁμοιομερές, 'alike in parts', i.e. having parts of all things, is very improbable: (a) it divorces the meaning of Anaxagoras from the meaning which Aristotle[1] himself gave to the word. I agree with Mr. Peck that in some of his comments Aristotle passes from his own sense to Anaxagoras' sense, but I do not think he could do so without a word of warning if the senses were so widely divergent; (b) it surely makes the word almost meaningless: if 'all things have a part of all things', then all things will 'have similar parts', and it is unnecessary to coin so strange a word to express a property which is common to everything. On p. 70 Mr. Peck seems to try to meet this difficulty by suggesting that it was only organic things of which there were 'parts': if then he holds that Anaxagoras only meant that 'all organic things contain parts of all organic things' he certainly expressed it oddly by saying 'there is a portion of everything in everything'. The limitation would help to give a rational meaning to the word ὁμοιομερές, but it wrecks the theory as a whole; (c) Mr. Peck has really dealt the most fatal blow to his own theory on p. 66. 'An ὁμοιομέρεια is not divisible. The whole doctrine falls to the ground unless we maintain this.' But nothing is clearer than that Anaxagoras did not regard the ὁμοιομέρειαι as 'indivisibles' beyond which you

[1] See below, pp. 551 ff.

cannot get. This was the view of the Atomists, but that Anaxagoras held the theory of 'infinite divisibility' is clear not merely from the evidence of Lucretius,[1] but of his own fragments: 'there is not a least of the small, but always a less'.[2] And on Mr. Peck's theory, if we divided up a piece of bread, one would, just as much as on the traditional view, arrive ultimately at a 'seed' of bread which was bread and nothing else. His explanation seems to me to do valuable service in insisting on the relation of the μεῖγμα and the ὁμοιομερῆ and the necessity of concentrating on the problem of physical change, but it breaks down on comparison with the evidence.

Is it possible then to give any other explanation of Anaxagoras' theory which will explain how all 'things' in a concrete sense are present in all things, and yet allow for infinite division and at the same time take due account of the idea of the σπέρματα? I think it is and that such a view can best be arrived at by an examination of Anaxagoras' idea of the macrocosm and the creation of worlds. It is there possible to see the problem 'writ larger', and moreover the view which I wish to propound will be tested by its applicability to the theory as a whole and not merely to one part of it.

In the beginning then 'all things were together, infinite in number and smallness: for even the small was infinite',[3] there was, that is to say, as Anaxagoras calls it elsewhere, a σύμμιξις[4] or μεῖγμα[5] of an infinite number of substances, each one of which, even the smallest, consisted of an infinite number of divisible parts. Was this μεῖγμα a mere jumble of particles of 'all things' placed side by side in σύνθεσις, or, as Anaxagoras says, σύγκρισις, yet each retaining its own individuality, as in the atomic theory, or was there some closer coalition? Two fragments throw light on this question: 'when all things were together no one of them was manifest (ἔνδηλον) owing to its smallness';[6] 'since it is impossible for a least to exist, no one thing could be separated, or exist by itself, but all things together'.[7] That is to say, that however small a particle of the μεῖγμα you might take, and there was no limit to the possibility of division, all things would always be present in it, but they were not ἔνδηλα, which means surely not merely 'seen', but 'capable of perception'. A very important comment on the notion is furnished by Aetius,[8] who in speaking of the μόρια or portions of 'things' in things, says using the expression of a later age that they were λόγῳ θεωρητά : you know, that is, that they are there, but you could

[1] i. 844.   [2] D.B. 3: cf. 6.   [3] D.B. 1.
[4] D.B. 4, § 2.   [5] Simpl. in Ar. *Phys.* A. 4. 187; D.B. 1.
[6] D.B. 1.   [7] D.B. 6.   [8] i. 3. 5; D.A. 46.

never perceive them. What then is the underlying notion? I believe that in the terms μεῖγμα and σύμμιξις Anaxagoras was really striving after the idea of a union closer than mere mechanical juxtaposition, and more like our notion of chemical fusion, a union in which things are not merely placed side by side, but are, as it were, completely merged in a new substance: it is in his own terminology a σύμμιξις and not a σύγκρισις.[1] In this μεῖγμα individual things could not be distinguished, for from the nature of their fusion they were not distinguishable (χωριστά),[2] but 'you know that they are there' and their presence in greater or smaller quantities influences the character of the whole. What then was the appearance and character of this original μεῖγμα? In the first place 'no colour was perceptible: for the mixture of all things prevented it';[3] the fusion was so complete that the character of no one thing could prevail to give a colour to the whole. Yet even so the μεῖγμα was not entirely homogeneous in all its parts: for 'each thing is and was most manifestly those things of which it has most in it'. Though in every part of it all things were present, yet in some parts one thing would dominate and give the prevailing character to its neighbourhood, and in others another thing. If this is so, we should expect the appearance of the whole μεῖγμα to be that of the elements of which in the whole universe there were most: and this is precisely what Anaxagoras says: 'nothing was manifest owing to its smallness: for mist and sky[4] prevailed, both being infinite: for these are the greatest things in the sum total both in bulk and size'.

So far at least the description of the μεῖγμα seems to tally exactly with the notion of a fusion of all things, each part of which and also the whole take their character from the prevailing thing. And at this point comes a curious confirmation of this idea. For there was one element which did not enter this combination, but remained pure, the corporeal substance νοῦς,[5] or, as we might say in the language of

[1] I believe that I owe the suggestion of this view originally to Professor J. A. Smith.

[2] Cf. D.B. 6. [3] D.B. 4, § 2.

[4] ἀήρ, the vaporous misty air which Anaximenes had selected as the one ultimate constituent, and αἰθήρ, the bright clear air of the sky, which was one of the 'elements' of Empedocles.

[5] The famous passage (*Phaedo* 97 b) in which Plato expresses his disappointment at finding that Anaxagoras' νοῦς was after all a physical existence, and not, as he had hoped, a non-material motive cause makes it clear that Burnet (*E. G. P.*3, p. 267) is right in regarding it as corporeal. Cornford too (p. 153) from his own point of view arrives at the conclusion that it was a 'soul-substance'.

a modern thinker, 'mind-stuff'. Anaxagoras' description of it and its relation to other 'things' is of great importance for the present purpose: 'all other things have a portion of everything, but mind is an infinite thing and self-governed (αὐτοκρατές) and is mixed with no other thing, but exists alone by itself. For if it were not by itself, but were mixed with anything else, it must have had a share of all things, if it were mixed with anything: for in everything there is a portion of everything, as I have already said. And the things mixed with it would have prevented it from controlling anything as well as it does alone by itself'.[1] It is essential to work out this notion closely and see its implications: how are we to conceive the position of νοῦς with regard to the μεῖγμα? It cannot be that it was outside the μεῖγμα, like Empedocles' Strife in the beginning of things, for firstly the μεῖγμα and νοῦς were both infinite, and secondly, since being corporeal it could only control things by contact, it must touch them. It must then have been spread throughout the μεῖγμα without entering into combination: as Anaxagoras says himself, 'it is in'[2] things (ἔνι) but 'it is not mixed (μέμεικται) with them'.[3]   Here then is a strong confirmation of the view that the μεῖγμα was a fusion: for if it had been merely a juxta-position (σύγκρισις), then νοῦς, spread about in it, was in fact just as much 'mixed' as were any other 'things'; but if it was a fusion, then and then only could νοῦς be in juxtaposition with any part of it, and yet remain pure. This I believe to have been Anaxagoras' meaning: in the μεῖγμα individual substances were 'lost' in the close mixture, νοῦς was in the μεῖγμα but never entered the mixture, however much it was disseminated through it.

It is now possible to follow the process of the creation of worlds. The μεῖγμα in itself is static, but at any point in it at which there is present a portion of νοῦς, there results a 'movement'[4] (κίνησις), which takes the form of a rotation (περιχώρησις),[5] first of all, as Anaxagoras carefully explains, 'of a small part, and then of more and more': the whirl and the amount of rotating matter is ever increasing. The result of this is that bits of the μεῖγμα are separated off (ἀποκρίνονται).[6] These bits which are separated off are in fact the 'seeds of all things', having all kinds of forms and colours and savours (ἡδονάς)'.[7] What then will be their constitution? In the first place they are not of course 'ultimate molecules', like the atoms, incapable of further division: they, just like all other things in the universe, may be divided up into

[1] D.B. 12.   [2] D.B. 11.   [3] D.B. 12.
[4] D.B. 9.   [5] D.B. 12.   [6] D.B. 9, 12, 13.
[7] D.B. 4, § 1.

smaller and smaller portions:[1] they are in fact just the bits of the μεῖγμα as they happen to be broken off by the rotation. Like the whole μεῖγμα too they each of them contain all things and so would any portions, however small, into which they might be broken, but they differ in an endless variety of 'forms and colours and savours', differ that is, in quality. How does this happen? They differ in form no doubt according as they happen to be broken off, and in colour and savour and other qualities owing to the constitution of the original μεῖγμα. For just as it, though in all its parts it contained all things, yet was not entirely homogeneous, for in different parts different things prevailed, so it is with the bits broken off from it. A bit which comes from a part of the μεῖγμα in which 'the moist' prevails will become a 'seed' of water, if it come from where 'the hot' dominates a seed of 'fire', and so on not only with the opposites, but with all concrete substances, gold, bone, flesh, blood, bread, &c.: the effect of the whirl is to break up tracts of the μεῖγμα into the 'seeds of all things'.

The next stage in the process is that these 'seeds' are 'separated apart'[2] (διακρίνεται), that is to say that from the miscellaneous jumble of the whirl, the unlike seeds, or to speak more strictly, those unlike in their prevailing 'thing', begin to move apart. Like then becomes attached (προσκρίνεται)[3] to like, and the result is the formation of a compound structure (συγκρινόμενον),[4] in which the majority of the seeds will be those in which the same substance prevails and so determines the character of the compound, but each of these seeds still contains all things, and there will be mixed with them, though not 'manifest', seeds in which other 'things' are dominant. But the compound made up of 'seeds' is not itself a fusion but a juxtaposition. The detailed process of the formation of a world contains nothing which throws further light on the main question and has been sufficiently considered in the text.[5]

It is not to the point here to enter into the details of Anaxagoras' astronomical and biological speculations, nor of his interesting theory of perception; there is nothing in them which at all prejudices the account given of his general notion of creation, but they are not essential for its understanding. It is time to return to the phenomena

---

[1] Note that a 'seed' is not a permanent entity: it is just a piece of the original μεῖγμα in which one 'thing' prevails and might at any moment be broken up into smaller particles, each of which then becomes a 'seed'.

[2] D.B. 13. [3] D.B. 14. [4] D.B. 4, § 1.

[5] I agree with A. L. Peck (C. Q., l.c.) that Anaxagoras' cosmology was traditional and stands apart from his main theory.

of physical and physiological change which take place in a world after its creation and to see whether any light is thrown on them by the larger theory. There is unfortunately in none of the fragments or references anything like a detailed account of the process: if there were, it would be possible to arrive at certainty on the main issue. There is however enough material to start the inquiry and the analogy of the fuller details of the larger process is of great value. It will have been observed that in the description of the process of world-formation Anaxagoras represented each stage by a carefully differentiated compound of κρίνειν (ἀποκρίνεσθαι, διακρίνεσθαι, προσκρίνεσθαι, συγκρίνεσθαι). In Simplicius'[1] commentary on Aristotle's *Physics* it appears that the phenomenon of birth or production in the created world is also described by its appropriate compound of κρίνω, different from any of those yet used. 'He said that all things were mixed in everything and that production (γένεσις) took place by separating out (ἔκκρισις).' A little later on he explains its meaning more fully: 'seeing therefore that from each of the things now separated apart (διακεκριμένων) all things were separated out (ἐκκρινόμενα), as for instance flesh and bone and the rest from bread, as though all existed already in it and were mixed together, from this he surmised that all existences were once mixed together before they were separated apart'. Is it possible on the analogy of the other compounds of κρίνω and from the idea already formed of the ἀποκεκριμένα to form a notion of the nature of ἔκκρισις? It will be easiest to attempt it in a concrete instance and Simplicius' example of food comes most readily to hand. What then is the constitution of the piece of bread before it is eaten? It is made up of a very large number of minute 'seeds' or particles in juxtaposition, each of which contains 'all things' in fusion: these 'seeds' were in origin bits of the μεῖγμα separated off (ἀποκρινόμενα) and separated apart (διακρινό-μενα) in the whirl, they subsequently came together (προσκριθέντα) and formed a compound body (συγκρινόμενον). What is the character of these 'seeds'? Must it be said that in every one of them bread 'prevails'? In spite of a serious difficulty,[2] I think, emphatically not. Though in the majority bread 'prevails', there are yet in the constitution of the bread 'seeds' of all things, of gold, fire, onions, &c. But not by any means in equal numbers: there are undoubtedly most 'bread-seeds', a large number, though not so many, of flesh, blood,

[1] In Arist. *Phys.* Γ. 4. 203; D.A. 45.

[2] That of the use of the terms ὁμοιομερῆ and ὁμοιομέρειαι: I hope however to show that the usual interpretation of these words is mistaken: see pp. 551–55.

and bone-seeds, of the things, that is, into which bread normally changes, and some examples at least of every kind of 'seed'. This is the constitution one would expect out of a compound formed in the whirl, and it is surely the meaning of the famous sentence from which the whole controversy starts, 'each thing is and was *those things*[1] of which it has *most* in it'. Not enough stress has hitherto been laid on the plural 'those things . . . most' ($\pi\lambda\epsilon\hat{\iota}\sigma\tau a$): it means surely that not only has the bread a majority of 'bread-seeds', but also many corresponding to those parts of the body which it may form when eaten: bread 'is and was' bread, but also potentially flesh, blood, and bones. But these secondary seeds in which flesh and blood, &c., prevail are so minute, and perhaps we may also say with Giussani so scattered, that they do not affect the character of the whole and could never be perceived. Indeed they cannot yet be described as pieces of bone, flesh, &c., but they are only, as Aetius[2] accurately calls them, 'portions capable of producing blood, &c.' ($\mu\acute{o}\rho\iota a$ $a\"\iota\mu a\tau os$ $\gamma\epsilon\nu\nu\eta\tau\iota\kappa\acute{a}$). And so it comes to pass that when we eat the bread, the processes of biting and digestion 'separate out' the latent 'seeds' in which flesh and blood prevail from the seeds in which bread prevails and then these join each other and the pre-existent flesh and blood in the body. But such separation does not, as in the ordinary view, cause the production of things which no longer contain all things, for in every 'seed', in whatever compound body it may be, there are always 'portions of everything' fused together.

Here then there is a complete parallelism between the macrocosm, the normal substance of things, and the microcosm of the 'seed'. Just as in the original $\mu\epsilon\hat{\iota}\gamma\mu a$ 'all things were together', but owing to their great prevalence 'in size and bulk' mist and sky determined the appearance of the whole, so in the 'seeds' all things are present in fusion, but the character of each is determined by that of which there is most, and in the compound body all the different kinds of 'seeds' are there, but the character of the whole is that of the majority of the 'seeds'. Just as in the $\mu\epsilon\hat{\iota}\gamma\mu a$ the rotatory motion instituted by 'mind' caused the 'separating off' of 'seeds' and like joined like, so now the extraneous force of the process of eating and digesting food causes the 'separating out' of the latent seeds in which flesh, blood, &c., prevail, which join 'the like' in the body. Nor of course is this a mere parallelism, but is all due to the fact that the ultimate constitution of the 'seeds' is just that of the $\mu\epsilon\hat{\iota}\gamma\mu a$, for they are nothing but portions of it. The view

[1] Simpl. in Arist. *Phys.* A. 2. 184; D.A. 41. The manuscripts have ὅτῳ, for which Usener's ὅτων is universally accepted as against a possible ὅτου.

[2] i. 3. 5; D.A. 46.

I have put forward satisfies, I believe, the requirements with which we started. It preserves the concrete nature of the 'things' of which everything has a part; it preserves the possibility of infinite division without reaching 'things' unmixed, for every 'seed' and every particle, however minute, into which it might be divided, will still contain all things fused together; it shows how the process of change may take place by a 'separating out' of 'seeds' already existent and latent in the previous body, and finally it accords, I believe, better both with the extant fragments of Anaxagoras and the accounts of his system.

But, it will be urged, the fatal objection to this view is the application by Aristotle and other later commentators to the theory of Anaxagoras of the words ὁμοιομερής and ὁμοιομέρεια, which it will be noticed I have hitherto neglected. These words must mean, it will be said, that, according to Anaxagoras, each part of a whole compound body, each 'seed', was exactly homogeneous in character both with all the other parts and with the whole. If so, it is impossible that there should be in bread, any 'seeds' in which anything else than bread prevails, for they would not be ὁμοιομερῆ either with the vast majority of the other 'seeds' or with the whole piece of bread. The objection is not, I think, by any means fatal, but it is serious, and it is necessary in conclusion to attempt to trace the meaning of these words and the idea which they imply. In the first place it must be remarked that the ordinary interpretation of their meaning is in any case a fatal one, because it *must* involve a deadlock and make change impossible. If *all* the parts of a compound body are exactly homogeneous and have the same prevailing 'thing', then nothing could ever change into something else without a dissolution which would produce some things in which 'all things' were not present. If bread prevails in every particle of a piece of bread, flesh and blood can only be 'separated out' from it pure, and then, as on the 'old view' of Anaxagoras' theory, things exist which do not any longer contain all things. As Burnet argues, and the least reflexion must cause agreement, such cannot have been Anaxagoras' meaning.

In other words the traditional idea of the homoeomeria cannot be right and a new inquiry into its meaning is demanded. At the outset a distinction must be drawn between the substantive (ὁμοιομέρεια) and the adjective (ὁμοιομερής). Only the adjective is used by Aristotle in his comments on Anaxagoras: the later commentators use the adjective when they are reproducing Aristotle and they also give us the substantive as though, contrary to modern belief, it were a term employed by Anaxagoras himself. It will therefore be best to consider them separately. Now the word ὁμοιομερής[1] had for Aristotle a very peculiar sense apart from his comments on Anaxagoras in association with his own physical theory. A substance that is in the Aristotelian sense ὁμοιομερής is the resultant of a μῖξις or fusion of the four elements or στοιχεῖα as opposed to the resultant of a mere σύνθεσις: such are the material substances of which things are composed. Thus, as Burnet[2] notes, the ὁμοιομερῆ, in Aristotle's biological theory, stand intermediate between the elements and the developed organs: they are, to take the example of the human body, bone, flesh, blood, &c., which are homogeneous in all their parts, as distinguished on the one hand from the στοιχεῖα, earth, air, fire, and water, which themselves have no component parts, and on the other from the formed ὄργανα, such as the hand, in which the parts are not ὅμοια. Now there is an *a priori* probability that when Aristotle applied a word of such distinctive connotation to the theory of Anaxagoras, he intended to use it, if not in exactly the same sense, at least, in a sense not widely different from his application of it to his own theory. If the account given above of Anaxagoras' theory be at all correct, there was in fact a double reason why Aristotle should have applied the epithet ὁμοιομερής to the substances and the particles of substance which Anaxagoras conceived as the underlying substratum of matter. In the first place the epithet would denote just the class of reality which Anaxagoras wished to express, the material substance of existing things and in particular the flesh, bone, blood, &c., in which, with his physical bias, he was mainly interested: in the second it would connote that these were the products of a μῖξις—not, of course, a μῖξις of the elements, as Aristotle held himself, but of a μεῖγμα such as Anaxagoras conceived as the original condition of the universe. This is what one would expect *a priori*: it is necessary to inquire how far it is actually the case. There are three main passages in which Aristotle uses the word in connexion with Anaxagoras.

1. In the *de Caelo*[3] Aristotle is contrasting Anaxagoras with Empedocles in his account of the elements. 'Empedocles', he says, 'maintains that fire and things in the same category with them[4] are the elements of bodies and that all things are compounded of them. But Anaxagoras says the opposite; for he makes the ὁμοιομερῆ elements, I mean flesh and blood and each of the things in this class: but air and

---

[1] See a paper by H. H. Joachim, *Journal of Philology*, xxix. 72 ff.
[2] *E. G. P.*3, p. 265. [3] Γ. 3. 302 a; D.A. 43 (b).
[4] The plural (τούτοις) suggests that καὶ ὕδωρ or something like it has dropped out after πῦρ.

fire are mixtures of these and of all other seeds, for all of these are composed of invisible ὁμοιομερῆ of all kinds.' This is exactly what we should expect. He is in the first instance using ὁμοιομερῆ in his own sense and describing the class of things to which Anaxagoras' elements belonged in opposition to the elements of Empedocles: in the second he applies the term in the same sense to the Anaxagorean imperceptible 'seeds' in compound things.

2. So in the Physics[1] in precisely the same way: 'Of those who make the elements infinite, Anaxagoras said that they were made of the ὁμοιομερῆ'—Aristotle's own sense of the term again.

3. The passage from the Metaphysics[2] has caused much difficulty:[3] 'Practically all the ὁμοιομερῆ (just like fire and water), Anaxagoras says, come into being by combination and perish by separation only, but in no other sense[4] do they come into being or perish at all, but remain everlasting.' The critics, who stumble chiefly over the parenthesis, have got into difficulties because they take ὁμοιομερῆ to refer here to the ultimate particles or else the 'seeds' in Anaxagoras' theory. It surely does not, but as in the two previous passages means 'the substances I call ὁμοιομερῆ', i.e. the flesh, bones, &c., in the human body. These, as I understand Anaxagoras' theory, come into being and perish owing to the combination and dissolution of 'seeds': but such birth and death are only illusory, for the 'seeds' themselves do not perish, but only enter into new combinations. Fire and water are, of course, on Anaxagoras' theory, compounds and so too are even the substances Aristotle regards as ὁμοιομερῆ, for they are all alike constructed by the juxtaposition (σύγκρισις) of 'seeds'. The meaning then is that in Anaxagoras' theory both substances which Aristotle calls ὁμοιομερῆ and also those which he regards as elements (fire and water) are compounds of 'seeds', created by combination and destroyed by separation. I do not at all agree with Burnet that 'the general sense is that Anaxagoras applies to the ὁμοιομερῆ what is really true of the στοιχεῖα'.[5]

---

[1] Γ. 4. 203 a; D.A. 45.   [2] A. 3. 984 a; D.A. 43 (a).

[3] See E. G. P.3, p. 265, n. 2.

[4] I do not think that Zeller's ἁπλῶς for ἄλλως, which is adopted by Burnet, improves the sense.

[5] Cf. Simpl. in Arist. Phys. A. 2. 184 (27. 2); D.A. 41 πάντα γὰρ τὰ ὁμοιομερῆ, οἷον ὕδωρ ἢ πῦρ ἢ χρυσόν, ἀγένητα μὲν εἶναι καὶ ἄφθαρτα, φαίνεσθαι δὲ γινόμενα καὶ ἀπολλύμενα συγκρίσει καὶ διακρίσει μόνον, which is obviously an echo of this passage of Aristotle, makes its meaning quite clear, and it is interesting to note that there water and fire are actually grouped with gold as ὁμοιομερῆ: on Anaxagoras' theory there is no difference in their constitution.

In passing from Aristotle to the doxographers it is impossible not to be struck at once with the curious fact that what is now found for the most part is not the Aristotelian adjective ὁμοιομερής, but the substantive ὁμοιομέρειαι. It is used clearly in a slightly different sense from Aristotle's adjective and spoken of as if it were a technical term of Anaxagoras'. Two passages are of great interest and must be considered in detail.

1. Simplicius [1] commenting on the passage in the Physics: 'Since Anaxagoras postulates the ὁμοιομέρειαι, and Democritus the atoms, both regarded as infinite in number, as first-beginnings, he (Aristotle) inquires first into the opinion of Anaxagoras and also explains the reason which led Anaxagoras to such a supposition, and shows ... that each ὁμοιομέρεια, just as much as the whole, has all things present in it, and that not merely infinite in number but infinite times infinite.' Here the ὁμοιομέρειαι are clearly something different from the ὁμοιομερῆ of Aristotle: they are not substances such as we know, but something underlying them which can be compared with the atoms of Democritus. In short they are the 'seeds' of which things are compounded and Simplicius explains clearly enough—what I have attempted to show is a necessary postulate for the explanation of change—that each of them too contains portions of all things: the passage is in fact the clearest and most convincing explanation of exactly what I believe to have been Anaxagoras' theory. The name ὁμοιομέρειαι, as applied to the 'seeds', is appropriate enough as on the one hand the 'seeds', like Aristotle's ὁμοιομερῆ, are the resultants of μῖξις, on the other they are each of them 'parts like to whole substances': a thing that is ὁμοιομερής has 'seeds' which are ὁμοιομέρειαι, for they are like to material substances: the adjective and substantive are correlative.

2. Aetius [2] after explaining that since Anaxagoras could not conceive the possibility of anything being created out of the non-existent, therefore supposed the existence in food of 'particles capable of creating' blood and nerves and bones, &c., which are only λόγῳ θεωρητά, goes on to say, 'from the fact then that the particles in the food are like the substances produced he called them ὁμοιομέρειαι, and he took the ὁμοιομέρειαι as the material cause'. Burnet [3] comments: 'Aetius, supposing as he does that Anaxagoras himself used the term (ὁμοιομέρειαι) gives it an entirely wrong meaning.' As to Anaxagoras' use something will shortly be said, but the meaning is not 'entirely' wrong: the ὁμοιομέρειαι are so called because they are like in substance to the

[1] In Arist. Phys. Γ. 4. 203 a; D.A. 45b. [2] i. 3. 5; D.A. 46.
[3] E. G. P.3, p. 264, n. 3.

material things of sense which they compose, and though Aetius goes too far, he is right in referring the term not only to the 'bread-seeds' in the bread, but also to its 'flesh-' and 'blood-seeds'. In other words his comment is an effective contradiction of the traditional view that all the 'seeds' in the piece of bread must be 'bread-seeds'. Aetius in another passage [1] says 'the ὁμοιομερῆ are of every kind of shape': here ὁμοιομερῆ is loosely used in the sense of ὁμοιομέρειαι and the statement is exactly parallel to Anaxagoras' [2] own affirmation that the 'seeds of all things' in the original μεῖγμα were of every form.

To these usages of ὁμοιομέρειαι by the doxographers in a way clearly independent of, though not inconsistent with, Aristotle's use of the adjective ὁμοιομερής, we must add the no less startling, and quite unique, application of the singular homoeomeria by Lucretius [3] to Anaxagoras' theory as a whole for which he claims Anaxagoras' authority. What then is to be said about the origin of these later uses? Clearly the doxographers did not get them from Aristotle: for he uses only the adjective in a sense applicable enough to Anaxagoras' ideas, but connected with his own biological theory. Did they then develop the substantive and its meaning from Aristotle's adjective? It is not probable that in that case they would have diverged quite so far from his usage: still less that they would have invented the rather strange formation ὁμοιομέρειαι to express the essentially concrete substance of the 'seeds'. Where then did they get the word and its sense? There is surely only one answer that Aetius and Lucretius are telling the truth, that Anaxagoras did call his ἀρχαὶ ὁμοιομέρειαι, that he did refer to his theory as the homoeomeria, and that in all probability he spoke of compound substances as ὁμοιομερῆ. None of these terms of course occurs in the extant fragments, but I cannot see how it is possible to explain their later uses except on the supposition, which is confirmed by the statements of the doxographers, that the terms were Anaxagoras' own. Aristotle, I imagine, adopted from him the adjective because it expressed exactly what he wanted to describe in his own theory—a substance homogeneous in its parts with the implication that it was the resultant of a μῖξις: in speaking of Anaxagoras' theory he used it to denote those substances to which it was applicable both on his own theory and Anaxagoras'—the substances of which the organs of the body and so on are composed. The later commentators returned to Anaxagoras' own use and spoke of the 'seeds' as ὁμοιομέρειαι, and the whole theory as ὁμοιομέρεια.

[1] i. 14. 4; D.A. 51. [2] D.B. 4, § 1 : see p. 547.
[3] i. 830, 834 'rerum *quam dicit* homoeomerian'.

Whether this surmise be correct or not, it is, I hope, clear that there is nothing either in Aristotle's use of ὁμοιομερής, or the later usage of ὁμοιομέρεια which is in any way a bar to the view here taken of the general theory. ὁμοιομέρειαι denotes the 'seeds' containing a fusion of all things, and like in substance to the bodies which they compose, ὁμοιομερῆ denotes bodies so formed, but there is nothing in the evidence which necessitates the conclusion that in *all* the ὁμοιομέρειαι of a given body, the same 'thing' prevailed: on the contrary the evidence tends to show that Anaxagoras conceived that in any one body there were 'seeds' corresponding to every substance, but they differed greatly in number, and the character of the body, present and future, was determined by those 'seeds' 'of which there were most in it'.

APPENDIX II

Other Views of Πρόληψις

THE scantiness of the evidence as to the exact nature of Epicurus' conception of πρόληψις has caused a certain divergence of opinion. Though I have no doubt that the interpretation given in the text, which is that of the great majority of modern critics, is right, it is worth while to chronicle some of the other views.

1. Cicero, *de Natura Deorum*, i. 17. 44, speaking of the προλήψεις which all men have of divine beings, describes them as *insitae vel potius innatae cognitiones*. It might be thought at first sight that he regarded them as 'innate ideas', concepts which are in the mind from birth and are not due in any sense to experience. But the divergence is more apparent than real: the Latin words do not necessarily imply this, but only that the 'anticipations' 'were implanted in or grew up' within the mind and were not—directly at least—given it from without. Cicero is capable of a good deal of misinterpretation of Epicurus, but the notion of 'innate ideas' would be wholly repugnant to Epicureanism and it is not necessary to suppose that he held it. See Mayor's note on the passage, and Tohte, *Epikurs Kriterien der Wahrheit*, p. 17.

2. Steinhart, in the article on Epicurus in Ersch and Grüber's *Encyclopaedia*, understands the προλήψεις to be the images of *individual* sense-perceptions, which remain in the mind and may be called up at will for purposes of comparison. Tohte (op. cit., p. 16) has shown that this view is sufficiently contradicted by the evidence of Diogenes (x. 33), and in particular by the phrases καθολικὴ νόησις and μνήμη τοῦ πολλάκις ἔξωθεν φανέντος, which must refer to a general concept founded on the repeated image and not to an individual image. We may add (1) that the operation which Steinhart conceives is simply that of the memory of a particular sense-perception, μνήμη τοῦ ἅπαξ ἔξωθεν φανέντος, (2) that, as such, it could have no validity in cognition as a 'criterion', for 'one sensation cannot correct another'.

3. A more important divergence from the ordinary view has (1909) been put forward by F. Merbach (op. cit., pp. 45 ff.), who, it must be remembered (see p. 232, n. 2), also denies that Epicurus' Canonice was thought out in terms of his physical theory: he is thus not hampered by the necessity of explaining the atomic psychology of its details. He holds (1) that the essence of the πρόληψις consists in the

connexion of name and thing: it would be of no value to us to have general concepts stored in our mind, unless we could also name them: (2) that we receive the προλήψεις not from repeated sensations, but from the instructions of parents, &c., in our childhood who tell us the names of things; (3) that the πρόληψις owes its validity as a test of truth to the fact that cognition, in which we use it, is an essential part of sense-perception and is therefore itself a department of αἴσθησις. Merbach seems to me to have done good service in emphasizing the place of πρόληψις in cognition, and still more in showing its connexion with the naming of things, and the assumption of the idea of πρόληψις in §§ 37, 38 of the Letter to Herodotus (see pp. 248, 267). But his divorce of the Canonice from the physical theory is to my mind a root-misconception of Epicurus and vitiates the details of his work, and he entirely neglects the evidence of Diogenes' definition, which he regards as a patchwork, unintelligible because we do not possess the context of the various explanations given of πρόληψις. Moreover, to come to his three main contentions, (1) admitting the importance of the name, as a label of the concept, and the close connexion of the idea of πρόληψις with Epicurus' theories both of the origin of language and the requisites of scientific terminology, I yet think that the name is not an essential part of Epicurus' notion of πρόληψις: even without a name, it would be possible for the individual to refer a new sensation to the general concept, and say 'this is that', which is the fundamental element in cognition; (2) we receive names from the instruction of others, but the concepts themselves, which are more important, must be due to sense-experience: further, it is, I think, clear that Epicurus regarded all the κριτήρια as closely connected in origin, αἴσθησις being the ultimate source of all; (3) cognition is indeed an essential part of sense-perception, but not of mere sensation, and could not be included by Epicurus, except very loosely, under αἴσθησις: it is ἐπαίσθημα. If the προλήψεις had validity as part of sensation, they would be ἀληθεῖς as well as ἐναργεῖς; but such validity, which did not rest on origin, would be assumed, not inferred. The whole theory is interesting and has called attention to important points, but it cannot, I think, be set up against the ordinary view. Merbach approaches the question with too great a desire to find in πρόληψις the explanation of Ep. i, §§ 37, 38, where it is not actually mentioned, and too little respect for Diogenes' definitions, which must after all come from Epicurean sources.

On the Meaning of ἐπιβολὴ τῆς διανοίας [1]

OF all the technical terms of the Epicurean philosophy none is nearly so obscure and elusive as ἐπιβολὴ τῆς διανοίας. We are confronted with it or its equivalent five[2] times in the Letter to Herodotus and once[3] in the Κύριαι Δόξαι; Diogenes[4] further tells us that the 'Epicureans' added it to Epicurus' three criteria of truth: yet each fresh context seems at first only to shed further obscurity on its meaning. Nor can it be said that modern critics and historians of philosophy have for the most part assisted much towards its elucidation: finding it in a prominent place in the Epicurean philosophy they have felt bound to give some equivalent for it, but most of them have been content to make wild guesses[5] without, as it seems, any careful consideration of the contexts in which it occurs: yet the very divergence of these guesses shows how little the phrase conveys a direct indication of its meaning. Only two[6] scholars, so far as I know, have made a really critical study of the subject, Tohte[7] and Giussani,[8] and they again differ widely in their conclusions. I should be loth to enter the discussion, but that I feel bound to justify the views assumed in my account of the *Canonice* and also believe that something may yet be said, which may help towards a solution.

It will be convenient, before entering the details of the discussion, to give in full the passages of Epicurus dealing with the subject, which

[1] I have for convenience of reference reprinted this Appendix from *Epicurus*, pp. 259–74.

[2] §§ 38, 50, 51 (twice), 62.   [3] xxiv.

[4] x. 31 (*Vit.*).

[5] We may instance Zeller, 'sensible impression'; Überweg, 'intuitive apprehension of the understanding' (which is nearer to part of the right idea than most conjectures); Ritter and Preller, 'a form of πρόληψις not differing from images seen in delirium or sleep'; Steinhart, 'the free activity of the imagination'.

[6] Brieger's contribution (*Lehre von der Seele*, pp. 19, 20) is so vague and uncritical that it does not really come into question, though, as will be seen, he has grasped one essential part of the full meaning. F. Merbach (*de Epicuri Canonica*, pp. 28–35) has some interesting pages on the subject, in which he agrees in the main with Tohte, but does not touch the crucial difficulty of § 62 of the Letter to Herodotus.

[7] *Epikurs Kriterien der Wahrheit*, pp. 20–4.

[8] *Stud. Lucr.* pp. 171–82.

will frequently be required for reference, and to state summarily the conclusions at which this note will arrive.

I. Letter to Herodotus:

A. § 38 ἔτι τε [1] κατὰ τὰς αἰσθήσεις δεῖ πάντα τηρεῖν καὶ ἁπλῶς ‹κατὰ› τὰς παρούσας ἐπιβολὰς εἴτε διανοίας εἴθ᾽ ὅτου δήποτε τῶν κριτηρίων, ὁμοίως δὲ κατὰ τὰ ὑπάρχοντα πάθη, ὅπως ἂν καὶ τὸ προσμένον καὶ τὸ ἄδηλον ἔχωμεν οἷς σημειωσόμεθα.

B. § 50 καὶ ἢν ἂν λάβωμεν φαντασίαν ἐπιβλητικῶς τῇ διανοίᾳ ἢ τοῖς αἰσθητηρίοις εἴτε μορφῆς εἴτε συμβεβηκότων, μορφή ἐστιν αὕτη τοῦ στερεμνίου, γινομένη κατὰ τὸ ἑξῆς πύκνωμα ἢ ἐγκατάλειμμα τοῦ εἰδώλου.

C. § 51 ἥ τε γὰρ ὁμοιότης τῶν φαντασμῶν οἱονεὶ [1] ἐν εἰκόνι λαμβανομένων ἢ καθ᾽ ὕπνους γινομένων ἢ κατ᾽ ἄλλας τινὰς ἐπιβολὰς τῆς διανοίας ἢ τῶν λοιπῶν κριτηρίων οὐκ ἄν ποτε ὑπῆρχε τοῖς οὖσί τε καὶ ἀληθέσι προσαγορευομένοις, εἰ μὴ ἦν τινα καὶ τοιαῦτα προσβαλλόμενα.

D. § 51 (immediately following the preceding) τὸ δὲ διημαρτημένον οὐκ ἂν ὑπῆρχεν, εἰ μὴ ἐλαμβάνομεν καὶ ἄλλην τινὰ κίνησιν ἐν ἡμῖν αὐτοῖς συνημμένην μὲν ‹τῇ φανταστικῇ ἐπιβολῇ›, διάληψιν δὲ ἔχουσαν.

E. § 62 ἐπεὶ τό γε θεωρούμενον πᾶν ἢ κατ᾽ ἐπιβολὴν λαμβανόμενον τῇ διανοίᾳ ἀληθές ἐστιν.

II. Κύριαι Δόξαι xxiv εἴ τιν᾽ ἐκβαλεῖς ἁπλῶς αἴσθησιν καὶ μὴ διαιρήσεις τὸ δοξαζόμενον κατὰ [1] τὸ προσμένον καὶ τὸ παρὸν ἤδη κατὰ τὴν αἴσθησιν καὶ τὰ πάθη καὶ πᾶσαν φανταστικὴν ἐπιβολὴν τῆς διανοίας, συνταράξεις καὶ τὰς λοιπὰς αἰσθήσεις τῇ ματαίῳ δόξῃ, ὥστε τὸ κριτήριον ἅπαν ἐκβαλεῖς.

To these passages of Epicurus must be added two others of great importance:

Diog. Laert. x. 31 ἐν τοίνυν τῷ Κανόνι λέγων ἐστὶν ὁ Ἐπίκουρος κριτήρια τῆς ἀληθείας εἶναι τὰς αἰσθήσεις καὶ προλήψεις καὶ τὰ πάθη· οἱ δ᾽ Ἐπικούρειοι καὶ τὰς φανταστικὰς ἐπιβολὰς τῆς διανοίας.

Clem. Alex. *Strom.* ii. 4, p. 157 (Usener, *fr.* 255) πρόληψιν δὲ ἀποδίδωσιν ἐπιβολὴν ἐπί τι ἐναργὲς καὶ ἐπὶ τὴν ἐναργῆ τοῦ πράγματος ἐπίνοιαν.

Briefly put, the line of argument which I propose to pursue is as follows: (1) The natural meaning of ἐπιβολή used of operations of the senses or the mind is a 'projection upon', and so 'attention to', and, with the added notion of the result, 'apprehension' and even 'view'. (2) Epicurus in several of the crucial passages implies an ἐπιβολή of

---

[1] For the text see my notes on the passages.

the senses, an 'apprehension' by 'looking' as opposed to passive seeing. (3) ἐπιβολὴ τῆς διανοίας corresponds exactly to this and means firstly (a) the immediate apprehension by an act of mental attention of certain subtle 'images', too fine to be apprehended by the senses, and, in particular, of the 'images' of divine beings; secondly (b) the immediate, or 'intuitive' apprehension of concepts, and in particular of the 'clear', i.e. self-evident concepts of scientific thought. With this preface, which may be of assistance in the course of a rather intricate and necessarily controversial argument, we may proceed to full discussion.

1. It was one of the cardinal principles of the *Canonice*[1] (§ 38) that words must be used in their first and obvious meaning, and though it may well seem to us at times that Epicurus has hardly succeeded in carrying out his principles, yet his intention suggests that the best starting-point for inquiry is to ask what is the natural meaning of the word ἐπιβολή. Proceeding from such literal usages as ἐπιβάλλειν τὰς χεῖρας it is natural to conclude that ἐπιβάλλειν (τὸν νοῦν or the like) will mean, like the commoner ἐπέχειν, 'to project the mind towards', 'to turn the attention to' an object: so Diod. Sic. xx. 43 has πρὸς οὐδὲν ἐπέβαλλε τὴν διάνοιαν, 'he paid no attention to anything'. In an absolute sense without the accusative we find τοῖς κοινοῖς πράγμασιν ἐπιβάλλειν in Plut. *Cic.* 4 as an equivalent of *rem publicam capessere*, and in a famous passage of St. Mark, xiv. 72 καὶ ἐπιβαλὼν ἔκλαιε. The verb is used in this way in an Epicurean passage of some importance, Aet. iv. 8. 10, p. 395 (Usener *fr.* 317) Λεύκιππος Δημόκριτος Ἐπίκουρος τὴν αἴσθησιν καὶ τὴν νόησιν γίνεσθαι εἰδώλων ἔξωθεν προσιόντων· μηδενὶ γὰρ ἐπιβάλλειν μηδετέραν χωρὶς τοῦ προσπίπτοντος εἰδώλου, and again in Iambl. *Protr.* 4. 56 ἡ ὄψις τοῖς ὁρατοῖς ἐπιβάλλει: for the moment we will suspend the question of the exact sense in these rather technical places.

ἐπιβολή, the substantive, should then mean 'a projection towards', 'attention to', and so with the added notion of the result of such attention, 'view' or 'apprehension': the substantive is thus used by Clem. Alex. 644 ἐπιβολὴ τῆς ἀληθείας, a 'grasp' or 'apprehension' of the truth. The simple ἐπιβολή without further qualification occurs six times in the Letter to Herodotus. (1) In § 35 Epicurus is speaking of the reason for writing an epitome, τῆς γὰρ ἀθρόας ἐπιβολῆς πυκνὸν δεόμεθα, τῆς δὲ κατὰ μέρος οὐχ ὁμοίως, 'for we have frequent need of the general view of the system, but not so often of the detailed exposition'. (2) In § 83 again, summing up the uses of the Letter, he says that even those who are working out the system in detail will be

[1] Ep. i, § 38.

able εἰς τὰς τοιαύτας ἀναλύοντας ἐπιβολὰς τὰς πλείστας τῶν περιοδειῶν ὑπὲρ τῆς ὅλης φύσεως ποιεῖσθαι, 'to carry out the greater part of their investigations into the nature of the whole by conducting their analysis with reference to such a survey as this'. (3) With these two passages goes the earlier of two instances in § 36 βαδιστέον μὲν οὐκ ἐπ' ἐκεῖνα καὶ συνεχῶς ἐν τῇ μνήμῃ τὸ τοσοῦτον ποιητέον, ἀφ' οὗ ἥ τε κυριωτάτη ἐπιβολὴ ἐπὶ τὰ πράγματα ἔσται, 'it is necessary to go back on the main principles and constantly to fix in one's memory enough to give one the most essential comprehension of the truth'. The meaning in these three passages is direct and clear. Slightly more technical are (4) § 69, where he is speaking of the properties (συμβεβηκότα) of compound things καὶ ἐπιβολὰς μὲν ἔχοντα ἰδίας πάντα ταῦτά ἐστι καὶ διαλήψεις, 'all these properties have their own peculiar means of being perceived and distinguished', and (5) § 70 κατ' ἐπιβολὰς δ' ἄν τινας ... ἕκαστα προσαγορευθείη, 'as the result of certain acts of apprehension ... they might each be given this name'. Here we are clearly approaching a more esoteric use, though still on the same lines, and the last passage, (6) § 36 τὸ ταῖς ἐπιβολαῖς ὀξέως δύνασθαι χρῆσθαι must wait for the results of the general discussion. Similarly the passage in Clement of Alexandria quoted above, in which it is stated that πρόληψις is an ἐπιβολή towards an ἐναργές, must be kept over for the present. ἐπιβολή then would appear to mean an 'act of attention', and so 'view' or 'apprehension'. Both Tohte and Giussani, however, believe that it has also in Epicurus the 'passive' or 'objective'[1] meaning of the 'impression' resulting from such an act of apprehension. It is true that there are close parallels in Epicurus' technical phraseology for this derivative passive sense: αἴσθησις is certainly used both for the act of sensation or perception and also for the passive sensation or perception received, and πρόληψις, which should strictly mean the 'act of anticipation' is never, I think, used in this sense by Epicurus,[2] but always of the 'general concept' or 'compound image', which is the basis of such an 'act of anticipation'. But, although it is sometimes possible that the passive sense rather than the active may be intended, it is never[3] necessary, and its indiscriminate introduction has, I believe, done a good deal to confuse issues.

2. We may get much light on the meaning of ἐπιβολὴ τῆς διανοίας if we ask first whether Epicurus contemplates any other kind of ἐπιβολή besides that of the mind. The answer is not far to seek,

---

[1] Giussani, loc. cit., p. 180.

[2] It seems, however, to be so used in the Epicurean passage from Clem. Alex. quoted above.   [3] Except possibly in § 38 : see p. 568.

though its importance seems not to have been sufficiently noticed:[1] Epicurus clearly recognizes an ἐπιβολή of the senses. They are not (at any rate, not always) the merely passive recipients of an impression, but by an 'act of attention' they apprehend the images which are flowing in upon them: they 'look' or 'listen' as opposed to merely 'seeing' or 'hearing'. In that case it is clear that ἐπιβολή[2] will be connected with the process of ἐπιμαρτύρησις, the close view of the ἐνάργημα, which is to check the rash inferences of δόξα, and tell us with certainty the true nature of the object. The passages in the Letter to Herodotus which mention or imply this ἐπιβολή of the senses are four in number, and it will be convenient to consider them in the order of their increasing difficulty.

B. § 50. The clearest and easiest of the passages is that in which Epicurus most emphatically and directly sums up his doctrine as to the value of ἐπιβολή in general. The idea here seems exactly to bear out what has been said. 'The image which we obtain by an act of attention or apprehension on the part of the senses (we must leave out the mind for the moment) of the shape or property (e.g. the colour) of an object, is in fact its shape (or property).' This is exactly the idea of ἐπιμαρτύρησις which Epicurus has just been expounding in the preceding context. Our first passive sensation of a distant object is 'true', for the image is a faithful representation of the successive 'idols', but it is not until we have 'looked at' the close, clear view (τὸ παρόν, τὸ ἐναργές) that we can be sure that the image exactly reproduces the shape and colour of the object. ἐπιβολή is required for the confirmation (or non-confirmation) of the δόξα founded on the original passive perception.

E. § 62, though a very difficult passage from the point of view of the ἐπιβολὴ τῆς διανοίας, strongly confirms this notion of the ἐπιβολή of the senses. Epicurus is considering the motion of the atoms in a moving compound body: by 'looking' we perceive that the motion of a whole body is the sum of the motions of all its perceptible parts in the same direction as the whole (e.g. an army). δόξα applies this analogy to the motion of the atomic parts of a moving body and infers

---

[1] Tohte remarks it (p. 21) and points out that it is in distinction from the ἐπιβολή of the senses that Epicurus speaks explicitly of ἐπιβολὴ τῆς διανοίας. So also does Merbach (pp. 31, 32). Giussani seems not to realize it at all, and is consequently driven to a very unnatural interpretation of some of the passages in which it is referred to.

[2] This connexion, which seems to me both necessary and extremely important, has escaped both Tohte and Giussani.

that it will be the same, whereas ἐπιβολὴ τῆς διανοίας shows that it is different. Here τὸ θεωρούμενον (what is seen by 'looking' as opposed to τὸ ὁρώμενον) is clearly equivalent in sense to τὸ ἐπιβλητικῶς λαμβανόμενον τοῖς αἰσθητηρίοις in B, and the general idea is the same as in the previous passage. The ἐπιβολή of the senses gives us the certain image of a σύμπτωμα (in this case movement) of a στερέμνιον.

We are now in a position to deal with the other two passages, where the sense is slightly more obscure.

A. § 38. After speaking of the necessity for keeping the terminology of our investigations in exact correspondence with the ideas which it represents, Epicurus proceeds to consider the methods of investigation. For clearness' sake we may extract the words which refer to the ἐπιβολή of the senses: κατὰ τὰς αἰσθήσεις δεῖ πάντα τηρεῖν καὶ ἁπλῶς ⟨κατὰ⟩ τὰς παρούσας ἐπιβολὰς . . . ὅτου δήποτε τῶν κριτηρίων, . . . ὅπως ἂν . . . τὸ προσμένον . . . ἔχωμεν οἷς σημειωσόμεθα: 'in order that we may have certain indications by which to judge the image awaiting confirmation (i.e. the original image of the distant object), we must keep everything under the control of the senses (i.e. free from the additions of δόξα), and in particular of the close apprehension (τὰς παρούσας ἐπιβολάς is equivalent to τὰς ἐπιβολὰς ἐπὶ τὸ παρὸν ἤδη κατὰ τὴν αἴσθησιν, cf. Κ.Δ. xxiv) of any of the standards of judgement'. The κριτήρια[1] here are clearly the individual senses, sight, hearing, &c., the αἰσθητήρια of B, which are indeed κριτήρια because they are the instruments of αἴσθησις: the expression is a little loose, but the meaning in view of the parallel passages quite unmistakable. The general notion of the passage is then exactly the same as that of the two preceding quotations, but it is much more clearly and elaborately stated. The ἐπιβολή of the senses, the προσμένον and the process of ἐπιμαρτύρησις are all brought into close connexion. The all-important matter for scientific investigation in the region of perception is the pure sensation, and in particular the observation of phenomena in the close view, which will give us the certainty that the sense-image corresponds to objective reality.

C. § 51. Epicurus is here arguing for the exact resemblance of the sense-images to the objects from which the 'idols' emanate. Extracting

---

[1] Giussani (p. 177), not realizing the ἐπιβολή of the senses, takes κριτήρια here to be 'signs' (σημεῖα as Epicurus ordinarily calls them), and, since he naturally feels that 'signs' could not be standards of reference, does not insert κατά, but leaves the ἐπιβολαί both of the mind and of the κριτήρια subordinate to αἴσθησις in general: but apart from all other objections (see my notes on the passage) the parallel of § 51 makes this impossible.

again the portions relating to the ἐπιβολή of the senses, we get: ἥ τε γὰρ ὁμοιότης τῶν φαντασμῶν οἷον εἰ ἐν εἰκόνι λαμβανομένων . . . κατὰ τὰς ἐπιβολὰς τῶν λοιπῶν κριτηρίων οὐκ ἄν ποτε ὑπῆρχε τοῖς οὖσί τε καὶ ἀληθέσι προσαγορευομένοις, εἰ μὴ ἦν τινα καὶ τοιαῦτα προσβαλλόμενα 'unless "idols" came to us, which are exact reproductions of the object, we could not be certain of the exact resemblance of the images obtained by the "apprehensions" of the senses', that is, the images seen by observation in the nearer view. The expression, as far as concerns the ἐπιβολή of the senses, is exactly parallel to what we have already met: the present passage adds no new ideas, but once more confirms our conclusion.

There is now no difficulty in interpreting the phrase of Iamblichus, which was noted on p. 261, ἡ ὄψις τοῖς ὁρατοῖς ἐπιβάλλει expresses clearly enough the act of ἐπιβολή on the part of the sense of sight in immediate relation to its own peculiar object, visible things. Before leaving the ἐπιβολή of the senses, we may notice that the whole notion of the act of attention on the part of the senses and the resulting apprehension is clearly brought out by Lucretius, iv. 807–10 (as an illustration of similar 'attention' on the part of the mind):

> nonne vides oculos etiam, cum tenvia quae sunt
> cernere coeperunt, contendere se atque parare,
> nec sine eo fieri posse ut cernamus acute?

The ideas of the ἐπιβολή and the 'clear view' could hardly be expressed more accurately.

3 (a). It is now time to pass to the consideration of the ἐπιβολὴ τῆς διανοίας, and it is clear that the first question to be asked is whether there is any act performed by the mind in Epicurus' psychology which is analogous to the apprehension of an image by an act of attention on the part of the senses? We are at once reminded of course of the very subtle 'idols' which, being too fine to be perceived by the senses, pass on into the mind and are there immediately apprehended by it, the images seen in sleep, the visions of dead persons, above all the 'images' of the gods. In these cases there seems to be a very close parallel: the act of apprehension by the mind is, as it were, a kind of fine sense-perception, and moreover we are informed by Lucretius[1] that such images are so fine, that, even when they have penetrated to the mind, they cannot be perceived by it except by a special act of attention, so that we see them most often in sleep, when the senses are dormant and the mind is undisturbed. This seems to be exactly

[1] Compare iv. 757–76 with 800–15.

what we should expect of the ἐπιβολὴ τῆς διανοίας, the perception of what is really a sense-image by an act of attention on the part of the mind. It is necessary to see how this notion tallies with the passages in Epicurus: it will again be convenient to take them in the order which will most naturally develop the idea.

D. § 51, the passage in which Epicurus is arguing for the exact correspondence of the sense-images to the object from which they come. We are now concerned with the list of 'images' whose likeness is guaranteed by that of the idols. They are 'the images perceived as a kind of likeness (i.e. the normal images of sensation) or those occurring in sleep, or owing to any of the other apprehensions of the mind . . .' It would be impossible to have clearer confirmation than this: the images of sleep are perceived by one kind of ἐπιβολὴ τῆς διανοίας, and there are others (such as the images of the gods and the visions of the dead) perceived by other similar ἐπιβολαί. All of these, just like the sense-images perceived by the ἐπιβολαὶ τῶν αἰσθητηρίων, require as the guarantee of their truth the correspondence of 'idols' to object.

B. § 50. 'Any image which we obtain by an act of apprehension on the part of the mind . . ., whether it is of shape or quality, is (i.e. exactly represents) the shape (or quality) of the object.' Is this true of our present notion of the ἐπιβολὴ τῆς διανοίας? It certainly is true of the images of the gods, for they are formed by a succession of 'idols' which come directly from the divine beings to the mind: the 'idol' is that which was once the 'body' of the god. It is equally true of visions of the dead, for again they are caused by 'idols' which came from their bodies when alive. But there are certain other kinds of images similarly perceived by the mind, which cannot here be passed over, for example, the συστάσεις, the strange, grotesque, compound images which form themselves in the air, and the visions of delirium. In neither of these cases does the 'image' correspond to an external reality. Epicurus saved himself in such cases by arguing that the image is 'true', because it corresponds to the 'idols', and [1] it is a mistaken inference of δόξα to assume that the 'idols' in their turn represent actual realities. But it would perhaps be the truest account of the case to say that Epicurus is in the present passage thinking primarily of the other kinds of 'mental apprehensions', and in particular, as Tohte[2] believes

---

[1] Sext. Emp. *adv. Math.* viii. 63 (Usener 253) ἡ μὲν αἴσθησις ὑπ' εἰδώλων κινουμένη ἀληθὴς ἦν (ὑπέκειτο γὰρ τὰ εἴδωλα), ὁ δὲ νοῦς οἰόμενος ὅτι στερέμνιοί εἰσιν Ἐρίνυες (he is taking the case of Orestes) ἐψευδοδόξει.

[2] Op. cit., p. 23.

he usually is, of the images of the gods. At any rate this passage again is a strong confirmation of the present view.

A. § 38 contains nothing which is inconsistent with this interpretation. The objects known to us by this mode of cognition, the immediate apprehension by the mind, are necessarily ἄδηλα, because they are imperceptible by the sense-organs. Selecting then the portion of the aphorism which concerns us, we get the principle: 'in order that we may have standards by which to judge the imperceptible, we must keep all under the control of the senses, and in particular of the close apprehension of the mind'. This suits well enough with our present idea, but seems to suggest that it is not yet complete: for there seems nothing in the perception by the mind of the subtle images to correspond to 'a judgement on the imperceptible by means of the close view', or at any rate to get it we should have to press facts a little. Here then there is no contradiction of our present position, but a distinct hint for the first time that the ἐπιβολὴ τῆς διανοίας covers something more.

D. § 51 and E. § 62 must still be left aside for the present, but we are now in a position to consider the reference in *Κύριαι Δόξαι* xxiv, and it will be seen to sum up admirably the account at present given of the ἐπιβολαί both of the senses and of the mind. In xxiii, which is closely connected with it, Epicurus has said: 'if you reject all sensations, you will have no standard by which to judge even those which you say are false'. In xxiv he pushes his argument still farther: 'if you reject any single sensation and fail to distinguish between the conclusion of opinion as to the appearance awaiting confirmation on the one hand, and on the other the close view made by sense-perception or feeling, or every kind of mental apprehension of an image, you will confound all other sensations as well by your groundless opinion, so that you will lose all standard of judgement'. This agrees excellently with what has been said: alike in cases of sense-perception and mental apprehension we must respect the validity of every sensation and attend to the close view, carefully distinguishing between the vague image of the indistinct view and the clear vision obtained by an act of apprehension. But here once again there is a suggestion of something more in the ἐπιβολὴ τῆς διανοίας than we have yet discovered: how does it obtain a clear vision in contrast to an image awaiting confirmation? and what is meant by 'every ἐπιβολή of the mind'? Surely something more than the apprehension of the various kinds of subtle image.

So far we have concluded that the ἐπιβολὴ τῆς διανοίας is a 'mental apprehension of an image perceived directly by the mind without the intervention of the senses', and we might naturally suppose that Epicurus insisted on its truth and, even if he did not quite class it as a κριτήριον,[1] yet named it so frequently among the κριτήρια, mainly in order to support his theological contention that our mental vision of the forms of the gods is evidence of their existence. This is in effect the view of Tohte, except that he leans (unnecessarily, as I think) to the passive interpretation, and would speak of the ἐπιβολὴ τῆς διανοίας as an 'impression received by the apprehension of the mind'. And if this were all the evidence we had, we might be content with his explanation. But it has already been noted that this view does not seem to cover the full meaning required either in A. § 38 or in K.Δ. xxiv: we have, moreover, been compelled at present to leave over D. § 51, as there seems nothing in what has been said to explain it, and an examination of E. § 62 in its context will show at once that it can have nothing whatever to do with mental apprehension of subtle images. If a complete explanation of ἐπιβολὴ τῆς διανοίας is to be discovered, it will be necessary to make further inquiry.

3 (b). We must ask then, can the ἐπιβολὴ τῆς διανοίας grasp or apprehend anything else besides these subtle images, exactly analogous to the images of normal sense-perception? At this point the passage quoted above[2] from Clement of Alexandria becomes of crucial importance. 'Epicurus', he says, 'explains "anticipation" as an apprehension of something clear or of the clear thought-image of the thing.' Now from our knowledge of the nature of πρόληψις this is not difficult to explain: the 'act of anticipation'—for πρόληψις[3] is here used, contrary to Epicurus' usual custom, in an active sense—is the apprehension of the general or compound image, made up of many individual sense-images. This 'apprehension' must be mental—must be an ἐπιβολὴ τῆς διανοίας, for the general image can only be perceived by the mind and not by the senses, and what now is its object? Not a sense-image, nor anything analogous to it, but a concept. An ἐπιβολὴ τῆς διανοίας then can grasp a concept, and with this new notion in mind we may turn to the examination of the difficult passage in the Letter to Herodotus, which has been left over for consideration.

E. § 62. The particular question at issue in the context is: What is the nature of the atomic motions in a compound body? 'We know', says Epicurus in effect, 'that the perceptible parts of a moving body are all moving in the same direction as the whole body: this is the truth guaranteed to us by an ἐπιβολὴ τῶν αἰσθητηρίων (τὸ θεωρούμενον is

---

[1] D.L. x. 31, quoted on p. 560.
[2] p. 560.   [3] See p. 247, n. 1.

clearly that which is grasped by the senses when "looking" at the close view, i.e. by an ἐπιβολή). By analogy we apply the same idea in thought to the imperceptible atomic parts and suppose that they too are all moving in the same direction as the whole: this is the work of opinion (δόξα) combining images and forming what Epicurus would call technically an ἐπίνοια κατ᾽ ἀναλογίαν. But we know as the result of scientific investigation that the atoms are really in a constant state of vibratory motion (πάλσις) in all directions, and this conclusion must be true as against our previous supposition, *because it is obtained by an* ἐπιβολὴ τῆς διανοίας.' What does this mean? how do we know this fact by an ἐπιβολὴ τῆς διανοίας and why is it therefore certainly true? Giussani, largely on the strength of this passage, but influenced also by his general theories of the process of thought in Epicurus, has argued for a far wider sense of ἐπιβολὴ τῆς διανοίας than that proposed by Tohte. 'The ἐπιβολὴ τῆς διανοίας for Epicurus comprehends both what Tohte supposes, but not that alone, and πρόληψις, as Brieger wishes, but not it alone, and scientific concepts in general, including the concepts of those ἄδηλα—be they real or *coniuncta* or *eventa*—which do not give off "idols". In fine the ἐπιβολὴ τῆς διανοίας is mental representation in general.'[1] The one fatal objection to this all-embracing view of the ἐπιβολή is to my mind just this passage (§ 62) on which it is based. Seeing that all mental operations, including δόξα itself, are carried on, according to Epicurus, by visualized images or 'mental representation', it is impossible that Epicurus could have said that 'everything that is grasped by mental representation is true'. Giussani went farther, I think, in this last clause than he really meant, and wished to distinguish the 'concepts of science' from the images formed by opinion, but that is just the crux of the whole matter.

Turn once more to the instance in § 62. We have a problem: What is the motion of the atoms in a moving compound body? Two solutions are offered, one that they are all moving in the same direction as the whole, the other that they are moving in imperceptible little trajects in all directions. The former is the solution of opinion based on the analogy of the perceptible, and it is false: the latter is the solution of ἐπιβολὴ τῆς διανοίας, and it is true. Why? What is the difference in process by which the two solutions are aimed at? 'Opinion', Epicurus himself tells us—for we may now make use of D. § 51—'is a movement of the mind closely connected with the ἐπιβολὴ τῆς διανοίας, but distinct from it?' What is the distinction? Why is one liable to produce false results, while the other can only give us what

[1] Loc. cit., p. 179 *fin.*

is true? If we could answer that question with certainty, we should have solved not merely the particular problem before us, but much of the difficulty of the Epicurean theory of knowledge. With some hesitation I venture to give an answer. So far what we know of ἐπιβολὴ τῆς διανοίας in the secondary sense is that it can apprehend concepts, as in πρόληψις (Clem. Alex.), and that its operation is in some way parallel to that of the ἐπιβολὴ τῶν αἰσθητηρίων in the process of ἐπιμαρτύρησις (A. § 38 and K.Δ. xxiv). Let us attempt to apply these ideas to the problem of atomic motion. Δόξα frames the theory that the atoms in the moving compound all move in the direction of the whole body, as do the perceptible parts of the body. How is this theory to be tested? According to the ordinary rule of the *Canonice* in dealing with ἄδηλα by reference to the senses. But in this case, either the senses would give us no criterion of judgement, or, as in the case of celestial phenomena, several possible theories might meet with no ἀντιμαρτύρησις and be equally true. Scientific theory requires a greater accuracy than this, and as a matter of fact Epicurus does not test the δοξαζόμενον by reference to the senses, but by reference to an ἐπιβολὴ τῆς διανοίας. Scientific thought then about the ultimate realities is conducted on some different lines, and results in a 'one and only' truth. I suggest that in Epicurus' view the concepts of science are built up step by step by the juxtaposition (σύνθεσις) of previous concepts, each in their turn grasped as 'clear' or self-evident by the immediate apprehension of the mind (ἐπιβολὴ τῆς διανοίας). What is important here is to show that this conclusion is forced upon us by the passage in question. Epicurus refers the δοξαζόμενον not to the senses, but to 'that which is grasped by ἐπιβολὴ τῆς διανοίας'. What is it that is thus apprehended? Clearly the 'vision' or 'image' or 'concept' of the atoms still, even inside the moving compound body, themselves moving in every direction. And how is that vision (ἐναργές) formed? Clearly by the juxtaposition of the previous concept of the movement of free or uncompounded atoms (itself similarly formed by the apprehensipn of other 'clear visions' in juxtaposition) with the concept of atoms enclosed in a moving ἄθροισμα; such a juxtaposition can only make one new image or concept—only form one picture and not several alternative pictures—and that concept, because it is 'clear' or, as we might say, 'self-evident', is immediately or, as we should say, 'intuitively' apprehended by the attentive mind in an ἐπιβολή. And the moment that concept is apprehended, is seen to be true, we know that the previous δοξαζόμενον, founded on an arbitrary analogy, is false. Here then is an exact illustration of what I conceive to be Epicurus' idea of the process of scientific thought. Moreover, we now see that this process is in reality exactly parallel to the ἐπιμαρτύρησις. The δοξαζόμενον of thought is tested, just as is the δοξαζόμενον with regard to a sense-impression, by the apprehension—now mental—of a 'clear' image, seen, as it were, in the nearer view: that apprehension declares against the supposition of opinion, and at the same time, as the near view should, gives the one and only truth. Finally, it is now possible to say that the difference between opinion and mental apprehension is that whereas δόξα arbitrarily combines many kinds of concepts with each other or with the images of sense, ἐπιβολὴ τῆς διανοίας immediately apprehends a new concept as the necessary result of the combination of concepts, themselves similarly apprehended. ἐπιβολὴ τῆς διανοίας then, as it plays its part in the highest mental operation of scientific thought, is the immediate 'apprehension by the mind of the concepts of scientific truth', which is conceived of as a chain of necessarily connected and self-evident visualizations.

It remains to test this idea by reference to the other passages in Epicurus.

B. § 50 deals solely with the form and qualities of στερέμνια. The secondary sense of ἐπιβολὴ τῆς διανοίας has no place here, and we may say confidently that Epicurus is thinking solely of the primary sense of the mental apprehension of 'subtle images'. C. § 51 is similarly concerned with the theory of 'idols'. Again the 'mental apprehension' involved there is solely the semi-sensational apprehension of the subtle images. But in A. § 38 the new conception supplies exactly the lack which was felt on the first examination of the passage. In it the parallel between the two kinds of ἐπιβολή, that of the senses and that of the mind, is very prominent, as also is the conception of the προσμένον and ἐπιμαρτύρησις. Including the second meaning of ἐπιβολὴ τῆς διανοίας it is possible to complete the parallel: ἐπιβολὴ τῆς διανοίας is a test by which to judge the ἄδηλα, not merely because some ἄδηλα give us direct mental impressions, but because by the process of the 'near view' of scientific concepts, hypotheses about the imperceptible may be tested and the truth 'clearly' perceived. The passage is given a fullness of meaning which was before notably lacking. Once again in Κ.Δ. xxiv the secondary sense is, though not perhaps so clearly, included. The ἀπορούμενον of scientific inquiry is, like the distant view, a προσμένον: as opposed to it is the 'near view', τὸ παρὸν ἤδη κατὰ τὴν ἐπιβολὴν τῆς διανοίας. If these be not kept distinct, science, like everyday life, will be confounded with groundless opinion.

I do not of course wish to substitute this new conception of the ἐπιβολὴ τῆς διανοίας for that of Tohte, but to add it to it: 'mental apprehension' is of course concerned with the subtle images, but also with the concepts of science. If we now turn back to Giussani's summary, and exclude the rash generalization of the final clause, we shall see that it precisely represents the conclusion we have reached, only that we now know the reason for the inclusion of all its parts. 'The ἐπιβολὴ τῆς διανοίας comprehends both what Tohte supposes (for there it is the immediate apprehension of an image perceptible only by the mind), but not that alone, and πρόληψις, as Brieger wishes (for the act of πρόληψις is again an immediate apprehension by the mind of an image that can exist only in the mind and is itself a criterion of truth), and (what Giussani wishes, but does not clearly express or explain) scientific concepts (for in their case ἐπιβολή is the act of apprehension in the nearer view of clear and self-evident concepts).' But ἐπιβολὴ τῆς διανοίας is not 'mental apprehension in general', for that would include also the operations of δόξα, which are liable to error. The result then of this long investigation is to confirm what I believe Giussani really meant, only I hope that the process of investigation has put his theory on a firmer basis: for parts of my argument I cannot, I fear, claim complete ἐπιμαρτύρησις in the authorities, but I fully believe there is no ἀντιμαρτύρησις; and as I may certainly claim that the whole subject is ἄδηλον, that is as much as can be demanded.

There remain over certain additional problems which are closely connected with the main question.

1. It is not difficult now to see that ἐπιβολαί in § 36 is used in a technical sense, but also in the widest possible meaning, including all ἐπιβολαί both of the αἰσθητήρια and of the διάνοια. 'The most essential thing', for a scientific inquirer, 'is to be able to conduct acutely his acts of observation or apprehension, both with the senses and in the mind.' Similarly we can now say that the passage from Aetius quoted on p. 561 is technical, and concerns ἐπιβολαί both of the senses and of the mind.

2. It will be noticed that in some of the extracts[1] there is prefixed to ἐπιβολὴ τῆς διανοίας the epithet φανταστική. The question has often been raised whether the φανταστικὴ ἐπιβολὴ τῆς διανοίας differs from any other form of ἐπιβολὴ τῆς διανοίας, and if so, what the difference is. Both Tohte and Giussani, though for different reasons, deny the difference, Tohte because it is obvious that the only ἐπιβολή he con-

---

[1] §§ 31, 51 *fin.*; *K.Δ.* xxiv.

ceives—the direct apprehension of the subtle images—is always necessarily φανταστική, Giussani because, since all thought is conducted by visual images, it is impossible to imagine an ἐπιβολή (or even a δόξα) which is not φανταστική. I should be inclined to agree in denying the difference, of course for Giussani's reason, but I also think that in the passages where the epithet is used, Epicurus is thinking primarily of the ἐπιβολή of the subtle φαντασία of the gods, &c., and not of that of scientific concepts, for it is more obviously and immediately φανταστική.

3. A more difficult and important problem is the question why 'the Epicureans'[1] made the φανταστικὴ ἐπιβολὴ τῆς διανοίας a criterion of truth, with its almost equally difficult corollary, why Epicurus, after his constant coupling of it with the other criteria, did not. I hope that the previous discussion has thrown some light on this point. In justice to 'the Epicureans' we must in the first place notice how exceedingly close Epicurus himself comes to calling it a criterion. In E. § 62 he affirms that the conclusions reached (or, as we should rather say, the images grasped) by ἐπιβολὴ τῆς διανοίας are always true: in B. § 50 he states similarly that the image of the form of a concrete object apprehended by ἐπιβολὴ τῆς διανοίας is in fact its form: in A. § 38 he speaks of the ἐπιβολαί 'of the mind or of any of the κριτήρια' (used here, as we have seen, in an active sense, of the senses which make the ἐπιβολαί, i.e. αἰσθητήρια), and in C. § 51 even more explicitly of 'the ἐπιβολαί of the mind or of the rest of the κριτήρια': finally in Κύριαι Δόξαι, xxiv the φανταστικὴ ἐπιβολὴ τῆς διανοίας is ranked alongside with αἴσθησις and the πάθη. The cumulative impression of these passages is certainly that of a tacit acceptance of ἐπιβολὴ τῆς διανοίας as a κριτήριον, and one feels that 'the Epicureans' had but a very small step to take. Yet Epicurus never in so many words states that the ἐπιβολή is a κριτήριον of truth and his authoritative list of the κριτήρια does not contain it. Can we explain his reluctance to make this identification as contrasted with the Epicureans' apparent insistence upon it? I think I can give an answer. Epicurus did not include the ἐπιβολή[2] mainly, I believe, for two closely allied reasons: (1) that he felt uneasy about the 'truth' of

---

[1] D.L. x. 31.

[2] Notice that all the passages in the Letter to Herodotus give us just as much justification for the inclusion of the ἐπιβολή of the senses as a criterion, as they do for that of the ἐπιβολὴ τῆς διανοίας: the passage in the Κύριαι Δόξαι alone places the φανταστικὴ ἐπιβολὴ τῆς διανοίας on a different footing.

certain of the images directly apprehended by the mind, about the visions, that is, of delirium, the συστάσεις and some of the images of sleep; (2) that in spite of all his insistence on the truth of αἴσθησις, he felt similarly uneasy about the passive sensation, and in particular about the 'distant view'. In other words, to put these two difficulties together, Epicurus did not wish to raise in any form the question of 'truth' involved in the relation of the image, the 'idol' and the real object, for any such 'stirring of the mind' might have imperilled his whole system. There are plenty of similar indications of the same hesitation at different points in his psychology. On the other hand, where their Master feared to tread, the Epicureans rushed in and included the ἐπιβολὴ τῆς διανοίας[1] in the criteria. Their reasons were, I believe, somewhat as follows: (1) They strongly maintained the truth of the 'image' on the ground of its correspondence to the 'idols': it was then necessary to admit that the 'idol' of the 'distant view' (e.g. the small round tower) was untrue as a representation of the concrete object: ἐπιμαρτύρησις and the 'near view' obtained by ἐπιβολή is then the only method of securing full truth, i.e. complete correspondence of object, 'idol' and image. (2) Similarly in the region of thought the only method of distinguishing the certain concepts of science from the false hypotheses of δόξα, was by insistence on the truth of ideas obtained by ἐπιβολὴ τῆς διανοίας. (3) They were anxious (as Tohte has suggested) to maintain the certainty of the knowledge of the gods as obtained by the immediate mental apprehension of their images. The Epicureans had already been denounced on the ground of atheism, and it was necessary to rebut the charge.

4. In conclusion we must consider certain expressions in Latin authors, which appear to have a connexion with the ἐπιβολὴ τῆς διανοίας. In one passage of Cicero and two (possibly three) in Lucretius such an echo seems clear: we must ask whether it is the result of mere coincidence or of translation, and if the latter, what is the exact relation of the Latin passages to Epicurus' theory.

(a) Cic. de Nat. Deor. i. 20. 54 'si immensam et interminatam in omnis partis magnitudinem regionum videretis, in quam *se iniciens animus et intendens* ita late longeque peregrinatur, ut nullam tamen oram ultimam videat, in qua possit insistere'. The mind is here 'projecting and straining itself towards (or into)' the infinity of space.

---

[1] It seems odd at first sight that they did not also put in ἐπιβολὴ τῶν αἰσθητηρίων, but the reason clearly is that it was already included under αἴσθησις, whereas in Epicurus' list there was no mental κριτήριον at all, under which ἐπιβολὴ τῆς διανοίας might be subsumed.

(*b*) Lucr. ii. 1044–7:

> quaerit enim rationem animus, cum summa loci sit
> infinita foris haec extra moenia mundi,
> quid sit ibi porro quo prospicere usque velit mens
> atque *animi iactus liber* quo pervolet ipse.

The mind is here similarly 'projecting itself freely' into infinite space to ask what there is outside our world.

(*c*) Lucr. ii. 739–44. The poet has stated that the atoms are colourless, and wishes to forestall the objection that we can have no mental pictures which can give us knowledge of such atoms:

> in quae corpora si nullus tibi forte videtur
> posse *animi iniectus* fieri, procul avius erras.
>
> .   .   .   .   .   .
>
> scire licet nostrae quoque menti corpora posse
> verti in notitiam nullo circumlita fuco.

We can 'project our mind' to bodies without colour: they can form a concept in our mind.

(*d*) Lucr. ii. 1080 would, if Winckelmann's conjecture

> in primis animalibus *inice mentem*

be right, offer us another example of the similar idea, 'turn your attention to the animals', but (*a*) *in* with the ablative *animalibus* as compared with *in* with the accusative in the other passages is not satisfactory, or indeed natural, (*b*) I doubt if the sense is right, as we may see subsequently. The MS. text *indice mente* should probably be kept.

(*e*) To these passages we must add, though the expression is different, another already quoted in connexion with the ἐπιβολή (iv. 802–17), and note especially:

> et quia tenvia sunt, *nisi quae contendit*,[1] acute
> cernere non potis est animus; proinde omnia quae sunt
> praeterea pereunt, *nisi si ad quae se ipse paravit.*   (802–4)

and

> et tamen in rebus quoque apertis noscere possis,
> *si non advertas animum*, proinde esse quasi omni
> tempore semotum fuerit longeque remotum.   (811–13)

It is clear in the first place that none of these passages (except the last, which has no phrase which can be a direct translation of ἐπιβολή

---

[1] Compare Cicero's 'animus . . . se *intendens*' in (*a*) above.

τῆς διανοίας) is concerned with the direct mental apprehension of subtle images. Tohte[1] therefore, who restricts ἐπιβολὴ τῆς διανοίας to this sense, though he admits that the Latin *animi iniectus*, &c., is a translation of Epicurus' term, yet concludes that 'Lucretius and Cicero have used these expressions in another sense from that in which Epicurus used the corresponding Greek'. But Giussani[2] has rightly insisted that the very oddness of the Latin phrases, the coincidence between the expressions of Cicero and Lucretius, and the occurrence of Cicero's term in a passage where he is obviously following his Epicurean text carefully, will make it certain that the Latin expressions were an intentional and careful translation of Epicurus' technical term. Giussani, who of course approached the whole problem from the point of view of Lucretius, was in fact largely influenced by the apparent width of ideas embraced in these Latin passages to conclude that ἐπιβολὴ τῆς διανοίας is a wide term for 'mental representation in general'. As we have seen, that contention will not hold and must be limited. Is there anything in these Latin passages which is inconsistent with our general conclusion about the ἐπιβολή?

In (*a*) and (*b*) the idea is the same, the 'projection of the mind' into the infinity of space: here we have exactly the notion of the ἐπιβολή, as we have explained it: it is the mental examination of a scientific concept. The Epicurean parallel is E. § 62. In (*c*) we have a particularly interesting instance of the same idea: we can have an ἐπιβολή of the colourless atoms, for again it is an image based on πρόληψις (*notities*, ii. 745, is always Lucretius' technical translation of πρόληψις). In (*d*) I think Winckelmann's emendation cannot be right, for we should not have an ἐπιβολὴ τῆς διανοίας of 'animals' either as a direct mental apprehension of a subtle image, or as a scientific concept (though we might of course have an ordinary πρόληψις of 'animal'). Lucretius would more naturally have said simply, 'look at animals', as he practically does in ii. 342 ff. If *inice mentem* is right, it is a loose use of the phrase. Finally, in (*e*) we have an instance without a technical term of the general idea of the ἐπιβολὴ τῆς διανοίας in the primary sense of the apprehension of subtle (*tenvia*) images.

It may fairly be said then that the Latin passages, so far from creating any difficulty or being in any way inconsistent with Epicurus' phraseology, strongly confirm the general view we have taken, and especially the second sense of ἐπιβολὴ τῆς διανοίας as the apprehension of a scientifically verified concept.

[1] p. 24.   [2] p. 171.

APPENDIX IV

On the meaning of ὄγκος cacumen and glomeramen

THE word ὄγκος occurs in six distinct passages in the course of the Letter to Herodotus, which in view of Giussani's theory that it is a technical term equivalent in sense to the 'molecule' of chemistry, it will be as well to examine in detail. In the first three of these passages Epicurus is dealing with the processes of sense-perception, in the first two with sound, in the third with smell.

1. Sound, he says (§ 52), is caused by an effluence (ῥεῦμα), i.e. a stream of material particles, given off from the things which originate the sound. It then becomes necessary for him to explain how several or many percipients can hear the same sounds at once: this is caused, he explains, because this effluence is split up into 'particles each resembling the whole' (εἰς ὁμοιομερεῖς ὄγκους διασπείρεται), that is, the original mass is subdivided, and smaller 'particles' go off in every direction, yet each 'particle' so exactly retains the characteristics of the whole that when it reaches its percipient it produces the same effect.

2. Continuing the same discussion he rejects (§ 53) the theory of Democritus that the voice-particles make an impression of themselves in the air, which is in its turn brought to the ear of the percipient, and reasserts his own belief that 'the blow which takes place inside us, when we emit our voice, causes a squeezing out[1] of certain particles (ὄγκοι), which produce a stream of breath of such a character as to afford us the sensation of hearing'. Here the ὄγκοι are the particles which unite to form the effluence, not those into which the effluence subsequently splits up, but the idea is not radically different.

3. In the immediately following discussion of smell (§ 53) we meet the same notion again: 'we must suppose that smell too, just like hearing, could never bring about any sensation, unless they were certain particles (ὄγκοι) carried off from the object of suitable size to stir this sense-organ'. The particles here are thrown off by the object and in this case directly penetrates the sense-organs of the percipient.

In all these three examples, which must be taken together, there is clearly no question of any idea comparable to that of a 'molecule', or indeed of any special or technical sense of the word. The ὄγκοι are

[1] ἔκθλιψιν, a correction of the manuscript readings ἐκλίθην and ἐκλήθην which has been made independently by several scholars—first probably by Brieger—may be regarded as certain.

merely particles of matter, agglomerations of atoms, of greater or less size, endowed with no special characteristics or powers, nor constituted by any particular atomic formation.

4. In the instances which it will be convenient to consider next (§§ 56, 57) the word ὄγκος has a very distinct technical sense—that in fact from which Giussani starts his theory. It is the passage already discussed (Chap. III, pp. 284–7) concerning the 'least parts' in the atom. Epicurus, as was seen there, argues from the analogy of the perceptible object: 'We must not suppose that in a limited body there can be infinite particles (ὄγκοι) or particles of every degree of smallness.' Throughout these two sections the word recurs several times, but always in the sense of a particle into which a body can be divided, and subsequently in the more technical sense of the *minimum visibile*, the smallest particle in the visible object, which is perceptible only as a part of that object, and to which are ultimately compared in § 58 the πέρατα or 'least parts' of the atom. It is in this sense that Lucretius uses *cacumen* in i. 599 and 749, but neither in Epicurus or Lucretius is there the faintest hint of Giussani's notion of the least particle which possesses the qualities of the 'thing': the meaning is merely that of the 'least visible particle'. It might be noticed incidentally that this conception is in itself of something much larger than the modern chemical 'molecule' which would never be visible.

5. So in § 54 Epicurus is explaining that change in things is caused by the alteration in arrangement of the component atoms and says: 'it is essential that the bodies which shift their position (*sc.* the atoms) should be imperishable and should not possess the nature of what changes, but parts (ὄγκοι) and configurations of their own'. Here by anticipation of § 58 ὄγκοι is again used in a technical sense, but now of the 'least parts' of the atom, which in the more exact discussion of § 56 and § 57 he calls πέρατα, as opposed to the ὄγκοι of perceptible things, the *minima visibilia* with which the πέρατα are composed. In this sense *cacumen* was probably used by Lucretius in a line which has dropped out after i. 599 (compare the use of *extremum* in the parallel passage, i. 752). But this time the ὄγκοι would be something far smaller than either Giussani's 'molecules' or those of modern chemistry.

6. The last passage (§ 69), again in a quite different context, is perhaps even more clearly decisive against the 'molecule' theory. Epicurus is explaining his notion of properties (see p. 302) and after saying that the whole body of a thing owes its own permanent existence to its properties, adds as a precaution against a misunderstanding, 'not in the sense that it is composed of properties coming together to form

it, as when, for instance, a larger structure is put together out of the particles which compose it, whether first particles or parts of the whole smaller than itself, whatever it is' (ὅταν ἐξ αὐτῶν τῶν ὄγκων μεῖζον ἄθροισμα συστῇ ἤτοι τῶν πρώτων ἢ τῶν τοῦ ὅλου μεγεθῶν τοῦδε τινὸς ἐλαττόνων). It is manifest that here the ὄγκοι are particles of matter of any size which go to compose a larger body: to restrict them to the *minima visibilia* they have to be qualified with the epithet 'the first particles', and the more general sense is explained by the perfectly vague phrase 'parts of the whole smaller than itself'. ὄγκος is clearly a quite indefinite word to be used of a particle of any size. In both cases here the ὄγκοι would be very much larger than the molecules of chemistry, and in the latter case larger than Giussani's molecules.

There does not then seem any justification for the idea that ὄγκος = 'molecule' in Giussani's sense: in some of the cases where it occurs in the Letter to Herodotus it is used in the technical sense of the *minima visibilia*, or by analogy of the least parts of the atoms: in the others it is an indefinite term for particles of matter of any size and any stage of atomic aggregation.

As to *glomeramen* it is a very rare word in Lucretius and in no case seems to be used either as a translation of ὄγκος or as an equivalent in idea of 'molecule'. In ii. 454 it is used to denote merely the 'round drops' which make up a stream of water, which Lucretius compares to the individual round seeds in a handful of poppy-seed: there is no trace of a meaning like the least parts, which retain the character of water. In ii. 686 atoms of different shape are said to unite *glomeramen in unum*, 'into one mass', in order to form a single thing, which explains why the same pasture-land can rear animals of different nature like cows and horses. This is a little nearer perhaps, but again it is quite vague and means no more than an 'aggregate'. In v. 726 *glomeraminis* is used of the round ball of the moon, than which few things could be farther from the notion of a 'molecule'. Similarly the verb *conglomerari* is used in iii. 210 of the soul gathering itself up, as it were, into a ball in a particular part of the body (as is the simple *glomerari* in iii. 541), and in iv. 871 he speaks of the *glomerata vaporis corpora*, 'aggregated nuclei of hot matter'. There is no sense approaching 'molecule' here. Lucretius' equivalent for ὄγκος in the technical sense is, as we have seen above, *cacumen*: for the idea which is expressed in ὄγκος in its indefinite sense he uses indifferently *elementa, corpuscula, particulae*, as well as, no doubt, in these instances *glomeramina*: but none of these words have any technical meaning, much less that which Giussani wishes to discover.

APPENDIX V

On the relation of the 'nameless' element and the 'mind'

I HAVE assumed in the text of the chapter on the Soul that both 'spirit' and 'mind' alike are composed of all four soul-elements, and that in both alike sensation or consciousness is started by the 'fourth element' and communicated to the other three: 'spirit' and 'mind' are thus wholly alike in material composition and differ only in place and function. I am entirely confident that this was the doctrine both of Epicurus himself and of his followers. Recent German critics of the Epicurean theory have however held a different view: this view has, to my mind, been answered most completely by Giussani (*Studi Lucreziani: Psicologia Epicurea*, pp. 183–217), but seeing that the problem is one of great importance for the understanding of Epicurean psychology, and that, while the arguments of the German critics are scanty and vague, Giussani's reply is rather diffuse and admits, I think, of some additional support, I have thought well to resume the controversy as briefly as possible. I shall attempt first to state the German theory and its consequences, then to deal with the arguments used by its supporters, then to add some general considerations which make for the view I believe to be right. The great bulk of my material is due to Giussani.

There are two varieties of the German view:

1. That supported by Woltjer (*Lucretii philosophia cum fontibus comparata*, pp. 69 ff.), by Eichner (*Adnotationes ad Lucretii Epicuri interpretis de animae noctura doctrinam*, a work I have not myself read), and most explicitly by Tohte (*Epikurs Kriterien der Wahrheit*). According to these critics the 'nameless element' or 'fourth nature' is confined to the 'mind'; the 'spirit' consists of the three other soul-elements, the 'mind' of these plus the 'fourth nature'.

2. That originally put forward by Reisacker (*Epicuri de atomorum natura*) and more recently maintained by Brieger (*Epikurs Lehre von der Seele*), who formerly held the first view. On this theory the 'nameless element' and the 'mind' are identical: 'the spirit' consists of the three other soul-elements: the 'mind' of the 'nameless element' alone. Seeing however that Brieger[1] believes that in the breast the 'mind', consisting solely of the 'fourth nature', yet moves 'among the

[1] p. 11.

coarser elements' of the soul, there is not in effect much difference between the two views and they may safely be treated together, and Brieger's exposition, which is the most argumentative, regarded as typical of the rest.

The real importance of this theory lies in the effect which it necessarily has on the account which is to be given of the process of sensation. If the 'fourth nature', which is universally acknowledged to be the sole element which has the capacity of sensation in itself, is not present in the 'spirit-atoms' in the sense-organs, it is obvious that the sense-organs have not of themselves direct and immediate perception. The process must be worked out on different lines, and must now be understood as follows. When the external stimulus[1] (be it a body in passive sensation or an 'idol' or effluence in sense-perception) touches one or more of the spirit-atoms (i.e. wind, heat, and air) on the surface of the body, these atoms are set in movement, but the movement is entirely mechanical and insensible. The movement is by their means communicated to the breast and there stirs the 'nameless element' (approaching it, of course, through the medium of the other three soul-elements in the breast, which according to Tohte are, according to Brieger are not, themselves a portion of the mind). The 'nameless element' is thus stirred by movements which are now 'sense-bearing' and thus translates the insensible movement of the spirit-atoms into sensation. It then, reversing the current of movement, 'retelegraphs' a second and now sensational movement to the 'spirit-elements' and they in their turn communicate it to the sense-organ or the portion of the body where the original contact took place: then, when this cumbrous process is complete, the body feels or the sense-organs perceive. The original contact produces a movement which is nothing in the sensible world; the real sensation lies in the mind, and it is only after the return of the now 'sensationalized' movement that in an indirect and secondary sense local sensation occurs.

The view of the German scholars rests practically on the evidence of one passage in Plutarch, and certain coincidences of language in Lucretius' exposition in Book III. It will be best first to deal with these arguments.

1. Plutarch, adv. Coloten, 20, 1118; U. 314 τὸ γὰρ ᾧ κρίνει καὶ μνημονεύει καὶ φιλεῖ καὶ μισεῖ καὶ ὅλως τὸ φρόνιμον καὶ λογιστικόν ἔκ τινος φησιν ἀκατονομάστου ποιότητος ἐπιγίνεσθαι. Epicurus is here reported as attributing to the 'nameless element' certain functions which are undoubtedly functions of the mind: therefore, it is argued, the two

---

[1] See Tohte, p. 6; Brieger, p. 17.

are identified. The conclusion is quite unjustified. The 'nameless element' is the only αἰσθητικόν *per se* and is therefore the ultimate cause of sensation and consciousness both in spirit and in mind. Plutarch is therefore quite right in attributing to it these functions of the mind, the movements of which it does in fact initiate. But he says nothing to preclude our also assigning to it the initiation of sensation in the 'spirit-atoms' in the body and sense-organs. He is thinking here solely of the mind and not of the spirit: his account is quite correct as far as it goes, but incomplete: it is not intended to be a summary of all the functions of the 'nameless element'.

2. (*a*) Lucr. iii. 138–42:

> caput esse quasi et dominari in corpore toto
> consilium quod nos animum mentemque vocamus.
> idque situm media regione in pectoris haeret.
> hic exsultat enim pavor ac metus, haec loca circum
> laetitiae mulcent: hic ergo mens animusquest.

compared with
iii. 241–6:

> quarta quoque his igitur quaedam natura necessest
> attribuatur.   east omnino nominis expers;
>
> .   .   .   .   .
>
> sensiferos motus quae didit prima per artus.

In the former passage the origin of certain feelings or emotions is attributed to the mind: in the latter the 'fourth nature' is said to 'send abroad the motions which bring sensation throughout the limbs': therefore, argues Brieger,[1] mind and 'fourth nature' are identified. It is hardly necessary to point out that in the former passage Lucretius is speaking of emotions, as distinct from mere passive sensations, and they are, of course, the function of the mind; in the latter he is speaking of immediate sensation in the body (*per artus*), which is due to the presence of the 'fourth nature' in the 'spirit'. As Giussani[2] argues, it does not follow, because the emotion of joy or fear starts in the mind, that the mind also initiates my sensation when I burn my finger.

(*b*) Lucr. iii. 138, 139:

> caput esse quasi et dominari in corpore toto
> consilium quod nos animum mentemque vocamus.

[1] p. 13.   [2] p. 202 *fin.*

compared with

279–81:

> sed tibi nominis haec expers vis facta minutis
> corporibus latet atque animae quasi totius ipsa
> proporrost anima et dominatur corpore toto.

Both mind and 'fourth nature' are said *dominari corpore toto*: they are therefore identical. Giussani replies that *dominari*[1] is used in slightly different senses: in the former passage it means 'holds sway', 'is monarch', in the latter 'is diffused': for this latter sense he compares vi. 224, where thunderbolts having struck a house *dominantur in aedibus ipsis*; also ii. 958 *leti dominantam in corpore motum*, and iii. 705, where the particles of soul (*animi* is used here in a loose sense, as so often, when Lucretius is not distinguishing 'spirit' and 'mind': see 421–4) *in nostro dominantur corpore*. It is hardly necessary, I think, to make so great a distinction in meaning: the mind 'is lord in the whole body', because it is the seat of emotion, thought, and will, the 'fourth nature' 'is lord in the whole body', because it is everywhere the cause of sensation: but they are not for that reason identical.

(c) Lucr. iii. 396–401:

> et magis est animus vitai claustra coercens
> et dominantior ad vitam quam vis animai.
> nam sine mente animoque nequit residere per artus
> temporis exiguam partem pars ulla animai,
> sed comes insequitur facile et discedit in auras
> et gelidos artus in leti frigore linquit.

compared with

252–5:

> nec temere huc (i.e. to the 'fourth nature') dolor usque
>   potest penetrare neque acre
> permanare malum, quin omnia perturbentur
> usque adeo ⟨ut⟩ vitae desit locus atque animai
> diffugiant partes per caulas corporis omnis.

In the former passage it is said that if the mind is destroyed, the spirit cannot remain in the limbs and life departs: in the latter that a severe hurt penetrating to the 'fourth nature' will cause the life to depart and the spirit to leave the body: therefore, once again, mind and 'fourth nature' are identical. Both statements of Lucretius are true, but are no evidence of identity. If the mind is destroyed, the body is left without *regimen* and *consilium*: it could not interpret any sensations,

---

[1] p. 202 *supra*.

or think or feel or will: in other words it would have no consciousness and so must die. The 'fourth nature' is deep[1] hidden within the other three soul-elements and they in their turn among the body-atoms: a hurt then which actually penetrated to the 'fourth nature' and dislocated its structure, would have caused so great disruption in the whole *concilium* as to destroy life. The causes differ in the two cases, though the result is the same. Woltjer[2] objects that the amputation of a limb, which nevertheless leaves the patient alive, ought, if this account of the second passage is right, to cause death. No, for though with the rest of the 'spirit' in the limb some portion of the 'fourth nature' is actually lost, the act of amputation did not produce a hurt which dislocating the whole structure, penetrated to and caused disruption in the 'fourth nature': the limb was taken off whole (Giussani[3] seems to me not fully to appreciate Lucretius' point here).

3. Lucr. iii. 273–4:

nam penitus prorsum latet haec natura subestque
nec magis hac infra quicquam est in corpore nostro.

It is perhaps hardly worth while to mention Woltjer's[4] idea that this refers to the position of the 'fourth nature' (i.e. the mind) in the breast, the central portion of the body, which he is obliged to support by altering *infra* in 274 to *intra*. It does of course refer to the position of the 'fourth nature' alike in spirit and mind as hidden deep beneath the other soul-elements, which meaning *infra*, recalling *penitus latet* exactly expresses.

Certain general considerations may now be suggested which tell strongly against the identification.

1. The evidence of the authorities.

(*a*) Epicurus. There is nothing in the Letter to Herodotus which makes for the identification of the 'nameless element' and the mind, but a good deal which is against it. Epicurus makes no distinction between the mind and the spirit, as he would be almost bound to, if there were a difference of material structure between them as well as of function. On the other hand he mentions the 'nameless element' immediately after the other two, as if it were an essential part of the general structure of the soul, which is, as he says, distributed through the whole structure. (The scholium on § 67 which distinguishes the rational and irrational elements is quite silent as to any material difference between them.)

---

[1] See Lucr. iii. 273, 274.   [2] Op. cit., p. 69.
[3] pp. 196, 197.   [4] Op. cit., p. 69.

(*b*) The evidence of Lucretius is quite unmistakable: he carefully explains the constitution of the 'soul' (mind and spirit) of the four elements and distinguishes *animus* and *anima* only in function. Besides the passages discussed above we may call attention to

(1) iii. 136, 137, where he states that mind and spirit 'form of themselves a single nature'—an impossible expression, if they were materially different.

(2) 231, where *haec natura* means as is clear from 228 *mentis natura animaeque* and is stated to consist of all the four elements.

(3) 262 ff., where he explains that the 'first-beginnings' (i.e. atoms) of all four elements in the soul 'course to and fro among themselves with the motions of first-beginnings, so that no single one can be put apart, nor can its powers be set in play divided from others by empty space, but they are, as it were, the many forces of a single body'—a most explicit statement of the invariable union of all four elements.

(4) 269–72:

> sic calor atque aer et venti caeca potestas
> mixta creant unam naturam et mobilis illa
> vis, initum motus ab se quae dividit ollis,
> sensifer unde oritur primum per viscera motus.

an even clearer expression of the same idea.

(5) 275, where it is stated that the 'fourth nature' is the 'soul of the soul' (*animae anima*). On Brieger's theory it might be called the soul of the mind (*animi*), but certainly not of the 'spirit' (*animae*), in which it is not even present. This is repeated in 280.

In fact Brieger[1] has to admit that the evidence of Lucretius is against him and tries to discredit it on the ground of the 'contradiction' between 136–60 and 231–57 (see 2 (*a*) above). He believes that Lucretius 'invented' the idea of the presence of the 'fourth nature' in the *anima*, but not only is Lucretius always scrupulous in following the authority of his master, but the whole of this passage on the nature of the soul bears the marks of very careful writing, which with Lucretius means very careful reporting of his text (the Μεγάλη Ἐπιτομή no doubt, as usual).

(*c*) The evidence of other writers is equally clear.

Aetius, iv. 3. 11 (=Stob. *Ecl. Phys.* 41); U. 315 Ἐπίκουρος (τὴν

---

[1] p. 13.

ψυχὴν) κρᾶμα ἐκ τεττάρων, ἐκ ποιοῦ πυρώδους, ἐκ ποιοῦ ἀερώδους, ἐκ ποιοῦ πνευματικοῦ, ἐκ τετάρτου τινὸς ἀκατονομάστου· τοῦτο δ' ἦν αὐτῷ τὸ αἰσθητικόν . . . τὸ δ' ἀκατονόμαστον τὴν ἐν ἡμῖν ἐμποιεῖν αἴσθησιν· ἐν οὐδενὶ γὰρ τῶν ὀνομαζομένων στοιχείων εἶναι αἴσθησιν. Here not merely is the 'nameless element' stated to be a portion of the soul, but it is said to be the sole source of αἴσθησις, which is the function of the spirit, not the mind. Brieger strangely enough without comment claims this passage in support of his own view.

2. If the German view is correct, there is no reason why objects[1] which touch only body-atoms should not be felt just as much as those which touch the spirit-atoms. For they too could start a mechanical insensible movement which might be transmitted to the mind and there translated into sensation, just as much as could the spirit-atoms: indeed there is no possible point in supposing these insensible soul-atoms to be distributed over the body at all. Therefore

3. The argument against the theory of Democritus that soul- and body-atoms are disposed alternately in the body, is quite futile, for the three grosser soul-elements have no more power of sensation than the body-particles, unless they contain the 'fourth-nature'. In fact

4. The 'spirit' is not really a part of the soul at all, for it is itself entirely devoid of sensation, except what it indirectly receives from the mind, just as the body does.

5. After the mind has, on the German view, 'retelegraphed' the new motion of sensation, why do we not feel the sensation or perceive the image at any part or all parts of our body? the movement would spread through the 'soul-atoms' wherever they were, and there is nothing to direct the current of sensation to the proper point, the place, that is, of the original contact.

6. By far the most important consideration. The German theory really destroys altogether the idea of local sensation. According to it all sensation really takes place not at the point of contact or in the sense-organs, but in the mind. But it is a cardinal point in Epicurean psychology that sensation is local and not in the mind. For this we have the direct statement in *Plac. Phil.* iv. 23 οἱ Στωικοὶ τὰ μὲν πάθη ἐν τοῖς πεπονθόσι τόποις, τὰς δὲ αἰσθήσεις ἐν τῷ ἡγεμονικῷ. Ἐπίκουρος δὲ καὶ τὰ πάθη καὶ τὰς αἰσθήσεις ἐν τοῖς πεπονθόσι τόποις, τὸ δὲ ἡγεμονικὸν ἀπαθές. Nothing could be more explicit than this: 'all sensation occurs in the places affected, but the mind has no sensation (πάθος, the passive sensation of pleasure and pain due to external contact)'. Tohte[2] is reduced to stating that this is an error of Plutarch's,

[1] See Lucr. iii. 381 ff. [2] p. 6.

and that the 'falsity of the statement is obvious': it is of course an exact reproduction of Epicurus' doctrine. This localization of sensation is emphatically affirmed by Lucretius, especially in 359–69, where he states with ironical scorn that 'to say that the eyes can see nothing, but that the mind looks out through them as when doors are opened, is madness, seeing that the feeling in the eyes cries out against it'. The feeling that it is the eyes which see, that the sensation is localized, is an immediate πάθος, which according to the very first principles of the *Canonice* cannot be gainsaid; yet it is just this 'madness', which the German critics wish us to accept as true Epicurean doctrine by denying the presence of the 'fourth nature' in the soul-atoms in the sense-organs and the whole body.

APPENDIX VI

Other Views of the Constitution of the Epicurean Gods

I HAVE attempted in the text to put forward the account of the constitution of the gods, as Epicurus conceived them, which seems to me most in accordance at once with the scanty and unsatisfactory evidence which we possess and with the general principles of Epicurean physics, and have followed in the main the theory first outlined by Lachelier and subsequently elaborated by W. Scott and Giussani. But so widely divergent have been the views of critics both as to the nature of the Epicurean gods and as to the interpretation of the famous passages in the *de Natura Deorum* and in the scholium on Diogenes, that it is necessary to examine some of the more important suggestions, if only to show—what I readily admit—that any theory which may be propounded is perforce tentative.

1. The first serious attempt to explain how the gods, being atomic compounds, could yet be immortal, was made by Schömann (*Opuscula*, iv. 336–59). His theory is not based on any very profound understanding of Epicureanism and shows little respect for the authorities and still less for their text, but it is worth considering partly because it brings out the difficulty of the problem and partly because 'it has recently been revived by Masson (*Lucretius, Epicurean and Poet*, pp. 273 ff.). Schömann starting with the general notion of the extreme fineness of texture of the forms of the gods and the statement of Cicero that they had not body but 'a kind of body' (*quasi corpus*), argues that since the images thrown off by the gods are perceptible by the soul, they, and therefore the bodies which give them off, must be like in texture to the soul. The 'bodies' of the gods are therefore composed of round, smooth, and very fine atoms. But this is not enough to make them immortal: the divine body must indeed be a *concretio*, but differ from other συγκρίσεις. This Schömann suggests may have been the case because the component atoms were all of the same shape (p. 341, n. 15)—an opinion which he bases on the mention by Plutarch of the ὁμοιότητες (*sc.* bodies made of similar atoms), as the fourth class of immortal things—and being all of the same shape would therefore be able to adhere in a strong permanent combination. Among many reasons which make it impossible to accept this view may be mentioned the following: (1) Its total disregard of evidence. (*a*) Schömann finally admits that he cannot understand the Cicero passage, and practically abandons it, except that he takes it to deal with the perception of the

divine images and not with the constitution of the divine body. Incidentally he takes *ad numerum* to mean 'so that they could be counted' and *similitudine* to refer to the likeness between the texture of the divine images and the recipient soul. (*b*) The statement of Diogenes as to the two classes of gods he maintains is wholly impossible: he gets rid of it by 'emending' οὓς μὲν ... οὓς δὲ to οὐ μὲν ... γνωστοὺς δὲ and then takes κατὰ ὁμοείδειαν to mean 'owing to the similarity' between divine bodies and the soul, like *similitudine* in Cicero. That this, and with it the interpretation of Plutarch's ὁμοιότητες, is impossible, is sufficiently proved by Scott's references to Aristotle and Philodemus, which show the notion in both cases to be that of bodies having 'identity of like' material. (2) An atomic compound of only one kind of atoms is not an impossibility, but we can gather from Lucretius, ii. 586–8, that it would have practically no 'powers' (*vis*) at all—which is improbable even for Epicurean gods. (3) No atomic compound could be more subtle than the 'fourth nature' in the soul, as is clear from the descriptions both of Epicurus and Lucretius. If the soul is far from immortal, how could the gods be immortal, whose texture so closely resembles it? (4) There is no reason for supposing that a compound of atoms of one kind should have any greater stability than any other compound—certainly it is impossible that it should be immortal. If it were made of round atoms, it would not even be stable to start with: once again the soul, its counterpart, is so little capable of cohesion, that it cannot remain together at all except in the στέγαζον of the body.

In fact Schömann's theory is at variance both with the evidence and with many fundamental principles of Epicurean physics. Yet it has been revived again by Masson with no further support than laudation and the quotation from Munro of the misinterpretation of a passage in Philodemus.[1]

2. Hirzel (*Untersuchungen zu Ciceros philosophischen Schriften*, i. 46–84) approached the question from the point of view of the interpretation of Cicero. He accepts Diogenes' distinction between the two classes of gods: these were, he interprets, the real gods who exist κατ' ἀριθμόν in the *intermundia*, and the images, which float about the

---

[1] μήτε γὰρ ἀτόμους νομίζειν τοὺς θεοὺς μήτε συγκρίσεις, Gomperz, *Herc. Stud.* 121, p. 136. Munro and Masson take this to be an exposition of atomic doctrine: a glance at the passage shows that it is really the objection of an opponent, which is subsequently answered. Even if the words meant what Masson supposes them to mean, they do not support Schömann's view, for according to it the gods are indubitably συγκρίσεις.

world, are perceived by men, and accepted by them as gods. He then supposes that this distinction caused confusion in Cicero's mind, that he identified the images of the gods which came to us with the gods themselves and in the second part of his description is speaking not of the gods but of these images (he reads of course *ad nos* following Lambinus for *ad deos*). The obvious objections[1] to this theory are (1) the improbability of this double doctrine of Epicurus (see pp. 459–61), (2) the difficulty of accounting for the nature of the 'real gods' in the *intermundia* on any consistent atomic basis, (3) the very serious charge of blundering made against Cicero, who was evidently trying to follow his Epicurean texts as carefully and closely as possible, (4) the extreme improbability that so careful a description of the process of perception of the images of the gods should be given, when it would differ in no way from the process of normal sense-perception. But Hirzel did good service to the elucidation of the problem in connecting the *ad numerum* of Cicero and the κατ᾽ ἀριθμὸν of Diogenes with the distinction made by Aristotle between existence κατ᾽ ἀριθμὸν and κατ᾽ εἶδος, and in pointing out that *soliditate quadam* is an independent ablative of quality and is not to be construed with *cernatur*.

Mayor in his edition of the *de Natura Deorum* follows Hirzel, except that he needlessly emends 'nec soliditate quadam nec *eadem* ad numerum *sit*', and believes that the gods κατ᾽ ἀριθμὸν in the *intermundia* are the popular anthropomorphic deities, while those of the image-streams are the esoteric divinities of the Epicureans, vague influences comparable to modern ideas of the 'stream of tendency which makes for righteousness'. His view seems open to all the objections which can be brought against Hirzel's, with the additional disadvantage that he has introduced a most un-Epicurean conception, which is immeasurably remote alike from what is described in the texts and the whole current of Atomic thought.

3. The theory of R. Philippson[2] stands rather by itself in that it deals not so much with the atomic constitution of the gods as with the means of their cognition by men, and with the interpretation of the Diogenes scholium and the passage in the *de Natura Deorum*. It is highly ingenious and contains many fruitful suggestions, but it seems to me to rest upon somewhat arbitrary assumptions as to the Epicurean psychology, which he does not sufficiently work out on atomic lines,

---

[1] See the criticisms of Scott, p. 227, and Giussani, pp. 230–4.

[2] *Zur Epikurischen Götterlehre.* Hermes, li, 1916, pp. 568 ff.: see also his dissertation 'de Philodemi libro qui est περὶ σημείων καὶ σημειώσεων', Berlin, 1881.

and to involve unnatural interpretations of the passages concerned. It is difficult to do justice to the theory in a summary, but, as it has attracted some notice, it is necessary to express an opinion on it.

Philippson holds in the first place that there are, according to Epicurus, two distinct departments of mind (νοῦς), διάνοια (Lat. *mens*) the faculty which perceives the single 'idols', and λόγος the faculty of reason, whose operations are described as λογισμός, ἐπιλογισμός, διαλογισμός, διαλόγισμα and its result as ἐπίνοιαι (ἔννοια is similarly the image resulting from sense-impressions and as such is used as an equivalent of πρόληψις (D.L. x. 32)). It has already [1] been pointed out that this distinction is too rigid: διάνοια is no doubt used in connexion with 'mind-perceptions' especially in the famous ἐπιβολὴ τῆς διανοίας, but it is also used in cases where reason is concerned: λόγος is not used by Epicurus except in the phrases διὰ λόγου θεωρητός or θεωρία, which must be subsequently examined, though its derivatives are certainly applied to rational operations of the mind.

Men's cognition of the gods has, according to Philippson, two sources. In the first place there is the direct perception of their 'idols' by διάνοια, in the second, they are known by reasoning, which makes certain inferences, e.g. that from the wonders of the heavens and their orderliness [2] (incidentally Philippson seems not to notice that in the eyes of Epicurus and Lucretius, to whom he refers, this is a false inference, a ψευδὴς δόξα): similarly according to Sextus [3] the immortality and complete happiness of the gods is deduced 'by an inference from men' (κατὰ τὴν ἀπὸ τῶν ἀνθρώπων μετάβασιν). Of these two sources it is διάνοια which gives the 'concept' [4] (πρόληψις) of the gods, derived from the succession of idols, and reason reinforces that immediate knowledge by argument (ἐπιλογισμός), as for instance in the double syllogism recorded in the *de Natura Deorum*,[5] 'the human form is the most beautiful', 'man alone has reason': 'the gods are beautiful and have reason:' 'therefore the gods are most like men'.

It is then this cognition of the nature of the gods by means of reasoning as opposed to the direct 'apprehension' of the idols which Philippson supposes to be expressed in the phrase λόγῳ θεωρητούς both in the scholiast and in the parallel passage of Aetius:[6] he translates 'durch

---

[1] Chap. VIII, p. 423, n. 3.

[2] Sext. *adv. Math.* ix. 26 and 44.   [3] Ibid. 45, 46.

[4] Also referred to in Ep. iii, § 123 as ἡ κοινὴ τοῦ θεοῦ νόησις.

[5] i. 18. 48.

[6] Aet. i. 7. 34; U. 355 Ἐπίκουρος ἀνθρωποειδεῖς μὲν τοὺς θεούς, λόγῳ δὲ πάντας θεωρητοὺς διὰ τὴν λεπτομέρειαν τῆς τῶν εἰδώλων φύσεως.

Vernunft erkennbar'. I find it impossible to accept this view. λόγῳ θεωρητός is a traditional phrase in Greek philosophy for what is mentally conceived as opposed to what is sensationally perceived, but it does not carry with it the idea of a process of reasoning or inference. When for instance the 'seeds' of Anaxagoras are spoken of as λόγῳ θεωρητά[1] it is not meant that the conception of them is reached by a train of thought, but that we can only 'imagine' them and never see them. And if the passages in which διὰ λόγου θεωρητός, &c., occur in Epicurus himself be examined the same result is reached. In § 62 οἱ διὰ λόγου θεωρητοὶ χρόνοι as opposed to ὁ ἐλάχιστος συνεχῆς χρόνος and are clearly the instants, the *minima* of time, which can be mentally conceived, or contemplated, as opposed to the continuous periods, however small, which alone can be noticed by the senses. In § 59 Epicurus comes nearer to Philippson's notion: from the analogy, he argues, of the minima of perception (the *extrema cacumina* of Lucretius) we infer similar minima of extension in the atom τῇ διὰ λόγου θεωρίᾳ ἐπὶ τῶν ἀοράτων. This may no doubt fairly be translated 'in our contemplation of the unseen by means of thought', but again the reference is not to a chain of argumentation resulting in a conclusion, but, as always in Epicurus' material psychology, to the contemplation of a mental picture: all mental processes are to him acts of visualization. It is indeed significant that the word coupled with λόγῳ or διὰ λόγου in all these instances is θεωρητός or θεωρία: that is not a word which denotes the result of a process of reasoning, it is the mental equivalent of the αἰσθητός and αἴσθησις of sensation.

To sum up: while no doubt inference by reasoning played some part in forming the conception of the nature of the gods in the system of the later Epicureans and even possibly of Epicurus himself, it is not the source of our knowledge of their existence. This is the direct information given by the 'idols' which enter the mind and it is to this 'mental perception' that λόγῳ θεωρητούς refers both in the scholiast and in Aetius. If this contention be right, it cuts at the root of Philippson's view of the two crucial passages, but it is necessary to follow his interpretation in further detail because it involves, to my mind, further improbabilities.

    1. Schol. ad Ep. *K.Δ.* i; D.L. x. 139.[2] (*a*) Philippson rightly rejects

Philippson incidentally would place the emphasis on πάντας; 'by reason they cannot be known as individuals but only universally as a class', a very unnatural interpretation.

  [1] See Part I, Chap. I, p. 37.
  [2] For the text see Chap. IX, p. 446, n. 1.

emendation of οὕς μὲν ... οὕς δέ, yet also refuses to believe that Epicurus supposed two categories of gods. He therefore proposes to translate 'partly ... partly' (teils ... teils), for which he quotes certain parallels elsewhere in Greek. But in those passages there could be no mistake as to the meaning intended, here it would be to say the least ambiguous and any straightforward reader would take the meaning to be that there were two classes of gods. (b) He rejects Scott's interpretation of κατ᾽ ἀριθμόν as opposed to κατ᾽ εἶδος ('in numerical identity'. ... 'in form'), and takes the opposition to be κατ᾽ ἀριθμὸν ἕν and κατ᾽ εἶδος ἕν, which he would translate 'one as an individual' and 'one as a member of a class' ('das der Art nach Selbige'). This is a less natural interpretation. (c) The clause οὕς δὲ ... ἀποτετελεσμένων he takes not as describing the constitution of the gods but the method of their cognition; the συνεχὴς ἐπίρρευσις is not that of the atoms which come together to form the bodies of the gods, but that of the 'idols' to the mind of the percipient. (d) ἐπὶ τὸ αὐτὸ ἀποτετελεσμένων he takes to mean either 'which lead to the same result' or 'which are of the same configuration': neither of these interpretations seem to me natural; (e) he regards ἀνθρωποειδεῖς as a later addition to the scholium, probably with justice.

We thus get the meaning, if I interpret Philippson rightly; 'Epicurus says elsewhere that the gods are cognizable by reason, partly as having individual existence, partly as like in form (i.e. as members of a clan), thanks to the unceasing flow of the idols which are of the same configuration', that is to say, reason tells us (a) that the gods exist as individuals (as opposed for instance to the general idea of a divine spirit held by the Stoics), (b) that the gods are like in form as we gather from the succession of similar 'idols'. The advantage of this version would be that it would enable one to take ἐκ τῆς συνεχοῦς ἐπιρρύσεως in its more natural sense of the flux of 'idols' from the gods to men's minds. But apart from the difficulties in detail referred to above I think the interpretation is made impossible by the sense given to λόγῳ θεωρητούς and by the connexion of this with the second clause. The information given by the constant influx of idols is certainly not information given λόγῳ in Philippson's sense, though I think it is so in reality.

2. Cic. N. D. i. 19. 49.[1] Philippson does not differ from the interpretation given in the text of the first clause down to στερέμνια appellat and agrees that soliditate quadam ... numerum is to be taken as descriptive and not with cernatur. After that he differs widely, (a) imaginibus

---

[1] For the text see Chap. IX, p. 445, n. 1.

similitudine et transitione perceptis, he renders 'by images grasped by induction'. *Similitudine et transitione* is a translation of μεταβάσει καθ' ὁμοιότητα, a phrase which he[1] believes to have been used by the later Epicureans to express the inductive method, 'inference according to similarity'. The sense then will be that we know the gods by images which we form by inference from the succession of similar idols. As regards this startling interpretation, even if it be admitted that μετάβασις was so used in later Epicurean logic, yet (1) if Cicero had μεταβάσει καθ' ὁμοιότητα before him, he translated it very oddly by the 'hendiadys' *similitudine et transitione,* (2) *perceptis* is the ordinary word for sense-perception and not for comprehension as a result of inference, (3) the parallel passage in *N. D.* i. 39. 109 *fluentium frequenter transitio fit visionum* shows conclusively that *transitio* meant to Cicero the succession of 'idols' passing from the persons of the gods to the mind. (*b*) The clause *cum infinita . . . ad deos affluat.* Philippson keeps *ad deos* and takes the clause rightly in my view to apply not to the flux of 'idols' to the mind but to the flow of matter to form the bodies of the gods. Rejecting, again, as I think, rightly, Scott's idea of the 'pre-formed' images, he would exclude *imaginum* as a gloss and substitute *rerum.* I have, I hope, shown in the text that emendation is not necessary, if a slight misunderstanding on Cicero's part be assumed, and that in any case *rerum* would not have been the word he would use.

Philippson has made a valuable contribution to the study of Epicurean psychology in calling attention to the meaning of the various terms employed by Epicurus and the Epicureans for the different mental processes, but he has not succeeded in solving the puzzle as to the nature of the constitution of the gods and his interpretations of the two crucial passages seem to me to rest on untenable suppositions.

None of the views here considered appear to satisfy the conditions or the evidence as nearly as that of Scott and Giussani. It may be that both of them, and especially Giussani, have elaborated the notion beyond what the extant information strictly warrants, and it is certainly true that the notion reached on their lines is grotesque and fantastic even for Epicurus, but as far as the evidence now available can take us, I believe that Epicurus' conception of the constitution of the gods cannot in its main outline have been far removed from the account which they have given.

[1] The evidence is set out in his dissertation, p. 34.

BRIEF BIBLIOGRAPHY

I. GENERAL

Beare, J. I., *Greek Theories of Elementary Cognition*, 1906.
Burnet, J., *Early Greek Philosophy*, 3rd edition, 1920.
Cornford, F. M., *From Religion to Philosophy*, 1912.
Gilbert, O., *Die meteorologische Theorien des griechischen Altertums*, 1907
Gomperz, T., *Greek Thinkers* (vol. i, translated by L. Magnus, 1901).
Lange, F. A., *Geschichte des Materialismus*, 1873.
Natorp, P., *Forschungen zur Geschichte des Erkenntnissproblems im Altertum*, 1884.
Ritter, H., and Preller, L., *Historia Philosophiae Graecae*, 4th edition, 1869.
Schwegler, A., *Geschichte der griechischen Philosophie*, 1870.
Ueberweg, F., *Grundriss der Geschichte der Philosophie*, 1871.
Zeller, E., *Philosophie der Griechen*, 1856.

II. THE ATOMISTS

Text:

Diels, H., *Die Fragmente der Vorsokratiker*, 3rd edition, 1912.
Heraclitus—Bywater, I., 1877.

Commentaries, &c.:

Brieger, A., *Die Urbewegung der Atome und die Weltentstehung bei Leukipp und Demokrit*, 1884.
Dyroff, A., *Demokritstudien*, 1899.
Goedeckemeyer, A., *Epikurs Verhältnis zu Demokrit*, 1897.
Lafaist, M., *Dissertation sur la Philosophie atomistique*, 1833.
Lasswitz, K., *Geschichte der Atomistik*, 1890.
Liepmann, H. C., *Die Mechanik der Leucipp-Democritischen Atome*, 1885.
Mabilleau, L., *Histoire de la Philosophie atomistique*, 1895.
Natorp, P., *Ethika des Demokritus*, 1893.
Pillon, F., *L'Évolution de l'Atomisme*, 1892.

III. EPICURUS

Texts:

Bailey, C., *Epicurus*, 1926.
Hicks, R. D., *Diogenes Laertius* (Loeb), 1925.
Usener, H., *Epicurea*, 1887.
von der Mühll, *Epicurus* (Teubner), 1922.
Sententiae Vaticanae—Wotke, C., in *Wiener Studien*, 1888.
Metrodorus—Körte, C., 1890.
Diogenes Oenoandensis—William, I. (Teubner), 1907.
Philodemus, &c.—Gomperz, W., *Herculanische Studien*, 1865.
Scott, W., *Fragmenta Herculanensia*, 1885.
Editions of separate treatises in Teubner Series.

Translations :

Bignone, E., *Epicuro*, 1920.
Ernout, A., in Introduction to *Commentary on Lucretius*, i, ii, 1925.
Hicks, R. D., *Diogenes Laertius* (Loeb), 1925.
Kochalsky, A., *Das Leben und die Lehre Epikurs*, 1914.

Commentaries, &c.:

Bailey, C., *Epicurus*, 1926.
Bignone, E., *Epicuro*, 1920.
Brieger, A., *De Atomorum Motu Principali* (in Martin Hertz zum Geburtstage), 1888.
Brieger, A., *Epikurs Brief an Herodot*, 1882.
Brieger, A., *Epikurs Lehre der Seele*, 1893.
Crönert, W., *Colotes und Menedemos*, 1906.
Giussani, C., *Studi Lucreziani*, and other essays in edition of Lucretius, 1896.
Guyau, M., *La Morale d'Épicure*, 1904.
Hicks, R. D., *Stoic and Epicurean*, 1910.
Joyau, E., *Épicure*, 1910.
Masson, J., *Lucretius, Epicurean and Poet*, 1907.
Merbach, F., *De Epicuri Canonica*, 1909.
Schömann, G. F., *De Epicuri Theologia*, 1864.
Taylor, A. E., *Epicurus*, 1911.
Thomas, P. F., *De Epicuri Canonica*, 1889.
Tohte, T., *Epikurs Kriterien der Wahrheit*, 1874.
von Arnim, H., *Epikurs Lehre von Minimum*, 1907.
Wallace, W., *Epicureanism*, 1880.
Woltjer, J., *Lucretii Philosophia cum Fontibus Comparata*, 1877.

INDICES

I. GENERAL

II. GREEK WORDS

III. PASSAGES QUOTED OR REFERRED TO

* Fragments marked with an asterisk are quoted from Stobaeus, *Ecl.* Bks.
ii, iii, iv.

* To save space references are mostly given to sections of the poem, within which the quotations made will be found.

DATE D

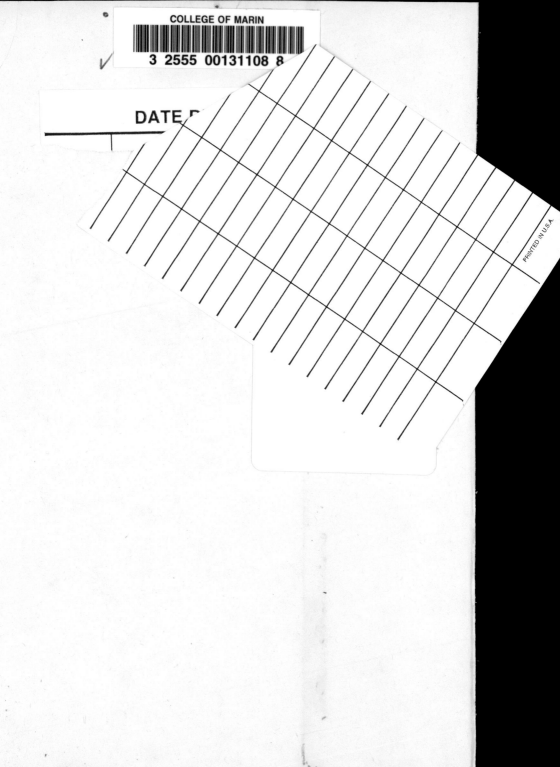

PRINTED IN U.S.A.